Outlook® 2010

ALL-IN-ONE

FOR DUMMIES®

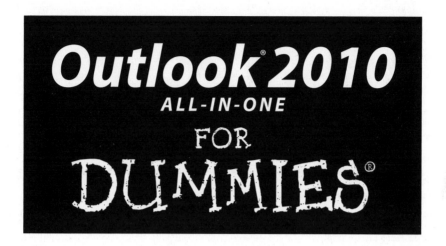

by Jennifer Fulton and Karen S. Fredricks

John Wiley & Sons, Inc.

Outlook® 2010 All-in-One For Dummies®

Published by
John Wiley & Sons, Inc.
111 River Street
Hoboken, NJ 07030-5774

www.wiley.com

Copyright © 2010 by John Wiley & Sons, Inc., Hoboken, New Jersey

Published by John Wiley & Sons, Inc., Hoboken, New Jersey

Published simultaneously in Canada

For general information on our other products and services, please contact our Customer Care Department within the U.S. at 877-762-2974, outside the U.S. at 317-572-3993, or fax 317-572-4002.

For technical support, please visit www.wiley.com/techsupport.

Wiley publishes in a variety of print and electronic formats and by print-on-demand. Some material included with standard print versions of this book may not be included in e-books or in print-on-demand. If this book refers to media such as a CD or DVD that is not included in the version you purchased, you may download this material at http://booksupport.wiley.com. For more information about Wiley products, visit www.wiley.com.

Library of Congress Control Number: 2010926850

ISBN 978-0-470-48773-0 (pbk); ISBN 978-0-470-87319-9 (ebk); ISBN 978-0-470-87320-5 (ebk); ISBN 978-0-470-87321-2 (ebk)

Manufactured in the United States of America

10 9 8 7 6 5 4 3 2

WILEY

About the Authors

Jennifer Fulton, iVillage's former Computer Coach, is an experienced computer consultant and trainer with over 20 years in the business. Jennifer is a best-selling author of over 100 computer books for the beginner, intermediate, and advanced user, ranging from the self-motivated adult business user to the college, technical, high-school, or middle-school student. Jennifer is also a computer trainer for corporate personnel, teaching a variety of classes, including Windows, Microsoft Office, Paint Shop Pro, Photoshop Elements, and others.

Jennifer is a self-taught veteran of computing, which means, of course, that if something *can* happen to a computer user, it has probably happened to her at one time or another. Thus, Jennifer brings what's left of her sense of humor to her many books, including *Outlook 2007 All-in-One Desk Reference, Adobe Photoshop Elements 4 in a Snap, How to Use Macromedia Dreamweaver 8 and Fireworks 8, Adobe Photoshop Elements 3 in a Snap, Digital Photography with Photoshop Album in a Snap, Paint Shop Pro 8 in a Snap,* and *Learning Microsoft Office 2007.*

Karen S. Fredricks began her life rather non-technically growing up in Kenya. She attended high school in Beirut, Lebanon, where she developed her sense of humor while dodging bombs. After traveling all over the world, Karen ended up at the University of Florida and is an ardent Gator fan. In addition to undergraduate studies in English, Theater, and Accounting, Karen has a master's degree in Psycholinguistics. Beginning her career teaching high school English and theater, Karen switched to working with the PC during its inception in the early '80s and has worked as a full-time computer consultant and trainer ever since.

Karen is an ACT! Certified Consultant, an ACT! Premier Trainer, a Microsoft Office User Specialist, and a QuickBooks Pro Certified Advisor. She is the author of four *For Dummies* books on ACT! In addition, she has written *Outlook 2007 Business Contact Manager For Dummies* and is completing work on *Microsoft Office Live For Dummies.* A true fan of the *For Dummies* series, she helped organize The Authors Unconference, the first ever gathering of *For Dummies* authors.

Karen resides in Boca Raton, Florida. Her company, Tech Benders, specializes in contact management software and provides computer consulting, support, and training services. She is also a regular guest on several syndicated computer radio talk shows. In her spare time, Karen loves to spend time with family and friends, play tennis, work out, road bike, and write schlocky poetry.

Karen loves to hear from her readers. Feel free to send her your comments about the book to dummies@techbenders.com or visit her Web site www.techbenders.com to learn more about the products listed in this book.

Dedication

Jennifer Fulton: To my husband Scott, who patiently and lovingly supports me in everything I do, and my daughter Katerina, who is my future and my life.

Karen S. Fredricks: To Gary Kahn, who loves and encourages me every step of the way!

Authors' Acknowledgments

Jennifer Fulton: I would like to thank all the wonderful people at Wiley Publishing who worked hard under a very tight deadline to guide this book through to its completion. I would especially like to thank Katie Mohr for giving me this opportunity and Paul Levesque for his keen eye as an editor.

Karen S. Fredricks: This is my sixth book for Wiley Publishing, and as usual, they've made writing this book a pleasure! Thanks to Katie Mohr, my acquisitions editor, for believing in me; I look forward to working with you on many more titles! Special thanks to my project editor, Paul Levesque. Laura Miller, the copy editor, had the unenviable task of making me look good; her edits were always right on! Technical editor Lee Musick's sharp eye helped to spot all the changes between the beta and final versions of Outlook 2010. It was an honor to work with Jennifer Fulton, my co-author; I hope we work on more titles together again in the future!

Rich Tennant is the coolest cartoonist ever. I am astounded by the thought, research and time that he devotes to each one of his cartoons. I'm not sure which is funnier — his cartoons or his stories about creating his cartoons!

The most important acknowledgment of all goes out to all of the readers of the *For Dummies* series and, more specifically, the readers of this book. I hope you'll enjoy *reading* this book as much as I enjoyed *writing* it!

Publisher's Acknowledgments

We're proud of this book; please send us your comments through our online registration form located at http://dummies.custhelp.com. For other comments, please contact our Customer Care Department within the U.S. at 877-762-2974, outside the U.S. at 317-572-3993, or fax 317-572-4002.

Some of the people who helped bring this book to market include the following:

Acquisitions, Editorial, and Vertical Websites

Project Editor: Paul Levesque

Executive Editor: Katie Mohr

Copy Editor: Laura K. Miller

Technical Editor: Lee Musick, Daniel A. Begun

Editorial Manager: Leah Cameron

Editorial Assistant: Amanda Graham

Sr. Editorial Assistant: Cherie Case

Cartoons: Rich Tennant
(www.the5thwave.com)

Composition Services

Project Coordinator: Sheree Montgomery

Layout and Graphics: Melanee Habig, Kelly Kijovsky

Proofreaders: Melissa Cossell, Rebecca Denoncour, Susan Hobbs

Indexer: Christine Karpeles

Special Help: Rebecca Senninger

Publishing and Editorial for Technology Dummies

Richard Swadley, Vice President and Executive Group Publisher

Andy Cummings, Vice President and Publisher

Mary Bednarek, Executive Acquisitions Director

Mary C. Corder, Editorial Director

Publishing for Consumer Dummies

Kathleen Nebenhaus, Vice President and Executive Publisher

Composition Services

Debbie Stailey, Director of Composition Services

Contents at a Glance

Table of Contents

Introduction

*L*ife in the digital age seems so complicated to me. When I was younger, life was simple: Go to school, do your homework fast, then play, play, play until Mom calls you in for dinner. Then go back out and play until just past dark. We didn't need a lot of fancy electronics — just something resembling a ball (even if it was a bit deflated), a set of ever-changing rules, and a big backyard.

As an adult, things have gotten much too hurry-up-and-wait, if you know what I mean. Sure, it's nice to have all the latest gadgets — I don't know what I'd do without my BlackBerry, or my notebook computer and its wireless Internet connection. But I find it ironic that the tools that were supposed to make life easier have made it more complex. Sure, having a cell phone means I can get through to my daughter when needed and get help in case of an emergency. It also means that my boss can find me even when I go out on the weekends, or that a client can track me down at all hours and give me new things to get done by the end of the day.

If your life runs nonstop like mine, you're probably overwhelmed with lists, lists, lists. You keep notes to remind you to pick up milk on the way home and to keep track of your client's cell-phone number, your best friend's new address, and directions to that restaurant where you're meeting your boss for an employee review. Rather than filling your purse, wallet, or pockets with a bunch of notes, I recommend turning the whole mess over to Microsoft Outlook. I'm pretty confident that Outlook is a much better organizer.

Outlook includes several parts, or *modules;* each module keeps track of an important aspect of your busy, busy life:

✦ **Mail:** Stores incoming and outgoing e-mail messages in folders you create. It also lets you quickly find e-mail based on content and re-sort messages however you want, and it provides a quick and easy way of previewing e-mail attachments without having to open them completely (and possibly infect your system with a virus).

✦ **Calendar:** Stores all your appointments, meetings, and day-long events and displays them in daily, weekly, or monthly format. It also displays the Daily Tasks List, in case you don't have enough going on in your day.

✦ **Contacts:** Helps you remember the important facts about the people you know, such as their names, phone numbers, addresses, e-mail addresses, cell-phone numbers, and Web page addresses. This module also helps you track important trivia, such as the names of a contact's spouse, children, and family pet.

✦ **Tasks:** Tracks all the things you need to get done, now or someday. Tasks are divided into two groups: To-Do items, which are basically quick notes about things to do, and tasks, which contain more detailed info (such as task start date, due date, number of hours spent on the task, status, percent complete, priority, and a reminder to do the task).

✦ **Notes:** Tracks small bits of stray info, such as your locker combination and super-secret decoder password. You can even post these notes on your Windows Desktop if you need them to be more in your face.

✦ **Journal:** A module wanna-be. Although the Journal was originally designed to track all sorts of activities, such as e-mails sent to and from a specific contact, appointments made with a contact, phone calls made to a contact, and Office documents associated with that contact (such as Excel workbooks and Word documents), most of this is done by automatically without the Journal's help, and displayed almost everywhere in Outlook, through something called the People pane. To learn what you might still use the Journal for, check out Book I, Chapter 1.

You may be completely satisfied with the group of six hard-working modules described in the preceding list. But if you're one of those people for whom nothing is ever enough, well, depending on your version of Office, Outlook comes with several companion programs that expand its functionality:

✦ **OneNote:** Notes on steroids. With this creature, you can create notebooks on any subject and fill their pages with text, graphics, sound recordings, screen captures, Web links, and links to Outlook items (such as appointments and tasks).

✦ **Business Contact Manager (BCM to its friends):** Can help you manage numerous hot and cold leads, important contacts and their accounts, and several money-generating projects.

About This Book

Even though Outlook is made up of a lot of parts, such as Mail, Contacts, and Calendar, most people use it at first only to manage e-mail. That's okay; Outlook's a big boy and can take the fact that you think it's only an e-mail program. After you get used to using Outlook, though, you may figure out that it's pretty handy for all sorts of things — except maybe taking out the garbage and clearing a drain.

Don't let all those Outlook modules overwhelm you at first; you can get to each of them in your own sweet time. And the way this book is organized can help you. Each chapter is written with a kind of "I don't know much" attitude, so if you want to jump over to one of the Calendar chapters and start there, you can. If something you need to know is located in a different chapter than the one you're reading, I'll tell you about it and point you in the right direction. Don't worry.

Along the way, I offer a lot of hand-holding. Steps are written clearly, with explanations and a lot of pictures to help you figure out whether you're getting it right.

Conventions Used in This Book

Discovering the Ribbon that runs along the top of the Outlook window may throw you at first, but Book I, Chapter 1, helps you get over any trepidations you may have. Frankly, I found the Ribbon a bit overwhelming at first because its purpose is to show you every command you might ever want to use. However, after a second or so, I found it the smartest design change Microsoft could have ever made, and I am ohhh so glad to see it incorporated throughout Outlook at last. The Ribbon makes it quite easy to locate the command you need, such as New E-Mail (for creating a message) or Reply (for replying to a message you've received).

The Ribbon doesn't just hang out in the Outlook window. Nope — whenever you try to create something, the Ribbon continues to stick around by using a special window that Outlook calls a *form*. So, if you create a message or an appointment, you see the Ribbon. If you're wondering what the Ribbon looks like, you can find a picture of it in Book I, Chapter 1, so the two of you can be properly introduced. Go ahead and take a look; the Introduction will still be here when you get back. On the Ribbon, the tabs along the top allow you to display different sets of buttons, and the group name appears below each group of similar buttons. And that big orange button on the far left edge of the Ribbon is called the File tab. The File tab is your gateway to something Microsoft calls the Backstage, where you can perform ancillary tasks, such as printing, creating e-mail accounts, and setting options.

Every book has its own way of showing you how to do stuff. In this book, if I want you to select a command on the Ribbon, I give you the sequence of things to do, like this:

> Click the New Items button on the Home tab and select Contact from the pop-up menu that appears.

Pretty clear, I think: Start by clicking the Home tab on the Ribbon, which causes the Ribbon to display the Home tab buttons. Scan from left to right, and you're sure to find the New Items button I'm talking about — the buttons are all generally large and easy to read. After you find the New Items button, click it to reveal a pop-up menu of items; select Contact from this menu by clicking it.

Occasionally, a button is so small that I don't think you're likely to locate it quickly. In such a case, I add the group name (the name that appears under a group of buttons on the Ribbon) to the instructions in order to help you find the particular button I mean:

> Click the Meeting button in the Respond group on the Home tab.

Foolish Assumptions

Well, maybe it's foolish for me to assume something about you because we've never actually met, but I'm betting that you're a Windows user and therefore at least a little familiar with basic Windows stuff, such as windows, minimizing and maximizing, and using menus. I'm also assuming that you know how to use a mouse and how to click and double-click.

I guess I wouldn't be far off in assuming that you have an e-mail account somewhere and that you want to send and receive e-mail messages. That's what Outlook is more or less known for. I don't assume, however, that you've set up Outlook to get messages; instead, I show you how to do that in Book I, Chapter 3.

Finally, when I show you something, I don't assume that you know anything about Outlook other than its name or that you know how to use Outlook to do anything.

How This Book Is Organized

Although Outlook is actually a pretty complex, full-fledged program, don't let its power overwhelm you. It's remarkable how little you actually need to know to get started, and I've stuck it all in Book I, "Getting Started." In fact, you don't even have to read all four chapters in Book I. I recommend at least glancing through Chapters 1 and 2, though, because they teach you the basics of how to navigate and use Outlook.

So, with two little chapters, you're off to the races. From there, you can skip around to whichever chapter deals with a topic of interest. Not sure where to find stuff? Don't worry; I have this book pretty well organized so that you can find what you need quickly. This book is divided into minibooks — ten of them, in fact, each focusing on a particular aspect of Outlook. Each book contains chapters, numbered from 1 to whatever. So, when I say to go look in Book II, Chapter 4, I mean the fourth chapter in the second minibook. You can always tell what book and chapter you're in by looking for that gray box on the right-hand page.

Book I: Getting Started

This minibook covers the basics of the Outlook window, such as how to use the Navigation pane, the Reading pane, the Ribbon, and Backstage. Chapter 2 shows you how to quickly create just about any item in Outlook, such as a quick message or appointment. Obviously, there's more to creating items than what's covered in Chapter 2, so from there, you can jump to the book that covers the item you're working with in more depth, such as Calendar. This minibook also includes stuff you might not need to do because someone's already done it for you, such as adding your e-mail account information and importing data from your old e-mail program.

Book II: E-Mail Basics

This minibook shows you how to use the Mail module. You can find out how to create more than just simple e-mail messages, read and reply to e-mail you get, make your messages look snappy, and repeat the same information (such as your name and phone number) in all outgoing e-mails without retyping it all the time.

Book III: Über E-Mail

This minibook covers more than the need-to-know stuff, moving into the cool-to-know area of e-mail. In this minibook, you can find out how to manage multiple e-mail accounts, control when e-mail is sent or received, use Outlook to send text messages (yes, you can!), and blanket the Internet with a single message. Don't worry, I don't show you how to generate *spam* (mass junk e-mail); I show you how to send a single message to multiple people in your Contacts list.

Book IV: Working with the Calendar

As you might expect, this minibook focuses on the part of Outlook that keeps track of appointments, meetings, and such: Calendar. You can find out how to display Calendar in a bunch of different ways; create appointments, meetings, and day-long events; make those items repeat in your calendar without retyping them; make changes to appointments, meetings, and events; share your calendar with other people in your company; add cool stuff, such as Internet calendars; and customize the way Calendar looks and operates.

Book V: Managing Contacts

This minibook focuses on the Contacts module, showing you the basics in adding contacts and displaying them in a variety of ways. You also can find out how to work your contacts, pulling up an associated Web site or a map of their location. I also show you cool stuff such as creating mock business cards and sharing contacts with colleagues and friends.

Book VI: Tracking Tasks, Taking Notes, and Organizing Life with OneNote

This minibook covers a lot of ground — the Tasks module, where you create tasks and To-Do items (think mini-tasks), and the Notes module, where you can create quick Post-It-like short notes. You can also find out how to use OneNote, a cool add-on program that allows you to gather Outlook items such as tasks and meeting details into one place, alongside your notes from the meeting, handouts, graphics, audio notes, and other minutiae.

Book VII: Working with Business Contact Manager

This minibook focuses on an Outlook add-on program called Business Contact Manager. You can find out how to use it to manage business contacts, business accounts, and the revenue they generate. You also can figure out how to keep track of the details surrounding large projects that involve multiple contacts, a myriad of tasks, and who knows how much record keeping.

Book VIII: Customizing Outlook

Jump to this minibook to see how to create categories for grouping Outlook items together; change your view of messages, tasks, contacts, appointments, and such; and customize the basic working window, the *form* (the window in which you create an item, such as an outgoing e-mail message or a new contact).

Book IX: Managing All Your Outlook Stuff

After you create tons of Outlook items, including contacts, e-mail messages, and tasks, you probably need to organize them. You can approach this problem in several ways, all of which are covered in this minibook. You can find out how to create new folders to put stuff in, move or copy items from folder to folder, and clean up your mailbox. You also can find out how to complete handy tasks, such as using rules to automatically sort incoming mail; deal with *spam* (junk e-mail); locate the stuff you've created; and make Outlook more secure.

Book X: Out and About: Taking Outlook on the Road

This minibook covers ways to manage the problem of getting e-mail when you're out of the office (or away from home), how to deal with incoming messages automatically when you're on vacation (or how to get someone to do it for you), and how to print stuff such as e-mail messages or contact info.

Icons Used in This Book

While you browse through this tome, your thoughts will occasionally be interrupted by little pictures (icons) in the margin. These icons point out important (or, in the case of Technical Stuff, simply fun) things you should know.

These paragraphs contain shortcuts and other tips that can help you get something done quickly and get back to enjoying life.

These icons point you toward other important information in the book, or they may just contain important things to make a note of.

Watch out for this information because it may very well prevent you from making a common mistake.

Technical Stuff paragraphs contain interesting but not vital information, such as the reasons behind a particular task or the ways to deal with a particular situation that applies to only a select few. Don't feel compelled to read these tidbits unless you're truly interested in the topic at hand.

Where to Go from Here

The best place to start if you're new to Microsoft Outlook is Book I, Chapter 1. Then, move on to Book I, Chapter 2. Those two chapters give you the basic stuff you need to know to start using Outlook right away. From there, just jump around to the chapters that interest you or that point you to the ways to solve the problem you're dealing with at the moment, such as how to get an appointment to appear somewhere else on your calendar (check out Book IV, Chapter 2) or change somebody's e-mail address in the Contacts list (flip to Book V, Chapter 1).

Book I

Getting Started

The 5th Wave   By Rich Tennant

"It's another deep space probe from Earth seeking contact with extraterrestrials. I wish they'd just include an email address."

Contents at a Glance

Chapter 1: An Insider's Look at the Outlook Interface

In This Chapter

✔ Getting comfortable with the Outlook interface

✔ Moving from place to place within Outlook

✔ Getting a handle on today's events

✔ Making everything the right size for you

✔ Moving Outlook out of the way while you do other work

Right now, I'm sitting here wondering exactly how much information a single adult needs just to get through any given day. I certainly need to keep track of a lot — phone numbers, cell numbers, e-mail addresses, meetings, appointments, and endless lists of things to do before anybody catches on that I haven't done them yet.

If ever a program was designed for the Information Age, it's Outlook. I bet that the people at Microsoft created Outlook just so they could see their desks every once in a while. As you discover in this chapter, Outlook is pretty handy for managing the tons of data that clutter your desk on a daily basis — the hundreds of messages, appointments you better not miss, names you better not forget, and things you better do.

What Can Outlook Do for Me?

There's no sense in letting Outlook sit around on your Windows desktop if it doesn't at least help you clean up your *real* desktop once in a while.

As you probably already know, Outlook handles e-mail messages, both coming and going. What you might not know, however, is that it integrates nicely with other forms of electronic communication, including instant messaging, text messaging, and electronic news feeds (RSS). All this communicating takes place within the confines of Outlook's Mail module — which happens to be the module that appears when you start Outlook, as shown in Figure 1-1. The Mail module is so handy that it takes two minibooks to tell you all about it: Books II and III. Not to mention what you learn about the Mail module in this minibook (Book I).

New Features

If you send a lot of e-mail (like I do), you will really, really (did I mention really?) appreciate a new feature that Outlook calls Mail Tips. I call it Silently Saving My Grateful Backside. Assuming that you use Outlook at work, Mail Tips questions your questionable choices *before* you make them. I'm talking embarrassing mistakes such as sending out an e-mail reply to 1,000 of your nearest and dearest colleagues when you meant to reply only to the sender. Or sending out a message to your boss after she already told you *three times* that she was going to be off today and to send stuff to Bob, instead. Or including an outsider in what should have been an inside-the-company-only discussion. Intrigued? See Book II, Chapter 2.

Another cool feature of Outlook is Quick Steps. Although it can't save your backside, it may very well save your hair (because you'll stop pulling it out so often). Quick Steps allows you to perform a series of steps by clicking a single button. Outlook comes with many of these handy things already programmed for you, such as quickly generating an e-mail to your team or your manager, moving an e-mail to a folder that you use often, and generating a meeting request by using the currently selected e-mail as a basis. But you can program more. The time-saving possibilities are endless, so jump over to Book I, Chapter 2 to find out more before you run out of hair.

Social butterflies will love the new People pane, which appears at the bottom of e-mail messages, contact cards, and other Outlook items. The People pane helps you stay connected to friends and colleagues through the information they post on social networks such as Sharepoint, Facebook, Windows Live, LinkedIn, MySpace, Twitter, and so on. In addition, it helps you find meetings, e-mails, and files you may have gotten from a particular person. See the upcoming section, "Viewing Mail with the Reading Pane," for more info.

There's one more new feature that you should get to know, and it's Backstage. To the folks at Microsoft, Backstage is the place where you go to perform behind the scene tasks such as printing, saving, opening files, and setting options. You get to Backstage through the File tab, which is bright orange and located in the upper left-hand corner of the Outlook window. You learn more about Backstage later in this chapter, in the section "Backstage Pass".

Outlook Modules

In addition to the Mail module, Outlook has five other modules, each one designed to help you manage a different part of your busy life:

+ **Calendar:** The life's work of the Calendar module is to keep track of all your appointments, meetings, and day-long events such as birthdays, holidays, and seminars. And the magic doesn't stop there. The Calendar can help you easily manage multiple calendars — from the busy schedules of your children to the central calendar for your department. You can find the nitty-gritty details about using the Calendar in Book IV.

File tab

Quick Access toolbar

Help button

Ribbon

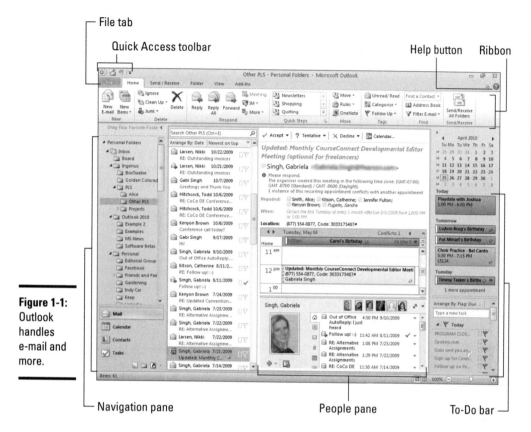

Figure 1-1:
Outlook handles e-mail and more.

Navigation pane

People pane

To-Do bar

✦ **Contacts:** The Contacts module organizes the details you need to remember about all the people in your life, from your favorite plumber's emergency phone number to the name of your boss's spouse. You can use it to keep track of important business contacts, even grouping people from the same company together. And when you're running late for a meeting, Contacts can quickly provide a map to the meeting's location. The Contacts module is the star of Book V.

✦ **Tasks:** In the Tasks module, you can find all those things that you need to do whenever you can find the time. You can quickly arrange tasks by due date, priority, or any other category you can think of (such as Pass On to Some Unsuspecting Fool). You master multitasking in Book VI.

✦ **Notes:** In the Notes module, you keep track of, well, your notes. I know you prefer little bits of scrap paper, the back of cash-register receipts, empty envelopes, and Kleenexes, but why not give the Notes module a shot? See Book VI for help.

✦ **Journal:** Playing a background role is the Journal (so much in the background that you don't see it initially on the Navigation pane). Its lowly status is due to the fact that most of what the Journal does is now done automatically for you in Outlook 2010! You see, the Journal was originally created to track your activities. I know you're thinking, "My busybody neighbor in the next apartment is already doing a pretty good job of that." Unlike your neighbor, however, the Journal tracks the e-mail, appointments, and To-Do items associated with a particular client. But Outlook itself now does this tracking business without your permission. The only thing you might tell the Journal to track now is which Office documents you work on, and when. When you return to the Journal at some later date, the documents you've created or changed since turning on this document-tracking feature appear in a long list.

To tell the Journal to track your Office document history, switch to the Journal by first adding its button to the Navigation pane (see the section "Building better buttons in the Navigation pane," later in this chapter, for details). A message appears, reminding you, silly person, that Outlook basically tracks all the normal Journal stuff automatically. But you want to turn the Journal on anyway, so click Yes in this message box. In the dialog box that pops up, select the Office programs whose documents you want to track from the Also Record Files From pane and click OK. That's it! Just return to the Journal when you want to view a list of documents that you've changed or created since turning on the Journal's document tracking feature. You can change to Timeline view to view these documents in a kind of historical timeline if you want by clicking the Timeline button on the Home tab. Double-click an entry to open it in Office.

Outlook is a part of Microsoft Office, so it's designed to play nicely with its brothers and sisters. Throughout this book, you can find many ways to use the various Office components — Word, Excel, PowerPoint, and so on — with Outlook. For example, you might want to use the addresses in Contacts to create form letters in Word, or you might want to insert Excel data into an e-mail message in Outlook. Whether your goal is to get data into or out of Outlook, you can find a simple way to accomplish your task within these pages.

You can jump between modules — Mail, Calendar, Contacts, Tasks, and Notes — by choosing the module that you want from the Navigation pane (see Figure 1-1), which is described in more detail later (in the section "Getting Around with the Navigation Pane," to be precise).

Heeeerrre's Outlook!

Like most Web pages, Outlook's window (refer to Figure 1-1) contains a navigation system on the left and a viewing area on the right. The viewing area changes a bit when you move from module to module, but basically items appear in a big, long list.

You can choose the view you want to use to display the items in the current module by clicking the Change View button on the View tab and selecting a view. For example, when you open the Mail module, it displays e-mail by using the Compact view, which probably sounds like Outlook has somehow reviewed all your messages and gotten rid of the meaningless ones, thus compacting the list of messages you need to read. Unfortunately, even Outlook can't decide for you which messages you should read. (To find out what Compact view actually does, read the Technical Stuff.) The point here is, if you don't happen to like Compact view you can choose a different view to display e-mail messages. After you choose a view, you can then sort the corresponding items (in this case, messages) by selecting a particular arrangement. Just choose the arrangement you want (such as From order, which arranges messages by sender) from the Arrangement section of the View tab.

Outlook initially arranges messages in Date order, which sorts your mail in the order in which you receive it, grouped by day. Although this is a pretty good arrangement, I recommend that you sort your messages in Date (Conversation) order, which is a slight variant. To do that, select the Show as Conversations option in the Conversations group on the View tab. This option keeps messages in date order, but arranges them in conversations, grouping e-mails that you've sent and received on the same subject together. Each conversation is compacted so that initially, only the most recent message in that group (the most recent e-mail in the conversation) is visible. This may alarm you at first, because all of your email is not displayed — only the most recent message in each conversation. As you'll quickly learn though, Date (Conversation) order (which is known by its nickname, Conversation view) instantly shrinks your Inbox into something more manageable, so this "hiding messages" trick turns out to be a good thing. In addition, it won't take you long to realize what a life-saver Conversation view is when you're trying to piece together who said what when. See Book II, Chapter 2 for more information about using Conversation view. In the meantime, I'm switching over to Conversation view, so expect that most of the figures in this book will feature it — but not all, since each Mail view is useful for its own reason, as you learn in Book II, Chapter 2.

So, to recap, the viewing area is located on the right, and it changes depending on which module you're in. The left side of the Outlook window is where the navigation system (known as the *Navigation pane*) resides. As you discover in the section "Getting Around with the Navigation Pane," later in this chapter, the Navigation pane helps you get around the various modules in Outlook.

At the top of the Outlook window, you find the File tab, Quick Access toolbar, and the Ribbon (again, refer to Figure 1-1). There are lots of buttons, buttons, buttons here — and you can figure out how to use them in the following section.

By the way, if you don't know what a button does, just hover the mouse over it for a second, and a ScreenTip appears, explaining it all to you patiently.

On the far-right side of the Outlook window, you can find the To-Do bar. This guy doesn't automatically show up in every module, although you can make him appear whenever you want. He's there to remind you of upcoming appointments and things that you need to get done. You can read more about the To-Do bar in the section "Your Week in a Nutshell: The To-Do Bar," later in this chapter.

A Ribbon in the Sky

When you start Outlook 2010 for the first time, you probably notice the horizontal string of buttons across the top of its window. Well, okay — you may have first noticed all those unanswered messages, and then the buttons. Anyway, this string of buttons is called the Ribbon, and my guess is that it looks pretty familiar, given that the Ribbon was introduced in Office 2007 (although not in Outlook).

Even if you're somewhat familiar with the Ribbon and its neighbors, the File tab and the Quick Access toolbar (refer to Figure 1-1), my other guess is that you probably still don't know some things about them, busy as you were actually *using* Office 2007, rather than exploring the nuances of its interface. So, indulge me a second while I babble on about these little wonders.

Backstage pass

First, the File tab provides access to the commands that you used to find on the old File menu, such as New, Open, Save, Print, and Exit. Microsoft thinks of these as "behind the scenes" kind of commands, so it grouped such commands into a single platform it calls the Backstage.

Backstage is also the gateway to Options (the program settings), Rules and Alerts, and your e-mail account setup, in case you were wondering where they were hiding (see Figure 1-2). When you click the File tab, the Backstage appears, displaying a list of commands on the left (Open and Print, for example.) Click one of these commands to make related options appear on the right. For example, in Figure 1-2, I clicked the Info command on the left to display the Account Information options on the right. Click one of the other tabs on the Ribbon to return to Outlook. Click the Close (X) button for the window (like I did the first time I saw this thing) and you exit Outlook. Grrrrr. You also exit Outlook if you select Exit from the list on the left, but that at least seems a bit more apparent.

I discuss the commands you access through Backstage (such as Print, account setup, and setting options) as we go along, but feel free to explore Backstage on your own if you can't wait.

Command list

File tab   Click a different tab to return to Outlook.

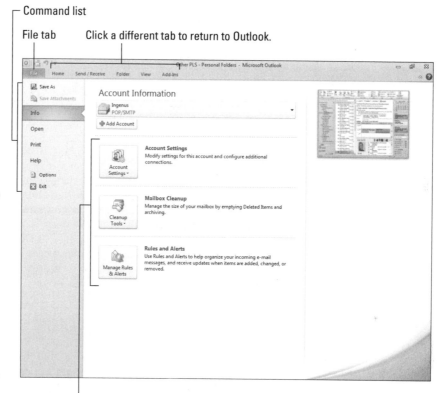

Figure 1-2:
The File tab
displays
Backstage,
through
which you
can access
common
program-
level
commands.

Options associated with the selected command

The Ribbon

The Ribbon (see Figure 1-3), located at the top of the window, contains buttons for just about every command you might want to perform. I have to confess — I love the Ribbon. Now, instead of searching through endless menus, I search through endless tabs for what I want. All kidding aside, it's very refreshing that after I select something, the very command I'm looking for seems to magically appear right on the Ribbon, without a lot of fumbling around.

The Ribbon is divided into *tabs,* and the buttons on each tab are arranged in *groups.* Click a tab to display its buttons. Most of the commands that you need appear on the Home tab, so you probably don't have to change tabs too often in Outlook. The buttons that appear on the Home tab change to reflect the module you're working in. For example, in Mail, the Home tab includes buttons such as Reply, Forward, and New E-mail. If you switch to the Calendar, you see New Appointment, New Meeting, and view buttons such as Week and Month.

Figure 1-3:
The Ribbon
provides
access
to the
commands
that you
need.

Tabs   Buttons   Dialog box launcher   Minimize button

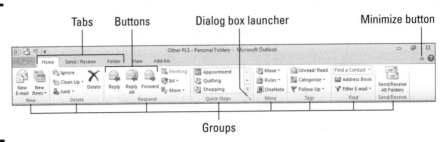

Groups

You can identify the button groups pretty easily because their names appear below the buttons in each group — names such as New, Respond, and Quick Steps. Occasionally, a group has so many related commands that Microsoft decided (thankfully) to not cram them all on the Ribbon. Instead, Outlook offers a tiny dialog box launcher button which appears at the bottom right edge of the button group, and which (not surprisingly) displays a dialog box with all the missing commands when you click it. In Figure 1-3, the dialog box launcher is located at the bottom right of the Quick Steps group. Clicking the launcher displays the Manage Quick Steps dialog box.

How buttons appear on the Ribbon depends on the actual width of the Outlook window. If your Outlook window is wider than the one used in the figures in this chapter — perhaps because you use a higher resolution than shown here — more or larger buttons may appear. If your Outlook is narrower, fewer or smaller buttons may appear.

When you change to a different module in Outlook, the buttons on the Ribbon (refer to Figure 1-1) change, as well. For example, if you jump to the Calendar, you can find buttons that you click to display today's schedule, change the view, create an appointment, or set up a meeting.

Now, just because the Ribbon is so useful, you don't need to stare at it all the time. To get it out of your way temporarily, double-click the currently displayed Ribbon tab or click the up-arrow thingy at the right end of the Ribbon. (Okay, okay, it's officially known as the *Minimize button;* refer to Figure 1-3.) For example, double-click the Home tab. Go ahead; I'll wait. After you minimize the Ribbon, the tabs still peak out; to redisplay the Ribbon, double-click the active tab again. You can temporarily redisplay the Ribbon by clicking the tab just once. After you click a button (or anything else, such as an unopened e-mail), the Ribbon hides itself again.

This Ribbon thing doesn't stop with a simple show of commands. Nope. Depending on what you're working with, a new tab may appear like an attentive waiter, offering you a tasty selection of related commands. For example, after you perform a search, the Search Tools tab offers you a perfect assortment of buttons that help you refine your search so that you can quickly find that e-mail from Mr. Big Client that you forgot to respond to.

The Quick Access toolbar (or QAT, as it's fondly known; see Figure 1-4) is located just above the Ribbon and the File tab, and it does just what its name implies — it provides quick access to the commands that you use often because it's always there, regardless of whether the Ribbon is fully displayed or which tab is active. Initially, the Quick Access toolbar doesn't have a lot on it, just the Send/Receive All button (which you can use to send and receive e-mail through all your e-mail accounts) and the Undo/Redo buttons (which you can use to undo something that you've done or to do it again).

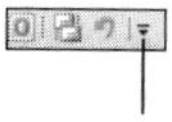

Figure 1-4:
The Quick
Access
toolbar
gives you
quick
access
to the
commands
that you use
the most.

Customize Quick Access
Toolbar button

You can move the Quick Access toolbar below the Ribbon, if you want; just click the Customize Quick Access Toolbar button at the right end of the QAT and select Show Below the Ribbon from the pop-up menu that appears. Add common commands such as Print or Save As to the Quick Access toolbar by selecting them from this same menu. Wanna add a command that you don't see? No problem; just select More Commands from the menu instead. A dialog box appears; select the command that you want to add to the toolbar from those listed on the left and click Add — it's that easy! Click OK to save your changes.

You can also right-click any button on the Ribbon and select Add to Quick Access Toolbar from the pop-up menu that appears to add that button to the toolbar without a whole lot of fuss.

Getting Around with the Navigation Pane

I don't know where they got the name because the Navigation pane (see Figure 1-5) definitely isn't a pain. In fact, it couldn't be simpler to use. To jump to a different module in Outlook, just click that module's button. For example, click the Calendar button to see all the appointments, meetings, and other things you have to do today. If you get depressed when you look at all the stuff that you have to get done by Friday, you can jump over to

Tasks (by clicking the Tasks button) and make a note to book a vacation —
soon. You can find buttons for most of the modules at the bottom of the
Navigation pane.

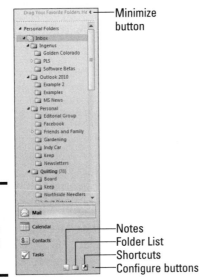

Figure 1-5:
The
Navigation
pane is full
of buttons.

Below the Tasks button (refer to Figure 1-5), a group of these small icons
appears:

✦ **Notes:** Takes you to the Notes module. You can find out how to take
notes in Book VI, Chapter 4.

✦ **Folder List:** Displays a list of Outlook folders. Did I mention that you
can create folders to organize your mail? See Book IX, Chapter 1 for the
lowdown.

✦ **Shortcuts:** Lets you easily access your pet folders from anywhere within
Outlook. You can find out how to take such shortcuts in the section
"Taking a Shortcut to Your Pet Folders," later in this chapter.

✦ **Configure Buttons:** Click this down-arrow button to see a menu that
includes commands that control the number and type of module buttons
on the Navigation pane and commands to perform other tweaks. You
can find out how to work with these buttons in the following section.

What's the Folder list? It's a handy list of all your Outlook folders — one for
each Outlook module, plus other special folders. You can use the Folder list
to perform neat tricks such as organizing your Outlook items (by creating
new folders or moving items from place to place) and jumping right to an
e-mail folder from any other module. You can investigate the Folder list in
the following section.

Although the bottom half of the Navigation pane remains constant, the top portion of the Navigation pane changes depending on which module you have open. In the Mail module, it displays a list of e-mail folders. In other modules, you see a list of alternate lists that you can display, such as shared calendars, suggested contacts you might want to add permanently, or the To-Do list.

Finding your way around the Navigation pane buttons

You can view Navigation pane buttons as either large buttons that run vertically up from the bottom of the pane, or as small buttons that run horizontally across the bottom of the Navigation pane. Initially, the buttons are a mix of sizes — a few of them (such as Mail and Calendar) are large, but others (such as Notes and Folder List) are small.

A horizontal splitter separates the Navigation pane buttons (bottom) from the Folder list (top). If you hover your cursor over the splitter and wait for the pointer to turn into a double-headed arrow, you can drag the splitter bar up as far as it'll go to expand the large button list, as shown in Figure 1-6.

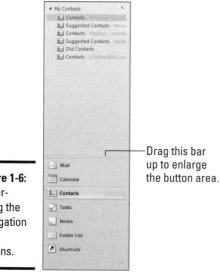

Drag this bar up to enlarge the button area.

Figure 1-6: Super-sizing the Navigation pane buttons.

You can make all the buttons small if you need to make more room for information to appear in the upper part of the Navigation pane. Just do the hovering thing and drag the border all the way down to minimize all the buttons. Figure 1-7 shows the buttons in their miniaturized state.

Building better buttons in the Navigation pane

You can add buttons to or subtract buttons from the Navigation pane. No matter how you view the Navigation pane, the Configure Buttons icon (cleverly disguised as a tiny arrow) appears at the bottom of the Navigation pane. If you click it, you have several options from which to choose:

✦ **Show More Buttons:** Each time you select this option, Outlook takes one minimized button on the pane and makes it super-sized.

✦ **Show Fewer Buttons:** Each time you select this option, Outlook takes one super-sized button and minimizes it on the pane.

✦ **Navigation Pane Options:** Opens the Navigation Pane Options dialog box, which enables you to select the buttons you want, as well as to place them in the order you want. You can even click the Reset button to set the buttons to their original states. Figure 1-8 shows the Navigation Pane Options dialog box.

✦ **Add or Remove Buttons:** Allows you to select the buttons that you want to appear on the Navigation pane by clicking them. For example, if you want to add the Journal button to the mix, select that option from the Add or Remove Buttons menu.

Playing hide and seek with the Navigation pane

If you feel that the Navigation pane is taking up a bit too much of your Outlook real estate, you can change the Navigation pane into a thin vertical bar (*minimize* it) so that you can see more of the viewing area. I use the Navigation pane a lot, but I still minimize it often because I like a lot of room in which to work. To make the Navigation pane skinny, click its Minimize button. (Refer to Figure 1-5.) The buttons for changing from module to module still appear even when the Navigation pane is minimized, so it's functional enough. When you need the little guy again, simply restore it by clicking just one button: the Expand button, shown in Figure 1-9.

Here are some tips for making the Navigation pane just the size you want:

✦ You can click the Navigation Pane button on the View tab and select Minimize from the pop-up menu that appears to minimize the pane.

✦ To restore the pane by using the Ribbon commands, click the Navigation Pane button on the View tab and select Normal from the pop-up menu that appears.

✦ To compromise between pane space and viewing space, resize the Navigation pane by first hovering your mouse pointer over its right edge. The cursor changes into a double-arrow; drag the border of the pane to the left or right, depending on whether you want to make the Navigation pane fatter or skinnier.

**Book I
Chapter 1**

An Insider's Look at the Outlook Interface

—Expand button

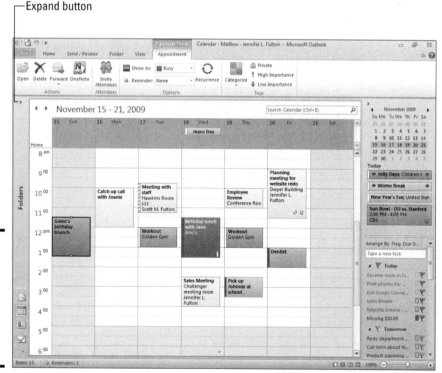

Figure 1-9:
Minimize the Navigation pane to make more viewing room.

There's no right or wrong way to position and size your Navigation pane —
just whatever works for you.

Getting turned off by the Navigation pane

If space is really a problem, you can remove the Navigation pane altogether
and then redisplay it when you want to switch modules. To banish the
Navigation pane from the screen, click the Navigation Pane button on the
View tab and select Off from the pop-up menu that appears, or just press
Alt+F1 enough times until the Navigation pane disappears. Reverse these
steps to redisplay the pane (this time choose Normal from the Navigation
Pane menu).

Having Fun with the Folder List

The Folder list displays all your Outlook folders — not only your e-mail f
olders, but also a folder for each Outlook module, such as Contacts. You
also find some special folders hanging around the Folder list, such as search
folders. Search folders are linked to specific search criteria; when you open
a search folder, it displays any e-mail that currently matches the criteria
— such as all your unread mail. You can find out how to create your own
search folders in Book IX, Chapter 4.

To make the Folder list appear within any module, just click the Folder List
button at the bottom of the Navigation pane, as shown in Figure 1-10. Your
folder listing then appears at the top of the Navigation pane.

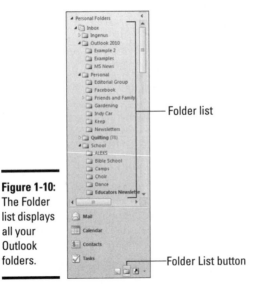

Figure 1-10:
The Folder
list displays
all your
Outlook
folders.

Folder list

Folder List button

You probably won't use the Folder list much because you can jump to most folders pretty easily without it. I tend to use the Folder list when jumping back and forth between other modules and my e-mail. I use a lot of e-mail folders to help me organize my mail. When I'm in Calendar or Contacts, I like to be able to jump right to the exact e-mail folder I need, instead of to whatever e-mail folder I was using last.

To figure out how to create your own folders for organizing e-mail, see Book IX, Chapter 1.

If you decide to use the Folder list, here are some things to remember:

✦ If you display the Folder list and then click a different module button on the Navigation pane (such as the Contacts button), the Folder list disappears.

✦ You can keep the Folder list on-screen by clicking the folder for the module that you want to use from those in the list. So, to keep the Folder list up and move to Contacts, click the Contacts folder.

✦ Like with any Windows folder listing, if you want to see subfolders, click a folder's plus sign. To collapse a folder and hide its subfolders, click the folder's minus sign.

✦ You don't see shared folders in the Folder list. So, to browse through your boss's Calendar, you have to click the Calendar button to access the link to the shared calendar.

✦ If you shrink the module buttons on the Navigation pane, you can make more room to display the Folder list.

✦ To remove the Folder list and return to normal, just click any of the module buttons. For example, click the Contacts button to remove the Folder list and replace it with the My Contacts and Shared Contacts lists.

Viewing Mail with the Reading Pane

If you get a lot of e-mail messages (and who doesn't these days?), you have to deal with them when they come in — otherwise, they quickly pile up. By using the Reading pane, you can preview the contents of a message without wasting time opening it. Here's how it works: In the normal view in the Mail module, several columns appear to the right of the Navigation pane, as shown in Figure 1-11. The first column lists the messages in the current e-mail folder; here, I'm using the default Date view, which lists messages in simple date order. (You can find out how to create e-mail folders in Book IX, Chapter 1.) The second column is the Reading pane, where you can preview messages.

Just click a message header to preview its contents in the Reading pane, as shown in Figure 1-11. To preview a series of messages one by one, use the down-arrow key to move down the message list, previewing while you go. If needed, use the Reading pane's scroll bars to scroll through the e-mail. While you preview the message, you can reply to it, forward it, open attached files, click included hyperlinks, and even cast a vote (assuming the sender asked your opinion) by using Outlook's voting buttons. You can do all these activities without actually opening the message.

To find out how to read and reply to messages, see Book I, Chapter 2. To discover how to view attachments without actually opening them, see the section "Sneaking a peek at attachments," later in this chapter. You can find out about hyperlinks in Book II, Chapter 3, and voting in Book III, Chapter 1.

Important stuff sometimes appears just above the sender and recipient names in what's known as the InfoBar. (Refer to Figure 1-11.) For example, the InfoBar might be telling you right now that Outlook *blocked* (didn't download and display) embedded images in the e-mail. In Figure 1-11, the InfoBar appears with text on a white background, but if you move the mouse pointer over the InfoBar, it changes to orange. So, be sure to glance at the InfoBar often to determine whether the message contains evil attachments, images, or audio files that Outlook blocked because they might cause problems on your system if they scurry about willy-nilly. Helpful little thing that it is, the InfoBar tells you what to do about this blocked content, too, although I can hold your hand through the process the first time if you feel like being extra cautious.

By now, you might be wondering, "What's so evil about a photo that I can't just look at it to judge its artistic merit for myself? Is Microsoft assuming the role of my parent? Because I have plenty of people in my life telling me what to do, thank you very much." In this case, Microsoft is just trying to help you keep your Inbox small because images and audio files tend to eat up a lot of room. Where I used to work, they kept the Inbox limit fairly small, and I can't tell you how annoying it was to have to clean out old messages before I could get any new ones. (My postman has stopped delivering mail for the same reason. Guess I should clean out my mailbox every once in a while.) If you're as determined as I am to waste space, you can use the InfoBar to download the images and audio files in messages that Outlook blocked; see Book II, Chapter 2 for how-to's.

Currently selected messsage

InfoBar

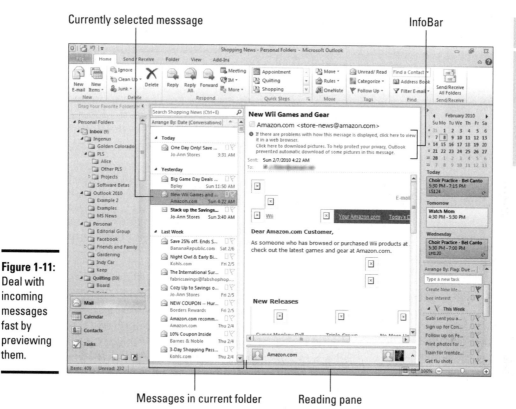

Figure 1-11:
Deal with incoming messages fast by previewing them.

Messages in current folder   Reading pane

When it comes to blocking attachments, however, Microsoft — the dutiful parent in this circumstance — might actually be doing you a favor. First of all, even the act of opening a message from someone you don't know might unleash an unruly virus on your computer, possibly causing damage to your files. Previewing a message isn't the same as opening it, so previewing allows you to keep the bad guys in their cages. By previewing a message, you might be able to tell whether the sender means you harm. If so, just delete the message without opening it.

Be careful of opening any attachments, even after you preview a message. Opening a file can set loose any monster inside it. See Book II, Chapter 2 for tips on how to safely open e-mail attachments; see the following section for details on previewing the contents of attachments without opening them (which can possibly let out a nasty virus).

Here are some tips for dealing with the Reading pane:

✦ You can hide the Reading pane if you don't want to use it by clicking the Reading Pane button on the View tab and selecting Off from the pop-up menu that appears.

✦ Bring the pane back out of hiding by clicking the Reading Pane button on the View tab and selecting Right (to position the Reading pane to the right of the message list) or Bottom (to position the Reading pane at the bottom of the Outlook window, below the message list) from the pop-up menu that appears.

✦ Enlarge the Reading pane by making the message list smaller. Hover the mouse pointer at the left edge of the Reading pane, and when it changes to a double arrow, drag this edge to the left. You can also hide the To-Do bar to enlarge the Reading pane. Yep, you guessed it — you can find out how to do just that in the section "Your Week in a Nutshell: The To-Do Bar," later in this chapter.

Previewing with AutoPreview

Even if the Reading pane is hidden, you can still preview the contents of unread messages, although in a slightly different way, by using a little gadget called AutoPreview. To turn on AutoPreview, click the Change View button on the View tab and select Preview from the palette that appears. Immediately, the Reading pane disappears, and the first three lines of each unread message appear just below the message's header, as shown in Figure 1-12. This display allows you to quickly scan the message list and decide which ones you want to open (see Book I, Chapter 2 for how to's on how to open messages). To change back to Compact view, select that option from the Change View button's palette. In AutoPreview, messages appear in date order. If you want them to appear in a different order, select that option from the Arrangement group on the View tab. To display messages in date order but grouped by conversation (so that only the most current message in each conversation appears), select the Show as Conversations checkbox on the View tab.

Staying connected with the People pane

You may have noticed that when you view a message (in the Reading pane or by opening it), that some interesting information about its sender appears at the bottom of the pane/window. (Refer to Figure 1-13.) The People pane is normally minimized, but here I show it expanded. To expand the People pane, click its Expand button (an up arrow located at the right end of the pane). To collapse the pane and reduce it to a thin strip that runs along the bottom of the message window/Reading pane, click its Collapse button.

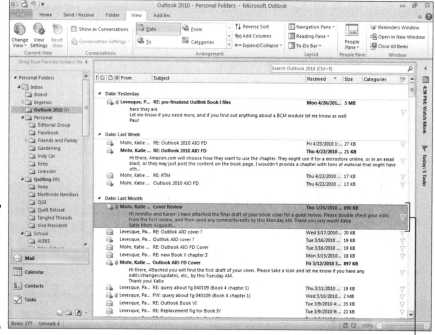

Figure 1-12: AutoPreview provides an alternative to using the Reading pane.

AutoPreview

By the way, I should mention here that the People pane also appears at the bottom of the Contact, Appointment, and Meeting windows. So when you open a particular contact, meeting, or appointment, you can easily catch up on the latest-greatest by scanning the People pane. You learn to open existing items to edit and view them in Book I, Chapter 2.

When it's expanded, the People pane shows you important information about not only the person who sent you the current message, but anyone who received it as well (including you). "What kind of information?" you ask? Well, the People pane pulls data (such as status updates, message posts, and profile changes) from the social networks (such as SharePoint, Facebook, Windows Live, LinkedIn, MySpace, Twitter, and so on) the sender belongs to, and displays that information right there in Outlook. In addition, Outlook scours its own data in search for relevant appointments, meetings, e-mails, and attachments the sender might have shared with you, and displays those in the People pane as well.

Collapse button — People pane

Toggle between People Pane Views —

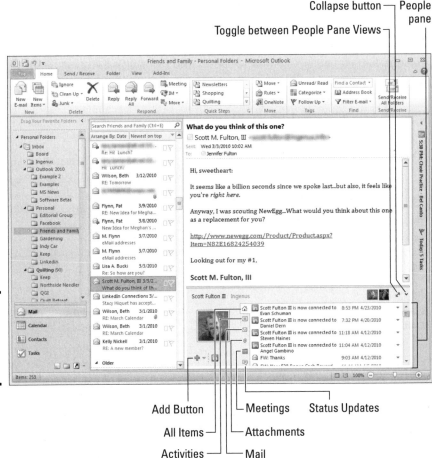

Figure 1-13:
Use the
People
pane to stay
connected.

Add Button — Meetings   Status Updates

All Items — Attachments

Activities — Mail

I say "sender" here because normally, the information displayed concerns the sender of the selected message. Above the People pane, there is a row of small photos, one for the sender and each recipient. To view info on someone other than the sender, click that person's photo. Can't see the photos because they are too small? No problem; just click the Toggle Between People Pane Views button on the far right.

Here's a breakdown of the info you find in the People pane. Click the appropriate tab (such as Activities) to see that information in the People Pane:

✦ **All Items** displays all available information about the person.

✦ **Activities** displays alerts, comments, RSS articles, and other postings regarding the person's current activities, as posted to any social network the person belongs to.

✦ **Mail** displays a list of recent e-mails you've exchanged with this person.

✦ **Attachments** displays a list of files you've shared with this person.

✦ **Meetings** displays a list of appointments or meetings you've scheduled with this person.

✦ **Status Updates** displays the most recent status updates this person has posted to his/her social networks.

To enable the People pane to show as much information as possible about the sender and receivers of a message, you need to install the Outlook Social Connector. Click the People Pane button on the View tab and select Account Settings from the menu that appears. The Microsoft Outlook dialog box pops up onscreen. Select the social networks you wish to monitor, type your account information in (you have to belong to the networks you select), then click Connect to add them. If you want to connect to a social network that's not listed, you can check online to see if they support Outlook Social Connector by clicking the View Social Network Providers Available Online link at the top of the Microsoft Outlook dialog box. Once you add a social network, Outlook scans for your list of friends and adds them to Outlook as contacts automatically, placing these contacts in a separate folder. See Book V, Chapter 2 for more information.

If you click a tab in the People pane (such as the Mail tab) and display a list of the sender's recent messages to you, you can view any one of the listed items by clicking it. This magic works not just for opening messages, but attachments, appointments, and meetings as well.

If a person uses a social network you've set up in the Outlook Social Connector, then you see that person's current status and related info in the People pane. In addition, a small icon representing each social network the sender belongs to appears just under their picture on the left. If you are not yet friends with someone, you can click the Add button which appears underneath the sender's photo in the People pane (refer to Figure 1-13) and send a request to become "friends" through any of the social networks you use from the popup menu that appears.

Change how often contact information is updated using the data pulled from social networks by clicking the Settings button in the Microsoft Outlook dialog box. The Settings dialog box appears; choose from these options: Prompt Before Updating, Update Without Prompting, or Never Update. You can also set how much data is retained by changing the Automatically Delete Activity Items From The Feed Folder After *XX* value, which is normally set to 30 days.

Sneaking a peek at attachments

Opening *attachments* (images, documents, and other files sent with an e-mail) can sometimes cause problems on your system because the attached files might contain macros, scripts, and ActiveX controls with evil on their minds. These potential monsters are basically an automated series of actions that might damage your files if you set them loose. You can help protect your computer by previewing an attachment, rather than opening it. When you preview an attachment in Outlook, Outlook automatically restrains any macros, scripts, or ActiveX controls so that the little monsters can do no damage.

Messages that have attachments appear in the message list with a small paper clip icon, as shown in Figure 1-14. To preview an attachment in an unopened message, just click the file's name (which appears just above the message contents in the Reading pane). If you see a warning in the Reading pane telling you that Outlook may not be able to display the file's full contents, click the Preview File button that appears below the warning to view the file's contents. If someone sends you a message that includes a lot of attachments, you might have to scroll the list to find the attachment that you want to preview. To view the message contents again, click the Message button which appears to the left of the filename.

When you preview an attachment, you might not see the complete, final contents of the file. To be absolutely sure that you're seeing everything, open the attachment. See Book II, Chapter 2 for details. There you can also learn how to save the attachment to your computer, if you are interested.

Paper Clip icon   Attachment name

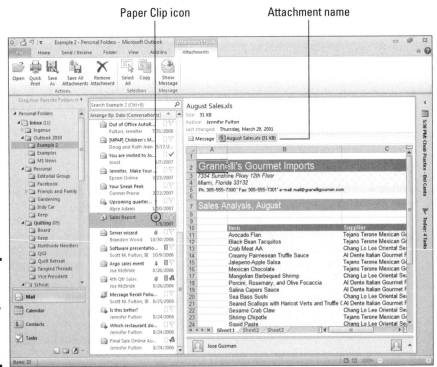

Figure 1-14:
Preview attachments, instead of opening them.

Of course, you can't preview some attachments because Outlook doesn't know how to properly decipher their contents. Outlook can easily preview Office documents (duh), image files, and PDFs, so you shouldn't have any problems with those files. To view the contents of other attachments, you must open them manually — after running your virus detector over them, of course. See Book II, Chapter 2 for help.

By the way, you can also preview an attachment in a message that's already open (assuming Outlook knows how to display the attachment, of course). You might actually want to open the message to preview some attachments because you can maximize the window, something you can't do in the Reading pane. Again, in the open message, just click the name of the attachment (which appears below the Subject box). To redisplay the message contents, click the Message button. In order to entice you to read more of this book, I've cleverly hidden the directions for opening messages in Book I, Chapter 2.

If necessary, you can easily display all your messages that have attachments so that you can find the message that contains the attachment you want to preview. See Book VIII, Chapter 2 for help.

Your Week in a Nutshell: The To-Do Bar

Nowadays it's common for a person to wear lots of hats: project leader, department head, soccer mom, PTA queen, party girl, and occasional community volunteer. Although Outlook doesn't provide a closet for all your hats, you might find that it does a good job of helping you keep track of them — plus all the meetings, appointments, events, and tasks that come with wearing so many. Outlook gathers your stuff together in one place on the To-Do bar, where you can find your due-soon-or-even-sooner list of appointments, meetings, and tasks.

You can also find tasks listed along the bottom of the Calendar and in the Tasks module.

The To-Do bar, shown in Figure 1-15, appears nightly in the Mail room, along its right side. Use these tips to change that behavior:

✦ You can make the To-Do bar appear in any other module by clicking the To-Do Bar button on the View tab and selecting Normal from the pop-up menu that appears.

✦ Turn the To-Do bar off again by clicking the To-Do Bar button on the View tab and selecting Off. This action turns the bar off only in the current module.

✦ To minimize the bar to a skinny column along the right side that you can instantly expand with a single click, click the bar's Minimize button. Minimizing the To-Do bar increases the viewing area.

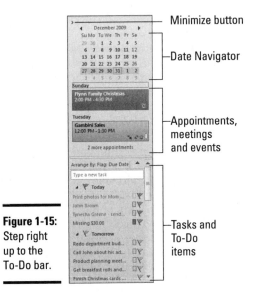

Minimize button

Date Navigator

Appointments, meetings and events

Tasks and To-Do items

Figure 1-15: Step right up to the To-Do bar.

Here's a closer look at the different parts of the To-Do bar, as shown in Figure 1-15:

✦ **Date Navigator:** You can use this navigator to jump over to the Calendar so that you can look at tasks and appointments for a different day, week, or month. You can find out how to navigate the Date Navigator in Book IV, Chapter 1.

✦ **Appointments:** This section is sorta where your next three appointments or meetings are listed in order by date. This section has three slots (unless you've changed the size of the section by dragging the bar between it and the Tasks list up or down), which are filled by the appointments and meetings for today that haven't already passed. For example, if you have only two appointments today and two tomorrow, the To-Do bar initially shows you the two appointments for today, and a note in the last space letting you know that you have two appointments tomorrow (lucky you!). After the first appointment time passes, though, it disappears from the To-Do bar, and all three appointments (the one left for today and the two tomorrow) appear.

Day-long events appear above of appointments/meetings on the Appointments list. They take up less room than appointments and meetings, so Outlook might list more than three appointments/meetings/ events. You might be alarmed that events appear on the To-Do Bar at all, because you might feel that you don't need to be reminded of day-long events, such as birthdays and anniversaries, as much as, say, a meeting with your firm's top client. As a wife, however, I applaud Microsoft on their insight — because forgetting certain events might cause the belongings of their clients to be thrown out on the lawn. Just a thought.

✦ **Tasks list:** Below the Appointments section, your complete list of things to do, arranged by due date, appears. The thoughtful folks at Microsoft added a scroll bar, just in case you have a long, long list of things to do.

When reviewing your long, long list of things to do, keep in mind that Outlook categorizes those things in two groups:

✦ **Tasks:** A task is something that you create, typically while in the Tasks module. It usually has both a starting and ending (due) date associated with it, and lots of other details such as how much work you've already done on the task, info you need to complete the task, the task's priority, and so on.

✦ **To-Do items:** You create a To-Do item by flagging some other Outlook item. For example, if an e-mail message comes in reminding you to bring that sales report to the planning meeting, you can flag the message and create an instant reminder in the To-Do list. By default, items flagged this way are considered due today, although you can tweak the due date as needed.

You can find out the nitty-gritty of flagging stuff to create To-Do items in Book VI, Chapter 1. Right now, just know that both your To-Do items and your tasks show up on the To-Do bar.

You can customize the To-Do bar to change the number of months shown and whether events and details for private items appear on the bar. You can also control whether the Tasks list appears on the To-Do bar. See Book VI, Chapter 1 for details.

Getting a Snapshot of Your Day with Outlook Today

Like with just about everything Microsoft creates, Outlook often offers you a thousand different ways to perform the same task. In other programs, this variety might provide you with many opportunities to mess something up. Luckily, Outlook is both flexible and childproof.

Outlook Today — a single page that displays upcoming appointments, meetings, events, tasks, and the number of unread messages — is just another example of such flexibility. You can display Outlook Today by following these steps:

1. **Click the Mail button on the Navigation pane to change to the Mail module, if you aren't already there.**

2. **Click the root folder for your mail.**

In most cases, the root folder shows up as Personal Folders in the Mail Folder list. (See Figure 1-16.) If you're on an Exchange network, the root folder often shows up as `Mailbox - Jennifer Fulton` or something similar. Regardless of the name, the root folder is typically the first folder in the Folder list.

Root folder   Outlook Today

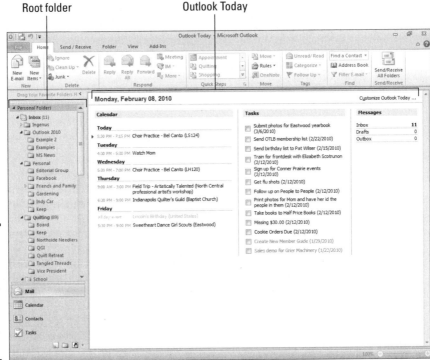

Figure 1-16:
The Outlook
for today is
a bit stormy.
Can I have
a few more
things to do,
please?

Although the To-Do bar is pretty good at giving you an idea of what you have coming up, it mostly focuses on what's going on today. Despite its name, Outlook Today actually presents you with more of a weekly overview of your upcoming appointments, meetings, all-day events, and tasks. It also kindly reminds you exactly how many e-mails in your Inbox you haven't read yet, how many saved but unsent e-mails in the Drafts folder you still need to finish, and how many e-mails in the Outbox await actual transmission to the mail server. What it doesn't show are your To-Do items (Outlook messages, contacts, and the like that you've flagged for follow-up).

You can use Outlook Today to open anything that it displays. Just click any event, appointment, meeting, or task that you see listed, and the associated item opens for you. To check your unread messages, click the Inbox link; to finish an e-mail, click the Drafts link; to check on unsent messages, click the Outbox link.

You can customize the Outlook Today page somewhat; you can even make it the first thing that you see when you start Outlook. Just click the Customize Outlook Today link at the top-right of the Outlook Today page, and select the options that you want from the page that appears. Click the Save Changes link at the top of the Options page to save your choices and return to the Outlook Today page.

Minimizing Outlook to a Taskbar Icon

In order to have Outlook automatically check for e-mail at periodic intervals, you need to keep Outlook open. But you don't have to let Outlook have the run of the place. If you need to get on with other tasks, you can minimize Outlook to remove it from the screen: Simply click the Outlook window's Minimize button, which is located in the upper-right corner. Clicking this button reduces the Outlook window to a button on the Windows taskbar. If you often run a lot of programs, however, putting one more button on an already-crowded taskbar is not always the best answer.

Outlook works a bit differently from other Windows programs, so it allows you to really get it out of the way (and off the taskbar) when you want. Whenever Outlook is running, it puts an icon for itself in the Windows system tray. When new mail arrives, a chime sounds, and an envelope icon (the New Mail icon) appears beside the Outlook icon on the system tray so that you know right away that you have new messages. See Figure 1-17. In addition, the Outlook icon on the Windows taskbar changes to show an envelope with the program icon. (Refer to Figure 1-17.)

Just in case you don't get the subtle hint of an envelope icon, a notification for each incoming message briefly appears. You can click one of these incoming notices to switch to Outlook and view that message. At any other time, even if the taskbar button for Outlook is removed, you can still access the program by clicking the Outlook system-tray icon or the envelope icon (whichever's visible).

You can change how Outlook lets you know that you have mail; see Book III, Chapter 1.

Figure 1-17:
You've got mail.

Outlook Taskbar icon   New Mail Indicator   Outlook System
                                                     Tray icon

To prevent the Outlook taskbar icon from glowing whenever the program is minimized, follow these steps:

1. **Right-click the Outlook system-tray icon.**

2. **Choose Hide When Minimized.**

With the Outlook taskbar icon disabled (non-glowing), you won't be able to click it to restore the Outlook window when it's minimized. Instead, you need to click the Outlook system tray icon and select Open from the pop-up menu to restore Outlook.

Taking a Shortcut to Your Pet Folders

Normally, several small icons appear along the bottom of the Navigation pane. On the far-right is the Shortcuts button (it features a right-pointing arrow), which provides quick access to your pet Outlook folders. Once you create shortcuts, you can quickly jump to a pet folder quick as a wink. To create a shortcut to a beloved folder, follow these steps:

1. **Click the Shortcuts button.**

Again, you'll find the button hiding on the far right, at the bottom of the Navigation pane. When you click the Shortcuts button, your shortcuts appear on the Navigation pane (see Figure 1-18.)

Even if you haven't created any shortcuts yet, Outlook has already created some for you — there's one to Outlook Today and another to Microsoft Office Online.

2. **Right-click the Shortcuts heading and select New Shortcut.**

The Shortcuts heading is located at the top of the Navigation pane. After you right-click it and select New Shortcut, the Add to Navigation Pane dialog box appears.

3. **Select a folder and click OK.**

Select a folder from the Folders list and click OK. The folder appears at the top of the Shortcuts list on the Navigation pane.

You can create new folders for special stuff, such as personal e-mail or your boss's calendar, and then add shortcuts to those folders. See Book IX, Chapter 1 for help.

To use the shortcuts that you've set up, click the Shortcuts button, located at the bottom of the Navigation pane. (Refer to Figure 1-18.) The list of the shortcuts you've created appear on the Navigation pane, as shown in Figure 1-19. As you might gather from the presence of the Work and Personal headings shown in the figure, you can group shortcuts to organize them. To create a shortcut group, follow these steps:

1. **Right-click the Shortcuts heading.**

2. **Select New Shortcut Group from the popup menu that appears.**

3. **Type a name for the group and press Enter.**

The group name appears just below the Shortcuts list. (See Figure 1-19.)

4. **Drag shortcuts into the group.**

To add a shortcut into the new group, drag and drop it on the group name.

After you create a few shortcuts and group similar ones together, here's how to work with them:

✦ To open a group (such as the Work group) and display its shortcuts, click the plus sign just in front of the group name.

✦ To hide a group's shortcuts (such as the Personal group) and make the shortcuts list smaller, click the group's minus sign.

✦ To use a shortcut, click it. The corresponding folder then appears. For example, if the shortcut points to an e-mail folder where you keep personal correspondence, Outlook jumps over to Mail and displays your personal e-mail.

Shortcuts heading

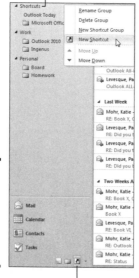

Figure 1-18:
Add a favorite folder to the Navigation pane.

Shortcuts button

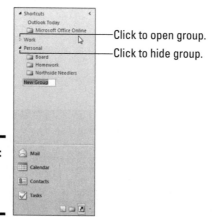

Click to open group.

Click to hide group.

Figure 1-19:
Why not take a shortcut?

Chapter 2: Outlook, Quick and Dirty

In This Chapter

✔ Seeing what all Outlook items have in common

✔ Adding a new contact and working with e-mails

✔ Scheduling an appointment

✔ Recording something to do or making a note

✔ Processing e-mail quickly with Quick Steps

✔ Using drag and drop to get almost anything done quickly

*I*t doesn't take long after you realize how Outlook can help you manage information — thousands of appointments, phone numbers, e-mail addresses, and tasks — that you start wishing I'd just shut up and show you how to get that pile off your desk and into Outlook. Well, in this chapter, I grant your wish . . . at least, kinda: I can't promise that I'll shut up, but I can promise that you can find out how to create every kind of Outlook item quickly.

Creating Outlook Items: The Common Factors

Even though Outlook manages many different kinds of data — appointments, tasks, and contact information — it does so in a strikingly similar way, regardless of what module you're working in. So, it won't be long before you can perform most functions in Outlook without asking for help. The other 750-plus pages in this book are for those rare times when you attempt something new and strange, or just want a friendly guide to help you along the way.

Wow! There's a New button!

You might have already met one element that unites all Outlook items: the New button — well, actually, Outlook now has two New buttons. They always hang out on the Ribbon. Click the New *Something* button whenever you want to create something new in the current module. For example, if you're in Mail, the New E-Mail button appears on the Home tab; clicking it starts a new message. If you're in Notes, the New Note button appears instead; click it to create a new note.

To create a new something that belongs in a module other than the one you're in, click the New Items button and select that something from the list that appears, as shown in Figure 2-1. For example, if you've been browsing through some incoming messages, you can create a new appointment without giving up your cozy spot in Mail. Instead of jumping over to Calendar, just click the New Items button and select Appointment from the drop-down list that appears. The Appointment form opens (more on this form later in this chapter), but you stay put in Mail.

Figure 2-1:
The New Items button helps you create new Outlook items.

The items that appear on the New Items list vary, based on the module you are working in. For example, in the Calendar module, All Day Event appears as an option. In the Mail module, the E-Mail Message Using option appears instead. This option allows you to choose the format for a new message (such as plain text or HTML; see Book II, Chapter 1 for more info) or a stationery (check out Book II, Chapter 3). The More Items option (which appears in every module) displays a longer list of items that you might want to create — typically, these items are lesser known than common items such as e-mails, appointments, and tasks, and include things such as contact groups, notes, and journal entries.

Using forms to create items

In order to create a new Outlook item, you obviously have to enter some details. You enter these details into a form, such as the Appointment form shown in Figure 2-2. Later, if you want to make changes to an item, you make changes to the information on the form. The form simply corrals all the details about a particular item into something that's manageable.

Quick Access toolbar

Insert tab Format Text tab

File tab │ Main tab   Review tab

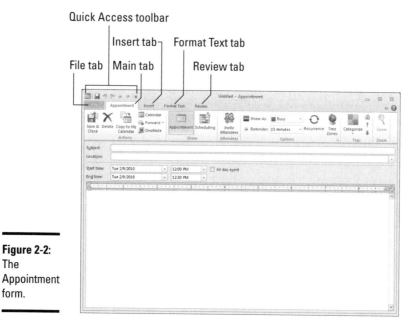

Figure 2-2:
The
Appointment
form.

Although — for obvious reasons — the fields (text boxes) on a form change
depending on the type of item you're trying to create or make changes to,
some parts of a form remain the same for all items. Here's a look at the
standard elements of a form (refer to Figure 2-2):

✦ **Quick Access toolbar:** You've probably met before, but this toolbar
   includes buttons for common form tasks such as saving, undoing, and
   viewing the next or previous item.

✦ **File tab:** Again, I probably don't need to introduce you. This tab which
   is really a button provides access to Backstage and its commands for
   saving, printing, and closing the form.

✦ **The main tab, Insert tab, Format Text tab, and Review tab** Every form
   features the Ribbon, which you should already be familiar with. The
   tabs on the Ribbon change, depending on the item that you're trying to
   create, but some common ones always appear. For example, the main
   tab, such as the Appointment tab shown here, contains the buttons
   most needed for creating that item. The Insert tab also always appears
   on the Ribbon, so you can insert stuff such as pictures and hyperlinks
   into the item or attach files. The Format Text tab allows you to format
   any text that you might enter into the form, while the Review tab
   provides tools for checking spelling, grammar, and performing other
   reviews of your text. You can find out how to use the Ribbon buttons in
   later chapters, when we get into the nitty-gritty details of creating various
   Outlook items.

One button I want to mention before moving on is the Save & Close button. This button appears on the main tab for a form. For the Appointment form shown in Figure 2-2, the Save & Close button is the first button on the Ribbon of the Appointment tab. After you enter data for a new item or make changes to an existing one, click the Save & Close button to save that data. The one exception to this Save & Close rule is e-mail; if you want to send the completed message, click Send. Clicking Save on the Quick Access toolbar (the e-mail form doesn't even provide a Save & Close button) in a message saves the message to the Drafts folder, where you can return and make further changes to the message at a later date.

To close a form and not save changes, press Esc or click the form's Close button (the X in the upper right-hand corner). Then, click No in the dialog box that appears, asking whether you want to save changes.

Editing an item

You sometimes need to change information that you've entered previously in an appointment, contact, or task. For example, a contact's phone number might change, or the due date for a task might be moved up (lucky you). In any case, you can easily go back to an item after you create it and make adjustments, as needed. Just follow these steps:

1. **Double-click the item to open it.**

   For example, in the Tasks list, double-click a task.

2. **Make your changes to the fields on the form that appears.**

   For example, set a new due date or change the amount of progress made on the task.

3. **Click the Save & Close button on the Ribbon to save the changes you've made; or press Esc to abort your changes and close the form.**

   The Save & Close button appears on the main tab for the form. On the Task form, for example, the Save & Close button is on the Ribbon for the Task tab.

You can change an e-mail message after you create it, assuming you haven't sent that message yet. If you create a message and click the Save button rather than Send, the message is saved in the Drafts folder. Go to that folder and double-click the message to open it, then make changes. If you clicked Send but the message is still awaiting delivery in the Outbox folder (which happens if you work offline and aren't connected to the Internet), go to that folder and open the message. Make your changes and click Send to put the revised message in the Outbox for delivery. See Book II, Chapter 1 for more information on the Outbox and the Drafts folder.

Deleting an item

If you finish with an item, such as a completed task or outdated contact, you can get rid of it. Just click the item to select it, and then click the Delete button on the Home tab. You can instead press the Delete key, if you prefer. Even if the item's open, you can get rid of it by clicking the Delete button on the main tab of the form.

Emptying the trash

Items that you delete aren't really removed; you can always get them back — at least, until you take out the trash. When you delete an item, the item is simply moved to Outlook's Deleted Items folder. And there it sits until you empty the trash. You take out the trash by following these steps:

1. **Click the Folder List button on the Navigation pane.**

The Folder list appears.

2. **Click the Deleted Items folder.**

3. **Click the Empty Folder button on the Folder tab.**

A dialog box appears, reminding you that choosing this command permanently removes any item that's sitting in the Deleted Items folder.

4. **Click Yes to confirm the deletion.**

You can also right-click the Deleted Items folder in the Folder list and then select Empty Folder from the pop-up menu that appears to empty it.

Okay, if you work in an office (and are therefore connected to an Exchange server that handles your e-mail), all is not lost, even after you empty the Deleted Items folder. Nope, you can still recover deleted items by selecting the Deleted Items folder and clicking the Recover Deleted Items buttons on the Folder tab. You can claw back those deleted e-mails for only a limited amount of time — how long is determined by the person in charge of your company's e-mail server, who gets to decide when your deleted e-mails are permanently removed from the company server.

Automating trash emptying

If you have more on your mind than trash collection, you can automate the process of taking out the trash. If you follow these steps, Outlook empties the Deleted Items folder every time you exit the program:

1. **Click the File tab to display Backstage and then select Options from the list on the left.**

The Outlook Options dialog box appears.

2. **Select Advanced from the list on the left.**

The Advanced options appear on the right in the Outlook Options dialog box.

3. **In the Outlook Start and Exit section, select Empty Deleted Items Folders When Exiting Outlook, and then click OK.**

Restoring an item

If you want to restore an item after you delete it, you must act before the trash man comes (before the Deleted Items folder is emptied). To restore an item, follow these steps:

1. **On the Navigation pane, click the Folder List button.**

   The Folder list appears.

2. **Click the Deleted Items folder.**

   Items in the Deleted Items folder appear in a list.

3. **Drag and drop any item that you want to restore back on its original folder.**

   For example, to restore a deleted appointment, drag and drop the appointment on the Calendar folder.

For help in permanently deleting IMAP mail messages or restoring messages marked for deletion, see Book X, Chapter 2. IMAP (Internet Message Access Protocol) is one kind of e-mail account — so, if you don't have that kind of account, don't worry about it. Not sure? See Chapter 3 of this minibook for the lowdown.

Adding a Quick Contact

Who knows how many people you might meet in any given day? Most of them are completely forgettable, but for those you shouldn't forget, add them quickly to the Contacts list before you do. Follow these steps:

1. **From any module, click the New Items button on the Home tab and select Contact from the drop-down list that appears.**

   If you're in the Contacts module, you can just click the New Contact button on the Home tab. The Contact form appears, as shown in Figure 2-3.

2. **Fill the Contact form's fields with any information that you have about the new contact, as shown in Figure 2-3.**

   Skip over any fields that you don't know, such as Job Title or Home phone. (For more information about what some of these fields mean, see Book V, Chapter 1.)

3. **Click Save & Close to save the contact.**

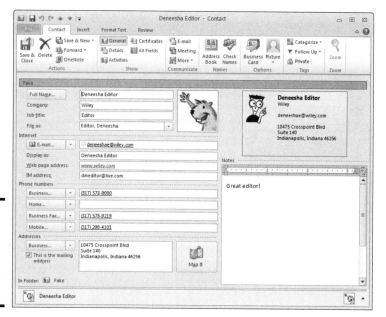

Figure 2-3:
Remember
even
forgettable
people with
Contacts.

Sending a Fast E-mail

Gotta get the word out? No problem; sending a basic e-mail message is pretty
simple. It helps if you already have the person you want to send the message
to set up in your Contacts list, but that's not necessary to send out a message.

Follow these steps to send a quick message:

1. **From any module, click the New Items button on the Home tab and
select E-mail Message from the drop-down list that appears.**

If you're in the Mail module, you can just click the New E-Mail button on
the Home tab. The Message form pops up, as shown in Figure 2-4.

2. **Click in the To text box and type the e-mail address of the person to
whom you want to send the message.**

If the person is already set up in your Contacts list, you can just type his
or her name and let Outlook look up the address.

The process of having Outlook look up an e-mail address based on a
name you type is called *resolving*. If Outlook successfully identifies the
person you're looking for, it underlines the name you've typed. If it can't
guess who you're talking about (for example, if you spell the person's
name incorrectly), Outlook puts a red, wavy underline beneath the
name. If the name you type isn't in the Contacts list, Outlook does nothing
(you won't see an underline). In that case, type that person's e-mail
address, rather than his or her name.

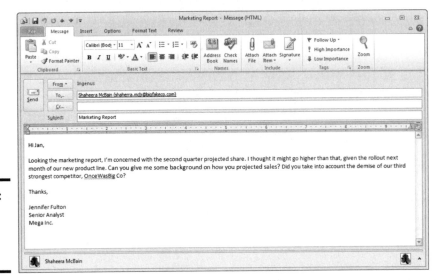

By the way, Outlook assumes that e-mail addresses are valid, even if they aren't in Contacts — thus, they're always underlined. If an e-mail address matches someone in Contacts, not only is the address underlined, but the person's name also appears to the left of the e-mail address. See Book II, Chapter 1 for more help in addressing e-mails.

3. **Type the topic of your message in the Subject text box.**

4. **Click in the big text box at the bottom of the form and type your message.**

5. **Click Send.**

Obviously, you can do more than simply enter a text when you send a message, or I wouldn't have devoted two minibooks to the process. For example, you might want to mark a message as urgent, format your text to make it easier to read, or include a recent photo of your kids. You can discover how to do all that and more in Books II and III.

Reading and Replying to Incoming Messages

In Chapter 1 of this minibook, I discuss the Reading pane and how to use it to review incoming messages. The Reading pane is convenient because it allows you to view the contents of messages without actually "getting out of your chair," as it were, and going through the lengthy business of opening, reading, and then closing them. The downside is that the Reading pane is notoriously small, and with some messages, you end up scrolling up and down and right and left to view the message contents. You might as well have "gotten up" and left the comfort of the main Mail window for the Mail form, which at least displays the message text in its entirety. (And hey, if you're heading to the kitchen, could you get me a soda?)Follow these steps to open and read a series of e-mails:

1. **Click the Mail button on the Navigation pane to change to the Mail module.**

2. **In the Folder list, click the folder that contains the messages you want to review.**

   This is probably the default mail folder, Inbox, although it might be a different folder if you've created others.

   To find out how to create and use e-mail folders to organize your messages, see Book IX, Chapter 1.

3. **Double-click the first message that you want to read.**

   The message opens in its own window, as shown in Figure 2-5. Use the vertical scroll bar or the Page Down key to scroll through long messages. If a message contains pictures, they're typically *blocked* (not shown). See Book II, Chapter 2 for help in viewing them.

Previous item   Next item

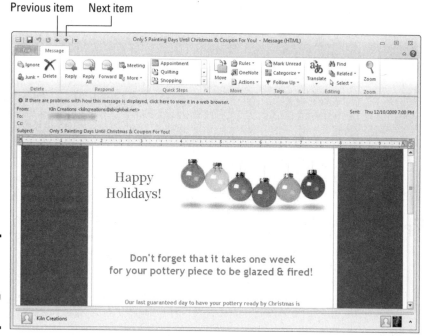

Figure 2-5:
Open long messages to read them more easily.

Don't open an e-mail message unless you know the sender and you're sure the message doesn't contain any viruses, macros, or scripts. See Chapter 1 of this minibook for help in previewing a message's contents without unleashing any monsters.

Because of the buttons on the Ribbon, you can perform a lot of tasks while viewing a message, such as instantly deleting it, flagging it for follow-up, or adding the sender to your stop-annoying-me list. You can also reply to a message, which is something I get to in a minute; the other tasks I cover in Books II and III.

4. **To view the contents of the next message in the list, click the Next Item button on the Quick Access toolbar at the top of the message window.**

   To view a previous message, click the Previous Item button instead.

5. **When you're done reviewing messages, you can click the Close button (the "X") on the message window to close it.**

If you're looking through a series of e-mails and you find one that requires a reply, click the Reply button on the Message tab to make a new message form appear, conveniently addressed to the sender. The content of the original message is copied to the new message, so if your sender has sent out more e-mails than he or she can remember, then he or she can at least identify what you're referring to. Type your reply above the copied text and click Send to send your reply on its way.

You don't have to have the original text copied to your replies; see Book II, Chapter 2.

You might notice a Reply All button sitting coyly next to the Reply button. Cute as it is, that button is one dangerous sucker. If you click that button, rather than Reply, what you thought was a private conversation can get shared with *thousands* of your nearest and dearest. See Book II, Chapter 2 for tips on how to use Reply All safely.

Creating a Simple Appointment

Client meetings, dates with the sales rep, doctor appointments, dentist appointments, parent-teacher meetings — the list goes on. To keep track of all these demands on your time, you can enter these various appointments in Outlook. After you enter them, you can quickly browse your daily, weekly, or monthly calendar to review how many appointments you have for that time period and then decide on the best time to head out of town. Luckily, the process of entering a new appointment is much less stressful.

Outlook keeps track of all your appointments, meetings, and events in the Calendar. *Appointments* are meetings that you have with people outside your company; *meetings* are appointments with your colleagues. By setting up a meeting in Outlook, you can use the company's shared Contacts list to invite attendees, book resources, and manage the whole meeting process. (*Events,* by the way, are day-long happenings, such as birthdays, seminars, anniversaries, and such. You can find out how to add events in Book IV, Chapter 1, and how to add meetings in Book IV, Chapter 4.)

You can make appointments fairly detailed when you need them to be, but you can create one quickly and easily by following these steps:

1. **Display the Date Navigator.**

You can display the Date Navigator in a lot of different ways, depending on where you're currently working:

- Display the To-Do bar (and its Date Navigator) in any module by clicking the To-Do Bar button on the View tab and selecting Normal from the pop-up menu that appears.

- If the To-Do bar is displayed but minimized, click the To-Do Bar button on the View tab and choose Minimized from the pop-up menu that appears to turn that option off and redisplay it in the module in which you're working. You can also click the Expand button to redisplay the bar.

- Switch to Calendar (which has its own Date Navigator) by clicking the Calendar button on the Navigation pane.

2. **On the Date Navigator, click the day on which you want to schedule the appointment.**

If need be, you can switch over to a different month by clicking the left or right arrow on either side of the month name. After you click a day on the Date Navigator, you are switched to Calendar. So if you are working in Tasks and you click January 10th on the Date Navigator, Outlook changes you over to Calendar, and displays the appointments, meetings, and events for January 10th.

3. **If needed, click the Day button on the Home tab.**

When you are switched over to Calendar from another module, your appointments, meetings, and events may appear using the view you selected the last time you were using Calendar. So if you are looking at an entire week of appointments for example, click the Day button on the Home tab to narrow the view to the day on which you are trying to set up an appointment.

You don't have to display a single day in order to create an appointment, but the technique I show you here is easier to perform if you are using Day view. After you get the hang of this however, you can create an appointment using this technique and any Calendar view.

The day that you selected appears, sliced and diced into handy, half-hour segments, as shown in Figure 2-6. Appointments, meetings, and events appear as rectangles on this day grid, blocking out the time they take up.

4. **Start a new appointment.**

   Hover the mouse over the half-hour time slot in which the appointment is scheduled to begin. Click when you see these words: *Click to Add Appointment.*

   For example, hover over the 9:00 time slot, and then click the Click to Add Appointment bubble when it appears. See Figure 2-6.

5. **Type the appointment description in the bubble and press Enter.**

   Type a brief name or description for the appointment, such as Coffee with Kyla. After you press Enter, Outlook creates your half-hour appointment. To find out how to lengthen the appointment or enter additional details, see Book IV, Chapters 1 and 2.

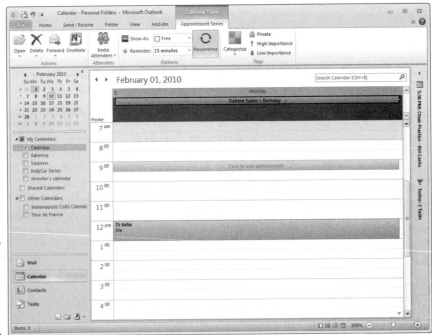

Figure 2-6:
Create an appointment with a single click.

Adding a Quick Task

We all have things to do — some are quick, easy, just-do-it things, whereas others are long, drawn-out, complicated affairs. Outlook can easily help you track both types of tasks. Of course, you still have to find the time to get them all done or assign them to some other poor sap.

Enter your quick, easy, just-get-it-done things on the To-Do bar by following these steps:

1. **Click the Type a New Task box on the To-Do bar.**

You can find this sucker in the bottom half of the To-Do bar, just above the list of tasks. Click this text box to add a task, as shown in Figure 2-7.

Figure 2-7:
The To-Do bar provides an easy way to add a task.

2. **Type the task description (such as** `Project X status report` **or** `Pick up laundry`**) and press Enter.**

That's it! Now, if only you could get the task done as easily.

The task you just created appears in the Tasks list, grouped with other things that you need to get done today. If you want to change the task due date or add other task details, see Book VI, Chapters 1 and 2.

Actually, Outlook assigns a due date to a new task that you create on the To-Do bar based on your current Quick Click setting — which, by default, is set to Today. If you typically create tasks that are due tomorrow or next week, you can change the Quick Click setting so that the tasks you create have the correct due date to begin with. See Book VI, Chapter 1 for all the details.

If you put off completing a task that you originally assigned to be due today, it continues to appear below the Today heading on tomorrow's task list. It changes, however, from calm, non-threatening black text to pay-attention-to-me red text. Any new task that you add appears below any red tasks for today.

You might want to know a couple of other things about tasks — first, you can complete them! Yes indeedy, if you finish a task and want to strike it off your list, you can do that pretty easily. Also, you can add tasks while looking at your Calendar by jotting them down on the Daily Task list (assuming it's visible, which it is initially, at the bottom of the screen). So, if you happen to be in Calendar view, you can create a task without having to display the To-Do bar or jump over to Mail, where the To-Do bar normally appears. I show you how to do all this stuff in Book VI, Chapter 1.

Taking a Note

Notes don't get a high priority in Outlook, and darned if I know why. Creating a note in Outlook couldn't be simpler, and most people I know (myself included) are constantly jotting down notes all over any conceivable surface, including palms and inner arms. Follow these steps to create a note without marking up your body parts:

1. **From any module, click the New Items button on the Home tab, select More Items from the pop-up menu that appears, and select Note from the other pop-up menu that appears.**

    Or you can switch to the Notes module (assuming that you can find its teeny-tiny icon, laying low at the bottom of the Navigation pane) and click the New Note button on the Home tab.

    A yellow box appears; this is your note.

2. **Type whatever you want in the box, as shown in Figure 2-8, and then click the form's Close button (the almost invisible X in the upper right-hand corner) to close the note.**

    If you want, you can keep the note on-screen and add to it throughout the day. Whatever you type is automatically saved periodically, so you shouldn't lose any notes, even if a sudden power outage takes down your computer.

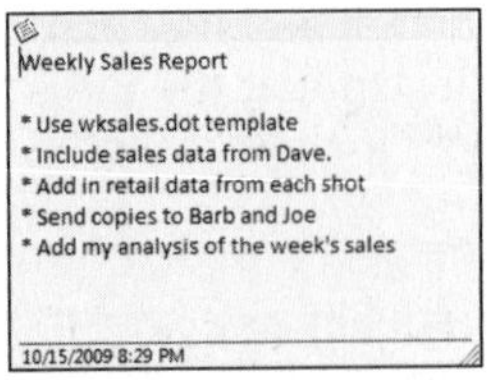

Figure 2-8:
Make a
note of that,
will ya?

Weekly Sales Report

* Use wksales.dot template
* Include sales data from Dave.
* Add in retail data from each shot
* Send copies to Barb and Joe
* Add my analysis of the week's sales

10/15/2009 8:29 PM

As you discover in Book VI, Chapter 4, you can do some pretty cool things with notes, such as:

✦ **Categorize them.** Group notes about the same project, client, or meeting together.

✦ **Put them on the Desktop.** That way, you can't lose or forget them.

✦ **Resize big notes.** Make them easier to read.

Constant note-takers might appreciate OneNote, an accessory program that comes with Office. OneNote allows you to create entire notebooks of notes, complete with drawings, images, charts, and even audio or video. You can link the notes that you take in OneNote to items in Outlook, such as client meetings, company seminars, important contacts, or tasks. See Book VI, Chapter 5 for help.

Learning the Quick Step

Ever wanted your own personal assistant? Wouldn't it feel good every once in a while to leave the dishes in the sink, drop your bath towel on the floor, and not work on the big presentation for that overbearing, boring client because you know that you have someone you can pawn it off on? And wouldn't it be really great to leave your e-mail in your Inbox and have someone else take over the responsibility of organizing it? Well, it doesn't do the dishes or the laundry, but Quick Steps do help you make quick work out of managing your incoming e-mail.

A *Quick Step* is a set of preprogrammed actions that Outlook can perform on a selected e-mail, with just the touch of a button! Outlook provides you with a set of common Quick Steps to start out with, which you can customize however you like. For example, Outlook gives you a Move To Quick Step, which you can customize so that it quickly moves e-mails into a chosen folder. You can also create your own from-scratch Quick Steps. To use one of the provided Quick Steps, follow these steps:

1. **Select one or more e-mails.**

   By select, I mean click. To select more than one e-mail, hold down Ctrl while you click. Grab a consecutive group of e-mails by clicking the first one, holding down Shift, and clicking the last one in the group.

2. **Select a Quick Step.**

   Click the Home tab, and then click any Quick Step, such as To Manager. Quick Steps appear around the middle of the Home tab, all grouped together. You may have to scroll through the list or click the More button to find the one that you want. If you selected multiple e-mails, you can click only Quick Steps that can be applied to a group.

If you've used one of the preset Quick Steps, you can create a similar one by clicking the More button in the Quick Steps group, selecting New Quick Step from the palette that appears, then selecting one of the Quick Step types (such as Forward To) from the pop-up menu. If you want to create a Quick Step completely from scratch, see the section "Creating baby Quick Steps," later in this chapter.

3. Provide the necessary info.

Most of the Quick Steps, by default, require you to supply some information (such as the name of the folder to which you want the e-mails moved) before they can work. (See Figure 2-9.) After this initial use, however, this Quick Step performs its duty without any further input from you.

In this example, I need to supply the e-mail address of my manager. I can click the To button and select a name from my Contacts list. Or I can type an address in the box and click the Check Names button to the right of that box to check what I typed against my Contacts list.

You don't have to take one of the provided Quick Steps at face value; you can tweak them all you want, either now (by clicking Options) or later. See the following section for help.

4. Click Save.

After you provide whatever info the Quick Step needs, click Save to save it.

5. Rinse and repeat.

Bet you expected something to happen just then, such as Outlook forwarding the selected email to my boss. I expected something to happen too, initially, but I got over it. After configuring a Quick Step, nothing actually happens except that it's added to the Quick Step list. At that point, you can use it any time by clicking its button. So, in this example, if I leave that e-mail selected, I just have to click the button to forward the e-mail as desired — voila!

Figure 2-9:
For most Quick Steps, you have to supply a bit of information before they can work.

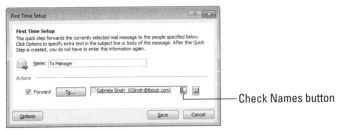

Changing your Quick Step

Nobody says that the Quick Steps you get from Outlook right out of the box are going to fit your working style like a glove. You're free to tinker with them as much as you like until they work the way you want them to. Just follow these steps:

1. **Click the More button on the Home tab and select Manage Quick Steps from the palette that appears.**

   The Manage Quick Steps dialog box appears, as shown in Figure 2-10. Before you move onto Step 2, however, let me point out what else this little box does:

   - You can rearrange the order in which a Quick Step appears in the Home tab list by selecting it from those listed on the left and clicking the up/down arrow keys. It may seem like a minor thing, but you want the Quick Steps you use most often at the top of this list so that you don't have to keep digging for them on the Home tab.

   - If you want to create a new Quick Step that's similar to an existing one, select that Quick Step and click Duplicate. Make any changes and click Finish to create the twin.

   - If it ain't workin', why stress out about it? Just remove the unwanted Quick Step by selecting it and clicking the Delete button.

   - You can also create a brand-new Quick Step from the Manage Quick Steps dialog box by clicking the New button. I talk about the how-to's for creating a new Quick Step in the following section.

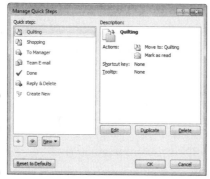

Figure 2-10:
Take charge
of your
Quick Steps.

2. **Select a Quick Step and click Modify.**

Okay, so we took a little side trip there down Manage Quick Steps Lane. Now it's back to Modify Street. Select a Quick Step from those listed on the left side of the dialog box, and click the Modify button. The Edit Quick Step dialog box appears; see Figure 2-11.

Figure 2-11: Choose the options for your Quick Step.

3. **Select the options that you want.**

A list of actions associated with the Quick Step you've chosen appear in the Edit Quick Step dialog box; you can do any of the following:

- To change any one of the actions, make a different selection from the drop-down list. You can also change the specifics associated with that action, such as which folder or e-mail address to use.

- If you see a Show Options link, click it to show additional options for that action. For example, when forwarding an e-mail, you can specify not only the person to forward to, but also the subject, e-mail flag, importance level, and default message text.

- Add a new action to the mix by clicking the Add Action button. Select an action from the list box that appears and set that action's options, as desired.

- Set a shortcut key for this Quick Step to eliminate the messy business of locating the Quick Step on the Home tab when you want to use it. Instead, you can just select an e-mail, laugh wholeheartedly at all the silly people who waste time searching for Quick Steps, and press your custom-made shortcut key. Just open the Shortcut Key list at the bottom of the dialog box and select the shortcut that you want to use to sic this Quick Step on the selected e-mail(s).

- If you create tons of Quick Steps (as you're likely to do), you might want to modify the text that appears when you hover the mouse pointer over each Quick Step's button on the Home tab — the Tooltip text. To do that, select the text in the Tooltip Text box and make any changes you want.

4. **Click Save.**

   Click Save to save your changes and return to the Manage Quick Steps dialog box. Repeat this whole process with a different Quick Step if you want, or just click OK to indicate that you're done.

If you create a Move To–type Quick Step, you can use it to jump right to that folder. Just right-click any of these moving Quick Steps and select Go to *Folder Name* from the pop-up menu that appears. You can also hold down Ctrl and click a particular Move To Quick Step to jump right to that folder.

Creating baby Quick Steps

I can pretty much bet that after you start using the provided Quick Steps, you'll start thinking, "I wonder what else these little things can do?" Follow these steps to create a custom Quick Step:

1. **Start the custom Quick Step.**

   You can create a custom Quick Step in several ways. If the Manage Quick Steps dialog box is already open (refer to Figure 2-10), you can click the New button and select Custom from the list that appears.

   If not, you can click the More button in the Quick Steps group on the Home tab, select New Quick Step from the palette that appears, then select Custom. The Edit Quick Step dialog box appears, as shown in Figure 2-11.

2. **Type a name for the new Quick Step.**

   Select the text in the Name box and replace it with the name that you want to give this new Quick Step.

3. **Select the first action that you want the Quick Step to perform.**

   Open the Choose an Action list and select the first action that you want performed. Set the options associated with the action. For example, you might have to select the folder, e-mail address, or category to use.

4. **Add more actions.**

   Click the Add Action button. Select an action from the list box that appears and set that action's options, as desired. Repeat this process to add more actions, as needed, until you get that Quick Step doing exactly what you want it to.

5. **Set a shortcut key to initiate the Quick Step.**

Wanna use the Quick Step without having to visit the Ribbon? Just assign a shortcut key by selecting one from the Shortcut Key list, and you can use that shortcut later to start the Quick Step. Look, Ma, no hands!

6. **Describe the Quick Step's purpose.**

   Enter the text in the Tooltip Text box that you want to appear when you hover the mouse pointer over this Quick Step's button on the Home tab.

7. **Click Finish.**

   The new Quick Step appears in the Quick Step list on the Ribbon.

Dragging and Dropping, and How It Saved My Life

Before drag-and-drop, I used to climb mountains of commands, clicking away until finally I got something done. Now, frankly, whenever I'm working in a program, I try dragging and dropping all sorts of things just to see what happens. And in a Microsoft program such as Outlook, you may discover a handy shortcut to a common task.

Understanding how drag-and-drop works

If you're perhaps a bit new to dragging and dropping, follow these steps to make it happen:

1. **Select something that you want to do something with.**

   To select something, you typically click it. For example, you can click a contact in your Contacts list.

2. **Drag that sucker somewhere.**

   To drag, you click and hold the mouse button down while you move the mouse somewhere. For example, you can click a contact and hold the mouse button down while you drag that puppy over to the Mail button on the Navigation pane.

3. **Drop it and see what happens.**

   To drop, you simply release the mouse button that you've been holding down. For example, after you drag the contact over to the Mail button, you can drop it right there by simply letting go of the mouse button. Next, just pop a cold one and watch what happens as a result of your little drag-and-drop experiment. In this case, Outlook instantly creates a new mail message, already addressed to the contact you chose. Pretty cool, eh?

To quickly send the same message to a bunch of people, just select all those folks in the Contact list (by holding down Ctrl and clicking each one), and then drag the whole kit and caboodle to the Mail button and let go. Poof! Up pops an e-mail addressed to all the contacts you selected.

Now that you have related commands so perfectly organized on the Ribbon, you don't need to do some of this drag-and-drop stuff. To continue the example, I can now select a contact and click the E-Mail button on the Home tab to create a message to that person, instead of dragging and dropping. Even so, Microsoft apparently can't read my mind, and so they don't provide buttons for all the things that I want to accomplish by dragging and dropping, so I'm betting that you'll also find these techniques useful.

Creating Outlook items with drag-and-drop

The following sections show you some of the ways that you can drag and drop to save time when you create messages, appointments, and the like.

If you don't want to create a new Outlook item by using another as its basis, but you want to link two similar Outlook items (such as a contact name and a task), you might want to use OneNote instead. OneNote can gather a lot of separate parts — text, drawings, charts, and various Outlook items — into a single container called a *notebook.* By using OneNote, for example, you might create a notebook for each project or special client, and keep related information in the notebook. See Book VI, Chapter 5 for help on working with OneNote.

Messages

To create a message by using drag-and-drop, use one of these methods:

✦ **Drag a contact name onto the Mail button.** Been there, done that, as described in the section "Understanding how drag-and-drop works," earlier in this chapter.

✦ **Drag an appointment onto the Mail button.** Essentially, this action forwards the appointment details to someone else. But if you want to invite someone to a meeting, you can find a better way than using drag and drop in Book IV, Chapter 4.

✦ **Drag a task onto the Mail button.** If you want to send a short status report to a supervisor, you can use this approach. But if you're looking to reassign the task, you can do that and continue to track its progress by performing other steps. See Book VI, Chapter 3.

✦ **Drag a note onto the Mail button.** This action forwards a note to someone else.

Appointments

To create an appointment with drag-and-drop, use one of these techniques:

✦ **Drag a message onto the Calendar button.** The text of the message is copied to the Notes area of the appointment, so you can refer to it as needed, as shown in Figure 2-12. This trick is especially useful if the message has the appointment details or other details about the person you need to remember, such as his or her address and phone number.

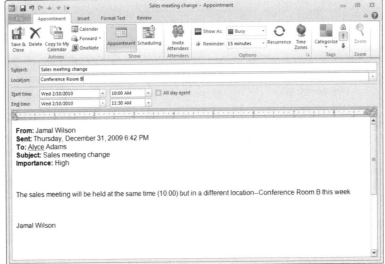

Figure 2-12:
Use a message to create an appointment.

✦ **Drag a contact onto the Calendar button.** This actually creates a meeting and not an appointment, which means that Outlook sends an e-mail message that invites the contact to the meeting. If you want to create an appointment instead, you can: It turns out that Outlook was only "suggesting" that you set up a meeting. Click the Cancel Invitation button on the Meeting tab to turn off the suggestion and change the item into an appointment.

If you're setting up an appointment or meeting with multiple people, you can start by selecting the multiple contacts you want to invite to the meeting (by holding down Ctrl and clicking each name), and then dragging the motley crew over to the Calendar button.

TIP

If you want to create an appointment and copy a contact's information into the Notes area of the appointment, *right-drag* (drag while holding down the right mouse button) the contact onto the Calendar. From the menu that appears, select Copy Here as Appointment with Text. By using the other commands on this menu, you can copy a shortcut to the contact information (so that you can quickly display it from the Appointment window by double-clicking the shortcut) or add the contact information as an attachment to the Appointment form.

✦ **Drag a task onto the Calendar button.** This procedure seems backward to me because I typically create an appointment first, and doing *that* creates a thousand things to do. But if you start out with a task, such as Project Status Report, and then finally schedule a time to meet with a client to go over that report, you can use this handy way to add the appointment to your Calendar. The details of the task are copied to the Notes area of the appointment.

✦ **Drag a note onto the Calendar button.** I don't use this action much, but if you jot down some key ideas for a product launch in a note, you can use the note to create the appointment for the launch meeting.

Contacts

To create a contact by using drag-and-drop, use one of these methods:

✦ **Drag a message onto the Contacts button.** This takes the contact's e-mail address right out of the message for you. If the message contains other contact information, such as a phone number or address, you can refer to it without switching between the Contacts form and the message window.

✦ **Drag an appointment or meeting onto the Contacts button.** This action has a strange outcome. If you drag an appointment, you end up being the new contact, but if you type contact details (such as address and phone number) into the Notes area of the appointment when you create it, you can use this technique to create a new contact. If you drag a meeting, then you create a new contact for the person who sent the meeting request.

✦ **Drag a task or a note onto the Contacts button.** The details of the task or note are copied into the Notes area of the Contact form. You may find using a note to create a contact useful when you have a note that pertains to a new contact. However, you probably don't want to use a task this way because the Contact is created by using the owner of the task, which is typically you. But if someone who's not already in the Contacts list assigns you a task, you can drag and drop the task to get his or her name in your Contacts list fast.

As useful as dragging and dropping is, *right-dragging* (dragging while holding down the right mouse button, rather than the left) provides a bit more control over the result. When you drag and drop something, such as an appointment, onto a button on the Navigation pane, the details of that something (the appointment) are copied into the Notes area of the new item that's created. When you right-drag, a menu of choices appears; instead of copying the text of the item you dropped, you can create a shortcut to the item or add it as an attachment, leaving the Notes area of the new item free for additional notes.

Tasks

To create tasks by using drag-and-drop, use one of the following methods:

✦ **Drag a message onto the Tasks button.** The message text appears in the Notes area of the task. You can use this approach when a message contains a lot of information related to the thing you need to do.

✦ **Drag an appointment onto the Tasks button.** Use this handy trick if you have to get several things done prior to the appointment because the details of the appointment appear in the Notes area of the task.

✦ **Drag a contact name onto the Tasks button.** Do this only if you're trying to reassign a task to someone else. See Book VI, Chapter 4 for the scoop on reassigning tasks. If you want to associate a task with a client, use the Business Contact Manager (discussed in Book VII, Chapter 2).

✦ **Drag a note onto the Tasks button.** Use this trick to quickly copy a note into a task so that you can refer to it while you work on the task. Keep in mind that the Task form includes a Notes area, so you can create a task first and add notes while you go along.

Notes

To create a note by using drag-and-drop, use one of these methods:

✦ **Drag a message onto the Notes button.** The text of the message is copied into the Notes form, where you can make your own additions.

✦ **Drag an appointment onto the Notes button.** I typically use OneNote to link Outlook items such as appointments to notes, but you might use this approach if the appointment contains notes that you refer to often or you want to save the details of the appointment in a note for some reason.

✦ **Drag a contact name onto the Notes button.** Copies all contact information into the note, where you can add more information.

✦ **Drag a task onto the Notes button.** Copies task details into the note, where you can add your own comments or notes about a task. This option seems pretty silly to me because the Tasks form has a place for taking notes.

Reorganizing Outlook items with drag-and-drop

You can use drag-and-drop techniques for other things besides creating Outlook items. I mean, after you create all those items, you have to deal with them, and what better way than by dragging and dropping?

Here are some things you might want to try:

✦ **Delete old items.** Use this technique to get rid of old tasks or contacts that you'll never need again. Drop them onto the Deleted Items folder. See the section "Creating Outlook Items: The Common Factors," earlier in this chapter, for more info on how to remove unwanted items from Outlook.

✦ **Shuffle appointments from one day to the next.** Drop them on the appropriate day on the Date Navigator.

✦ **Rearrange the order of tasks for any given day.** Drag and drop them where you want them in the list. If you drag and drop a task into a group of tasks that you've set for another day, you change the due date for that task, as well.

Chapter 3: Setting Up Your E-Mail Accounts

In This Chapter

✔ **Understanding the various types of e-mail accounts**

✔ **Automating the e-mail setup process**

✔ **Configuring e-mail manually**

✔ **Setting up an e-mail connection**

Some people are content to use Outlook as a fancy address book and calendar, but most folks rely on Outlook as their e-mail handler. If you're lucky enough to have a full-time IT person on staff at work — or a geeky friend who's easily bribed with chocolate chip cookies — you may not have to read this chapter, which is about setting up your e-mail account(s). Also, if you upgraded from a previous version of Outlook, everything is probably running smoothly. If you're forced to wear that IT hat, however — or are a lousy cookie baker — you can use this chapter to help get your e-mail up and running, as needed.

This chapter covers the various types of e-mail accounts and shows you how to coax Outlook into setting them up automatically. After you're up and running, you need to know how you can change your settings or add new ones. Finally, you can see how to change the type of connection you're using to access the Internet.

Understanding the E-Mail Process

Just in case you didn't know, the *e* in e-mail stands for electronic. It's no coincidence that e-mail includes the word *mail* — e-mail and its more traditional counterpoint share a lot of similarities. Understanding these similarities helps you better grasp the overall concept of e-mail. As simple as the process of mailing a letter is, you must still take several steps in order to ensure its success. First, you must properly address the letter or package, then take it to a qualified mail service provider, who charges you a fee for processing and sending the letter (or package) on its way. At some point, your letter arrives at a different mail service provider, who delivers the letter to its intended recipient based on the address that you provided. In almost all cases, however, the recipient must remember to go out to his or her mailbox and pick up the mail to actually receive the letter.

E-mail works in a remarkably similar way: You choose an e-mail provider and address your message, and that provider routes the message to the proper e-mail server for the recipient. The recipient has to start his or her e-mail program and go through what's called a sending/receiving process to receive e-mail from the server, then open the message and read it.

Obtaining an e-mail account

The first thing you need for e-mail is an e-mail account. Outlook doesn't create or issue e-mail accounts; it merely provides you with a way to use one. You can get an e-mail account from your Internet service provider (service provider), your employer, an online service (such as AOL), or from an HTML e-mail service (such as Yahoo! Mail, Google's Gmail, and Windows Live Mail). You generally must pay for e-mail service with cold, hard cash or put up with annoying advertising that appears while you use a free e-mail program.

When you obtain an e-mail account, you receive a username and password. If you forget them, you need to contact your e-mail provider for this informa-tion; even the savviest of Outlook gurus can't get this information for you. You probably also received setup instructions that include cryptic words such as POP3 or SMTP, but don't worry — I decipher those terms in the following section.

Don't discard your e-mail setup instructions because they provide the info you need to plug into Outlook to get it to work — and you need this info again if you ever have to reconfigure Outlook (such as when you buy a new computer). By using your setup instructions, instead of waiting for other people to help solve problems with your account, you can take a shot at solving the issues yourself. If that fails, then you can suffer through automated telephone services and wait times.

Knowing the e-mail flavors

Most things that you purchase — from ice cream to ovens — come with a variety of flavors and options. E-mail accounts are no different. Although e-mail service providers typically offer only one type of e-mail account, armed with the info in this list, you can at least have a basic understanding of what you're getting and why your e-mail works the way it does:

✦ **POP3:** Post Office Protocol 3 (POP3) is the most common e-mail account type on the Internet. A POP3 account works just like traditional mail. Your e-mail messages arrive at the mail server (post office) and then are downloaded to your computer (mailbox). In general, after you receive your mail, it's no longer available on the mail server — just like copies of your letters aren't available at the post office after they're delivered to you.

POP3 accounts have one disadvantage, which is that e-mail generally gets deleted from the server after you receive it. If you check your e-mail on several different computers however, you may prefer to have your e-mail stick around a bit on the server so that you can receive it in more than one place. In the section "Configuring your e-mail account manually," later in this chapter, I show you how to do just that.

✦ **IMAP:** With an Internet Message Access Protocol (IMAP) account, you can store and process mail and optionally download it to the computer you're working on (or just leave it on the server). You're also somewhat safer from viruses with an IMAP account because you can view the *headers* (the sender and subject) of your e-mail messages before you download them. However, not all IMAP accounts work with software designed to manage business e-mail such as Outlook, and thus IMAP accounts have fallen out of favor.

✦ **Microsoft Exchange:** You commonly find this type of account in a medium-size or large business environment. E-mail is stored on the Exchange server, not downloaded to each employee's computer. This setup allows a business to process e-mail for viruses, phishing attempts, suspect attachments, and the like. It also allows the business to control how much e-mail each employee can retain by limiting each user's e-mail folder on the server.

The server provides an employee Contacts list, enabling you to bug your teammates with endless messages right away. Because everyone's calendar is also on the server, you can easily schedule meaningless meetings that eat up your company's resources (meeting rooms, media equipment, and so on) — which are often included in the company's Contacts list, so you can schedule these resources just like people. Because all this stuff stays on the server, you can access your Outlook info from any computer (assuming your company gives you permission to do that) without fear of missing some e-mail you looked at previously.

✦ **HTTP:** These accounts use a Web protocol to view and send e-mail. HTTP (Hypertext Transfer Protocol) accounts include services such as Windows Live Mail, Gmail, Yahoo! Mail, and AIM Mail. Although you should be able to use most HTTP accounts with Outlook (because they often provide POP and IMAP access to the HTML account), certain providers require you to install an add-on first.

In general, your ISP provides you with one or more e-mail accounts, typically POP3. You may have several free e-mail addresses as well (such as Windows Live Mail and Gmail) that use HTTP, but provide alternative access to Outlook through POP3 or IMAP. In addition, you may have an Exchange e-mail account at work that you want to access. In this chapter, you learn how to setup Outlook for all of these different types of e-mail accounts.

Configuring Your E-Mail Accounts

In order to send and receive e-mail messages by using Outlook, you need to add your e-mail account information to it. For most accounts, Outlook can automatically detect and configure the account with a name, e-mail address, and password. Alternatively, your Internet service provider (ISP) or other e-mail service provider (such as a free HTML service) can provide you with configuration information if you need to manually set up your e-mail account in Outlook.

If you're trying to set up an Exchange account on your home computer, you probably don't have to do anything beyond logging into the company network. After you log in, Windows most likely detects the Exchange server and asks you whether you want to set up this e-mail account, after which you can pop a cold one and just watch because the process is basically automatic.

When you run Outlook for the first time, it automatically creates an Outlook profile. A profile tells Outlook what e-mail accounts you use and the username, e-mail server name, and password for each account. Each profile is like a separate Outlook program, with the e-mail, contacts, tasks, and calendar associated with that profile. Typically, you need only one Outlook profile. But if more than one person uses the same computer (or if you want to completely separate work mail, contacts, tasks, and so on from your personal stuff), you might want to create a separate Outlook profile. Then, when you start Outlook, you choose the profile you want to work with. To create a profile, exit Outlook, choose Start⇨Control Panel⇨Mail, and then select Show Profiles in the Mail Setup dialog box that appears. Click Add to add a new profile, type a name for the profile, and click OK. You can choose a default profile or arrange for a prompt to always ask you which profile to use when starting Outlook.

Having Outlook do the heavy lifting

Often, Outlook has both easy and hard ways to accomplish the same goal. And, if you're like I am, you opt for the easiest method whenever possible. Follow these steps to let Outlook automatically detect your e-mail account setting (to set up an Exchange account, see the following section):

1. **Click the File tab to display Backstage and then select Info from the list on the left.**

   The Account Information options appear on the right.

2. **Click the Add Account button, located at the top of the window on the right.**

   The Add New Account wizard, shown in Figure 3-1, appears.

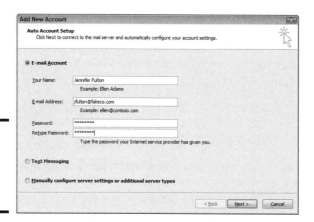

Figure 3-1:
The Add
New
Account
wizard.

3. **Select the account type.**

   You can choose to set up an e-mail account or a text-message account. Select the E-mail Account radio button. (You can find out about text-message accounts in Book X, Chapter 2.) You can also choose to do everything manually, which we discuss in the following section.

   The Text Messaging option isn't an e-mail type, it's a service that allows you to send (and receive) text messages from within Outlook. The service can also send reminders for meetings/appointments from Outlook to your cell phone so that you don't forget them, even if you're out of the office. You can get the lowdown on this type of service in Book III, Chapter 2.

4. **Fill in your basic e-mail information in the text boxes.**

   You need to provide three tidbits of information:

   - **Your Name:** As you want it to appear to all your recipients. Hopefully, you know what to enter in this text box without prompting of any sort.

   - **An e-mail address:** Provided to you by your service provider.

   - **A password:** Provided to you by your service provider. Just for good measure, you need to type it twice.

5. **Click Next.**

   Hold your breath while Outlook tries to connect to your e-mail account. To make the time go faster, you can look at the search screen that appears.

6. **Do a congratulatory dance if you receive a message telling you that your e-mail account is now set up.**

Curse up a storm if you receive the message shown in Figure 3-2. After you calm down, read the following section to figure out how to configure this account manually. Sometimes, try as it might, Outlook can't detect your settings, which can happen for a number of reasons:

- Your service provider uses special encryption.

- You're using an HTML e-mail account that requires an add-on to work with Outlook (or it simply doesn't work with Outlook at all).

- You typed your e-mail address or password incorrectly.

7. **If the setup didn't work and you want Outlook to try again without changing anything, click Next.**

   If you think you typed something wrong, click Back, verify what you typed, and click Next to try again. Otherwise, click Back, and check out the following section for help in resolving this problem before you click Next.

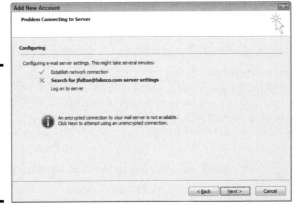

Figure 3-2:
Cause for annoyance: Outlook couldn't detect your e-mail settings.

Configuring your e-mail account manually

If Outlook can't configure your e-mail account for you, you just have to bite the bullet and do it yourself. Follow these steps:

1. **Open the Add New Account wizard (refer to Figure 3-1).**

   You can get there by doing one of the following:

   - Click the Back button when Outlook prompts you that it can't configure your e-mail account automatically.

   - Click the File tab to display Backstage, select Info from the list on the left, then click the Add Account button on the right.

If you want to set up an Exchange account, you have to close down Outlook first, then start the setup program by choosing Start–>Control Panel➪Mail, selecting E-mail Accounts in the Mail Setup dialog box that appears, and then clicking the New button in the Account Settings dialog box to display the Add New Account wizard. (Again, refer to Figure 3-1.) In Outlook 2010, by the way, you can now add multiple Exchange accounts to a single profile, so don't go thinking you need to create another Outlook profile to manage your extra Exchange e-mail account.

2. **Fill in your name, e-mail address, and password in the text boxes.**

   If you already filled in this information when you tried to have Outlook automatically configure your e-mail account, then your information is already sitting there waiting for you.

3. **Select the Manually Configure Server Settings or Additional Server Types option and click Next.**

   The Choose Service screen appears.

4. **Select Internet E-Mail, and then click Next.**

   You can't select Microsoft Exchange; to add a Microsoft Exchange account, you must first exit Outlook (as described in the preceding section). For help setting up a text-messaging account, see Book X, Chapter 2.

5. **Fill in your vital statistics on the screen that appears, shown in Figure 3-3.**

   You need all that confusing information about POP, SMTP, and passwords that your service provider gave you, which you (I hope) wrote down legibly and stored in a safe spot. If you didn't save this information, you have to contact your service provider to get it. Here's a brief description of each field:

   - **User Information:** Fill in your name and e-mail address.

   - **Server Information:** Select your account type and fill in your incoming (POP3) and outgoing (SMTP) information for your service provider.

   - **Logon information:** Fill in your e-mail username and password. Your username is generally the portion of your e-mail address that comes before the @ sign.

   - **Remember password:** If you're working in a reasonably safe, spy-free environment, check this option so that you don't have to reenter your password each and every time you want to send or receive e-mail.

You can use the Deliver New Messages To option to store your e-mail for this account in a new data file. This option provides you with another way to keep your e-mail organized, kind of like storing special computer files on a separate hard disk. You might, for example, create a new data file while adding your work account to Outlook. You can open both data files in Outlook and set up separate folders within each; you can also close a data file when you don't want to view its contents, which doesn't prevent Outlook from receiving e-mail for that account and saving the e-mail in that data file.

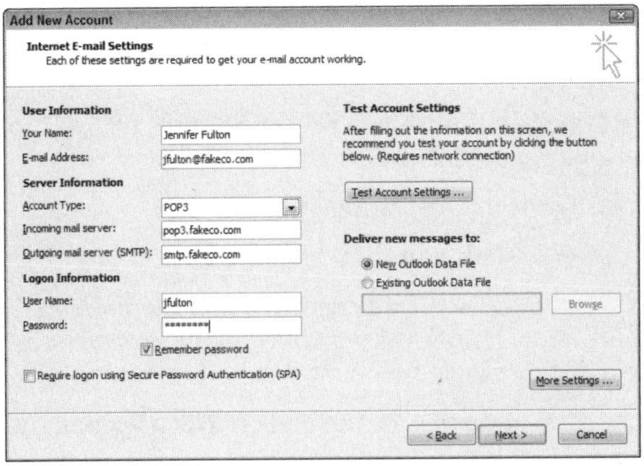

Figure 3-3:
Configuring
your e-mail
account.

6. **Click More Settings to open the Internet E-Mail Settings dialog box (see Figure 3-4), where you can enter advanced account settings.**

   Typically, your service provider lets you know if you have any other settings that you need to enter for your account. Make your selections in these tabs:

   - **General:** Change the name of the e-mail account so that you can more easily identify it. You can also list your organization name and a different e-mail address if you want Outlook to send all replies for this account to that address, rather than the e-mail address you enter in Step 2.

   - **Outgoing Server:** Typically, a service provider requires some way to make sure that it's you getting your e-mail; on this tab, you might set additional safeguards, such as the use of Secure Password Authentication (SPA).

   - **Connection:** If you're on a network, Outlook assumes that you want it to use the network connection to get your mail. If you need it to dial up instead, you can indicate that fact on this tab.

- **Advanced:** Your mail server may want Outlook to connect to it through a different port than the normal 110 for incoming and 26 for outgoing e-mail. Just type whatever port number your service provider provides you into the appropriate box.

On the Advanced tab, you can tell Outlook to leave your e-mail on the server after it downloads that e-mail. Doing so allows you to retrieve the same messages on another computer until a specified time has passed or you manually delete the messages yourself.

Figure 3-4:
Your service
provider
doesn't
require most
of these
settings.

7. **Click OK.**

   You return to the Internet E-mail Settings page of the Add New Account wizard (refer to Figure 3-3).

8. **(Optional) Click the Test Account Settings button to open the Test Account Settings dialog box.**

   It's always nice to make sure that things work now, instead of finding out later they don't. As soon as you click the Test Account Settings button, Outlook sends a test message to you and makes sure that you can receive it. The Test Account Settings dialog box displays the progress of all this testing stuff. If all systems are go, Outlook gives you a high five. For additional excitement, you can race over to your Inbox and read the test message that Microsoft sent you.

9. **After all the testing is done, click Close to exit the Test Account Settings dialog box, and then click Next in the Add New Account wizard to advance your way to the last page.**

   A very large congratulatory message opens. Outlook realizes the importance of positive feedback — particularly if it initially let you down when you tried to configure your e-mail account automatically.

10. **Click Finish to close the congratulatory message.**

Maintaining Your E-Mail Accounts

After you create your e-mail account(s), you can sit back and let the good times roll — or, at least, let the e-mail roll in. You probably seldom (if ever) have to make changes to your e-mail account. However, like with the best laid plans of mice and IT people, things do go wrong, and so you have to be ready to don your red cape and pocket protector at a moment's notice.

Fixing a lost password

The trouble with most passwords is that they're so darn picky. Unlike in horseshoes, close doesn't count — passwords have to be letter-perfect when you use them. Passwords are often case-sensitive, so capital letters have to appear in the correct spot.

You may start to see the message in Figure 3-5 often.

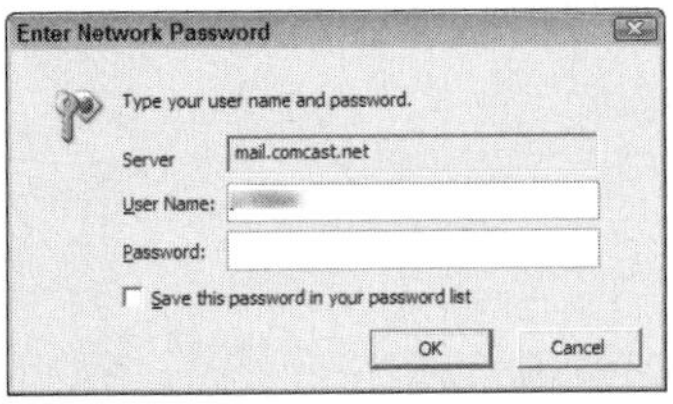

Figure 3-5:
A really annoying Outlook message.

You may see that message continuously pop up for a number of reasons:

✦ You entered an incorrect password — or left the password blank — when you set up your e-mail account.

✦ You failed to check the Remember Password check box when you set up your e-mail account.

✦ You forgot your password and your service provider has assigned you a new password to replace the old one.

Even more annoying than the message in Figure 3-5, the one shown in Figure 3-6, which tells you that Outlook is having trouble sending and/or receiving your e-mail.

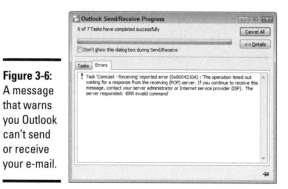

Figure 3-6:
A message
that warns
you Outlook
can't send
or receive
your e-mail.

At this point, you reenter your password into Outlook (so it will hopefully
remember it and stop bugging you) by following these steps:

1. **Click the File tab to display Backstage and then select Info from the
   list on the left.**

   The Account Information options appear on the right.

2. **Click the Account Settings button on the right, then select Account
   Settings from pop-up menu that appears.**

   The Account Settings dialog box, shown in the background in Figure 3-7,
   appears.

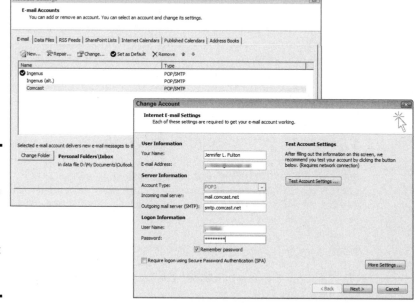

Figure 3-7:
Make
adjustments
to an
existing
account in
the Account
Settings
dialog box.

3. **Select the e-mail account that you want to change, and then click the Change button.**

   The Change Account wizard opens. (See the foreground in Figure 3-7.)

4. **Type your password in the Password text box in the Logon Information area.**

5. **Select the Remember Password check box.**

6. **Click Next.**

   The final page of the wizard appears.

7. **Click Finish to close the Change Account wizard.**

8. **In the Account Settings dialog box, click Close.**

Setting the default account

One of your e-mail accounts acts as the default for Outlook. It's not like it can stroll in and get a table ahead of the other accounts, but Outlook does treat it as the leader. Outlook uses the default account when you send e-mail, which means that replies to those e-mails automatically return to that default account. Now, you can easily select a different account that you want to use with a single e-mail just prior to sending it, but unless you feel like doing that all the time, set your default account to the one you use the most.

If you set up multiple e-mail accounts and aren't sure which one is the default, return to the Account Settings dialog box by clicking the File tab to display Backstage, selecting Info from the list on the left, clicking the Account Settings button on the right, and selecting Account Settings from the pop-up menu that appears. After all this selecting, the Account Settings dialog box appears. (Refer to the background in Figure 3-7.) One of the e-mail accounts is flagged with a checkmark icon, which indicates that the account is the currently designated default. If you want to change which account is the default, select the account from those listed in the Account Settings dialog box, and then click the Set as Default button.

Changing your account information

Once in a while, the mail server that you connect to in order to receive and send e-mail might change. For example, the cable company in your area may change from Adelphia to Comcast. Or you might receive a notice from your service provider telling you that they've upgraded their servers and your POP3 has changed from `mail.isp.com` to `incoming.isp.com`.

Follow these steps to change your account information:

1. **Click the File tab to display Backstage and then select Info from the list on the left.**

   The Account Information options appear on the right.

2. **Click the Account Settings button on the right, then select Account Settings from the pop-up menu that appears.**

   The Account Settings dialog box appears. (Refer to the background in Figure 3-7.)

3. **Select the e-mail account that you want to change and click Change.**

   The Change Account wizard appears. (Refer to the foreground in Figure 3-7.)

4. **In the Server Information section, enter the complete name of the incoming server provided by your service provider in the Incoming Mail Server text box.**

5. **Enter the complete name of the outgoing server provided by your service provider in the Outgoing Mail Server (SMTP) text box.**

   The incoming server address controls the way in which you receive e-mail. Conversely, the outgoing server controls the way you send your e-mail. Theoretically, your service provider supplies both server addresses. However, the outgoing server may come from a different source. If you're traveling, for example, you may need to connect to a different network than the one you normally use. If so, you may be able to receive new mail, but none of your outgoing messages leave your Outbox.

   If your service provider has made changes to your mail server address, it may have changed your e-mail address, as well. If so, you can make the appropriate change in the wizard.

6. **Click Next.**

   The final page of the wizard appears.

7. **Click Finish to close the Change Account wizard.**

8. **Click Close in the Account Settings dialog box.**

Changing your connection type

You can connect to the Internet in two ways: through a network connection or through a phone line. When you first purchased your computer, you were probably prompted to reveal the type of Internet connection you have. However, if you're having trouble connecting to the Internet — or you change the type of connection that you have — you need to pass that information along to Outlook. Follow these steps:

1. **Click the File tab to display Backstage and then select Info from the list on the left.**

   The Account Information options appear on the right.

2. **Click the Account Settings button on the right, and select Account Settings from the pop-up menu that appears.**

The Account Settings dialog box appears. (Refer to the background in Figure 3-7.)

3. Select the e-mail account that you want to change and click Change.

The Change Account wizard appears. (Refer to the foreground in Figure 3-7.)

4. Click More Settings.

The Internet E-mail Settings dialog box appears.

5. Click the Connection tab.

Your Connection options spring into view, as shown in Figure 3-8.

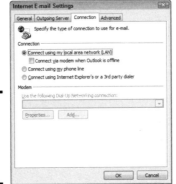

Figure 3-8:
Changing
Outlook's
connection
type.

6. Select the correct Connection option.

You have three connection options to choose from:

- **Connect Using My Local Area Network (LAN):** Use this option if you get your Internet connectivity courtesy of a network. (If you connect to the Internet using a DSL/cable modem, then this is typically the option you want to select.) Optionally, you can select the Connect Via Modem When Outlook Is Offline check box if you want to use a dialup connection when you're not connected to your network.

- **Connect Using My Phone Line:** This option is for instances when you're dialing into the Internet through your telephone line. After selecting this option, click Add, select a dialup type from the Set Up a New Connection wizard, then enter the information provided to you by your service provider when prompted by the wizard.

- **Connect Using Internet Explorer's or a 3rd Party Dialer:** Select this option if you want to use the dialer that pops up when your dial-up connection (phone line) is not yet initiated, and you want to use Internet Explorer or another Web browser to handle the dial-up connection to the Internet for you, even reconnecting automatically if the connection is broken).

7. **Click OK to close the Internet E-Mail Settings dialog box.**

8. **Click Next in the Change Account wizard.**

   The last page of the wizard appears.

9. Click Finish in the Change Account wizard to save your changes.

10. **Click Close in the Account Settings dialog box.**

Chapter 4: Importing Data into Outlook

In This Chapter

✓ Importing old e-mails from other e-mail programs

✓ Importing other e-mail programs' e-mail account information

✓ Grabbing names and addresses from other e-mail programs

✓ Importing data from other sources

*A*fter you install Microsoft Outlook and set up your e-mail account, you're ready to send and receive e-mail. If you've been using a different e-mail program in the past, though, you may not have set up any e-mail accounts in Outlook yet, in hopes that maybe somehow you can get those accounts out of that lousy e-mail program you've decided never to use again. As it turns out, you may be able to import your e-mail account information from your old e-mail program without a lot of fuss and bother.

But even if you already set up your e-mail accounts in Outlook, you may want to take one more step and import that old e-mail data into Outlook. You might import old messages so that you can still refer to them from time to time, for example. Or you might import your old contact data so that you can avoid having to retype e-mail addresses. You can import e-mail data from a variety of sources, including other popular e-mail programs and database files, such as Access or Excel files.

First, a little background: Outlook Express is an e-mail program that used to come free with Windows, and so it's a pretty popular solution for handling e-mail. Windows Mail is basically Outlook Express from a different planet (Windows Vista). Outlook Express/Windows Mail don't include Calendar, Tasks, Notes, or Journal, or anything even close to all the features and functionality of Outlook — just e-mail and a simplistic Contacts list. So, since Santa has put Outlook 2010 under your tree, you probably want to leave its clunky cousins far behind. Outlook, not too surprisingly, makes the transition from Outlook Express/ Windows Mail fairly painless.

In Windows 7, you don't exactly get a free e-mail program, but you do get a link to Windows Live Mail (also called Windows Live Hotmail, Hotmail, or Windows Live Essentials). Although Windows Live Mail now includes a Web calendar and task keeper, it's still not as feature-rich as Outlook. However, unlike other HTML e-mail accounts, you can *synch* Windows Live Mail with Outlook (display your Live calendars and contacts in Outlook, and update Windows Live with any changes you make) and continue using both, if you like.

Importing E-Mail Data from Outlook's Cousins

When you installed Outlook, it asked you whether you wanted to import data from your old e-mail account, and you probably clicked Yes, Ma'am! (okay, Outlook doesn't actually have a Yes, Ma'am! button — but the Yes button can get the job done). But if you weren't sure at the time whether you wanted to import that stuff until you tried out Outlook and decided it wouldn't bite, you're stuck with a problem: You want that data and hope it's not too late to get it. In this section, you learn how to grab old e-mail messages from Outlook's cousins: Outlook Express, Windows Mail, and Windows Live Mail.

Importing Outlook Express/Windows Mail messages

If Outlook and Outlook Express/Windows Mail are on the same computer, follow these steps to import Outlook Express/Windows Mail e-mail into Outlook:

1. **Click the File tab to display Backstage and then select Open from the list on the left.**

The Open options appear on the right.

2. **Select Import from the options on the right.**

The Import and Export wizard appears, as shown in Figure 4-1.

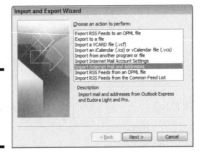

Figure 4-1:
The Import and Export wizard.

3. **Select Import Internet Mail and Addresses, and then click Next.**

   The Outlook Import Tool wizard makes its appearance. (See Figure 4-2.)

Figure 4-2:
Import
Outlook
Express or
Windows
Mail e-mail.

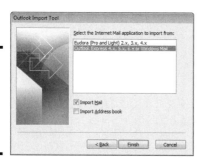

4. **Select the Outlook Express 4.x, 5.x, 6.x or Windows Mail option.**

5. **Select just the Import Mail check box, and then click Finish.**

   You can import contacts at the same time by checking the Import Address Book check box. If you select this additional option, the wizard changes a bit and you have another step to complete. See the section "Importing Contacts," later in this chapter, for help.

   A summary of what was imported and what wasn't appears. Usually Outlook imports everything, but if it had a problem with a particular message, it might not be able to grab it. Typically though, the only thing Outlook won't import is duplicate contacts (again, see the section, "Importing Contacts" for help with that.) If you want to save this summary, click Save in Inbox. Otherwise, just click OK.

Grabbing Outlook Express/Windows Mail account info

E-mail is only one part of Outlook Express/Windows Mail that you might want to transfer to Outlook. Another part is your e-mail account info. After all, who wants to sit there and manually type in POP3 and SMTP addresses? I know I don't.

You can grab your e-mail account stuff out of Outlook Express/Windows Mail if you have Outlook on the same computer as Outlook Express/Windows Mail. Follow these steps:

1. **Click the File tab to display Backstage and then select Open from the list on the left.**

The Open options appear on the right.

2. **Select Import from the options on the right.**

   The Import and Export wizard appears. (Refer to Figure 4-1.)

3. **Select Import Internet Mail Account Settings, and then click Next.**

   The Internet Connection wizard appears. (See Figure 4-3.)

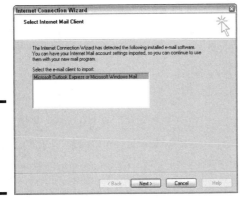

Figure 4-3:
Grab that
e-mail
account
info.

4. **Select the Outlook Express or Microsoft Windows Mail option, and then click Next.**

   Outlook pulls your old account info from Outlook Express/Windows Mail and displays it for you, one page at a time, so that you can verify it and make changes.

5. **Confirm the Display Name (see Figure 4-4), and then click Next.**

   The Display Name is pulled from your old e-mail account. It's the name that shows up in the From field in an e-mails you send, so it should reflect the name you want to be known by. Make any changes you want to the Display Name and click Next.

6. **Confirm your e-mail address and click Next to advance to the next page of the wizard.**

7. **Confirm that the incoming and outgoing mail servers are correct and click Next to advance to the next page of the wizard.**

Figure 4-4:
Verify the
name by
which you
want to be
known.

8. **Confirm your login info. Click Next to advance to the next page of the wizard when you're done.**

   You need to confirm the Account Name (username) and Password that you use to log into your e-mail account. Select the Remember Password option if you don't want to enter that data each time you check mail.

   If you need to use SPA (Secure Password Authentication) with this account (check with your service provider), be sure to select the Log In Using Secure Password Authentication (SPA) option.

9. **Confirm how you connect to the e-mail server, then click Next to advance to the last page of the wizard.**

   You connect either through a modem, by using a network, or over the Internet.

10. **Click Finish.**

    The account information is imported into Outlook. If you want to verify it, click the File tab to display Backstage, select Info from the list on the left, click the Account Settings button on the right, then (you guessed it) select Account Settings from the pop-up menu that appears.

Synching Windows Live Mail with Outlook

If you have a Windows Live Mail account, you can set it up in Outlook and use Outlook to send and receive from that account. (For help in setting up e-mail accounts in Outlook, see Book I, Chapter 3.)

In addition, with the help of a little gizmo called Outlook Connector, you can import your Live Mail contacts and calendars into Outlook and use its tools to organize and manage them. Outlook Connector updates any changes you make in Outlook to your Windows Live Mail account (and vice-versa) so both are always kept in synch. That way, you get the best of both worlds. On one hand, you get access to your appointments, meetings, and contacts from, well, anywhere you can access the Internet. On the other hand, you get to take advantage of Outlook's stream-lined features and sophisticated tools to make fast work of any e-mails you need to send or contacts/appointments you need to add. Not bad for a free e-mail account!

To work this little magic, you need to first download and install the nifty Windows Live Mail–Outlook synchronizer gizmo, otherwise known as Outlook Connector. Follow these steps:

1. **Connect to the Internet, start your Web browser, and search for** `Outlook Connector` **using a search engine such as Google.**

2. **Once you find the program OutlookConnector.exe, download it to your computer.**

   A dialog box appears, asking whether you want to save the program file or open it.

3. **Click Open.**

   After the program is downloaded to your computer, a dialog box appears, asking whether you want to run it. Yep, you do.

4. **Click Run to install the program.**

   After the program is installed, a dialog box appears, prompting you to enter your Windows Live Mail account info.

5. **Type your e-mail address, password, and your name (as you want it to appear when you send e-mail by using this account) in the appropriate text boxes. Click OK.**

   Your Windows Live account is added to Outlook.

6. **Start Outlook.**

   Your Windows Live Mail account appears in the Navigation pane. (Just scroll down until you see it.)

7. **Review your Windows Live Mail information.**

   For example, click the Inbox folder for your Windows Live Mail account in the Navigation pane to view your e-mail messages. Send or receive messages to your Live Mail account just as you would any other Outlook e-mail account.

Change to the Calendar module, and click your Live Mail calendar(s) in the Navigation pane to view them (they should be listed in the My Calendars group). Add or delete appointments, meetings, or events as you like. Outlook Connector will update your changes to your Live Mail account automatically.

Change to the Contacts module, and click your Live Mail contacts in the Navigation pane to view them. You should find them in the My Contacts group, labeled Contacts – `yourname@live.com` or something similar. Add or remove contacts from this group, and your changes are automatically updated to your Live Mail account.

Importing E-Mail Data from Eudora

If you've used Eudora for a while, you've probably accumulated more than a few contacts and messages that you just don't feel like losing — at least, not yet. Moving from Eudora Pro or Eudora Light (versions 2.0 to 4.0) is fairly straightforward. Just follow these steps:

1. **Click the File tab to display Backstage and then select Open from the list on the left.**

The Open options appear on the right.

2. **Select Import from the options on the right.**

The Import and Export wizard appears, as shown in Figure 4-5.

Figure 4-5:
Go get those Eudora messages and addresses.

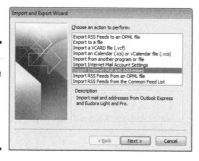

3. **Select Import Internet Mail and Addresses, as shown in Figure 4-5, and then click Next.**

The Outlook Import Tool dialog box appears (refer to Figure 4-2).

4. **Select the Eudora (Pro and Light) 2.x, 3.x, 4.x option.**

5. **Select the Import Mail check box, and then click Next.**

   You can, if you want, import contact info from Eudora when you grab old messages by selecting the Import Address Book check box. See the following section for help.

6. **Click Finish.**

   A summary of what got imported and what didn't appears. If you want to save this summary, click Save in Inbox. Otherwise, just click OK.

If you use a newer version of Eudora (5.0 or higher), you can't easily get that data into Outlook because Outlook offers no option for importing it, as Figure 4-2 makes abundantly clear. If you're using Windows XP, then you're in luck because that means you have Outlook Express. Basically, with Windows XP, you can import your Eudora data into Outlook Express, and then import the Outlook Express data into Outlook. If you use Windows Vista or Windows 7, however, it no longer includes Outlook Express — it uses Windows Live Mail, instead. In such a case, you can try exporting a CSV (Comma Separated Values) file from Eudora and importing it into Windows Live Mail.

Importing Contacts

Importing requires more than just grabbing ancient e-mail messages from your old e-mail client. For me, at least, I need to get my contacts into Outlook (so that I don't have to type them back in) more than I need to be able to peruse dusty old messages. Regardless, you can easily import your old addresses from Outlook Express, Eudora Light, or Eudora Pro (2.0 to 4.0).

If you have Eudora 5.0 or higher, you can use the same technique that you use to import Eudora messages. See the preceding section for more info.

To import addresses from Outlook Express or Eudora Light/Pro (versions 2.0 to 4.0), follow these steps:

1. **Click the File tab to display Backstage, and select Open from the list on the left.**

   The Open options appear on the right.

2. **Select Import from the options on the right.**

   The Import and Export wizard appears. (Refer to Figure 4-5.)

3. **Select Import Internet Mail and Addresses, and then click Next.**

   The Outlook Import Tool wizard makes its appearance. (Refer to Figure 4-2.)

4. **Select either the Outlook Express 4.x, 5.x, 6.x or Windows Mail option, or the Eudora (Pro and Light) 2.x, 3.x, 4.x option.**

5. **Check just the Import Address Book check box, and then click Next to move to the next page of the wizard.**

   You can import contacts at the same time by checking the Import Address Book check box. See the section "Importing Outlook Express/Windows Mail messages," earlier in this chapter, for more info.

6. **Decide what to do with duplicates.**

   When you import contacts, you probably have information for several people who have the same name. These names might represent unique contacts who just so happen to share the same name, or they might be duplicate entries that have either newer or older information. In any case, in the Import Addresses dialog box (refer to Figure 4-6), you can have Outlook do one of the following if it finds duplicate contacts during the import process:

Figure 4-6:
Dealing with contact copy cats.

   - To remove existing contacts and replace them with the ones you're importing, select Replace Duplicates with Items Imported.

   - To keep existing contacts and also import duplicates, select Allow Duplicates to Be Created.

   - To keep existing contacts and skip over duplicate entries in the import file, select Do Not Import Duplicate Items.

7. **Click Finish.**

   A summary of what got imported and what didn't appears. For example, if you told Outlook to skip over duplicate entries, the summary tells you how many contacts were skipped.

8. **If you want to save the summary, click Save in Inbox. Otherwise, click OK.**

Importing Other Data

Some people store contact information everywhere, and not just in an e-mail program. For example, you might have names and addresses stored in Excel or Access that you now want to use in Outlook. You might have an Act! client list or a Lotus Organizer contacts list that you want to grab. You use a similar process for various types of data files.

You can't import an Excel 2007 or Excel 2010 file directly into Outlook 2010, as silly as that sounds. But you can save your Excel 2007/2010 workbook in Excel 2003 format, and then import that. Before you do anything, though, you need to name the range of Excel data that you want to grab.

If you are a fan of RSS (Really Simple Syndication, a newsfeed) you might want to import your old list of feeds. Start the Import and Export wizard; select Import RSS Feeds from an OPML file or Import RSS Feeds from the Common Feed List and click Next; if importing an OPML (*Outline Processor Markup Language*) file — an XML file format popular with bloggers — select the file to import and click Next; select which feeds within the file that you want to subscribe to and click Next; then click Finish to close the wizard.

Follow these steps to import data into Outlook:

1. **Click the File tab to display Backstage, and select Open from the list on the left.**

   The Open options appear on the right.

2. **Select Import from the options on the right.**

   The Import and Export wizard appears, as shown in Figure 4-7.

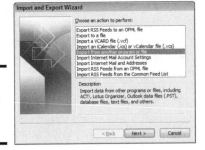

Figure 4-7:
The Import
and Export
wizard.

3. **Select the Import from Another Program or File option, and then click Next.**

   The Import a File wizard makes its appearance. (See Figure 4-8.)

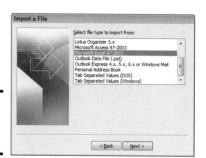

Figure 4-8:
Pick a
program.

4. **Select the type of file that you need to import, and then click Next.**

   The File to Import page of the wizard appears.

   If you don't find the file type that you're looking for in the list, don't despair. Go back to your original program and save the data in either comma-separated values (CSV) or tab-separated values format. You can then import the CSV or tabbed file into Outlook.

5. **Click Browse, locate the file to import, and click OK to return to the wizard.**

6. **Decide what to do with duplicates, and then click Next.**

   While Outlook imports these new items, it may discover that one of them has the same information as an existing item. In the File to Import page of the wizard, you tell Outlook what to do in such cases:

   • To remove existing items and replace them with the ones you're importing, select Replace Duplicates with Items Imported.

   • To keep existing items and also import duplicates, select Allow Duplicates to Be Created.

   • To keep existing items and skip over duplicate entries in the import file, select Do Not Import Duplicate Items.

   After making a selection, click Next to continue to the Select Destination Folder page of the wizard, as shown in Figure 4-9.

Figure 4-9:
So, where
should this
stuff go?

7. **Select which folder in Outlook you want the data to go into from the Select Destination Folder list, and then click Next.**

   For example, if you're importing a name and address list, select the Contacts folder (refer to Figure 4-9). After you click Next, the Following Actions Will Be Performed page of the wizard appears, as shown in the background of Figure 4-10.

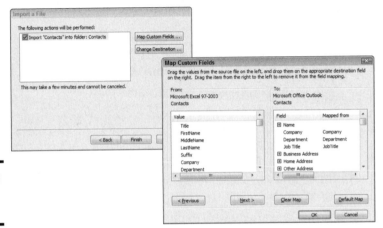

Figure 4-10: Map your data.

8. **Click the Map Custom Fields button.**

   The Map Custom Fields dialog box appears, as shown in the foreground of Figure 4-10.

9. **Match up fields.**

   For database-like files, such as Excel, Access, or CSV files, you need to select a table or worksheet, and then map the fields, a process that involves selecting a field (such as Name) in the import file and providing Outlook with the field (such as Last Name) in the folder to which you're importing data (such as Contacts).

   Basically, you select a field from the list on the left, which represents the import file, and then drag that field onto an Outlook Contacts field, listed on the right. This dragging-from-the-left-over-to-the-right thing is called *mapping,* and it's basically sophisticated finger pointing. You're pointing the way from the import file to Contacts for all the imported file's data fields.

10. **When you finish making your map, click OK to return to the wizard.**

    Back in the wizard, a Finish button has now appeared. This is looking good!

11. **Click Finish.**

    The data is imported into Outlook.

Book II

E-Mail Basics

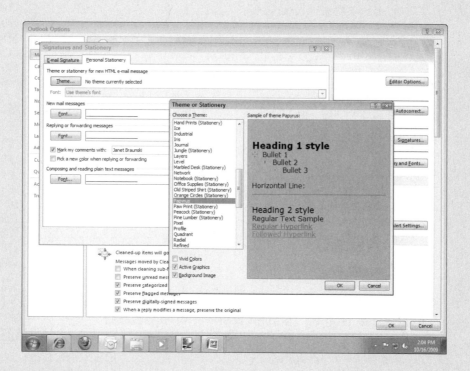

Contents at a Glance

Chapter 1: Creating New Messages: Beyond the Basics

In This Chapter

✔ Understanding the steps involved in sending e-mail

✔ Getting e-mail that others send to you

✔ Dealing with multiple address books

✔ Sending copies and blind copies of messages

✔ Formatting message text and attaching files

✔ Saving a draft of a message for later

Sending a simple message — such as "Hey, how are you? Where's the ten bucks you owe me?" — is fairly straightforward (although I review that process in this chapter, just in case you missed something in the whirlwind tour in Book I, Chapter 2). However, it takes a little more work to make your text look distinctive enough to stand out from the crowd of other messages most people receive in a day. And maybe even a little more effort to include an image or a file with the message. And perhaps you have to do some actual thinking when you need to fish for an address hidden deep inside one of your address books. No matter — you can find out how to deal with all these things and more in this chapter.

Creating a Message, Step by Step

In Book I, Chapter 2, you can discover a lot of quick and dirty tricks for using Outlook, including how to send a quick e-mail message. Sending a message isn't all that complex, but if you've never done it before, you might appreciate a little more info which I provide here.

Step 1: Display the message form

This step is probably no mystery; you can use the New Items button, located on the Home tab of the Ribbon, from anywhere in Outlook to create a new *something*. To create a new e-mail message, follow these steps:

1. **Click the New Items button on the Home tab.**

   A long list of options appears.

2. **Select E-Mail Message from the list.**

If you're in the Mail module, just click the New E-Mail button instead. Whichever way you do it, a new message form appears. Continue to the next section to learn how to address your new message.

You can create e-mails that have fancy colorful backgrounds by using templates that you can get from Microsoft's Web site. See Book II, Chapter 4 for more information.

Like most programs, Outlook offers about a billion ways to do everything. Typically, I like to start by showing you the normal way to do something, such as clicking the New Items or New E-Mail button to create an e-mail message. (See, you have two ways already!) Back in Book I, Chapter 1, I show you how to drag and drop a contact onto the Mail button to create an e-mail. Well, this next approach is so cool, so simple, that I just have to show you how to use it, too. To send an e-mail to someone who has sent you an e-mail, just click one of those e-mails, and in the Reading pane, hover the mouse pointer over the sender's address. A Contact Card appears, covered in lots of cool buttons (See Figure 1-1.) To send an e-mail to that person (and not a reply to the message you're viewing), click the little envelope-like button on the far left. The message form appears. (The Contact Card features other buttons; I talk about them in other chapters. Don't worry; I won't forget.) There are a couple of things I want to mention, though, before I move on — if you want to examine the Contact Card closely, you can pin it open by clicking the Pin button (refer to Figure 1-1). This pinned card, by the way, remains on top of all your windows, not just Outlook. Click the Pin button again and click anywhere else to make the Contact Card disappear. You can also click the Close button (the X) to close the card immediately. Click the Expand button to display more info about the contact, such as phone numbers, office, department, and location. Notice that with the Contact Card expanded, you can make changes to the contact's info by clicking the Open Contact link, located at the bottom of the expanded card.

Step 2: Address the e-mail

You have to address the message so that Outlook and all those e-mail servers on the Internet know who to pass the message on to. You see, there are special computers, located throughout the Internet, whose purpose is to handle incoming and outgoing e-mail for a group of people — such as all the people who work for your company. An *e-mail server* is kind of like a local post office; using the e-mail address attached to a message, the server sorts e-mails and passes them on. If a message comes in for someone working at your company, then the message is transferred to that person's computer whenever he or she logs on and requests e-mail. If a message arrives addressed to someone who uses a different e-mail server, then that message is passed along the Internet chain till it gets to its destination.

E-mail button   Pin button   Expand/Collapse button

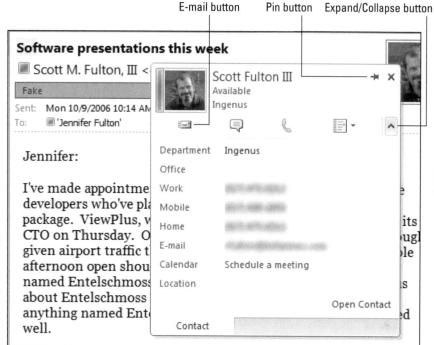

Figure 1-1:
Use the
Contact
Card to
send a quick
e-mail.

Basically, an e-mail address is broken down into two parts, separated by an @ sign: The first part identifies the person to whom the message is being sent, and the second part identifies the e-mail server. For example, the e-mail address `joebrown@fakeco.com` tells an e-mail server that the message is meant for Joe Brown, who gets his e-mail from a server at Fake Co. Likewise, `tenesha.j.ruiz@aol.com` identifies an e-mail for Tenesha J. Ruiz who gets her mail from AOL.

After you're armed with an e-mail address, you simply type that address in the To box of the Message form, as shown in Figure 1-2. If this person is somebody you think you'll be writing often, you might want to enter the e-mail address in your Contacts list (see Book V, Chapter 1 for the how-to). Entering the address in Contacts makes it much easier to address e-mails; you simply have to type a contact's name in the To box, like this: `Scott Thompson`. If your Contacts list has only one Scott, or only one to whom you send e-mail on a frequent basis, try typing just `Scott`.

Outlook then checks the Contacts list for a match and, assuming it finds one, it displays a list of matches — in this case, all the Scotts. Just click a name in the list that appears to select it. If you type the whole name, such as Scott Thompson, and then move on to type the message or subject or whatever, Outlook doesn't mind. It looks up the contact name that you typed while you continue to work, and (assuming it finds a match) it underlines the name you typed. This process is called *resolving* the e-mail address, and I discuss this topic in more detail in the section "Resolving to Find the Right E-Mail Address," later in this chapter. For now, just know that the magic works, assuming you type the name in a way that matches how it's entered in Contacts.

In Figure 1-2, Outlook underlined the e-mail address that I manually typed in. Outlook underlines all manual addresses, working under the assumption that if you took the time to type it in, you did so *carefully.* In other words, this underline doesn't reassure you that the e-mail address you typed in is valid. So, be careful when you're typing in e-mail addresses.

Names found in Contacts   Names not found

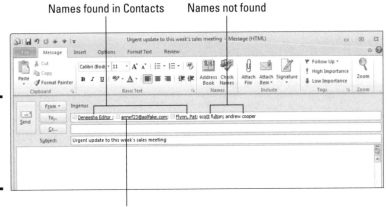

Figure 1-2:
Type an
e-mail
address in
the To box.

Typed e-mail address

If you type a short message, Outlook may not have looked up *(resolved)* the names that you typed in the To box. If those names aren't underlined or if you see a red, wavy underline, then Outlook may not know who are talking about. If you're not sure if Outlook has tried to resolve the names or not, you can nudge Outlook into checking them now by clicking the Check Names button in the Names group on the Ribbon's Message tab.

If, somehow, the name you type doesn't get matched with an entry in Contacts, you can go searching for the name by clicking the To button. What happens next depends a lot on your e-mail setup and requires a broader understanding of the Contacts list and something called an address book. So, for the time being, I'll leave the clicking the To button business alone and let you read up on it in the next section.

In Figure 1-2, you may have noticed the From button, located just above the To button. This button appears if you have multiple e-mail accounts, and it lets you choose which account you want to use when sending this message. (Replies to the message also come to the account that you select — if anyone replies to the message, that is.) Get all the details in Book III, Chapter 5.

Step 3: Send extra copies of the message

If you need to get the word out to multiple people, you can go about that in several ways:

✦ **Type ; (semicolon) after the first e-mail address in the To box, and then type another e-mail address.** For example, the To box might look like this:

       scott.thompson@fakeco.com;tenesha.j.ruiz@aol.com

✦ **Type an address in the Cc or Bcc fields.** Cc stands for *carbon copy,* and it literally sends a copy of the message to the people you designate. Bcc stands for *blind carbon copy,* and it secretly sends a copy of a message to someone without letting the others in the To or Cc fields know that you've done it. (See the section "Sending Carbon Copies (Cc's) and Blind Carbon Copies (Bcc's)," later in this chapter, for help in using these fields.)

Step 4: Enter a subject and a message

Before you type the message, you should enter a subject or description of that message's content. Just click in the Subject text box and type a brief description. Your recipient can then glance at the subject when the e-mail comes in and decide whether to ignore you now or later.

You don't actually need to type a subject, but most people enter one — and the right subject can make all the difference in whether your message gets read. You might type Update on Sales Meeting Today or What you been up to?. Both subjects identify the content of the message and help the reader identify the e-mails that need to be read right now.

The Subject becomes even more important with Outlook 2010 because of its Conversation view, which groups e-mails with the same subject (which are probably part of the same back and forth conversation) together so that you can quickly review them.

After entering a subject, click in the big text box at the bottom of the Message form and type your message. (See Figure 1-3.) Even when I'm just sending a file, I always type something about the attachment in the body of the message so that the reader doesn't think the e-mail's empty and some kind of strange prank. (You find out how to add file attachments in the section "Attaching a File to a Message," later in this chapter.)

InfoBar

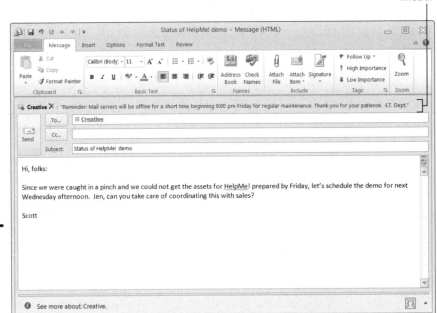

Figure 1-3:
Type your
message in
the big text
box.

Follow the normal word-processing procedures for typing your message:
Just type, and the words flow automatically between margins. Follow these
other tips for entering text:

✦ **Press Enter to begin a new paragraph.** As you may have noticed, when
you type text into the Message area of the form, the text wraps between
the left and right edges of the window automatically. You don't have to
do anything to get text to appear on the next line but fill that line up,
letting excess text flow down. If you want to begin a new paragraph,
press Enter, and text is automatically placed on the next line. To leave a
bit of eye space (white space) between paragraphs, press Enter twice.

✦ **Press Backspace to back up and erase characters to the left of the
cursor; press Delete to erase characters to the right.** To delete a large
section of text, drag over it to select it first, and then press Delete.

✦ **Select text, then drag and drop it to move it.** To select text, just drag
over it. Selected text is highlighted. After selecting text, move the mouse
pointer over it, click and hold the mouse button to drag. As you drag,
a horizontal line marks where the text will be placed once you drop it
(release the mouse button).

✦ **Press Home to move to the beginning of a line; press End to move to
the end of a line.** Press Ctrl+Home to jump to the top of the message or
Ctrl+End to move to the end of the message.

✦ **In most cases, you can add formatting to the text before or after you type.** See the "Formatting Text to Make Your Messages Stand Out" section, later in this chapter, for the scoop.

If you're wondering what to say, you might begin like you're typing a regular letter, with a *Hi, Hello,* or *Hey there.* For a closing, you can add *Sincerely* or *Thanks,* and then your name. A lot of people include an e-mail address, postal address, Web address, IM address, and phone number after their name to make it easy for the reader to contact them. If you want to get fancy, you can save your basic contact information in a file called a *signature* that Outlook adds to your outgoing e-mails automatically. (For the word on how to create a signature, see Book II, Chapter 4.)

Step 5: Send it off

When you finish creating the perfect message, check the InfoBar, located just below the Ribbon, for special warnings. (Refer to Figure 1-3.) You typically see warnings only if you work in an office under Exchange, where MailTips pop up to warn you of various faux pas such as e-mailing large groups of people, e-mailing someone who's on vacation, or replying all to a message you received as a blind carbon copy (and thus, revealing to everyone that you got the message too). If you don't see any warnings (or you want to ignore them and continue anyway), click the Send button to send your message off. After you click Send, the message is placed in your Outbox, where Outlook immediately sends it up to your e-mail server for processing, assuming that you're connected to the Internet or your company network.

As I mentioned, if you work on a company Exchange network, you may see warnings about the message you're about to send in the InfoBar, along the lines of "This person is out of the office," or "You're about to send this message to 493 of your nearest and dearest" — which begs the obvious question, "Do you want to send this message anyway?" Well, do you? If so, click Send.

If, for some reason, the e-mail isn't sent immediately, you can press F9 or click the Send/Receive All Folders button on the Quick Access toolbar to coax it along. Both the F9 key and the Send/Receive All Folders button start a send-and-receive cycle that sends e-mail, checks for new e-mail on the mail server, and downloads any new messages. If you only want to send e-mail right now, click the Send All button on the Send/Receive tab, instead.

You probably want to check your spelling and grammar before you send off a message, if for no other reason than to prevent embarrassment over a simple mistake. See Book II, Chapter 3 before clicking Send.

If you're not ready to send the message right now, you can save it in the Drafts folder, make changes later on, and then send it (which we discuss in the section "Saving a Message So You Can Send It Later," later in this chapter).

After sending an e-mail message, if your mail server or one of the mail servers along the path to your recipient can't find the e-mail address you used for some reason, an e-mail server sends you a message that tells you it didn't actually deliver the e-mail. When you receive that message, check the address you tried to send your e-mail to carefully, make changes to it as needed, and resend the message.

Retrieving Your Mail

Periodically, Outlook checks your mail server for new mail. Typically, it does this check every 15 minutes, assuming you're connected to the Internet all the time (or to your company's network). If you're not always connected to the Internet, then Outlook probably checks e-mail when you ask it to — whenever you click the Send/Receive All Folders button on the Quick Access toolbar.

You can make Outlook get your mail at any time by clicking the Send/Receive All Folders button. To change how often Outlook checks e-mail, click the File tab to display Backstage and select Options from the list on the left to summon the Outlook Options dialog box. In that dialog box, select Advanced from the list on the left and, in the Send and Receive section, click the Send/Receive button. The Send/Receive Groups dialog box appears; select the All Accounts group from the Group Name list, and then select the Schedule an Automatic Send/Receive Every "Number of" Minutes option. Set "Number of" to the number of minutes you want to wait between send/receive cycles. (See Book III, Chapter 1 for more information.)

Regardless of how it's set up, at some point, Outlook contacts your e-mail server — which looks to see whether you have any new messages. You can watch the process of downloading e-mail by staring intently at the status bar, where you can view a series of messages such as Send/Receive Status 40% and Send/Receive Complete.

When e-mails come in, Outlook does everything it can to gain your attention, short of bopping you in the head. First, for each e-mail (unless they're coming in too fast), Outlook flashes a Desktop Alert. This alert briefly displays the sender's name, the subject, and the first few lines of the incoming message so that you can instantly see whether you need to read this message now. You can do a lot of things with these alerts:

✦ **Get a longer look at the Desktop Alert.** Just hover the mouse pointer over the alert.

✦ **Read the message.** Move the mouse pointer over the bubble and click the message header, as shown in Figure 1-4.

✦ **Delete the e-mail without reading it.** Simply click the X that appears under the Mail icon on the left side of the bubble.

Figure 1-4:
When new
mail arrives,
you're
alerted.

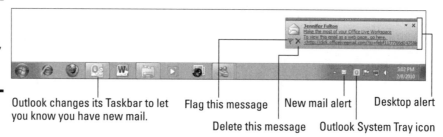

Outlook changes its Taskbar to let
you know you have new mail.

Flag this message

New mail alert

Desktop alert

Delete this message

Outlook System Tray icon

✦ **Create an instant to-do item.** Click the flag that appears under the mail icon on the left side of the bubble. See Book VI, Chapter 1 for help with to-do items.

✦ **Mark the message as already read.** Click the down arrow located in the upper right-hand side of the bubble, and select Mark as Read from list that appears.

If you do nothing when a Desktop Alert appears, it fades away slowly on its own, to be replaced by the next alert if you receive more mail. If you're slow on the uptake like me (without coffee, at least), you can lengthen the time that alerts stay on-screen; see Book III, Chapter 1 for details on how to adjust Desktop Alert display time.

In addition to displaying a series of Desktop Alerts, Outlook plays a sound to let you know you have mail, as well as placing a closed-envelope icon in the Windows System Tray, as shown in Figure 1-4. In addition, Outlook also changes its Taskbar icon (adding a small envelope) to tell you, "You've got mail!" After alerting you in every way it can think of, Outlook places those new messages in your Inbox, which is the main e-mail folder. The System Tray New Mail icon sits next to the normal Outlook icon (which is always there); the New Mail icon continues to appear until you switch to Outlook and review at least one of the new messages. Likewise, the Taskbar icon continues to display that little envelope until you review the new messages. At that point, the New Mail icon disappears and the Taskbar icon returns to normal (much the same, just minus the envelope).

Finding new messages is easy since the Inbox is the only e-mail folder that you have, until you create other folders to organize your messages. I highly recommend creating folders to keep similar messages together, such as personal e-mail. See Book IX, Chapter 1 to find out how to create Mail folders.

Going through the mail

To read the new messages you receive, you need to switch to Mail by clicking the Mail button on the Navigation pane, and then click a message header to view its contents in the Reading pane, as shown in Figure 1-5. If (like me) you've created various e-mail folders, then click the folder first in the Navigation pane to see its list of messages, and then click a message header.

Figure 1-5:
Reading the
mail.

Messages that you haven't read appear with a bold message header. In
addition, e-mail folders that contain unread messages appear in bold, so you
know that you need to check those folders, not just your Inbox. Outlook also
kindly lists how many unread items are in each folder.

Sometimes, I click a message header to read an e-mail, only to find that my
attention span is shorter than I thought. I then mark the e-mail as unread so
that I know to go back and actually read it (with full attention) later on. To
mark a message as unread, select it and then click the Unread/Read button
on the Home tab. If the message is open, click the Mark Unread button on
the Message tab.

Fast ways to review mail

Obviously, clicking a header here or there and then reading the message in a
tiny Reading pane may not be a very fast way to review a lot of messages —
but it *is* selective. You can speed up the process by displaying only the
messages you haven't read yet and widening the Reading pane so that you
can read the message content without scrolling (which cuts down on the
time it takes). Follow these steps:

1. **Click the Filter E-mail button on the Home tab, then select Unread
from the pop-up menu that appears.**

The view changes to display only unread messages in the current folder. At this point, you can start reviewing those long lost puppies, or you can take a minute to widen the Reading pane just a bit.

The Filter E-mail button basically initiates a search (in this case, for unread messages) and displays the result. Thus, when you use the Filter E-mail button, the Search Tools tab appears. To learn how to use these search tools to refine your search, see Book IX, Chapter 4.

2. Click the Reading button on the Status bar.

The Status bar is located along the bottom of the Outlook window, and you will find the Reading button there, just to the left of the Zoom button. See Book II, Chapter 2 for help in using these view buttons.

When you click the Reading button, the Navigation pane and Ribbon are automatically minimized, and the Reading pane is expanded to maximize your reading pleasure, as shown in Figure 1-6.

3. Click the first message header.

The contents of the message appear in the Reading pane.

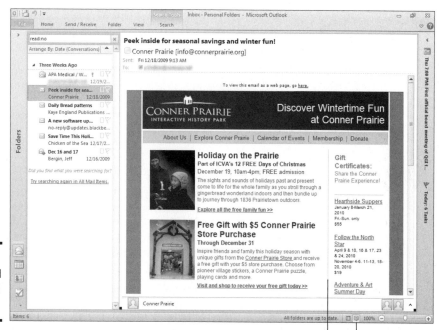

Figure 1-6: Quickly read your unread messages.

Reading pane ⎯

Reading button

Book II
Chapter 1

Creating New
Messages: Beyond
the Basics

4. **To read the next message, press the down-arrow key.**

   The contents of the next unread message appear in the Reading pane.

5. **When you're done reviewing your unread messages, click the Close Search button on the Search tab.**

   The Search tab isn't exactly showing right now, since the Ribbon is minimized, but you know what to do — just click Search, and the tab appears so you can click the Close Search button. If you want the Ribbon to remain displayed, double-click the Search tab.

If you'd rather review your mail in a window so that you can see its contents even more easily, follow these steps, instead:

1. **Click the Filter E-Mail button on the Home tab, then select Unread from the pop-up menu that appears.**

   Unread message headers appear in a long list.

2. **Double-click the first e-mail to view it in a full window.**

   The message opens in its own window which you can maximize if needed.

3. **To view the next item, click the Next Item button.**

   The Next Item button appears on the Quick Access toolbar. To review a previously viewed e-mail message, click the Previous Item button.

See Book II, Chapter 2 for more help in reviewing and replying to incoming e-mail.

Working with Address Books

You might not have noticed, but Outlook checks e-mail addresses you type in the Message form to see whether they're valid prior to sending any e-mail you create. Outlook checks e-mail addresses by looking through the Outlook *Address Book,* which was created when Outlook was installed. The Address Book contains your personal contacts.

As it so happens, you might actually have multiple address books. If so, Outlook checks all of them in order to find a match for the e-mail address you typed. Here's a description of the type of address books you might be using:

✦ **Outlook Address Book:** Outlook stores the contacts you personally add to Outlook in its Address Book. If you create multiple Contacts lists (which happens automatically as you add different e-mail accounts to

Outlook, although you can add a Contacts folder manually if you want), then these multiple Contacts lists are all stored in the Outlook Address Book. If your Outlook is set up to use a Global Address List (see below for a description), then you have two address books.

✦ **Global Address List:** If you work with Outlook at a company that uses Microsoft Exchange (an e-mail and groupware server program), Outlook is probably set up to use the company's *Global Address List,* which contains the names and e-mail addresses of all company employees. If you're a college student, you might have access to the university's Global Address List, which contains the e-mail addresses of professors and staff. Still, if you add a new contact to Outlook, it's stored in the Outlook Address Book.

✦ **Other address books:** Regardless of whether you use only the Outlook Address Book (and Contacts) or throw in a Global Address List as well, you might want to mix it up a little by adding other address books. For example, you could add an Internet address listing that uses LDAP (Lightweight Directory Access Protocol). Basically, you can access such a listing through the Internet to obtain directory information, such as e-mail addresses; you might receive access to an LDAP through your college or university, for example. You might also add a mobile address book to Outlook. For example, a mobile address book is added to Outlook when you sign up for Outlook Mobile Service, a service that enables you to send instant messages using Outlook. See Book III, Chapter 2 for more information on instant messaging. The mobile address book keeps track of cell phone numbers and allows you to send and receive text messages through the service.

Book II
Chapter 1

Creating New
Messages: Beyond
the Basics

When you set up Outlook to use multiple address books, you designate one as the main address book, which means that Outlook searches it first when it's verifying names. The main address book also appears first when you click the Address Book button on the Home tab or click the To button in a message form to look up someone's e-mail address manually. (For more on verifying e-mail addresses and looking up names, see the section "Resolving to Find the Right E-Mail Address," later in this chapter) If you tend to search for names in the Contacts list, rather than in a Global Address List, you might want to change which address book Outlook searches first. You can find out how to do so in the section "Choosing which address book is the boss," later in this chapter.

Attaching a new address book to Outlook

Companies typically set up their employees' computers, so if your company uses Exchange, your Outlook at work is probably already connected to the company's Global Address List. However, if you need to attach a university's Global Address List or some kind of Internet list to Outlook, follow these steps:

1. **Click the File tab to display Backstage, and select Info from the list on the left.**

The Account Information options appear on the right.

2. **Click the Account Settings button, and select Account Settings from pop-up menu.**

The Account Settings dialog box pops up.

3. **Click the Address Books tab and click New.**

The Add New Account wizard, shown in Figure 1-7, appears.

Figure 1-7: What's one more address book between friends?

4. **Select the address book type that you want to attach.**

You have these two options:

- **Internet Directory Service (LDAP):** This option adds an Internet directory list. Select this radio button and click Next. a new page of the Add New Account wizard opens, displaying the Directory Service (LDAP) Settings page, as shown in Figure 1-8. Continue to Step 4.

- **Additional Address Books:** To add a Global Address List or similar address book, select this option and click Next. Another page of the Add New Account wizard appears, displaying the Other Address Book Types page. Select the type of list you want to add and click Next. The last page of the wizard opens. Click Finish. You're done (so skip the remaining steps in this list)!

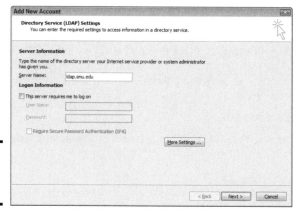

Figure 1-8:
Enter LDAP
settings.

5. **Enter the server and logon information.**

   The Add New Account wizard asks for this info:

   • In the Server Information box, type the server name of the computer that contains the Internet directory list.

   • If you need to use a password to access the list (you usually do), select the This Server Requires Me to Log On check box, and then type your username and password in the appropriate text boxes.

   • Select the Require Secure Password Authentication (SPA) option if your service provider asked you to do so.

6. **Click the More Settings button. You see a warning telling you that you must restart Outlook for these changes to take effect. Click OK to continue.**

   The Microsoft LDAP Directory dialog box, shown in Figure 1-9, magically appears, begging for more information.

Figure 1-9:
Tell Outlook
how to find
the LDAP
directory.

7. **Type the port number for the connection in the Port box.**

I assume that the service provider (perhaps a university) provided detailed instructions for installing its LDAP, including the port number they want you to connect through. Enter that port number in the Port box. Select the Use Secure Sockets Layer option if the service provider asked you to do so.

8. **Click the Search tab.**

A whole new set of stuff to fill in appears, as shown in Figure 1-10.

Figure 1-10:
Outlook
wants just
a little more
info, please.

Microsoft LDAP Directory

Connection Search

Server Settings

Search timeout in seconds: 60

Specify the maximum number of entries you
want to return after a successful search: 100

Search Base

○ Use Default

● Custom: o=smu.edu

Browsing

☑ Enable Browsing (requires server support)

OK   Cancel   Apply

9. **Change any of the Search tab options, as needed.**

The tab features these options:

- **The Search Timeout in Seconds option:** Change this value if you want to extend the amount of time Outlook will search for the list.

- **The Specify the Maximum Number of Entries You Want to Return After a Successful Search option:** Change this value if you want to limit the number of address books Outlook lists after searching.

- **The Use Default or Custom radio button:** If you select Custom, type the name that the owner of the list gave you.

- **The Enable Browsing check box:** Select this check box if you want to try searching for the list manually.

10. **Click OK to close the Microsoft LDAP Directory dialog box.**

You're returned to the Add New Account wizard.

11. **Click Next to advance to the last page of the wizard, and then click Finish to create a connection to the LDAP list.**

After you add an address book, you must exit Outlook and restart it in order to make the new address book available.

Importing personal address books

In previous versions of Outlook (Outlook 2003 and older), you could create multiple personal address books (for separating personal and business e-mail addresses, for example), but in Outlook 2010 (like in Outlook 2007), you can have only one Outlook Address Book for storing the contacts you create yourself. You can (and should) import the addresses from these extra personal address books into the one Outlook Address Book. Just follow these steps:

1. **Click the File tab to display Backstage, and select Open from the list on the left.**

   The Open options appear on the right.

2. **Select Import from options on the right.**

   The Import and Export wizard appears.

3. **Select Import from Another Program or File from the Choose an Action to Perform list, and then click Next.**

The Select File Type to Import From page of the wizard appears.

4. **Select Personal Address Book and click Next.**

   The File to Import page of the wizard appears.

5. **Click Browse, and then select the file that you want to import. Click Next.**

   The Select Destination Folder page of the wizard appears.

6. **Select the Contacts folder to which you want to import (if you have more than one Contacts folder) and click Next to move to the last page of the wizard.**

7. **Click Finish.**

Choosing which address book is the boss

If you have more than one address book, such as a Global Address List and an Outlook Address Book, you can boss Outlook around and tell it which address book you want it to search first when it's verifying e-mail addresses. Follow these steps:

1. **Click the Address Book button in the Find group on the Home tab.**

   The Address Book dialog box snaps open.

2. **Choose Tools⇨Options.**

   The Addressing dialog box appears, as shown in Figure 1-11.

3. **Select the address book that you want Outlook to search first.**

   You can choose to have Outlook start with the Global Address List, the contact folders in the Outlook Address Book, or to search your addresses in some kind of custom order.

If you choose Custom, then arrange the address books in the order in which you want them searched. To move an address book up in the list, select it and click the up arrow button on the right. To move it down, click the down arrow button instead.

You can change which one of your address books appears first when you click the Address Book button. Just select the one that you prefer from the When Opening the Address Book, Show This Address List First drop-down list.

4. **Click OK to finalize your choices, and then close the Address Book.**

Figure 1-11:
Choose which address book you want Outlook to search first when resolving e-mail addresses.

Resolving to Find the Right E-Mail Address

Ever have a problem trying to find the e-mail address for someone you just have to send a message to *right now?* You can find this desperate search especially frustrating if you know that darn e-mail address is right there, hiding somewhere in Outlook. In the following sections, I explain how Outlook verifies e-mail addresses prior to sending a new message and what to do if Outlook doesn't have any idea to whom you're trying to send a message.

Understanding how Outlook verifies addresses

To explain how Outlook verifies e-mail addresses, I need to remind you how to properly address an e-mail. Contrary to what you might think, you don't actually need to type an e-mail address to send a message. Nope. As I explain in the section "Creating a Message, Step by Step," earlier in this chapter, you can just type a name and let Outlook do all the work of finding the matching e-mail address for you. Of course, Outlook can't find what isn't there, so this magic assumes you've added the name (and a matching e-mail address) to your Contacts list. (See Book V, Chapter 1 for help on that one.)

Sometimes, you can confound Outlook somewhat — causing it to place a red, wavy underline below the name you type in the To text box. This line means that you've come close to spelling the person's name right, but not close enough for Outlook to find a matching e-mail address. It might also mean that the name you typed has several e-mail addresses associated with it. If you stump Outlook completely, it doesn't underline the name at all. (See Figure 1-12.)

Figure 1-12:
Outlook
resolves
e-mail
addresses
by checking
your various
address
books and
underlining
the names it
finds.

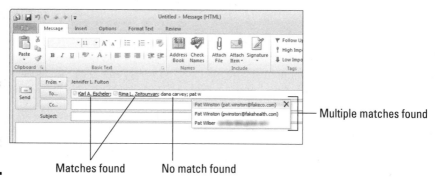

Matches found   No match found

Multiple matches found

Assuming you know someone well enough to remember his or her name, I'm guessing you'll find this process pretty easy. Follow these steps:

1. **Type the name in the To text box of a message form.**

   After just a few letters, the e-mail address of the recipient should appear automatically, courtesy of the AutoComplete feature.

2. **Press Enter to accept Outlook's suggestion.**

I say that an address *should* automatically appear in the To field while you type because, in fact, AutoComplete keeps track of only those people you e-mail frequently. If a list of addresses appears, rather than just one address, use the arrow keys to highlight the correct person, and then press Enter. (You can also click the address that you want in the list.) If AutoComplete pops out an address that you no longer plan to use (or presents you with the result of some earlier typing mistake), just highlight the address by using the arrow keys, and then press Delete. The address is history.

Any feature so fancy that all it needs for looking up an e-mail address is a few measly letters has got to have an equally fancy name, and this one is no exception. The process of matching a name to an e-mail address is called *resolving*. And guess what? You can actually misspell a person's name, and as long as you're close enough, Outlook should find the address for you. When Outlook resolves a name, it underlines that name so that you know it's okay to go.

AutoComplete, as great as it sounds, can't always come up with the right e-mail address, or it might come up with too many (and tell you so with that red wavy underline thing). If Outlook didn't find any match to what you typed, you might have to type the complete name and wait a second or two to see whether Outlook can resolve the name for you (locating the matching e-mail address in one of your address books). If Outlook finds too many possibilities, you can force it to try to resolve the address by clicking the Check Names button on the Message tab. The Check Names dialog box jumps up, as shown in Figure 1-13; it probably doesn't have any suggestions to make about the missing name unless the problem is that it found several matches for the same name in your address books. But if Outlook did find several matching names, select the name that you want from the list and click OK. Otherwise, click the Show More Names button to display your address books, where you can select the name manually. You can also click the New Contact button to add the contact right then and there, if you come up completely empty.

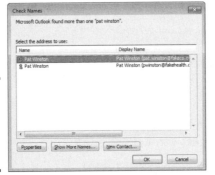

Figure 1-13:
Resolve the disputed name yourself.

If you get tired of looking up contacts because you can't get Outlook to understand whom you're talking about when you type a name, you can try drag and drop to create a message, as described in Book I, Chapter 2. You can also use the Contact Card, which we talk about in the section "Creating a Message, Step by Step," earlier in this chapter.

Searching for an address in your address books

Unfortunately, if you type a name and Outlook can't resolve it, you have to address your e-mail the old-fashioned way — by searching for the e-mail address in your address book. Follow these steps:

1. **Click the To (or Cc or Bcc) button in the Message form.**

The Select Names dialog box appears, as shown in Figure 1-14.

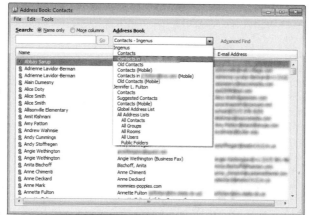

Figure 1-14:
If necessary, search your Address Book for a name.

2. **Select an address book from the Address Book drop-down list.**

Assuming you have more than one address book, specify which one you want to search. If the address book has multiple Contacts lists (refer to Figure 1-14), you need to select the specific Contacts list you want to display.

3. **Type a name in the Search box.**

While you type, Outlook obligingly highlights a matching name for you. By the way, contacts are typically listed first name first, so you should start by typing part of the person's first name.

If you need more than a name to find a person's information, you can search any column that appears in the Select Names dialog box. Click the More Columns radio button, and then type the information you want to search for. For example, type `fulton` to find everyone with that last name. Type `nfulton` to display anyone with the characters "nfulton" in the first part of e-mail address (the part before the @ sign). Use multiple criteria, if you want; just separate them with a space. Type `n fulton` to find people whose first names begin with N and whose last name is Fulton.

4. **Click the To (or Cc or Bcc) button.**

Outlook adds the highlighted name to the To/Cc/Bcc text box, depending on which button you click. (See the following section for more on sending cc's and bcc's.) Repeat Steps 2 to 4 to add other e-mail addresses, as needed. (Yes, you can select people from different address books and e-mail a single message to them.)

5. **Click OK.**

The Address Book closes and the e-mail message form reappears, now including the recipients' addresses.

You can type any e-mail address that you want to use into the To, Cc, or Bcc fields of a message form. You can use this approach to send an e-mail to someone you don't want to add permanently to your Contacts list. Outlook tries to verify that the address is valid by matching it with a name in one of your address books. Failing that, Outlook slaps an underline below the mystery name — which does not mean that the e-mail address is valid, just that it looks like a valid e-mail address because it uses the right format. Underline or no underline, you can still send the e-mail. As an FYI, if you go this manual route, remember to separate addresses with a semicolon (;).

You can access any of your address books at any time (not just in a message form), either by clicking the Address Book button on the Home tab from within any module or by clicking the Address Book button on the Message tab from within a message form.

Sending Carbon Copies (Cc's) and Blind Carbon Copies (Bcc's)

If you've already sent some messages, the To field should seem pretty familiar (even if you haven't finished your second cup of coffee for the day) because you use it in pretty much every e-mail. The To field of every e-mail message contains the e-mail addresses of those people you consider the message's main recipients.

In addition to the To field, the message window contains two other address fields, as shown in Figure 1-15:

Figure 1-15:
The To field, along with the Cc and Bcc fields.

✦ **Cc:** Use the Cc field (*cc* is short for *carbon copy*) when you want to send a copy of an e-mail message to someone — not so much for them to read it, study it, and maybe even reply, but more as a simple FYI.

For example, maybe you want to cc your boss on a message that you're sending to a supplier who's jeopardizing a critical project because his delivery is already two weeks late. Everyone who gets the e-mail sees that it was sent to the people listed in the To field and also to those people listed in the Cc field. In other words, your supplier will soon be sweating when he reads your message because he'll know that your boss is aware of his failure.

✦ **Bcc:** If you type an e-mail address or a name for Outlook to resolve into the Bcc (short for *blind carbon copy*) field, that person receives a copy of the message, but no one else knows it. The people whose addresses appear in the To and Cc fields are completely unaware that you sent a copy to the person or persons listed in the Bcc field because any address that you type in the Bcc field is hidden from the other recipients of the message.

So, if you want to send the same message to a bunch of people and make it look as if each and every one of them is the only one who got this special message, just type their e-mail addresses (or names) in the Bcc field.

As you might have guessed, if you type addresses in the Bcc field, you don't have to type any address in the To field if you don't want to. The Bcc field doesn't ordinarily appear on the Message form, so you might have to click the Bcc button on the Options tab to make it come out of hiding.

Spammers like to use the Bcc field to send messages to tons of people. Therefore, a lot of e-mail systems are pretty unfriendly to messages that use the Bcc field, flagging them as junk mail. If your Bcc recipient knows to expect your message, he or she can easily fish it out of the junk pile if it lands there, but otherwise, your message might go unheard. As an alternative, you can use Word to send out a mass mailing — creating a lot of individually addressed e-mails from a single sample. (See Book III, Chapter 4 for details.)

If you're blind carbon–copied on a message, don't click Reply All to reply to the message, or you reveal your secret presence. However, you can safely click Reply to send a comment to the sender, who obviously knows you got the message — so no secret there. By the way, assuming you work on Exchange network, the InfoBar (which appears just below the address area of a message form, when needed) stops you before you commit such a travesty by displaying a warning there, telling you that you're about to reveal your secret presence.

Formatting Text to Make Your Messages Stand Out

Time was, communicating electronically was novel and new; nowadays, receiving an e-mail is more business as usual than an exciting event. To grab your audience's attention, you might want to employ various formatting techniques to make your text stand out. Even if you're not worried that your message will go unheard, it's kinda fun to shake things up a little and enhance a message with cool formatting.

Understanding message formats: HTML, RTF, and plain text

Outlook supports three message formats. To see what format a message is using, look at the message window's title bar. Here's a list of the formats and what distinguishes each one:

✦ **HTML (default):** What makes formatting possible in an e-mail message is HTML, the same thing used to format Web pages. Outlook can easily read HTML messages, so all you need to worry about is whether your recipients also have this capability. Unless they're using really dusty e-mail programs, chances are that anyone you want to send a message to can handle HTML. If not, they'll see a simple text version of your message; keep that in mind when you send out formatted e-mail. Also, keep in mind that if you're sending a message to someone's cell phone (not a text message, but e-mail to a Blackberry, for example), your formatting may not all appear — colored text and bold formatting should show up, but weird fonts probably won't.

By default, Outlook messages use HTML format, which means that you can fancy them up as much as you like. You can add text formatting (such as bold and italics), insert professional-looking numbered and bulleted lists, and apply paragraph formatting (such as alignment, indentation, shading, line spacing, and borders). I run through the basics of applying text formatting in the following section. I show you how to fancy up text with paragraph formatting, stationery, and styles in Chapter 2 of this minibook.

✦ **Rich Text Format (RTF):** RTF format is like HTML in that it supports a certain amount of formatting options. The trouble with RTF format is that few e-mail programs support it, including Outlook (of course), Outlook Express/Windows Mail, Windows Live Mail, and Microsoft Exchange Client (an old Exchange e-mail program that eventually became Outlook). So, you can use RTF, I suppose, if you want to send a formatted message to other people in your company over an Exchange network. I don't know why you'd want to because if you're using Outlook, chances are everyone else in your company also is, so why not just use HTML?

If you send an RTF-formatted message over the Internet, Outlook converts it to HTML format to make sure it's readable by whatever e-mail program receives it. So, the bottom line is that RTF isn't worth bothering with. Suppose, for some reason, you do send an RTF message without knowing whether a recipient can read it. (Some people just have to try everything.) Your recipient might tell you that he or she didn't see your message, but did get an odd `winmail.dat` attachment. You have your answer — your recipient's e-mail program can't decipher RTF format. So, stop using the silly thing and resend the e-mail by using HTML or plain text.

✦ **Plain-text format:** True to its name, plain-text format is, well, pretty plain. You don't find any formatting here, no sir — just text characters. Plain text is the format to choose if you're sending an e-mail to someone who refuses to upgrade his or her e-mail program to something from the 21st century.

By default, Outlook creates outgoing messages in HTML format. If you prefer to use another format, you can change the format you use for most of your messages by following these steps:

1. **Click the File tab to display Backstage, and select Options from the list on the left.**

The Outlook Options dialog box appears.

2. **Select Mail from list on the left to display the Mail options.**

3. **In the Compose Messages section, select the format you prefer from the Compose Messages in This Format list.**

Your format choices are HTML, Rich Text, and Plain Text.

4. **When you finish, click OK to save your changes.**

To select the format for a single message, click the New Items button on the Home tab, select E-Mail Message Using from drop-down menu, and select the format to use from the pop-up menu that appears. If you've already started a message, you can still change its format. Just click the HTML, Plain Text, or Rich Text button on the Format Text tab in the message form.

Applying formatting to a message

You apply text formatting to message text in the same way you format text in Word, so I don't go into too much detail. If you're unfamiliar with Word, you can look over *Word 2010 For Dummies,* by Dan Gookin, to brush up. Basically, to format text in an Outlook e-mail, click the appropriate buttons on the Home tab in the message form. Want more options? Click the Format Text tab instead (shown in Figure 1-16), and select a formatting tool.

You can apply formatting while you type; for example, you might select a new font or font size, or apply bold format by clicking the Bold button. Anything you type after you make a format selection uses the new formatting. You can change the formatting back when you don't want to use it anymore. For example, click the Bold button again to turn off the Bold format.

Instead of formatting while I type, I prefer to apply most of my text formatting after the fact — by selecting text and then making selections to apply to it. Some of the advantages to using this technique might come as a surprise to those of you with previous Outlook experience. For one thing, when you format after typing, you can browse choices in any list (such as the fonts on the Fonts list) and actually preview how the selected text will look before making your decision. For example, you might select some text and then browse the Font Color list to see how various colors look when applied to that text.

Clear formatting ⌐   ⌐ Font dialog box launcher

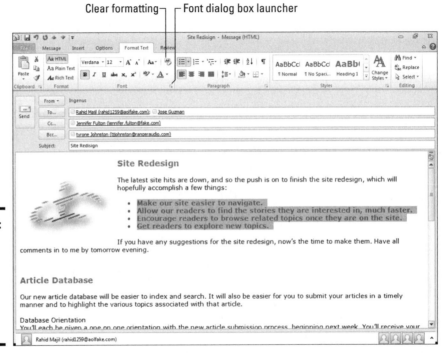

Figure 1-16:
Use the
tools on
the Format
Text tab
to format
message
text.

You figure out the second reason for formatting after you first type some text: Select that text and move the mouse pointer up just a little to make a mini-toolbar appear right next to the selection (as shown in Figure 1-17), offering popular text options, such as font and font size.

To use the Text Highlight Color button, you must type the text first and then select it because you can apply the highlight only to existing text.

You probably recognize the buttons in the Font section of the Format Text tab, but if you don't, you can always hover the mouse pointer over a button to display a ScreenTip. The Clear Formatting button is kinda new. Use it to remove formatting from selected text — it's a bit like using the Format Painter, only in reverse. If no text is selected, Outlook removes formatting from the current paragraph. You can find the Format Painter button hiding in the Clipboard group over on the left side of the screen.

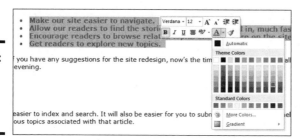

Figure 1-17:
A mini-
bar of
formatting
tools.

I have no idea why you'd want to do the following because, frankly, I prefer toolbars over dialog boxes. But if you feel more at home in a box, you can display the Font dialog box by clicking the Font Dialog Box Launcher button, and then you can use that dialog box to apply a bunch of font changes all at the same time.

On the Message tab — the tab that shows up by default when you create a message — Outlook has put quite a few of the most frequently used tools for formatting text. If the tool you want to use is there, don't feel obligated to visit the Format Text tab. For example, if you want to change the font size, you can find the Font Size list right there on the Message tab. You can also make use of some paragraph formatting buttons, such as Left Alignment and Bullets. I go over these formatting options in Chapter 3 of this minibook.

Attaching a File to a Message

Whenever you like, you can send along a file with a message. This file is called an e-mail *attachment*. Recipients can preview, open, and save attachments. The following sections explain how to send a file to a recipient. (You can find out how to deal with attachments that you receive in Chapter 2 of this minibook.)

Best practices for working with attachments

Here are some things you should keep in mind when sending attachments:

+ **Compress large files.** If the file you want to send is large, you might want to compress it first (zip it) to make it as small as possible. If the recipient connects to the Internet by dialup and not by broadband, restrict yourself to sending only very small files; large files take forever to download over a dialup connection.

Some companies block zip files because they believe that these compressed files might contain a hidden virus, so be sure that your recipient can receive such files before attempting to send them.

Need some help understanding file compression and how to go about it? Come on over to our house and read all about it:

> www.dummies.com/WileyCDA/DummiesArticle/id-3086.html

Be sure to type this in your Web browser exactly as it appears here — initial caps and all — or you might get a message telling you the article can't be found!

✦ **Contact the recipient before sending files that might potentially exceed maximum loads.** You might not be able to send a large file to some people because a lot of companies stop the big guys at the entrance. When trying to figure out who to stop and who to let in, e-mail servers take the total of the message size plus all attachments. To add insult to injury, your message might not even get that far. It might be stopped by your own e-mail server, which sets its own message limitations. You can't guess what a company might decide is too large, so your best bet is either to ask first, or to send and wait for an error-message reply. You can, however, find out what your ISP considers the maximum load and try not to go over it.

If you and your recipient work on an Exchange network, Outlook warns you (via a message on the InfoBar) that your attachment is too large for the recipient's Inbox. You also see warnings if your own e-mail server dislikes the size of the attachment. So, be sure to watch the InfoBar!

✦ **Avoid sending file types that might be flagged as potential viruses.** As I mentioned in the Warning box earlier, some attachments are stopped at the door because they aren't welcome. These file types include ones that might contain nasty visitors, such as viruses, macros, and scripts: Look for extensions such as `.exe`, `.vbs` (Visual Basic script), `.prg` (program file), `.ws` (Windows script), and sometimes even `.doc` and `.zip` files. You might not know what file types won't get to their destination because they're stopped by the recipient's e-mail server.

Outlook tries to protect you by warning you whenever you try to attach a file that might be stopped at the door: `.exe`, `.bat`, `.vbs` (Visual Basic source file), and `.js` (Java script). It's up to you, however, to decide whether to send the file anyway, despite the warning.

✦ **Don't send your personal info unless you want to.** Office documents, as a matter of routine, embed personal info into your documents, such as your name, company name, and so forth. If you don't want to share such information, then strip it before you send a document along. To remove such data in Word 2010, for example, click the File tab to display Backstage, select Info from the list on the left, click the Check for Issues button from the options on the right, and select Inspect Document from the pop-up menu. In the Document Inspector dialog box that opens, click Inspect to check for hidden info and even remove it, if you like.

Attaching files

To send a file along with a message, follow these steps:

1. **Click the Attach File button on the Message tab.**

The Insert File dialog box pops up, as shown in Figure 1-18.

You can also use the Attach File button on the Insert tab to display the Insert File dialog box. However, unless you're inserting other things, as well, such as pictures, tables, or hyperlinks, it's not really worth the trip to the Insert tab.

**Book II
Chapter 1**

**Creating New
Messages: Beyond
the Basics**

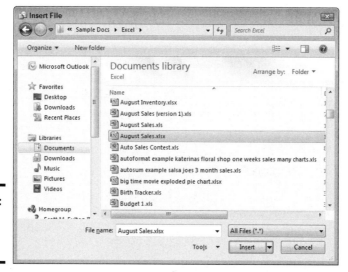

Figure 1-18:
Pick out
the file to
attach.

2. **Select the file(s) that you want to send along with the message.**

You can select multiple files by holding down Ctrl and clicking each one, or holding down Shift and clicking the first and last files in a group.

You can probably zip your large file prior to attaching it, right there within the Insert File dialog box, because most zip utilities support this process. To see whether it works for you, simply select the file(s) that you want to attach, and then right-click. In the pop-up menu that appears, select the name of your zip utility; or in Windows 7, select Send To from the menu, then select Compressed (Zipped) Folder from pop-up menu that appears. On the pop-up menu of choices that appears when you right-click, you might see an option that allows you to zip and mail the file(s) immediately. Now, that's convenient! Outlook might try to prevent the utility from working, however. (It's a control thing.) If so, click the File tab to display Backstage, select Options from the list on the left to display the Outlook Options dialog box, then select Add-Ins from the list on the left, and select COM Add-Ins from the Manage list and click the Go button. From the COM Add-Ins dialog box that appears, select your zip utility's check box, then click OK.

3. **Click Insert.**

   How an attached file appears within the message form depends on the message format you used:

   • For HTML and plain-text messages, the name of the selected file appears in the Attach box below the Subject line, as shown in Figure 1-19.

   • For RTF messages, you see a clickable icon within the body of the message. Don't let the icon fool you; the file is still attached separately from the message, and it's not *embedded* (inserted) into the message itself.

   The filenames are followed by the file's approximate size. This information can prevent you from accidentally trying to send too large a file or files.

Attached file   File size

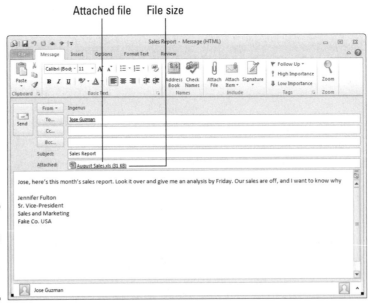

Figure 1-19: Attachments and their file sizes are listed.

Saving a Message So You Can Send It Later

Sometimes, in the middle of composing a missive, you discover that you don't have all the information you need to finish it. You don't need to lose all your hard work; you can easily save what you've written so far, and then change or add to the message later on.

If you're looking for how to resend a message that you've already sent (and not how to save one you haven't), just skip over to Chapter 2 of this minibook for help.

Saving a draft

To save what you've written so far, along with any files you might have attached and anything you might have inserted, follow these steps:

1. **Click the Save button on the Quick Access toolbar.**

2. **After the message is saved, you can close it by clicking its Close button.**

The saved message is placed in your Drafts folder. Follow these steps to open the message at a later time:

1. **Switch to Mail, if you aren't already there.**

2. **Select the Drafts folder on the Navigation pane.**

3. **Double-click the message to open it.**

4. **Make whatever changes you want and click Send to send it on its way.**

If you repeat certain messages a lot (*Hey, sorry, but uh, you're fired. Be sure to leave the stapler on your way out.*), you can save the text in a reusable form. See Chapter 4 of this minibook for the lowdown.

Changing the Drafts folder

Actually, Outlook saves your messages every three minutes while you work on them, just in case the power goes out right when you're about to finish the Great American Novelette. You can change the folder that Outlook uses to save unsent messages (normally, it uses the Drafts folder) and how often Outlook saves messages while you work. Just follow these steps:

1. **Click the File tab to display Backstage, select Options from the list on the left.**

   The Outlook Options dialog box jumps up.

2. **Select Mail from the list on the left.**

   The Mail options are displayed.

3. **In the Save Messages section, select the folder to which you want to save unfinished messages from the Save To This Folder list.**

4. **Change how often drafts are saved by typing a value in the Automatically Save Items That Have Not Been Sent After This Many Minutes box.**

   You can type a value from 1 to 99 minutes, although why you'd want to work over 90 minutes on an e-mail and *not* save it yourself is beyond me.

5. **Click OK a bunch of times to close all the dialog boxes.**

Chapter 2: Reading and Replying to E-Mail

In This Chapter

- ✏ **Switching to a different Mail view**
- ✏ **Dealing with images in an e-mail**
- ✏ **Opening and saving an e-mail's attached files**
- ✏ **Replying to or forwarding an e-mail you receive**
- ✏ **Keeping your eye on MailTips**
- ✏ **Sending an e-mail again**

I used to think that getting e-mails was fun; it was nice to know that some-body cared enough to send me a special note. Alas, the fun didn't last long because I quickly became overwhelmed with the stack of e-mails that I needed to read and reply to. And those people who insisted on sending images and other files along with their notes only made the mess bigger and my life more difficult. In this chapter, you can find out how to wade through it all.

Finding the Messages You Want to Read: Changing the View

When you change from the Mail module to the Contacts module (or to Calendar or whatever), the information in that module appears in a particular way, called a *view*. For example, your e-mail initially appears in Compact view, arranged by date. You don't have to stay with Outlook's way of look-ing at things. You can, instead, change to a different view by clicking the View tab, clicking Change View, and then selecting the view you want from palette that appears. After you select a view, you can arrange (sort) the items in that view by selecting an option from the Arrangement group on the View tab. You can also apply Conversations "view" on top of any of the Mail views, in order to group messages by conversation. You can find out more about Conversations view in the upcoming section, "Dealing with Long Conversations."

In the Mail module, you have several view options:

✦ **Compact:** This is the default Mail view. Compact view displays Messages in a long skinny list, with the Reading pane to the right, as shown in Figure 2-1. In addition, messages are arranged by date, although you can easily arrange them in Conversations "view" by selecting the Show as Conversations checkbox on the View tab. Normally, Compact view displays messages in Date order, but in the Conversations arrangement, messages are not only displayed by date, but grouped by subject. Outlook decides which messages are in the same conversation by looking at the message Subject. In Compact view, messages are arranged by date but when you add the Conversation arrangement, only the header for the latest message in the conversation is initially displayed. In addition, the conversation appears in the listing using the date of the latest message. See the next section, "Dealing with Long Conversations" for information on working with conversations.

If you select the Show as Conversations option, then messages are grouped by conversation.

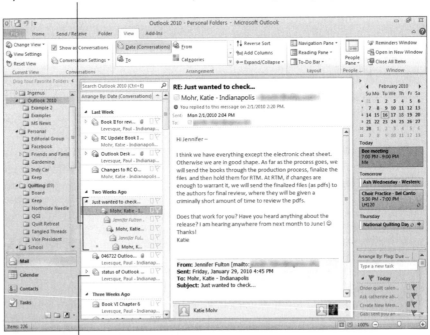

Figure 2-1:
Compact
view.

Message header is displayed on two lines.

✦ **Single:** Compact view uses two lines to display info about each message; on the first line it displays the message subject and icons for category, flag, importance, and attachments. On the second line, Compact view displays the name of the sender and the date/time the message was sent. In Single view, each message appears on a single line, making the list of messages shorter, as shown in Figure 2-2. In order to view all this information though (such as the sender's name and subject) you might need to widen the message list by dragging its right edge to the right as I have done (refer to Figure 2-2). This also makes the Reading pane a bit smaller, but I can live with that. You can once again add the Conversations arrangement, in which case each conversation appears in the listing using the date of its latest message.

Message header is displayed on a single line

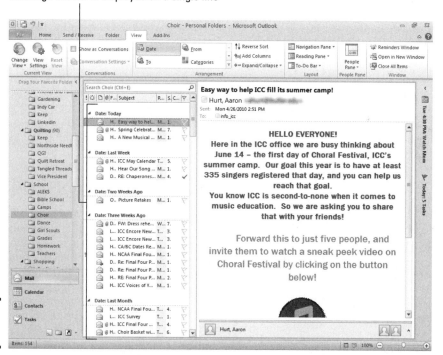

Figure 2-2:
Single view.

✦ **Preview:** Displays the first few lines of each unread message below the message header, as shown in Figure 2-3. The Reading pane is automatically hidden when you choose this view. By default, this view lists messages in date order, although you can use Date (Conversations) arrangement if you like.

Some views, like the one shown in Figure 2-3, are list (table) views in which data appears in various columns. Items in a list view are typically arranged in groups (like the messages shown in Figure 2-3, which are arranged by the date on which they were received). To hide the items in a particular group, click the group's downward triangle. To redisplay the items in a hidden group, click the group's right-facing triangle.

Click to display messages in this group.

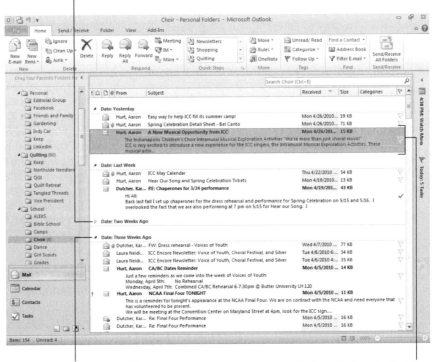

Figure 2-3:
Preview
view.

Click to hide messages in this group.

Outlook displays the first few
lines of each unread message.

You can do some pretty fun things with the columns in a list view, including the following:

✦ Arrange (sort) the items by one of the columns, just by clicking the column header.

✦ Make a column very skinny (by dragging its border) so that you can get more columns onscreen without scrolling. Similarly, you can make a column wider in order to display what's in it.

✦ Add, remove, and rearrange columns to show exactly what you want by clicking the Add Columns button on the View tab.

You can discover how to perform these tricks and more (including creating custom views that display only the information you want to see) in Book VIII, Chapter 2.

Dealing with Long Conversations

Conversations view was present in previous versions of Outlook, but Microsoft tweaked it in Outlook 2010 to make it more useful. I use the term "view" loosely; I really mean Conversation *arrangement,* so look for the Show as Conversations checkbox on the View tab. It shows related back-and-forth messages in an e-mail conversation. Basically, Conversation view groups e-mails by Subject. When you reply to a message, your reply keeps the same Subject, only adding RE: in front of it, so you can easily identify that your message is a reply to something that came before. For example, if someone sent you a message with the Subject Lunch Today, your reply would appear with the Subject RE: Lunch Today. Outlook uses this same logic to group messages together in Conversation view.

Now, I don't know about your company, but when someone in mine sends out a message asking about where we all want to go to lunch, it starts an endless chain of back-and-forth replies until someone finally makes a decision. What's cool about this new incarnation of Conversation view is that it not only groups all these messages together, but it also includes your own replies (even though they're in the Sent Items folder) and any other related e-mails (even though you may have filed them in a different folder), so you can easily review the flow of the conversation, as shown in Figure 2-4. Conversations appear with a white right-pointing triangle to the left of the message header (see Figure 2-4.) To expand a conversation, click this triangle.

If you accidentally try to reply to an e-mail that falls earlier in the conversation (and not the most recent contribution), a warning appears on the InfoBar. Even cooler — the InfoBar includes a clickable link to the most recent e-mail in the conversation so you don't have to go rooting around for it.

What's even more cooler about Conversation view is what you can do with it:

Book II Chapter 2

Reading and Replying to E-Mail

✦ **Condense.** First of all, just switching to the Conversation arrangement in Mail condenses your long list of messages into something that looks almost manageable — because each conversation gets only one header, and you have to click that header to expand the listing and view the back-and-forth e-mails in that conversation. When you click the white triangle to the left of the conversation header, e-mails directly associated with the conversation are displayed. (Side conversations, if any, are hidden.) Click the triangle again to fully expand a conversation. For example, in Figure 2-4, I sent out an invitation to the family Christmas party on December 10th, which my sister Beth replied to, twice. My other sisters replied just to me as well, causing four splits in the conversation, each with its own back and forth business as we nailed down the menu and what each of us should bring. When I clicked on the white triangle, the conversation initially expanded to just four headers — the last message in each of the four splits in the conversation. After clicking on the white triangle again, the conversation is expanded fully. Optionally, you can change your conversation settings to always expand conversations with a single click. See the Change those settings bullet coming up.

✦ **Who replied to whom?** Well, you can answer this question by using Conversation view because when you expand the listing for a conversation, little lines connecting the currently replied-to message with its replies appear along the left edge. That way, you can easily identify side conversations, because the little line doesn't connect to splits in this particular conversation. In Figure 2-4, you can see that Beth's message is a reply to my original invitation on December 10th.

✦ **Change those settings** Initially, the Conversation arrangement displays all e-mails in the conversation, regardless of the folder in which those e-mails are stored. To exclude e-mails in other folders, click the Conversation Settings button on the View tab and select Show Messages in Other Folders from the pop-up menu to turn that option off. There are other options on the Conversation Settings menu you can turn on or off: Show Senders Above the Subject (displays the sender's name above the subject line on the message header), Always Expand Conversations (fully expands a conversation with one click on the top message header), and Use Classic Indented View (which displays side conversations within a larger conversation using indention).

✦ **So, done with that?** To rid yourself of the entire conversation, you can just click its header (which, in turn, selects all the e-mails in the conversation) and press Delete. Confirm by clicking the Delete Selected Messages button in the dialog box that appears. Take this one step further by clicking the Ignore button on the Home tab; clicking the Ignore button not only dumps the entire conversation in the trash (the Deleted Items folder), but any future e-mails in the conversation are automatically dumped in the Deleted Items folder, as well. When you're so done with that endless discussion about where to go for lunch, just click Ignore. You can always check out the final decision by flipping over to the Deleted Items folder, but at least you don't have to put up with any more of that nonsense until lunchtime.

These lines connect replies to the original.

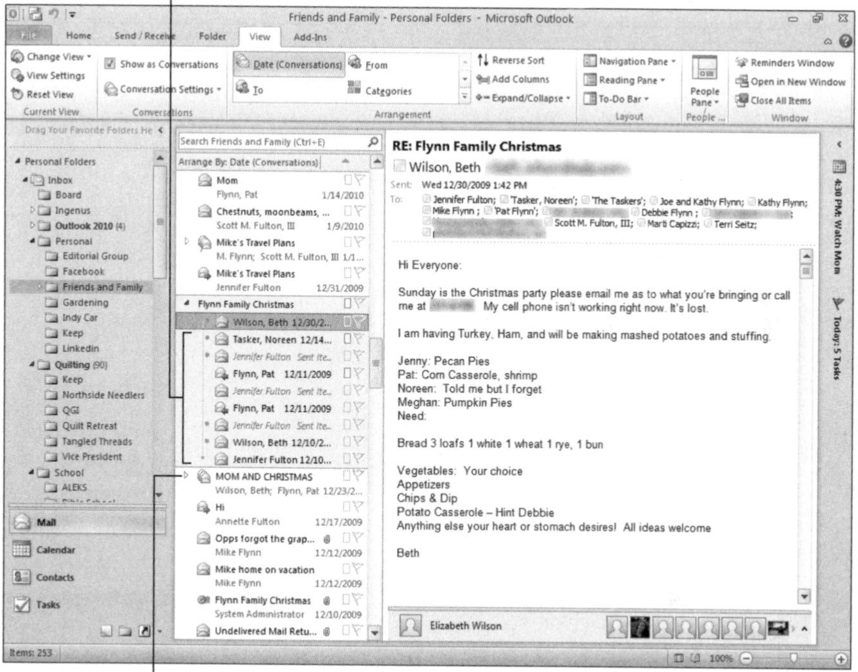

Figure 2-4:
Can
someone
make a
decision
already?

Click here to expand the conversation.

✦ **Take advantage of the group.** You can click the conversation's header and perform any other batching function, such as marking all the e-mails as read (by clicking the Unread/Read button on the Home tab), applying a category (you can find out about categories in Book VIII, Chapter 1), and moving them into a different folder using drag and drop.

✦ **Clean up.** When you create a reply to a message, Outlook normally copies the contents of that message into a new message form, where you can then type your reply. Reply to the reply, and your new e-mail contains not only the original message, but the reply, and of course whatever you wanted to say about it all. At some point, it becomes painfully obvious that the latest e-mail in the chain contains everything that's been discussed, so hey, you don't need those dusty old e-mails anymore. Just follow these steps:

1. **Click the Clean Up button on the Home tab and select Clean Up Conversation from the pop-up menu that appears.**

   The Clean Up Conversation dialog box jumps to attention. (See Figure 2-5.) If you want, you can change the options related to this clean up by clicking Settings.

Figure 2-5:
You done
with that?

2. **Click Clean Up.**

Outlook keeps only the latest e-mail in the chain and any unread
e-mails (and any that seemed so important to you that you went
ahead and messed with the Settings option I mention in Step 1;
e-mails that are digitally signed or that you've flagged or assigned a
category, could conceivably fall into that group.)

Here's how the whole Settings business works. If you click Settings in the
Clean Up Conversation dialog box, the Outlook Options dialog box appears,
as shown in Figure 2-6. In this dialog box, you can change the folder to which
Outlook sends cleaned up e-mails and set other options, such as whether
Outlook can remove flagged messages. Make your choices and click OK to
save them.

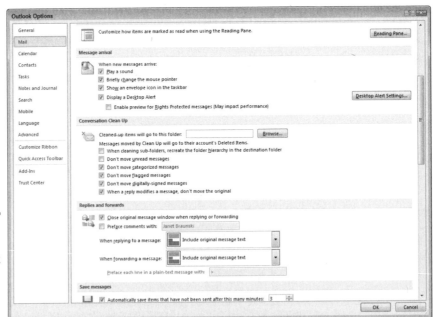

Figure 2-6:
Customize
your Outlook
conver-
sation
cleanup.

Outlook offers you other options when it comes to cleaning up. When you click the Clean Up button's arrow on the Home tab, a menu featuring three options opens. The preceding steps tell you about one choice — the Clean Up Conversation option. Here's the low-down on the other two:

✦ **Clean Up Folder:** Performs a clean up on all the conversations in the current folder. What an easy way to clean house!

✦ **Clean Up Folder & Subfolders:** Takes the clean up thing to its highest heights, cleaning up not only the current folder, but any subfolders, as well.

Dealing with E-Mails That Use Pictures

It seems like everybody is slipping little pictures into their e-mail messages these days. I guess plain ol' words just don't make it anymore — at least, not in newsletters, sales notices, and the like. As nice as e-mails look when they're dressed up with some photos or a few nice graphics, messages that contain downloaded images might act as a scout for spammers, which is why Outlook stops these strangers at the door and lets you decide whom to invite in.

E-mails that have attached images aren't a danger to you, because images themselves are harmless. But if a message contains a link to an image instead of the actual image, there could be a danger. Just like a home invader who knocks at every door until he finds someone dumb enough to let him in, such messages might actually be searching for valid e-mail addresses. When you download images from the Internet into a message, you might be sending a signal that you're at home and your e-mail address is a working one. Armed with such info, the home invader can now confidently flood your valid e-mail box tons of *spam* (unwanted junk e-mail). So, download images only from people you know or sources you trust. An innocent-looking link to an image file may turn out to be anything but innocent.

When an e-mail arrives that contains linked images, a message appears in the InfoBar telling you so. Also, the places where the images should appear are marked by a small, white square with a red X, as shown in Figure 2-7.

If the image represents a link to a particular page on the Web, you don't have to download the image; just click the link to visit the page. If you do want to download the linked images in an e-mail message, click the InfoBar and then select Download Pictures from the pop-up menu, as shown in Figure 2-7. Outlook copies the images from the Internet, and those images appear in the message in place of the empty boxes.

InfoBar tells you how to download the images in this message.

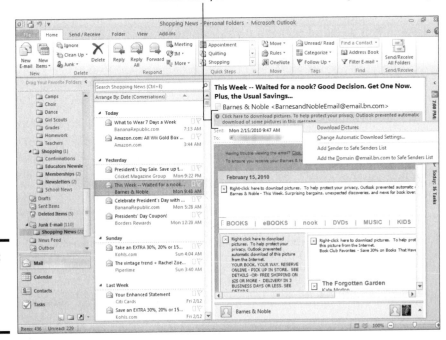

Figure 2-7:
The Xs
represent
linked
images.

If you regularly get e-mail that includes linked images from a source that you trust, you can add that person or source to your list of safe senders. That way, Outlook doesn't block the images, so you don't have to waste time downloading them. Click the InfoBar and on the pop-up menu, just click either Add Sender to Safe Senders List or Add the Domain *Domain Name* to Safe Senders List (refer to Figure 2-7). See Book IX, Chapter 3 for more about spam and the ways in which you can protect your privacy.

Although I advise against it, you can stop Outlook from preventing linked images from automatically downloading. Click the File tab to display Backstage, and select Options from the list on the left to display the Outlook Options dialog box. Select Trust Center from the list on the left, and click the Trust Center Settings button on the right. The Trust Center dialog box appears. Deselect the Don't Download Pictures Automatically in HTML E-Mail Messages or RSS Items check box to turn off the option. Click OK a few times to save your changes.

Opening E-Mail Attachments

An *attachment* is a file that's sent along with an e-mail message. If someone sends you an attachment, Outlook definitely lets you know: You see both a paper clip icon in the message header and the name of the attachment listed just above the message text.

Opening a message from someone you don't know might unleash a pack of brats (macros, scripts, and ActiveX controls) that can cause damage to the files on your computer. Previewing a file allows you to view a file's contents without danger. (See Book I, Chapter 1 for details.) However, Outlook can't preview all file types, and you can't make changes to a file that you're only previewing. So, if you decide you simply *must* open a file from someone you aren't sure you can trust, my advice is to save it to your computer first and then run an antivirus program before opening it. See the following section for help in saving an attachment to your hard drive.

To protect you, Outlook blocks some file types at your front door — file types that might contain macros, viruses, scripts, or commands with mayhem on their minds. Common file types that Outlook blocks include .exe, .vbs, .prg, .ws, .asp, .cmd, .com, and .js, among others. If an attachment is blocked, a message telling you so appears on the InfoBar.

Book II
Chapter 2

Reading and
Replying to E-Mail

If you don't want Outlook to block a particular file with one of these extensions, you can have the sender resend the file, possibly renaming the file's extension to something that Outlook won't block. For example, if somebody tries to send you a JavaScript file, 2muchfun.js, you could have them rename it 2muchfun.ok. After you get the file attachment, you must rename it again (2muchfun.js), or you can't use the file properly.

You can find out how to preview a file without actually opening it in Book I, Chapter 1. But keep in mind that previewing limits your viewing area to the size of the Reading pane. If a person you trust sends you a file, do either of the following to open the file for viewing in a larger window:

✦ Double-click the attachment's name in the Reading pane.

✦ Right-click the attachment's name in the Reading pane and select Open from the pop-up menu that appears.

To quickly locate all the e-mails that have attachments, use a Search folder. See Book IX, Chapter 4 for details.

Saving E-Mail Attachments

Because you have the capability to easily preview or open attached files, you might wonder: Why would I want to save an attachment to my already crowded hard drive? Well, the answer isn't so you can while away half of a work day searching for the file later on. (I mean, when would you be able to shop on the Internet and play online poker?) No, you do so in order to check the attachments for viruses, open them, and then make changes to the files, if you want.

If an e-mail contains multiple attachments, you can either save all the attachments in a single step (provided that you want to save all of them to the same folder) or save just one attachment at a time.

To save any or all files, follow these steps:

1. **Select the message that contains the attachment(s) you want to save.**

2. **Click any attachment.**

The list of attachment(s) appears above the message text. Click any one of them to select it. The Attachment Tools tab appears on the Ribbon, as shown in Figure 2-8.

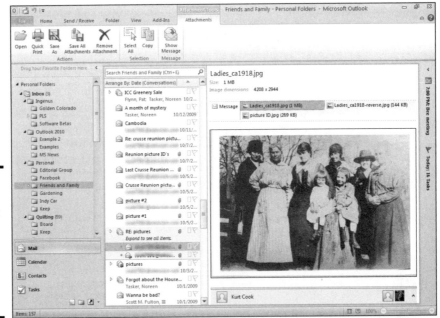

Figure 2-8:
The
Attachment
Tools tab
helps you
work with
e-mail
attach-
ments.

3. **Click either the Save As or Save All Attachments button on the Attachments tab.**

To save the one selected attachment, click the Save As button. To save all the attachments to the same folder, click Save All Attachments, instead.

4. **(Optional) If needed, select the attached file(s) that you want to save, and then click OK.**

If you're saving a single attachment, you can skip this step. If you're saving all the attachments, the Save All Attachments dialog box opens, with all the files selected, as shown in Figure 2-9. If you want to save only a few attached files, hold down Ctrl and deselect the ones you do not want to save right now.

Figure 2-9:
Select
which
attachments
to save.

**Book II
Chapter 2**

**Reading and
Replying to E-Mail**

Files that you select to save are saved to the same folder. To save attachments to different folders from an open message, repeat all these steps for each attachment.

After you click OK in the Save All Attachments dialog box, the Save Attachment dialog box opens so you can select the folder in which you want to save these files.

5. **Select a folder where you want to save the file(s) and click Save.**

If you're saving multiple attachments, but you selected a particular group of files in Step 4 (because you wanted to save only the ones in this group to a particular folder), you return to the Save All Attachments dialog box, where you can select the remaining file(s) and save them, as well, but to a different folder this time. If you're done, click Close instead of choosing more files.

After you save an attachment to the hard drive, scan it with your antivirus program, even if you know the person who sent you the file. Even your best friend can accidentally pass on a file that contains a virus, so it's better to be safe than sorry.

Copy the contents of an attachment directly to the Clipboard by selecting the attachment (as explained in Step 2) and clicking the Copy button on the Attachments Tools tab.

Replying versus Replying to All

This topic is a big one for me. I have to confess that I just hate it when somebody clicks Reply All and sends an e-mail to the original 200 recipients of a message, when all he or she wanted to do was pass on a comment to the sender.

True story: I'm on a parents list for my daughter's school, and last year, the president of the parents group sent an e-mail to everybody letting them know that the parent social was coming up. One parent sent a reply to everyone, asking if anyone knew of a good babysitter. Next, various parents used Reply All to answer that message, and before I knew it, my Inbox was filled with chatty e-mails on the trials and tribulations of finding a good babysitter, tips on baby care, recipes, and other trivia.

So, let me say this loud and clear: If you want your comments to go to everyone — count 'em, everyone — who got the original e-mail, click Reply All. If you want to send a comment to just the original sender of the e-mail (and to no one else), click Reply. Basically, before clicking Reply All, stop, look both ways, and then cross the street.

Watch that InfoBar! It can save you if you accidentally click Reply All on a message that has tons of original recipients. But this magic works only if you use an Exchange network at work and are replying to other people on the network. See the section "Letting MailTips Save Your Grateful Backside," later in this chapter, for more info.

Okay, class, lecture's over. Now, I move on to the details of replying:

✦ **If you're viewing the message in the Reading pane:** Click the Reply or Reply All button that you can find on the Home tab.

✦ **If you're viewing the message in a message window:** Click the Reply or Reply All button on the Message tab.

When you click Reply or Reply All, the text of the original message is copied to the new message, as shown in Figure 2-10. The message is also automatically addressed — either to the original sender or to everybody in the known universe (the sender and the original recipients). Outlook keeps the original subject, but adds a RE: to the beginning so the recipient(s) can easily see that your message is a reply. Type your response above the copied text and click Send.

Messages that you've already replied to appear in the messages list with a special icon — an envelope with a left-pointing arrow. Also, when you view such a message, the InfoBar displays a reminder that you've already replied to this message — along with the date and time when you replied.

In the following sections, I show you how to control whether text from the original message is copied to the reply, as well as how to change the font, font size, and color of your reply text. In addition, you can discover how to prefix the comments that you type within the reply with your name, so you can easily type your annotated comments within the original message, just like you were having a conversation with the sender.

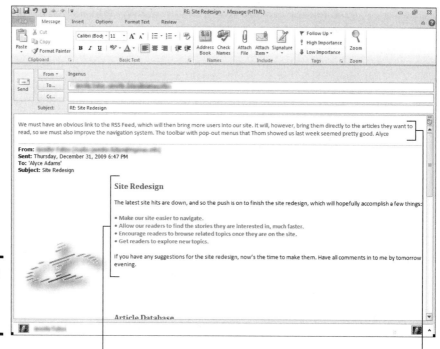

Figure 2-10:
The favor
of a reply is
requested.

Original text message   Type your reply above the original text.

 If you use Outlook on an Exchange network (in which case, the status bar says `Connected to Microsoft Exchange`), a colleague can reply to messages you receive when you're on vacation. See Book X, Chapter 1 for details.

Controlling how text is quoted in a reply

Copying the text of the original message in a reply helps everybody involved remember what they were talking about. (After all, it's probably been at least a minute ago, and you might have gotten another 50 messages in the meantime.) For this reason, Outlook normally copies the original text when it creates your reply, but you don't have to do that, as the following section makes clear.

Changing the formatting of the copied text

If you agree with me that copying the text into a reply is probably a good idea, you can still change how that copied text is formatted so that it suits your taste. Follow these steps:

1. **Click the File tab to display Backstage, and select Options from the list on the left.**

The Outlook Options dialog box appears.

2. **Select Mail from the list on the left.**

The Mail options appear on the right, as shown in Figure 2-11.

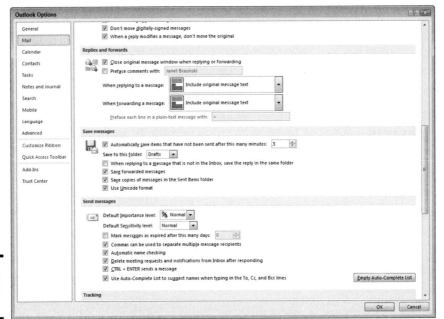

Figure 2-11:
How should
you reply?

3. **Choose how you want original text to appear in a reply.**

In the Replies and Forwards section, select an option from the When Replying to a Message drop-down list. Here are your choices:

- *Include Original Message Text.* The default, which copies the text to the bottom of the reply.

- *Do Not Include Original Message.* Creates the reply without copying any of the original text.

- *Attach Original Message.* Sends the original message in the form of an attachment, along with your reply. This option keeps the text out of the way but available is the recipient needs to refer to it.

- *Include and Indent Original Message Text.* Copies the original text but indents it so that the reader can more easily identify the original.

- *Prefix Each Line of the Original Message.* Copies the original text and indents it, putting a little character in front of the text. Outlook makes your reply blue to further distinguish it from the original text. If you select this option, in the Prefix Each Line With text box, type the character that you want to precede each line of the original text, such as >.

4. **Click OK to save your changes.**

Changing the color of your reply text

If you have Outlook copy the original text in a reply, you might want to distinguish it from your text by changing the color of your text. You can make this change manually by applying an alternative color while you type your reply, but why not let Outlook do it for you? Just follow these steps:

1. **Click the File tab to display Backstage, and select Options from the list on the left.**

   The Outlook Options dialog box appears.

2. **Select Mail from the list on the left.**

   The Mail options appear on the right.

3. **Click the Stationary and Fonts button.**

   It's hiding in the Compose Messages section.

   The Signatures and Stationery dialog box opens, as shown in Figure 2-12.

4. **On the Personal Stationery tab, select the Pick a New Color When Replying or Forwarding check box, and then click OK.**

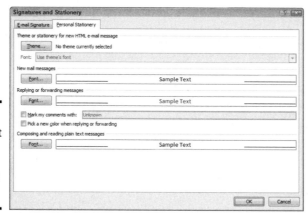

Figure 2-12:
Select a font
and other
text styles
to use when
replying.

Of course, this "pick a color for my text" thing works only if the reply is in HTML or RTF format, and not in plain text. You can use the Font button in the Signatures and Stationery dialog box to set the font and font size of the text that you use in a reply, regardless of whether you decide to have Outlook automatically change its color. (See Chapter 1 of this minibook for more on message formats.)

Adding your name to a reply

Sometimes, you can more easily type your reply within the original text of a message, as if you were directly responding to a question or concern, rather than typing your reply above the original text and trying to make recipient understand exactly what you're commenting on. Still, typing your comments within the original text can be a bit of a pain because when you type your text next to the original stuff, it's kinda hard to distinguish it from what the sender said. So, if you're like me, you probably go to the trouble of formatting your reply text a bit differently so that the reader can easily distinguish both sides of the conversation.

Outlook can help you accomplish this with a whole lot less sweat equity than typing comments within the original text and manually formatting them. Follow these steps:

1. **Click the File tab to display Backstage, and select Options from the list on the left.**

   The Outlook Options dialog box appears.

2. **Select Mail from the list on the left.**

   The Mail options appear. (Refer to Figure 2-11.)

3. **In the Replies and Forwards section, select the Preface Comments With option.**

4. **Type the something (such as your name or your initials) that you want to precede your comments in the text box.**

   When you create a reply and type any text within the original message text, your text is preceded by the something. Figure 2-13 shows an example of a reply with inline comments.

   By the way, if you type your reply above (rather than below) the copied text, it isn't preceded by your name.

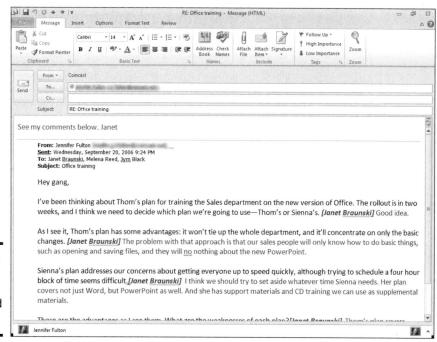

Figure 2-13:
Inline
comments
are included
in this reply.

Letting MailTips Save Your Grateful Backside

MailTips are warnings that appear in various e-mail messages, with the aim of preventing you from creating a seriously embarrassing error. For example, a MailTip appears when you attempt to Reply All with a message that has a hundred original recipients. Not that you never want your reply to such a message to actually go back out to everyone who got the original, but most times, you don't want to send a reply to everyone — and you'd be oh-so grateful to anyone who stops you before you click Send.

MailTips work only on an Exchange network because Outlook uses the information that the Exchange server provides to work its MailTip magic.

MailTips appear on the InfoBar as shown in Figure 2-14, so look there before clicking Send. Here's a list of the types of things MailTips can catch:

✦ **Messages being sent to a lot of people.** MailTips catches this potential misstep not only when you click Reply All, but even when you initiate the original message yourself. You see, in a large corporation, you can easily choose a group such as Sales Department from the company's Contact list, and not realize that the Sales Department consists of 325 people in various states.

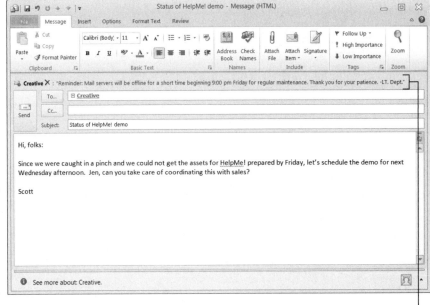

Figure 2-14:
The InfoBar
displays
warnings
when you
are about to
make a boo-
boo.

InfoBar

✦ **Replying to All on a message which you were blind-copied on.** When someone includes your address in the Bcc field of a message (the Blind Carbon Copy field), they probably intend for you to get the message in secret, unbeknownst to the other recipients. If you then Reply All on such a message, well, the jig is up.

✦ **Sending a message to someone outside your organization.** Every company has its secrets — and it wouldn't go over very well if you let some of them out by accidentally including someone outside your organization in an e-mail that includes private company info (or snide comments). So, a MailTip gives you a "heads up, this e-mail is being sent to an outsider" warning to help prevent such a situation.

✦ **The person you're trying to e-mail is out of town, has a full mailbox, or (like Elvis) has left the building.** Exchange knows when mailboxes are full or people have been fired, or if someone has set up an Out of the Office message, so MailTips can easily notify you of such situations before you send that useless e-mail. MailTips also flag any message that you might be trying to send to a person or group that's restricted for you. For example, perhaps you are not allowed to send e-mail outside of the company for security reasons and you have addressed an e-mail to a non-employee, or perhaps you are sending an e-mail to an employee of a company that does not allow outside e-mails to be sent to certain employees.

✦ **Trying to send super-large attachments.** If a message exceeds company limits, you get a "no way, Ray" MailTip warning.

Forwarding an E-Mail

If you get a message that you think other people should see, you can forward the message to them. Forwarding saves you the trouble of running to a copy machine; instead, when you forward a message, Outlook copies the original message text into a new message and doesn't even charge you a quarter. It also forwards the original attachments, free of charge. Outlook keeps the original subject line, adding a quick FW: to the beginning of it to let the recipient know that you're forwarding a message that you got from someone else.

To forward a message that you're viewing in the Reading pane, click the Forward button on the Home tab. If you're viewing the message in a message window, click the Forward button on the Message tab, instead. After Outlook copies the message for you, just address it normally and click Send. You can, prior to sending the message, add a quick note above the copied text (perhaps to explain what the forwarded message is about or why you're sending it on).

You can control how text appears in a forwarded message; just follow the same procedure for changing reply text. See the section "Controlling how text is quoted in a reply," earlier in this chapter, and mentally switch out "when replying to a message" with "when forwarding a message."

Resending an E-Mail Message

Yes, I admit it: Not only do I send messages once, but I sometimes send them twice. The main reason I send messages twice isn't because I like to overwhelm people with a lot of notes from *moi,* but because I sometimes forget to add the attachment.

So, when I click Send and discover that — oops — the attachment's missing again, I just jump over to the Sent Items folder, open the message, click the Actions button on the Message tab, and select Resend This Message from the pop-up menu that appears. Contrary to what you might think, Outlook doesn't just resend the message. Instead, Outlook copies the message, including its text, subject, recipients, and attachments, into a new message.

Basically, you get a Get Out of Jail Free card. You can add recipients (in case you forgot someone), change your text however you want, add attachments, and do basically anything you could have done originally, before your trigger finger clicked Send. When you're satisfied that this time you haven't forgotten anything or anyone, click Send to resend the message in its new form.

If you actually need to retrieve a sent message and replace it, you might be able to, provided you work on an Exchange network. Anyway, it's worth a try! See Book III, Chapter 1 for more details.

Chapter 3: Making Your E-Mail Look Professional and Cool

In This Chapter

✔ Removing misspelled words from your messages and the egg from your face

✔ Dressing up your e-mails

✔ Adding and manipulating images or illustrations in a message

✔ Inserting a hyperlink in an e-mail

✔ E-mailing an Outlook item

✔ Getting the text of your message just the way you want it

Frankly, there's nothing more embarrassing than revealing your ignorance. Perhaps you've hemmed and hawed your way through a conversation whose subject was only roughly familiar to you. You nodded at the right times and added vague comments that simply repeated what was already said. If so, then I say: Good for you, you faker! One thing you can't fake, however, is Spelling Champion. If you send messages that contain misspelled words, people will soon catch on that the spelling trophy on your desk is your brother's. You have no reason to get caught, however, because in Outlook, you can automatically spellcheck messages before you send them.

If your goal is to look smart, cool, and professional, I show you several ways to easily convince everyone that you are in this chapter. For example, you might use decorative stationery or a Quick Style to dress up a message. I show you how to add just about any kind of doodad you can think of: images, shapes, SmartArt (pre-drawn diagrams), horizontal lines, the current date and time, charts, tables, numbered and bulleted lists, hyperlinks, and bookmarks.

You can add images, charts, tables, shapes, hyperlinks, SmartArt, and just about anything that's fun only to messages that are in HTML format. By default, messages are already in HTML format, but if you've set Outlook to send plain text or RTF messages, you can change a single message to HTML by clicking the HTML button on the Format Text tab in the message form.

Checking Your Ignorance at the Door with Spelling and Grammar Checking

Outlook, like Word, automatically checks the spelling of words while you type. You can, if you want, have it step out of the way and stop hitting you over the head with its dictionary. Follow these steps to stop Outlook from checking spelling while you type an e-mail message:

1. **Click the File tab to display Backstage, and select Options from the list on the left.**

The Outlook Options dialog box appears.

2. **Select Mail from the list on the left.**

The Mail options appear on the right.

3. **In the Compose Messages section, click the Spelling and AutoCorrect button.**

The Editor Options dialog box appears.

4. **Select Proofing from the list on the left.**

The Proofing options appear on the right.

5. **In the When Correcting Spelling in Outlook section, deselect the Check Spelling as You Type check box, and then click OK twice to save your changes.**

Because Outlook won't be watching for mistakes while you type, you probably should check the spelling of a message right before you send it by pressing F7 or clicking the Spelling & Grammar button on the Review tab.

Because you can so easily just type and click Send, I like the check-as-you-go option, followed by a healthy dose of the automatically-check-this-again-before-sending option. Follow these steps to set up Outlook to spellcheck your e-mails right before sending:

1. **Click the File tab to display Backstage, and select Options from list on the left.**

The Outlook Options dialog box appears.

2. **Select Mail from the list on the left.**

The Mail options appear on the right.

3. **In the Compose Messages section, select the Always Check Spelling before Sending check box, and then click OK to save your changes.**

You can also have Outlook check your grammar while you type, but this option can be a bit annoying, in my opinion. (However, if you want Outlook to check grammar with spelling while you're composing a message, see the section "Checking grammar," later in this chapter, for how to get Outlook to check your grammar.) English is a fairly flexible language, and I tend to be a bit colloquial in my usage, so the Grammar checker and I sometimes find ourselves at odds. If you decide not to check grammar while you type, you can check grammar, along with spelling, right before you send a message.

The Outlook Grammar and Spelling checkers work within all Outlook items except notes. Of course, Outlook might check a message, but how and why might it check a contact, appointment, or task? Well, Outlook doesn't actually check the data that you enter for each item, but it does check the *notes* — anything you type in the big Notes area of an item. If you make a typo while typing in a Notes section, just follow the directions in the following section to correct it.

Checking spelling

The automatic spellcheck occurs while you type. (If you've turned that option off, you can start the Spelling checker by pressing the F7 key or clicking the Spelling & Grammar button on the message form's Review tab.) When you misspell a word, Outlook quickly underlines it with a red, wavy line. You can right-click the word and instantly correct it by selecting a suggestion from the pop-up menu that appears, as shown in Figure 3-1.

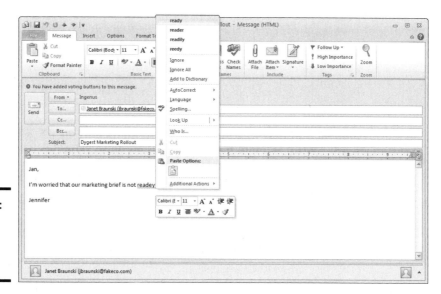

Figure 3-1:
Correct spelling while you type.

Here are the other options on that pop-up menu that Outlook gives you to deal with potential misspellings when you right-click a word that has a red, wavy underline:

+ **Ignore and Ignore All:** If the word isn't misspelled at all (so there, smartypants!), you can click Ignore to ignore this instance only; click Ignore All to ignore this word throughout the text.

+ **Add to Dictionary:** Use this option when the selected word is simply one that Outlook doesn't know (such as your name). If you click this option, the word is added to the dictionary, and Outlook never bothers you about it again.

+ **AutoCorrect:** Select a correction from this submenu to add the misspelling and its correction to the AutoCorrect list. Or select AutoCorrect Options to open the AutoCorrect in E-Mail dialog box. Type the misspelling in the Replace box and the correction in the With box, and then click Add. Click OK to close the dialog box.

You can use AutoCorrect to correct what you type; it's especially handy for the types of errors that the Spelling checker flags but can't correct (because it doesn't know what you meant to type). AutoCorrect works like this: You type a misspelled word, and if that word is in the AutoCorrect list, Outlook looks up the correction — and ZIP, POW, BANG! — Outlook replaces the misspelled word automatically. Outlook has a lot of common misspellings and their corrections (such as *thier* and *their*) already in its AutoCorrect list. But you can use the AutoCorrect option on the pop-up menu that appears when you right-click a word (refer to Figure 3-1) to add to this list so that it includes the types of spelling errors you often make, along with their corrected spellings. AutoCorrect uses what you add to correct your errors while you type.

+ **Language:** Allows you to select the language that the word is in. If you've set up Office to operate in more than one language, then the Spelling checker uses the language that you select from this menu to check the spelling of the selected word.

+ **Spelling:** Select this option if you agree that the word is misspelled, but Outlook has failed to provide a suggestion to correct it. The Spelling dialog box that appears displays a longer list of suggestions (where you might find the correction). In addition, if your message has a lot of misspellings, then by displaying the Spelling dialog box, you can review and correct these errors more easily than right-clicking and fixing each individual error manually. When the Spelling dialog box is displayed, the spelling error appears in red in the top window; select the correction you want to use from the Suggestions list at the bottom of the dialog box and click Change to change the text in the message form. The Spelling checker automatically moves to the next error and displays it in the top window. If the Spelling checker doesn't suggest the right correction, you can type the correction yourself (assuming you know how to correct the error) in the top window and click Change.

✦ **Look Up:** Displays a list of research sites that you can use to look up a term on the Internet. Outlook sends the search request out and displays the results in the Research pane. If you don't find what you want, you can select an option from the Can't Find It? section at the bottom of the pane. You can also search all the research sites and all the reference books (such as Encarta Dictionary and the English Thesaurus) in one stroke by clicking the All Reference Books or All Research Sites links in the Other Places to Search section at the bottom of the pane. See Figure 3-2.

**Book II
Chapter 3**

Making Your E-Mail
Look Professional
and Cool

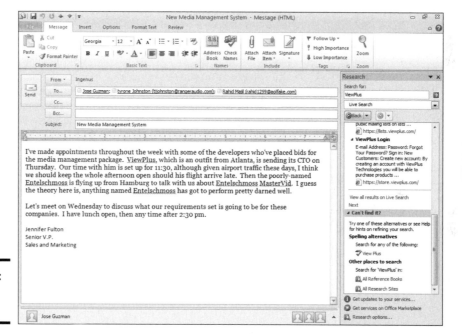

Figure 3-2:
Do a little
research.

✦ **Who Is:** Opens the Check Names dialog box and looks up a misspelled Contact name. See Chapter 1 in this minibook for how to check names.

The Spelling checker doesn't normally catch mistakes that aren't misspellings, although you might wish it did sometimes. For example, if you type `This is you're responsibility`, the Spelling checker doesn't flag the mistake. By default, however, Outlook turns on an option that allows the Spelling checker to check for errors in context, which causes it to flag the use of a wrong, but similar-sounding, word.

Although contextual checking is cool — gosh knows, it would catch a lot of common mistakes I make — it does slow down the computer, especially if you're running less than 1GB of RAM. So, if you want to turn the option off, click the File tab to display Backstage, and select Options from the list on the left to display the Outlook Options dialog box. Select Mail from the list on the left, and in the Compose Messages section, click the Spelling and Autocorrect button to display the Editor Options dialog box. Select Proofing from the list on the left, and in the When Correcting Spelling in Outlook section, disable the Use Contextual Spelling option. Click OK several times to save changes.

Checking grammar

Although, by default, Outlook doesn't check grammar, you can still have Outlook do it. After you turn on the Grammar checker, if you make a grammar mistake, the offending passage is underlined with a green, wavy line. If you see a blue, wavy underline, it's because you made a mistake in punctuation or capitalization. If you understand what's wrong (for example, the sentence is a fragment and not a complete thought), you can just type a correction.

Otherwise, you can right-click the wavy underlined text to see a pop-up menu that tells you why the grammar police stopped you, as shown in Figure 3-3. You can select one of the following options from the pop-up menu for further assistance:

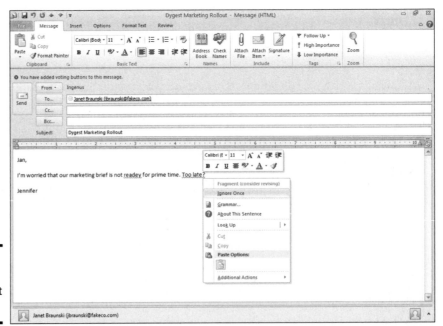

Figure 3-3:
Don't know nuttin' about grammar.

✦ **Ignore Once:** Select this option when the Grammar checker puts its nose where it doesn't belong. This option ignores the "error" in this instance only.

✦ **Grammar:** If you don't like the way the Grammar checker is pointing out your mistakes, you can display the Grammar dialog box, where you can promptly tell it to ignore this rule just this one instance (Ignore Once) or throughout the text (Ignore Rule). (See Figure 3-4.) To understand the rule more thoroughly before you decide what to do, click Explain. If you like one of the suggested fixes, select it and click Change to apply it. If you're doing a full grammar check on the whole message and that message includes another grammatical error, you can jump to that error by clicking Next Sentence. You can also change the Grammar options from this dialog box by clicking Options; see the following section for help in understanding them.

Book II
Chapter 3

Making Your E-Mail Look Professional and Cool

Figure 3-4:
Let Outlook help you improve your grammar.

✦ **About This Sentence:** Opens the Outlook Help window, which helps you understand your error by providing examples of that type of error.

✦ **Look Up:** Opens the Research pane and allows you to look up the grammatical phrase on the Internet. See the section "Checking spelling," earlier in this chapter, for help in using the Research pane.

You can turn off automatic spelling and grammar checking. If you do, check your Outlook message, contact, appointment, or task right before you save it or send it off. Just press F7 or click the Spelling & Grammar button on the Review tab. Keep in mind that the Spelling & Grammar command, despite its name, checks only spelling unless you set the option to always check grammar and spelling at the same time.

To control how and when Outlook checks grammar, follow these steps to make changes to your grammar settings:

You can make these same changes while checking spelling, if you display the Spelling dialog box (by right-clicking a misspelled word and selecting Spelling, as described in the section "Checking Spelling") and then click the Options button in the Spelling dialog box.

1. **Click the File tab to display Backstage, and select Options from the list on the left.**

   The Outlook Options dialog box appears.

2. **Select Mail from the list on the left.**

   The Mail options appear on the right.

3. **In the Compose Messages section, click the Spelling and AutoCorrect button.**

   The Editor Options dialog box appears.

4. **Select Proofing from the list on the left.**

   The Proofing options appear on the right.

5. **In the When Correcting Spelling in Outlook section, select the grammar options you want.**

   Select from any of these options:

   - *Mark Grammar Errors as You Type:* Select this check box to have Outlook check grammar while you type.

   - *Check Grammar with Spelling:* Select this check box to check grammar any time you check spelling (when you press F7 to start the Spelling checker or when Outlook automatically checks your spelling after you click Send).

   - *Show Readability Statistics:* Select this check box to have Outlook give you some idea of how easy your text is to read. Readability statistics, if you choose to use them, appear only after a manual spelling and grammar check. This option isn't the automatic, check-while-you-go kind.

    To calculate the readability statistics, Word calculates the Flesch Reading Ease and Flesch-Kincaid Grade Level scores. Both analyze your text using a number of factors such as word length and sentence length to determine how easy the text is to read. You should shoot for a Flesch Reading Ease score between 80-90, and a Flesch-Kincaid Grade Level of 11-12 if your audience is mostly adults.

6. **Click OK twice to save changes.**

Using Stationery to Add Flair

To dress up your messages and add some fun, you can choose from a variety of Outlook *stationery* that provides a colorful background or pattern on which to rest your words. If you're looking for something more high-tech and professional, you can choose an Outlook *theme,* which not only provides a background but also a matching set of bullets, fonts, text colors, china, and stemware.

Outlook provides its stationery and themes through a dialog box that you use at the start of a new message. If you find an Outlook stationery or theme that you want to use most of the time, you can set it up as the message default. Word provides some extra themes to Outlook through the Ribbon on a message form, making those themes available even after you start creating a message. (See the section "Applying a Word Theme," later in this chapter, for help.)

You can use stationery and themes only for HTML messages, not for plain text or RTF-formatted messages. Also, you can't add stationery or a theme to a reply or a forwarded message. See Chapter 1 of this minibook for help with message formats.

Taking a stationery out for a test run

To select an Outlook stationery or theme for a new message, follow these steps:

1. In the Mail module, click the New Items button on the Home tab, select E-Mail Message Using from the pop-up menu that appears, and then select More Stationery.

The Theme or Stationery dialog box, shown in Figure 3-5, appears.

By the way, if you want to use the same stationery that you've used recently (the last five types, to be exact), just select it from the E-Mail Message Using menu and skip the rest of this stuff.

Figure 3-5:
Stationery that makes your text look good.

2. **Select a stationery or theme, select other options, and click OK.**

When you make a selection from the Choose a Theme list, a sample appears on the right. Some selections are marked as stationery; the others are themes. Basically, themes provide consistent styles for various kinds of text, such as headings or bulleted lists, and a stationery provides a background. If you select a theme, you have three more options to choose from:

- *Vivid Colors:* Select this option to brighten up text, sometimes by adding color to black text or by making text bold.
- *Active Graphics:* Omit animated `.gif` files by disabling this option.
- *Background Image:* Select this option to bypass a graphic background.

If you select an Outlook theme, the text that you type in the message is automatically formatted by using that theme's body text style. If you format your text as a bulleted list, hypertext link, or heading, or you add a horizontal line (as explained in the section "Adding headings and other styles," later in this chapter), those elements look like the sample you saw in the Theme or Stationery dialog box.

If you select an Outlook stationery, the text is formatted in the default style for that stationery, but it probably doesn't have a fancy horizontal line or bullet style. If the stationery has a graphic that you want to type below, just double-click where you want to start the message, and then start typing.

A stationery provides you with a graphic background, whereas a theme provides a set that includes heading, bullet, and link styles, along with a background color (in most cases).

Selecting your everyday stationery

After you test-drive a few Outlook stationery choices and themes, you might come across one that fits you perfectly. If so, you can set that stationery or theme as your default. Just follow these steps:

1. **Click the File tab to display Backstage, and select Options from the list on the left.**

The Outlook Options dialog box appears.

2. **Select Mail from the list on the left.**

The Mail options appear on the right.

3. **In the Compose Messages section, click the Stationery and Fonts button.**

   The Signatures and Stationery dialog box appears, as shown in the background of Figure 3-6.

4. **Click the Theme button.**

   The Theme or Stationery dialog box appears, as shown in the foreground of Figure 3-6.

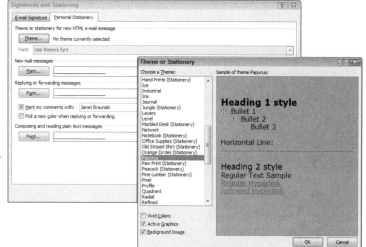

Figure 3-6:
Select your
favorite
stationery or
theme.

5. **Select your favorite theme or stationery from the list and click OK several times to close all dialog boxes.**

Even after setting a default, you can still pick and choose whatever stationery you want to use for an individual e-mail by following the steps so carefully outlined by *moi* in the preceding section. To go without your usual stationery, just click that ol' New Items button on the Home tab, choose E-Mail Message Using from the pop-up menu that appears, then choose a format: Plain Text, Rich Text, or HTML.

Applying a Word Theme

So as not to be left out, Word provides its own set of themes to Outlook, available only after you start a message. You can add a Word theme on top of an Outlook stationery or theme, although the result is often a rather surprising mix of colors and fonts.

In a Word theme, you get custom-colored and -styled fonts for body text, headings, bulleted lists, hyperlinks, and other text elements. You even get a style for horizontal lines. In addition, you get a set of colors: four text/background colors and six accent colors. After you select a theme, you see the first two text/backgrounds and the first two accent colors on the Colors button on the Options tab. The entire color palette appears anytime you try to colorize text, shapes, and other objects. You learned how to colorize text in Chapter 1 of this minibook; you learn how to colorize shapes and other objects in the sections "Formatting objects and playing around" later in this chapter.

Every HTML or Rich Text message uses the theme, Office, unless you choose a different theme to use. You can choose a theme or stationery (a message theme with a graphic background) when you begin a new message (see the section, "Taking a stationery out for a test run" for help in choosing a theme or stationery from the start). To apply a Word theme to an existing HTML or Rich Text message, click the Themes button on the Options tab to make a fat palette of Word themes appear, as shown in Figure 3-7. When you hover the mouse pointer over a theme, you can audition it (assuming you have some text in the message to use for the audition). Click a theme to select it. If you can't decide, select a theme based on its thumbnail — and if it turns out badly, simply repeat these steps to select a different theme. When you click a theme, existing text is reformatted to fit the new theme, quick as a wink.

If your text doesn't seem to change much when you preview a theme, don't worry — nothing's wrong with your monitor. The theme colors, for example, are only applied to colored text. (You learned how to apply text colors in Chapter 1 of this minibook.) So, if you haven't colored any text yet, then you don't see much of a change when you preview — other than the font, which typically changes from theme to theme.

At the bottom of the Themes menu, select Save Current Theme to save your current set of fonts and colors. See the section "Customizing your look," later in this chapter, for the scoop on creating themes. Select Browse for Themes to open one of these saved themes. Select Reset to Theme from Template to reapply the original message theme, which was probably the standard Office theme.

After you select a theme, just type. The font, size, and color of the theme's body text style are applied to what you type (as well as to existing text). The theme's heading style is applied to headings, the bullet style to bullets, and so on. (For the word on how to format text as a heading, a bulleted list, or whatever, see "Playing with Text," later in this chapter.) The fun doesn't stop there: If you create shapes, charts, tables, and the like, they're programmed by default to use the various colors built into the theme. That way, if you change to a different Word theme, your entire message stays color-coordinated.

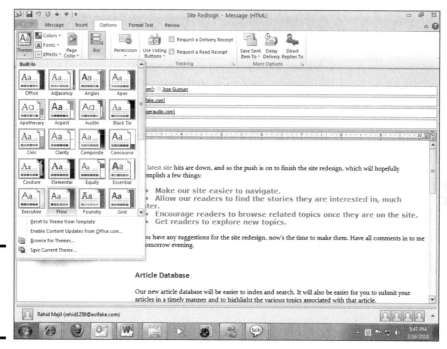

Figure 3-7:
Outlook,
move over
for Word
themes.

Applying a Color, Font, or Effects Set

Okay, is a theme too much decorating for you? No problem. If you want to
keep the fonts you use in a message and apply a different set of colors to bullets, headings, and the like, you can select just a color set. No guilt, no com-
mitment, no phone calls you have to avoid. You can do the same thing with
font types — switch them out without switching the colors you might have
already used in the message. If you've added lines and shapes to your message, you can pick out a set of fills and effects to apply to them.

Follow these quick steps to select a color, font, or effects set to a message:

1. **In the message form, click the arrow on the Colors, Fonts, or Effects
   button on the Options tab (depending on the element you want to
   change).**

   A menu or palette of choices pops up. Briefly, here's what each button
   is for:

   - *Colors:* You select the set of colors that can be applied to a variety
     of objects in your message, including text, headings, bulleted or
     numbered lists, shapes, SmartArt, charts, hyperlinks, text boxes, and
     horizontal lines. You insert most of these items by clicking buttons
     on the Insert tab (not surprisingly), which you can figure out how to
     do in the section "Illustrating Your Point," later in this chapter.

- *Fonts:* Each set includes two fonts — one for regular body text and the other for headings, although you can apply the fonts to text however you want.

- *Effects:* Each set includes a shape style, a color fill, shadow effects, and 3-D effects that provide a coordinated look to objects in your message. What objects, you ask? Good question. I'm talking about objects such as arrows, rectangles, stars, and so on, which you insert by using the Shapes button on the Insert tab. (See the section "Illustrating Your Point," later in this chapter.) You can also apply effects to SmartArt, charts, text boxes, and horizontal lines, which I discuss in various sections throughout this chapter.

2. **Click the Color, Font, or Effects set that you want to use.**

   When you slide the mouse pointer around the palette or down the list, the elements in your message change accordingly. For example, when you slide down the Fonts list, your text changes styles so that you can preview the option before you select it. If your message features a drawn object (such as a star), then it changes when you sweep down the Effects list. Colors you've applied to text or objects change when you preview the choices on the Colors list.

Creating a custom set of colors or fonts

Normally, the sets of colors, fonts, and effects that come with Outlook satisfy most people. And hey, you can easily select and apply the Fonts, Colors, and Effects sets, so what else could you want? Well, maybe you wish that one of the colors was a bit lighter or darker. Then, it would be just perfect. Or maybe you like the heading font, but you want to use something else for your body text. Or maybe your boss has instructed you to use only company colors in e-mails to clients. (Yippee.)

In any case, you can easily create your own set of custom colors and fonts. (You can't do anything about creating your own set of effects, so your boss is just gonna have to live with that.)

To create your own set of colors, start by modifying the set you're currently using. Haven't selected a set? Well, then you're using the Office default set of colors. But unless that generic set of colors represents all you want in the world, I'd recommend jumping back to the preceding section to figure out how to select a color set that's at least close to what you want to end up with. Then, follow these steps to change it:

1. **Click the Colors button on the Options tab, and then select Create New Theme Colors from the pop-up menu that appears.**

   The Create New Theme Colors dialog box peeks out, like the one shown in Figure 3-8.

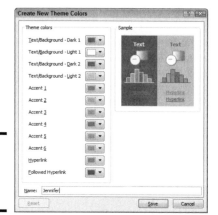

Book II
Chapter 3

Making Your E-Mail
Look Professional
and Cool

Figure 3-8:
Why
settle for
ordinary?

2. **Select the color that you want to change by clicking the button for that color.**

3. **Select a new color, either lightening or darkening the color from the palette that appears, or select one of the standard colors from the bottom of the palette.**

   To select a color that isn't on that palette, click the More Colors link and select one from the color palette that pops up. If you need help figuring out how to use the More Colors dialog box, you can find it in the section "Simply Colorizing the Background," later in this chapter.

4. **Repeat Steps 2 and 3 to change other colors.**

   You can look at the sample provided to decide whether the new color works with the existing colors or whether you need to select something different.

   If you decide that you don't like the colors you select, before you click Save, you can click the Reset button to return to all the original colors in the theme.

5. **Type a name for the theme in the Name text box.**

   If you can't think of a name, you can just add a number to the existing theme name and call it quits.

6. **Click Save.**

   The colors that you selected are applied automatically. For example, if a blue color appeared in the original color set, and you changed it to a nice green, then any text that used the blue changes to green. The set now appears in the Colors list, so you can select it again for a different message.

To create your own set of fonts, you basically follow the preceding steps, but you start by clicking the Fonts button on the Options tab, selecting Create New Theme Fonts from the pop-up menu that appears, and moving on from there. And no, you don't have to select a font set for your message first, although you're using one (even if you didn't choose one): the Office font set, which features Cambria for heading text and Calibri for body text. After clicking the Fonts button and selecting Create New Theme Fonts, a simple dialog box appears that allows you to select the Heading Font and Body Text font that you want. In the Sample area, you can see how your selections look together. When you're done looking in the mirror, type a name for your set in the Name box and click OK.

Customizing your look

After you select a Word theme, you can just type your message. The fonts and colors defined by the theme are applied automatically, and what could be easier than that? Still, sometimes you just need to express your own style. Luckily, even Word themes allow room for individuality.

Although you can't actually change the colors, fonts, or effects used in a theme, you can use the theme as your starting point and create a new theme to reuse however you want. Follow these steps:

1. **Select a Word theme that contains at least some of the elements you like, such as a rough set of colors and fonts.**

2. **Modify the color or font set (as described in the preceding section), and select a set of effects that you like.**

3. **To save your current Font, Color, and Effects selections as a new theme, click the Themes button on the Options tab and select Save Current Theme from the pop-up menu that appears.**

The Save Current Theme dialog box appears.

4. **Type a name for the theme in the File Name box and click Save.**

You can now use the theme in other messages. When you click the Themes button, your theme appears at the top, in the Custom section. Just click it to apply the custom theme to the current message.

Simply Colorizing the Background

If the thought of selecting a theme and using its heading, body text, and bullet styles seems like overkill for a simple message to a friend or colleague, you can opt for something simpler but equally as impressive: a colorful background. You can choose a solid color, gradient, texture, pattern, or image.

Keep in mind that if you select a dark-colored background, the normal body text (which is black) doesn't show up well on it. You should probably change your text to a lighter color to provide some contrast and make it easy to read. You probably want to use a sans-serif font, such as Calibri or Arial, as well, because its simple structure looks less fuzzy, even in a small size and with little contrast against the message background.

Color is a solid choice

To select a background color, click within the text area of the message form, then the Page Color button on the Options tab. A palette associated with the current theme appears (and yes, a theme is associated with your message, even if you didn't choose one — it's called Office). You can select any of those ten basic colors listed across the top of the palette, or their associated *tints* (white added to the basic theme color) or *shades* (black added). At the bottom of the palette, the set of ten standard colors from which you can choose appear.

Book II
Chapter 3

Making Your E-Mail
Look Professional
and Cool

The ten basic colors and their variations that appear on the Color palette come from the color set associated with the theme. The ten standard colors listed at the bottom of the palette represent the colors of the rainbow; the standard colors are always available in every theme.

If you overdo your choices and want to return to a plain message that has a white background, select No Color from the Page Color menu.

If you don't see a color that you want to try, click the More Colors option and select a color from the Colors dialog box that appears, which offers all the colors of the rainbow. (If you're overwhelmingly curious about that Fill Effects option, jump to the following section for all the details.) The Colors dialog box has two tabs for selecting colors:

+ **Standard:** Click a color from the large hexagon to select it. If you like black, gray, or white, you can click a color from the small group of hexagons that appear below the color hexagon.

+ **Custom:** Click the Custom tab, as shown in Figure 3-9, to custom blend your own color.

To create your own color in the Custom tab, follow these steps:

1. **Drag the four-pointed white marker within the Colors palette.**

   Dragging this marker selects a general color. In the figure, I selected a nice adobe brown by dragging the white pointy thing to the adobe brown area in the Colors palette on the left. The band to the right changes to show a range of this color, from tints to shades.

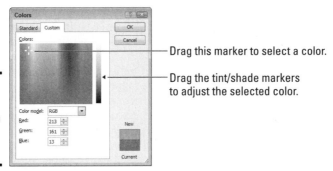

Drag this marker to select a color.

Drag the tint/shade markers
to adjust the selected color.

Figure 3-9:
Mix your
own color in
the Colors
dialog box.

2. **Drag the tint/shade marker to the color that you want and click OK.**

   To the right of the Colors palette, refine the vertical band of the current
   color by dragging the tint/shade marker up or down.

You can mix a color by the numbers if you want. Select the color model that
you're using, either RGB or HSL; then, enter the appropriate values from 0
to 255. *RGB* is short for *red, green, blue,* and it's one approach to creating
color on a computer monitor. If you set all values to zero, you get pure black;
if you set all to 255, you get white. Another approach to mixing color is HSL,
or *hue, saturation, luminance.* The hue value represents the color's position
on the color wheel; the saturation value controls the amount of gray that's
added to muddy the pure color; the luminance value controls the amount of
white added. Here, 0, 0, 0, gets you pure black; 0, 0, 255, gets you pure white;
and 0, 0, 127 gets you a perfect middle-gray.

Why not try a gradient, texture, pattern, or image?

If you don't want to use a pure color as your background, you can use a
fill, instead. You have several choices, such as a *gradient* (a slow blending
from one color to another), texture, *pattern* (an ordered arrangement of two
colors), or picture (such as a company logo). You're probably familiar with
this process because just about everything in the Office universe uses it, so I
cover it at warp speed. Follow these steps:

1. **Click within the text area of the message form, then click the Page
   Color button on the Options tab and select Fill Effects from the pop-up
   menu that appears.**

   The Fill Effects dialog box pops up, as shown in Figure 3-10.

2. **Select a gradient.**

   Click the Gradient tab and select a Colors option: One-Color, Two-Color,
   or Preset. Select the one, two, or preset color(s) that you want to work
   with. Adjust the amount of transparency in the gradient (if this option is
   available). Then, select a direction in the Shading Styles area.

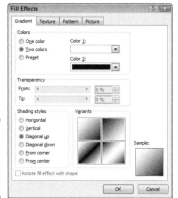

Figure 3-10:
Fill a
message's
background.

3. **OR select a Texture.**

    Click the Texture tab, and then select a texture. Pretty brainless.

4. **OR select a Pattern.**

    Click the Pattern tab, select a Foreground and a Background color, and then select the Pattern that you want. Not too difficult.

5. **OR select an Image.**

    Click the Picture tab. Click Select Picture, select the picture that you want to use, and click Insert. Images are tiled to fit the message form. They're not adjustable in Outlook, so do your resizing, cropping, and lightening (if you want to make it easier to see your text on the image) in a photo editor before you import the image into a message.

If you're looking for more control over an image that you use as a message background, you might be happier just inserting the image in the way explained in the following section. You can then format the image to allow text to flow over it (if that's what you're looking for), rather than around it. You can also crop, lighten, and adjust the level of contrast in Outlook, as needed, to make the image a proper background.

Inserting an Image

When it comes to adding pictures to an e-mail message, you have several choices: You can use an image as a message background (as explained in the preceding section), insert one of your own images and wrap text around it, or use one of Microsoft's images from its Microsoft Clip Organizer. You can also attach an image file, but that's different from actually placing an image within a message; see Chapter 1 of this minibook for help on attaching a file. To insert an image or a clip in a message do either of the following:

+ **To insert an image:** Click the Picture button on the Insert tab, select the image that you want from the Insert Picture dialog box that appears, and click Insert.

+ **To insert a clip:** Click the Clip Art button on the Insert tab to display the Clip Art pane. Type a search term (such as `gold fish`) in the Search For text box. You can include online clipart in the search by turning on the Include Office.com Content option.

  You can limit the results by selecting particular file types from the Results Should Be list. Click Go to display images that match your search criteria. Click an image to insert it into the message.

You can select, resize, move, and rotate an image the same way that you manipulate objects. See the section "Manipulating Objects," later in this chapter, for the lowdown.

One of the coolest things about the new Office programs is that they really make formatting fun. Take images, for instance: When you select one, up pops the Picture Tools Format tab; click it to see more buttons (on the Ribbon) than you find on a home theater remote control. (See Figure 3-11.) Here's what those buttons can do:

Figure 3-11:
Make any image look the way you want by using the Picture Tools Format tab.

+ **Corrections:** This button displays a palette of adjustments, such as sharpness, softness, brightness, and contrast of an image. Just click a sample to apply that correction to the picture.

To adjust the picture more precisely, select Picture Corrections Options from the bottom of the palette. In the dialog box that appears, you can drag Soften-Sharpen, Brightness, and Contrast sliders to adjust the softness/sharpness or brightness/contrast, or enter precise values.

+ **Color:** Displays a palette that allows you to adjust the amount of color in a picture *(saturation)* and its *tone* (the warmth or coolness of the colors — whether the colors are overly reddish or bluish). Click a sample to apply that adjustment, or select Picture Color Options from the bottom of the Color palette to display a dialog box in which you can make fine adjustments.

The Color palette also allows you to add a colored tint to a picture. Select a variation to recolor the image to that shade from the three rows in the Recolor area of the palette. The first row of options allows you to quickly create a black and white, grayscale, sepia, or washed-out image. The variations in the next two rows are all based on the current template colors, which helps you create a unified look easily. However, you can select More Variations from the bottom of the palette to choose a different color for tinting from the additional palette that appears.

Click the Set Transparent Color option on the Color palette, and then click in the image to change all pixels of that same color to transparent pixels so that you can see text through that part of the image. Use this option to remove the background around the subject, assuming that background is basically one color.

This Set Transparent Color business works only with particular images and clip art, but it's always worth a try. If you're dealing with a picture, you can use a cooler way to remove its background. See the section "Removing an image's background," later in this chapter, to find out the technique all the cool kids are using.

✦ **Artistic Effects:** Displays a palette of effects that make the picture look like it's drawn with markers, pencils, chalk, paint, watercolors, pastels, and so on. Click a sample to apply that effect to the picture. Click Artistic Effects Options at the bottom of the palette to display a dialog box where you can fine-tune the effect.

✦ **Compress Pictures:** This option *compresses* (reduces the file size) of all images in the message so that the message isn't too big to send. It also, however, reduces the quality of the images. In the dialog box that appears after you click the Compress Pictures button, you can select the quality level *(resolution)* you're willing to live with. You can also choose to apply the compression to selected images (rather than all images in the message), and to remove the cropped part of an image permanently (from the message only; this cropping doesn't affect the actual image file).

✦ **Change Picture:** Allows you to swap the current selected image with one of your own (and not one from Microsoft Clip Organizer), without losing the formatting that you applied to that image.

✦ **Reset Picture:** Resets the image to its original state (removing all formatting).

The Remove Background, Picture Styles, Picture Border, Picture Effects, Picture Layout, Wrap Text, Bring Forward, Send Backward, Selection Pane, Align, Group, Rotate, Crop, Shape Height, and Shape Width buttons also apply to a variety of other objects, such as shapes and text boxes. You can find descriptions for them in the section "Manipulating Objects," later in this chapter.

Illustrating Your Point

They say that pictures are worth a thousand words, and when you're trying to make a point, I guess that's true. Outlook provides several ways in which you can put your money, so to speak, where your mouth is: tables, charts, shapes, and SmartArt graphics.

SmartArt is a special graphic that you can use to illustrate a set of related data, such as a list of items or a series of steps. You can also find graphics that illustrate a cycle (such as a monthly process), hierarchy (such as an organization chart), relationship between items, *matrix* (parts that relate to a whole), or *pyramid* (proportionate relationships).

Most often, you will use tables, charts, shapes and SmartArt graphics to illustrate your documents, worksheets, and presentations, and not e-mail messages. This book doesn't focus on Word, Excel, or PowerPoint, however; so I'll just be touching on the basic how-to's in the following sections. If you want all the info you can stand about working with tables, charts, shapes, and SmartArt, check out *Microsoft Office 2010 All-in-One Desk Reference For Dummies,* by Peter Weverka.

To insert a symbol, such as £ or ¥ or ©, click the Symbol button on the Insert tab. In the palette that appears, select a symbol. If you don't find what you need, select More Symbols. In the dialog box that appears, select a character set, and then click a symbol to insert it in the text.

Tabling the notion

A table is a collection of related data, presented in rows and columns. The rows and columns intersect to form *cells.* You might use a table to show your wife how you plan to pay for a new multimedia room in three months, using the extra income you save by packing both of your lunches every day, not eating out for dinner during the week, and limiting her clothing allowance. (Okay, maybe even a table can't help that cause. . . .)

Here's the quick and easy way to insert a table: Click the Table button on the Insert tab. Drag over the grid that appears to select the number of rows and columns that you want. A table appears in your message. To enter data, click in the first cell on the left, type something, and then press Tab to move to the cell to the right of the first cell in the same row. Press Tab at the end of a row to move down a row, to the first cell on the left. If you press Tab in the last cell in a table, you automatically add a new row. Format the table quickly by clicking inside the table and selecting a table style from the Table Styles palette that appears on the Table Tools Design tab. Use the More button to display more table styles than you can figure out what to do with.

The check boxes to the far-left of the Table Tools Design tab control which table styles you see. For example, if you enable the Header Row, Total Row, and Banded Rows options, you see formatting tailored to make the headings in the first row of your table and the totals in the last row stand out. Because of the Banded Rows option, the colors for the body of the table alternate rows.

Use the Table Tools Layout tab to select a table element such as a row, and then format it by using the Shading and Borders buttons on the Table Tools Design tab. The Layout tab also includes buttons for adding and removing rows and columns, merging two cells together, and changing text alignment.

Charting the way

A *chart* is a graphical representation of a table. Instead of expecting your boss to pore over the latest boring sales data, why not show her graphically why she pays you the big bucks? And if she doesn't pay you the big bucks, maybe a chart that clearly shows how you consistently outsell everyone in the department can convince her why she should.

To insert a chart, click the Chart button on the Insert tab. The Insert Chart dialog box pops up; select a chart type on the left and a sample on the right, and then click OK. A chart appears in the message, based on the fake table data that appears in a separate worksheet window. Change this worksheet data in this separate window to change the chart (see Figure 3-12). (See the preceding section for some help with entering data into a table.) When you finish, close the worksheet window by clicking its Close button.

You can redisplay this worksheet at a later time if needed, by clicking the chart and then clicking the Edit Data button on the Chart Tools Design tab.

You can't create a chart based on a table that's already in a message — at least, not automatically. You can, however, select the table and paste its data into the worksheet after you create the chart.

Click in a chart, and then select a chart style from the Chart Styles palette on the Chart Tools Design tab to quickly format the chart. Use the More button at the right end of the Chart Styles group to display the entire palette of styles. On the Chart Tools Design tab, you can also change the chart type and apply a chart layout to rearrange the various chart elements, such as the chart legend. On the Chart Tools Layout tab, you can add chart elements, such as a legend, a title, and labels. You can also change how often the gridlines appear and rearrange the vertical and horizontal axes of the chart.

Chart

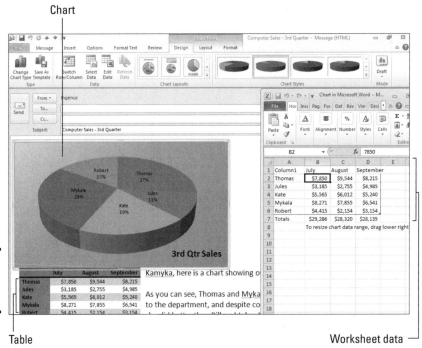

Figure 3-12:
Sales are
up.

Table

Worksheet data

You can format the elements of a chart (the bars, key, title, and so on) separately. For help with most of the buttons on the Chart Tools Format tab, see
the section "Manipulating Objects," later in this chapter.

Getting your message to take shape

The best way to call attention to critical information is to draw a big, fat
arrow pointing to it. Using the Shapes tool, you can insert not only arrows,
but rectangles, circles, lines, stars, flowchart symbols, and other interesting
shapes. You use the same process that you do within any other Office program; just click the Shapes button on the Insert tab, click a shape on the palette that appears, and then drag in the message form — from the upper-left
corner down to the lower-right corner — to position and size the shape.

At this point, you can insert more shapes by clicking a shape in the Insert
Shapes section on the Format tab. After you insert a shape, you can resize,
move, and format it. See the section "Manipulating Objects," later in this
chapter, for help in getting your shape just the way you want it.

To add text within a shape, just click the shape and type. To edit that text, click the shape, which makes the cursor appear within the text. Make your changes like you would within Word — press Backspace to erase characters to the left of the cursor or Delete to erase characters to the right. If you resize a shape, the text inside doesn't change, but you can select the text and resize it manually.

Getting smart with SmartArt

You might want to make your point by illustrating it with *SmartArt,* a set of graphics similar to charts. SmartArt helps to tell the story of a set of data in a graphically fun way that keeps your audience interested while you bamboozle 'em. Need to keep up department morale during another sense-less reshuffling of company personnel? Hide the news with a cool-looking Organization chart. Want to convince your boss that a big project can still get done on time, despite several critical setbacks? Illustrate your ideas by using a step-by-step plan and a process graph. Follow these steps to insert a SmartArt graphic:

1. **Click the SmartArt button on the Insert tab.**

The Choose a SmartArt Graphic dialog box jumps out.

2. **Select a SmartArt category from the list on the left (such as Process), and then select a graphic type from those shown on right.**

When you click each graphic type, a description that explains the intended use of that type appears on the far-right.

3. **Click OK.**

Some SmartArt graphics are better suited for illustrating particular ideas, processes, or data. Select List as your SmartArt type for items that can appear in any particular order, such as a grocery list. Select the Process type to show the steps in a task; select the Cycle type to show the steps in a task that repeats itself. Select the Hierarchy type when you want to create an organization chart or illustrate a series of decisions and where they might lead. Select the Relationship type when the most important point you need to make relates to the connections between items; select the Matrix type to highlight how various components relate to the whole unit. Select the Pyramid type to show how items relate proportionately, with the biggest or most important item in the largest part of the pyramid. Select the Picture type to show the relationship between items by using pictures.

The SmartArt graphic appears in the message, as shown in Figure 3-13. Click each bullet and type the appropriate text in the Type Your Text Here pane that appears. For example, type each item in a list or each step in a process. You enter each item in your process or list in the Type Your Text Here pane, as a bulleted list; just press Enter at the end of a line to add another bullet (which automatically creates another symbol in the SmartArt graphic) or press Tab to create a sub-bullet. To remove a bullet, select the text and press Delete.

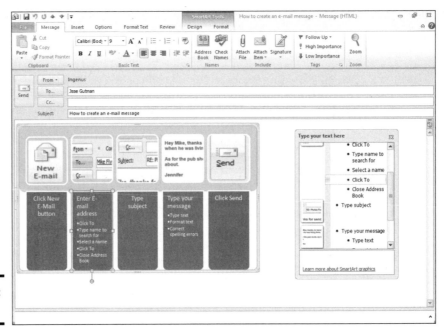

Figure 3-13:
Get smart.

If you press Enter to add another bullet but the item is marked with a red X in the Type Your Text Here pane, then Outlook is telling you that you can't type data there. But you might be able to add those extra items if you switch to a different layout.

You can format the text in the Type Your Text Here pane, although the formatting doesn't appear in that pane. It appears in the SmartArt graphic. Close the Type Your Text Here pane when you finish entering and formatting text; if you need it to stick its head back up, click the Text Pane button on the SmartArt Tools Design tab.

Now that you have a SmartArt graphic, you can do a lot of things to it:

✦ **Switch layouts.** If you select the Alternating Hexagon style, List type graphic but it just isn't working for you, you can change to a different style List type graphic by selecting one from the Layouts section of the

SmartArt Tools Design tab. If you want to change from a List type to a Process type, or to something else entirely, click the More button in the lower-right corner of the Layouts section of the Design tab and click More Layouts from the palette that appears to redisplay the Choose a SmartArt Graphic dialog box.

✦ **Colorize.** At the start, your SmartArt is as blue as a suede shoe. But you don't have to leave it like that; select one of the SmartArt Styles on the SmartArt Tools Design tab to dress up the blue look or click the Change Colors button on the SmartArt Tools Design tab to, uh, change colors from the palette that appears.

✦ **Add images.** Some SmartArt graphics contain a picture holder, which you can use to illustrate a step or process, or to provide some icon to help the reader remember what you said, even after ten seconds. Click the picture holder, search around for a graphic, and then click Insert.

✦ **Change the order of things.** On some SmartArt graphics, you can flip the order of shapes in the graphic by clicking the Right to Left button on the SmartArt Tools Design tab. To change the order of an item in the list, click it, and then click the Move Up or Move Down button on the SmartArt Tools Design tab.

SmartArt is similar to other objects such as shapes, text boxes, and images, and thus you can format and manipulate it just like other objects. See the section "Manipulating Objects," later in this chapter, for more ideas on changing your SmartArt.

Showing exactly what you mean

If you've ever tried to explain to someone, such as a tech specialist, exactly what problems you're seeing on your computer, then you know that both of you can quickly get frustrated by the lack of understanding on both sides. You speak normal-talk; the specialist speaks tech-talk, and never the twain shall meet.

You can easily get your point across in a message by including a screenshot of what you're seeing on your computer. I use screenshots all the time in this book to show you dialog boxes, the Ribbon, and the various parts of Outlook. You can do the same thing by following these steps to insert a screenshot in a message:

1. **Set up your screen so that it displays what you want to show.**

2. **In a message form, click the Screenshot button on the Insert tab.**

A palette of images appears. Each thumbnail image represents each of the windows you have open. (See Figure 3-14.)

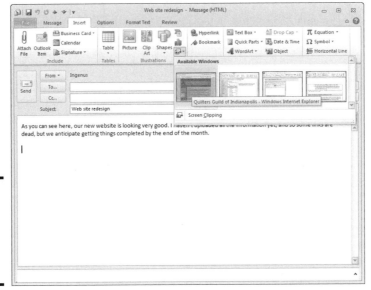

Figure 3-14:
Capture a
screenshot
to explain
what you
mean.

3. **Click one of the Screenshot images to insert it in the message form.**

   If you want to grab only part of the screen, select Screen Clipping from
   the palette, instead of clicking an image. The screen turns a semi-trans-
   parent white. Click at the upper-left point of the screen that you want
   to capture, and then drag the mouse pointer down and to the right, to
   outline the area you want. When you release the mouse pointer, the area
   you selected is inserted into the message.

4. **Make adjustments to the screenshot, as needed.**

   The inserted screenshot is automatically selected in your message form,
   and the Picture Tools Format tab appears. Use the tab's buttons to
   make adjustments to the image, as described in the section "Inserting an
   Image," earlier in this chapter, and the section "Manipulating Objects,"
   next in this chapter. For example, you might resize the image.

Manipulating Objects

A shape is just an object, meaning that you can manipulate it separately
from the message text. In Outlook, you can insert and manipulate several
types of objects, such as images, clipart, shapes, SmartArt, or text boxes.

Selecting, resizing, and other basic techniques

Use some of these common techniques to manipulate an object:

✦ **Select an object.** Click it to make white squares, called *handles,* appear around the object so that you can get a handle on what to do next. (See Figure 3-15.)

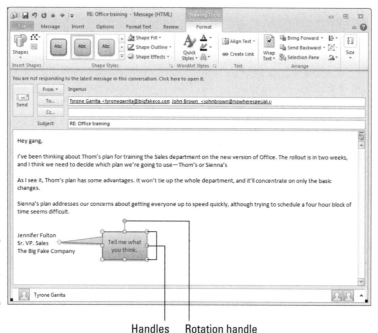

Figure 3-15: Get a handle on it.

Handles   Rotation handle

✦ **Resize an object.** Drag it by a handle. Drag by a corner handle to keep the object in proportion so that you don't distort it.

✦ **Move an object** by clicking in its center and dragging. Be careful; you can only move the object as you might a selected word, by dragging and dropping it within a paragraph.

✦ **Rotate an object.** Click the green dot connected to the top handle and drag right or left. (Refer to Figure 3-15.)

Formatting objects and playing around

After you select the object, you can use any of the tools that appear on the object's Format tab to pretty it up. You can't use buttons that are grayed out on the current object.

Here are some things you can do to format an object:

✦ **Format an object.** After you select an object, tools for formatting it appear on the Format tab. Apply a style to the object by selecting that style from the Styles list; click the More button below the scroll bar to display all the styles on a large palette. Fill the object with color, gradient, texture, or pattern by selecting one from the Shape Fill palette. (See the section "Simply Colorizing the Background," earlier in this chapter, for help in choosing a color or effect.) Like with any other formatting palette, just hover your mouse pointer over a style or color to preview it before you buy. Change the object's outline (its color, width, and style) by selecting a new one from the Shape Outline/Picture Border palette. Click No Outline to remove the border.

When sending a message to someone who doesn't use Outlook 2010 or Outlook 2007, keep in mind that some of your formatting may not appear in the recipient's e-mail in the way that you see it. For the most part, your formatting should arrive intact, but if you format shapes, they appear in a light blue rectangle.

✦ **Add a special effect.** Add shadows, reflections, glows, soft edges, and 3-D effects by selecting effects from the Shape Effects/Picture Effects palette. (See Figure 3-16.) If you want to refine the effect, select the Options command at the bottom of the palette. For example, to refine a shadow effect, select Shadow Options from the bottom of the Shadow palette. The Format Shape dialog box appears so you can customize the shadow effect.

✦ **Wrap text around an object.** The Wrap Text button controls how text runs alongside or over the object. Click the button and make a selection from the pop-up menu that appears; for example, select Square. Selecting In-Line with Text causes text to flow beside the bottom edge of the object like it's one really big word; selecting this option also causes the object to move left or right with the text when you add or delete text from the paragraph. The other options allow text to flow around all sides of the object, top and bottom only, or through the object.

If you change the text wrap to anything other than In-Line with Text, you can stack the object with other objects in the message (such as another shape, image, or text box) so that the object either is partially obscured by the other objects or partially obscures them.

✦ **Change the object's shape.** Click the Edit Shape button on the Format tab, then select Change Shape to select a different shape for the object. For example, you can change the object from a rectangle to an oval. Hold still, my beating heart! You can twist and turn the shape by moving one of its edit points (black dots that appear at each corner). Just select Edit Points from the Edit Shape menu to display small black points (handles) around the shape, and drag one of the black handles to a new location. Two wings appear on either side of the black handle; drag the white dot on one of these wings to curve that side of the object. (See Figure 3-17.)

Figure 3-16:
Manipulate
objects so
that they
look the way
you want
them to.

Add an effect.   Wrap text.

Stack objects on top of each other.

Edit shape button

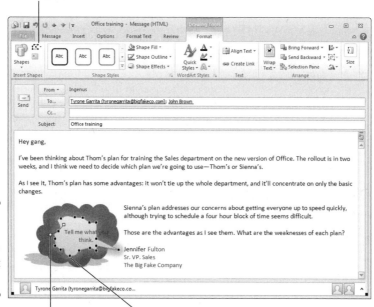

Figure 3-17:
Twist and
turn a shape
by using edit
points.

Bend object's side   Drag an edit point to change
with this handle.   an object's shape.

✦ **Rotate the object.** You can find out how to rotate an object by dragging its green handle in the preceding section. If you click the Rotate button on the Format tab, you can rotate a shape 90 degrees left or right, or flip it (mirror it). Select More Rotation Options to rotate an object by the exact amount you enter.

✦ **Crop a picture.** This option is available only for images. Click the Crop button on the Format tab to make *crop handles* (thick dashes) appear around the image's border. Drag a handle inward to crop off that part of the image (to prevent that portion from showing). You're not actually doing anything to the real image, and you can undo whatever you crop, so don't worry. When you're done, click outside the image.

You can compress the images in a message to reduce their size. One option in the compression process allows you to remove the cropped areas from an image from memory, reducing the size of an image even more. If you do that, however, you can't restore the original cropped areas of the image to your message. But you can always reinsert the image because this compression thing doesn't hurt the original image file.

✦ **Resize an object.** Using the Size boxes on the Format tab, you can enter the exact vertical and horizontal dimensions that you want.

Making an image significantly larger than its original size reduces its quality.

Arranging objects

If you have more than one object in your message, you can arrange them in various ways. First, you have to select the objects that you want to deal with. To do that, just hold down Ctrl while you click each one. After you rope them, here's what you can do with 'em:

✦ **Stack 'em:** Imagine a bunch of objects as a stack of pancakes. Some pancakes are beneath others in the stack and are partially or fully obscured. Other pancakes are on top of the others, and you can see more of each pancake. You can move an object in the stack of objects you've selected so that it appears on top of certain "pancakes" and beneath others. (Refer to Figure 3-16.) To move an object to the top of the stack (so that it moves in front of all other objects), first select the object, click the arrow on the Bring Forward button on the Format tab, and then select Bring to Front from pop-up menu that appears. To move the object up in the stack one "pancake" at a time, click Bring Forward as many times as needed.

To move the object behind all objects, do the selecting business, click the arrow on the Send Backward button on the Format tab, and then select Send to Back from pop-up menu that appears. To move an object down the stack one object at a time, click Send Backward as many times as needed. By the way, the Bring in Front of Text and Send Behind Text commands on these buttons are the same as the In Front of Text and Behind Text commands on the Wrap Text button.

✦ **Line 'em up:** Select your candidates, then click the Align button on the Format tab to arrange them. First, choose whether to align the object(s) to the page edge or the margin by selecting Align to Page or Align to Margin on the pop-up menu that appears when you click the Align button. Then click the button again, and choose a vertical (left, center, right) or horizontal (top, middle, bottom) alignment from the pop-up menu. If you have multiple objects selected, your vertical or horizontal alignment choice results in having those objects lined up along the edge you choose. For example, if you have two shapes selected, and you choose Align Top, then both shapes are lined up along their top edge. If you have only one object selected, these choices line the object up against the page edge or the margin. You can also distribute multiple objects evenly between the page or margin borders by choosing either Distribute Horizontally or Distribute Vertically from the pop-up menu.

✦ **Group 'em:** Outlook allows you to group multiple selected shapes and/ or text boxes together in order to move, resize, and format them in one step. Hold down Ctrl and click each object to select it, then click the Group button on the Format tab and select Group from the pop-up menu that appears. To ungroup objects and treat them separately, click the Group button on the Format tab and select Ungroup from the pop-up menu that appears.

Removing an image's background

Sometimes, when you look at an image, you think, "Lose the background." For example, you might have found a real scary pumpkin just right for a Halloween party invitation, but perhaps it loses its effectiveness when it's framed inside a nice rectangle filled with a cheery blue sky. Well, turns out you can remove the sky from just such a photo, without using a surgical knife. Follow these steps:

1. **Click the image to select it.**

2. **Click the Remove Background button on the Picture Tools Format tab.**

Outlook analyzes the image and attempts to identify its subject. It then highlights everything else (what it thinks is the background) in purple. It also places a rectangle around the general area of the subject, as shown in Figure 3-18.

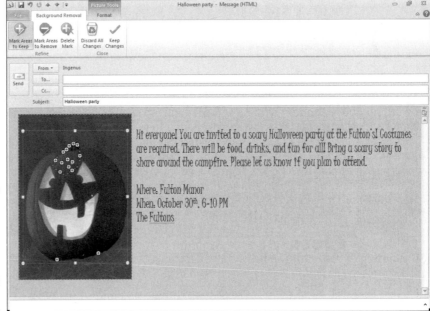

Figure 3-18:
Outlook
makes a
guess about
what to
remove from
an image.

3. **Adjust the rectangle that marks the subject area by dragging it around and/or resizing it (by dragging one of the white handles).**

4. **Indicate the areas that you want to mark as background by clicking the Mark to Remove button on the Background Removal tab.**

   Click a few times on the area that you want to mark as background, and Outlook should make the adjustment.

   You don't need to mark the outline of an area, although that might help. Just click around the area, let Outlook make its guess, and then refine the edge by clicking or dragging along it, if needed.

5. **Mark the subject area by clicking the Mark to Include button on the Background Removal tab.**

   Again, just click the subject area, especially on large patches of the same color, and Outlook should be able to figure out what you mean.

6. **Remove the background.**

   When you're through making adjustments, click the Keep Changes button on the Background Removal tab to do the deed. The image background is removed.

After removing an image's background, you may want to crop the image to hide those empty areas and allow you to place an image closer to your text. See the section "Formatting objects and playing around," earlier in this chapter, for the lowdown on how to make these changes.

Linking to the Outside World

Yes, there is a world outside your computer, and Outlook attempts to keep you connected to it, mostly by dumping a lot of messages on your desktop. It's a bit ironic, because if you weren't tied to your computer reading tons of e-mail, you'd be able to actually experience the world outside. Anyway, if you're on the Internet and you find an interesting Web page, you can provide a clickable link to the page within an e-mail message. You can also insert a link to any file on your computer or your company's network, assuming that the file is in a shared folder and that your recipient has access to the shared folder. In addition, you can link to another spot in that same message, which is a really neat way to allow someone to jump around a lengthy communiqué. And if that's not enough, you can link to an e-mail address. This kind of link creates an automatically addressed e-mail message when the user clicks it.

**Book II
Chapter 3**

Making Your E-Mail
Look Professional
and Cool

To insert a link, select the text in your message that the user must click to activate the link. Then, follow these steps:

1. **Click the Hyperlink button on the Insert tab.**

The Insert Hyperlink dialog box, shown in Figure 3-19, appears.

The text you selected appears in the Text To Display box. You can change this text, if you want, and you can even click the aptly named ScreenTip button to add a ScreenTip that appears when the user hovers the mouse pointer over the link.

Figure 3-19:
Add a link to
a Web page
or file.

2. **From the Link To pane, click the button that best describes where the page or file you want to link to is located.**

   The list on the right changes, depending on what you select.

   Here are your Link To choices:

   - **Existing File or Web Page:** Select the file or Web page that you want to link to. You can browse files in the current folder or files you've recently used, or you can go searching for a file located elsewhere. If you're linking to a Web page, you can look through a list of recently browsed pages or simply type the Web page address.

   - **Place in This Document:** This option assumes that you've pre-marked the places within the message you want the reader to navigate to by either bookmarking them or formatting them as headings. (See the "Adding headings and other styles" section, later in this chapter, for more info.) Select the bookmark or heading to link to from the Select a Place in This Document list.

   To create a bookmark in a message, select the text to bookmark and then click the Bookmark button on the Insert tab. Enter a name (no spaces, please) into the Bookmark Name field, and then click Add.

   - **Create New Document:** Enter a name for your new document in the Name of New Document field, and then click the Change button to change the folder in which you want to store this new file. In the When to Edit section, select when you want to actually start working on this new file — now or later.

   - **E-mail Address:** Type the e-mail address that you want to link to or select from the list of recently used e-mail addresses. Most of the time, you use this option to help the recipient send you some kind of related message, in which case, type your e-mail address. Type a subject for the e-mail message that this link creates in the Subject field; use something that helps recipient (possibly you) remember what this message is about.

3. **Click OK in the Insert Hyperlink dialog box.**

   The hyperlink is created. The text for the link is formatted according to the current template that you're using. See the sections "Using Stationery to Add Flair" and "Applying a Word Theme," both earlier in this chapter, for help.

4. **To test the link, hold down Ctrl and click it.**

You can also type the hyperlink text in the message, instead of inserting it. The only problem with that process is that the format for most hyperlinks is pretty difficult to type in manually and get right. If you get it wrong, you send your recipients into la-la land when they click the resulting link.

(I have no qualms, though, when it comes to copying a link to a Web page from the Address box of my browser, and then pasting it into a message when needed.) Whether you type a link or paste it, as soon as you press the spacebar, Outlook recognizes that you've typed a link and formats it appropriately. If (for some reason) the magic doesn't work, put the link text in between < and >, and then press the spacebar or hit Enter.

Inserting an Outlook Item

You might want to share a certain contact or the details of an appointment with someone without actually sharing your full Calendar or Contacts list. You can find out how to share parts of Outlook (such as the Calendar) later in this book, but if the person you want to pass the information on to isn't a part of your shared network, well, then you might think you're out of luck. As it turns out, your luck is about to turn: You can, when needed, send along any Outlook item with an e-mail message to just about anyone.

Attached Outlook items come out as gibberish to anyone who doesn't have Outlook, so don't bother. You can, however, send part of your calendar to even a non-Outlook user. See Book IV, Chapter 3.

To attach an Outlook item to a message, follow these steps:

1. **Click the Attach Item button on the Message tab.**

From the menu that appears, select the item that you want to send, such as a business card (an address card), a section of your calendar (such as today's appointments), or another Outlook item.

2. **Make additional selections, as needed.**

If you select Business Card, for example, you need to select the card from the menu that appears, which lists cards that you've sent in previous messages. If the card you want to send doesn't appear, select Other Business Cards, then select the card from the dialog box that appears and click OK.

The recipient can later save the attached business card, by the way, to his/her Outlook Contacts list. He or she just has to right-click the card and select Add to Outlook Contacts from the pop-up menu that appears.

If you select Calendar, the Send a Calendar via E-Mail dialog box appears. If you have more than one calendar, select the one from the Calendar list that you want to pull from. Select a section to include from the Date Range list (such as Today or Next 7 Days). Next, select the level of detail you want to send out, such as your availability during certain time slots or the full details of each appointment/meeting. To limit the calendar details to working hours only (by default, Outlook has working hours set for 8 a.m. to 5 p.m., but you can click Set Working Hours to change that), select the Show Time within My Working Hours Only option. Click OK when you're done making all these choices.

Click the Show button at the bottom of the Send a Calendar via E-Mail dialog box to display more options, such as including items that you've marked as private (yeah, that's likely) or attachments within calendar items. (These options aren't available if you select Availability Only from the Detail list). You can also select the layout for the calendar section that you send. If you select to attach the calendar items, they're sent in iCalendar format, which means that the recipient can then add those items to his or her Calendar.

If you select the Another Outlook Item option, then the Insert Item dialog box appears. Open the folder that contains the item you want to send from the Look In list. The list of items in that folder appears in the Items box at the bottom of the dialog box. Click the item that you want to send. Select whether to send the item as an attachment or as text only, and then click OK.

When a recipient receives a message that has an Outlook item attached, he or she can just open the attachment normally to view it. The attachment is displayed just like any other Outlook item. The recipient can also add it to his or her Outlook.

Playing with Text

You can do a lot more with text in Outlook messages than simply typing it. You might have already played with formatting; if not, skip over to Chapter 1 of this minibook for help. You have, I hope, discovered the spellcheck feature; it's saved me from embarrassment more times than I care to admit. If not, skip back to "Checking Your Ignorance at the Door with Spelling and Grammar Checking," earlier in this chapter. This section is kind of a catchall for other things that you can do with text, such as formatting it with Word styles and creating bulleted and numbered lists.

From time to time, you might want to insert the date and/or time into a message, if for no other reason than to remind your recipient just how long he or she has sat on it without responding. You can insert the date as text or as a field; you can update a field to reflect the current date or time, as needed, such as after creating a long, detailed message that took several days or weeks to finish. To insert the date or time, select the Date & Time button on the Insert tab. Select the format that you want; select Update Automatically to enter it as a field, and then click OK. If you don't enter the date/time as a field, then Outlook inserts the current date/time, which can't be updated as you continue to work. Assuming you entered the date/time as a field, then to update the field, click it and an Update button magically appears just above the text. Click the button to update the field (change the text to display the current date/time).

Adding headings and other styles

You can use themes to quickly dress up an e-mail so that it actually looks like you know what you're doing. In a theme, you instantly get a package of formats that apply to body text, bulleted lists, headings, horizontal lines, hyperlinks, and a variety of other elements. (See the section "Applying a Word Theme," earlier in this chapter, for the details about themes.)

If you want the formats in a selected theme to work, you have to identify the elements of a message, such as the headings and hyperlinks. Outlook identifies some elements, such as hyperlinks, by the way you insert them. Other elements, such as headings, are just ordinary text until you apply a style. You probably don't use headings in most e-mail messages; but if you're composing a relatively long message, you might want to break up the text with headings that help your reader jump to important information. Look at me; I add headings in this book to break up the text and to allow you to find your place again after you're rudely interrupted by the people stuck behind you at the stoplight waiting for you to look up from this book and notice that the light has changed. Can't they see that you're trying to better yourself here?

To apply a style, follow these steps:

1. **Select the text that you want to format.**

   Just drag over the text to select it.

2. **Select a style from the Styles palette on the Format Text tab.**

   You can scroll through the styles or click the More button to display the entire palette of styles. See Figure 3-20.

3. **Click a style.**

   While you hover the mouse pointer over a style type, the selected text changes to that style. For example, hovering over Heading 1 or Heading 2 (a subheading in a Heading 1 section) immediately displays your selected text in that style. If you like what you see, click the style to apply it to the selected text.

While you switch from theme to theme, various elements (such as headings) change to match the formats in the theme. Obviously, other text elements change, as well, including many that you identify with a style, such as Title, Subtitle, Quotations, and the other elements that you see listed in the Styles pane and on the Styles palette.

Book II
Chapter 3

Making Your E-Mail
Look Professional
and Cool

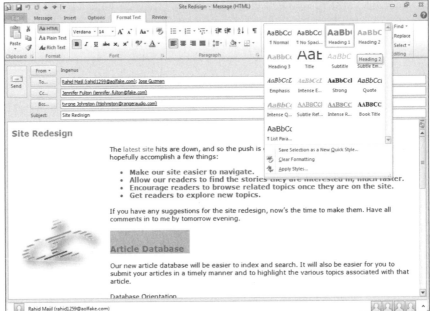

Figure 3-20:
Apply
various
styles to
text, such as
headings.

You can break up text into sections by adding horizontal lines. The current theme formats these lines, and the lines change when you change the theme. To insert a line, click the Horizontal Line button on the Insert tab. To change the line's size, click and drag its handle. To change a line's alignment, width, height (thickness), or color, right-click it and select Format Horizontal Line from the pop-up menu that appears. Make your adjustments in the Format Horizontal Line dialog box that appears, then click OK to save them.

Dealing with bulleted and numbered lists

A bulleted list contains items that can appear in random order, such as a list of things to bring to the quarterly sales meeting or stuff that you have to get done before you leave on vacation. A numbered list must appear in a specific order; typically, you use a numbered list to take you through the steps in a procedure. (I use a lot of both these list types in this book, if you want to see some examples.)

To create a bulleted or numbered list, follow these steps:

1. **Click either the Bullets or the Numbering button on the Message tab.**

If you click either of these buttons, text is formatted using the standard bullet/numbering style. You can instead click the arrow on either button to select the bullet/numbering style you prefer from the palette that appears.

2. **Create the list.**

   To create your bulleted/numbered list, just type the first item, and then press Enter to create the next item. End the list by pressing Enter twice.

Placing text exactly where you want it with a text box

Outlook's basically an e-mail program designed to send lots of text messages, and so you probably aren't surprised that its editor treats text just like Word does, wrapping text while you type between the borders of the message form. Sure, you remove a word or two or add a sentence, and everything moves over in a nice orderly fashion. But what do you do if you want text to appear in a specific spot? Do you add a bunch of spaces to move it over from the margin? That approach works, up to a point, but when you add or remove text elsewhere after adding those spaces, you might affect the perfect alignment of that special text.

You can easily solve the problem by adding your text within a text box. To Outlook, a text box is just an object, subject to its own rules, and so you can easily resize or move it at will. Follow these steps to create a text box:

1. **Click the Text Box button on the Insert tab and select Draw Text Box from the pop-up menu that appears.**

2. **Draw the box.**

   Click in the message to establish the upper-left corner of the box and drag downward and to the right to draw the text box.

3. **Type your text.**

   The cursor automatically appears within the text box; just type your text and click outside the box to finish.

You can format your new text box by using the buttons on the Drawing Tools Format tab; see the section "Manipulating Objects," earlier in this chapter, for help.

Chapter 4: Repeating Yourself Easily with Signatures and Templates

You can so easily send e-mail messages that you might be surprised just how many you send in a single day. If you're anything like me, you probably repeat a lot of the same information at the end of each message, such as your name, e-mail address, and other contact information. You can save such text in a reusable signature that's applied to all outgoing messages (or just the ones you choose). Or maybe you're in regular contact with new clients or sales prospects, sending along the same new-client tips or sales pitch. In any case, if you find yourself repeating the same text in a lot of messages, you can save that text and pop it into a new message whenever you need to. You can also take your recycling to the next level by creating a message template, which saves not only text, but formatting and other elements such as images, shapes, SmartArt, and so on. In this chapter, I show you how to do as much recycling as you want — minus that annoying kitchen odor.

Adding Your Signature

E-mails aren't traditional letters, so they often don't contain the elements of a formal letter, such as a salutation or a date. But even if you start all your e-mails with "blah, blah, blah" and leave out even a measly "Hey, you!" greeting, you probably still sign your messages with at least your name. You might even conclude all your business e-mails with detailed contact information, such as your address, phone number, cell number, IM address, and so on.

Rather than type all that stuff at the end of every business e-mail, you can create a reusable signature that Outlook automatically appends to your messages. Want to include some of that stuff in personal e-mails, too? No problem; Outlook lets you create as many different signatures as you like and choose which signature to use when.

Signatures can contain text (formatted however you want), images, and electronic business cards. (See Book V, Chapter 3 for the lowdown on business cards.) You might even include a hyperlink to a personal or company Web site or to your own e-mail address. If needed, you can include a privacy notice stating that the material in the e-mail is confidential. You're pretty much free to add whatever you want to a signature; whatever you include, the signature is added at the end of whatever e-mails you want.

If you have other stuff you repeat often, such as directions to your office or an off-site meeting room that you use frequently, you can type the text once and save it in a reusable format called a Quick Part. You can save images for reuse, as well; see the section "Repeating the Same Stuff Over and Over," later in this chapter, for more information.

Creating a signature

To create a signature, start out in a message, and then follow these steps:

1. **Click the Signature button on the Insert tab and select Signatures from the pop-up menu that appears.**

The Signatures and Stationery dialog box appears, as shown in Figure 4-1.

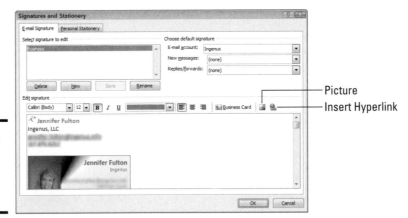

Figure 4-1:
Create
your own
signature
e-mails.

2. **Click the E-Mail Signature tab and click the New button.**

The New Signature dialog box pops up.

3. **Type a name for the new signature in the text box, and then click OK.**

A signature file is created, and you are returned to the Signatures and Stationery dialog box so you can enter the information you want to include in the signature.

4. **In the Edit Signature text box, type the text you want to reuse in your e-mails.**

The Edit Signature text box is that big white box at the bottom of the Signatures and Stationery dialog, and it's where you enter the information (text, business card, photos, hyperlinks) you want to appear in your signature. Begin by typing the text you want to use in your signature, such as your name, company name, and phone number.

5. **Use the formatting tools just above this text box to format the text so that it's nice and pretty.**

For example, change the font, font size, or color.

6. **Add a business card, if you want.**

Assuming you've created an electronic business card for yourself (see Book V, Chapter 3), you can insert that card in your signature. Recipients can use the card to create a Contact record for you in their Contacts list.

Follow these steps to include the business card:

a. *Click the Business Card button located just above the Edit Signature text box. (Refer to Figure 4-1.)*

The Insert Business Card dialog box appears, as shown in Figure 4-2.

**Book II
Chapter 4**

**Repeating Yourself
Easily**

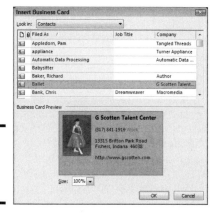

Figure 4-2:
Add your
card to the
signature.

b. *If you have more than one Contacts list, select the one to search from the Look In drop-down list.*

c. *Scroll through the list and select the contact whose card you want to use. (Uh, that would be you.)*

A preview of the card appears in actual size.

d. *If you want, select a different size from the Size drop-down list to make the card appear in your e-mail at less than 100 percent of its normal size. Click OK.*

You are returned to the Signatures and Stationery dialog box. The card appears in the Edit Signature text box, along with the text you typed in Step 4.

7. **Add a picture, if desired.**

To add a picture to your signature, follow these steps:

a. *In the Edit Signature text box , click the spot where you want the picture to go.*

b. *Click the Picture button (located to the right of the Business Card button, refer to Figure 3-1) to display the Insert Picture dialog box.*

c. *Use the Browser to select the image to insert, and then click Insert.*

Surprisingly, you don't have to limit yourself to only Web-friendly graphics such as JPEG, GIF, and PNG. You can select any graphic format for the picture you want to insert. You are returned to the Signatures and Stationery dialog box, and the picture you selected is inserted in the Edit Signature text box.

The Signatures and Stationery dialog box doesn't offer any tools for resizing or correcting the image you select, so use a graphics editor to make any adjustments prior to inserting the image. Also, you can't change how text wraps around the image using the tools in the Signatures and Stationery dialog box, but you can resize the image, move it, or add spaces around it, if you want. See Chapter 3 of this mini-book for help.

8. **Insert any hyperlinks.**

You might insert a hyperlink to a Web site, a document in a shared folder, or your e-mail address. When the user clicks the link, one of three things happens: he or she opens a Web page, views a document, or creates a new message that's automatically addressed to you. To create a hyperlink, select the text in the Edit Signature text box that you want to use as the link, and then click the Insert Hyperlink button. See Chapter 3 of this minibook for help with inserting hyperlinks.

9. **Set options for the signature.**

Now that you have a basic signature, you need to tell Outlook when to use it by setting options in the Choose Default Signature section, which is hiding on the upper-right of the E-Mail Signature tab of the Signatures and Stationery dialog box. (Refer to Figure 4-1.) To tell Outlook when to use this signature, follow these steps:

a. *Select an e-mail account from the E-mail Account drop-down list.*

You might have only one e-mail account, in which case, hey, this choice is pretty easy. (For information on how to set up and manage multiple e-mail accounts in Outlook, see Book III, Chapter 5.)

b. *If you want to attach a signature automatically to all new messages generated by the e-mail account that you selected, select the signature to use from the New Messages drop-down list.*

If you don't want to add a signature to all new e-mails from this account, select None.

c. *To attach a signature automatically to replies and forwarded messages sent from the account you selected, select the signature to use from the Replies/Forwards drop-down list.*

Again, if you don't want to add a signature when sending replies or forwarding messages from this account, select None.

**Book II
Chapter 4**

Repeating Yourself Easily

10. **Click OK to save the signature.**

Well, now that you have a signature, you might as well use it. Jump to the following section to find out how.

Adding the signature to e-mail messages

After you create a signature or two, you can add them to e-mail messages. You have two choices: You can add your signature yourself to each message, or you can tell Outlook to add your signature for you to all messages:

✦ **Manually add a signature to a message.** Click in the message text where you want the signature to appear, click the Signature button on the Insert tab, and then select the signature that you want to add from those listed in the drop-down menu that appears. The signature instantly appears within your message, as shown in Figure 4-3.

✦ **Have Outlook automatically add a signature to messages.** Use the options that appear in the upper right corner of the E-mail Signature tab of the Signatures and Stationery dialog box, as explained in the preceding section, to tell Outlook when you want it to automatically insert a signature. If you select to automatically add a signature to new messages and/or to your replies and forwards, that change doesn't happen until the next e-mail you send. For example, if you just created a new signature and designated that you want to add it to all new messages, that signature is added to the next new message you create (not the current message; you need to take care of that one manually).

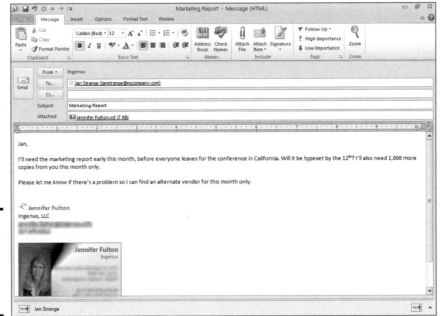

Figure 4-3:
Add your
John
Hancock to
an e-mail
message.

If you add formatting to signature text and insert the signature into a plain text message, you keep the signature text but lose the formatting. Other things get dropped if you insert a signature into a plain text message, including images, hyperlinks, and business cards. The business card still appears as an attachment, it just isn't included in the message itself. So, when you use signatures, use HTML or RTF format for your messages whenever possible. See Chapter 1 of this minibook for more information on message formats.

What if you want to remove a signature for a single message? Well, after Outlook inserts a signature into a message, it's just like any other text and/or graphic. So, you can edit it, removing stuff that you don't want to send this time (such as your phone number or address). To remove text, drag your cursor over it to select the text and press Delete. To remove an image or a business card, click it and press Delete.

Repeating the Same Stuff Over and Over

With Quick Parts, you can save any ol' thing you use over and over, and insert it quickly into any Outlook item — not just messages, although that's probably where you'll find the most use for this feature. For example, if your company insists that you include a little disclaimer or confidentiality statement at the end of any e-mail containing company information that you send to non-employees, you can type the text just once, select it, and save that text as a reusable Quick Part. The next time you send out an e-mail that contains company info, you can quickly insert the statement. (If you're just swapping recipes with your sister, you can leave out the statement, though.)

Saving reusable text and images as a Quick Part

Quick Parts can include images, hyperlinks, text, shapes, and anything else you might ordinarily use in an item. To create a Quick Part, open any item that contains the content you want to save and follow these steps:

1. **Select the reusable content.**

The content you want to reuse must be in an Outlook item to begin with (such as a message or an appointment), so if necessary, copy and paste your content into one. To select text, just drag over it. To select an image, shape, or other object, click it. Select multiple objects by holding down Ctrl and clicking each one.

2. **Click the Quick Parts button on the Insert tab, and then select Save Selection to Quick Part Gallery from the palette that appears.**

The Create New Building Block dialog box appears, as shown in Figure 4-4.

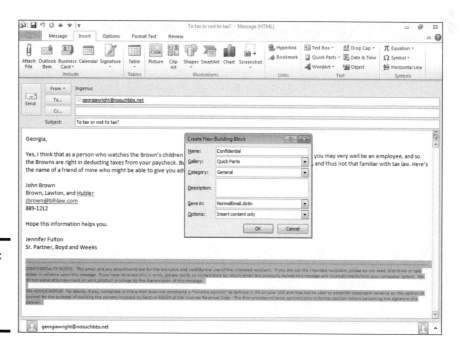

Figure 4-4:
Why type
the same
stuff over
and over?

3. **Enter a name for the Quick Part in the Name field.**

4. **Select a category from the Category drop-down list.**

   You can save the Quick Part in the General category, or you can create a different category in which to store it. For example, if you use a series of different texts to explain company policies to new employees, you can save each text as a Quick Part in a category called New Employees. Then, when you're searching for some text that you normally send to new employees, you can look in the New Employees category on the Quick Steps palette.

   To create a category, select Create New Category from the Category list to display the Create New Category dialog box, then type a name for the new category in the Name box and click OK. You're returned to the Create New Building Block dialog box.

5. **Type a description in the Description text box.**

   Make your description something that helps you remember what the Quick Part contains and why you might reuse it. This description appears when you hover the mouse over the Quick Part in the Quick Part palette.

6. **(Optional) Select a place to save the Quick Part from the Save In drop-down list.**

   Select a template to which to attach the Quick Part. Normally, all new messages are created based on a simple, generic message template called `NormalE-mail.dotm`. You can design your own templates so that you can easily create messages that have a custom look. If you do, you might want to attach your Quick Parts to your custom template so that you can use them within the items you create by using that template. If you want to know how to create a template, see the section "Using a Template to Create a Reusable Message," later in this chapter.

7. **Select an insert option from the Options list.**

   Select the way you want the Quick Part to be inserted when you use it. You can have the contents inserted at the cursor, within its own paragraph, or on its own page.

8. **Click OK to save the Quick Part.**

Inserting a Quick Part into an Outlook item

After you create and save some reusable content, it's time to put this baby in drive and see what it can do. To insert a Quick Part into any Outlook item, follow these steps:

1. **Click where you want the data to go.**

   In a message, you can pretty much click anywhere; in other items, you can insert a Quick Part only into the Notes section.

2. **Click the Quick Parts button on the Insert tab.**

   A palette of saved Quick Parts appears, organized by category.

3. **Select the Quick Part that you want to insert.**

   Your Quick Part magically appears within your Outlook item. Pretty painless.

To make changes to a Quick Part, right-click it in the Quick Parts palette and select Edit Properties from the pop-up menu that appears. The Modify Building Block dialog box appears; make your changes and click OK. To get rid of a Quick Part, right-click it in the Quick Parts palette, and select Organize and Delete from the pop-up menu. In the Building Blocks Organizer dialog box that appears, select the Quick Part that you want to delete and click Delete. Click Close to close the Building Blocks Organizer dialog box when you're through.

Using a Template to Create a Reusable Message

As a parent, it seems that I'm always repeating myself. Too bad I can't save what I'm always saying and then resend it to my kid whenever I feel she needs to hear it again. Actually, I suppose I could do that, but she's only six and doesn't have an e-mail address yet. I guess Outlook can't solve every problem.

If you find yourself repeating the same thing in several messages, you can save it in a template that you can use to repeat yourself as often as you like. You can save repeatable content in other ways, but with a template, you can save not only text, but formatting, graphics, and anything else that happens to be in the message.

Follow these steps to create a template for e-mail:

1. **Open a new message.**

   If you want to start your template out with some style, use Outlook stationery. (See Chapter 3 of this minibook for help in selecting a stationery.)

Well, okay, if you have an old message that you want to use as a template, you can start there, too, by simply opening it and then making whatever changes you want before saving the message as a template. First, locate the old message in your Sent box, double-click to open it, click the Actions button in the Move group on the Message tab, and then select Edit Message to make the message editable so that you can make changes. If you want to save the old message as a template without making changes, then skip the Edit Message part — simply open the message and jump to Step 3.

2. **Add the reusable text.**

    Don't add anything that you wouldn't use in each version of this kind of message. Add graphics, formatting, a subject line, whatever. You can even attach file(s), if you want. Apply a theme or colorize the background. Go all out because, hey, you only have to do this once! (See Figure 4-5.)

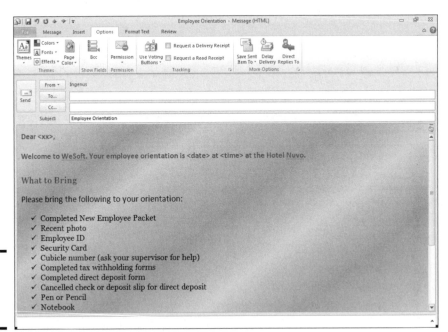

Figure 4-5:
Create a
reusable
message.

If you find yourself stuck for words, why not turn to the word expert, Microsoft Word? Word offers a plethora of templates that include text, designed to help you compose letters, memos, and the like, for specific situations, such as a rent increase, approving customer credit, collecting an overdue amount, and sales and marketing offers. After you use a Word template to generate the reusable text that you want for your e-mail, just select and copy it to an Outlook message. After that, you can create the template you need.

3. Click the File tab to display Backstage and select Save As from list on the left.

The Save As dialog box appears.

4. Type a name for the message template in the File Name box, such as New Product Release.

5. Select Outlook Template (*.oft) from the Save as Type drop-down list.

6. Click Save.

The template is saved, and ready for you to use.

To use the template to create a message, follow these steps:

1. Click the New Items button on the Home tab, select More Items from the pop-up menu that appears, and select Choose Form.

The Choose Form dialog box appears, as shown in Figure 4-6.

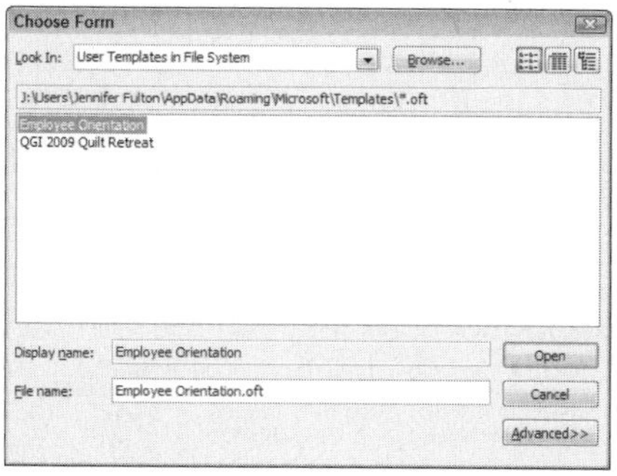

Book II
Chapter 4

Repeating Yourself
Easily

Figure 4-6:
Find your
template in
the Choose
Form dialog
box.

2. From the Look In drop-down list, select User Templates in File System.

Your templates should appear in the list; if not, click Browse and travel to the folder in which you saved the template.

3. Select a template and click Open.

A new message, based on your gorgeous template, appears in a message form. You know what to do; add the text applicable to this version of the message, make any other changes you want, and then address and send the message on.

Book III

Über E-Mail

Contents at a Glance

Chapter 1: Controlling the Sending and Receiving of Messages

In This Chapter

✔ Finding out whether someone actually reads your e-mails

✔ Conducting a poll via e-mail

✔ Delaying, recalling, and replacing messages

✔ Stopping an e-mail download

*B*y now you're probably feeling pretty confident about using e-mail, and rightly so. E-mail in and of itself is not a terribly complicated affair, although it can be. For example, suppose you start a new job, and you have to e-mail everyone in several departments about an upcoming meeting that you're hosting. You've managed to gather all the addresses that you need, and even though you're new, you're already aware of how many e-mails people get each day. How do you know whether everyone actually got the e-mail and then took the time to read it? Can you make sure that they grasp the strategic importance of your e-mail so that hopefully they don't simply ignore it? Can you delay delivery of the message until you get the exact meeting location and other details nailed down? Can you discover who's been stealing your lunch out of the refrigerator?

You'll probably never get to sleep because of all the worries about the many things that could go wrong with a simple e-mail. So, because you'll be up anyway, I invite you to read this chapter — it answers all these questions and more.

How Can I Tell Whether You Read This?

Sometimes, after you send an e-mail message, you find yourself checking the Inbox frequently, wondering when you'll get a response. After a few hours of this nonsense, you may even find yourself wondering whether the recipient got the e-mail at all. Well, you don't need to sit there and worry that your e-mail may have dropped into the Twilight Zone. Instead, you can flag important messages so that their recipients can't so easily ignore them. You can also track when messages have been successfully delivered, and when they've been opened and read.

Making what you send look really important

Tired of having e-mail ignored? Worried that your message will land in the Inbox with hundreds of other messages, in a hopeless battle to be read? You can easily make an important message stand out by flagging it as such, prior to sending it off. In addition to a flag, you can add a reminder that appears above the message text on the message's InfoBar, poking the recipients to take action.

Because a message that's flagged only for the recipient shows up as any ol' message in your Sent Items folder, you may want to flag the message for yourself, as well. Flagging a message for yourself adds the flag to the To-Do bar. See the following section for help in flagging a message for yourself.

To add a flag and a reminder for the recipient to an outgoing message, follow these steps:

1. **In the message form, click the Follow Up button on the Message tab and select Custom from the pop-up menu that appears.**

The Custom dialog box pops up, as shown in Figure 1-1.

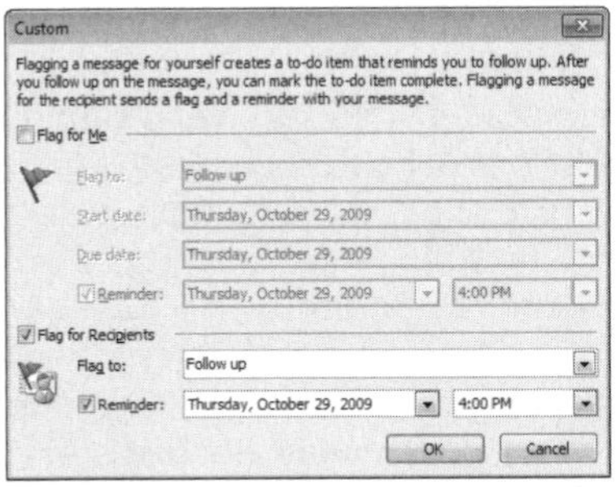

Figure 1-1:
Add a reminder to an outgoing message.

2. **Select the Flag for Recipients checkbox.**

The Recipient Flag options become available.

Notice the Flag for Me option. This option sets a flag for you, the sender. You can turn this option on if you want; to learn more about how to set this option correctly, see the upcoming section, "Flagging messages for yourself".

3. **Select a flag for the recipient from the Flag To drop-down list.**

You can select a flag such as Follow-Up or No Response Necessary. You can also replace the text by typing something more specific of your own in the Flag To text box, such as `Call me after you read this`.

4. **(Optional) Set a reminder date and time by selecting the Reminder checkbox, and then selecting a date and time for the reminder to go off from the appropriate drop-down lists.**

5. **Click OK.**

The details of the flag you just set appear in the message's InfoBar.

Using your time zone as a basis, the reminder time you select is adjusted accordingly after the message arrives at its destination. For example, if you live in the Eastern time zone and select 2:00 p.m., then the time is adjusted to 1:00 p.m. when the message arrives in the mailbox of someone in the Central time zone.

When the recipient gets a message that you've flagged, the flag appears in Outlook to the right of the message header, as shown in Figure 1-2. In the InfoBar for the message, the recipient can view the text of the flag (in this case, the words Follow Up) and the date and time of the reminder (assuming that you set one). Also, a recipient flag doesn't create a To-Do item on that person's To-Do bar. If you did indeed set a reminder, then at the appropriate time, the message header in the message list changes from its ordinary black text to a much more urgent red text. No, a reminder window doesn't appear and a buzzer doesn't go off. Hopefully, this gentle red nudge is all that the recipient needs to spur him or her into action. (If not, a club that pops out of the screen and hits the recipient over the head is available for a small additional fee.)

Another way in which you can make your messages look important to a recipient is to simply mark them that way. Messages marked as important appear with an exclamation icon to the right of the message header. (Refer to Figure 1-2.) To send a message and mark it as important, just click the High Importance button on the Message tab. When you turn on the High Importance flag for a message, it's highlighted on the Ribbon so that you can easily see whether you've set the flag, as shown in Figure 1-3. If you want to let your boss know that this message contains a routine report that he or she can safely put off reading until later, click the Low Importance button instead. Low importance messages appear in the Inbox with a down arrow to the right of the message header. (Refer to Figure 1-2.)

**Book III
Chapter 1**

**Controlling the
Sending and Receiving
of Messages**

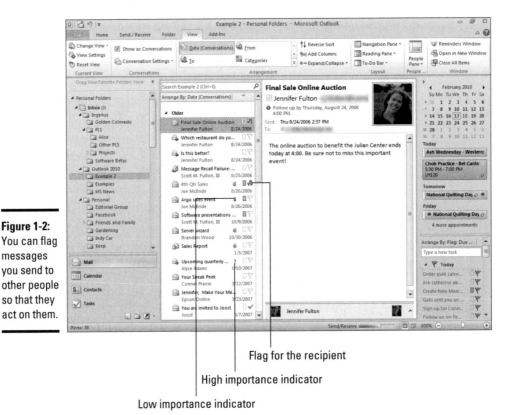

Figure 1-2:
You can flag messages you send to other people so that they act on them.

Flag for the recipient

High importance indicator

Low importance indicator

Figure 1-3:
The High Importance button makes an outgoing e-mail look urgent.

Flagging messages for yourself

If you're sending a message that corresponds with something you need to do, you can flag it before you send it so that it creates a To-Do item in your To-Do bar. If you have a long list of things to do, you may want to set a reminder that makes a lot of noise until you remember to do that something. For example, if you're sending a reply that promises your boss you'll pick up an important client at the airport tomorrow, you may want to flag the message and create a reminder so that you don't accidentally leave the client feeling terminal at the terminal. Follow these steps:

1. **In a message form, click the Follow Up button on the Message tab, and then select Custom from the pop-up menu that appears.**

   The Custom dialog box, shown in Figure 1-4, appears, with the option, Flag for Me, already set.

If you just want to set a flag that creates a To-Do item (and not a flag and reminder), then in the message form, click the Follow Up button on the Message tab and select a flag from the drop-down list, such as Tomorrow. If the message contains important information that you don't want to lose but nothing you need to do, you can select No Date from the Follow Up drop-down list on the Message tab to set a flag that still appears in the To-Do bar, but without a date that bugs you. Book VI, Chapter 1 shows you ways to deal with all these flags that you keep setting!

2. **Select a flag type from the Flag To list, such as Read or Reply.**

   You can also replace the text in the Flag To text box and type something of your own, such as `If Ron doesn't reply by 2, check with Anita`.

3. **Select a Start Date and a Due Date for the task.**

   If you're planning to start and finish the task on the same day, you can use the same date for both.

4. **(Optional) Set a reminder by selecting the Reminder checkbox, and then selecting from the drop-down lists the date and time when you want to be clubbed over the head.**

5. **Click OK.**

   The details of the flag you just set appear in the message's InfoBar.

6. **Finish the e-mail and click Send to send it.**

The subject for the message is used to create a To-Do item, which appears on the To-Do bar below its due date.

Tracking when messages are delivered and read

Have you ever wasted time checking e-mail every five minutes, wondering why you haven't gotten a response to an urgent message? Well, wonder no more. Outlook provides a simple way in which you can find out whether a particular message got to its intended destination and whether your recipient has opened and read that message:

✦ To track when a message gets delivered, select the Request a Delivery Receipt checkbox in the Tracking group on the Options tab in an open e-mail form.

✦ To track when a message is read, select the Request a Read Receipt checkbox in the Tracking group on the Options tab.

✦ You can turn on both the delivery and read options for a message, if you like, by selecting both the Request a Delivery Receipt and the Request a Read Receipt checkboxes.

Assuming you select both options, after your message is delivered, you receive an e-mail to let you know that your message reached the address to which you sent it. After the message is opened, you receive another e-mail.

No system is perfect, however. Before the outgoing messages are sent from the recipient's system, Outlook asks the recipient whether it can generate the delivery or read receipts. If the recipient refuses permission, Outlook doesn't create the outgoing messages, and you may still end up not knowing whether your message got there.

If you need to, you can quickly scan your incoming mail to see whether you've gotten a delivery or a read receipt. Just open the original message you sent (it's in the Sent Items folder), and click the Tracking button in the Show group on the Message tab. (The Tracking button doesn't show up on the Ribbon until you actually get a read or delivery receipt, so if the button isn't there, then either your recipient didn't get your message or blocked his or her e-mail program from sending a response.)

Wanna automate the process of dealing with delivery and read receipts? Then click the File tab to display Backstage, and select Options from the list on the left to display the Outlook Options dialog box. Select Mail from the list on the left to display the Mail options. After all that effort, you can finally select the options that you want from the Tracking section (shown in Figure 1-5):

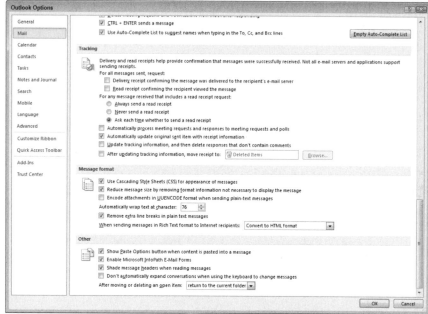

Book III
Chapter 1

Controlling the
Sending and Receiving
of Messages

Figure 1-5:
Set options
to control
how Outlook
tracks your
outgoing
messages.

✦ **To automatically delete receipts after you get them:** Select the Update Tracking Information, and Then Delete Responses That Don't Contain Comments checkbox.

✦ **To move receipts to some other folder after you read them:** Select the After Updating Tracking Information, Move Receipts To checkbox, and then select a folder by clicking the Browse button, selecting a folder, and clicking OK.

✦ **To add a read and/or delivery receipt for all messages you send:** Select the Read Receipt Confirming the Recipient Viewed the Message checkbox and/or the Delivery Receipt Confirming the Message Was Delivered To the Recipient's E-mail Server checkbox.

✦ **To automatically send a read receipt when it's requested:** Select the Always Send a Read Receipt radio button. If you never want to send a receipt, select the Never Send a Read Receipt radio button.

After you select whatever options you want to use to automatically track outgoing messages, click OK.

Getting Out the Vote

Voting is one of the most important rights granted to a democratic society. After voting, people can leave the voting booth knowing that their voices are being heard and that their opinions matter, even though the government will just do what it wants anyway. With Outlook, you can gather opinions from coworkers and automatically tally their votes (and then do what *you* want anyway).

To use Outlook to ask for a vote, follow these steps from inside a message form:

1. **Click the Use Voting Buttons button in the Tracking group on the Ribbon's Options tab and select a button type from the pop-up menu that appears.**

Yes;No is always a good choice. If you select Custom, you can create your own button types. For example, you can create buttons marked The Palomino, La Hacienda, and Saturn Grill if you're asking recipients to choose a restaurant for the quarterly staff meeting. When you click Custom, the Properties dialog box rears its head, as shown in Figure 1-6.

2. **If you selected Custom in Step 1, replace the text in the Use Voting Buttons field in the Properties dialog box with the button text that you want to use, such as** `The Palomino;La Hacienda;Saturn Grill.`

You separate button names by using a semicolon and no spaces.

3. **Click Close.**

The dialog box closes, and your message form reappears. A reminder appears in the InfoBar, informing you that you've added voting buttons to this message.

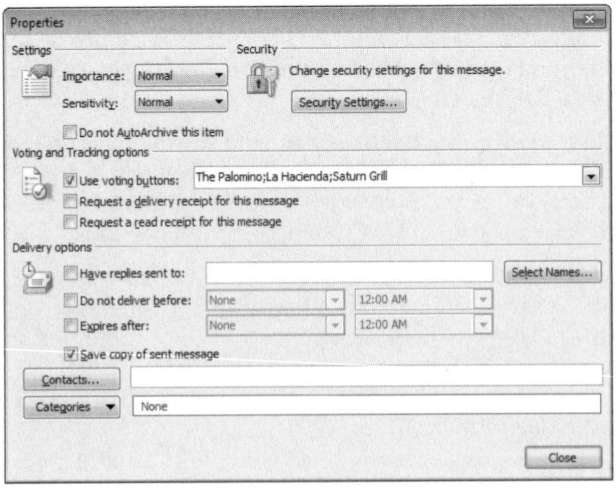

Figure 1-6: Setting up the voting booth.

After a recipient gets your special voting message, he or she simply needs to click the message's InfoBar in the Reading pane, as shown in Figure 1-7, to display the menu of voting options. After the recipient makes a choice from the list, a dialog box appears, asking him or her whether it's okay to send the response now. He or she can choose instead to edit the response, maybe to add a comment or explain his or her choice.

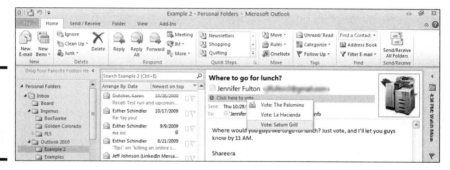

Figure 1-7: Click the InfoBar to cast your vote.

The recipient can also cast a vote by opening the message and clicking the Vote button on the Message tab and making a selection from the pop-up menu that appears.

After several people have exercised their civil right to have their choices ignored by you, you start getting e-mail responses in your Inbox. To tally the votes, you can look at each individual response (the user's choice appears in the Subject of the response message as in `Saturn Grill: Where should we hold our lunch meeting?`) and add the votes manually, or you can use your computer (imagine that!) to tally them up for you. Open your original voting message (you can find it lurking in the Sent Items folder), then click the Tracking button on the Message tab. The names of the people to whom you sent a voting message appear in a list; their responses appear in the Response column. (See Figure 1-8.) The Response column is blank for people who haven't responded yet. Voting totals appear in the InfoBar.

You can select and copy the voting response list and paste it into an Excel worksheet if you need to play with the totals a bit more. For example, you might want to analyze responses by department or office location by adding department/office data to the list and then sorting it.

Book III Chapter 1

Controlling the Sending and Receiving of Messages

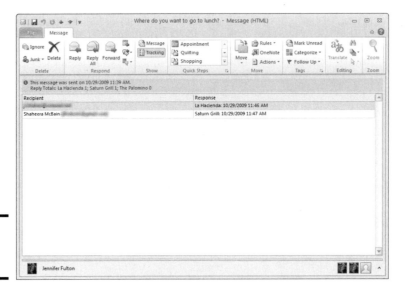

Figure 1-8:
Tally the
votes.

Just like the reading and delivery receipts that I talk about in the preceding section, you probably don't want all those voting receipts cluttering up your Inbox. To have Outlook handle those receipts automatically, click the File tab to display Backstage, and select Options from the list on the left to display the Outlook Options dialog box. Select Mail from the list on the left to display the Mail options. Select the options that you want from the Tracking section. (Refer to Figure 1-5.) Here's a description of the options you can choose from:

✦ **To automatically delete receipts after you get them:** Select the Update Tracking Information, and Then Delete Responses That Don't Contain Comments checkbox. This option affects read receipts (as discussed in the preceding section), as well as meeting responses.

✦ **To move receipts to some other folder after you read them:** Select the After Updating Tracking Information, Move Receipts To checkbox, and then select a folder by clicking Browse, selecting a folder, and clicking OK. This option also affects read receipts (as discussed in the preceding section) and meeting responses, so choose carefully.

✦ **To automatically record the voting responses in the original message:** Select the Automatically Process Meeting Requests and Responses To Meeting Requests and Polls checkbox. Obviously, this option also affects meeting responses.

Controlling Message Delivery

One of the best reasons for using Outlook is that it puts you in complete control over your e-mail. Wanna hold messages until the end of the day because sending them over your dial-up connection ties up your computer? Can do. Wanna set messages to expire after their content no longer applies? No problemo. Wanna take back what you said and say something else? No worries, be happy. Wanna change that annoying sound that alerts you to new mail? No big deal.

Delaying when messages are sent

Sometimes, you just can't gather all the information you need to put into a message at the time you're thinking about sending it. If you've already created a message, only to realize that you can't really let everyone know about Brad's new promotion just yet, you don't have to scrap the message. And you don't have to save it to the Drafts folder and hope you remember to send it later. Instead, you can just delay sending it.

To delay the delivery of a single message, click the Delay Delivery button in the More Options group on the Options tab. The Properties dialog box appears, as shown in Figure 1-9. Because the Do Not Deliver Before checkbox is already selected, you just have to enter the date and time you want the message to be delivered, click Close. The Delay Delivery button is highlighted on the Ribbon, not just because it looks cool that way, but to remind you that you've chosen to delay delivery of this message, and thus Outlook won't do anything with it when you click Send. When you're ready to place the message in the Outbox, click Send. Outlook will not actually send it however, until the time you selected.

Figure 1-9:
Choose
when you
want an
e-mail
delivered.

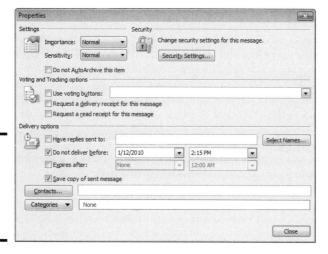

Yes, you can!

If you routinely need to delay the delivery of certain messages (say, all the ones to your picky boss, as you madly double- and triple-check their contents), you can! Just use Outlook to create a rule that does that for you. Rules and their creation are discussed in detail in Book IX, Chapter 2, but I'll give you a hint here so that you know how to set the rule up right. To create a rule that delays delivery of all messages, apply the rule so that messages are checked by Outlook after sending (after you click Send), then select the Defer Delivery by a Number of Minutes action. You can delay delivery for up to two hours (120 minutes) after you click Send.

If you are sending this message through a non-Exchange account (POP2 or IMAP), then you must keep Outlook running until the message is sent. If you are using an Exchange account, you can go ahead and close Outlook — Exchange ensures that your e-mail is sent when you designated.

Setting messages to expire after a certain date

A lot of things expire — driver's licenses, coupons, milk. After something expires, you have to first notice that it has expired (Sorry, officer, I forgot my birthday was this month, honest!), and then throw it away and get a new one. Well, messages can expire, too — for example, you might receive a voting message that you must reply to by Friday. When a message expires, nothing particularly bad happens; the message header simply changes to strikethrough text. The message itself isn't deleted, and you can still read it. Message expiration just makes it a bit more evident to your reader that he or she has missed the boat.

To set a message to expire, follow these steps inside a message form:

1. **Click the Properties dialog box launcher on the Options tab.**

The launcher, by the way, is that right arrow thingy located at the right end of the More Options group.

The Properties dialog box appears, as shown in Figure 1-10.

2. **Select the Expires After checkbox, then select a date and time for the message to expire from the drop-down lists.**

3. **Click Close to return to the message form.**

Properties dialog box launcher

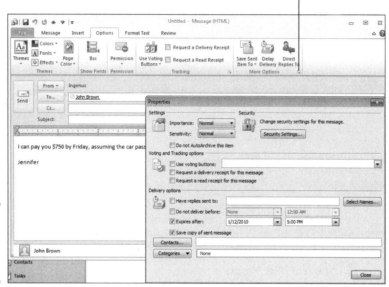

Figure 1-10:
Even
messages
can expire.

Recalling and replacing messages

Have you ever sat there after clicking Send, watching a message being pre-pared and sent, and then realized, "Oops, I shouldn't have sent that!" or "Darn, I forgot to attach the file and now I'm going to look like I shouldn't have refused that fourth cup of coffee this morning." Well, if you e-mail through a Microsoft Exchange network, then lucky you, because Outlook provides a way in which you can take your words back — literally.

In order for Outlook to recall or replace an e-mail message, both you and your recipient must use a Microsoft Exchange network. How you know whether your recipient uses Exchange, I haven't a clue, so my advice is to simply attempt to recall or replace messages, as needed, and then see whether it works. I can tell you one thing — home e-mail addresses typically don't use Microsoft Exchange. Exchange is mostly used by large corpora-tions and universities to handle e-mail.

When you need to chase down an e-mail message and stop it at the door, Outlook provides you with two choices: You can recall the message, which essentially deletes it from the server so that it's not actually delivered, or you can replace the message, which removes the original e-mail from the server and replaces it with the new one.

To recall a message (and possibly replace it), follow these steps:

1. **Open the Sent Items folder and double-click the message you want to recall.**

2. **Click the Actions button in the Move group on the Message tab, and then select Recall This Message from the pop-up menu that appears.**

   The Recall This Message dialog box appears (see Figure 1-11).

Figure 1-11:
This you can
recall.

3. **Select a Delete option.**

   To simply recall the message and not replace it, select the Delete Unread Copies of This Message radio button. To recall the message and replace its text or add attachments, select the Delete Unread Copies and Replace with a New Message radio button.

4. **(Optional) If you want to know whether the recall works or not, make sure the Tell Me If Recall Succeeds or Fails for Each Recipient checkbox is selected.**

   However, if you're recalling a message sent to everyone in your company, then you might want to turn this option *off* (by deselecting the checkbox) to avoid flooding your Inbox with thousands of return receipts.

5. **Click OK to close the dialog box.**

   The message is recalled.

6. **If you're replacing the message, make changes as needed to the copy of the message that appears, and then click Send.**

   For example, you might want to attach that file you forgot to attach the first time you sent the message.

If the recall fails, you can always resend the message (with changes) and beg the recipient to ignore the original transmission. See Book II, Chapter 2 for info about resending a message.

Changing how Outlook tells you e-mail has arrived

When a new message arrives, Outlook lets you know by sounding its "You've got mail!" chime and briefly flashes the e-mail's header just above the Windows system tray. In addition, Outlook briefly wiggles the mouse pointer to alert you, and adds an envelope to the Outlook button on the Windows taskbar. If you get a lot of e-mail (and who doesn't nowadays?) you can easily become immune to the constant chiming of the Outlook postman and all this wiggling and flashing business. If you need something really annoying to draw your attention (or something less annoying so that you can ignore all those messages and get some work done), why not change Outlook's behavior?

To change the sound Outlook plays on message arrival, you have to exit Outlook and have a suitable `.wav` file prepared. After exiting Outlook, open the Control Panel in Explorer, select Hardware and Sound, and select Sound to open the Sound dialog box. (See Figure 1-12.) Click the Sounds tab and select New Mail Notification in the Program Events area. Click the Browse button in the lower-right of the tab, select a `.wav` file from the Browse for New Mail Notification sound dialog box that appears, and click Open to return to the Sound dialog box. Click OK to save your changes. As soon as new mail arrives in Outlook, the new sound that you chose plays.

Figure 1-12:
Change how Outlook sounds.

Book III Chapter 1

Controlling the Sending and Receiving of Messages

You can create a rule to play a unique sound whenever e-mail arrives from a particular person or for e-mail that has other certain characteristics. You learn how to create this kind of rule in Book IX, Chapter 2.

To turn off the sound alerts completely, follow these steps in Outlook:

1. **Click the File tab to display Backstage, and select Options from the list on the left.**

The Outlook Options dialog box appears. (See Figure 1-13.)

2. **Select Mail from the list on the left.**

   The Mail options appear on the right.

3. **In the Message Arrival section, deselect the Play a Sound checkbox to turn off the sound alerts.**

   In that section, you can also disable the mouse wiggle (the change to the mouse pointer) and prevent the Envelope icon from crowding your Windows system tray when new mail comes in by deselecting the appropriate checkboxes.

4. **Click OK to save changes.**

While we're on the topic, you can disable the Outlook taskbar icon so that you must use the Outlook system tray icon to restore the Outlook window if minimized. See Book I, Chapter 1 for more info.

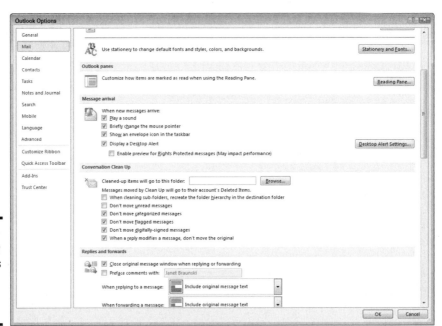

Figure 1-13:
Control how Outlook tells you e-mail is "in the house."

Outlook also lets you know "You've got mail!" through its Desktop Alerts — the quick flash of an e-mail message just above the Windows system tray when that message arrives in the Inbox, as shown in Figure 1-14. You can meet these guys in Book II, Chapter 1, so if you need to figure out how they work, jump back to that chapter.

Figure 1-14:
Summaries
of incoming
messages
appear on
the taskbar
when they
arrive.

Desktop Alerts notify you of e-mail incoming to only Exchange or POP3 accounts. In addition, the alerts appear only for e-mail coming into your default Inbox, no other folder. You can, however, set up a rule to alert you of messages incoming to other folders or messages that meet other conditions, such as "sent by my boss." If you use an IMAP account, you can get alerts, too; just set up a rule that handles that condition. See Book IX, Chapter 2, for more information on setting up rules.

The alerts go by really quickly, so don't be surprised if you miss one. You can adjust how long the alerts appear on-screen, and even how transparent (and less eye-catching) they appear. You can also turn alerts on or off however you want. Follow these steps to adjust your Desktop Alerts:

1. **Click the File tab to display Backstage, and select Options from the list on the left.**

The Outlook Options dialog box appears.

2. **Select Mail from the list on the left.**

The Mail options appear on the right.

3. **(Optional) In the Message Arrival section, turn off Desktop Alerts by deselecting the Display a Desktop Alert checkbox.**

4. **To adjust how Desktop Alerts appears, click the Desktop Alert Settings button.**

The Desktop Alert Settings dialog box appears, as shown in Figure 1-15.

5. **Adjust the amount of time the alerts appear by dragging the aptly named How Long Should the Desktop Alert Appear? slider.**

6. **Adjust whether the alerts appear more or less transparent by dragging the How Transparent Should the Desktop Alert Be? slider.**

7. **Click Preview to view your choices; click OK to accept them. Click OK again to close the Outlook Options dialog box.**

**Book III
Chapter 1**

Controlling the
Sending and Receiving
of Messages

Figure 1-15:
Test your new Desktop Alert.

Stopping a Long E-Mail Download

Nothing is more interesting than watching the progress of an e-mail download than possibly, um, watching grass grow. So, frankly, I don't bother to watch the progress of Outlook getting my mail from its electronic mailbox out in cyberspace, even though a Send/Receive progress bar shows up right there on the Outlook status bar. But if you notice that Outlook is taking an extraordinarily long time to complete a particular Send/Receive, you may want to figure out why Outlook's acting so sluggish.

To view the progress of a Send/Receive that's underway, click the Show Progress button on the Send/Receive tab. The Outlook Send/Receive Progress dialog box appears, as shown in Figure 1-16. I should note here that this Send/Receive Progress dialog box automatically appears if you initiate a send/receive manually (by clicking the Send/Receive All Folders button on the Quick Access Toolbar, for example).

When an automatic send/receive is underway, a Send/Receive progress bar appears on the Outlook status bar. You can also display the Send/Receive Progress dialog box by clicking the Send/Receive Progress button on the Outlook status bar.

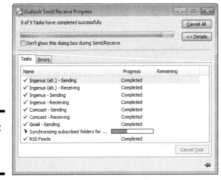

Figure 1-16:
Now, that's progress.

If you want to stop the download — maybe Outlook's stuck on a large file attachment or maybe the mail server's stuck in some endless loop — select the task that's hanging things up from the Tasks list in the Outlook Send/ Receive Progress dialog box, and click the Cancel Task button. To cancel all tasks, click the Cancel All button.

Chapter 2: When You Have to Know Now: Instant Messaging

In This Chapter

✔ IMing or texting someone when Outlook e-mail isn't fast enough

✔ Finding an IM or SMS text service that Outlook likes

✔ Sending instant messages or text messages through Outlook

✔ Keeping up with everybody's online status

Sometimes, e-mail feels so old-school. When you want to carry on a real back-and-forth conversation with someone, you can feel like you have to wait forever for your e-mail to upload to the server, and then for your recipient to download it so that he or she can finally read it. Wouldn't it be great if you had a way to communicate instantly — judge a person's mood, share information, debate, confer, argue, and deliberate in real time? Besides using the telephone, I mean. (Talk about old-school!)

Understanding the Magic

By using instant messaging, you can communicate instantly — assuming the person you want to communicate with is also online and receiving visitors." After someone "picks up" your call, you can exchange instant text messages and, depending on the instant messaging service that you use (such as Google Talk or Windows Live Messenger), utilize real-time audio and video, file sharing, and *remote help* (a help desk situation in which you can take over someone else's computer and guide him or her through a solution or simply fix a problem).

SMS (Short Message Service) text messages are another form of instant communication. SMS text messages can contain only 160 characters. Instant messages, by contrast, are not typically limited in length, and they can contain more than text, unlike SMS text messages which are text only. SMS is designed to be sent between cell phones, or from a PC to a cell phone.

Outlook is basically about sending e-mail, but it can help you communicate more instantaneously in one of two ways:

✦ **Outlook can "initiate" instant messages.** Outlook basically wakes up your instant message program so that you can IM someone in your

Contacts list. When you receive an e-mail from someone, Outlook alerts you that the person is also online (receiving visitors), so you can stop the e-mailing madness and talk live via a compatible instant messaging program.

✦ **Outlook can send a text message to someone's cell.** If you want to be able to track your text conversations within Outlook, sign up for an Outlook Mobile Service provider. For a fee (of course), the provider not only allows you to send and receive SMS text messages through Outlook and your cell phone provider, but to send the same message to both cell phone numbers and e-mail addresses at the same time. You can also forward meeting reminders or e-mail messages to your cell phone by using rules. (See Book IX, Chapter 2 for the rules about rules). In addition, you can send copies of appointments, contacts, tasks, and even your daily calendar to your cell phone.

Instant messaging is by no means secure, despite the attempts by many services to make it so. In theory, using Windows Live Messenger, you should receive messages only from people you've added to your Allow list, but a determined hacker can bypass that list and send you messages anyway. Sending unsolicited SMS text messages to someone's phone is even easier, since all someone needs is a phone number. To protect your privacy, don't view or respond to instant messages or SMS text messages from people who you don't know, because it might be someone phishing for a valid IM address or cell phone number so they can flood you with spam or to phish for additional information from you.

Using Instant Messaging

Outlook cannot send instant messages, but it can make it easier for you to do so by enabling you to view someone's online status and to initiate an instant messaging conversation if that person is online. So when you need to discuss something with someone, rather than send lots of back and forth e-mails, you can use Outlook and your IM service to get the answers you need quickly. Start by choosing an IM service that's compatible with Outlook.

Compatible IM Services

A lot of instant messaging services out there offer pretty much the same things, but only a few are compatible with Outlook. So, if you want to be able to initiate an IM from within Outlook, as well as check whether someone's logged into his or her IM program, then choose one of these compatible services:

✦ **Microsoft Windows Live Messenger:** Allows you to chat via text and also talk and use live video. It also supports help-desk tasks such as taking over a computer. It supports communication with Yahoo! Messenger, as well.

✦ **Microsoft Office Communicator:** Some offices install Communicator in order to connect Microsoft Windows Live Messenger with the company's phone service so that you can send IMs, have video conferences, share documents, and manage your online status easily. For example, with Communicator, if you pick up your office phone, your status changes to Busy automatically. Now, if only Communicator could answer the phone, take a message, and call the person later !

For best results, sign up for the same instant messaging service used by the people you want to contact. How you sign up varies (obviously), but no money changes hands. If you want to sign up for Microsoft Windows Live Messenger, go to `http://download.live.com`. After downloading the instant messaging software, you install it and then create an IM address for yourself. To install Windows Live Messenger, supply an e-mail address and sign up for a Windows Live ID. A wizard leads you through all the steps, I promise. The address you supply to Windows Live Messenger for login doesn't have to be a Microsoft e-mail address (Hotmail, MSN, Live Mail, or any others Microsoft may invent) — you can use any e-mail address you want, and it becomes your IM address channeled through Windows Live Messenger. After you install the IM program, just log onto it, then switch to Outlook to use your Contacts to send instant messages through your IM program.

You can install Windows Live Messenger on your cell phone, too, and never be out of touch. Windows Live for Mobile Phones is available for iPhones, BlackBerrys, Nokias, and Windows phones.

Adding IM contacts

After installing a compatible instant messaging program, you are almost ready to have Outlook initiate IMs using information in your Contacts list. But first you need to add some IM contacts by following these steps:

1. **Add some contacts to the IM program.**

How you add contacts varies by instant messenger, but look for a button somewhere in the IM program called Add a Contact (or something similar). Adding contacts in your IM program allows you to send instant messages using that program and also to initiate instant messages within Outlook.

2. **Add IM addresses to Outlook by first locating a person in your Contacts list that you want to exchange instant messages with, and opening the contact by double-clicking it.**

3. **In the Contacts form that appears, type the person's IM address in the IM address field, as shown in Figure 2-1.**

4. **Click Save & Close to save the change.**

IM address field

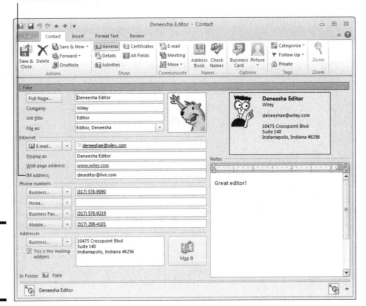

Figure 2-1:
Add IM
addresses
to Outlook.

Initiating an IM through Outlook

Now that you have somebody to IM, you're ready to send your first message.
Follow these steps:

1. **Check the online status of the person you want to IM.**

   When you get an e-mail message from someone you have set up in your IM
   program as a contact, Outlook automatically checks the sender's online
   status. You can view it yourself in the message header, along with the
   online status of others who also received the message. Simply hover the
   mouse pointer over the sender's name in the message header to bring up
   the person's Contact Card, as shown in Figure 2-2, which lists his or her
   online status. If someone is online (if the Contact Card features a green dot
   icon), then you can reply to his or her e-mail by sending an instant message.

2. **Click the Send an Instant Message To XXX button (it looks like a cartoon text bubble) on the Contact Card.**

   Your instant messaging program opens, and a conversation window
   appears, as shown in Figure 2-3. The window that appears varies,
   depending on the IM program you use; the one shown in Figure 2-3 is for
   Windows Live Messenger.

   You can send an instant message to someone even if they are offline.
   However, they will not get the message until they log on to their instant
   messaging program. You might do this if you have reason to believe that
   the person will get your IM before he/she might get your e-mail.

Contact Card

Send an Instant
Message To button

Figure 2-2:
To IM or not
to IM.

3. **Type your message and press Enter.**

Type what you want to say in the box at the bottom of the conversation
window and press Enter. What you type appears in the upper window;
when the user replies, you see the reply just below your text in the
upper window.

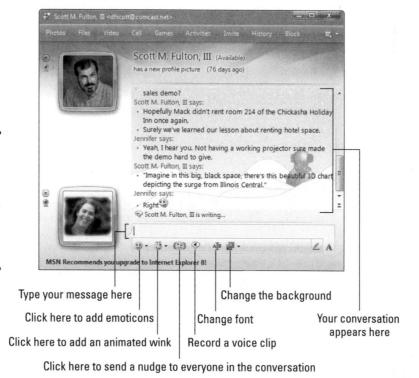

Figure 2-3:
Outlook
IMing gives
you yet
another way
to bother
people
instantly.

Type your message here

Click here to add emoticons

Change the background

Change font

Click here to add an animated wink

Record a voice clip

Your conversation
appears here

Click here to send a nudge to everyone in the conversation

You can't guarantee a secure conversation over the Internet, including while instant messaging. Don't share confidential information through instant messaging, just in case someone is hacking into your online connection.

4. **Repeat Step 3 as many times as necessary to have your online conversation,**

   Eventually, your conversation may scroll off the screen, but you can use the scroll bars to revisit anything you said earlier.

5. **When you finish your IM discussion, click the Close button.**

   Clicking Close (unsurprisingly) closes the conversation window, which ends that conversation. If you keep the conversation window open, you can scroll back through the conversation if you like.

Windows Live Messenger provides *emoticons* (small icons that you can use to express your feelings throughout a message), *winks* (animated greetings), and nudges (which shakes the conversation window of everyone participating in the conversation), along with buttons for recording and sending a voice clip, changing your text font, and selecting a background for the conversation window. For example, to add a surprise face to your text, click the Select an Emoticon button and select the Surprised Smile emoticon from the palette that appears. Still, Live Messenger is always changing, and who knows what other buttons Microsoft might add? Be sure to check the bottom of your conversation window for buttons you can use to spice up your conversation.

Viewing someone's online status

SMS text messages are sent to a person's cell phone, and they are received whether or not that cell phone is currently on. There is no way for you to know for sure that someone has read your SMS text message until that person responds. Such is the world of text messaging.

Instant messages, however, are sent between IM clients, such as Google Talk or Windows Live Messenger. When you log into you instant message program, the program automatically broadcast's your presence online to everyone in your friends list. If you use a compatible IM client, then Outlook receives this information and lets you know that a specific message sender is online by putting a green square icon in front of his or her name in the message header, as shown in Figure 2-4. In addition, if you hover the mouse pointer over the sender's name in an e-mail message, you'll see that person's availability listed on his or her Contact Card. Depending on the IM service you use, you might see additional status icons, such as a red dash (for Busy) and a pinkish circle (for Offline).

For Outlook to be able to show someone's online IM status, you must first use a compatible messaging service (see the following section for information on compatible services) and, second, add the person to your instant messaging program's Contacts list before you can view his or her online status in Outlook. You can find out how to add people to your IM list in the section "Using Instant Messaging", earlier in this chapter.

Status icon   Status icon   Status text

Figure 2-4:
Is anybody
there?

Controlling your online status

When you are logged into your instant messaging program, your status typically says something like "Online" or "Available." If you aren't actively using your computer, then your instant messaging program senses that and automatically changes your status to something like "Offline" or "Away." You can change your online status from Online to Offline immediately by simply logging out of your instant messaging program; Live Messenger also allows you to fake being offline by changing your status to appear as if you are.

In addition, if you don't want to be shown as offline (you're still working and may even want to send an instant message or two), you can change your status to Busy, instead. Busy means just that; you're online, but you don't want to be bothered right now with instant messages (although that may not stop some people).

You change your online status in your instant messaging program, not within Outlook. To give you some idea how this process works, follow these steps to change your online status within Windows Live Messenger (if that's the program you use):

1. **Click the arrow next to your name at the top of the Windows Live Messenger window.**

A list of status options appears.

2. **Select the status you want to display.**

Windows Live Messenger gives you only limited options here, such as Available, Busy, Away, or Appear Offline.

3. **(Optional) Leave a personal message.**

You can add a personal message that all your contacts can see. For example, if you're on the phone, why not tell everyone so that they stop trying to get you involved in two conversations at the same time? Follow these steps to add a personal message:

a. *Click on your personal message, which appears just below your name in the Windows Live Messenger window.* (See Figure 2-5.)

Leave a personal message

Update your status

Figure 2-5:
Explain your
absence.

The text of your current personal message becomes selected.

b. *Type your message. For example, you could type* Be back at 2 P.M.

c. *Press Enter.*

The new message appears below your Name in the Windows Live Messenger window.

Using SMS Text Messages

You'll probably find that not everyone you want to communicate instantly with will also happen to use the same instant messaging program as you do. I use Windows Live Messenger and Google Talk just to be able to IM most of my friends. For the rest, I use SMS text messaging when I need to "chat" because most everyone else has a cell phone. If you want to send SMS text messages using Outlook however, you need to use an Outlook Mobile Service provider. Your Outlook Mobile Service provider (for a fee) enables you to not only send SMS text messages to cell phone numbers in your Contacts list, but to forward meeting reminders, e-mails, and other info to your cell phone as well.

Choosing an Outlook Mobile Service provider

If you, like me, Google everything in order to research it before you buy, you may be surprised to know that you don't have to go shopping for an Outlook Mobile Service provider. At least, you don't go shopping the Google way. Instead, you start by setting up the text messaging account in Outlook (much the same way that you set up an e-mail account), and then Outlook hooks you up with providers that are compatible with your cell phone service. It couldn't be simpler. Just follow these steps:

1. **Click the File tab to display Backstage, and select Info from the list on the left.**

   The Account Information options appear on the right.

2. **Click the Account Settings button, then select Account Settings from the pop-up menu that appears.**

   The Account Settings dialog box appears.

3. **Click the New button.**

   The Add New Account dialog box appears.

4. **Select the Text Messaging radio button and click Next.**

   The Add New Outlook Mobile Service Account wizard appears. (See Figure 2-6.)

5. **Select a provider.**

   If you've somehow already chosen an Outlook Mobile Service provider, well, then good for you — you can skip this step.

   Otherwise, click the Find a Text Messaging Service for Your Mobile Operator link. A Web site opens in a browser window. Select your country and mobile carrier. At that point, a list of compatible Outlook Mobile Service providers appears. Shop to your heart's desire. After you select a service and sign up for it, that provider gives you the info you need to continue onto Step 6.

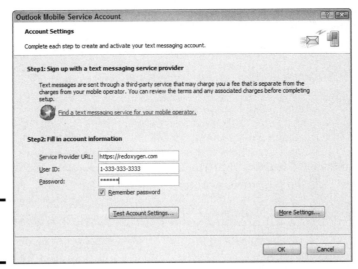

Figure 2-6:
Select a
provider.

6. **Enter your account info at the bottom of the wizard.**

   After selecting an Outlook Mobile Service provider and signing up for
   their service, switch back to the wizard window. The sign up process
   may have caused the following information to be automatically completed for you, or you may need to type it in manually yourself. You
   need to provide Outlook with three tidbits of information about the
   Outlook Mobile Service provider you've selected:

   - **Service Provider URL:** The service provider's Web site address.

   - **User ID:** Your mobile phone number.

   - **Password:** Your service provider gives you this information when
     you sign up for the service. Select the Remember Password option,
     unless you want to be bothered with entering it every time Outlook
     sends an IM or checks for new ones being sent to you.

7. **Click OK.**

   You're returned to the Add New Account Wizard.

8. **Click Finish to add the account, then click Close to close the Account
   Settings dialog box.**

   You're set up and ready to send text messages using Outlook to the
   mobile phone numbers stored in your Contacts list and to your cell
   phone (stuff like appointment reminders and forwarded e-mails).

Controlling your online status

Unlike an IM program such as Windows Live Messenger in which you can change your online status from Available to Busy when needed, if you use an Outlook Mobile Service provider to send text messages, then your status is pretty much always Online because, as long as Outlook is running, it can forward messages to your cell phone. Whether you choose to view them is up to you. If you close Outlook, then messages will not be forwarded to your cell phone, so be sure to leave it running when you leave the office.

Adding mobile phone numbers

Now that you've signed up with an Outlook Mobile Service provider, you are ready to send text messages. The only thing that might be missing is the addition of mobile phone numbers for the people you want to send text messages to. Follow these steps to add a mobile phone number for a contact:

1. **Change to the Contacts module, locate a person you want to exchange instant messages with, and open the contact by double-clicking it.**

The Contact form for the selected contact appears.

2. **In the Contacts form, type the person's phone number in the Mobile Phone Number field. (Refer to Figure 2-7.)**

3. **Click Save & Close to save the change.**

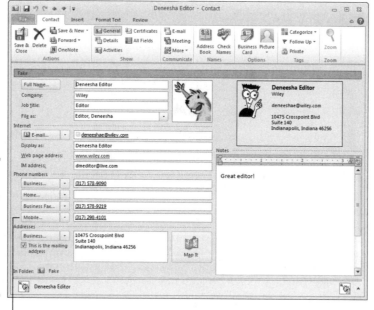

Figure 2-7:
Enter a
mobile
phone
number for
contacts
you want to
text.

Mobile phone field

Sending a text message through an Outlook Mobile Service provider

Okay, now that you have someone to text message, you can get to bothering them. Follow these steps:

1. **In the Mail module, click the New Items button on the Home tab and select Text Message (SMS) from the pop-up menu that appears.**

The Text Message form appears. (See Figure 2-8.) If you aren't in the Mail module, then click the New Items button on the Home tab, select More Items, and then select Text Message (SMS) to display the Text Message form.

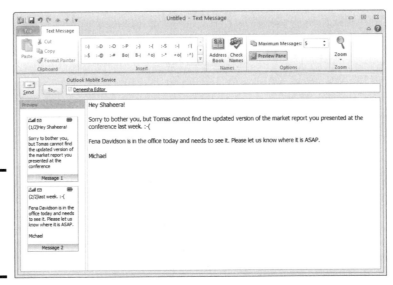

Figure 2-8:
Send an SMS message by using Outlook.

2. **Click the To button and select an address from the Select Names: Contacts (Mobile) dialog box that appears.**

The contacts that appear include only those for whom you've entered a mobile phone number.

You can type the person's last name or cell phone number to address a text message to him or her. In addition, you can type e-mail addresses and send a text message and an e-mail message that contain the same content to various recipients. Also, you can schedule the delivery of your text message for a later time, if you want. (Kind of takes the "instant" out of instant communicating though, doesn't it?)

3. **Type your message in the big text box.**

   You can actually send only 160 characters in a single message, so Outlook breaks up long messages into what it considers logical units. These separate messages appear in the preview boxes on the left, where you can edit them into something that makes more sense.

   You can insert common emoticons by going to the Insert group of the Text Message tab and clicking the one you want to place.

4. **(Optional) To limit the number of text messages into which Outlook breaks up your text, type a value in the Maximum Messages box on the Text Message tab.**

5. **Click Send.**

Outlook treats text messages that you send and receive through an Outlook Mobile Service provider just like regular e-mail. For example, text messages that you send appear in your Sent folder so that you can review what you said later on, if you want. In addition, Outlook saves text messages forwarded to your cell phone in the Inbox, where both you and your boss can clearly see the content, in case your boss forgot that bonus he promised in that text he sent.

Other cool things to do with an Outlook Mobile Service provider

Your Outlook Mobile Service provider allows you to automatically forward contacts, tasks, appointments, and meetings to your cell phone when you're out of the office. You can even send these special texts to multiple cell phones, if you want. Follow these steps:

1. **Click the File tab to display Backstage, and select Options from the list on the left.**

   The Outlook Options dialog box pops up, as shown in Figure 2-9.

2. **Select Mobile from the list on the left.**

   The Mobile options appear on the right.

3. **Set your options, and then click OK.**

   Your choices in this dialog box include the following:

   - **Send Calendar Summary to Mobile Phone.** Select this option if you want to send a summary of your appointments, meetings, and events for the next 12, 24, 36, or 48 hours to your cell phone. If you're routinely in and out of the office, you can use this option to ensure you don't miss that big meeting with your best client. Click the Calendar Summary Settings button to display the Calendar Summary dialog box, where you can select exactly what you want sent and how often.

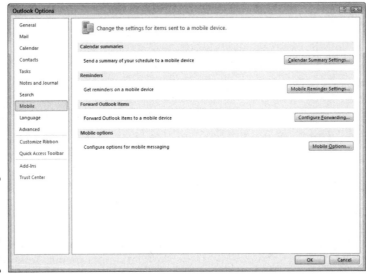

Figure 2-9:
Stay in
touch, even
when you're
out of touch.

- **Send Reminders to Mobile Phone.** Select this option if you want
  to send Outlook reminders to your cell phone so that you don't
  miss out on an important appointment or meeting. Click the Mobile
  Reminder Settings button to display the Reminder dialog box, where
  you can set options that identify which reminders you want Outlook
  to bug you with.

- **Forward Outlook Options.** Select this option if you want to forward
  messages to your cell phone. Click the Configure Forwarding button
  to display the Mobile Notification dialog box, where you can set
  options to have Outlook forward only messages you're likely to care
  about, such as those from a particular person or group that you identify as highly important or those giving you meeting updates.

- **Mobile Options.** Click this button to display the Mobile Options
  dialog box, where you can set the format for all these Outlook items
  that you keep having sent your way. For example, you might want to
  limit the number of texts that Outlook breaks a long message into.

Chapter 3: Getting the Latest News Delivered Right to Your Inbox

In This Chapter

✔ **Getting the lowdown on RSS, weblogs, podcasting, and syndicated content**

✔ **Getting coffee and the latest news**

✔ **Adjusting your list of RSS feeds**

✔ **Poring over the content of your RSS feeds**

✔ **Sharing the news**

*I*n this electronics-driven world, news is all around us — on our cell phones, TVs, laptops, grocery carts, shopping malls, and sports stadiums — and, oh yeah, in actual newspapers. So, you're probably not surprised to find out that you can also get your news within Outlook (by using something called RSS).

RSS is short for Really Simple Syndication, and it's a way for news content providers and *bloggers* (people who run online Web journals) to keep their readers updated on the latest goings-on. After you subscribe to an RSS *feed* (channel), news articles from that source arrive in your Inbox in a special folder. You view these articles just like you do any other e-mail. Typically, these articles contain only headlines that, when clicked, take you to a particular Web page where you can "read all about it."

Sometimes, rather than just links, the articles themselves arrive in the message. An article might also contain links or attachments for audio (or even video) versions of news articles. A *podcast* is an RSS feed that contains MP3 audio and sometimes video files, which you download and then play on an iPod or compatible multimedia player. You might hear news feeds referred to as RSS feeds, Web feeds, or XML feeds (because XML is the format used). Among its other capabilities, Outlook serves as an *RSS aggregator* — a program that receives and displays your feeds and the links or attachments they contain. Outlook supports all the most popular RSS feed types, including RSS, Atom, and HTML.

More and more, you may see the word "Atom" associated with a news feed. Atom is a refinement to RSS, and it's treated the same by Outlook and your Web browser, so the processes of adding such a feed to Outlook are the same as described here for RSS.

Adding News Feeds

You can add RSS feeds (news feeds) to Outlook either with the help of Outlook's Account Settings or with the help of your Web browser. Using Account Settings, which is spelled out in the following section, is similar to the process of setting up an e-mail account, only here you are adding a link to a specific RSS feed. The process of using your Web browser (as described in the section "Adding a news feed through your Web browser," later in this chapter), involves clicking a bright orange button (called a *chicklet,* by the way) displayed in some prominent place on a Web page. Figure 3-1 shows some typical chicklets in all their orange glory.

If you use Internet Explorer, when IE detects an RSS feed on a Web page, it highlights the RSS button on the Command bar and probably rings a chime to call your attention to it. Firefox, on the other hand, proudly displays an orange RSS icon at the right end of its address box.

You can also share your favorite RSS feeds with friends in two ways: by inviting friends to join in on the fun via a special e-mail, or by exporting a bunch of feeds at the same time to an RSS file (which you can identify by its `.opml` extension) and sending on that file. See the "Sharing News Feeds" section, later in this chapter, for help with these two options.

Figure 3-1:
Want a
chicklet?

When you subscribe to an RSS feed, it doesn't ask you to give a lot of personal data, such as your name, Social Security number, or e-mail address. The RSS provider isn't sending stuff *to* you or your computer; instead, your computer is collecting articles from the RSS provider when you tell it to. So, the process is pretty anonymous and thus a bit more secure than signing up for an e-mail newsletter. Also, most RSS feeds are free (although sometimes you have to pony up for their content). If you have to pay for something, you're given a chance to decide whether it's worth the fee.

Adding a news feed through Outlook's Account Settings

Probably the simplest way to add a news feed to Outlook is through your Web browser, as discussed in the following section. Sometimes, however, an RSS feed on a Web page is not detected by your browser because the page was not coded with the additional metadata needed by your browser to help it detect the presence of the feed. In other words, the feed is there, but your Web browser doesn't detect it. In such a case, the Web page usually shows a generic link to the feed, typically at the bottom of the page. Use this URL to add the news feed to Outlook by following these steps:

Occasionally, a news source such as CNN will offer podcasts (video and audio news) in an RSS format. This means that you can add these podcast links to Outlook, and use the podcast's RSS articles to view the videos/ audios created for the podcast. If you choose to automatically download enclosures (see options for that listed here in these steps), then the video/ audio files will be automatically downloaded to your computer.

1. **From within Outlook, click the File tab to display Backstage, and select Info from the list on the left.**

The Account Information options appear on the right.

2. **Click the Account Settings button, and select Account Settings from the pop-up menu that appears.**

The Account Settings dialog box pops up.

3. **Click the RSS Feeds tab and select New.**

The New RSS Feed dialog box appears.

4. **Enter the URL of the RSS feed you're interested in, and then click the Add button.**

The RSS Feed Options dialog box opens, as shown in Figure 3-2.

5. **Type a name for your feed in the Feed Name text box.**

6. **Set your options.**

You have several ways to go:

- *Change Folder:* If you want to change where Outlook stores the feed articles, click this button and select a different Outlook folder from the New RSS Feed Delivery Location dialog box that appears.

- *Automatically Download Enclosures for This RSS Feed:* Select this checkbox to download media files *(enclosures)* within the feed.

Figure 3-2:
Add a feed
through
Account
Settings, if
necessary.

- *Download the Full Article as an .html Attachment:* Select this checkbox if you want to download full articles, rather than just links to articles. (Before you select this option, make sure that you have enough free space on your hard drive to accommodate all those RSS articles.)

- *Use the Publisher's Update Recommendation:* Leave this checkbox selected. It prevents you from trying to get articles too frequently — which might lead to you getting dumped by the RSS provider.

7. **When you're done selecting options, click OK to return to the Account Settings dialog box, and then click Close.**

    The feed is added to Outlook.

See the section "Reading News Feeds," later in this chapter, for help in slogging through the news articles for your new feed.

Adding a news feed through your Web browser

Web pages today typically come embedded with metadata (descriptors) that help a Web browser detect the presence of an RSS feed on that page. Once your Web browser detects the feed, it tells you by displaying a chicklet in its Address box or on a toolbar. When you see one of these chicklets appear, you can use it to instantly add a news feed to Outlook.

There are many Web browsers out there, but two of the most commonly used are Internet Explorer and Firefox, so I provide the steps to add an RSS feed to Outlook using either one.

Keeping your RSS feeds in sync

If you use Internet Explorer, then when you add an RSS feed, it is added to Internet Explorer's RSS feed list only. To synchronize Internet Explorer's list of RSS feeds with Outlook (so you can access the feeds in Outlook as well), you have to turn on the option. From within Outlook, click the File tab to display Backstage, and select Options from the list on the left to display the Outlook Options dialog box. Select Advanced from the list on the left to display the Advanced options, and in the RSS Feeds section, check the Synchronize RSS Feeds to the Common Feed List (CFL) in Windows checkbox. Click OK to save your change.

If the Synchronize RSS Feeds to the Common Feed List (CFL) in Windows checkbox is checked, the feeds in both programs stay in synch — if you add a feed to Outlook, it also appears in IE's list of feeds. Likewise, remove

a feed from Internet Explorer, and you remove it from Outlook, as well. Uncheck this option to prevent changes in Outlook from affecting IE and vice versa.

If you want to keep your RSS feeds in Outlook only, make sure you do not turn on the Synchronize RSS Feeds to the Common Feed List (CFL) in Windows checkbox. Then add the RSS feeds manually, by following the steps in the earlier section, "Adding a news feed through Outlook's Account Settings." You may be able to automate the process a bit, using something called USM (Universal Subscription Mechanism). If you see USM offered as an option for subscribing to an RSS feed, choose it, and then choose Outlook as the program to send the data to. You might be asked a few times to confirm that you want to add a subscription, but that's it!

You can find RSS feeds at most news sources, such as CNN.com (www.cnn.com) and MSNBC.com (www.msnbc.com). You can also find them at RSS source sites, such as syndic8 (www.syndic8.com/index.php), Moreover Technologies (www.moreover.com), NewsIsFree (www.newsisfree.com), RssFeeds.com (www.rssfeeds.com), and RSSTop55 (www.masternew media.org/rss/top55).

To add a feed to Outlook using Internet Explorer, follow these steps:

1. **Navigate to a Web page that has a news feed.**

After browsing a page that contains a link to a news feed, the chicklet button (okay, Microsoft calls it the RSS Feeds button) on the Command bar magically lights up next to the Home button at the top of the Internet Explorer window.

2. **Click the downward-pointing arrow on the RSS Feeds button and select the particular feed on that page that you want to add from the drop-down list that appears, as shown in Figure 3-3.**

**Book III
Chapter 3**

Getting the Latest
News Delivered
Right to Your Inbox

If the button doesn't have an arrow, IE has only one feed, so just click the button. You can also click the RSS, XML, or whatever-they're-calling-it button located on the Web page.

A Web page appears, displaying a sample of some of the articles associated with this feed.

RSS Feeds button

Figure 3-3:
Add a
feed from
Internet
Explorer.

3. Click the Subscribe To This Feed link.

The Subscribe to This Feed dialog box appears, as shown in Figure 3-4. If you don't see the Subscribe To This Feed link, you might see icons that represent various places to which you can send the feed. Select USM (Universal Subscription Mechanism).

4. Type a name for the feed in the Name field.

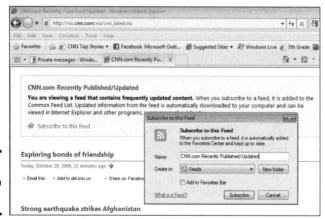

Figure 3-4:
Subscribe to
the feed.

5. **Select which Internet Explorer folder you want to save the feed in.**

   You can select one from the Create In drop-down list. Or click the New Folder button, which makes the New Folder dialog box appear. There, you can type the name for the new folder in the Folder Name text box. Click Create to create the folder and return to the Subscribe to This Feed dialog box.

6. **Click Subscribe.**

   A new Web page appears, telling you that you've successfully subscribed. Click the View My Feeds link at the top of this page to review your news feeds in Internet Explorer. Switch over to Outlook to read articles from your new feed. See the section "Reading News Feeds," later in this chapter, for help.

To add a feed to Outlook using Firefox, follow these steps:

1. **Navigate to a Web page that has a news feed.**

   After browsing a page that contains a link to a news feed, a chicklet button (Firefox calls it the Subscribe To This Page button) magically appears at the right end of the Address box, located at the top of the Firefox window.

2. **Click the Subscribe To This Page button and select the particular feed on that page that you want to add from the drop-down list that appears, as shown in Figure 3-5.**

   If the button doesn't have an arrow, then Firefox has found only one feed, so just click the button. You can also click the RSS, XML, or whatever-they're-calling-it button located on the Web page.

   A Web page appears, displaying a sample of some of the articles associated with this feed.

Book III
Chapter 3

Getting the Latest
News Delivered
Right to Your Inbox

Subscribe To This Page button

Figure 3-5:
Add a feed
from Firefox.

3. **Open the Subscribe To This Feed Using drop-down list, and select Microsoft Outlook.**

   If you want to always send your RSS feeds to Outlook, select the Always Use Microsoft Outlook to Subscribe to Feeds checkbox.

4. **Click the Subscribe Now button.**

   The Microsoft Outlook dialog box appears, as shown in Figure 3-6.

Figure 3-6:
Subscribe to
a new feed.

5. **Click Yes to add the feed.**

   If you want to set options for the new feed, click the Advanced button in the Microsoft Outlook dialog box to display the RSS Feed Options dialog box. (Refer to Figure 3-2.) Set your options as described in the earlier section, "Adding a news feed through Outlook's Account Settings," then click OK to return to the Microsoft Outlook dialog box.

   After you click Yes, the feed is automatically added, and you're switched over to Outlook so you can read articles from your new feed. See the section "Reading News Feeds," later in this chapter, for help.

Changing or Removing a Feed

After adding a feed to Outlook, you can change its options in just a few steps:

1. **Click the File tab to display Backstage, and select Info from the list on the left.**

   The Account Information options appear on the right.

2. **Click the Account Settings button, and select Account Settings from the pop-up menu that appears.**

   The Account Settings dialog box pops up.

3. **Click the RSS Feeds tab.**

A list of your current RSS feeds appears in the Account Settings dialog box, as shown in Figure 3-7.

If a news feed proves annoying with its frequent articles (or just proves uninteresting), you can remove it altogether by selecting the feed in the Account Settings dialog box and clicking Remove.

4. **Select the feed that you want to modify and click Change.**

   That RSS Feed Options dialog box opens (refer to Figure 3-2).

5. **Make your changes, click OK in the RSS Feed Options dialog box, and then click Close in the Account Settings dialog box.**

Change button

Remove button

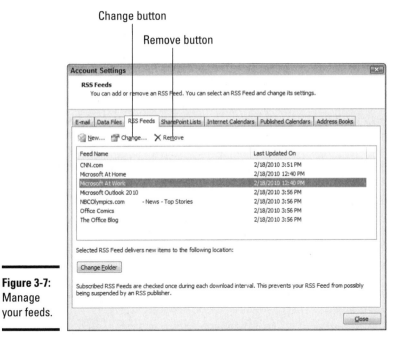

Figure 3-7:
Manage
your feeds.

Reading News Feeds

Reading news feeds is actually nothing *new.* You simply do what you already know how to do — read messages. Outlook typically collects all the news feeds in one spot for you — its RSS Feeds folder. To view a news feed, open the RSS Feeds folder in the Navigation pane, and then click the folder for that news feed.

The articles for the feed appear as ordinary e-mail messages, so you have several ways to view them:

✦ If you have the Reading pane open, you can click a news article and view its contents in the Reading pane.

✦ Double-click the article to open it in a separate window.

✦ If the article contains a link to the entire article online, you can click that link to view the entire article in your Web browser. You can also click the View Article button in the RSS group on the Home tab to view the article associated with the message online. Click the Download Content button on the Home tab and select Download Article from the pop-up menu that appears to download the article to your system (as an HTML attachment to the RSS article in Outlook) for your viewing pleasure.

✦ If the feed didn't automatically download enclosures and you want to see them, click the Download Content button on the Home tab and select Download All Content from the pop-up menu that appears.

✦ If you have a long list of articles to scan, you may prefer Preview view; it displays the full message header and a few lines of the message contents for every unread article, as shown in Figure 3-8. (See Book II, Chapter 2 for help in changing message views.)

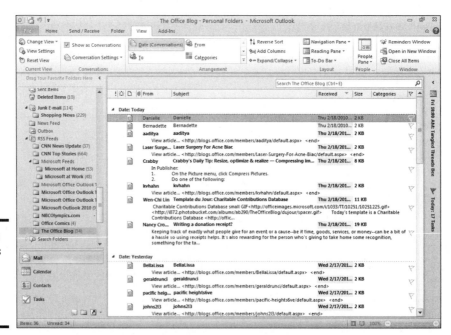

Figure 3-8:
View news feeds by using Preview view.

Sharing News Feeds

You can share your news feeds in one of two ways: by sending an invitation via e-mail to subscribe to the news feed or by exporting your feeds in a file. If you choose to export, you can select which feeds you want to share. The following sections detail these different approaches.

Sharing a feed by e-mail

After you add a news feed to Outlook, if you find that you like its articles, you can forward the URL for the news feed in the form of an invitation to your friends and colleagues so that they can share the fun. Just follow these steps:

1. **Click any article within the feed that you want to share.**

2. **Click the Share This Feed button in the RSS group on the Home tab.**

   If the article is open, the Share This Feed button appears on the RSS Article tab. After you click the button, a new message is created. Just below the Subject, in the header area, the RSS feed is listed, along with the URL to the feed.

3. **Address the message, add any comments that you want in the text area, and click Send to send the invitation.**

If someone sends you an invitation to subscribe to a news feed, you can add the feed to Outlook pretty easily. Start by simply viewing the invitation e-mail. Information about the RSS feed appears in the e-mail message, as shown in Figure 3-9. Click the Add This RSS Feed button on the Share tab, and the Microsoft Outlook dialog box appears. (Refer to Figure 3-6.) Click Yes to add the feed, and it appears in the RSS Feeds folder in Outlook.

**Book III
Chapter 3**

**Getting the Latest
News Delivered
Right to Your Inbox**

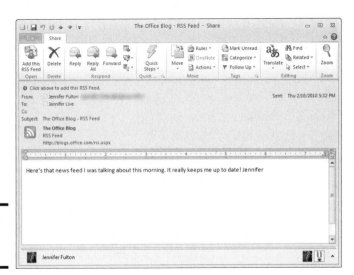

Figure 3-9:
Feeding
frenzy.

Importing/exporting a news feed list

If you want to share multiple news feeds, export a selected list of news feeds (or all of them) into a file, and then send that file as an attachment in an e-mail message to anyone with whom you want to share the feeds. To create an export file, follow these steps:

1. **Click the File tab to display Backstage, and select Open from the list on the left.**

   The Open options appear on the right.

2. **Select Import.**

   The Import and Export Wizard appears.

3. **Select Export RSS Feeds to an OPML File and click Next.**

   The Export to an OPML File page of the wizard appears.

4. **Select which feeds to export, and then click Next.**

   All your feeds are checked off initially, so just uncheck those that you don't want to share. After you click Next, the Save Exported File As page of the wizard appears.

5. **Click Browse and select a folder in which to save the file from the OPML File dialog box.**

6. **Type a name for the feeds list in the File Name box, and click Save to return to the wizard.**

7. **Click Next to save the selected news feeds in a file.**

8. **To send the list onto someone else, create a new message and attach the file.**

   See Book II, Chapter 1 for more on attaching files.

If you receive an e-mail that has an RSS feed list attached, save the file, and then import the list into Outlook. Follow these steps:

1. **From within Outlook, click the File tab to display Backstage, and select Open from the list on the left.**

   The Open options appear on the right.

2. **Select Import.**

   The Import and Export Wizard appears.

3. **Select Import RSS Feeds from an OPML File and click Next.**

   The Import an OPML page of the wizard appears.

4. **Click Browse, select an RSS feed file to import, and click Open to return to the wizard.**

   RSS feed files have the .opml file extension.

5. **Click Next.**

   The Select RSS Feeds page of the wizard appears.

6. **Select the feeds you want to import, and then click Next.**

   All the feeds in the file are listed, so just select the ones that you want to import into Outlook.

   After you click Next, the confirmation page of the wizard appears.

7. **Click Finish.**

   Outlook adds the feed to the RSS Feeds folder and downloads articles to that folder.

Chapter 4: Sending Mass Mailings

In This Chapter

✔ Grouping contacts in a distribution list

✔ Pulling contacts into Word to create a massive mailing

The invention of electronic messaging has made getting the word out incredibly easy. Using *contact groups* (distribution lists), you can easily send the same message to a group of your friends or colleagues. I mean, you have a list of personal and business contacts, so why not use it? Outlook lets you leverage your Outlook Contacts names and addresses to personalize a letter or other document that you create in Word. You can also leverage your Contacts list to create printed envelopes or labels for mass paper mailings. And if that lever isn't high enough yet, you can leverage your Contacts again to create a professional-looking mass e-mailing that you create by using Word templates and send by using Outlook.

You can also get the word out by using Business Contact Manager, a program that comes with Outlook in the Office 2010 Professional Plus package. Basically, you can use Business Contact Manager to track the mass mailing and the responses that you get from your customers or potential sales contacts. (In a not-so-strange coincidence, you can find out more about Business Contact Manager in Book VII.)

Creating a Distribution List

Do you often find yourself sending messages to the same group of people? Do you find yourself wandering aimlessly around the office trying to remember what it was you got up for? Well, I can't help you with the last one, but I can make sending group messages easier. If you have a group of people you like to bother regularly with meaningless correspondence (uh, I mean *really important messages*) — such as your departmental colleagues, best clients, brothers and sisters, or the members of your Mommies and Me group — you can create a contact group (distribution list). You can create as many contact groups as you want and bother people easily with a single click. You can even attach a contact group to an e-mail message so that others can use the list to bother people (uh, send really important messages).

To create a contact group, follow these steps:

1. **Click the New Items button on the Home tab, select More Items from the pop-up menu that appears, and select Contact Group.**

The Contact Group form appears. (You can see it in the background in Figure 4-1.)

Search box

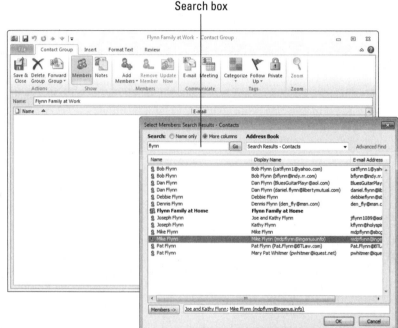

Figure 4-1:
Create a contact group to bother a lot of people with a single click.

2. **Type a name for the contact group in the Name text box.**

You have to give your contact group a name so that Outlook can keep track of it. Use a name that helps you to identify the purpose of the contact group, such as My Department, My Family, or Soccer Moms.

3. **Click the Add Members button on the Contact Group tab.**

Select either From Outlook Contacts or From Address Book — depending on where the people you want to add to the group are hiding — from the pop-up menu that appears. People from your company are probably in your Exchange address book (so choose From Address Book to see them), and people you've added to Outlook manually are in your Contacts list (so choose From Outlook Contacts to see them).

You can add someone to Contacts and to this group at the same time; skip to Step 6 to see exactly how.

Assuming you select either From Outlook Contacts or From Address Book, the Select Members dialog box appears. (You can see it in the foreground in Figure 4-1.) The contacts in your default address book appear in a large list. If needed, change to a different address book by selecting one from the Address Book list.

4. **Add members to the contact group by selecting a name from those listed and clicking the Members button.**

   You can also double-click a name to add it to the contact group. The members that you select appear in the Members box at the bottom of the Select Members dialog box.

   To search for someone in a large list, type a few letters of the person's first name in the Search text box and click the Go button. To search by first name, last name, or e-mail address, click the More Columns radio button, then type something to search for in the Search text box and click the Go button.

5. **When you're done adding names, click OK.**

   The Select Members dialog box disappears. The names you selected appear in the Contact Group form.

6. **(Optional) Add someone to the list who's not already in Contacts, if you want.**

   Follow these steps:

   a. *Click the Add Members button on the Contact Group tab and select New E-mail Contact from the pop-up menu that appears.*

   The Add New Member dialog box appears. (See Figure 4-2.)

Figure 4-2:
The
Contacts
list always
has room for
one more.

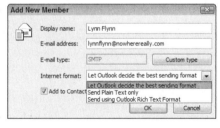

   b. *Type the person's name in the Display Name text box.*

   c. *Type the person's e-mail address in the E-Mail Address text box.*

   d. *From the Internet Format drop-down list, select the e-mail format (plain text or RTF) that you prefer to use when sending e-mail to this person.*

   You can also let Outlook choose the format to use.

e. *Select the Add to Contacts check box to add this name to your Contacts list.*

Not selecting this option means that you can add people manually to a contact group while keeping them off your Contacts list (although why you'd want to do that is a mystery to me).

f. *Click OK to add the new member.*

The Contact Group form reappears.

7. Click the Save & Close button on the Contact Group tab.

Your new contact group appears within the Contacts list, with a special icon that helps to identify it, as shown in Figure 4-3. If you view your Contacts as Business Cards, then look for the word Group just under the name on the card to help you identify that card as a contact group.

Contact Group icon

Sort by Icon button

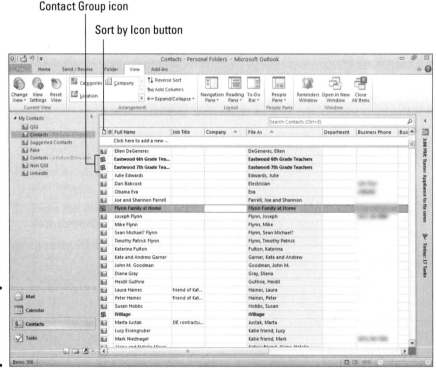

Figure 4-3:
Look for
this Contact
Group icon.

If you're having trouble finding a contact group (because maybe you forgot the name that you used to create it), keep this in mind: You can force contact groups to appear at the top of any list view by clicking the Sort by Icon button at the top of the first column on the left. (Refer to Figure 4-3.) For more help in sorting a list, see Book VIII, Chapter 2.

Using a contact group to send e-mails

Contact groups give you a lot of options for efficient e-mailing:

✦ **To send an e-mail message or meeting invitation to everyone on the list:** Follow the same steps that you would to send any other message — just type the name of the list in the To text box of an e-mail/meeting invitation form.

✦ **To send an e-mail to each member without the other members knowing:** Type the contact group name in the Bcc text box.

✦ **To send an e-mail message or meeting invitation to almost everyone on the list:** Address the message/invitation to the contact group, then expand the list (by clicking the plus sign in front of the list name in the To text box of your message/invitation). Expanding the list converts it from just a name to a listing of the actual e-mail addresses in the list. After expanding the list, select any address that you don't want to include and press Delete.

If you select a contact group in the Contacts list, then you can click the E-Mail or Meeting button on the Home tab to send a message or a meeting invitation to everyone in the group.

Making changes to a contact group

Sadly, the members of a contact group may leave the department, change e-mail addresses, or simply fall off your favored-friends roster. To change a contact group, jump over to Contacts and double-click the contact group name. In the Contact Group form that appears, you can make a range of changes:

✦ **Add someone.** Use the processes I describe in the section "Creating a Distribution List," earlier in this chapter:

• To add someone from the Contacts list, click the Add Members button on the Contact Group tab and select either From Outlook Contacts or From Address Book from the pop-up menu that appears.

• To add someone who isn't in the Contacts list, click the Add Members button on the Contact Group tab and select New E-Mail Contact from its pop-up menu.

✦ **Remove someone.** Select the name in the list, and click the Remove Member button on the Contact Group tab.

✦ **Update old e-mail addresses.** If you know that someone in the list is using a new e-mail address, you can update the list with that new address. Click the Update Now button on the Contact Group tab. Outlook searches your address books for new addresses.

✦ **Make the list private.** To prevent others who have permission to see your Contacts list from viewing or changing this contact group, click the Private button on the Contact Group tab.

✦ **Send the list to someone.** To share your list with someone, click the Forward Group button on the Contact Group tab and select a format from the pop-up menu that appears: In Internet Format (vCard) — a format that's compatible with most e-mail programs, or As an Outlook Contact (a format that allows the receiver to add the contact group directly to his/her Outlook).

✦ **Annotate the list.** Having trouble remembering whom you have in the list and why? Click the Notes button on the Contact Group tab and type a reminder for yourself in the large text box that appears. Your note appears in the Contacts list when you use Card view. You can also redisplay the note by clicking the Notes button again when you have the contact group open.

To remind yourself about something that you want to do with the list, add a reminder, rather than a note. Click the Follow Up button on the Contact Group tab and select a follow up flag from the pop-up menu that appears. See Chapter 1 of this minibook for help.

✦ **Categorize the group.** Group the list with similar items by adding categorie(s) to it. For example, if this contact group contains a list of bowling buddies, you might add a category "Friends" to it. You could then sort the Contacts list by category, and quickly locate all your friends and your bowling buddies contact group because they would be next to each other in the Contact list. To add a category to a group, click the Categorize button on the Contact Group tab and select the category to which you want to add the list from the pop-up menu that appears. (See Book VIII, Chapter 1 for help in creating categories.)

Creating a Mass Mailing in Word Using Your Contacts

You can get the same message to a lot of people by creating a single Word document, printing it a bunch of times, and then printing matching labels or envelopes for everyone you want to reach. Okay, you know this isn't a book about Word, so you may be wondering what Word has to do with Outlook. Well, first off, you can use the names, addresses, and other information that you keep in Outlook Contacts to create hundreds of personalized printed letters in Word — in a matter of minutes. You can then reuse that same Contacts information to create labels or envelopes so that you can send your personalized letters to all your nearest and dearest. You can also use the power of Word — and its templates, if you want — to create a mass e-mailing that's professionally formatted and personalized with information that you pull from Contacts (for example, each person's first name).

For the juicy details of *mail merge* (the Word term for this magic) and other advanced Word techniques, see *Word 2010 All-in-One Desk Reference For Dummies,* by Doug Lowe. Instead of wading through all that, you can follow these basic steps to create a mail merge with your Contacts, and create a series of e-mail messages with Word's Mail Merge feature:

1. **Start a document.**

   If you have a document ready to use, open it now in Word. Close any other open documents that you are not going to use. If you don't have a document you want to use; that's okay, because you get the opportunity to create a brand new document to use in Step 4.

2. **Click the Start Mail Merge button on the Mailings tab and select Step by Step Mail Merge Wizard from the pop-up menu that appears.**

   The Mail Merge Wizard task pane appears on the right.

3. **Select a Document Type, such as letters or e-mail messages, and click Next: Starting Document.**

   The Select Starting Document page of the wizard appears.

4. **Select the document that you want to use.**

   Select the Use the Current Document radio button. If you have an existing document that you want to use but haven't yet opened it, select the Start from Existing Document radio button, instead. To use a template to create the document, select the Start from a Template radio button, then click the Select Template link, which opens the Select Template dialog box, where you can select a template and click OK to return to the wizard.

   Because the templates online change often and you can probably find a template out there designed to do exactly what you want (maybe a newsletter or sales brochure), why not check them out?

5. **(Optional) Select the label or envelope type.**

   If you selected labels as the document type in Step 3, click the Label Options link and select the label type from the Label Options dialog box and click OK to return to the wizard.

   Word needs to know which type you're using so that it can format everything correctly. Similarly, if you selected envelopes in Step 3, click the Envelope Options link, select an envelope type from the Envelope Options dialog box and click OK to return to the wizard.

6. **Click Next: Select Recipients.**

   The Select Recipients page of the wizard appears.

7. **Select the Select from Outlook Contacts radio button.**

8. **Click the Choose Contacts Folder link (assuming you have more than one folder), select the Contacts list that you want to use from Select Contacts dialog box that appears, and then click OK to return to the wizard.**

   The Mail Merge Recipients dialog box appears, similar to the one shown in Figure 4-4.

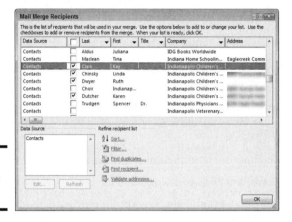

Figure 4-4:
So, who do
you want?

9. **Use the Mail Merge Recipients dialog box to narrow your Contacts list to the people you actually want to send the Word document to.**

   You can select recipients manually, sort the list, or filter the list to narrow it down. To sort, click a column heading; to filter, click the arrow on a column heading and select an option from the pop-up menu that appears.

10. **Click OK when you have the list the way you want it.**

    The Mail Merge Recipients dialog box closes.

11. **In the wizard, click Next: Write Your Letter/E-Mail Message/ Labels/ Envelope.**

    The Write Your Letter/E-Mail Message/ Labels/Envelope page of the wizard appears.

12. **Create your sample letter, label, envelope, or e-mail message.**

    Type the text you want to appear in every copy of your letter, label, envelope, or e-mail message in the document window. At a point in the text where you want to insert information from your contacts (such as a contact's address), you insert a placeholder. Word calls these place-holders "items". Later, when you complete the merge, a copy of the document you create now is made for every contact you select in Step

9, and the actual information for a contact is used in place of the place-holder. For example, in place of the address placeholder, the address of a selected contact will appear.

Add items within the text by clicking the item you want to insert from those listed on the Write Your Letter page of the wizard. For example, click the Address Block link to insert a placeholder for a contact's address in your document.

If you don't see a field that you want to add, click More Items to display the Insert Merge Fields dialog box. Select a field and click Insert to insert the placeholder into the document. To return to the document, click Close to close the Insert Merge Fields dialog box.

13. **(Optional) If you're creating labels, after inserting the fields that you want on the first label, click Update All Labels button on the wizard to copy the information to each label on your sample label sheet.**

14. **Click Next: Preview Your Letters/Labels/Envelopes/E-mail Messages.**

The Preview page of the wizard appears, where you can view how your letter, labels, envelopes, or e-mail message will look when you merge them with the contact information that you inserted. Use the left and right arrow keys on the wizard to scroll through each merged item.

15. **Click Next: Complete the Merge.**

The Complete the Merge page of the wizard appears.

If you're creating a form letter or e-mail message, each letter/message starts on its own page, but they're all contained in one Word document.

16. **If you want hard copies of your new documents, click the Print link on the wizard to print all the letters, labels, or envelopes.**

17. **If you're sending a series of e-mails, click the Electronic Mail link on the wizard to e-mail your messages.**

The Merge to E-Mail dialog box appears.

18. **If you are sending a series of e-mails, type a subject in the Subject Line text box, select a format from the Mail Format list, and click OK.**

The Merge to E-Mail dialog box closes, and an email is immediately sent to each contact you selected.

19. **Save your document by clicking the Save button on the Quick Access Toolbar, selecting a folder to save to, and clicking Save.**

Save your merged document if you think you'll reuse it again as-is; otherwise, skip this step.

20. **Close the document.**

Chapter 5: Managing Multiple E-Mail Accounts

In This Chapter

✔ Controlling e-mail coming and going

✔ Choosing which e-mail account to use when sending e-mail

✔ Setting up Outlook for multiple people and multiple e-mail accounts

*N*owadays, a lot of people have multiple e-mail addresses. Even though I work from home, I still have multiple e-mail addresses for personal versus business mail. I even have one address that I use strictly for Web sites that require my address — I find it helps me deal with the inevitable junk mail that results. This chapter shows you how to deal with the issues that crop up when you're using several e-mail accounts. For example, maybe you don't want to get your personal e-mail as often as your work mail. Or maybe you want the opportunity to review e-mail headers and weed out the junk before you take the time to download it all. Maybe you want to select the e-mail account that you use for sending a specific message so that replies go back to that address. Maybe your issue is organization — finding an easy way of directing e-mail for a particular account into a special folder. If you have multiple people using the same computer, the problems seem to multiply — how do you keep your contacts, calendar info, and e-mail separate from those of your kids or coworkers? In this chapter, I tackle all these issues and more, to boot.

If you need to set up a second (or third) e-mail account and want to know where I cover that, see Book I, Chapter 3.

Controlling Sending and Receiving

If you have only one e-mail account — and you're not interested in downloading news feeds into Outlook or displaying Internet calendars — then you can control the sending and receiving of e-mail pretty straightforwardly. If you have multiple e-mail accounts, one or more news feeds, and some Internet calendars that need updating every once in a while, well, it gets a bit more complicated. Still, if you use Send/Receive groups, as outlined in the following section, you can soon have things under control.

You can find out how to set up news feeds in Outlook in Chapter 3 of this minibook. For pointers on adding Internet calendars to Outlook, see Book IV, Chapter 5.

Creating Send/Receive groups

You start Outlook life with a single Send/Receive group called All Accounts. As you might expect, even if you have multiple e-mail accounts, a bunch of news feeds, and several Internet calendars, the All Accounts group controls them all. You use the All Accounts group to send and receive *everything*. So, if you want to use the same schedule to send and receive all your messages and update your news and calendar subscriptions, then hey, skip the stuff in this section; you don't need it. But if you want to send and receive messages for each e-mail account at different intervals — or want to update your news feeds more often (or your Internet calendars less often) than you get e-mail — then setting up multiple Send/Receive groups helps you establish separate schedules.

You can't remove the All Accounts group, but you can remove e-mail, news, and Internet calendar accounts from it, if you want, and then include those accounts in some other Send/Receive group that you create. By the way, you can include accounts in multiple Send/Receive groups, so you don't actually have to edit the All Accounts group if you don't want to. And by accounts, remember that I mean not only e-mail accounts, but also news feeds and Internet calendars.

You can't update some news feeds and Internet calendars more frequently than at specific intervals, so even if you try to send/receive them, you might not see any new messages.

Send/Receive groups are a pretty useful way to control a lot of stuff:

✦ **Sending and receiving:** This one's a *duh*. By using Send/Receive groups, you can control when a particular account receives e-mail, news updates, or calendar changes. You can also control when messages that you create by using a particular account are sent. (See the section "Sending from a Specific E-Mail Account," later in this chapter, for help.)

✦ **Frequency:** Control how often Outlook actually sends and receives e-mail, news updates, or calendar changes for this group.

✦ **Limitations:** Limit the size of messages that are downloaded. This option prevents you from downloading messages that have really large attachments.

✦ **Folders:** Update specific folders on your corporate Exchange account as frequently as you desire.

✦ **What you get:** You can download only headers from the mail server so that you can mark the ones you want or get everything without reviewing.

✦ **Offline:** Control what Outlook does when you're *offline* (not connected to the Internet).

To create a new Send/Receive group, follow these steps:

1. **Click the File tab to display Backstage, and select Options from the list on the left.**

   The Outlook Options dialog box appears.

2. **Select Advanced from the list on the left.**

   The Advanced options appear on the right.

3. **In the Send and Receive section, click the Send/Receive button.**

   The Send/Receive Groups dialog box appears.

4. **Click New.**

   The Send/Receive Group Name dialog box opens.

5. **Type a name for your new group, such as Personal, in the Send/ Receive Group Name text box and click OK.**

   The Send/Receive Settings dialog box jumps up. (See Figure 5-1.)

**Book III
Chapter 5**

**Managing Multiple
E-Mail Accounts**

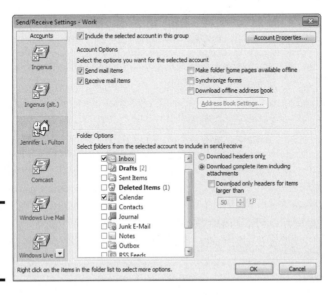

Figure 5-1:
Who
belongs in
this group?

The Accounts list on the left of the dialog box shows all the accounts that you have set up: e-mail, news, and Internet calendars.

6. **From the Accounts list, select an account to include in this new group; then select the Include the Selected Account in This Group checkbox.**

   The icon for that account changes: Rather than a red X, it now includes a blue double-arrow Send/Receive thingy. So, if you glance down the Accounts list, you can quickly see which accounts are associated with this group.

7. **Set the account options.**

   The options you see vary, depending on the type of account:

   - *Send Mail Items:* Do you want Outlook to send e-mails created for this account when you activate this Send/Receive group?

   - *Receive Mail Items:* Do you want to receive e-mails sent to this e-mail account?

   - *Make Folder Home Page Available Offline:* For Exchange accounts, you can create a home page for each Outlook folder (such as Inbox, Calendar, and so on) to help users get to subfolders quickly. Assuming the owner of the folder (typically, the system administrator) has created a home page for a folder (which you see when you click the folder's name in the Folder list), you can have Outlook copy the home page to your computer so that you can use it to navigate folders when you're offline.

   - *Synchronize Forms:* For Exchange accounts, if your company provides Outlook forms for creating certain items and you want to access them from the server, even when you're offline, you can select this option to update your computer's copy of the forms.

   - *Download Offline Address Book:* For Exchange accounts, selecting this option allows you to pull up e-mail addresses and such even when you're not connected to the network (when you're offline).

   - *Folder Options:* If you're on an Exchange network, select from the folder list which folders on the Exchange server (such as Calendar and Inbox) you want updated (downloaded) during the Send/Receive action.

   - *Download Options:* Select whether to download just the headers (by selecting the Download Headers Only radio button), download the complete item, including attachments (by selecting the Download Complete Item Including Attachments radio button), or download only headers for those items larger than a size you've set by selecting the Download Only Headers For Items Larger Than checkbox, and typing a size in the text box.

If you routinely receive e-mails that have large file attachments and you're tired of them clogging up your machine, the Download Only Headers For Items Larger Than XX option lets you still get all your regular, slender e-mail. But for large e-mails that have bulky attachments, you get headers only. You can then pick and choose which of these large-attachment e-mails you want now and which ones can wait until you've nothing better to do than twiddle your thumbs while they download.

- *Include Published Calendars:* Select this option to include Internet calendars in the group so they can be updated with the latest changes. After you select the Include Published Calendars in This Send/Receive Group checkbox, select the exact calendars you want updated with this group from the Published Calendars list. See Book IV, Chapter 5 for more info on Internet calendar publishing.

- *Feeds:* For RSS accounts, you can select the specific feeds that you want included in this Send/Receive group. First, select the Include RSS Feeds in This Send/Receive Group checkbox, then select the exact feeds you want updated with this group from the Feed Name list.

8. Click OK.

The Send/Receive Groups dialog box reappears (see Figure 5-2).

9. Set Send/Receive options for this group.

These options control the automatic sending and receiving of e-mail for this account:

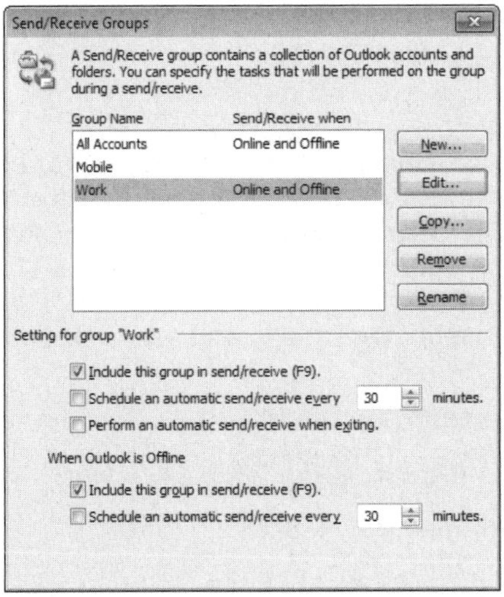

Book III
Chapter 5

Managing Multiple
E-Mail Accounts

Figure 5-2:
Set other
options.

- *Include the Group in Send/Receive (F9):* Tells Outlook to send and receive e-mail for the accounts in this group whenever you say "Go get 'em, boy!" by pressing F9.

- *Schedule an Automatic Send/Receive Every XX Minutes:* Tells Outlook to automatically send and receive messages for this account at regular intervals every number of minutes that you specify. Normally, the interval for automatic Send/Receives is set to 30 minutes, but you can change the interval by clicking the up or down arrow to the right of the number text box.

- *Perform an Automatic Send/Receive when Exiting:* Tells Outlook to do one last Send/Receive for this account right before you shut down the program.

You can also select options to control what happens when you're offline:

- *Include This Group in Send/Receive (F9):* When you press F9 while working offline, Outlook reconnects you, gets the messages for your account, and disconnects you again. (For an extra $50, it picks up your laundry and orders take-out.)

- *Schedule an Automatic Send/Receive Every XX Minutes:* While you're working offline, Outlook automatically reconnects you every number of minutes that you specify (by clicking the up or down arrow to the right of the number text box), and then disconnects after it gets the messages for this group.

10. **Click Close.**

You are returned to the Outlook Options dialog box.

11. **Click OK.**

The Outlook Options dialog box closes.

You can edit a group to add or remove accounts from it. For example, you can remove accounts from the All Accounts group if you don't want those accounts controlled by that group's settings, or you can make changes to a group that you created. To edit a group, follow these steps:

1. **Click the File tab to display Backstage, and select Options from the list on the left.**

The Outlook Options dialog box appears.

2. **Select Advanced from the list on the left.**

The Advanced options appear on the right.

3. **In the Send and Receive section, click the Send/Receive button.**

The Send/Receive Groups dialog box appears. (Refer to Figure 5-2.)

4. **Select the group that you want to change from the list.**

5. **Click Edit.**

   The Send/Receive Settings dialog box appears (Refer Figure 5-1.)

6. **Make your changes and click OK to save them.**

   The Send/Receive Groups dialog box reappears (see Figure 5-2).

7. **Click Close.**

   You are returned to the Outlook Options dialog box.

8. **Click OK.**

   The Outlook Options dialog box closes.

Now, go get that mail!

Even if you don't create new Send/Receive groups, you still have the good ol' All Accounts group. And it has settings (which you can change, using the steps in the preceding section) that control how often it does a send/receive. Other Send/Receive groups have their own settings that control when they do their thing. So — one way or the other — you get e-mails, updated news feeds, and online calendars whenever you've scheduled those groups to go off.

If you're waiting anxiously for an important e-mail, you aren't at the mercy of the various Send/Receive groups because you can poke 'em to make them do a send/receive whenever you feel like it. Your options include

✦ **Send/receive everything.** To do a send/receive for all groups, press F9 or click the Send/Receive All Folders button on the Quick Access Toolbar.

   If you're in Mail, you can click the Send/Receive All Folders button on the Home tab. In other modules, you can click the Send/Receive All Folders button on the Send/Receive tab if the Quick Access Toolbar isn't visible.

   The preceding section discusses a setting in the Send/Receive Groups dialog box that can *prevent* Outlook from doing a send/receive when you press F9. If you've activated this setting for a particular group, then that group opts out of the F9 business; it doesn't go get mail when you press F9, but it does if you select the Send/Receive All Folders button.

✦ **Send and receive e-mail for one folder only.** Select a folder in the Folder list (such as e-mail folder or a calendar) and click the Update Folder button on the Send/Receive tab or press Shift+F9 to update the contents of that folder only. This command applies to Exchange users only, since it can only be used on folders in that type of account.

+ **Send but don't get.** To send messages for all groups without receiving anything, click the Send All button on the Send/Receive tab.

+ **Send/receive all the accounts in one group.** Click the Send/Receive Groups button on the Send/Receive tab, and choose a group from the pop-up menu that appears. The group names appear at the top of the menu. For example, if you created a Work Send/Receive group, you'd choose Work from the Send/Receive Groups menu to send and receive messages, calendar updates, and news feed updates for the accounts in that group.

+ **Send/receive for a particular e-mail account only.** Click the Send/Receive Groups button on the Send/Receive tab, and select an account from the pop-up menu that appears. The accounts are listed at the bottom of the menu. After you select the account you want to play with from Send/Receive Groups menu, you select the specific Send/Receive action from the pop-up menu that appears. Your choices include Inbox (which gets everything), Download Inbox Headers (which gets message headers only), and Process Marked Headers (which downloads or deletes messages from the server, depending on how you've marked the headers on your end). To learn how to mark headers, read the upcoming Technical Stuff sidebar, "The heady business of message headers." You can process the headers in a single folder by selecting that folder first and then clicking the Process Marked Headers button on the Send/Receive tab, and selecting Process Marked Headers from the pop-up menu that appears.

+ **Get headers for a particular folder.** Select in the Folder list the folder from which you want to download headers, and then click the Download Headers button in the Send/Receive tab.

+ **Download the Exchange Address Book.** If you want to make sure that your Global Address Book is updated with the most recent contacts on your Exchange network, click the Send/Receive Groups button on the Send/Receive tab and select Download Address Book from the pop-up menu that appears. The Offline Address Book dialog box appears; select the Download Changes Since Last Send/Receive checkbox if you only want to update changes. If you don't select this option, then all contacts are downloaded even if they haven't changed since the last update. Next, select which information you want updated: Full Details or No Details (which updates the minimal information about each contact, including the display name, primary SMTP address, office location, surname, and mail nickname. If you use more than on address book, select the address book to update from the Choose Address Book list and click OK.

You can cancel all regular send/receives temporarily by clicking the Send/Receive Groups button on the Send/Receive tab, and selecting Disable Scheduled Send/Receive from the pop-up menu that appears. You can then send/receive messages for a single account or Send/Receive group. Just follow the steps in this section. Resume your regularly scheduled program by clicking the Disable Scheduled Send/Receive button again.

The heady business of message headers

If you download message headers only, you can mark the ones that pique your interest enough to want to see the full message and use the Process Marked Headers command to get those messages. To mark a header for download, click the Mark to Download button on the Send/Receive tab, and select Mark to Download from the pop-up menu that appears. To get a copy of the message and leave it on the server, select Mark to Download Message Copy from the Mark to Download menu. Unmark headers by selecting them first and

clicking the Unmark to Download button on the Send/Receive tab, and selecting Unmark to Download from the pop-up menu that appears. Unmark all headers by clicking the Unmark to Download button on the Send/Receive tab and selecting Unmark All Headers from the pop-up menu that appears. To mark a header so that its message is removed from the server the next time you connect, click the message header and press Delete. A red X appears on the header to remind you that it's a goner the next time you process headers.

Selecting Your Default E-Mail Account

If you've ever worked on a team, you're used to the concept of a team leader, otherwise known as the "person to blame if something goes wrong." If you have multiple e-mail accounts, one of them has to be the boss. Outlook basically needs to know which account to treat as the *default* (the one used for sending new e-mails if you don't specify another account).

When you reply to or forward an e-mail that you've received, Outlook doesn't send that message by using the default e-mail account, but instead uses the account to which that e-mail was sent originally (although you can override this option when needed). Outlook uses your default account whenever you create a new e-mail, and so if the recipient clicks that ol' Reply button, the reply is sent back to your default account. Because replies come back to the e-mail account you use when you send e-mail (and that account is typically your default account), take pains to make sure that the default account is the one that you want people to address you by most often. When needed, you can always send a new e-mail from any one of your accounts, rather than from the one you've crowned as king.

To set the default account, follow these steps:

1. **Click the File tab to display Backstage, and select Info from the list on the left.**

The Account Information options appear on the right.

2. **Click the Account Settings button, and select Account Settings from the pop-up menu that appears.**

The Account Settings dialog box appears, as shown in Figure 5-3.

Default Account   Click these arrow buttons to change the account order.

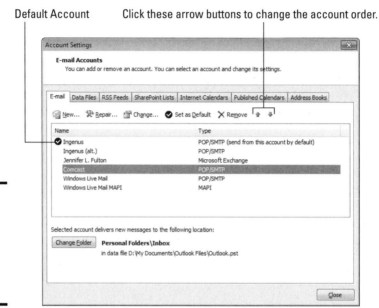

Figure 5-3:
Here's
where you
crown the
king of
Outlook
accounts.

3. **Select the account that you want to act as your default e-mail account from the list.**

The current default is marked with a check mark.

4. **Click Set as Default, and then click Close.**

The selected account becomes your default, and is marked by a check mark.

Changing the Order in Which Accounts Are Checked

When multiple accounts are lumped together in a group (such as All Accounts or a Send/Receive group that you've created), Outlook sends and receives e-mail for the accounts in the group, in a specific order — the order in which the accounts appear in the Account Settings dialog box. If you happen to display the Send/Receive Progress screen during a send/receive, you see this order on-screen while Outlook checks each account in that group, one by one.

If you want, you can change the order in which accounts are checked — not within a specific group, but within all groups — by changing the order in which accounts appear in the Account settings dialog box. Follow these steps:

1. **Click the File tab to display Backstage, and select Info from the list on the left.**

   The Account Information options appear on the right.

2. **Click the Account Settings button, and select Account Settings from the pop-up menu that appears.**

   The Account Settings dialog box pops up. (Refer to Figure 5-3.)

3. **Select an account from the list.**

   When you have multiple accounts placed in a particular group, Outlook sends and receives accounts in the order in which you see them listed. Change this order to send and receive information from the accounts in a different order.

4. **Use the arrow buttons to move the account.**

   To move an account up in the listing, click the up-arrow button. To move an account down in the listing, click the down-arrow button, instead.

5. **Repeat Steps 3 and 4 until you have all the accounts positioned in the way you want.**

6. **Click Close.**

Sending from a Specific E-Mail Account

When you set up multiple e-mail accounts in Outlook, one of them acts as the default, meaning that all messages you send from Outlook are sent from that account (see the section "Selecting Your Default E-Mail Account," earlier in this chapter, for help in setting the default account). Because e-mail providers don't limit the number of e-mails that you can send and receive (if only I could talk my cell phone provider into that kind of plan!), it probably doesn't matter to you which of your accounts you use to send a particular e-mail (especially if all of your accounts are personal). But it does make a difference. When a user replies to your message, the reply is sent to the e-mail address that you used to send the initial message — which may cause problems for you. For example, if you send an e-mail using your Windows Live account and Outlook isn't set up to check it often, then you might miss that reply you thought would come back immediately. Or perhaps you sent an e-mail to a friend by using your work account and a reply comes back over the weekend, you might not know it until you get back to work and check the account again.

Even if the user doesn't reply to a particular message, the e-mail address that you used to send that message appears in the message header. Ordinarily, this setup works perfectly fine. However, if you accidentally sent the message to your kid brother by using your business account, he might not reply, but he may send it on to a few hundred of his closest friends (and their closest friends), and because a bunch of strangers now have your work e-mail address, you might mysteriously start getting a lot of junk mail at work.

To send a message from an e-mail account that's not the default, follow these steps from within a message form:

1. **Click From.**

As long as more than one e-mail account has been set up in Outlook, the From button appears above the To button in an open message form. Clicking it reveals a list of your accounts, as shown in Figure 5-4.

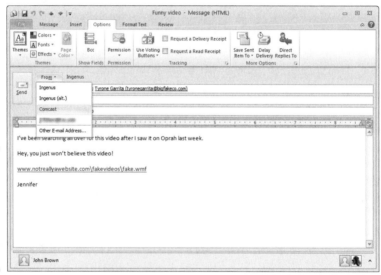

Figure 5-4:
Select which account you want to use for sending a message.

2. **Select the account to use.**

The account that appears to the right of the From button is the default account — the one that Outlook uses to send this message if you don't choose anything else. If you do make an alternate choice, that e-mail account appears next to the From button instead, so you can be sure that you've selected the right account before you click Send.

On the From menu, you may notice the option, Other E-mail Address. If you select this option, the Send from Other E-mail Address dialog box appears. Type an e-mail address in the From text box, or click the From button to display the Contacts list (Address Book) from which you can select an address, then click OK to return to the Send from Other E-mail Address dialog box. Click the Send Using button and choose one of your e-mail accounts to send the message from, and then click OK to return to the message form. When you send such a message, it arrives in the recipient's Inbox, the header indicates that it was sent by you on behalf of the other e-mail address you selected. If the recipient clicks Reply, his or her message is automatically addressed to the other email address and not yours.

Directing Incoming Mail to a Specific Folder

For anyone, keeping e-mail organized is an ongoing job. But when you add multiple e-mail accounts and the tons of e-mail they generate to the mix, the problem increases dramatically. When you add multiple e-mail accounts to Outlook, Outlook unceremoniously dumps the e-mail for each account in the Inbox folder. To redirect incoming mail to a different folder, you need to create a rule.

I cover rules in detail in Book IX, Chapter 2, so in this section, I go over things pretty quickly. For example, if you want all your personal e-mail to go into a folder called *Personal* or *Family,* create a rule by following these steps:

1. **In the Mail module, click the Rules button in the Move group on the Home tab and select Create Rule from the pop-up menu that appears.**

The Create Rule dialog box appears.

2. **Click Advanced Options.**

The Which Conditions Do You Want to Check page of the Rules Wizard appears. (See Figure 5-5.)

**Book III
Chapter 5**

**Managing Multiple
E-Mail Accounts**

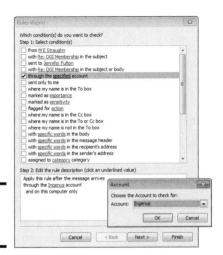

Figure 5-5:
Select an
account.

3. In the Step 1: Select Condition(s) section at the top of the window, select the Through the Specified Account checkbox.

4. In the Step 2: Edit the Rule Description section at the bottom of the window, click the Specified account link.

The Account dialog box appears.

5. From the Account drop-down list, select the account whose incoming mail you want to reroute.

6. Click OK to close the Account dialog box.

You're returned to the wizard.

7. Click Next in the wizard.

The What Do You Want to Do with the Message page of the wizard appears.

8. In the Step 1: Select Action(s) section at the top of the window, select the Move It to the Specified Folder checkbox.

9. In the Step 2: Edit the Rule Description section at the bottom, click the Specified folder link.

The Rules and Alerts dialog box appears.

10. Select the folder in which you want all incoming mail from this account placed. (See Figure 5-6.)

11. Click OK to return to the wizard, and then click Next.

The Are There Any Exceptions page of the wizard appears.

Figure 5-6:
Select a
folder.

12. **Create any exceptions and click Next.**

If you don't want all mail from this account dumped in the folder that you select in Step 10, you can create an exception on this page of the wizard. Select the exception that you want to use from the Step 1: Select Exception(s) section at the top of the window, and then refine it by using the Step 2: Edit the Rule Description section at the bottom of the window. For example, maybe you want all your personal mail rerouted except stuff from your spouse. If you don't want to create any exceptions, you don't have to. Simply click Next to move to the last page of the wizard.

You can create multiple exceptions by repeating this step. (For more help with rules, see Book IX, Chapter 2.)

13. **In the Finish Rule Setup page that appears, type a name for the new rule in the Step 1: Specify a Name For This Rule text box. (See Figure 5-7.)**

14. **In Step 2: Setup Rule Options, select the Run This Rule Now on Messages Already in "XX" checkbox, if you want to run this rule now on existing e-mails.**

In Step 3: Review Rule Description, you can review the details of your new rule.

15. **Click Finish.**

If you specify that you want Outlook to run the rule right now in Step 14, after you click Finish, Outlook moves the appropriate e-mails to the folder that you select in Step 10.

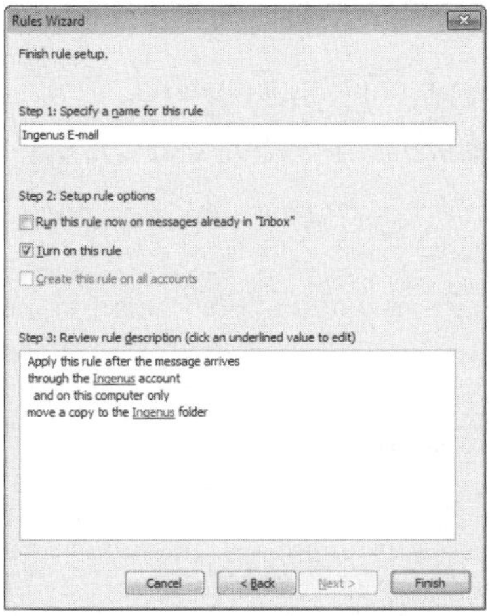

Figure 5-7:
Finishing
touches.

> Rules Wizard
>
> Finish rule setup.
>
> Step 1: Specify a name for this rule
>
> Ingenus E-mail
>
> Step 2: Setup rule options
>
> ☐ Run this rule now on messages already in "Inbox"
>
> ☑ Turn on this rule
>
> ☐ Create this rule on all accounts
>
> Step 3: Review rule description (click an underlined value to edit)
>
> Apply this rule after the message arrives
> through the Ingenus account
> and on this computer only
> move a copy to the Ingenus folder
>
> Cancel   < Back   Next >   Finish

Directing Sent Messages to a Different Folder

When you send an e-mail to someone, a copy of that e-mail is placed in the Sent Items folder. So, you can go back and check what you sent and to whom, any time you like. You can also easily locate a message that you've sent and resend the e-mail when you need to. (See Book II, Chapter 2 for details.) In addition, if you change to Conversation view (by selecting the Show as Conversations checkbox from the Conversations group on the View tab), you can view your sent e-mails in line with related e-mails (the e-mails to which you replied), in a sort of threaded conversation.

Still, if you're originating a new message thread (rather than replying), you may want to direct the sent message to some folder other than the Sent Items folder. For example, when I zip off an e-mail to one of the editors of this book, I tell Outlook to save my sent message in a special folder devoted to my book correspondence.

To save a message that you're sending to a folder other then Sent Items, first create the message, and then follow these steps in the message form:

1. **Click the Save Sent Item To button on the message form's Options tab.**

2. **From the pop-up menu that appears, select where you want a copy of the message saved.**

   You can choose not to save a copy at all by selecting Do Not Save. Otherwise, select a folder from those listed (the menu lists folders you saved to before) or select Other Folder from the menu to save a copy of the message somewhere else.

   If you choose Other Folder, the Select Folder dialog box appears. Continue to Step 3.

3. **Select a folder from the Folders list and click OK.**

   A copy of the message is saved to the folder you selected.

   The message isn't saved in the Sent Items folder, so don't freak out when you don't see it in that folder.

4. **Finish your e-mail message as usual and click Send to send it along.**

Having Replies Sent to another Address

Sometimes, you want replies to go to an e-mail address other than the one you're using to send a message. For example, you might want replies to a company training invitation to go to your assistant so that he or she can keep track of the number of people expected and order enough food and party hats.

You can send a single e-mail on someone's behalf and have replies automatically directed to that person's e-mail address. See the earlier section, "Sending from a Specific E-Mail Account" for more information on this technique. If you work on an Exchange network, a coworker can designate you as a delegate, which allows you to act on their behalf in various matters, including sending and responding to meeting requests (which is the typical use of a delegate). See Book X, Chapter 1 for help.

To have replies for a message sent to a different e-mail address than the one from which you send that message, first create a message, and then follow these steps in the message form:

1. **Click the Direct Replies To button on the Options tab.**

The Properties dialog box appears. See Figure 5-8.

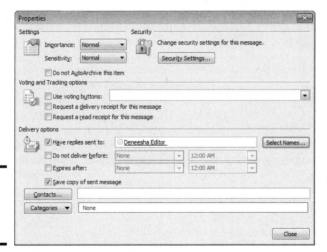

Figure 5-8:
Redirect
your
messages.

2. **Highlight the address that appears in the Have Replies Sent To text box and press Delete to remove it.**

3. **In the text box, type the e-mail address to which you want replies to this message sent.**

Alternatively, if the address you want to use is in Contacts, click Select Names, select a name from the Have Replies Sent To dialog box that appears, and click Reply To. You can select several addresses from this list if you want replies sent to more than one address; when you're through picking names, click OK to close the dialog box and return to the Properties dialog box.

4. **Click Close in the Properties dialog box.**

   The message form reappears. The Direct Replies To button remains highlighted on the Ribbon so that you don't forget you've redirected the replies for this message.

5. **Finish your e-mail message as usual, and click Send to send it along.**

Dealing with Multiple People, Multiple Accounts, and One Little Ol' Computer

If you have kids fighting over the one computer in your household — or if you and the sales team are duking it out over the one laptop for your department — you might be able to end the arguments by setting up e-mail profiles. Basically, a *profile* contains all the e-mail accounts used by a single person. If you set up multiple profiles, everyone in your family/department/ group can instantly live in peace and harmony while sharing the one lousy computer you're stuck with. (Or you can get a start on peace and harmony, anyway.)

Even if you're the only person who uses your computer, you might still find e-mail profiles useful — they not only keep track of e-mail accounts, but they also record where Outlook stores the incoming mail (on the server or locally in an Outlook .pst file), as well as where Outlook stores Contacts, Calendar, Notes, Tasks, Journal, rules, search folders, and so on. For example, if you want to keep your personal contacts and calendar separate from your business ones, you can create two e-mail profiles. When Outlook starts, you select which profile to use (such as your Home profile), and you see only that e-mail, Calendar, Contacts, and such. To change to a different profile, make a hasty exit and then restart Outlook.

An e-mail profile can contain information for multiple e-mail accounts, but all data is stored in a single .pst file.

You start out with one e-mail profile. To create another e-mail profile, follow these steps:

1. **Click the Start button on your computer's desktop, select Control Panel from the pop-up menu that appears, and select Mail.**

   If your Control Panel opens in a dialog box, select User Accounts and Family Safety, then select Mail. The Mail Setup dialog box peeks out.

2. **Click the Show Profiles button.**

   The Mail dialog box pops up. See the background of Figure 5-9.

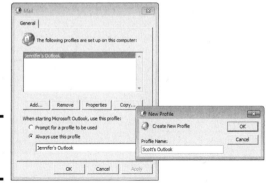

Figure 5-9:
Create a
new profile.

3. **Click Add.**

The New Profile dialog box appears. See the foreground of Figure 5-9.

4. **Type a name for your profile in the Profile Name text box, then click OK to create the profile.**

A wizard appears to step you through the process of setting up an e-mail account for this profile. See Book I, Chapter 3 for help. When you finish the wizard, the Mail dialog box reappears, and your new profile is listed in the Mail dialog box.

5. **To get Outlook to prompt you for the new profile, select the Prompt for a Profile to Be Used option in the Mail dialog box. (Refer to the background of Figure 5-9.) Click OK.**

The next time you start Outlook, it asks you which profile you want to use, as shown in Figure 5-10.

6. **Select a profile from the Profile Name list and click OK.**

The Mail, Contacts, Calendar, and other modules associated with that profile appear. Having multiple accounts is all about choices.

**Book III
Chapter 5**

**Managing Multiple
E-Mail Accounts**

Figure 5-10:
Nice to have
a choice —
so select
a profile to
use.

Book IV

Working with the Calendar

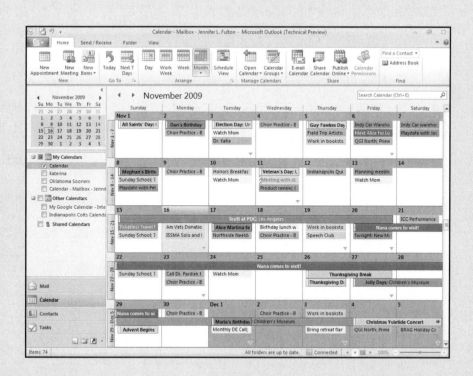

Contents at a Glance

Chapter 1: Getting Familiar with the Calendar

In This Chapter

✔ Getting the lowdown on appointments, meetings, and events

✔ Displaying daily, weekly, or monthly calendars

✔ Changing to a different day, week, or month

✔ Keeping an appointment

✔ Setting reminders and then dealing with them

✔ Entering all-day events

*W*hen people think of Outlook, mostly they think of e-mail and maybe Contacts because the two are so closely tied together. Me, I think of Calendar. Without something to help me keep track of all the lunch meetings, doctor appointments, soccer games, choir practices, hair appointments, and special school events I have to attend, I would literally lose my mind. (Now, if I can only find a way for Outlook to keep my appointments for me while I take a nap.)

Appointments, Meetings, and Events — What's the Difference?

Because people tend to use the word *appointment* to describe "any ol' thing that interrupts my day," here's a breakdown of how Outlook differentiates among these three ol' things — appointments, meetings, and events:

✦ **Appointment:** Set up between yourself and someone whose calendar you can't access, such as friends and family, or service people such as doctors, plumbers, roofers, carpenters, and so on.

✦ **Meeting:** Set up with someone in your company, assuming that your company uses Microsoft Exchange and that you want to hold this meeting with people who have shared their Calendars with you. When you create a meeting, you can check people's schedules to find the best time for everyone to get together. For more information on meetings, including how to create them in Outlook, see Chapter 4 of this minibook.

Okay, technically speaking, you can set up a meeting with anyone whose e-mail address you've entered in Contacts because Outlook needs only e-mail addresses to send invitations to the meeting. However, if you're on an Exchange network, not only can you send invitations, but you can also view other participants' schedules and suggest a time that's free for most people. Also, if you use an Exchange network, Outlook helps you schedule meeting resources such as meeting rooms, multimedia equipment, and so on. In addition, you can create a Meeting Workspace where meeting participants can share files (such as the meeting agenda and handouts) and keep current on meeting details (such as attendees and location). A Meeting Workspace is a company SharePoint site where materials for one or meetings can be found. So, all in all, I personally consider meetings useful for Exchange users only — although, like I said, you can technically create a meeting for anyone whose e-mail address you have, even if you don't share an Exchange network.

✦ **Event:** An all-day happening that may or may not interfere with your ability to attend appointments or meetings that day. Typical events include birthdays, holidays, conferences, and seminars.

You can find out how to create detailed appointments in the section "Creating a Complete Appointment" and how to set up all-day events in the section "Planning an All-Day Event," both later in this chapter. (For help with meetings — scheduling them, anyway — jump over to Chapter 4 of this mini-book.)

Understanding Calendar Views

A *view* is simply the way in which Outlook decides to lay out the data in a particular module. The default view for Mail is Compact view in Date order, which lists messages in the order in which they were received, grouping replies to messages with the original one.

For the Calendar module in Outlook, the default view is Calendar, meaning that appointments appear graphically on the right, organized by day, week, or month, rather than in a long list. In addition, the Daily Task List appears along the bottom of the Calendar by default. There are other views besides Calendar view that you might choose — to change to a different view, click the Change View button on the View tab and select a view from the palette that appears: Preview (similar to Calendar view, but displays not only an appointment's name and location, but also any notes), List (displays all Calendar items in a long list, grouped by category), or Active (displays in a long list Calendar items that have not yet occurred, grouped by frequency of occurrence).

Figure 1-1 shows Week view, which isn't really a view so much as an *arrangement* — in other words, items are displayed using Calendar view but *arranged* to show only one week at a time. Because Microsoft calls these arrangements different views (as in Week view or Month view), I do, too. But to be clear, when I say Week view, I actually mean Calendar view, using the Week arrangement. By the way, I explain each view (meaning arrangement) in a moment, along with how to change your Calendar to that view.

When you first look at Calendar, pay particular attention to these features:

✦ Appointments and meetings appear as rectangles that graphically depict the amount of your day that they consume. Items appear in half-hour segments; if an appointment lasts one hour, it blocks out two of these segments.

To change the scale used to block out appointments and meetings, click the Time Scale button on the View tab and select a scale, such as 15 Minutes, from the pop-up menu that appears.

✦ Events appear in that little blue-gray area at the top of each day in Day, Work Week, Week, and Schedule view. In Month view, events appear at the top of the list of items for a given day. In Figure 1-1, a lot of different events, such as Washington's Birthday and Circle the State with Song, appear in the blue-gray area that runs across the top of each day in the week.

When I say that events show up in that blue-gray area at the top of each day's timeline, I assume that you're using the default color with Calendar. In this chapter, I describe other items as blue-gray, but again, that's only because my calendar is using the default color scheme. You can change the color associated with each of your calendars to make them easier to identify (for example, you might display your Calendar and the Calendar for each of the members of your team in different colors). To change the color associated with the current Calendar, click the Color button on the View tab and select a color from the palette that appears. If you change your calendar to green, for example, then the event area at the top of each day appears in dark green.

✦ To view some of the details (time and location) of an appointment, meeting, or event, hover the mouse pointer over that item's rectangle, as shown in Figure 1-1.

The Daily Task List typically appears at the bottom of the view window in Calendar, because it's part of the default view (Calendar view). By default, the To-Do bar doesn't appear in Calendar view, although you can make it show up if you want. You can also turn on the Reading pane and use it to view all the details of any selected appointment, meeting, or event: But, frankly, I think it takes up too much space, so I leave it off. Here's what you need to know about these elements:

✦ The Navigation pane, To-Do bar, Reading pane, and Daily Task List are all elements that you can turn on or off, using the buttons on the View tab. For example, to display the Daily Task List, click the Daily Task List button on the View tab and select Normal from the pop-up menu that appears.

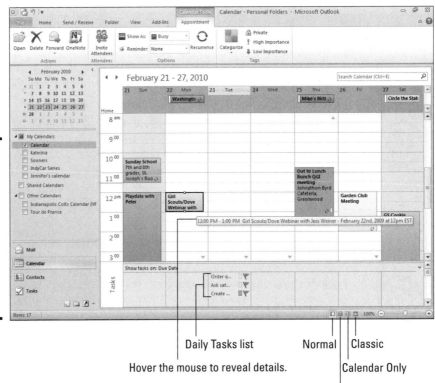

Figure 1-1: The Calendar is full of information about what you have to do today, this week, or this month.

Daily Tasks list   Normal   Classic

Hover the mouse to reveal details.   Calendar Only

Calendar and Tasks

✦ If you display the Navigation pane, Daily Task List, or the To-Do bar, keep in mind that you can easily minimize them when needed. For example, to minimize the To-Do bar, click its Minimize button, or click the To-Do bar button on the View tab and select Minimized from the pop-up menu that appears.

✦ You can quickly display these elements by using a different set of View buttons, which run along the bottom of the Calendar window:

  • *Normal view:* Displays the Calendar with the Daily Task List below.

  • *Calendar and Task view:* Similar to Normal view, but the Navigation pane is minimized to maximize the area for viewing.

- *Calendar Only view:* Displays just the Calendar, with the Navigation pane minimized.

- *Classic view:* Displays the Navigation pane on the left, the Calendar in the middle, and the To-Do bar on the right.

Day view

You can change from view to view by clicking the Change View button on the View tab and selecting a view, such as Calendar, from the palette that appears. (See Book I, Chapter 1.) In any view that's not a list view (Calendar view and Preview view are the two non-list views), you have various options for arranging items. One of those arrangement options is known as Day "view".

So, assuming you're in Calendar or Preview view, to display a single day's worth of appointments, meetings, and events (as shown in Figure 1-2), click the Day button on the View tab. (You can also find the Day button on the Home tab, so don't feel like you have to change tabs just for me.) While you have your Calendar in Day view, keep the following in mind:

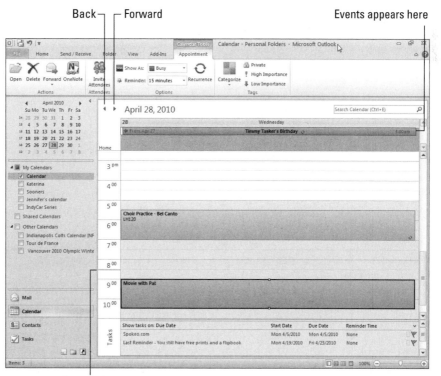

Back ── ┌─ Forward   Events appears here

Figure 1-2:
Day view.

Current time

✦ **Events appear at the top of the day.** When you add events, the events area expands. But at some point, it stops expanding, and you need to use the small scroll bar on the right to scroll.

✦ **The current time is displayed.** It shows up with an orange band on the left, on the Time bar.

✦ **You can change from day to day.** Click the Forward button (to see the next day) or Back button (to see the previous day).

✦ **Scroll through the appointments for the day by using the scroll bar.** If some appointments or other items are out of view, a blue-gray up or down arrow appears at the top or bottom of the appointment section. Click the arrow to jump to the previous (or next) item for that day. In Figure 1-2, for example, the small down arrow appears at the bottom-right of the appointment section. This arrow indicates that I have another appointment or meeting later than 4 p.m. that day, and I can click this down arrow to view that item.

✦ **If you have no appointments, events, or meetings for the currently displayed day, two blue-gray tabs appear on either side of the day's timeline.** Click either the Previous Appointment or Next Appointment tabs to jump to the previous or next day that contains an appointment, meeting, or event (see Figure 1-3).

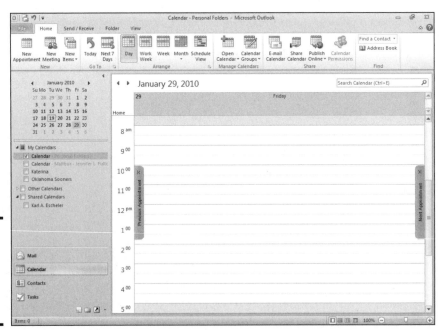

Figure 1-3:
Jump to the previous or next appointment.

Displaying just the days you work

Not everybody's work week is Monday to Friday; if needed, you can select other days to show in the Work Week view. Click the File tab to display Backstage, and select Options from the list on the left to display the Outlook Options dialog box. Select Calendar from the list on the left to display the Calendar options and, in the Work Time section, select the checkboxes in the Work Week area for the days you work during the week. You don't have to choose consecutive days, by the way. Also, you can change the day on which your week starts (by default, it's Sunday), the week that starts the year (by default, it's the week that contains January 1), and the time that you start and end each work day (by default, each work day is from 8 a.m. to 5 p.m.). Hours and days outside these normal work times appear in blue-gray when you use Day, Week, Work Week, or Next 7 Days view. (Refer to Figures 1-2 and 1-4.) Click OK close the Outlook Options dialog box.

✦ **Hours that fall outside the normal work day appear in blue-gray.** You can change the start and end time for your day, if you want — for help, see the sidebar "Displaying just the days you work," in this chapter.

To change to Day view quickly while in Week, Work Week, or Month view, click that day's header (the blue-gray or orange bar that has the date on it). For example, in Figure 1-1 (which shows Week view), you can jump to Day view and display the appointments for January 20 by clicking the 20 Wed header.

Week, Work Week, and Next 7 Days views

I must look at my schedule a hundred times a day: not because I'm *that* busy, but because I seem to have a rather short-term memory. Like a lot of moms, I keep not only my personal and work schedules, but the schedules for my daughter and my husband, so I need to constantly remind myself what's next.

Somehow, viewing the appointments for a single day doesn't work for me. I guess I just need to see everything in context so that I can plan my free time. So, displaying a week's worth of appointments suits me just fine. A lot of users must agree because Microsoft offers three different weekly view variations — Week, Work Week, and Next 7 Days.

To display a week's worth of appointments, meetings, and events, click either the Week, Work Week, or Next 7 Days button on the Home tab:

✦ **Week view:** Displays items for an entire week, from Sunday to Saturday (although you can change what constitutes the first day of your week — see the sidebar "Displaying just the days you work," in this chapter). Figure 1-4 gives you a glimpse at Week view.

**Book IV
Chapter 1**

**Getting Familiar
with the Calendar**

✦ **Work Week view:** Displays items for an entire work week, which is typically Monday to Friday. But if you work Tuesday to Thursday, for example, you can set up Outlook to recognize that as a work week (if only I could get my boss to do the same). The sidebar "Displaying just the days you work," in this chapter, explains how.

✦ **Next 7 Days view:** Displays items for the next seven days, beginning with today's appointments.

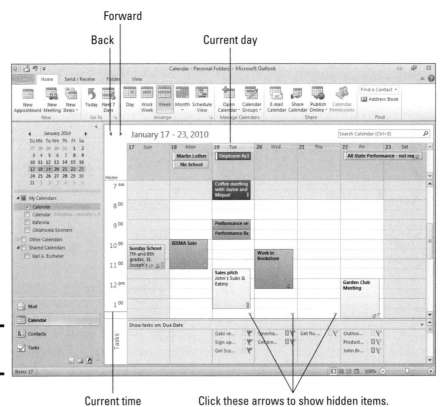

Forward

Back

Current day

Figure 1-4: Week view.

Current time

Click these arrows to show hidden items.

When using Week, Work Week, or Next 7 Days view, please note the following:

✦ **Events appear at the top of the day on which they occur.** If you have a lot of events for a particular day, you may need to use the scroll bar on the far-right to scroll so that you can see them all.

✦ **The current day is marked in orange.** The current time is marked with an orange band on the left, on the Time bar.

✦ **Hours that fall outside the normal work day appear in blue-gray.** Sunday and Saturday show up in blue-gray in Figure 1-4 because they're not part of my work week. In the figure, the hours after 5 p.m. each week-day also show up in blue-gray. You can change the start and end time for your day, if you want — for help, see the "Displaying just the days you work" sidebar, in this chapter.

✦ **You can move back and forth from week to week.** Click the Forward button (to see the next week) or Back button (to see the previous week).

✦ **Scroll through the appointments for the weekday by using the scroll bar.** If you can't see some appointments or other items for a particular day, a blue-gray up or down arrow appears at the top or bottom of that day's timeline. Click the up or down arrow to jump to the previous or next item for that day. For example, in Figure 1-4, a down arrow appears at the bottom of the appointment section on Wednesday the 20th. Click the down arrow to view whatever's hidden at the moment.

✦ **If you have no appointments, events, or meetings for the entire week, two blue tabs appear on either side of the view window.** This doesn't happen to me, but if you find a week in which nothing's going on, click the tabs marked Previous Appointment and Next Appointment to jump backward or forward to a week that has something going on.

Month view

To display a month's worth of appointments, meetings, and events, click the Month button on the Home tab and select a level of detail from the pop-up menu that appears: Show Low Detail, Show Medium Detail, or Show High Detail. Low detail shows only day-long events. Medium detail shows day-long events and busy time blocks. Day-long events are labeled and easy to see in Medium Detail view (such as Martin Luther King Day and Employee Appreciation Day in Figure 1-5). The busy time blocks appear as colored horizontal bands, whose thickness graphically depicts the length of that appointment or meeting. (Refer to Figure 1-5.) In Medium Detail view, you might notice a thin blue line that divides each day in half; it helps you gauge where in your day a particular appointment or meeting falls — colored bands appearing above the blue line represent items that fall before noon; below the line indicates an item that falls after noon.

By the way, the colors used in depicting each appointment, meeting, or event are based on the categories you've assigned to each item. Assigning colored categories to each item lets you quickly gauge the type of activities that you have going on each day. You can find out how to assign categories to appointments and events in the sections "Creating a Complete Appointment," and "Planning an All Day Event" later in this chapter.

Book IV
Chapter 1

Getting Familiar
with the Calendar

Events   A blue line divides each day in half.

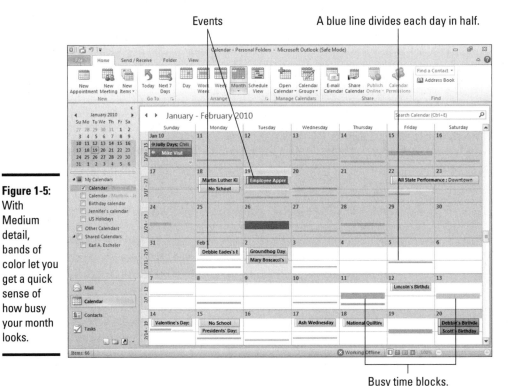

Figure 1-5:
With
Medium
detail,
bands of
color let you
get a quick
sense of
how busy
your month
looks.

Busy time blocks.

High detail shows all events, appointments, and meetings in horizontal bars that display the subject (description) and location (when there's room). In High Detail view, events, appointments, and meetings tend to look alike, but if you look closely, you notice that events appear with a small white band on the left edge of their horizontal bar. (See Figure 1-6.) Here are some items to make a note of when using Month view:

✦ **Items appear on the day on which they occur.** Because High detail displays events, appointments, and meetings, events appear first in the listing.

✦ **The current day is marked in orange.** In Figures 1-5 and 1-6, Tuesday the 19th is the current day.

✦ **You can easily change from month to month.** Click the Forward button (to see the next month) or Back button (to see the previous month).

✦ **Scroll through the items for a particular day, if needed.** When you use High detail, if you can't see some appointments or other items for a particular day, a blue-gray down arrow appears on that day's square. Click this down arrow to scroll through the hidden items. For example, in Figure 1-6, a down arrow appears on February 1, which I can click to view whatever's hiding.

Forward

Back

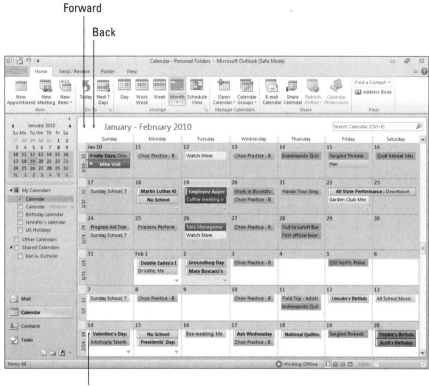

Figure 1-6:
Month view,
High detail.

Events appear with a white band.

+ **If you have no appointments, events, or meetings for the entire month, two blue tabs appear on either side of the view window.** Click either the Previous Appointment or Next Appointment tab to jump to the previous or next month (respectively) that contains an appointment, meeting, or event.

To discover how to change to a different day, week, or month, see the section "Navigating Around the Calendar," later in this chapter.

If you're on an Exchange network, you can view other people's calendars within Calendar, if those people choose to share their calendars with you. See Chapter 3 of this minibook for information on how to share.

Schedule view

Schedule view allows you to display multiple calendars side by side, in individual horizontal timelines. For example, if several coworkers are sharing their calendars with you (see Chapter 3 of this minibook for how-to's), you can display those calendars in Schedule view and quickly find a time to meet. (You can also easily spot the slackers when you put schedules against each other, but hey, that's just a bonus.) Even if you use Outlook at home, you can use Schedule view to compare your various calendars side-by-side. For example, I keep a calendar that track's my daughter's many activities, and then I've imported several Internet calendars that list sporting events I don't want to miss. By changing to Schedule view, I can quickly see which television shows I might need to Tivo because I will either be taking Katerina somewhere or going somewhere myself. To change to Schedule view, click the Schedule View button on the Home tab. Here are some things to make a note of:

✦ **The date appears on the top bar.** Schedule view displays either a single day's or a week's schedule in a long, horizontal bar. If you were viewing your calendars using Day or Month view, then when you change to Schedule view, only the current day's items are displayed in a series of horizontal bars. If you were using Next 7 Days, Work Week, or Week view, then a week's worth of items is displayed instead. While you scroll from left to right, you scroll through the day or week. If weekly schedules for each calendar are displayed, then you can tell where you are in that week because the date for the displayed day appears at the top of the window. (See Figure 1-7.)

Date being displayed   Time slot when someone is busy

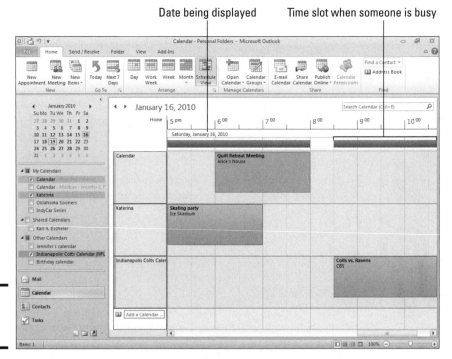

Figure 1-7:
Schedule
view.

✦ **The timeline appears along the top.** While you scroll, each day is broken into equal units (typically, half-hour segments).

You can change the default time scale from half-hour segments to something else if you like; see the earlier section, "Understanding Calendar Views" for help.

✦ **Appointments and meetings appear in large time blocks.** If more than one appointment or meeting occurs at the same time, they appear as thinner horizontal bars, rather than fat time blocks.

✦ **Most events don't appear.** The focus here is on scheduling, so day-long events (which are typically birthdays and holidays) don't often appear. Such events don't take up your work time (unless you actually block out that time for cake eating and general frivolity), so Outlook shows you as Free when such events occur. If you marked an event as Busy, Out of Office, or Tentative when you created it, it appears on the timeline. For example, you might add a two-day conference to your schedule and mark your time during that period as Out of Office or Busy so that people don't think you're taking a two-day vacation (even if you plan to snooze during the keynote). If you want to show Free events anyway, click the File tab to display Backstage, and select Options from the list on the left to display the Outlook Options dialog box. Select Calendar from the list on the left to display the Calendar options, and in the Display Options section, enable the When in Schedule View, Show Free Appointments checkbox. Click OK to save your changes.

✦ **Busy times appear in blue at the top of the window.** Outlook summarizes all the displayed calendars into busy time blocks, which appear at the top of the window. (Out of Office or Tentative appointments and meetings show up in other colors or patterns.) This summary enables you to quickly spot a timeslot in which everyone is available.

Outlook allows you to mark your availability during any event, appointment, or meeting that you add to the Calendar. Availability is only important if you share your Calendar with others so that they can know when you're busy and when you're free to meet. When you create an event, Outlook assumes you're free, but you can select other options: Busy, Out of Office, or Tentative (which means you might be available to talk because you don't know right now whether you're going to attend the event for sure). Busy time blocks show up in blue on the timeline; Out of Office, Tentative, and Free show up in other colors, as you can read about in Chapter 3 of this minibook.

You can most effectively use Schedule view to compare several other people's calendars. See Chapter 3 of this minibook for info on how to add other people's calendars to Outlook.

**Book IV
Chapter 1**

**Getting Familiar
with the Calendar**

Navigating around the Calendar

After you choose a view, you aren't stuck with whatever's currently displayed. You can quickly change to a different day, week, or month from the one listed at the top of the viewing window. Figure 1-8 shows the meetings, appointments, and events for the week of January 17 to 23. In views that show more than one day (Next 7 Days, Week, Work Week, and Month), the current day is highlighted in orange. In Schedule view, the current day doesn't appear orange, but just above the timeline, you see the date associated with the portion of the timeline being shown so that you can quickly figure things out.

The day of the week also appears with the day's date, so you can't confuse Tuesday with Wednesday (if you're prone to that kind of thing). Here's how to browse through your Calendar:

✦ **To change to the next day, week, or month (depending on the view):** Click the left or right Back or Forward navigation arrows at the top of the viewing window.

✦ **To jump back to today:** Click the Today button on the Home tab. If you're using Day view, today's appointments appear. But if you're using a different view — Week view, for example — that view's period of time (the current week, in our example) appears, with today highlighted.

In the Date Navigator (that calendar thing at the top of the Navigation pane), Outlook highlights the current day, week, or month that appears in the viewing area. For example, in Figure 1-8, the current week (January 17 to 23) is highlighted in dark gray in the Date Navigator. The current day is marked on the Date Navigator with a red outline.

Here are some techniques for using the Date Navigator to browse your Calendar:

✦ **If you're using Day view:** Click any day in the Date Navigator to display that day's appointments, meetings, or events.

✦ **If you're using Week or Work Week view:** Click any day in the Date Navigator to display that week's appointments, meetings, or events.

✦ **If you're using Month or Next 7 Days view:** Click a day in the Date Navigator to display that day in Day view. So, for example, if you're using Month view and you click January 2, the view changes from Month to Day in order to show the items for that day.

✦ **If you want to create a modified Month view:** Select the days that you want to display by dragging over them in the Date Navigator.

Date Navigator

Change to a different month

Current week being displayed

Back

Forward

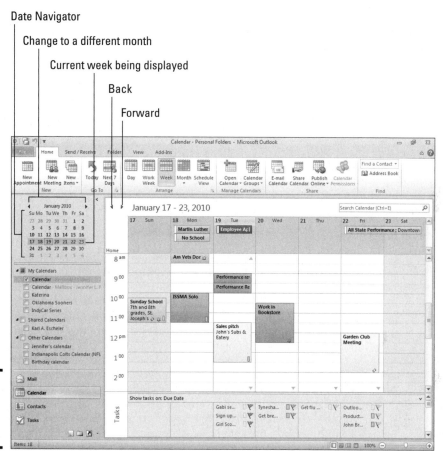

Figure 1-8:
Your typical
Calendar
view.

✦ **If you want to create a modified Day view:** Hold down Ctrl and click those days in the Date Navigator.

✦ **If the day you want to review isn't displayed in the Date Navigator:** You can change to a different month by clicking the left or right arrows on either side of the month name at the top of the Date Navigator.

✦ **If you want to change to a particular month:** Click the current month's name in the Date Navigator and select a month from the pop-up menu that appears. If you're in Month view and you change to a different month, all the items for that month appear on-screen. If you're in Day, Week, Work Week, or Next 7 Days view, the corresponding day or week for that month (respectively) appears. For example, if you're currently looking at October 16 and you change to August, August 16 appears (or the week of August 16th). If you're in Next 7 Days view, the corresponding week appears. For example, suppose today is January 19, and you choose Next 7 Days view to display the week of January 19-25. If you change to February, then the week of February 19-25 appears.

For a quick display of consecutive days, beginning with the current day, press Alt plus any number from 0 (the current day plus nine more days) to 9 (the current day plus eight more days). For example, if the currently displayed day is October 10th, if you press Alt+9, you see October 10 to 19 in a crowded Week view. If you press Alt+1, you display the current day only, but Alt+3 gets you the current day plus two more.

Jump to a specific day quickly by using Go To. Click the dialog box launcher in the Go To group on the Home tab, or press Ctrl+G to display the Go to Date dialog box. Type the date that you want to view in the Date text box, select a view (such as Week) from the Show In drop-down list, and click OK. The selected date is shown in the view you selected.

Creating a Complete Appointment

You can easily create a quick appointment (as discussed in Book I, Chapter 2): Change to the day on which you want to create the appointment, hover the mouse pointer over the time for the appointment, and click when the words Click to Add Appointment appear in a small bubble. Type the description for the appointment in the white bubble and then click outside the bubble to create a half-hour appointment. To lengthen the appointment, drag its bottom edge. (See Figure 1-9.)

Sometimes, appointments appear in your Calendar without you actually creating them. For example, someone may forward an appointment to you in an e-mail message (basically, sending a copy of the appointment to you). You can then easily add that appointment to your Calendar, essentially copying it from the e-mail. Also, if you work on an Exchange network, a colleague might invite you to a meeting, and if you accept, Outlook automatically adds that meeting to the Calendar. See Chapter 3 of this minibook for more info.

To create a more detailed appointment, use the Appointment form by following these steps:

1. **Click the New Appointment button on the Home tab.**

If you're not in Calendar, click the New Items button on the Home tab while in any module, then select Appointment from the pop-up menu that appears. The Appointment form opens.

You can save time if you go to the date for the appointment (by scrolling through the Calendar or selecting that date from the Date Navigator), and then click the appointment time *before* you click the New Appointment button, but you don't have to do it that way.

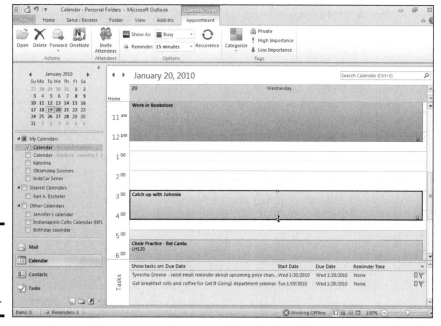

Figure 1-9:
Drag to
expand an
appoint-
ment's time.

If you want to create appointments from other Outlook items, you can do so quickly by dragging and dropping an item onto the Calendar button on the Navigation pane. For example, you can create an appointment from an incoming e-mail — or copy related contact information into an appointment — by dragging and dropping the e-mail or contact onto the Calendar button. (See Book I, Chapter 2 for more drag-and-drop tips.)

2. **In the Subject field, enter a basic description for the appointment.**

   Figure 1-10 has a Subject of Dr. Feld.

3. **(Optional) In the Location field, make a note of where the appointment is taking place.**

   The appointment in Figure 1-10 is happening at 100 W. Washington, Suite 202.

4. **Select the date of the appointment from the Start Time drop-down list, and then select a time of day from the drop-down list to the right of the Start Time list.**

**Book IV
Chapter 1**

**Getting Familiar
with the Calendar**

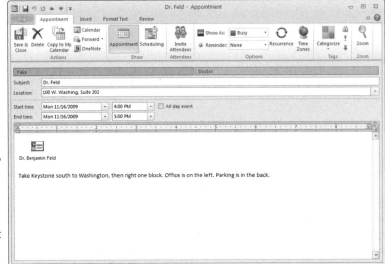

Figure 1-10:
Create an
appointment
with the
Appointment
form.

5. **If the appointment ends on the same day, select only a time of day from the drop-down list to the far-right of End Time drop-down list.**

If the appointment spans more than one day, you need to select an end date from the End Time drop-down list first, then select a time of day.

The drop-down lists offer only half-hour intervals; you can type an exact start or end time in the boxes if you can't find what you want on the lists.

You can type words in the date boxes instead of selecting an actual date. For example, you can type `today` or `tomorrow`, or `three days from now`. Some holidays are recognized as well, such as `Fourth of July`, `New Year's Day`, or `Christmas`.

Also, you can set the appointment's start and end times in relation to a specific time zone (other than your normal time zone). For example, suppose you live in the Eastern U.S. time zone, but you're currently attending a conference in California. You want to set up an appointment for noon tomorrow to meet up with a vendor, but your brain is too jet-lagged to do the proper math. First, click the Time Zones button on the Appointment tab. Two time zone drop-down lists appear, one for the start time and one for the end time. Select the time zone that you want to use for these times (such as Pacific Time) from the drop-down lists, then select a start or end time from Start Time or End Time drop-down lists, such as 12:00 PM.

Outlook lets you schedule overlapping appointments; I can only assume that the folks at Microsoft have worked out how to be in two places at the same time. Anyway, if you want to preview this appointment within your current Calendar before you decide to adjust its time, click the Calendar button on the Appointment tab. This unfinished appointment appears in your actual Calendar, identified by a dark black rectangle. If you want to review your Free and Busy time without leaving the Appointment form, click the Scheduling Assistant button on the Appointment tab, instead.

6. **Set a reminder.**

   By default, the reminder goes off 15 minutes before the Appointment Start time. If you need longer than that to get to the appointment, select an interval from the Reminder drop-down list in the Options group of the Appointment tab. For example, open the Reminder list and choose 1 hour to be reminded of this appointment one hour ahead of time. You can also type something, such as 25 minutes, 2.5 hours, or 5 days in the Reminder text box. Don't want to be reminded? Just select None from the Reminder drop-down list. (The following section offers details about what the reminder does when it goes off and what you should do about it.)

7. **If you've set up categories, select as many as you want, one at a time, from the Categorize drop-down list on the Appointment tab.**

   One of the easiest ways to keep your appointments organized and easy to identify within Outlook is to use categories. (See Book VIII, Chapter 1.)

8. **Set other options.**

   A lot of the other options have to do with creating a meeting, such as marking your Free and Busy time (these options are covered in Chapter 4 of this minibook). If you want this appointment to repeat at regular intervals, see Chapter 2 of this minibook for help. In the meantime, here are a few options for appointments that you might set:

   • Mark an appointment as "gotta keep" by clicking the High Importance button in the Tags group on the Appointment tab.

   • Click the Low Importance button in the Tags group on the Appointment tab to mark appointments that you can blow off if you have to (such as your gym time, right?).

   Appointments marked as High Importance or Low Importance don't appear that way in any view. In addition, you can't add the Importance field to a view in order to make it appear, so I'm stumped as to why you should bother to mark the importance of an appointment at all. But the High and Low Importance buttons are highlighted on the Appointment tab when you click the item while viewing your Calendar or if you open the item, so keep that in mind.

Book IV
Chapter 1

Getting Familiar
with the Calendar

- Type any notes for the appointment (for example, `Bring new project schedule and timeline`) in the large Notes area at the bottom of the form.

- If you don't want to look like a silly-willy to anyone who views your Calendar, spellcheck your notes by clicking the Spelling & Grammar button on the Review tab.

- Format the note text by using the buttons on the Format Text tab.

- Insert related files or attach Outlook items to the appointment by using the buttons on the Insert tab. (For example, you might attach a related e-mail, contact, or task to make that item easily accessible from within the appointment.) See Book II, Chapters 1 and 3 for help with inserting files, graphics, or Outlook items. Granted, in those chapters, I talk about inserting things into an e-mail message, but the process is the same for all Outlook forms. Trust me.

9. **When you finish setting options, click the Save & Close button on the Appointment tab.**

   The appointment appears in your Calendar.

Wanna make a change already? No problem; appointments, by their nature, are flexible. (For the word on how to make changes, see Chapter 2 of this minibook.)

Dealing with a Reminder When It Rears Its Ugly Head

When you create an appointment, you have an option to set a reminder. Actually, if you do nothing when you create an appointment, a reminder is automatically set that goes off 15 minutes before the appointment. Of course, you can change this interval (or remove the reminder altogether) when you create the appointment. Assuming you set a reminder, at the right time, Outlook bops you on the head. Figure 1-11 shows what the bop looks like.

You can set reminders when you create meetings, events, tasks, and To-Do items as well; those reminders work exactly as described in this section.

At the top of the Reminder window, the date and time of the original appointment appear. If you need to review the rest of the appointment details, click Open Item. You can click Dismiss to simply get rid of the reminder — after that, you're on your own to get to the appointment on time. If you want to be reminded again before the appointment, select an interval from the Click Snooze to Be Reminded Again In XX drop-down list and click the Snooze button.

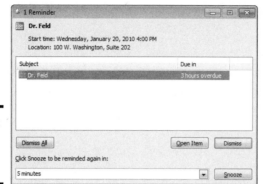

To redisplay the Reminders window, click the Reminders Window button on
the View tab.

Planning an All-Day Event

An event takes up the whole day. Events include things such as birthdays,
anniversaries, conferences, vacations, and Saturday naps. The idea behind
scheduling an event in Calendar is that you're reminded about a special day,
but you can still schedule appointments and meetings on that day, if you
want. For some events, such as conferences, vacations, and all-day meetings,
you might not want to schedule other things to occur at that same time.
Well, okay, maybe your boss wants you to keep appointments during your
vacation, but that's not Outlook's problem. Based on what you manage to
work out with your boss, Outlook can mark your time during the event as
Busy or not.

You can actually schedule as many appointments or meetings as you want
during an event day, regardless of how you mark your time within Outlook
(meaning whether you mark it as Busy or Free). Mark your time as Busy
during an event only to prevent people who might also have access to your
Calendar (such as an overeager assistant) from scheduling appointments or
meetings that you can't actually attend.

To add an event to your Calendar, follow these steps:

1. **With the Calendar module open, click the New Items button on
the Home tab and select All Day Event from the pop-up menu that
appears.**

In Day, Week, Work Week, or Next 7 Days view, you can also change to
the date on which the event will occur and double-click the blue-gray
area at the top of that day to create an event.

An Event form appears.

2. **Type a subject in the Subject field.**

   Enter a basic description for the event, such as `Professional Developer's Conference`. (See Figure 1-12.)

3. **(Optional) Type where the event is taking place in the Location field.**

   You might need to enter information in this text box for events that actually occur in a different place, such as conferences or seminars.

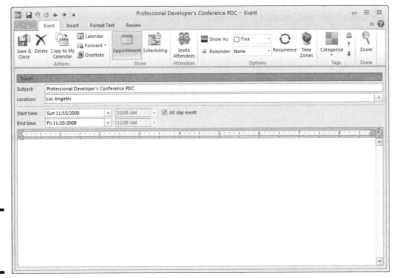

Figure 1-12:
Add an event.

Outlook lets you schedule events even if you already have appointments or meetings on that day; it assumes that most events are just holidays and such — not something you actually have to attend. Chapter 3 of this minibook explains how to designate your time as busy during an event, rather than free. If you change the event's time to Busy and you want to take a look at what's causing the conflict in your Calendar, click the Calendar button on the Event tab.

4. **If needed, select the start date for the event from the Start Time drop-down list.**

5. **If your event will take more than a single day, set an end date for the event from the End Time drop-down list.**

   You don't enter any times when setting up an event because events take all day. If the activity you're recording won't take all day and you want to show part of your day as Free, you can change this event into an appointment by deselecting the All-Day Event check box.

You can type words in the date boxes instead of selecting an actual date. For example, you can type today or tomorrow, or three months from now. Outlook recognizes some holidays, as well, such as Fourth of July, New Year's Day, or Christmas.

A lot of events recur. For example, birthdays and anniversaries reoccur on the same day each year. For help in setting up recurring events, see Chapter 2 of this minibook.

6. **Set a reminder.**

By default, the reminder goes off 18 hours before the event's start date. If you need longer than that to get prepared, select an interval from the Reminder drop-down list. You can also type a specific amount of time, such as 25 minutes, 2.5 hours, or 5 days, in the Reminder text box. Don't need to be reminded about your brother's birthday because you're not getting him anything? Just select None from the Reminder drop-down list. To find out how to deal with reminders after they pop up, see the preceding section.

7. **After you set up some categories, select the ones that apply to this event, one at a time, from the Categorize list.**

Book VIII, Chapter 1 gives you details on keeping your Outlook items organized by using categories.

8. **Set other options.**

Most of the other options on the Ribbon have to do with creating a meeting, which you can find out about in Chapter 4 of this minibook; however, you can set a few more options for an event:

- Mark this event as "better not forget" by clicking the High Importance button on the Event tab.

- Click the Low Importance button on the Event tab to mark events that don't require your presence and that you can even forget about if you get too busy — such as your anniversary (kidding, kidding . . .)

Events marked as either high or low importance appear as ordinary events in any Calendar view because the Importance field doesn't normally appear. To see whether an item is important, you must click it and look to see whether the High or Low Importance button is highlighted on the Event tab.

- Type any notes for the event, such as Flight #2047, leaving at 10:02 a.m., arriving 12:37 p.m. Shuttle to conference on lower level., in the large Notes area at the bottom of the form. You can spellcheck your notes by clicking the Spelling & Grammar button on the Event tab.

- Format the note text by using the buttons on the Format Text tab.

- Insert related files or attach Outlook items to the event by using the buttons on the Insert tab. For example, you might attach an e-mail that details the conference schedule, the contact who made your hotel arrangements, or the tasks that you need to finish before the event. (See Book II, Chapters 1 and 3 for help with inserting files, graphics, or Outlook items.)

9. **When you finish setting options, click the Save & Close button on the Event tab.**

The event appears in your Calendar at the top of the selected day(s).

Events often happen anywhere but at work. If you type some critical information in the Event form that you want to take with you (such as your flight info, conference agenda, or emergency phone numbers), you can print the Event form and take it with you to the event. See Book X, Chapter 3.

You can change an event later, if needed; see Chapter 2 of this minibook for the steps that do the job.

Chapter 2: Going Further with the Calendar

In This Chapter

✔ Making appointments, meetings, and events repeat

✔ Changing (or removing) an existing appointment or event

✔ Adding holidays to the calendar

I wish I could tell you that after adding an appointment, meeting, or event to your Calendar, you're done. But life doesn't work that way; all too often, you have to make adjustments. In this chapter, you can find out how to navigate those changing waters with ease — copying, moving, and deleting appointments or events; changing appointment times; making appointments, meetings, or events occur multiple times automatically; and much more!

Scheduling a Recurring Appointment, Meeting, or Event

Some appointments, meetings, and even events just won't go away. Like a stubborn stain, they keep coming back, even after repeated washings. Well, you don't have to manually copy an item repeatedly just to get it to appear in your Calendar multiple times. If an item's recurrence has a pattern, you can get Outlook to do the hard work for you and copy the item throughout your Calendar at regular intervals.

To make an appointment, meeting, or event recur on a regular basis (such as every Wednesday), follow these steps:

1. Click the Recurrence button.

If the item is open, the Recurrence button appears on the Appointment/ Meeting/Event tab. If you've already created the item and you just want to make it recur, click the appointment, meeting, or event in the Calendar. The Recurrence button appears on the Appointment/Meeting/ Event tab that pops up. After you click the Recurrence button, the Recurrence dialog box appears, as shown in Figure 2-1.

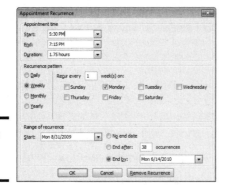

Figure 2-1:
Rinse and
repeat.

> **2.** **Select the Recurrence Pattern for the basic interval at which you want the appointment, meeting, or event to repeat.**
>
> You can select the Daily, Weekly, Monthly, or Yearly radio button.
>
> **3.** **Set recurrence options.**
>
> Depending on the frequency that you selected in Step 2, a set of options appears on the right. Set those options to match the pattern of repetition:
>
> - *Daily:* Enter a number in the Recur Every *Number of* Day(s) text box. Or, if this activity happens every day during the work week, you have the option of setting it to repeat every weekday, skipping weekends, by selecting the Every Weekday radio button.
>
> - *Weekly:* Enter a number in the Recur Every *Number of* Week(s) On text box. Then, select the check box for the day on which the activity recurs, such as Monday.
>
> - *Monthly:* You can choose a particular day of the month or a particular day every so many months (such as the 10th of every third month) by typing the day and month you want in the *Day of the Month* of Every *Number of* Month(s).
>
>   Or you can choose the first, second, third, fourth, or last weekday of every month (or so many months), such as the second Thursday of every other month, by selecting the values you want from The *Number of Weekday Name of Weekday* of Every *Number of* Month(s).
>
> - *Yearly:* Like the Monthly option, you can select either a particular date to repeat each year, such as October 16, or a particular day within a certain month, such as the last Friday of November. This repeating business doesn't have to repeat every year — just enter a number in the Recur Every *Number of* Year(s) text box. Then choose

either the On *Month Day* radio button and select a month from the drop-down list and type a day in the text box, or choose the On the *Number Weekday* of *Month* radio button, and select a number from the first drop-down list (such as third), a weekday from the second list (such as Monday) and a month (such as January) from the last list.

If you can't find a pattern in the Recurrence dialog box that fits the actual pattern for your appointment, meeting, or event, you might have to create multiple items and select a pattern for each one that, when combined, create the pattern for the actual activity. For example, if your garden club meets on the last Friday of every month except during January through April, when it meets on the second Tuesday, you need to create two recurring items: one that recurs every last Friday from May to December, and another that recurs on the second Tuesday from January to April, as explained in Step 4.

4. **Set limits to the recurrence in the Range of Recurrence section at the bottom of the dialog box.**

   Will the appointment repeat forever? Then select the No End Date radio button. Will it recur a certain number of times (say, five) and then stop? If so then select the End After radio button, and type the number of occurrences in the text box. Or will it repeat until the end of November, and then no more? If so, then select the End By radio button and select an end date from the drop-down list.

5. **Click OK to close the dialog box and return to the appointment, message, or event form.**

   After you make an appointment, meeting, or event recur, the pattern that you establish appears in the InfoBar of the item's form. The Recurrence button is also highlighted on the Ribbon as kind of a visual reminder that this item repeats.

6. **Click Save & Close to save your changes.**

   The item is automatically copied throughout your Calendar, using the recurrence pattern that you set. Recurring appointments, events, or meetings appear with a special Recurrence icon (as shown in Figure 2-2).

Figure 2-2: Recurrent items use a special icon.

Recurrence icon

Making Changes to a Recurring Item

After you create a recurring appointment, meeting, or event, Outlook treats the repeating items as a series. Basically, if you make a change to one of the recurring items, Outlook often expects that you want to make the same change to all of them. To be sure, whenever you open a recurring item, Outlook asks you if you want to make the same change to all occurrences.

However, as explained in the following section, "Changing Appointments or Events," you can make changes to an appointment, meeting, or event *without ever opening it*. For example, you can drag an appointment to another start time. If you do that with a recurring item, however, you might not get the changes you want because Outlook assumes that because you didn't open the item, you want to make changes to only that one occurrence, and not the whole series of appointments/events.

To know whether a change you have made has affected a single occurrence of a recurring item, select the item and then look at the Ribbon: If the Edit Series button appears on the Appointment/Event/Meeting Occurrence tab, then Outlook is trying to tell you, "Hey, the change you just made applied to only one of the occurrences. To make that change to all the occurrences, click me, click me." If you then click the Edit Series button, the button changes to the Recurrence button, which displays the Recurrence dialog box when you can click it, so you can make changes to the recurrence pattern.

If you open a recurring appointment, meeting, or event (by double-clicking it), instead of trying to make changes without opening the item, then Outlook asks you whether you want to affect the related items, as well. (See Figure 2-3.) To affect only this particular appointment, meeting, or event, select Open This Occurrence. To affect all items in a recurring series, select Open the Series. When you click OK, the appointment, meeting, or event form opens.

Figure 2-3:
Repeating
yourself?

In this open form, you can make any changes you like. However, the Recurrence button appears on the main tab only if you're making changes to all items in the series. If you indicated earlier that you wanted to make changes to only this occurrence but you've changed your mind, you don't need to start over — just click the Edit Series button on the main tab in the form. The Edit Series button changes into the Recurrence button, which you can click to display the Recurrence dialog box and make changes to the recurrence pattern.

Here are the changes you can make to all items in a series:

✦ **Subject, Location, Categories, Reminder, Free/Busy time, and similar changes:** Make these changes in the form — see the following section for helpful hints.

✦ **Start/End time, Duration, Recurrence Pattern, and Range of Occurrence:** To change these things, click the Recurrence button on the Appointment/Meeting/Event Series tab. The Recurrence dialog box appears — refer to Figure 2-1. Make changes as described in the section "Scheduling a Recurring Appointment, Meeting, or Event," earlier in this chapter.

To remove a recurrence (in other words, to change a recurring appointment into a single one), click the Recurrence button on the Appointment/ Meeting/Event Series tab, then click the Remove Recurrence button in the Recurrence dialog box that appears.

If you're changing just this occurrence, however, here are the changes you can make:

✦ **Subject, Location, Categories, Reminder, Free/Busy time, and similar changes:** Make these changes in the form — see the following section for helpful hints.

✦ **Start/End time and Duration:** You can change the Start/End Time and Duration in the form, for this occurrence only.

Make your changes and save them by clicking the Save & Close button on the main tab.

If you delete an item that's part of a series, Outlook asks you the question again: Do you want to remove just this occurrence or the entire series? (Not sure how to delete an appointment or event? See the section "Removing an Appointment or Event," later in this chapter. Meetings are a whole different animal; for help in removing them, see Chapter 4 of this minibook.)

Changing Appointments or Events

It seems that the only thing constant in life is change. So, if you make an appointment and later the doctor's office calls asking whether you can come an hour earlier because Mrs. Hoover was a no-show, you can make that change, and others, in Outlook.

Book IV Chapter 2

Going Further with the Calendar

Changing an appointment/event without opening it

Make changes to the appointment or event *without opening it* by following these steps:

1. **Click the appointment or event that you want to change.**

The item is highlighted with a dark border. The Calendar Tools tab appears, as you can see in Figure 2-4.

Date Navigator   A highlighted item

Figure 2-4:
Change an item without opening it.

2. **Make changes.**

You can make just about any change you want:

- *Change the item's subject.* Click the item twice, with a pause between clicks. The subject becomes editable. Click inside the item's box and edit the text that appears there. End this process by clicking outside the box. Click the box again if you want to make other changes to the item.

Although the location for an item appears in the Calendar, you cannot change it unless you double-click to open the item.

You can also edit the subject of an appointment, meeting, or event by clicking the item just once and then pressing F2. The cursor appears within the item so that you can edit its text.

- *Change the time at which an appointment occurs.* Drag and drop the appointment within the Calendar. For example, to change a 1 p.m. appointment to 3 p.m., change to Day or Week view, drag the appointment to the 3 p.m. time slot, and then drop it.

- *Change the date on which the item occurs.* Drag and drop the item onto any visible date in the Calendar area. For example, you might drag an appointment from Monday to Thursday. You can also drag and drop an item onto a date in the Date Navigator to move it to that date at the same time of day.

  If you want to drag the appointment to a different date and time, drag it onto the Date Navigator and drop it on a date. The Calendar changes to display that date for you. Move back into the viewing window and drag the item to the appropriate time slot.

  If you need to move an appointment or event pretty far, you can use the Cut and Paste to move it. First, click the appointment or event to select it, and then press Ctrl+X to Cut the Appointment/Event. Change to the day on which you want to move the item and click the time slot where you want the appointment or event to appear. (Don't click when it says Click to Create Appointment or you end up moving the appointment inside the small white bubble that results.) Press Ctrl+V to Paste and make the item appear at the slot where you clicked.

- *Lengthen an appointment.* Drag its bottom edge down; drag up to shorten the appointment.

- *Make other changes by using the buttons on the Appointment/Event tab.* For example, change the Free/Busy time by opening the Show As drop-down list and selecting how you want this time slot to appear to others who might look at your Calendar.

- *Change the reminder time.* Open the Reminder drop-down list and make a selection.

- *Add or remove a category.* Click the Categorize button and select a category from the drop-down list that appears to add it. Select an already applied category (it appears with an orange border around its color box) to remove the category. Select Clear All Categories from the drop-down menu to remove all categories from the item.

- *Set privacy and importance options.* Click the Private, High Importance, or Low Importance button.

Book IV Chapter 2

Going Further with the Calendar

- *Make changes to a series.* For example, change the recurrence pattern or range of occurrence. Click the Recurrence button to display the Recurrence dialog box, and check out the section "Scheduling a Recurring Appointment, Meeting, or Event," earlier in this chapter, for the how-to.

Copy an appointment or event, by clicking it, and then pressing and holding down Ctrl as while you drag the copy where you want it. After you make a copy, you can click the item and make changes if needed by following the steps given here.

Changing an appointment/event by opening it

To make changes to an appointment or event other than the ones described in the preceding section, you need to open that appointment or event. Follow these steps:

1. **Double-click the appointment or event that you want to change.**

   The Appointment/Event form appears, as you can see in Figure 2-5.

2. **If the appointment or event is part of a recurring series of appointments/events, select an option from the Open Recurring Item dialog box. (Refer to Figure 2-3.)**

   Select Open the Occurrence if you want to make changes to just this particular occurrence in the series; if you want to make changes to all occurrences, select Open the Series. Click OK and the Appointment/ Event form appears.

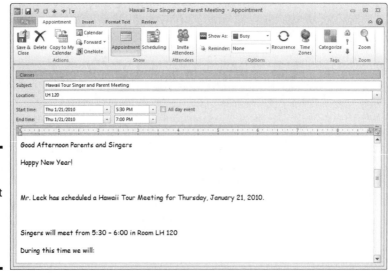

Figure 2-5:
Open an appointment or event to make certain changes.

3. **Make changes.**

Make the changes you want:

- *Change the subject or location.* Click in the appropriate text box and edit the text.

- *Change the Start/End time or date.* Select an option from the appropriate list. If you're editing a recurring series, these lists don't appear; you need to make changes to the Start/End time or date in the Recurrence dialog box, which means you need to click the Recurrence button on the Appointment/Event Series tab to display the Recurrence dialog box so you can change the Start/End date or time.

- *Make other changes to a series, such as the recurrence pattern or range of occurrence.* Click the Recurrence button to display the Recurrence dialog box, and read the section "Scheduling a Recurring Appointment, Meeting, or Event," earlier in this chapter, for what to do.

- *Add notes about the appointment/event.* Type notes in the large text box or edit the existing notes.

- *Make other changes by using the buttons on the Appointment/Event tab.* For example, change the Free/Busy time by opening the Show As drop-down list and, selecting how you want this time slot to appear to others who might look at your Calendar.

- *Change the reminder time.* Click Reminder drop-down list and make a selection.

- *Add or remove a category.* Click the Categorize button and select a category from the drop-down list that appears to add it. Select an already applied category (it appears with an orange border around its color box) to remove the category. Select Clear All Categories from the drop-down menu to remove all categories from the item.

- *Set privacy and importance options.* Click the Private, High Importance, or Low Importance button.

Make these special changes, if needed:

- *Remove a reminder.* Click Reminder and select None from the drop-down list that appears.

- *Change an appointment into an event.* Select the All Day Event option. The Start and End times disappear, but you can still change the End date. If you're making changes to a recurring appointment, you have to remove the recurrence first (by clicking the Recurrence button to display the Recurrence dialog box and clicking the Remove Recurrence button), then change the appointment into an event and reapply the recurrence.

- *Change an event into an appointment.* Simply deselect the All Day Event option. When you do, the Start and End times appear so that you can change them.

- *Change an appointment into a meeting.* Click the Invite Attendees button on the Appointment tab. The Meeting Suggestions pane appears, and the Appointment form is changed to a Meeting form so you can invite attendees. To find out more about creating meetings, see Chapter 4 of this minibook.

- *Copy the appointment or event into your main Calendar.* If the appointment/event you opened is currently contained in a different calendar (such as an extra calendar you created or a shared calendar) then you can copy the item to your main Calendar by clicking the Copy to My Calendar button on the Appointment/Event tab.

4. **Click the Save & Close button to save your changes.**

Removing an Appointment or Event

Sometimes, an appointment or event gets cancelled; sometimes, you just get uninvited. (Okay, that never happens to me, but I've heard it happens to other people.) If it happens to you, you can easily remove the unneeded appointment or event from your Calendar:

✦ **To remove a nonrecurring appointment or event:** Click it to select it. (You can remove multiple appointments or events at one time by holding down Ctrl and clicking each one to select them.) After selecting what you want to remove, click the Delete button on the Appointment/Event tab or press Delete.

✦ **To remove a recurring appointment or event:** Click it to select it, and then click the Delete button on the Appointment/Event tab or just press Delete on your keyboard. A dialog box appears; to delete all occurrences of the recurring appointment or event, select Delete the Series. To delete this occurrence only, select Delete This Occurrence.

You don't have to delete a recurring appointment or event to get it to stop. Instead, you can simply change the date the recurrence ends. See the section "Scheduling a Recurring Appointment, Meeting, or Event," earlier in this chapter, for help in making changes to an item.

You don't necessarily have to delete items in your desire to keep Outlook tidy. *Archiving* is a process of *backing up* (saving) older items, such as appointments and events, and then removing them from Outlook. Archiving allows you to reduce the size of your Outlook data file without losing important data; you can always search for, view, and even restore any archived item. (See Book IX, Chapter 1 for details.)

Adding Holidays to the Calendar

Whoever installed Outlook on your computer probably added common holidays, such as New Year's Eve and Halloween during the installation process. (If you installed Outlook yourself and can't remember whether you added the holidays, you're probably in great need of one.)

Outlook has a set of holidays common to various countries or religions, and you can add as many holiday sets as apply to you. To check if you already have holidays installed, follow these steps to look for them in your calendar:

1. **Click the Change View button on the View tab and select List from the palette that appears.**

The items on your Calendar appear in a long list.

2. **Click the header at the top of the Location column to sort the events by location.**

Holidays for your country appear together in a group. If you live in the United States, for example, then after sorting the list by location, the holidays in your calendar appear in the United States group. If you add religious holidays, they're listed together under that religion in the Location column. For example, if you added Christian holidays to your calendar, they appear in the Christian Religious Holidays group. In addition, Outlook holidays appear with the word *Holiday* in the Categories column.

If holidays haven't been added to Outlook, you can add them to the Calendar by following these steps:

1. **Click the File tab to display Backstage and select Options from the list on the left.**

The Outlook Options dialog box appears.

2. **Select Calendar from the list on the left.**

The Calendar options appear on the right.

3. **In the Calendar Options section, click the Add Holidays button.**

The Add Holidays to Calendar dialog box opens, as shown in Figure 2-6.

4. **Select the holidays that you want to add.**

The check boxes for the holiday sets that Outlook already has installed are selected, so deselect them to prevent installing duplicates.

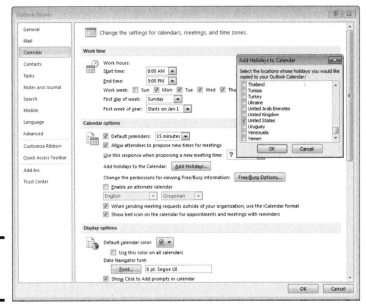

Figure 2-6:
Add a
holiday set.

5. **Click OK.**

   The holidays that you selected are added to the Calendar. Holidays are the gifts that keep on giving; after you add them, they appear year after year automatically — at least, from 2009 to 2028 (which is as far as the Outlook Calendar goes).

If, despite carefully checking, somehow you still manage to select a holiday set that's already installed in Outlook, a warning appears, telling you so — and asking whether you really want to install the holidays again. Click No to prevent creating duplicate holidays on your Calendar.

Creating Your Own Holiday List

I love holidays. I mean, what's not to love? You get the day off (assuming you turn off the phones so that your boss can't reach you). You get to sleep in. (The kids can reach the cereal boxes if they just stand on the countertops.) And you have a great excuse to eat too much. (Woo hoo, Columbus Day! Pass me another turkey leg!)

If you're in human resources and you want to issue a list of official company holidays so that all the employees can update their Outlook Calendars easily, Microsoft provides a way for you to do that. Remember, holidays are simply events, so if you don't happen to work in human resources, you can still create a list of family birthdays, school holidays and events, or club meetings and outings — and easily distribute the whole set. Follow these steps:

1. **Open the** `outlook.hol` **file.**

To create this list, you edit a file that Microsoft provides for this purpose. To do the editing, you need a simple text editor, such as Notepad. (Using Word is a bit of overkill.)

Exit Outlook and start My Computer (or just Computer, as Microsoft's now calling it). The file is carefully hidden in the `C:\Program Files\ Microsoft Office\Office 14\`*LCID* folder, where *LCID* is actually your local identification number, which identifies the language you speak. The United States version of English (in which we do *color* and not *colour*) is LCID #1033.

2. **After locating the file, make a copy of it by right-clicking the file and choosing Copy from the pop-up menu that appears. Right-click again and choose Paste to create the copy.**

Microsoft doesn't say what can happen if you mess up the file and don't have an original copy to go back to, but I'm sure it's ugly. So, just back up the file before you do anything. Personally, I copied the file and named the copy `orig outlook.hol` (so I could remember that it contained the original data and none of my edits) and then opened `outlook.hol` to edit. Keep the copy in a safe place, just in case the `outlook.hol` you're working with somehow starts acting kooky.

3. **Right-click the copy and select Open With from the pop-up menu that appears, then Notepad from additional pop-up menu.**

The file opens in Notepad.

4. **Press Ctrl+End.**

The cursor moves to the end of the file.

5. **Type a heading.**

Press Enter to begin a new line. Then, type a heading for your holiday list, like this: `[Marketing Department Events]` 6. Type the name of your holiday list in square brackets, then add a space followed by a number. The number you type represents the total number of holidays on the list you are about to enter into the file.

6. **Press Enter to begin a new line, and then type the first holiday.**

For example, you could type `AdCon 2011, 2011/03/10` (for March 10, 2011). (Figure 2-7 shows how that looks.) A comma separates the holiday name from its date, and you need to put the date in *yyyy/mm/dd* format (where *yyyy* is the four-digit year, *mm* is the two-digit month, and *dd* is the two-digit day).

Book IV Chapter 2

Going Further with the Calendar

7. **Repeat Step 6 until you've added all the holidays, then press Enter one last time to add a blank line at the end of the file.**

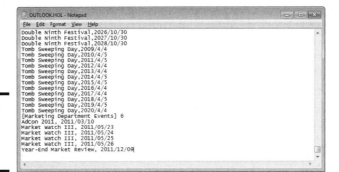

Figure 2-7:
Create
your own
holidays.

8. **Save the file by choosing File⇨Save, and then exit Notepad.**

   A sample holiday list might look like this:

   ```
   [Marketing Department Events] 6
   AdCon 2011, 2011/03/10
   Market Watch III, 2011/05/23
   Market Watch III, 2011/05/24
   Market Watch III, 2011/05/25
   Market Watch III, 2011/05/26
   Year-End Market Review, 2011/12/09
   ```

9. **Restart Outlook.**

10. **Import the dates by clicking the File tab to display Backstage and selecting Options from the list on the left.**

    The Outlook Options dialog box appears.

11. **Select Calendar from the list on the left.**

    The Calendar options appear on the right.

12. **In the Calendar Options section, click the Add Holidays button.**

    The Add Holidays to Calendar dialog box opens.

13. **Select the holiday list that you just created from the dialog box's listings, and then click OK to add those holidays to your Calendar, as shown in Figure 2-8.**

    When you add your custom holiday set, be sure to uncheck the holiday sets that you've already added; otherwise, you add them again and end up with duplicates in your Calendar.

Figure 2-8:
Add custom holidays.

To share the holiday list with friends or colleagues, simply attach the file to an e-mail message or place the file in a shared folder. Mention to your friends and colleagues that they should save the file in their Outlook folder, after first making a copy of their original `outlook.hol` file.

You can also share events and holidays by creating a special calendar just for the holidays and placing that calendar in a shared folder. (See Chapter 3 of this minibook for details.)

**Book IV
Chapter 2**

Going Further with the Calendar

Chapter 3: Calendar Collaboration

In This Chapter

✔ Sharing what's on your calendar

✔ Taking a peek at someone else's calendar

✔ Controlling your available time

✔ Playing well with a group's schedule

✔ Sharing appointments via e-mail

*I*f you're a fairly private person, it may come as a shock that of all the data you keep in Outlook, the Calendar is probably the least private thing. At least, it should be. As much as you might prefer letting everyone in the office guess whether you'll be in today, letting other people have access to your Calendar has some advantages. If you're lucky enough to have an assistant, for example, you can instantly delegate the responsibility of looking up your schedule and then explaining to Mr. Please-give-me-that-product-demo-again-even-though-there's-no-chance-I'm-ever-going-to-buy-it-I'm-just-no-good-at-making-decisions that you simply have no room in your schedule this week for another appointment, sorry. It's also much easier to corner Kenny and Jen so that you can schedule that group project meeting if you can see their calendars and they can see yours.

So, this sharing Calendar thing is not all that bad, and being able to view your calendar may just convince your boss that you're way, way, underpaid. Even so, you don't have to share everything. I mean Jen, Kenny, and Nora (your boss) don't need to know that you're skipping out early on Thursday to get your nails done, or that you're seeing *Hairspray* for the third time this month on Saturday. When needed, you can keep certain appointments private.

Live, let-me-see-what-you're-doing kind of sharing happens over a Microsoft Exchange network. So, if your company uses Exchange, you can share your calendar with your colleagues, and they can share theirs with you. If you aren't on an Exchange network, you can share your calendar in other ways: through e-mail or over the Internet. You can find out all the fascinating ways to share in this chapter.

Sharing Your Calendar via Exchange

If you're on an Exchange network, you can share your Calendar, live and up-to-date, with everybody you know or just the select people on your team. Likewise, they can share their calendars with you, and you can view those calendars in Outlook just as easily as you can view your own. While sharing a calendar, you can designate whether users can only view your calendar, or make changes to it, as well.

Even when you share your calendar, you can mark particular meetings, appointments, or events private so that no one else can see them. You can also create a separate calendar for sharing and keep only the kinds of appointments you want to share in it. For example, you can create a team calendar and keep all your team-related appointments in it. Or you can create a personal calendar, keep all your private appointments in it, and share only the default Calendar.

To make an appointment, meeting, or event private, select the item by clicking it and then click the Private button on the Appointment/Meeting tab. If the item is already open, you can click the Private button on the main tab to make it private.

When you share a calendar, other people can view the appointments, meetings, and events in it (at least, those items that you don't mark as private). Other people, however, can't update your calendar for you or accidentally delete an appointment. If you want to grant them that kind of freedom, you need to delegate your supreme and magnificent authority. See Book X, Chapter 1 for the lowdown.

When it comes to sharing your calendar over an Exchange network, you have two choices. You can either

✦ **Share the main calendar with basically everyone on the network.** You can designate what people are allowed to do on your calendar, such as View Only, or View and Edit. See the following section for more info.

✦ **Share either the main or a custom calendar completely with only the specific people you select.** See the section "Sharing a calendar with specific people," later in this chapter.

If you decide that you want to create a new Calendar folder and put either the private or the not-so-private appointments, meetings, and events in it, then flip to Chapter 5 of this minibook for the necessary help.

Sharing a calendar with everyone

By default, your main calendar is already shared with everyone on the network, but that doesn't mean everyone can rework your calendar willy-nilly. The damage (uh, activities) that someone can perform on your calendar is controlled by his or her permission level. By default, everybody on the Exchange network has Free/Busy Time access level, as described here. Following these steps, you can bump up that level to show more detail to anyone who decides to view your calendar. If you want to bump up the level of detail for only selected users, see the following section for help. In addition, if you want to share a calendar you added to Outlook, see the following section because you can't do that by following this procedure.

To share the main Calendar folder with everyone on the network, follow these steps:

1. **Click the Calendar Permissions button on the Home tab.**

The Calendar Properties dialog box pops up.

2. **Click the Permissions tab, and then click Default in the Name list. (See Figure 3-1.)**

Figure 3-1:
Why not share?

**Book IV
Chapter 3**

**Calendar
Collaboration**

3. **From the options that appear in the Permission Level drop-down list, select the one that describes the kind of things you want visitors to be able to do.**

Here are the options you can choose from:

• *Publishing Editor:* Lets a user create, edit, delete, and view Calendar items. Publishing Editors can also create subfolders within the shared folder.

- *Editor:* Same as Publishing Editor, except the user can't create subfolders.

- *Publishing Author:* Lets users create and view Calendar items, create folders, and edit or delete Calendar items that they've created themselves.

- *Author:* Same as Publishing Author, except that the user can't create subfolders.

- *Nonediting Author:* Same as Author, except that the user can't edit existing Calendar items, even if he or she created them.

- *Reviewer:* Lets a user view Calendar items only.

- *Contributor:* Lets a user create and edit new Calendar items, but the user can't view existing ones unless he or she created them.

   I don't recommend that you use Contributor access because it prevents users from scheduling meetings with you (because they can't view items — existing meetings and appointments that might interfere with the meeting they're trying to set up).

- *Free/Busy Time:* Allows a user to view your Free and Busy time so that he or she can determine the best time for a meeting. Calendar always has this initial setting.

- *Free/Busy Time – Subject Location:* Similar to Free/Busy Time, except that it allows a user to view not only the Free or Busy status of an appointment, meeting, or event, but also a few more details, such as the items' subjects and locations.

- *None:* Prevents all users from accessing the folder at all — a user can't even view the Calendar items in the folder. You might use this setting to specifically block everyone from viewing even your free/busy time.

 4. Click OK.

   Your main Calendar folder appears in the Navigation pane with a special Welcome icon (a hand holding a business card), showing that it's now shared.

Well, okay, you've shared your main Calendar, and although you don't need to send everybody an invitation to come to the party, you may want to so that they know they can access your calendar. All someone on your Exchange network needs to know right now is your name in order to gain access to your shared calendar. See the section "Viewing Someone Else's Calendar," later in this chapter, for more info on how your recipient gains access to your main Calendar folder.

Sharing a calendar with specific people

When it comes to sharing, I'm probably like most people. I don't mind sharing as long as I can be selective. There's just no sense sharing a piece of pie with Aunt Minnie, for example, because she'll just smile and then turn around and give the pie to someone else. It's not that Aunt Minnie doesn't like pie, she just has a problem accepting presents. This makes our family Christmas a fairly strange event, because we all have to check our boxes before we head out, just in case we have any presents that were originally tagged "Aunt Minnie."

If you have a bunch of Aunt Minnies at your office who share their calendars fully with everyone, that doesn't mean you have to return the favor. You can share exactly what you want to share with only those you want to share it with. To share the details of your calendar with selected people, you need to set those users up with their own personal access. You can most easily provide this access by sending such users an invitation to view your calendar. If you're sharing your main calendar in this way, you can provide visitors with only Free/Busy Time, Free/Busy Time – Subject Location, or Reviewer status — at least, initially. After the sharing invitation goes out, you can always change a particular person's access level as you see fit — see the following section for details.

To share a calendar with a select few, first select it in the Navigation pane. You can share your main Calendar with just a few people by following these steps, or a calendar you've added to Calendar. (If you want to share your main Calendar with everyone, see the preceding section.) After selecting a Calendar folder, follow these steps to share it:

1. **Click the Share Calendar button on the Home tab.**

   A message form appears, as shown in Figure 3-2. The form in the background of Figure 3-2 appears if you share your main Calendar; the form in the foreground appears if you share a calendar you added yourself.

2. **In the To box, type the addresses of the people with whom you want to share your calendar.**

3. **Edit the Subject text if you like.**

   Normally it shows Sharing invitation: *Your Name – Folder Name.*

4. **(Optional) In the large text box at the bottom of the form, type a short message explaining the invitation, if you want.**

5. **(Optional) If you are sharing your main Calendar, select the Request Permission to View Recipient's Calendar check box.**

   If you select this check box, you request specific permission to view each addressee's calendar, in return.

6. **If you're sharing your main Calendar, make sure that the Allow Recipient to View Your Calendar check box is selected.**

   Otherwise, well, you won't actually be sharing your calendar.

Share your main calendar with a select few.

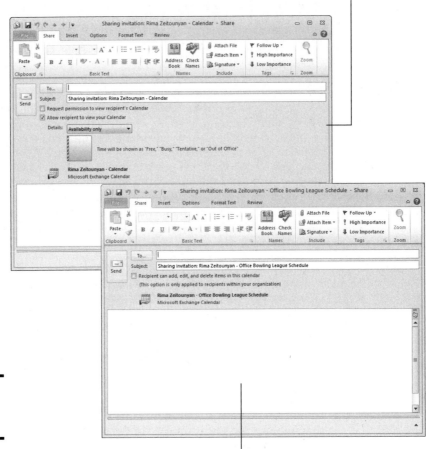

Figure 3-2:
Message
sent, sir!

Share a custom calendar.

7. **If you are sharing your main Calendar, from the Details drop-down list, select the amount of detail you want them to be able to see.**

   You have these options:

   - *Availability Only:* Allows the user to see only your Free/Busy status, which is the default for Calendar.

   - *Limited Details:* Allows the user to see your Free/Busy status and the Subject line for each Calendar item.

   - *Full Details:* Allows the user to see basically everything having to do with each Calendar item (such as your notes, the location, and so on).

8. **If you're sharing a calendar that you added and want users to only view appointments, meetings, or events (Reviewer access), deselect the Recipient Can Add, Edit, and Delete Items in This Calendar check box.**

   If you want them to be able to mess things up (by granting them Editor access), select the check box, instead.

9. **Click Send.**

   A dialog box appears, in which Outlook asks whether you really want to grant access to your calendar to those silly people you work with; if you do, click Yes. Outlook displays another dialog box with a message saying that your calendar is shared.

10. **Click OK.**

The folder you chose appears in the Navigation pane with a special icon of a hand holding a business card, which is supposed to indicate that folder is now shared. After one of your recipients gets your sharing invitation, he or she needs to perform a few quick steps to view your calendar. See the section "Viewing Someone Else's Calendar," later in this chapter, for details.

Changing permissions or stopping sharing

After you decide to share a calendar, you don't have to keep sharing it forever. For example, if you're sharing the folder with selected colleagues, you can change what they're allowed to do. On the other hand, if you're sharing the folder with everyone on the network, you can simply stop sharing it or change everyone's level of access.

To change permission to use a shared folder, follow these steps:

1. **Select the shared calendar in the Navigation pane.**

2. **Click the Calendar Permissions button on the Home tab.**

   The Calendar Properties dialog box pops up. (See Figure 3-3.)

3. **Change permissions, as desired.**

   You have two options:

   - *To make a change that affects everyone:* Select Default from the Name list. Then, make a selection from the Permissions Level list or, to completely revoke all access, select None.

   - *To make a change to a particular user's permissions:* Select the user's name from the Name list. Then, from the Permission Level drop-down list, select the level of access that you want to grant this user.

4. **Click OK.**

   The permissions are changed right way.

Figure 3-3:
Changing
permissions
for a shared
calendar.

If someone is viewing your calendar at the moment that you change his or her level of access, the change takes place immediately — or, at least, as soon as the network traffic allows.

Viewing Someone Else's Calendar

When you hear it on the grapevine or you're otherwise notified that someone has been kind enough to share their calendar, you can easily gain access to it. After you access the calendar for the first time, it's added to the list of calendars that appear in the Navigation pane, in the section called *Shared Calendars*. After that, you can switch between your calendar and theirs as often as you want. Viewing someone's calendar is the same as viewing your own; you can change from day to day, change the view, and even search the calendar, just like it was your own personal calendar.

Accessing someone's main Calendar folder

To open and view somebody's default Calendar that he or she has already shared on an Exchange network, follow these steps:

1. **Click the Open Calendar button on the Home tab, and then select Open Shared Calendar from the pop-up menu that appears.**

   The Open a Shared Calendar dialog box jumps to attention, as shown in the background in Figure 3-4.

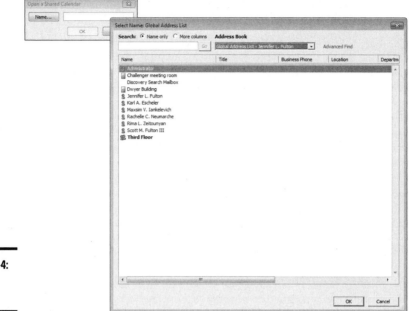

Figure 3-4:
Open
sesame.

2. **In the Name box, type the name of the person whose calendar you want to view.**

If you don't know the name, click the Name button. The Select Name: Global Address List dialog box appears. (Refer to the foreground of Figure 3-4.) Select a name from this dialog box and click OK. You're returned to the Open a Shared Calendar dialog box.

3. **Click OK to open the calendar in Outlook.**

Assuming you've been granted permission to open the calendar, it's added to the Shared Calendars list on the Navigation pane and tucked in next to your open calendars, as shown in Figure 3-5. The names of the calendars currently displayed appear in the Navigation pane with their check boxes selected. If you don't want to display this calendar right now, just uncheck its check box. The next time you want to view the calendar, click the check box.

If the folder is shared but you haven't been given access to it just yet, you'll be asked if you want to beg permission.

4. **Click Yes in the dialog box if it appears.**

A message form appears, asking for permission to use the folder.

**Book IV
Chapter 3**

**Calendar
Collaboration**

5. **Make sure to select the Request Permission to View Recipient's Calendar option.**

   If you want to offer access to your main calendar in return, select the Allow Recipient to View Your Calendar check box.

6. **Click Send to send the request.**

Although you can view someone's calendar, you can't view his or her tasks unless you gain access to his or her Tasks folder. Even so, those tasks don't show up in Calendar like yours do, right there on the Daily Tasks list or the To-Do bar (assuming either one is displayed). Nope, to see this person's tasks (again, assuming they've been shared with you) you need to jump over to the Tasks module (by clicking its button on the Navigation pane) and select that person's Tasks folder from those listed in the Shared Tasks section on the Navigation pane.

If you see an item in someone's shared calendar that you want to copy to your calendar (such as the company Jeans Day coming up next week, or a trade conference), open that item and click the Copy to My Calendar button on the main tab. If you copy a meeting, then in a dialog box that appears, you are given a choice between accepting, tentatively accepting, or simply copying the meeting. If you copy the meeting, you are *not* added to the attendees list.

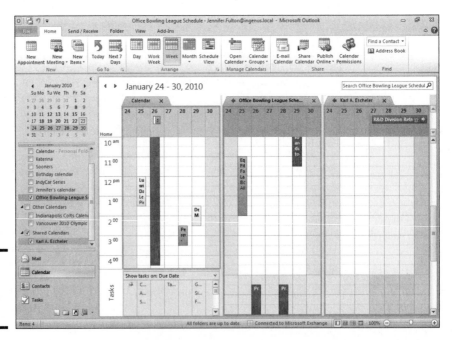

Figure 3-5:
Snug as some bugs in a rug.

You can view up to 30 calendars side-by-side, although unless you have a really big monitor and a very high resolution, you just end up with a bunch of too-skinny-to-read calendars full of mish-mash if you try. The best view for displaying multiple calendars alongside your own (such as three or more in total) is Schedule view, which displays calendars as horizontal timelines for easy comparison. (See Chapter 5 of this minibook for help.)

You can remove a shared calendar from the Shared Calendars list if you don't think you'll need to open it again. Simply select the shared Calendar you want to remove and click the Delete Calendar button on the Folder tab. By the way, this action doesn't actually delete the Calendar from the owner's system, regardless of your level of access.

Accessing someone's custom calendar

When someone shares a calendar that he or she has created, you receive a special e-mail invitation telling you so. You might also get an e-mail granting just you or a limited number of your colleagues, access to someone's main Calendar. Regardless, you can use that invitation to gain access to the specified calendar. The folder's owner determines your level of access; you were probably granted either Reviewer (view only) or Editor (create, edit, and delete tasks) access to the calendar. Regardless of your level of access, after you gain access to the calendar, you can easily view its contents any time you want.

To access someone's shared, custom calendar or main Calendar shared with a selected few, follow these steps:

1. **Click the Mail button on the Navigation pane to change over to Mail, and then either select the sharing invitation to view it in the Reading pane or double-click it to view it in a separate window, as shown in Figure 3-6.**

2. **Click Open This Calendar button.**

This button appears at the top of the Reading pane or on the Share tab in the message window.

You are automatically switched over to the Calendar module, where the folder now appears in the Shared Calendars group on the Navigation pane. The contents of the shared calendar is automatically displayed for you.

**Book IV
Chapter 3**

Calendar
Collaboration

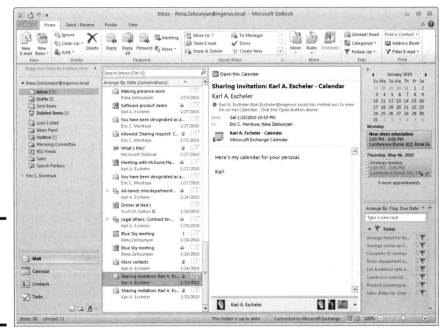

Figure 3-6:
Accessing
a custom
calendar's
sharing
invitation.

Managing Your Time

After you begin sharing your calendar, it becomes pretty important that people respect what you've scheduled. For example, if you add a new employee interview to your schedule, your colleagues need to understand that although you're in the office, no one should disturb you. Or maybe you want people to interrupt if they have an important reason, and you want to indicate that exception on your calendar, instead.

The trouble, my friend, begins with you. When you create an appointment, Outlook automatically lists you as Busy. That designation probably fits most appointments, but sometimes, it just doesn't. For example, maybe you list your son's football practice on your calendar, and it takes place at 4 p.m. every Thursday. You want to go, but you may not be able to make it each time. And if you do go, people at the office can certainly reach you by cell phone if something really important comes up, so you're not exactly Busy. If you change the appointment to show that you're Tentative or Out of the Office, at least people know more about the nature of the appointment. Although you can't create a label that says Busy but Reachable, you can add that phrase to the appointment notes, or you can create a special color category to indicate that particular status. Events, on the other hand, are typically shown as Free, but you may not be if the event is a conference or marketing event that requires your full attention.

To indicate whether you're still available while at an appointment, meeting, or event, follow these steps:

1. **Select the meeting, appointment, or event in your calendar by clicking it.**

The Appointment or Meeting tab appears, as shown in Figure 3-7.

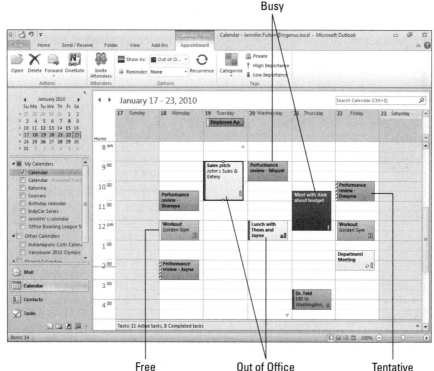

Busy

Free   Out of Office   Tentative

Figure 3-7:
So what are
you: free,
tentative,
out of office,
or busy?

2. **To change your availability from the default Busy to something else, click Show As in the Options group on the Meeting or Appointment tab, and then select an option from the drop-down list that appears.**

You can choose from these options:

- *Free:* You're still available, despite what your schedule might imply. For example, maybe you schedule some time to go over the employee reviews. You need to do it, which is why you schedule time to get it done. But someone can interrupt you if they need to.

- *Tentative:* The appointment, meeting, or event isn't definite yet and may very well change.

Be sure to mark a tentative appointment, meeting, or event as Busy after you know it's definitely going to happen.

- *Busy:* Indicates that you're busy and no one should interrupt you with questions and concerns during this time block.

- *Out of Office:* Indicates that you, like Elvis, have left the building. You may want to either set a standard that Out of the Office means don't call or add something in the notes of such appointments/meetings/ events to indicate whether your coworkers can contact you by cell phone during this time.

The marker on the selected appointment, meeting, or event is changed to reflect the status you selected. Continue reading to learn how to identify each marker type.

The Free, Busy, Out of Office, and Tentative markers may not tell the whole story. For example, you might be out of the office in a private meeting and don't want to be disturbed. Or you might be at a conference in which you can discretely accept calls of an urgent nature by putting your cell phone on vibrate. To help you and your coworkers sort out this mess, I recommend creating two categories, Do Not Disturb and Urgent Calls Only, and assigning the appropriate category to related appointments, meetings, or events. The consistent use of the High Importance and Low Importance markers might do the same thing, if you're category-phobic.

After you mark an appointment, meeting, or event as anything other than Busy, a special marker appears in the calendar to help you identify an item's Show As status, as shown in Figure 3-7.

Here's how the markers show up:

- ✦ **Busy:** For appointments and meetings, busy is normal, so they show up without a marker. For events, the color of the category assigned to the event is used to color the day(s) on which the event occurs. If there is no color assigned to the event, then the color of the calendar (typically, blue-gray) is used instead.

- ✦ **Free:** For appointments and meetings, a white banner appears along the left side of the appointment or meeting rectangle. For events, free is normal, so they also show up with a white banner along the left side just like appointments and meetings.

- ✦ **Tentative:** A diagonal striped banner appears along the left side of the appointment or meeting rectangle, or is used to color the day in the case of an event.

- ✦ **Out of Office:** A solid purple banner appears along the left side of the appointment or meeting rectangle, or is used to color the day in the case of an event.

Your normal work schedule plays an important role in determining whether you're free or busy. For example, if you normally work on Tuesday, Wednesday, and Thursday, you need to set up Outlook so that it shows Mondays and Fridays as non-work days to anyone who views your calendar. For help setting up your actual work days and hours, see Chapter 5 of this minibook.

Creating a Group Schedule

After you start sharing, it's hard to stop. Loan your hedge clippers to a neighbor, and he'll be back soon for your ladder. Still, it's hard to complain because he still hasn't remembered that three months ago, you borrowed his snow blower, chipper/shredder, and tiller. In any case, when you get accustomed to the give and take of calendar sharing, you may want to try group schedules. You have to be on an Exchange network for group schedules to work, though.

A *group schedule* is simply a collection of the combined appointments, meetings, and events in a series of shared calendars. These calendars don't have to represent just people. On an Exchange network, resources (such as multimedia equipment and conference rooms) can also have calendars that display when those resources are being used. So, for example, your group schedule might help you quickly identify not only the available time slots for all the members of your team, but also the available meeting rooms and equipment.

To create a group schedule, follow these steps:

1. **Click the Calendar Groups button on the Home tab, and then select Create New Calendar Group from the pop-up menu that appears.**

   The Create New Calendar Group dialog box appears.

2. **Type a name for the new group schedule in the Type a Name for the New Calendar Group text box and click OK.**

   The Select Name: Global Address List appears. (See Figure 3-8.)

3. **To add someone's calendar or a company resource (such as a meeting room that the group typically uses), select the calendar or resource from the Name list, and then click Group Members to add it to the Group Members box at the bottom of the Select Name: Global Address List dialog box.**

4. **Repeat Step 3 to add other calendars or resources.**

5. **Click OK.**

   The group schedule is added to the Navigation pane, and the schedules in that group appear alongside any currently displayed schedules (such as yours). See Figure 3-9.

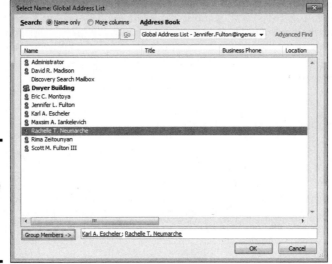

Figure 3-8:
Group together the schedules you reference often.

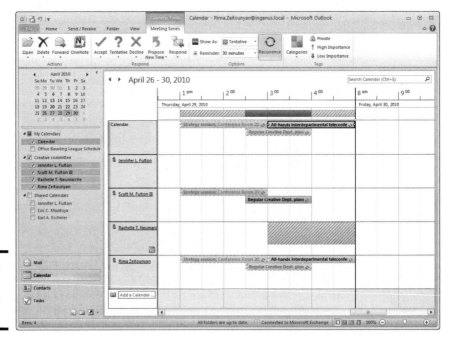

Figure 3-9:
Here's your group schedule.

You can create a group schedule using shared calendars you are already displaying in your Calendar. First, select the calendars you want to group by pressing Ctrl and clicking each one of their tabs. Then click the Calendar Groups button on the Ribbon's Home tab and select Save As a New Calendar Group from the pop-up menu that appears. The group, and the selected calendars, appear on the Navigation pane.

You can hide the group schedule by just deselecting its check box on the Navigation pane. Select the check box that appears to the left of the group's name to redisplay the schedules in that group. Likewise, you can display or hide an individual schedule within a group by selecting or deselecting that schedule's check box on the Navigation pane.

Working with group schedules

Thanks to your new group schedule, you can easily poke around someone's schedule, create a group meeting, or simply send a mass e-mail:

- ✦ **To send a meeting request to one member of the group:** Select that member's calendar, then click the New Meeting button on the Home tab and select New Meeting from the pop-up menu that appears.

- ✦ **To send a meeting request to all the members of the group:** Select any member's calendar, then click the New Meeting button on the Home tab and select New Meeting with All from the pop-up menu that appears. For more help with meetings, see Chapter 4 of this minibook.

- ✦ **To schedule a resource:** For example, you can schedule a conference room. Select the resource schedule from those listed in the group (assuming you included a resource schedule in your selections when you created the group) then click the New Meeting button on the Ribbon's Home tab and select New Meeting as Resource from the pop-up menu that appears.

If you suspect that maybe someone's schedule in the group isn't updated in your Calendar, right-click the group's name in the Navigation pane and select Refresh Free/Busy from the pop-up menu that appears.

To remove someone's schedule from the group schedule, right-click the schedule in the Navigation pane and select Delete Calendar from the pop-up menu that appears.

Forwarding Appointments to Others

If you're not on an Exchange network, you can't share your calendars in the traditional way. But you can share the details of an appointment, meeting, or event by forwarding them in an e-mail message. You can forward a Calendar item in one of two formats — Outlook (which the recipient can then add to his or her Outlook Calendar) or iCalendar (which the recipient can add to any calendar that supports that format — such as Google Calendar and Apple's iCal).

Of course, forwarding an appointment, meeting, or event in Outlook format to someone only does him or her some good if he or she has Outlook 2010. Likewise, forwarding an item to someone in iCalendar format doesn't help if that person doesn't use a calendar program that supports the format. In such a case, you can send your contact the same information as simple text. See the following section, "Sharing a Calendar via E-Mail".

To forward an appointment, meeting, or event to someone, follow these steps:

1. **In Calendar, click the appointment, meeting, or event to select it.**

   You can even forward a recurring appointment, meeting, or event, if you want.

   The Appointment/Meeting tab appears.

2. **Click the Forward button on the Appointment or Meeting tab and make a selection from the pop-up menu that appears.**

   You have several choices:

   • If you want to send a recurring appointment, meeting, or event, then select Forward Series from the menu that appears to forward the item in Outlook format. If you're sending a non-recurring appointment, meeting, or event, select Forward from the menu to forward the item in Outlook format.

   • To forward the item in iCalendar format instead, select Forward as iCalendar. If the item is recurring, you can choose to send just this occurrence or the series from the additional pop-up menu that appears by selecting either Forward Occurrence or Forward Series.

   The iCalendar format is supported by a lot of programs, including Windows Live Calendar, Apple's iCal, Google Calendar, and Lotus Notes.

   Regardless of which selection you make, a new message form appears, as shown in Figure 3-10. The Calendar item is physically attached to the message.

3. **In the To box of the message form, type the address of the person to whom you want to forward the appointment, meeting, or event.**

   The subject has been neatly typed in for you; it's based on the item name. Still, you can change the subject, if you want.

4. **Click Send.**

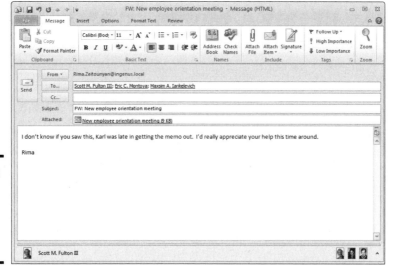

Figure 3-10:
Hold
the salt,
pass the
Calendar
item.

When your friend or colleague receives your package, he or she has a few options:

✦ **To simply view the Calendar item:** When he or she opens the attachment (by double-clicking its name at the top of the message in either the Reading pane or the message form), the familiar appointment, meeting, or event form appears, only if you check the title bar, you'll see that the item is marked Read-Only.

✦ **To add the appointment, meeting, or event to his or her Outlook Calendar:** Regardless of whether it's in Outlook or iCalendar format, the recipient should open the attachment, and click the Copy to My Calendar button on the Appointment/Meeting tab. The item is added to the main Calendar immediately.

✦ **To add the appointment, meeting, or event in iCalendar format to a calendar program that supports iCalendar format:** The recipient should first save the iCalendar file to his or her computer, and then import the file into that calendar program. If the calendar program happens to be Outlook (and the sender didn't know so he/she used iCalendar format), then to add the iCalendar item to Outlook, the recipient should open the item (by double-clicking its name at the top of the message in either the Reading pane or the message form) and click Save &Close on the Appointment/Meeting tab. The item is added to the main Calendar immediately.

**Book IV
Chapter 3**

**Calendar
Collaboration**

Sharing a Calendar via E-Mail

You can share your calendar by using Outlook in so many ways that, after a while, you start to think there can't be anybody anywhere who doesn't know you have a doctor's appointment tomorrow and that your boss is giving you a performance review on Friday. However, if you're not on an Exchange network (where you could share your calendar by simply granting someone permission), or if your friends or colleagues don't use Outlook or an iCalendar-compatible program (and thus, you can't forward an appointment, meeting, or event to them using the Forward command described in the preceding section), then sharing your calendar may have seemed a dream, based on what you've learned so far in this chapter.

Even so, you're not out of options yet. As you learn later in the upcoming sections, "Publishing a Calendar to Microsoft Office Online" and "Sharing a Calendar Through Google," you can share your calendar by publishing it online, but perhaps (even with the security measures in place) you don't feel comfortable with that. Well, you are still not out of options: you can share your calendar by using regular e-mail. The e-mail message itself contains the calendar data, in HTML format, so your recipient needs to be able to handle HTML (almost every e-mail program today handles HTML easily, but some people turn that option off). The procedure here might be a good one to try if you want to send your calendar to a cell phone, since Internet-capable cell phones should have no problem with HTML.

The calendar data is also attached to the e-mail in a pretty universal format called iCalendar. You learn how to forward a single appointment/meeting/ or event in iCalendar format using the Forward command described in the previous section; here, you are forwarding a larger portion of your calendar (even the entire thing if you want).

To share a calendar via e-mail, follow these steps:

1. **In Calendar, select the calendar that you want to share from the Navigation pane.**

2. **Click the E-Mail Calendar button on the Home tab.**

   The Send a Calendar via E-Mail dialog box appears, as shown in Figure 3-11.

3. **Select the portion of the calendar that you want to share from the Date Range drop-down list.**

   You can select Today, Tomorrow, Next 7 days, Next 30 days, or Whole Calendar. If you want to specify a unique portion of the calendar to share, first select Specify Dates from the Date Range drop-down list and then enter a Start and End date in the drop-down Start and End lists that appear.

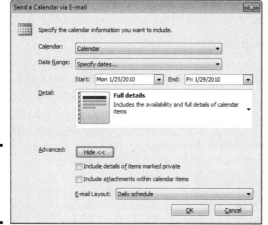

If you select a large portion of your calendar to include, the e-mail message that you create may be so large Outlook has difficulty sending it. Another way in which you might want to share a calendar is online. See the following sections for how to post your Outlook calendar on the Web.

4. **From the Detail drop-down list, select the amount of detail that you want to include in the e-mail.**

You have these options:

- *Availability Only:* Shows only your Free/Busy status. In addition, to limit the detail to your working hours only, select the Show Time within My Working Hours Only option.

- *Limited Details:* Shows Free/Busy and Subject information.

- *Full Details:* Includes basically everything.

5. **Click Show to display the advanced options in the bottom of the dialog box.**

6. **Select the options you want.**

You have these options:

- *To include details from private appointments, meetings, or events:* First, you must set the Detail level to either Limited Details or Full Details, and then select the Include Details of Items Marked Private check box.

- *To include any attachments to the included items:* First you must set Detail level to Full Details, and then select the Include Attachments within Calendar Items check box.

7. **From the E-Mail Layout drop-down list, select a format for your calendar.**

   You can choose from these options:

   - *Daily Schedule:* Includes a mini calendar at the top that features links to each day's details. Each day includes the entire schedule, including free periods, which are marked as Free in the calendar included in the e-mail message.

   - *List of Events:* Includes a mini calendar at the top that features links to each day's details. Each day includes only the time periods in which you have some item scheduled.

8. **Click OK.**

   The detail for the portion of the calendar that you selected appears in the e-mail message, as shown in Figure 3-12. In addition, an iCalendar format file is created and attached to the e-mail.

9. **Enter the addresses of the people you want to send your calendar to in the To text box of the message form.**

10. **(Optional) Type a message in the large text box, above the calendar text.**

11. **Click Send to send the e-mail.**

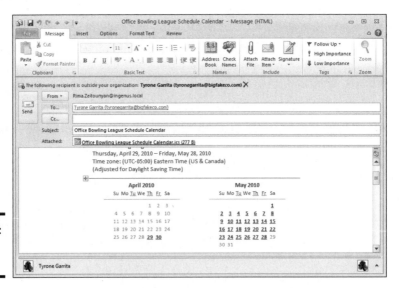

Figure 3-12:
Here's my
calendar.

Okay, you're still not out of options if your contact uses only text-based e-mail, not HTML. Instead of sending the calendar information in HTML format, you can send the details of individual appointments as text: Start an e-mail message and click the Other Outlook Item button on the message form's Insert tab. Select Calendar from the Look In list at the top of the dialog box, and then select the calendar item that you want to share from those listed in the Items list. Before you click OK, however, be sure to select the Text Only option. The calendar item's details are copied into the message as text.

Publishing a Calendar to Microsoft Office Online

Just about everyone can easily access the Internet, which makes it a good place to share a calendar with a large group of diverse people. The only thing that might give you pause is the idea that although you want to be able to share your calendar with your friends, you don't want to share it with *the world.* With Microsoft Office Online, you don't have to make your calendar public — you can keep it private, if you want.

You might also wonder how to keep your online calendar up-to-date. But Outlook can synchronize the online calendar with any changes you make, without bothering you at all.

To complete this procedure, you need to sign up for a free Windows Live account. If you already have one, great — pass Go! and collect your $200.

If you follow the basic steps in this section but select WebDAV Server from the Publish Online pop-up menu, you can publish your calendar to a Web server with perhaps more privacy, such as a company Web site. The dialog box that appears when you select WebDAV Server from the pop-up menu is similar to the one shown in Figure 3-13, except that it provides a space for you to type the Web address of the server to which you want to publish.

To publish your calendar online, follow these steps:

1. **In Calendar, select a calendar to publish from those listed in the Navigation pane.**

2. **Click the Publish Online button on the Home tab and select Publish to Office.com from the pop-up menu that appears.**

The Publish Calendar to Office.com dialog box pops up, as shown in Figure 3-13.

3. **Specify what you want to include in your online calendar.**

Select options that determine how much you want to share:

**Book IV
Chapter 3**

**Calendar
Collaboration**

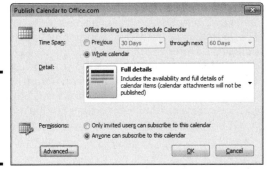

Figure 3-13:
How much
detail do
you want to
share?

- *To set the date range that's included:* Select either the Previous *Number of* Days through Next *Number of* Days or the Whole Calendar radio button. If you select the first option, then set the date range by selecting numbers of days from the two drop-down lists. For example, select Previous 30 Days through Next 60 Days.

- *To set the level of detail:* Select an option from the Detail list: Availability Only, which only shows your Free/Busy status; Limited Details, which shows Free/Busy and Subject information; or Full Details, which includes basically everything. In addition, if you select Availability Only, you can limit the detail to your working hours only by selecting the Show Time within My Working Hours Only option.

4. Determine who can see your calendar by selecting an option from the Permissions section.

You have these options:

- *To allow only selected users to view the calendar:* Select the Only Invited Users Can Subscribe to This Calendar radio button.

- *To allow anyone who searches for your calendar to view it:* Select the Anyone Can Subscribe to This Calendar radio button.

5. If you want to set advanced options, click Advanced.

The Published Calendar Settings dialog box appears, as shown in Figure 3-14.

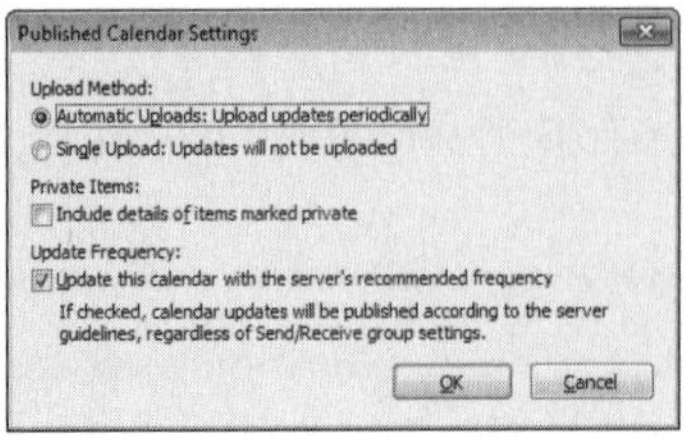

Figure 3-14:
Set some
advanced
options.

6. **Set the options that you want.**

   The advanced options allow you to

   - *Have the online calendar updated automatically.* Select the Automatic Uploads radio button. Then, select the Update this Calendar with the Server's Recommended Frequency check box to let Microsoft determine how often to update the calendar.

   - *Never update the calendar.* Select the Single Upload radio button.

   - *Include details for any private items.* Select the Include Details of Items Marked Private check box.

7. **After you set all your options in the Published Calendar Settings dialog box, click OK.**

   The Publish Calendar to Office.com dialog box reappears.

8. **Click OK to actually publish the calendar.**

   A confirmation dialog box appears, saying that the calendar was published correctly. Whether or not you choose to share calendars with only selected people in Step 4, you're asked whether you want to send the invitations right now to your friends and colleagues.

   If you do not choose to send invitations right now, you can do so later by selecting the published calendar in the Navigation pane, clicking the Publish Online button on the Home tab, and selecting Share Published Calendar from the pop-up menu.

9. **Click Yes.**

   A message form appears so you can send sharing invitations, as shown in Figure 3-15.

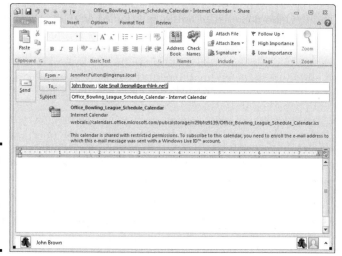

Figure 3-15: Be sure to e-mail your online-calendar invitations.

10. **In the To box, type the addresses of the people you want to invite.**

11. **(Optional) Type a message in the large text box, while you're at it.**

12. **Click Send to send the sharing invitation.**

When you send a sharing invitation, the recipient clicks the Subscribe to This Calendar button, located at the top of the Reading pane or on the Home tab of the message (it it's open), to add this calendar to his or her Other Calendars list, which is then updated along with other subscriptions (such as RSS news feeds and Internet calendars). With this option, the user can view the calendar right in his or her Outlook Calendar. See Book III, Chapter 3, and Chapter 5 of this minibook for more information on RSS feeds and Internet calendars.

Recipients of your invitation need to log on to Office.com to preview or subscribe to your calendar. They will be walked through the process when they accept your invitation to subscribe. Your calendars are published to calendars.office.microsoft.com, through its calendar sharing service. To remove a calendar from sharing, select it in the Navigation pane, click the Publish Online button on the Home tab, and select Remove From Server.

Sharing a Calendar through Google

For a lot of people, the Internet is synonymous with Google. If you've seen something interesting on the Internet lately, you've probably *googled* it (meaning you searched for it online by using the Google search engine). So, if you have a calendar that you want to share with the general Internet community, Google seems as good a place as any to do it. For example, maybe you compiled a calendar that lists the football and basketball games for your old high school. Put it online and update it with final scores every once in a while so that your old alums can easily keep up with the Fighting Tigers.

By using Outlook, you can export a calendar to Google and share it on Google Calendar. You can also import somebody else's Google Calendar and have it automatically updated or not — your choice. Keep in mind that you have to have a Google account to view and share Google calendars — but the registration is free and painless.

Exporting one of your calendars to Google Calendar

If you design a calendar that you want to share with other Google Calendar users, you can easily upload it from Outlook. Along the way, you get to choose whether to include certain details. Just follow these steps:

1. **In Calendar, select the calendar that you want to share from the Navigation pane.**

2. **Click the File tab to display Backstage and then select Save Calendar from the list on the left.**

   Your standard-looking Save As dialog box appears, as shown in the background of Figure 3-16. You're creating an iCalendar format file, and that option is already selected for you from the Save as Type drop-down list.

3. **Type a name for the file in the File Name box.**

4. **Click the More Options button.**

   Another Save As dialog box pops up (I'll call it Save As Jr.), as shown in the foreground of Figure 3-16.

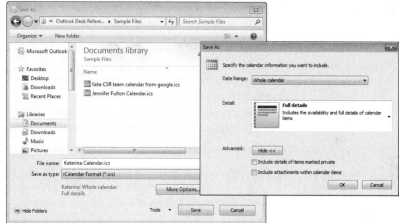

Figure 3-16: Set limits for the exported calendar in the Save As dialog boxes.

5. **Select options that determine how much you want to share.**

   You can make these specifications:

   - *To set the date range that's included:* Select either Whole Calendar or Previous *Number of* Days through Next *Number of* Days from the Date Range drop-down list. If you select the latter option, then set the date range by selecting numbers of days from the two drop-down lists that appear. For example, select Previous 30 Days through Next 60 Days.

   - *To set the level of detail:* Select an option from the Detail list. You can choose Availability Only, which shows only your Free/Busy status; Limited Details, which shows Free/Busy and Subject information; or Full Details, which includes basically everything. In addition, if you select Availability Only, you can limit the detail to your working hours only by selecting the Show Time within My Working Hours Only option.

6. **Click Show.**

   The Advanced settings appear. (Refer to Figure 3-16.)

**Book IV
Chapter 3**

**Calendar
Collaboration**

7. **Set the options that you want.**

   You can set these options:

   - *To include details for any private items:* Set Detail to either Limited Details or Full Details, and then select the Include Details of Items Marked Private check box.

   - *To include attachments:* Set Detail to Full Details, and then select the Include Attachments within Calendar Items check box.

8. **After you set all your options in the Save As Jr. dialog box, click OK to return to the Save As Sr. dialog box.**

9. **Click Save to save the calendar in iCalendar format.**

10. **Point your Web browser to** `http://calendar.google.com` **and log on to Google by using your account info.**

    If you haven't signed up yet for a Google account, a link appears on calendar.google.com. Click it to have Google guide you through the signup process. After you sign up and log onto Google Calendar, continue on to Step 11.

11. **Click the Create link in the My Calendars section over there on the left of the main Google Calendars account page.**

    A Calendar Details tab appears, like the one shown in Figure 3-17.

    Yep, you heard right. You import your iCalendar file into an existing Google calendar. So, you want to create a new Google calendar to act as the receiver of all that iCalendar data.

12. **Type a calendar name, description, and location in the appropriate text boxes.**

13. **From the drop-down lists, select the country that applies. Select a specific time zone that applies or select the Display All Time Zones check box.**

14. **Specify with whom you want to share this calendar.**

    You can allow any Google Calendar user to view your calendar, or you can restrict access to specific people:

    - *To allow anyone to see your calendar and all its details:* Select the Make This Calendar Public check box.

    - *If you make this calendar public, then to allow anyone who sees your calendar to view only the Free/Busy information:* Select the Share Only My Free/Busy Information check box.

    - *To restrict access to the calendar to a select few:* Type someone's e-mail address in the Person text box and select a level of access from the Permission Settings drop-down list. Click Add Person to add the user. Repeat this process to add each person with whom you want to share the calendar.

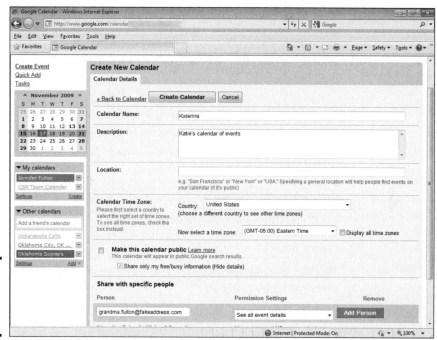

Figure 3-17:
Create a
new Google
calendar.

15. **Click Create Calendar.**

If you chose to make your calendar public, you see a dialog box asking to confirm that decision; click Yes to continue. The calendar is created and added to your list of calendars on the left side of your Google Calendar page.

If you added a specific user to your permissions list and that user doesn't currently have a Google Calendar account, Google prompts you to send him or her an invitation. Click Invite.

16. **Click the Settings link at the top of the page, on the right-hand side.**

The Calendar Settings page appears.

17. **On the Calendar Settings page, click the Calendars tab and click the Import Calendar link at the bottom of the page.**

The Import Calendar dialog box appears, as shown in Figure 3-18.

Figure 3-18:
Import your
calendar
into Google
Calendars.

18. **Click Browse.**

The Choose File to Upload dialog box opens.

19. **Navigate to the folder that holds your iCalendar file, then select the file and click Open.**

The Import Calendar dialog box reappears.

20. **From the Calendar drop-down list, select a Google calendar into which you want this calendar data imported.**

Select the blank, empty calendar you just created in Step 15.

21. **Click Import.**

Your calendar is imported into Google Calendar. The Import Calendar dialog box appears, telling you how many events (items) were imported successfully.

22. **Click Close.**

The Import Calendar dialog box disappears and the main Google Calendar page is displayed.

Keep in mind that your Google calendar is static; if you make changes to the one in Outlook, those changes aren't updated automatically to Google. Instead, you need to repeat these steps to create an updated iCalendar file and upload it.

The calendar appears in Google Calendar similarly to how calendars appear in Outlook. Appointments appear as rectangles that block out the time associated with that item; daily events appear in a band across the top, as shown in Figure 3-19.

Importing a Google calendar

When you invite a Google calendar into your Outlook home, you can choose to let it sit quietly and never get updated, or you can let it jump up and down, run around, and change itself as often as the online copy gets changed.

To import a Google calendar so that it updates whenever its online copy changes, you need to subscribe to it. See the following section for how to subscribe.

To copy a static, non-changing Google calendar to Outlook, follow these steps:

Event

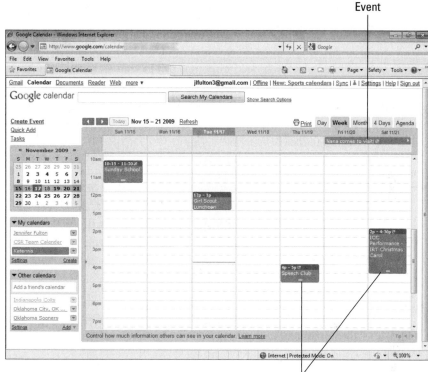

Figure 3-19:
Here's your
new Google
calendar,
for all the
world to see
(or not).

Appointments appear as time blocks

1. **Point your Web browser to** `http://calendar.google.com` **and log on to Google Calendar by using your account info.**

2. **Click the arrow to the right of the calendar's name, and then select Calendar Settings from the drop-down list that appears.**

The Calendar Details tab appears for the chosen calendar.

You can perform this task only with calendars listed in the My Calendars section of your Google Calendar page.

3. **Click the ICAL button in the Private Address section, located at the bottom of the Calendar Details page.**

4. **When the Private Address dialog box jumps out at you, click the Internet address for the calendar that appears as a link. (See the bottom part of Figure 3-20.)**

The iCalendar file is located, and a dialog box appears (refer to the foreground of Figure 3-20), asking what you want to do with that file.

REMEMBER

Book IV
Chapter 3

Calendar
Collaboration

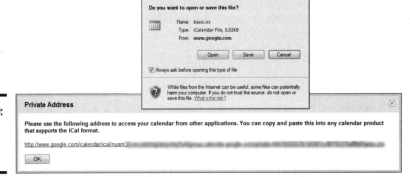

5. Click Open to import the calendar into Outlook.

The calendar is snuggled next to the currently open calendar, in a side-by-side view. The Google calendar is added to the Other Calendars list, where you can switch back to it anytime you want by selecting it in the Navigation pane.

If you want to update your calendar at some later time, you need to repeat these steps to import it again.

Subscribing to a Google calendar

Sometimes, the people who share calendars come back and actually update them. Of course, you have no idea going in whether the guy who posted the Bergersville Cloggers dance schedule is ever going to return and add more dates, but that's a chance a true fan has to take.

To subscribe to a Google calendar so that it updates automatically, follow these steps:

1. In your Web browser, go to `http://calendar.google.com` **and log on to Google Calendar by using your account info.**

2. Click the arrow to the right of the calendar's name and select Calendar Settings from the drop-down list that appears.

The Calendar Details tab appears for the chosen calendar.

You can perform this task only with calendars listed in the My Calendars section of your Google Calendar page.

3. Click the ICAL button in the Private Address section, located at the bottom of the Calendar Details page.

The Private Address dialog box jumps out at you. (Refer to Figure 3-20.)

4. **Right-click the Internet address for the calendar and select Copy Shortcut from the pop-up menu that appears to copy that address to the Clipboard.**

Don't go clicking that calendar address link, as tempting as it might seem. If you do, you create a static, non-changing calendar in Outlook, rather than the self-basting-and-automatically-updating one you're hoping to create.

5. **In Outlook, click the Open Calendar button on the Home tab and select From Internet from the pop-up menu that appears.**

The New Internet Calendar Subscription dialog box pops up.

6. **Right-click in the Enter the Location of the Internet Calendar You Want to Add to Outlook text box and select Paste from the pop-up menu that appears to paste in the calendar address that you copied to the Clipboard, and then click OK.**

The Microsoft Outlook dialog pops up, asking you to confirm your subscription to this calendar. Before clicking Yes, however, you might want to check out some options.

7. **Click Advanced to configure your calendar subscription.**

The Subscription Options dialog box, shown in Figure 3-21, appears.

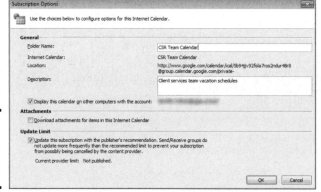

Figure 3-21:
Complete your subscription.

8. **Edit the name that appears in the Folder Name text box to match how you want it to appear in Outlook.**

9. **Set other options, if you want.**

You can type a description for the calendar in the Description text box. You can also set these options:

- *Display this calendar on other computers with this same account:* If you are on an Exchange network, you can have this calendar stored on the Exchange server with your other calendars, so you can display its contents anytime you log in to your company network regardless of which computer you use to do so (such as your home computer). Simply select the Display This Calendar on Other Computers With the Account check box.

- *To download any attachments:* Select the Download Attachments for Items in This Internet Calendar check box.

- *To update the calendar regularly:* Select the Update This Subscription with the Publisher's Recommendation check box.

10. Click OK to return to the Microsoft Outlook dialog box.

11. Click Yes to subscribe to the calendar.

The calendar is added to the Other Calendars list, and displayed side-by-side with any other open calendars. To hide/view the calendar, click its check box.

Periodically, Outlook checks the calendar online to see whether any changes have been made, and if it finds changes, it imports those changes into your copy of the calendar automatically.

Chapter 4: All About Meetings

In This Chapter

✓ **Finding the best time for a meeting**

✓ **Changing or cancelling a meeting**

✓ **Inviting people to a meeting**

✓ **Dealing with meeting requests when they come in**

✓ **Handling meeting invitation responses painlessly**

✓ **Enabling a meeting room to have its own meeting schedule**

*I*n Outlook, a *meeting* is an appointment that takes place between you and somebody else at your company — at least, most of the time. The main difference in Outlook between creating an appointment and creating a meeting is that with a meeting, e-mail requests to attend the meeting automatically go out when you create it. With Outlook, you can schedule meetings with people within and outside your organization. However, the true power of creating meetings with Outlook only comes alive when you involve just the people in your company.

Assuming that you work on an Exchange network, prior to creating a meeting and sending the invitations to attend, you can quickly scan people's Free/Busy time on their calendars and select a meeting time that you know is open. That way, Rene can't claim that she has an appointment she can't cancel, just so she can get out of that boring planning meeting on Friday. And Marcus can't slide out of the quarterly budget meeting on the flimsy excuse of being too busy with that new Hardwick account, when his calendar actually shows the exact opposite. In addition, on an Exchange network, you can schedule company resources needed for the meeting at the same time that you enter meeting details — resources such as the meeting room or any multimedia equipment.

So, if you're on an Exchange network, you can be sure that the meeting is pretty well set up before you even send the meeting invitations. For non-Exchange users, you can use the Meeting feature to easily send invitations for the meeting to everyone who's invited, as well as track the replies. This chapter gives you the rundown on how to get it all done.

Scheduling a Meeting

Creating a meeting when you work on an Exchange network has all sorts of benefits. You can peek at your colleague's schedules to find a time when most people can attend. You can also grab a meeting room, the cool new data projector, and a digital whiteboard. If you're not on an Exchange network, you can still schedule a meeting because meeting invitations are sent by using regular e-mail. But you can't know in advance whether the time you've selected works for everyone involved. And you have to let your legs, rather than your fingers, do the walking down to the receptionist's desk to schedule that meeting room you need.

Scheduling a meeting on an Exchange network

If you want to quickly schedule a meeting with someone whose calendar you're currently viewing (because he or she shared it with you, as covered in Chapter 3 of this minibook), change to the Calendar module, click the New Meeting button on the Home tab, and select New Meeting with All from the pop-up menu that appears. A meeting request is created from any shared calendars that you're currently displaying. Yep, it's not enough that some-one has shared his or her calendar with you, and that you have to load it into Outlook; you also have to be displaying that calendar. By the way, the new Schedule view is just perfect for displaying all the calendars for the members of your team because it shows them in a timeline, which allows you to quickly see when everyone might be available. See Chapter 1 of this minibook for more info.

If you're sharing several of your colleagues' calendars, you can collect them together in a group schedule. With a group schedule, you can quickly create a meeting and invite the members of the group. See Chapter 3 of this mini-book for the lowdown on group schedules.

To schedule a meeting in the regular (quick, but not super quick) way, follow these steps:

1. **Click the New Items button on the Home tab and select Meeting from the pop-up menu that appears.**

   If you happen to be in Calendar, you can also click the New Meeting button on the Home tab, instead. In either case, the same thing results: A new Meeting form appears, as shown in Figure 4-1.

   If you're in Mail, you don't need to jump over to Calendar to schedule a meeting. Granted, Step 1 here says you can always click the New Items button, but there's an even easier way, if you happen to be viewing an e-mail from the person you now want to have a meeting with: Just hover the mouse pointer over the sender's name to display the Contact Card.

Click the View More Options button (it's on the right, and it looks like a menu that's been shrunken) and select Schedule a Meeting from the pop-up menu that appears.

REMEMBER

Back at the Meeting window now: You may have noticed the Appointment button is highlighted on the Meeting tab the moment it comes up on your screen. So, what's up? Is this a meeting or not? Well, the information for a meeting in Outlook is divided into two sections: the general appointment-like info (such as date, time, and location) and the meeting info (such as invitees and meeting resources). To access the general appointment info for a meeting, you click the Appointment button on the Meeting tab to see the data that's shown in Figure 4-1. Outlook is pretty good at suggesting a meeting time that works for all participants, but if you want to examine the individual schedules of the people invited to a particular meeting, click the Scheduling Assistant button.

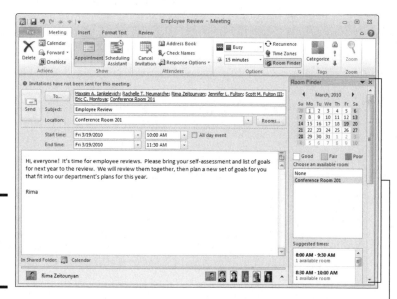

Figure 4-1:
Arrange a meeting through Outlook.

Room Finder panel

Book IV
Chapter 4

All About Meetings

2. **In the To box, enter the people you want to invite.**

You can add people in several ways:

- Type all or part of a person's name and let Outlook suggest an e-mail address, based on addresses you've typed before or added to Contacts.

- Type a complete e-mail address.

- Click the To button to display the Address Book, select someone, and click either Required or Optional (depending on whether that person must attend).

Repeat this step (whichever method you use) to add more invitees. Outlook looks up the schedules of the people you've invited and displays several workable meeting times in the Room Finder pane, under Suggested Times. (Refer to Figure 4-1.)

You can invite people who aren't on your Exchange network; you just can't see their schedules, so you can't figure out what meeting time will work for them without asking them personally.

If you've managed to invite someone to your meeting who has restricted Exchange network access or an invalid e-mail address, Outlook shows you the error of your ways by displaying an appropriately worded MailTip at the top of the meeting request.

3. **Click in the Subject text box and type a description for the meeting, such as** PhotoFinder 2.0 Planning Meeting.

4. **Click the Scheduling Assistant button on the Meeting tab.**

The Scheduling Assistant page of the Message form appears, as shown in Figure 4-2. If you want to return to the Appointment page at any time during this process, just give that Appointment button on the Meeting tab a click.

5. **Select a Start date and time from the Start Time drop-down lists, and select an End date and time from the End Time drop-down lists.**

Here's how to decipher what the Scheduling Assistant is trying to tell you:

- *Bands of color indicate meetings, appointments, or events that are already scheduled.* The colors of these bands have meaning as well: Blue means busy, striped means maybe busy, while purple means out of the office and therefore not available at all.

- *The green and red vertical bands mark the Start and End times for your meeting.* These bands extend downward through all the calendars, so you can visualize where your meeting fits into everyone's schedule.

6. **Book a conference room by clicking the Add Rooms button, selecting a room from the Select Rooms dialog box that appears, and clicking the Rooms button.**

Click OK to return to the meeting form. You can also schedule a room in Step 2 when you are adding invitees, although it makes more sense to me to book a room once you've settled on a time for your meeting. Anyway, from the Appointment page of the Message form shown in

Figure 4-1, click the Rooms button, select a room in the Select Rooms dialog box that appears, click the Rooms button to add the room you've chosen, then click OK to return to the Message form. If you want to schedule a room you've used recently, open the Location drop-down list and make a selection.

Figure 4-2: What time is convenient for you?

Another way to book a conference room is to use the Room Finder, shown on the right on either the Appointment or Scheduling Assistant page of the Message form. If it's hiding, click the Room Finder button on the Meeting tab to display it. Here's how to use the Room Finder:

- *The colors on the Date Navigator at the top of the pane indicate which days work best when trying to book a room.* White days are good for the majority of the conference rooms, but light blue days are only fair to partly cloudy. Dark blue days indicate that you may have real trouble finding a place to hold your meeting. Using the date you selected in Step 5, information is already displayed for you on the Room Finder pane. If that day is blue (indicating that not a lot of conference rooms are available), select a different day from the Date Navigator by clicking it.

- *After selecting a day, Outlook lists the best times to meet in the Suggested Times section of the pane.* The Room Finder pane lists the number of open conference rooms just below each suggested time slot. To select one of these times, simply click it.

**Book IV
Chapter 4**

All About Meetings

- *After selecting a time slot, available conference rooms appear in the Choose an Available Room list.* To choose an available conference room, select one from the Choose an Available Room list.

It may seem silly to invite a meeting room to your party, but with Exchange, meeting rooms and other resources (such as projectors, sound equipment, screens, and so on) have e-mail addresses and calendars, just like you do. Therefore, you can check their schedules, and then book the room or resource for your meeting. The meeting request gets sent to the resource in the same way that it gets sent to each invitee, and Exchange automatically processes it and adds it to the calendar. Pretty cool, don't you think? Now, if only all your employees would greet your meeting requests so cheerfully.

7. **To book other resources, such as a projector, click the Appointment button on the Meeting tab to return to the text of the invitation. Then click the To button, select the resource from the list in the Select Attendees and Resources: Global Address List dialog box, and click the Resources button. Click OK to continue.**

8. **In the big, blank message area in the center, type a message or describe the meeting further.**

9. **To attach a separate document such as an agenda, click the Attach File button on the Insert tab, select the file from the Insert File dialog box, and then click Insert.**

10. **Click the Categorize button on the Meeting tab and select a category from the list that appears.**

11. **To have Outlook signal you, and everyone else in the meeting, when it's time to think about going, set a reminder time from the Reminder list on the Meeting tab.**

12. **If you want to make the meeting recur every so often — for instance, at the same time every week — click the Recurrence button on the Meeting tab, and in the Appointment Recurrence dialog box set a recurrence pattern (daily, weekly, every other Tuesday, etc.).**

You can set an option to prevent attendees from proposing a time change for the meeting. See the section "Preventing time change proposals for a meeting request," later in this chapter. You can also prevent them from responding at all and overwhelming you with too many e-mails. Of course, if you prevent responses, you don't get a summary of who's coming and who's not, but if it's a really big meeting, you may not even want to deal with that detail. See the section "Preventing replies for a meeting request," later in this chapter.

If you frequently find yourself setting up a meeting with whomever it is who's sent you an e-mail, you can create a Quick Step for generating a meeting with the sender(s) of your open e-mail automatically. See Book I, Chapter 2 for help with the Quick Step feature.

If you use OneNote, you can create an instant page in a OneNote note-book where you can gather information about the meeting by clicking the OneNote button on the Meeting tab. See Book VI, Chapter 5 for help.

13. Click Send to send the invitations.

Outlook calls these invitations *meeting requests*. No matter what you call them, they're essentially e-mail messages.

Right away, the meeting is added to your calendar. After each attendee receives the meeting request, he or she can either accept, decline, or propose a different meeting time (assuming that you've allowed that option). See the section "Checking on Meeting Responses," later in this chapter, for help in processing these return e-mails. You, in the meantime, can't do much except catch a movie, do some Internet surfing, and — oh yeah — prepare for the meeting.

Scheduling a meeting when you don't use Exchange

As it turns out, you don't need to work on an Exchange network to send meeting requests. The process is very similar to creating an appointment, but with a twist: When you're done, meeting requests go out to each invitee, and your recipients can then respond by accepting or declining.

To schedule a meeting without using Exchange, follow these steps:

1. Click the New Items button on the Home tab and select Meeting from the pop-up menu that appears.

If you happen to be in Calendar, you can also click the New Meeting button on the Home tab, instead. A new Meeting form appears, as shown in Figure 4-3.

2. Enter the people you want to invite in the To text box.

Here are your options:

- Type all or part of a person's name and let Outlook suggest an e-mail address, based on addresses you've typed before or added to Contacts.

- Type an e-mail address.

- Click the To button to display the Address Book. Select someone, and click either Required or Optional, depending on whether that person must attend.

Repeat this step (whichever method you use) to add more invitees.

3. Click in the Subject text box and type a description for the meeting, such as Employee Orientation Meeting.

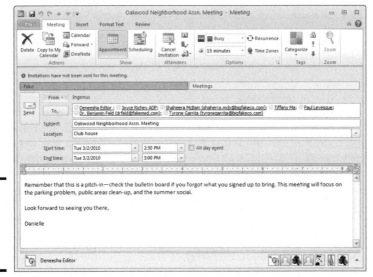

4. **Select a Start date and time from the drop-down lists to the right of Start Time, and select an End date and time from the drop-down lists to the right of End Time.**

If you want to consult your calendar before selecting a time, click the Calendar button on the message form's Meeting tab, in the Actions group, to open your calendar in a separate window, displaying in Day view the date you chose. You can also click the Scheduling button on the Meeting tab to view your schedule, but unlike the Scheduling Assistant discussed in the previous section, don't expect to see anybody else's calendar.

5. **Type a location in the Location text box.**

To choose a location you've used before, click the arrow to the right of the Location text box to open the Location drop-down list and make a selection.

6. **In the message area in the center of the form, type a message or describe the meeting further.**

7. **If you want to attach a separate document such as an agenda, click the Attach File button on the Insert tab, select its file from the Insert File dialog box, and click Insert.**

8. **On the Meeting tab, select a category from the Categorize list (something that will color-code the meeting when it appears on people's calendars).**

9. **To have Outlook signal everyone in the meeting when it's nearly time to start or time to go, set a reminder time from the Reminders list on the Meeting tab.**

10. **If you want to make the meeting recur every so often — for instance, at the same time every week — click the Recurrence button on the Meeting tab, and in the Appointment Recurrence dialog box set a recurrence pattern.**

You can prevent attendees from proposing a time change for the meeting, as spelled out in the "Preventing time change proposals for a meeting request" section, later in this chapter. You can also prevent them from responding at all so that you don't become overwhelmed with too many e-mails. Of course, preventing responses means that you can't view a summary of whose coming and whose not, but if you're having a really big meeting, you may not want to deal with that detail, anyway. See the section "Preventing replies for a meeting request," later in this chapter.

If you use OneNote, you can create an instant page in a OneNote notebook where you can gather information about the meeting by clicking the OneNote button on the Meeting tab. See Book VI, Chapter 5 for help.

11. **Click Send to send the invitations.**

The meeting requests are sent as e-mail messages to each attendee, and the meeting is added to your calendar. After each attendee receives the meeting request, he or she can either accept, decline, or tentatively accept (assuming the recipient uses Outlook). If the recipient doesn't use Outlook, he or she gets the message but can't see the Accept, Decline, or Tentative buttons. Outlook users, on the other hand, can even propose a different meeting time. (See the section "Dealing with Meeting Requests," later in this chapter.) You, in the meantime, have the wonderful job of simply waiting — and maybe snacking on some chocolate.

Changing a Meeting

Even before you get any replies, you can make changes to a meeting, and Outlook kindly lets everyone know how forgetful you are. For example, you may have forgotten to set a reminder, invite a particular attendee, mark the meeting private so that it doesn't show up on your shared calendar (only the people you invited know about it), or make a meeting recurring. No matter what you need to change, you can easily make the necessary changes and leave the updating thing to Outlook. After all, you're busy planning meetings. . .

To change a meeting, follow these steps:

1. **In your calendar, click the meeting to select it.**

The Calendar Tools Meeting tab appears, as shown in Figure 4-4. If the meeting is a recurring one, select either the Open This Occurrence (to change just this occurrence of the meeting) or the Open the Series radio button (to change all occurrences) from the dialog box that appears, then click OK.

2. **Make changes to an appointment that concerns only you.**

When the event you clicked on concerns just you, the tab that opens up automatically will be called Appointment (or Appointment Series if the event is recurring). Use the buttons on the Calendar Tools Appointment tab to make simple changes to events that other people in your office aren't part of. When you make the alterations described as follows, the attendees don't receive a change notice.

- *To change how the meeting appears in your schedule:* Select an option from the Show As drop-down list. This is to tell you (and the world) whether you're free or busy.

- *To set a reminder:* Select one from the Reminder drop-down list.

- *To mark an appointment as private:* Click the Private button.

- *To apply a category:* Select one from the Categorize drop-down list. See "Creating a Simple Appointment" in Chapter 2 of this minibook to review how you create an ordinary appointment for just yourself.

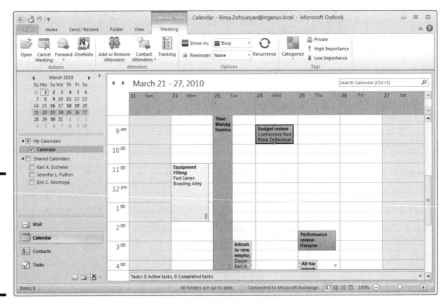

Figure 4-4:
You can change a meeting without messing things up.

3. **Make changes that affect your appearance in a meeting that someone else has organized to which you've been invited.**

   When the event you clicked on is something to which you've been invited — in other words, you're not the organizer — then the tab that opens up is called Meeting. You can use the buttons on the Calendar Tools Meeting tab to initiate the same kind of changes as for a personal appointment.

   Outlook will let you change the time of an event that someone else has organized, but that time will only apply to *you*. You won't change what everyone else sees. This way, for instance, you can set yourself up to arrive early or late, or to leave early. A dialog box will warn you that when you make a change like this, then if the meeting organizer makes his or her own change, you won't be notified because you did your own little adjustment. Click Yes if that's okay with you, or No to revert back to where the meeting was.

   Here are the easy ways you can change the time and duration of a meeting or appointment on the calendar:

   - *To change the date or start time of the meeting:* Just drag the meeting to a new location on your calendar.

   - *To change the length of a meeting:* Drag the meeting's lower edge downward.

   - *To make a meeting recur, or to change its recurrence:* Click the Recurrence button. Make the changes you want in the Recurrence dialog box that appears; see Chapter 2 of this minibook.

   - *To send a message asking the organizer to change a meeting's time:* On the Meeting tab, click the Propose New Time button, and from the pop-up that appears, select Decline and Propose New Time. To tell the organizer you will show up but you'd like to move the time anyway, select Tentative and Propose New Time.

4. **Make changes that may affect the times or locations that other people attend a meeting that you organized.**

   When you're the one who started this meeting in the first place, then Outlook can broadcast the changes you make to it, to everyone else you've already invited. They'll be notified that the meeting has changed, and they'll get an opportunity to accept or decline; their meeting won't just mysteriously float to a new spot on their calendars.

   - *To invite (or uninvite) someone:* Click the Add or Remove Attendees button on the Meeting tab. The Select Attendees and Resources dialog box pops up, as shown in Figure 4-5. Select someone and click Required or Optional to add him or her to the attendee's list. To remove someone, select his or her name in the Required or Optional list, and then press Delete. Click OK.

WARNING!

After you've moved around one of these meetings that you've organized, and you click outside the meeting box on the calendar to show that you're done making changes, Outlook shows you a dialog box asking whether it can send out an update. From here, you can either approve the changes and send the update to everyone else, or cancel the changes and start over. So the lesson here is, don't click outside the meeting box until you're sure it's where it needs to be.

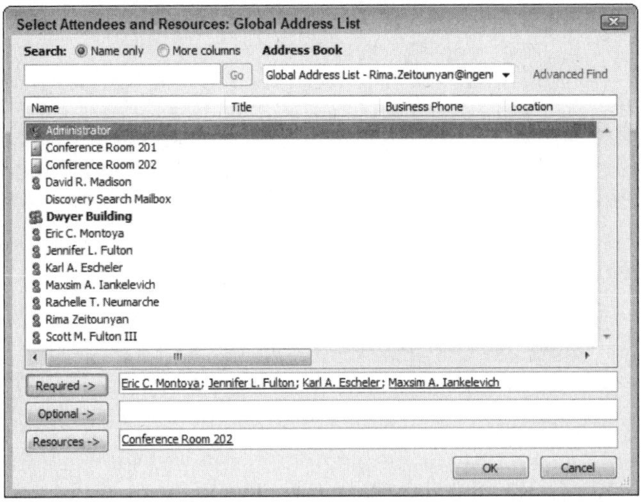

Figure 4-5:
You can invite someone to a meeting — and uninvite him or her just as easily.

5. **If you made changes that affect invitees in Step 4, confirm the change by clicking Save Changes and Send Update in the confirmation dialog box that appears.**

   To undo your change, click Don't Save Changes then click OK to continue.

   If you save the change, and other people are affected by this change, the Meeting form opens again, as shown in Figure 4-6.

6. **Review the change and make any other changes you want.**

   For example, you can type a message to let everyone know what was changed or why, or to apologize for the inconvenience. To remove an attendee, delete the person's name from the To text box. To add a last-minute attendee, click the To button, choose that person's name from the list, and click OK.

7. **Click Send Update.**

   If you haven't made any adjustments to the attendees list, then the message containing your explanation and proposed adjustments will be sent.

8. **If the attendees list has changed, then select whom to notify in the dialog box.**

   When you've been monkeying around with the attendees list, Outlook wants to know at this point, do you tell the uninvited people they've been axed? Do you tell the new folks they're expected?

   - *Send Updates Only to Added or Deleted Attendees:* Send e-mail notifications only to those people you invited (or uninvited) to the meeting in Step 4.

   - *Send Updates to All Attendees:* Notify every invitee of the change, regardless of whether they're original attendees, newly added invitees, or uninvited attendees.

9. **Click OK.**

   Your message of explanation is sent to those you've designated.

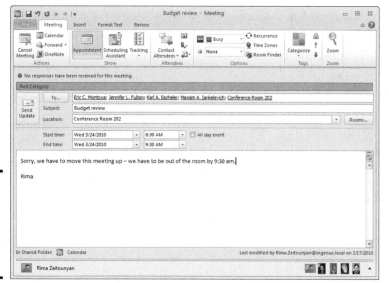

Figure 4-6:
Notify
everyone of
a change
you make to
a meeting.

Canceling a Meeting

It's hard to imagine right now, what with all that hard work you've put in creating the meeting, sending meeting invitations, and sharpening all those pencils, but there may come a time when you might actually have to cancel a meeting. Sigh. At least Outlook makes it easy for you to let everyone know the meeting's been cancelled.

To cancel a meeting, follow these steps:

1. **In your calendar, click the meeting to select it.**

   The Calendar Tools Meeting tab appears.

2. **Click the Cancel Meeting button on the Meeting tab.**

   If this is a recurring meeting, when you click the Cancel Meeting button, a pop-up menu appears. Select either Cancel Occurrence (to cancel this one meeting) or Cancel Series (to cancel all these meetings). The Meeting form appears. (See Figure 4-7.)

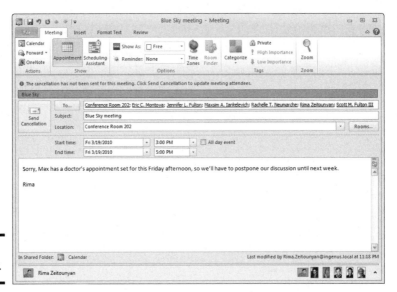

Figure 4-7: Cancel that.

3. **(Optional) If you want, type an explanation for the cancellation in the message area.**

   Even though you can't select this option, the cancellation is automatically marked High Priority, so hopefully your invitees will give it more than a passing glance when it ends up in their Inboxes.

4. **Click Send Cancellation.**

   The meeting is removed from your calendar. Meeting cancellation notices are sent to each attendee. When the attendee views the notice, he or she can click the Remove from Calendar button at the top of the Reading pane to remove the meeting from his or her calendar. (See Figure 4-8.) If the attendee opens the meeting, he or she can click the Remove from Calendar button on the Meeting tab instead.

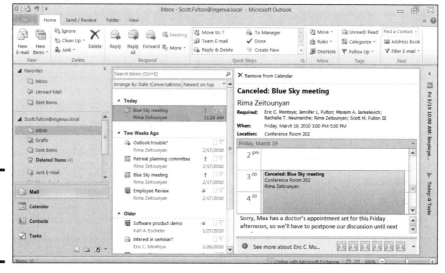

Figure 4-8:
Remove
a meeting
from your
calendar.

Sending a Message to All Attendees

Even if you haven't changed the meeting time or place, you may need to get a message to all attendees. For example, maybe you want to forward the meeting agenda so that they can review it before attending. Or perhaps you want to send directions to an out-of-office meeting venue. Because Outlook keeps track of who you've invited, you can easily get it to send out a message for you.

To send out a message to people attending one of your meetings, follow these steps:

1. **In your calendar, click the meeting to select it.**

   The Calendar Tools Meeting tab appears.

2. **Click the Contact Attendees button on the Meeting tab, and select New E-Mail to Attendees from the pop-up menu that appears.**

   A new message form appears, already self-addressed and stamped for you, as shown in Figure 4-9. People who have declined the meeting are still included in the list of addresses for some odd reason. Guess Outlook just doesn't feel good about leaving anyone out. The Subject shows the name of the meeting; you can change the subject, if you want.

   You can select Reply to All with E-mail from the Contact Attendees pop-up menu, instead, which creates a message form that includes the details of the meeting in the text area.

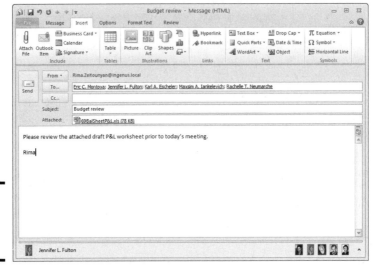

Figure 4-9:
Get the
message
out.

3. **Type your message in the message area.**

4. **Add any attachments you want.**

   For instance, to attach an Excel worksheet to the message, on the Insert tab under Include, click on Attach File (the little paper clip all by itself). Then from the dialog box, select the file(s) you want to attach and click Insert.

5. **Click Send.**

   Outlook sends out your message to all invitees.

Dealing with Meeting Requests

Just because you're busy, your colleagues won't stop asking for your help and advice. In fact, I venture to guess that your good work is one reason why you're so busy, in the first place. Given your busy schedule, you simply can't accept every request to attend a meeting. Luckily, you can choose whether to attend or decline a meeting request when it comes in. You can even propose a different meeting time that works better for you. And if you're really busy, you can automate your responses to meeting requests, rather than deal with them one at a time.

When a meeting request comes in, it appears as an e-mail message in your Inbox; Outlook assumes that you plan to accept the request, so it also places the meeting in your calendar. Until you formally respond, however, Outlook displays the meeting with dimmed text, with a "barber pole" left border, as shown in Figure 4-10.

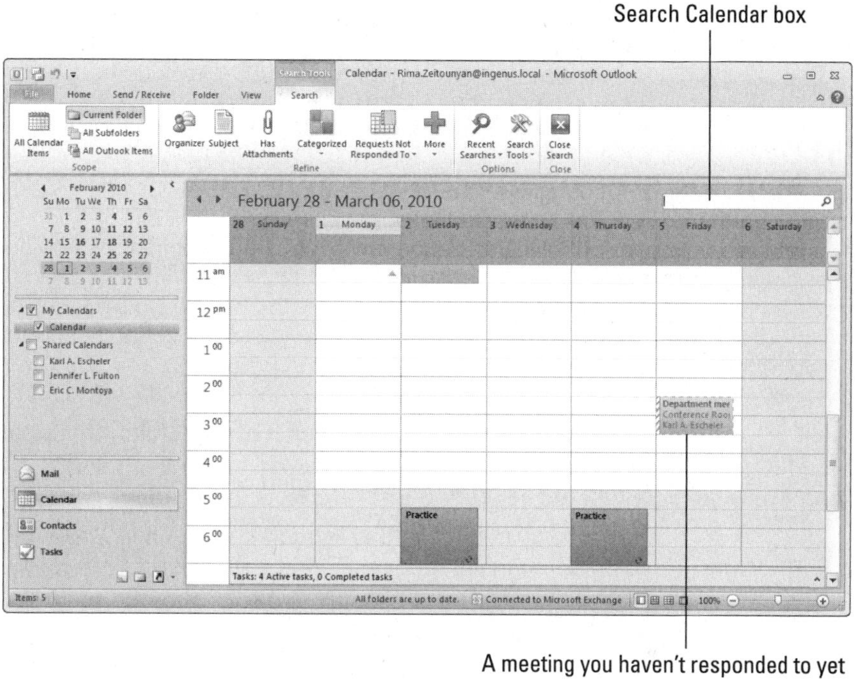

Search Calendar box

Figure 4-10:
Meetings whose invites you haven't responded to have dimmed text.

A meeting you haven't responded to yet

If you get a lot of e-mail, you can easily forget to respond to meeting requests, so they can pile up quickly. To easily display your meetings, follow these steps:

1. **In Calendar, at the top right corner of the window, click in the Search Calendar text box.**

The Search tab appears.

2. **Click the Requests Not Responded To button on the Search tab.**

3. **Select an option from the pop-up menu that appears.**

You have these options:

- *Accepted Appointments:* Displays meeting requests that you've responded to with an acceptance

- *Tentative Appointments:* Displays meeting requests that you've responded to tentatively

- *Requests Not Responded To:* Displays meeting requests to which you've not responded.

**Book IV
Chapter 4**

All About Meetings

A list of meetings matching your selection appears. To respond to any meeting you haven't responded to yet, or to change your response, click that meeting in the list and change to the Home tab. Now, follow along for a bit, because I'm going to show you another way to select meeting requests in Mail to which you haven't responded yet. Then I'll show you what to do with this Search list and the one in Mail as well, to take care of all your pending requests.

Accepting, tentatively accepting, or declining a meeting

When a meeting request arrives in your Inbox, you have a choice: You can accept, decline, or accept kinda, at least for now.

To deal with a meeting request when it arrives, follow these steps:

1. **Select the meeting request.**

You can select the meeting request e-mail in the Mail module or click the meeting request in Calendar.

If you select the meeting request in Mail, the details appear in the Reading pane. In addition, your schedule for the day of the meeting, snipped from your Calendar, appears in the Reading pane. This information should help you to decide whether you can attend this meeting.

There are three or four main buttons you can use to send your response to this request: Accept, Decline, and Tentative, and if the meeting organizer has allowed it, Propose New Time. If you select the meeting request in Calendar, these same buttons appear on the Calendar Tools Meeting tab.

Figure 4-11 shows a typical meeting request displayed in the Reading pane.

In the Reading pane, you'll see a snippet from your calendar in the message area — a little window that you can scroll up or down through that day, centered on the event in question. That snippet has a title bar with the meeting date in the middle. If the request is for a recurring meeting, there will be a set of arrows to the left of the date in the title bar. Those arrows let you move through your calendar so that you can view each instance of the meeting. If the proposed recurring meeting conflicts with several of your other prescheduled meetings and appointments, then there will be a second set of arrows to the right of the date in the title bar. This second set lets you move through the calendar, as well, but only to the other instances that conflict with other items in your calendar (the title bar will also show you how many conflicts there are, and which one this is in the sequence). Double-click this calendar snippet to open your calendar so that you can view your schedule more fully.

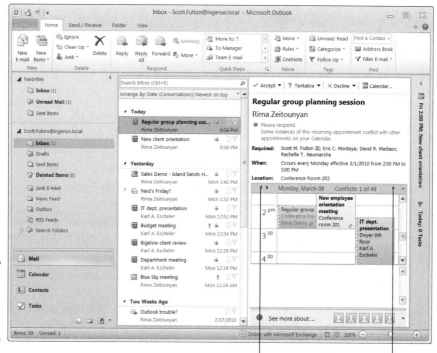

Figure 4-11: Reviewing a request for a meeting.

Use the arrows here to review each instance.

Use the arrows here to review only conflicting instances.

2. **Click the appropriate button to let the meeting organizer know whether you can attend the meeting.**

   You can choose from three or four buttons to send your request:

   - *Accept:* Accept the invitation and attend the meeting.

   - *Decline:* Respectfully decline the meeting.

   - *Tentative:* Indicate that you might be able to attend, but you're not sure right now.

   - *Propose New Time:* Indicate that you might be able to attend if only the organizer were to accept an alternate time that you provide in your response.

   - *Please Respond:* This link only appears on the InfoBar (it appears as a Respond button on the Calendar Tools Meeting tab if you open the meeting request) if you select the not-yet accepted/rejected meeting in your Calendar. If you click it, you can simply send a message back to the organizer, perhaps asking for clarification, without you having to commit yet one way or the other.

Book IV Chapter 4

All About Meetings

If you click Tentative, Propose New Time, or Please Respond, you can later review the request and send a more definite answer, such as Accept or Decline.

If you want to suggest a different meeting time, see the following section for help.

If you clicked Accept, Tentative, or Decline, then a pop-up menu appears, with choices of how you'd like to attach a comment to the reply.

3. **Select an option from the menu.**

   - *Edit the Response Before Sending:* Add a comment to your response. A message form appears, addressed to the meeting organizer; add your comment in the large text box and click Send.

   - *Send the Response Now:* Simply send the response without adding any comments. The e-mail response is sent immediately to the meeting organizer.

   - *Don't Send a Response:* Have Outlook record the meeting in your calendar, without sending a response to the organizer.

Proposing a new meeting time

If a meeting request arrives that you want to accept but the meeting time simply isn't the best one for you, you can propose a new meeting time. When you send your proposal for the time change, you can decline the current time or tentatively accept, depending on your schedule.

By default, Outlook assumes that when you propose a new time for a meeting, you're still tentatively accepting the invitation to attend. To select a new default setting for the Propose New Time button, click the File tab to display Backstage, then select Options from the list on the left to display the Outlook Options dialog box. Select Calendar from the list on the left to display the Calendar options on the right. In the Calendar Options section, select either Tentative, Accept, or Decline from the Use This Response When Proposing a New Meeting Time drop-down list. Click OK to save the change.

To propose a different date or time for a meeting you've been invited to, follow these steps:

1. **Select the meeting request in Mail or Calendar.**

2. **Click the Propose New Time button.**

   It appears at the top of the Reading pane in Mail or on the Meeting tab in Calendar.

3. **From the pop-up menu that appears, select one of the options shown in Figure 4-12.**

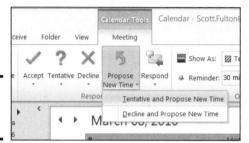

Figure 4-12:
Pick one,
only one.

This menu lets you choose from these responses:

- *Tentative and Propose New Time:* Tentatively accept the current time, while also proposing a change.

- *Decline and Propose New Time:* Decline the current meeting time and propose a different time.

The Propose New Time dialog box peeks out, as shown in Figure 4-13.

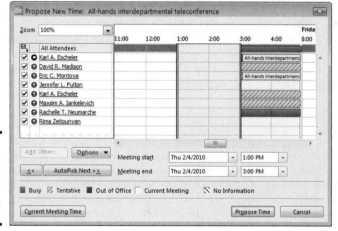

Figure 4-13:
Hmmmmm.
Now what
time works
best for me?

For employees sharing an Exchange network, the dialog box displays the schedule for all attendees. A time block's color tells you whether the item is marked as Busy, Tentative, or Out of the Office. The current meeting time is marked with a yellow vertical band.

4. Propose a new time.

You can make your suggestion in a number of ways:

- *To manually select a time:* Click in your row on any time slot that's open. The proposed time is flanked by green and red bars on the left and right, respectively. You can also select a new Meeting Start and Meeting End date and time from the drop-down lists provided.

- *To have Outlook propose a new time:* Click the AutoPick Next button. Outlook finds the first available free time slot for all attendees. Click the << button to locate the first free time slot available in the vicinity of the original appointment, usually later, within the same day if possible. The suggested meeting time is flanked by green and red bars.

- *To reset the suggested time to the current meeting time:* Click Current Meeting Time.

5. **Click Propose Time.**

   A meeting reply (message) is created. The InfoBar of the message form displays the current meeting time and the one you're proposing.

6. **In the message form, add any message you want in the message area.**

7. **Click Send.**

   The message is sent to the meeting organizer. The meeting changes in your Calendar, using your proposed time. Until your attendees respond to it, there will be a "barber pole" along the left side of the meeting box, to indicate that the new time may still be up in the air.

Checking on Meeting Responses

As it turns out, the fun doesn't end with you sending a meeting request; no, you have to do tons of things to get ready for the meeting, such as creating and copying the agenda, programming the PowerPoint presentation, and locating that silly laser pointer you keep misplacing. You definitely don't want to be constantly nagging attendees to find out who's really coming so that you can have enough agendas and color copies of your slides printed, and order enough donuts and coffee. Luckily, Outlook can do all the nagging for you. Whenever the need arises, you can easily check on each attendee's response to your invitation to get a quick head count.

To check on responses to your meeting request, follow these steps:

1. **Select the meeting in Calendar.**

   You can also open any of the e-mail replies you've gotten to your meeting request, if that's more convenient for you. The InfoBar at the top of the message form displays the total number of responses, divided into three categories: Accepted, Tentative, and Declined.

2. **Click the Tracking button on the Meeting tab.**

A list that shows each attendee's name, his or her status (as a required attendee or an optional one), and his or her response (if any) appears in a separate window. See Figure 4-14.

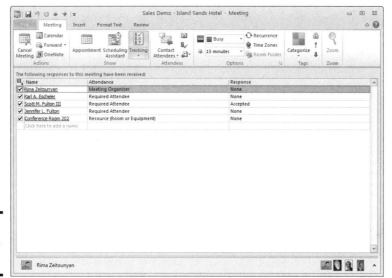

Figure 4-14:
So who all's
coming?

3. **Copy the tracking info, if desired, by clicking the Tracking down-arrow button on the Meeting tab and selecting Copy Status to Clipboard from the pop-up menu that appears.**

Obviously, you can review the tracking info in the listing. However, if the meeting has a lot of attendees, you might want to copy the tracking data to another program, such as Excel or Word, where you can sort it, total it, or use it for other purposes (such as creating name tags).

4. **Start the program to which you want to copy the data, paste the data, and save the file.**

For example, start Excel. Click in the worksheet where you want the data to appear, then click the Paste button on the Excel Home tab. Manipulate the data, as desired.

5. **Back in Outlook, when you finish viewing the meeting responses, close the meeting form by clicking the window's Close button.**

**Book IV
Chapter 4**

All About Meetings

Accepting or declining a time proposed by others

Well, it's bound to happen. Even though you've checked everybody's schedule twice (and made a note of who's naughty or nice), someone somewhere
is gonna have a problem with the time or the date you picked for your meeting. And that somebody is going to ask, "Hey, could we change that perfectly
good time to one that's harder for everyone to make?"

In reality, one of your attendee's may actually suggest a time that's better for
everyone, so it pays to at least listen to suggestions. Even while reviewing
time-change proposals, you still reserve the right to stick with the original
time, of course.

To review time change proposals for a meeting you created, and accept or
decline any of them, follow these steps:

1. **Change over to the Mail module by clicking the Mail button on the
   Navigation pane and double-click the meeting response that contains
   the proposed change, to open it.**

   You can easily identify such messages because the message header says
   something like New Time Proposed: *Meeting,* where *Meeting* is the name
   of the meeting.

   In the InfoBar of the Message form, below the subject line, you see the
   current time of the meeting and the proposed new time. You also see a
   summary of responses to the meeting.

2. **Click the View All Proposals button on the Meeting Response tab to
   check out any proposals to change the meeting time.**

   The form changes from a meeting response form (which is basically the
   e-mail response from one of your participants) to a meeting form (so you
   can review all the proposals and make changes to the actual meeting).

   In the meeting form, the proposed times appear in a list. In fact, all
   proposed times from all tentative responders appear in Scheduling
   Assistant, in a list above the scheduling grid. If you're on Exchange, then
   the grid will show you the schedules for everyone you've invited. See
   Figure 4-15.

   If you don't want to view all the responses first, you can accept or reject
   an individual proposal from within the message reply. To accept the
   proposal, click the Accept Proposal button on the Meeting Response
   tab. A new message appears so that you can let everyone know about
   the meeting change; click Send Update. The meeting is changed in your
   calendar. To reject the proposal, click Reply instead. Type a message
   explaining why you still like the guy but it's just not working out, and
   click Send.

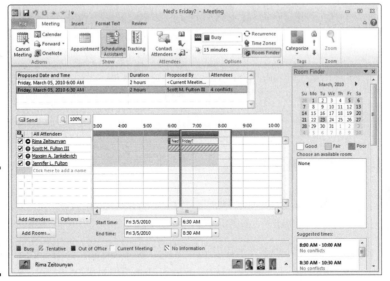

Figure 4-15:
View the
proposed
time
changes for
a meeting.

3. Select the time when you want to have the meeting.

If you want to stick with your original time, then select it. If you select a different time that's only slightly different from your original time (for example, postponing a two-hour meeting for a half-hour), then Scheduling Assistant may tell you the new time "conflicts" with the old one, so pay close attention to the scheduling grid.

4. Click the Contact Attendees button on the Meeting tab, and select Reply to All with E-mail from the pop-up menu that appears.

A message form appears.

5. Type an explanation for any change in the form's message area, if you want, and then click Send.

The message explaining why you may be accepting or rejecting the proposed change, is sent. The attendees receive your message, though at this point, they have not yet received any actual time change from you.

6. If you've accepted a time change request or made a time change of your own, then in the Scheduling Assistant, click Send.

The attendees receive your reply. If you accepted a time change request from someone else, the other invitees still need to accept, decline, or tentatively accept the new time — even the person whose time change you accepted; yep, he or she needs to accept the time change notice from you.

Book IV
Chapter 4

All About Meetings

Automatically handling meeting responses

By my way of thinking, it makes little sense to have a computer if it makes life harder. Well, okay, if I want to be truthful, Windows does sometimes make me wonder why I use a computer at all, but on most days (when Windows is behaving itself), I look around for ways to keep life running smoothly and peacefully, and the other day, I found one: a way to get Outlook to handle on my behalf all those annoying meeting responses from everyone to my similarly annoying meeting requests, so I don't have to interrupt my harmonious day by actually reading them. Follow these steps:

1. **Click the File tab to display Backstage, and select Options from the list on the left.**

The Outlook Options dialog box shown in Figure 4-16, pops up.

2. **Select Mail from the list on the left.**

The Mail options appear on the right.

3. **In the Tracking section, select how you want Outlook to handle meeting replies when they arrive in your Inbox.**

These two options pertain to tracking responses to meeting requests:

- *Automatically Process Meeting Requests and Responses to Meeting Requests and Polls:* Select this check box to just record somebody's response to your meeting request — Outlook doesn't wait for you to read it. If someone accepts your meeting request, for example, Outlook records that acceptance in the Meeting form without waiting for you to read the message reply.

- *Update Tracking Information, and Then Delete Responses That Don't Contain Comments:* Select this check box to automatically delete meeting responses after you read them when they don't contain any text in the body of their messages.

4. **Click OK to save your changes.**

Preventing replies for a meeting request

If you're planning a meeting for 50 people and you don't want to keep track of who can come and who can't (you just want to notify everyone), you can prevent attendees from bothering you with replies.

Regardless of whether you choose to track meeting replies, you can prevent people from trying to propose alternate meeting times. See the following section for details.

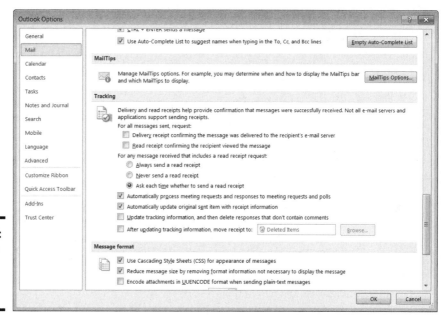

Figure 4-16:
Let Outlook
track
meeting
responses.

You can set up Outlook to handle meeting replies automatically, if replying manually is too tiring for you. See the preceding section.

Follow these steps to request a meeting, but prevent your attendees from sending you a reply:

1. **Click the New Items button on the Home tab and select Meeting from the pop-up menu that appears.**

The Meeting form appears.

2. **Use the Meeting form to select attendees, enter a Start and End date and time, choose a location, and set other options.**

See "Scheduling a Meeting" earlier in this chapter for details on how you perform these functions.

3. **Click the Response Options button on the Meeting tab and click Request Responses from the pop-up menu that appears to deselect it.**

Turning off Request Responses also turns off the ability for the recipient to bother you with alternate time proposals.

When you turn off the Request Responses option, you can't use Outlook to check whether individual invitees can attend.

4. **Set any other options that you want, and then click Send to send out the meeting invitations.**

Book IV
Chapter 4

All About Meetings

Preventing time change proposals for a meeting request

When creating a meeting, you don't have to listen to endless gripes about the meeting time or date. Nope, you can just put the kibosh on the idea that everybody can push you around and propose different times for your meeting. What do they think you are, anyway, a great big pushover? Just because you gave your Employee of the Year parking space to Rianna because she suffers from tenderfeetiatius and yet can still wear those expensive Jimmy Choo spike heels doesn't mean you're gullible. This time you're gonna really put your foot down and not even accept time change suggestions. That'll show them who's not the boss.

Just because you've prevented invitees from proposing a different time for your meeting, attendees can still accept, decline, or tentatively accept your original time, and you can still track their responses. See the section "Checking on Meeting Responses," earlier in this chapter, for the how-to.

To prevent your recipients from proposing time changes, follow these steps:

1. **Click the New Items button on the Home tab and select Meeting from the pop-up menu that appears.**

   A Meeting form pops into view.

2. **Use the Meeting form to select attendees, enter a Start and End date and time, choose a location, and set other options.**

   See "Scheduling a Meeting" earlier in this chapter for details on how you perform these functions.

3. **Click the Response Options button on the Meeting tab and click Allow New Time Proposals from the pop-up menu that appears to deselect it.**

   Turning off Allow New Time Proposals allows the recipient to respond to the meeting request (so that you can know whether he or she is coming), while preventing him or her from proposing an alternative time.

4. **Set any other options you want, and then click Send to send out the meeting invitations.**

Automatically Managing Resources

You may be working in an office where what happens in a particular meeting room every day, and at what time, may be of the utmost importance. You've seen how you can schedule meetings to make sure people can be available, but in some offices, you have to take account of the meeting *rooms* as well. It's almost like they were people with their own itineraries and busy lives.

So you can set yourself up to manage a room as a *resource* in Outlook, and then you can kinda let the resource do its own thing — almost like the room is its own person. When you set up something to be done in that room, you generate a meeting request that not only goes out to the attendees, but also *to the room.* ("Hi, room. Say, would you have a half-hour open Friday afternoon? You're not being vacuumed or something that time, are you?") When a meeting time needs to be changed, rather than wait for the room to get back with you on its BlackBerry or something equally weird, you can set up your resource to automatically say "Yes." But the key here is to remember that the room resource, like a person, has its own calendar. So when you do set the room up to make automatic responses, other people need to have access to that calendar to see those changes because, well, the room is not a person after all.

To set up Outlook so that resources you manage handle meeting change requests automatically, follow these steps:

1. **Click the File tab to display Backstage, and select Options from the list on the left.**

The Outlook Options dialog box appears.

2. **Select Calendar from the list on the left.**

The Calendar options appear on the right.

3. **In the Resource Scheduling section, click the Resource Scheduling button.**

The Resource Scheduling dialog box appears.

4. **Select the check box for the option that describes how you want Outlook to handle meeting requests.**

You have the following options — as shown in Figure 4-17:

Figure 4-17: Let Outlook manage those resources for you.

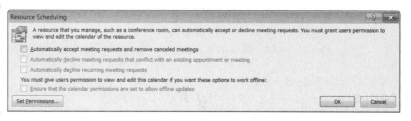

- *Automatically Accept Meeting Requests and Remove Cancelled Meetings:* Select this check box to have resources you manage accept any meeting requests they receive that pertain to them, and also accept any meeting cancellations they receive.

- *Automatically Decline Meeting Requests That Conflict with an Existing Appointment or Meeting:* Select this check box to have resources that you manage simply reject any meeting requests that conflict with items already in your calendar. Note you can only select this if you've first checked Automatically Accept Meeting Requests.

- *Automatically Decline Recurring Meeting Requests:* Select this check box to have the resources you manage always decline requests to attend recurring meetings. This is to avoid a situation where a room gets booked every Tuesday at 2:00 for several years running. Note you can only select this if you've first checked Accept Meeting Requests.

5. **To make sure the resource's calendar still functions when Exchange is offline, select the Ensure that the Calendar Permissions Are Set to Allow Offline Updates check box.**

6. **Click Set Permissions.**

   The Calendar Properties dialog box appears.

7. **Choose the permissions for only the people you want to see and use a resource's calendar.**

   Choose what you want real people to be able to do with the resource's calendar (for example, to see whether it's "busy" or "free," to delete meetings from its calendar, or create new meetings for it) by setting the corresponding options in the Permissions frame.

8. **Select the people to whom you want to delegate the permissions you've just chosen.**

   Click the Add button; then from the Add Users dialog box, double-click on the people you want to permit to use the resource's calendar, and click OK. The people you chose are now shown in the Calendar Properties dialog box, with each entry showing the level of permissions you've just assigned to it.

9. **Click OK to return to the Outlook Options dialog box, then from there, click OK to finalize your changes.**

   The changes you made to users' permissions are immediately applied. No messages will be sent to them automatically, so you may want to write them a separate message.

Chapter 5: Making the Calendar Your Own

In This Chapter

✔ Creating calendars for each of your kids, departments, or whatever

✔ Adding Internet calendars to the mix

✔ Changing how Calendar looks and acts

As a busy working mother, I frankly don't know where I'd be without Calendar to prod me into being where I should be. Add my busy schedule of deadlines, club meetings, and social obligations, and my kids' busy schedules of regular hair, dental, and doctor's visits, and you have one fat mess. If your kids are old enough to get themselves around town, perhaps things become a bit easier; but still, you need to know where everyone is and when they'll be home for dinner. One way to solve this problem is to create a calendar for each child and display the calendars in Calendar whenever you need to refer to them.

Okay, say you're not a mom. Instead, you're a busy manager left to cope with not only your impossible schedule, but also that of the department. As much as you want to attend *every* marketing rollout, training session, and group hug, you can't. Yet you still need to know when all these things occur. You can create a separate calendar for the department, which you can review whenever you like. You can even copy the appointments, meetings, and events that you intend to actually grace with your presence from the department calendar into your own calendar.

In case I haven't given you enough reasons to add another calendar to Outlook, maybe you're not a mom or a manager, but you still have a life (sorta), and you want to create a second calendar for personal appointments so that you can keep them away from prying eyes at work.

Keep in mind that you can share any calendar that you create. Not sharing a calendar keeps it private (meaning for your eyes only). You may want to create a separate calendar for personal appointments, for example, so that if you share your work calendar, your coworkers can't see your personal appointments. See Chapter 3 of this minibook for help in sharing.

You can add other third-party calendars to Outlook, as well — such as published company, family, or school calendars, and specialty calendars such as horoscopes and lunar calendars. You can customize Calendar in other ways — such as changing the number of days in your work week, the length of a work day, and the time intervals throughout a day (for example, showing each hour broken into 15-minute intervals, rather than 30-minute intervals). You can display multiple months on the Date Navigator, rather than just one, change the default reminder time so that you don't have to keep changing it yourself every time you make an appointment, and adjust the size of Calendar's text for those tired eyes of yours. You can search a calendar to create a custom view that displays only certain items. If you travel a lot — or if you deal with people in other times zones throughout the day — you can easily adjust your Calendar view to suit the time zone you're in or working with.

Creating Multiple Calendars

In the intro to this chapter, I spout off several reasons why you might want to create multiple calendars in Outlook, including

✦ It's an easy way to keep track of your kids without getting their schedules mixed up with yours.

✦ It's a simple way to manage the schedule for a department and keep it separate from your own.

✦ It's a manageable way to keep your personal appointments separate from your work ones.

You might have any number of reasons for creating a lot of calendars, and you may have no more complicated reason than, hey, it's easy to do. Follow these steps to create a new calendar:

1. **Change to Calendar by clicking the Calendar button on the Navigation pane, click the Open Calendar button on the Home tab, and select Create New Blank Calendar from the pop-up menu that appears.**

The Create New Folder dialog box pops up, as shown in Figure 5-1.

Figure 5-1:
Create
your own
calendar.

2. Type a calendar name in the Name text box.

Also, make sure that Calendar Items is selected in the Folder Contains drop-down list.

3. Click OK.

The new calendar appears in the My Calendars section of the Navigation pane. To find out how to work with this new calendar, see the section "Displaying Multiple Calendars," later in this chapter.

You can share your new calendar with other people in one of two ways: through an Exchange network or through e-mail (either as a static *snapshot* — a graphic that looks like your calendar — or as a piece of your actual calendar that the recipient can view within Outlook, just like any other calendar). The recipient can view the snapshot of your calendar within the e-mail but not within Calendar (because the snapshot is basically a picture graphic, not an Outlook file). As for sending on a piece of your actual calendar, check out Chapter 3 of this minibook for more on how to do that.

Adding Internet Calendars

You can find Internet calendars all over the Web. Without even trying, you can find tons of programs that can help you publish an Internet calendar to your Web site. Not much of a self-publisher? No problem — many Web sites can publish your calendar for you, also providing the software you use to create it. But this section isn't about publishing your Internet calendar; it's about adding other people's Internet calendars to Outlook. For example, suppose someone publishes the game schedule for the Indianapolis Colts (my team) on the Internet and updates it with the scores from each game while the season progresses. You can subscribe to this Internet calendar and keep up with your favorite football team, even if you live in California. (Go Colts!)

Outlook allows you to publish any of your calendars online, using an Internet calendar (iCalendar) format that allows others to subscribe to it. So, after you subscribe to an Internet calendar or two, you can jump on the bandwagon and publish your own Internet calendar to share. You can also share your calendar with your colleagues on an Exchange network. See Chapter 3 of this minibook for help in publishing or sharing your calendar.

As popular as the Internet is, think of how many calendars you might be able to find out there, simply by searching — for instance, the entire schedule for the South Flagston Amateur Sledding Association, the Junior Frog Comics Collectors Club meeting dates, and the Recent Elvis Sightings Calendar. If you want some help in tracking down some Internet calendars, check out these sites:

+ **iCalShare:** An extensive listing of online calendars at `www.ical share.com`.

+ **CalendarData.com:** A great listing of online calendars you might want to try at `www.calendardata.com`.

+ **The Internet Public Library:** Contains a listing of Web sites that provide Internet calendars at `www.ipl.org`.

+ **Yahoo! Sports:** Offers many Outlook-compatible calendars for national sporting teams and events at `sports.yahoo.com`.

+ **f!ogs:** Located at `www.f!ogs.com`, you can register for free and search its extensive database of calendars for whatever you need, then import them into Outlook if you like.

+ **Microsoft's Office Outlook's official Web site:** Find calendars published by Microsoft and its partners, and calendars shared by Microsoft users like you, at `http://office.microsoft.com`. Just search for `Internet calendars`.

These sites are pretty good, but most of the time I simply search for what I'm looking for such as `vancouver olympics internet calendar outlook` or `indianapolis oolts internet calendar outlook`. Good luck in your search!

Although you can find tons of calendars through Google Calendar, you can't import these calendars into Outlook — you can only import your main Google calendar. To work around this problem, copy the data from these other calendars into your Google calendar, then import it. See Chapter 3 of this minibook for help.

A link to an Internet calendar may begin with `webcal://` (rather than `http://`), although both are okay; the filename for the calendar ends in `.icf` (for *Internet calendar format*).

After you locate an Internet calendar, follow these steps to subscribe to it:

1. **Click the link to the Internet calendar.**

You might have received a link to an Internet calendar in an e-mail, or you might find a link on a Web page. After you click the link, a dialog box might appear, asking whether you want to open or save it; you want to open it. Another dialog box might then ask you whether it can add something to Outlook; if so, click Allow. The Microsoft Outlook dialog box jumps out. See Figure 5-2.

You can add an Internet calendar manually, if you know its address. Click the Open Calendar button on the Ribbon's Home tab and select From Internet from the pop-up menu that appears. Type the calendar's address in the text box provided and click OK.

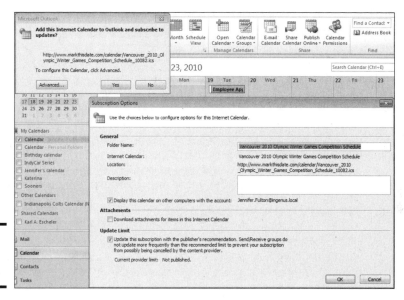

Figure 5-2:
Our best
subscriber.

2. **In the Microsoft Outlook dialog box, click Yes to subscribe or Advanced to set additional options first.**

   After you click Yes, the Internet calendar is added to Outlook.

   If you click Advanced, you see the Subscription Options dialog box (refer to Figure 5-2).

3. **If you clicked Advanced in Step 2, type a description in the Description text box of the Subscription Options dialog box.**

4. **Select the Download Attachments for Items in This Internet Calendar check box if you want Outlook to automatically download attachments.**

5. **Permit automatic updates to the calendar by selecting the Update This Subscription with the Publisher's Recommendation check box.**

6. **After making selections, click OK.**

   The Microsoft Office Outlook dialog box reappears.

7. **Click Yes to subscribe to the calendar.**

After you subscribe to an Internet calendar, that calendar appears in the Other Calendars section on the Navigation pane. In addition, the Internet calendar automatically opens and appears beside your private calendar(s). Outlook checks for updates to the calendar periodically and adds them for you automatically based on the options you selected when you subscribed. You can copy the items in the calendar to your private calendar, if you like; see the following section for help.

To remove an Internet calendar, right-click it in the Navigation pane and select Delete Calendar from the pop-up menu that appears.

Displaying Multiple Calendars

You may find it hard not to add extra calendars to Calendar; for example, you can easily add extra calendars for the people in your family or to keep your personal and business appointments separate. You can also add Internet calendars that are automatically updated by the publisher and calendars shared by your colleagues over an Exchange network. After adding a few calendars to Calendar, managing the whole bunch might seem overwhelming. Turns out, it's not.

When you have more than one calendar installed, each calendar appears in the Navigation pane, as shown in Figure 5-3. Your original calendar and any extra calendars that you've created yourself appear below the My Calendars heading, Internet calendars appear below Other Calendars, and calendars from other people typically appear below Shared Calendars.

You can create your own calendar groups and use those groups to quickly display or hide calendars, as well as to perform group tasks such as sending out meeting requests. See Chapter 3 of this minibook for help.

To display a calendar, select its check box in the Navigation pane. Up to a certain point, calendars are automatically snuggled side by side, as shown in Figure 5-3. In addition, each calendar gets a color that matches its color in the Navigation pane. This color coding helps you keep track of which calendar you're looking at. The main calendar normally appears blue-gray, but you can change the color assigned to it. (See the "Customizing the Calendar" section, later in this chapter, for more info.)

When you activate calendars for display by selecting their check boxes, Outlook places those calendars side by side. However, if you display more than four calendars, Outlook automatically displays them horizontally in Schedule view. Outlook switches back to the vertical arrangement when you display a single calendar. You can change these limits by clicking the File tab to display Backstage, selecting Options from the list on the left to display the Outlook Options dialog box, selecting Calendar from the list on the left, and in the Display Options section of Outlook Options dialog box, changing the value in either the Automatically Switch from Schedule View to Vertical Layout When the Number of Displayed Calendars is Greater Than or Equal To *Number of* Calendar Folder(s) option or the Automatically Switch from Schedule View to Vertical Layout When the Number of Displayed Calendars is Fewer than or Equal to *Number of* Calendar Folder(s) option, and clicking OK.

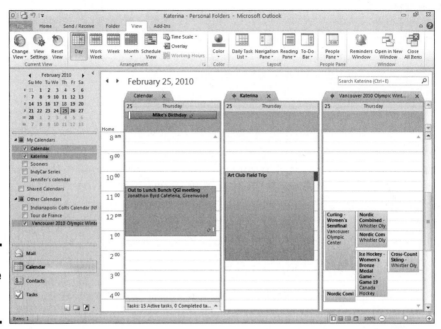

Figure 5-3:
Side-by-side
calendar
view.

To change the order in which calendars appear in side-by-side view, drag the calendar name up or down in the Navigation pane's list.

Displaying a calendar in its own window

The trouble with side-by-side view is that if you want to view more than two or three calendars, you really can't make out the details because they're so crammed together. Instead of displaying calendars side by side, you can display each one in its own window and then simply switch from window to window to view the calendar that you want to work with. Just right-click the calendar and select Open in New Window from the pop-up menu that appears. The calendar appears in a new Outlook window, separate from the main window. You can arrange the two windows on-screen however you like; that's the beauty of, well, Windows. And the fun doesn't end there; you can open as many calendars in separate windows as you like. When you're done with one of them, click its Close button, just like you would for any other window.

Overlaying calendars

Outlook offers you a final alternative for viewing calendars, and it involves only one Outlook window. The alternative is called Overlay view, in which the appointments, meetings, and events in one calendar are overlaid (like a clear sheet of film) on top of the other calendar. You can overlay as many calendars as you want, although overlaying more than a few may create a mess that you can't decipher. Overlaying the calendars allows you to see right away where free time exists — so you can quickly eliminate said free time with a new appointment, meeting, or event.

To overlay a calendar, follow these steps:

1. **Display the calendars that you want to overlay.**

   If needed, select the check box in front of any calendars that you want to overlay. You don't need to hide any calendars that you don't want to overlay, but you may want to reposition them.

2. **Click the Overlay button on the View tab.**

   The calendar on the far left is overlaid by the calendar on the far right (regardless of how many calendars are in between.)

   Alternatively, you can click the left arrow on tab of the calendar you want to serve as your overlay. When you go this route, the calendar on the far left is overlaid by the calendar whose arrow you clicked.

3. **Repeat Step 2 to overlay additional calendars.**

To get the configuration shown in Figure 5-4, I positioned my main calendar on the left, the calendar for Katerina in the middle, and the Indianapolis Colts calendar on the right. Then, I clicked the left arrow on Katerina's calendar to overlay it on top of the main calendar. If I wanted to overlay the Colt's calendar on top of the main calendar instead, I'd click the Overlay button or the left arrow on its tab.

When you overlay calendars, the appointments, meetings, and events of the lead calendar (the one whose tab is currently selected and appears in front of the other tab) appear in full color; items in the other calendar are semitransparent. So, in Figure 5-4, an appointment from the main calendar (Lunch with Dwayne and Performance Review) appears in full color, and the appointment from Katerina's calendar (Choir Practice) appears in semitransparent color. If I wanted to see the items in Katerina's calendar more clearly, I could click the tab for that calendar to bring it up front (and to display its items in full-color).

Repeat these steps to overlay more calendars. To remove a calendar so that it's no longer laid over another, click the calendar's right arrow, located on the calendar's tab.

Overlay button

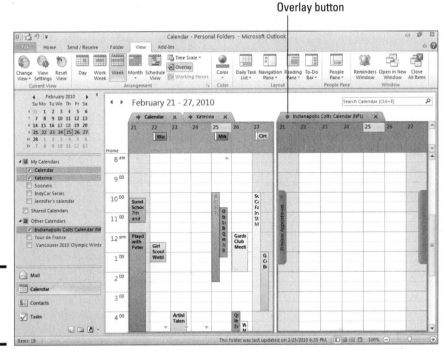

Figure 5-4:
Overlay
calendar
view.

Searching the Calendar to Create Custom Views

You can create custom views to suit your exact calendaring needs. For example, you might create a view that displays appointments, meetings, and events based on a category you've assigned them. Suppose you have a category called New Client, and you apply it to every new client meeting, appointment, or event; you can create a custom view to quickly see how much hand-holding you have to do this week by displaying all your New Client items. Or you might create a view that displays only Calendar items that contain particular bits of text, such as Sales or Big Important Company. Or you might want a view that displays only meetings organized by a particular person or with a particular person attending.

You can do a lot with custom views, as you can find out in Book VIII, Chapter 2. But if you just want to quickly display a select group of Calendar items, and you can't see yourself displaying this same group at some later date, why go to the time and trouble of creating an actual *view* (a saved set of View options accessible through the Change View button on the View tab) when you can just search Calendar and create a one-time customized view?

To search the currently displayed calendar, and create a customized view of its contents, follow these steps:

1. **Click in the Search Calendar text box.**

   The Search Tools Search tab appears, as shown in Figure 5-5.

Use these buttons to refine your search results.   Search results

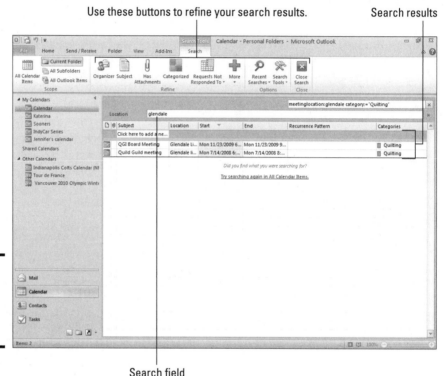

Search field

2. **If desired, type the text that you want to search for and press Enter.**

   You can search for items in the Calendar using just the buttons on the Search Tools Search tab if you want, instead of searching for items that contain certain text. For example, if you are searching for all the items that have attachments, you can do that without typing any search text. You learn how to use the Search Tools buttons in the next steps, so if you don't want to search using specific text, skip this step.

   If, however, you're looking for all the meetings that you have set up with your software vendor, LilSoft, then type lilsoft in the text box and press Enter. Items that contain the keyword(s) you typed (whether those words appear in the Subject, Location, or Notes section, or the To/From fields) are displayed in a list. (Refer to Figure 5-5.)

If you're looking for all the items you've marked with the category New Client, then you can type new client; however, you might get results that include appointments in which you talk about a new client, but which you haven't actually marked that way. Again, another reason to skip this step if you want.

To repeat a text search that you've performed recently, click the Recent Searches button on the Search Tools Search tab, and select the search that you want to repeat from drop-down list.

3. Use the buttons on the Search Tools Search tab to refine your current view of the Calendar.

As you make more and more selections using the buttons on the Search Tools tab, the results list reduces to display only those items that match all the criteria you specify. Here's what each button is for:

- *Organizer:* Displays **Organizer: (Sender Name)** in the text box. If you type Scott for example, then Outlook displays meetings organized by anyone named Scott. It doesn't, however, display meetings to which someone named Scott has been invited.

- *Subject:* Displays **Subject: (Keywords)** in the text box. If you type sales, then Outlook displays any items that contain the word sales in the Subject line.

- *Has Attachments:* Displays items that contain attachments, such as a meeting that has an agenda file attached.

- *Categorized:* After clicking this button, select a category from the drop-down menu. Outlook then displays only items that fit that category.

- *Requests Not Responded To:* After clicking this button, you select the types of meeting requests you want displayed from drop-down list. Your options include meetings you've accepted, those you've accepted tentatively, or those you haven't responded to yet.

- *More:* Clicking this button opens a drop-down list, from which you can select a field, such as the Start or End date, or required attendees. After you select a field a text box appears on the Search bar (refer to Figure 5-5); select an option from its drop-down list or type a search term in the text box to narrow the search results.

4. (Optional) Change the scope of the search, if you want.

By default, Calendar displays only items from the active calendar. You can change this setting by making a selection from the Scope section, located at the left end of the Search Tools tab:

- *All Calendar Items:* Clicking this button after performing some kind of search displays matching items from all Calendar folders.

- *Current Folder:* This button is on by default; it displays matching items from the current calendar only.

**Book IV
Chapter 5**

Making the
Calendar Your Own

- *All Subfolders:* Clicking this button after performing some kind of search displays matching items from any folder in the same group as the current folder.

- *All Outlook Items:* Clicking this button after performing some kind of search displays matching items from any Outlook folder, including Mail, Tasks, and Contacts.

You can also limit the scope of a search to include all of your calendars by clicking the Try Searching Again in All Calendar Items link, located at the bottom of the Search Results list.

You can refine the search further by using the tools that you can access by clicking the Search Tools button. See Book IX, Chapter 4 for help.

5. **To cancel the view and return to displaying all items, click the Close Search button on the Search Tools Search tab.**

Customizing the Calendar

For some people, vanilla ice cream works just fine; hamburgers with mustard, ketchup, and pickle work just fine. The last seat in the stadium, right up by the ceiling ("Hey, I can almost see Sting, and at least I can say I was there!") works just fine. I guess I'm not a "just fine" girl — at least, not when it comes to Outlook. I figure, if I'm going to use something every day, I'm gonna get comfortable and make it work the way I do. In case you feel the same way, the following sections show you how to make Calendar more comfortable for you.

Establishing the work week and work days

When you choose Work Week view in Calendar, Outlook displays a single week from your calendar — Monday through Friday. In addition, Outlook assumes that your work day lasts from 8 a.m. to 5 p.m. Now, this schedule probably applies to most people, but it may not mirror your actual work schedule.

To change the work week, follow these steps:

1. **Click the File tab to display Backstage, and select Options from the list on the left.**

   The Outlook Options dialog box jumps up. (See Figure 5-6.)

2. **Select Calendar from the list on the left.**

   The Calendar options appear on the right.

3. **In the Work Time section under the Work Week option, check the days that you want to include in Work Week view.**

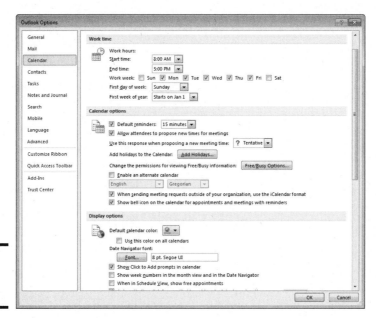

Figure 5-6:
Calendar
options.

Uncheck any days that you don't want included. For most people, Monday starts the work week; if that's true for you, make it the first day you select in the Work Week section.

4. **Change the start of the week (the full week) by making a selection from the First Day of Week drop-down list.**

   Normally, Sunday starts the full week; if that's true for you, too, choose it from the First Day of Week list.

5. **To change your normal work hours from the default (8 a.m. to 5 p.m.) to something else, select a new Start Time and/or End Time from the drop-down list(s).**

   Time slots outside this range appear with a light blue background in Day, Week, Work Week, Next 7 Days view. In Schedule view, time slots outside this range do not appear at all. Likewise, if you are sharing your free/busy time with your colleagues, they will not be able to see what's going on in your calendar outside the normal work hours you designate here.

6. **(Optional) Select a week from the First Week of Year drop-down list if your company starts its year on a date other than January 1.**

   You need to set this year-beginning date correctly if you also display week numbers, which you can find out about in the following section.

7. **Click OK when you finish making changes.**

Changing the time grid

A single day in your calendar is divided into 48 half-hour time slots. Half-hour time intervals work for most people because most people schedule appointments and meetings at either the top of the hour or at the half-hour mark, and not at (say) 1:45. However, if you're a regular 1:45 or 2:15 scheduler, the half-hour time slots may drive you crazy because to enter an appointment that starts at 1:45 or 2:15, you have to enter the start time manually. You may also have to enter the end time if, for example, the appointment lasts an hour and 15 minutes. Multiply this manual business by the number of appointments or meetings you create each day, and you can see what I mean when I say it'll drive you crazy — until you change the default time interval, anyway.

To change the time interval, follow these steps:

1. **Change to Day, Week, Work Week, Next 7 Days, or Schedule view by clicking the appropriate button on the Home tab.**

In Schedule view, the time grid runs along the top; for the other views, it runs along the left side. Vertical bands mark each hour on the grid; thin lines divide each hour into equal intervals. Normally, only one line appears in each hour, dividing the hour into two equal half-hour parts, as shown in Figure 5-7.

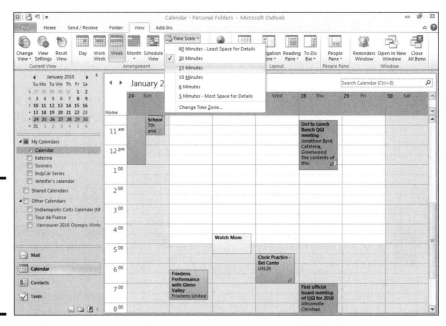

Figure 5-7: Change the time interval to fit the way you make appointments.

2. **Click the Time Scale button on the View tab.**

3. **Select the interval that you want from the pop-up menu that appears.**

   For example, select 15 Minutes. The grid changes to divide each hour into the interval you choose. (Refer to Figure 5-7.)

On the left of each week in Month view, you normally see a range of dates for that week — for example, you might see 1/3-9 to the left of the first week in January. A lot of companies use week numbers to control when particular events happen — most notably, payday. I don't know about you, but I've always had a special place in my heart for payday. If you feel the same way, display the week numbers in Month view (instead of the date ranges), so you can track when payday is coming. Follow these steps:

1. **Click the File tab to display Backstage, and select Options from the list on the left.**

   The Outlook Options dialog box appears. (Refer to Figure 5-6.)

2. **Select Calendar from list on the left.**

   The Calendar options appear on the right.

3. **In the Display Options section, select the Show Week Numbers in the Month View and in the Date Navigator check box.**

4. **Click OK.**

   The week numbers, rather than a range of dates, appear along the left side of each week in Month view, as shown in Figure 5-8. And as a special bonus to you, the week numbers appear along the left side of the Date Navigator, as well.

You might want to make one final change to the time grid, and it involves travel — at least, cyber-travel. If your work involves dealing with people in different time zones or traveling between time zones with a laptop computer, you may want to display another time zone next to the main time zone on the time grid. Adding a time zone display doesn't affect the main calendar, which normally bases the time for appointments and meetings on the current time zone only. Follow these steps to display a second time zone on the left side of the calendar:

1. **Click the Time Scale button on the View tab and select Change Time Zone from the pop-up menu that appears.**

   The Outlook Options dialog box jumps up, cued up to the Time Zones section. (See Figure 5-9.)

2. **Label your current time zone.**

   In the Label text box in Time Zones section, type a name for your current time zone. (This name appears at the top of the time zone grid.) For example, type the name of the city in which you live, such as New York.

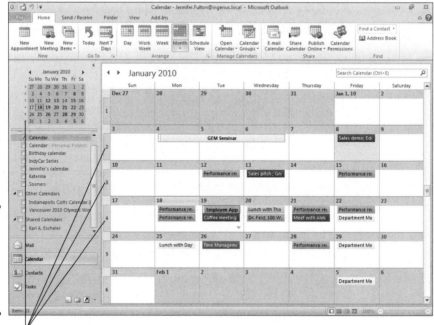

Figure 5-8:
You can make week numbers appear in Month view.

Week numbers

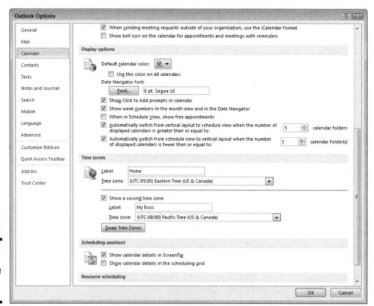

Figure 5-9:
You're in the Time Zone.

If you change your base time zone (the Windows time zone), the server on your Exchange network may change it back (assuming you're on an Exchange network, of course).

3. **Select the Show a Second Time Zone check box.**

4. **In the Label text box below the Show a Second Time Zone option, type a label for this second time zone, such as** `Los Angeles`.

5. **Select the time zone that you want to display from the Time Zone drop-down list below the Label text box.**

6. **Click OK.**

   In Day, Work Week, Week, or Next 7 Days view, the current time zone appears to the left of the calendar, and the second time zone you added appears to the left of the current time zone, as shown in Figure 5-10. A small gold line on the current time zone grid highlights the current time, based on your normal time zone. In Schedule view, time zones appear along the top of the Calendar window; the second time zone appears on top with the current time zone immediately below it. The time zones do not appear in Month view.

   Appointments and meetings that you create are still based on your current time zone, but you can easily convert that time to the second time zone simply by looking at the time listed on the second time grid.

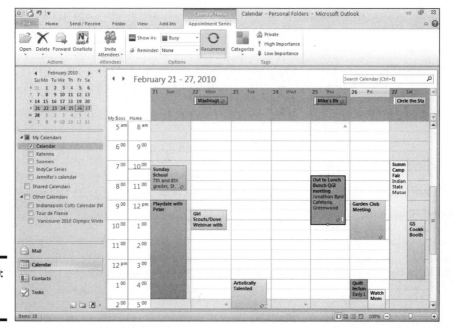

Figure 5-10:
Get in the zone!

**Book IV
Chapter 5**

**Making the
Calendar Your Own**

If you travel a lot between two zones, you can flip the times in Calendar just like you adjust your watch. Just redisplay the Outlook Options dialog box as described in the steps, and in the Time Zones section of the Calendar options page, click the Swap Time Zones button to change your Windows time zone, until you decide to swap it back. When you flip time zones, you can easily schedule new appointments or meetings in that new time zone, knowing that if you schedule something to happen at (say) 1 p.m. in this new time zone, you want to use local time and not your own time.

By the way, when you're setting up meetings with people who live in a different time zone, when the meeting request arrives in their Inbox, the time for the meeting is automatically adjusted to their local time without you doing a thing.

Setting the default reminder time

When you create an appointment, meeting, or event, Outlook creates an automatic reminder. For appointments or meetings, this reminder beeps about 15 minutes before it's gonna happen. For events, the reminder comes about 18 hours beforehand. You can't change the default for events, but you can change the reminder time for a particular event when you create it. You can also change the reminder time for a particular appointment or meeting, assuming you know in advance that you're going to need more time. If you often find that 15 minutes just isn't enough time to get to an appointment or meeting on time, you can change the default reminder to give you more time to break into a run.

To change the default reminder time for appointments and meetings, follow these steps:

1. **Click the File tab to display Backstage, and select Options from the list on the left.**

   The Outlook Options dialog box appears.

2. **Select Calendar from the list on the left.**

   The Calendar options appear on the right.

3. **In the Calendar Options section, make sure the Default Reminders check box is selected, then select when you want the reminder to appear from the drop-down list.**

4. **Click OK.**

You may be thinking, "Hey what about tasks? I get reminded about tasks all the time." Well, I can't stop your boss from nagging you, but if you're getting reminded about tasks *by Outlook,* it's because you set up a reminder when you created the task. It's not typically an automatic thing, so if you don't want to be bugged all the time about the stuff you haven't gotten around to yet, well, then don't set a reminder when you create the task. (Maybe you could set a reminder to remind yourself not to do that.) On the other hand, if you need someone to bug you to get stuff done, you can set up tasks so that they have an automatic reminder, just like appointments. See Book VI, Chapter 2 for help.

Changing the calendar color

By default, your main calendar is blue-gray. The normal working hours appear in white, and hours outside the work day appear in a lighter shade of blue-gray (at least, in Day, Week, Work Week, Next 7 Days, and Schedule view). Appointments, meetings, and events, regardless of when they occur, appear in light blue-gray (unless you assign a color category to them). Refer to Figure 5-10. In Month view, which doesn't break the day down into intervals, the entire day appears in white, although any days not in the current month appear in light blue-gray.

Maybe blue just isn't your color; or maybe you've added other calendars and want to assign colors that make sense to you. You can change the color of a calendar by following these steps:

1. **Select the calendar whose color you want to change by clicking it in the Navigation pane.**

2. **Click the Color button on the View tab and select a calendar color from the palette that appears.**

   If you select Automatic, then Outlook selects the color for that calendar. (Outlook chooses a color not currently assigned to any other calendar, starting with blue-gray and moving down the Color palette to the next un-assigned color.)

Customizing the Date Navigator

You can use the Date Navigator to jump to any date in your calendar. The Date Navigator appears at the top of the Navigation pane (on the left) in Calendar. It also appears on the To-Do bar. Initially, Outlook shows only one measly month on the Date Navigator. If you're often going back to a previous month or jumping ahead, you might approach the problem in several ways:

+ **Show more than one month on the Date Navigator.** Drag the right border of the Navigation pane to the right, making the Date Navigator wider. When it's wide enough to show more than one month, a second month appears. Of course, this approach narrows the viewing area for your calendar, so you may not want to do this unless you're using Day, Week, Work Week, Next 7 Days, or Schedule view.

**Book IV
Chapter 5**

**Making the
Calendar Your Own**

✦ **Display the To-Do bar and have it show more than one month.** To display the To-Do bar in the Calendar, click the To-Do Bar button on the View tab and select Normal from the pop-up menu that appears. The Date Navigator is then removed from the Navigation pane because you don't need to see two of them. Now, to show more than one month on the To-Do bar, you could drag the left border of the To-Do bar to the left, widening the To-Do bar and getting it to display more than one month. Making the To-Do bar that wide, however, will seriously reduce the area in which your Calendar appears. Instead, to display more than one month on the To-Do bar's Date Navigator, click the To-Do Bar button again and select Options from the pop-up menu that appears. Then, in the To-Do Bar Options dialog box that appears, enter the number of months to display in the Number of Month Rows text box and click OK.

Your changes affect the To-Do bar in all the Outlook modules, by the way, not just in Calendar.

After you display both the Navigation pane and the To-Do bar, you considerably narrow the viewing area. To remove the Navigation pane, click the Navigation pane button on the View tab and select Off from the pop-up menu that appears. To remove it temporarily, click its Minimize button. To redisplay the To-Do Bar, click the Expand button.

✦ **Jump from month to month without changing a thing.** Chapter 1 of this minibook discusses using the Date Navigator in detail, but if you want a hint, here it is: You can show a list of months adjacent to the currently displayed month by clicking the month name at the top of the Date Navigator. Assuming the month you want to jump to is a recent one, just click its name in the list.

Now that I have that "need more months on the Navigator" problem solved, I have another bone to pick. Okay, I'm getting older. I know it because I'm starting that trombone thing with the newspaper, trying to get it exactly in focus. Sure, I could get my eyes checked, but I'd rather live in denial a little bit longer, thank you very much. Still, when I'm chatting with a colleague, trying to check a particular date in my calendar to see if it's a good time for a meeting or a lunch date, and I keep fumbling around the Date Navigator because I can't see the dates clearly, it's getting harder and harder to keep my colleagues from figuring out that maybe I'm not really 29. So, I've decided that I should dye my hair and change the Navigator font so that I can read its text more easily. Follow these steps to do the latter thing:

1. **Click the File tab to display the Backstage, and select Options from the list on the left.**

The Outlook Options dialog box pops up.

2. **Select Calendar from list on the left.**

The Calendar options appear on the right.

3. **In the Display Options section, click the Font button.**

The Font dialog box appears (see Figure 5-11).

4. **From the Font and Font Size lists, select a font and size that are easy on the eyes, then click OK.**

Try to keep the font clean (no serifs) and relatively small (no bigger than 12-point).

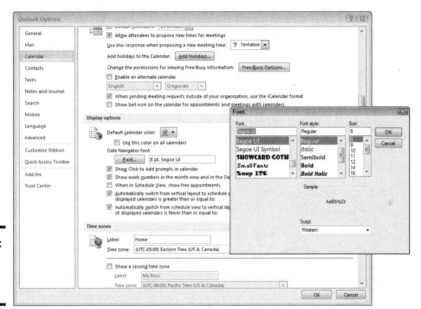

Figure 5-11:
Change the
Calendar
font.

You can change your default message font, as well, making what you type easier to read. (Changing the default message font doesn't affect the size of the text in e-mails you receive, however — but who knows, maybe you'll start a trend and get everyone to adjust their message font size!) To change the font and size of the text used in outgoing messages, click the File tab to display Backstage, select Options from the list on the left to display the Outlook Options dialog box, click Mail from the list on the left, and in the Compose Messages section, click the Stationery and Fonts button. The Signatures and Stationery dialog box appears. Then, in the New Mail Messages section, click the Font button and select the font and size you prefer to use most of the time from Font dialog box that appears. (In HTML and RTF messages, you can still change the font manually when you create each message.) You can change the font for replies and forwards that you send — as well as the font for composing text messages — by clicking the other Font buttons in the Signatures and Stationery dialog box. When you're through having fun, click OK to return to the Outlook Options dialog box, then click OK again.

**Book IV
Chapter 5**

**Making the
Calendar Your Own**

Days on which you have appointments or meetings scheduled appear in the Date Navigator in bold so that you can quickly identify them. Days that include events appear normally, without the bold accent. If you want all the dates to appear unbolded, you can turn that feature off by customizing the view. You get further into customizing views in Book VIII, Chapter 2, but follow these basic steps:

1. **Click the View Settings button on the View tab.**

   The Advanced View Settings: Calendar dialog box appears.

2. **Click the Other Settings button to display the Format Day/Week/ Month View dialog box, and then deselect the Bolded Dates in Date Navigator Represent Days Containing Items check box.**

3. **Click OK to close the Day/Week/Month View dialog box. Click OK again to close the Advance View Settings: Calendar dialog box.**

Book V

Managing Contacts

The 5th Wave   By Rich Tennant

"Your mail program looks fine. I don't know why you're not receiving any personal e-mails. Have you explored the possibility that you may not have any friends?"

Contents at a Glance

Chapter 1: Getting in Contact

In This Chapter

✔ Keeping track of trivia about your friends, family, and colleagues

✔ Picking new contacts out of your mail

✔ Taking Outlook's contact suggestions

✔ Creating more than one contact from the same company

✔ Tracking down duplicate contact entries

*I*f you think about it, Outlook is all about contacts — keeping in contact via e-mail, keeping in contact through appointments and meetings, and uh, keeping contacts. As you can find out in this chapter, you can record whatever information you want to remember about a contact, including a photo (if it's not too ugly). Outlook provides a lot of timesavers for you, so you can create contacts in a jiffy; if you get carried away, Outlook also makes it easy to track down duplicate contacts and get rid of them.

Malicious e-mails typically target your contact list, using it to send spam and viral messages to everyone you know. To protect yourself (and your friends, family, and colleagues), be very careful about which e-mails you open. Be especially careful about opening file attachments; as a general rule, you should run a virus scanner on such files first, prior to opening them. See Book I, Chapter 1; Book II, Chapter 2; Book IX, Chapter 3; and Book IX, Chapter 5 for more information on file attachments, viruses, and phishing expeditions.

Adding a Complete Contact

Contacts have no rules; you can record as little or as much information as you want about each contact you create. If you record an e-mail address, you can use the contact to send e-mail messages. Record an IM address, and you can exchange instant messages. Record a phone number, and you can ring 'em up. Record a Web page address, and you can display it in your browser with a single click. Record a street address, and you can get directions to a contact's location instantly.

For tips on working with your new contact, such as calling, viewing an address, or viewing a Web site, see Chapter 2 of this minibook. For info on how to send an e-mail, see Book II, Chapter 1. Looking to IM someone? See Book III, Chapter 2.

Create contacts in a list view

You can quickly add a new contact by first selecting a list view in Contacts, such as List or Phone. Just above the listing, an area marked Click Here to Add a New Contact appears. Go ahead, it doesn't hurt: Just click and type the data (such as the Full Name, Company, and Business Phone) for the contact in each field. Skip any fields that you don't know or don't feel like entering. For help changing your view, see Book VIII, Chapter 2.

You can create a contact quickly by simply pulling his or her name and e-mail address from a message he or she sent you. (See the section "Basing a Contact on an Incoming E-Mail," later in this chapter, for help in creating a contact with this method.) In addition, Outlook tracks e-mails you get from people and creates a Suggested Contacts list that includes anyone (actually, any e-mail address) you've communicated with who's not already in your Contacts list. See the section "Adding a Suggested Contact," later in this chapter, for how to convert these suggestions into reality. You can also create a contact by using other Outlook items — simply drag the item to the Contacts button on the Navigation pane and drop it. For example, you can drag an appointment onto the Contacts button. (We talk about dragging and dropping in Book I, Chapter 2.) Finally, you can create an instant contact by using the Electronic Business Card that someone thoughtfully included in an e-mail to you. See Chapter 3 of this minibook for help on that one.

To create a new contact, follow these steps:

1. **Click the New Items button on the Home tab and select Contact from the pop-up menu that appears.**

   If you're already in Contacts, just click the New Contact button on the Home tab to create a new contact.

   Either way, the Contact form pops up, as shown in Figure 1-1.

   If you have multiple Contacts lists — such as your personal list and a work list, or your company list and a list of key contacts — then your life is more complicated than most. Adding a new contact still doesn't have to be complicated, but you do need to make sure you select the right Contacts list from the Navigation pane before you click the New Contact button. Otherwise, you add the contact to the wrong list.

Add Contact Picture button

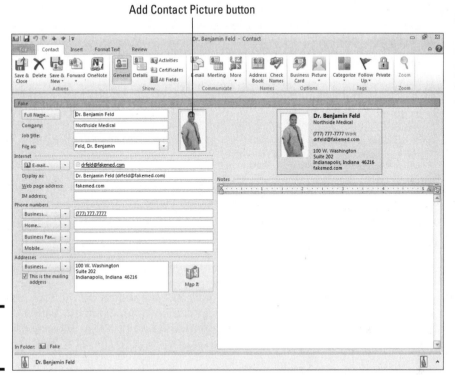

Figure 1-1:
Keeping in
contact.

2. **Type what you know about this contact in the appropriate fields.**

   Here's an explanation of some of the more common fields:

   - *Full name or not:* If the contact is a person, type his or her name (such as `Cameron McNichol`) in the Full Name text box. If the contact is a business, not a person, leave the Full Name text box blank, and type the company's name in the Company text box, instead.

   - *Select how you want the contact sorted with other contacts:* Select an option from the File As drop-down list — last name first or first name last, for example. You can also type something in the File As text box; the option you specify here determines not only how Outlook sorts this contact, but also how it locates the contact when you search, and how it resolves the contact's e-mail address.

   Resolving is the process that Outlook goes through to make sure an e-mail address is valid prior to sending a message. See Book II, Chapter 1 for the lowdown.

If you have multiple contacts from the same company such as Gladys Brown and Jorge Suento, you might want to select `Big Company (Gladys Brown)` and `Big Company (Jorge Suento)` in the File As text box so that Outlook groups those contacts together under "B" for Big Company. See the section "Creating Another Contact from the Same Company," later in this chapter, for help in creating multiple contacts who work for the same company.

- *You can store up to three e-mail addresses for a contact:* After entering the first one, click the arrow on the E-Mail button and select E-Mail 2 from the drop-down list that appears.

- *Choose how to contact your contact:* The name that you enter in the Display As text box appears in the To field of any outgoing messages, so if you want the name to look a bit less formal than `Tyra Jones` `(tjones@nowhere.com)`, you might want to type just `Tyra` or `T Jones` in this text box.

- *The fields that have downward-pointing arrows:* Use these fields (Business, Home, and so on) for any phone numbers that you want to store for this contact. For example, click the arrow to the right of the Home button and select Assistant from the drop-down list that appears to enter an assistant's phone number, rather than a home number. You can enter up to four phone numbers for a contact.

- *The mailing address:* Type the contact's address in the Address text box. Select the type of address from the drop-down list (it's initially set for Business); you can enter up to three addresses. If the address you're typing is the contact's mailing address, select the This Is the Mailing Address check box.

- *Add a contact picture:* If you have a photo of the new contact, you can add it by clicking the Picture button on the form's Contact tab and selecting Add Picture from the pop-up menu that appears (or by simply clicking the Add Contact Picture button). Select the photo that you want to use from the Add Contact Picture dialog box that appears and click OK. The photo appears where the Add Contact Picture button was; double-click the picture to change it if needed. The photo also appears on the Electronic Business Card sample, located on the right (see Chapter 3 of this minibook for more on Electronic Business Cards) and on the header of any message sent to you from this contact. Thus, the picture you add to a contact's form helps you to put a face on the name of the sender. You can double-click the photo in a message header to display that contact's information.

You don't have to use a photo of a person; if the contact works for a particular company and that's what you want to remember, you can add the company logo as the photo.

- *To add more details not shown:* Click the Details button on the form's Contact tab. Additional fields appear, as shown in Figure 1-2. You can add work-related information, such as the department or specific office that the contact works for, and his manager's or assistant's name. You can also add personal info, such as a contact's nickname, spouse's name, birthday, and such. If the contact keeps his or her calendar online and wants you to access it to see when he or she is free or busy, you can type that online address into the Internet Free/Busy Address text box. To redisplay the main fields, click the General button on the Contact tab.

You can find even more fields available for entering contact data if you want 'em. See the following section for the scoop.

3. **When you finish recording information about this contact, click the Save & Close button on the Contact tab.**

   The new contact is sorted with existing contacts by using the name that you typed in the File As text box.

For help in locating a contact, see Chapter 2 of this minibook.

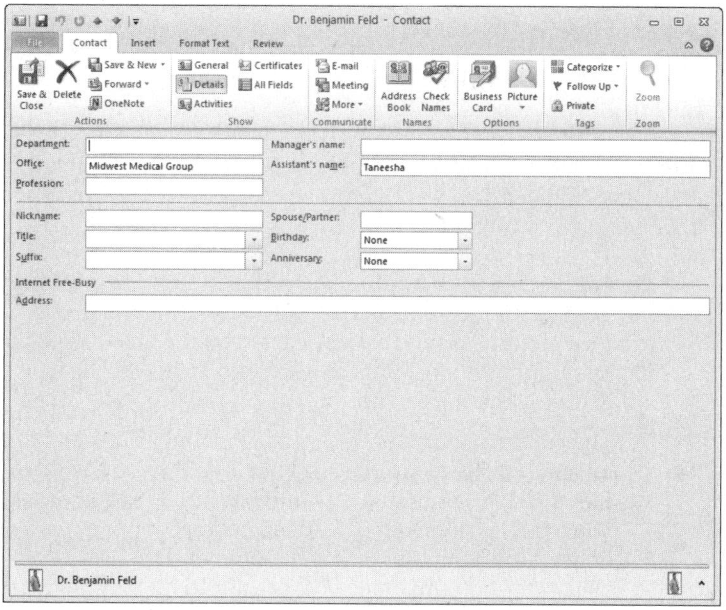

Figure 1-2:
Add more detail.

Changing Contact Information

You probably don't have many (or any) contacts whose information never changes. People change jobs, phone numbers, home and work addresses, and e-mail addresses often. Or, instead of changing some bit of information, you may have new stuff that you've just found out about a contact, such as a related Web site address or a cell phone number, that you want to add to his/her Contact information.

To change a contact, first locate him or her. Typically, the Contacts list appears alphabetically, so if you're looking for Alfonso Duerre, just look in the Ds. However, if you selected Alfonso Duerre instead of Duerre, Alfonso from the File As list you should look in the As; or if you selected `Fakeco (Duerre, Alfonso)` from the File As list, look in the Fs with the other Fakeco employees. In Chapter 2 of this minibook, you can find a lot of tips for locating a contact.

If you display contacts in a list view, such as Phone or List, you can click in any field and edit the data right there. For example, in Phone view, click in the Business Phone field for a particular contact. Then, either type a new phone number (if the field is empty) or edit the one that's already there. To replace existing data (such as a phone number), click in the field, select the phone number by dragging over it, and then type the new phone number. Don't know how to change views? No problem, see Book VIII, Chapter 2 for the lowdown.

After you locate a contact, simply double-click it to reopen the Contact form. Make any changes you want, and then click Save & Close to save them. Here are some tips to help you:

✦ **To swap a contact's photo for a different one:** Double-click the photo or click the Picture button on the Contact tab and select Change Picture from the pop-up menu that appears, select a new image file from the Change Contact Picture dialog box, and click OK. To remove the photo altogether, click the Picture button on the Contact tab and select Remove Picture from the pop-up menu that appears.

✦ **To edit the contact's Electronic Business Card:** Double-click it in the Contact form. See Chapter 3 of this minibook for help in making changes.

✦ **To add a second e-mail address:** Click the arrow on the E-Mail button and select E-Mail 2 from the pop-up menu that appears. You can also add a third e-mail address in a similar manner.

✦ **To add another street address:** Click the arrow to the right of the Business button and select Home or Other from the drop-down list that appears. Then, type the address in the text box to the right. Even though you may fear Outlook has lost the Business address, it hasn't. To redisplay that address, click the arrow to the right of the new address designation (either Home or Other) and select Business from the drop-down list that appears.

✦ **Add a *lot* of detail:** Outlook can store just about anything you can think of about a contact in its own proper little place. In the preceding section, you work with the general Contact page (Figure 1-1) and the Details page (Figure 1-2). But if you still need to locate the proper place for a particularly interesting bit of information on a contact, check out All Fields. Click the All Fields button on the Contact tab to display the All Fields page. Funny as it seems, you don't suddenly see all the fields that Outlook can track, but at least you get to choose *which* ones you want to see. Select the set of fields that you want to show from the Select From drop-down list to make those fields appear, like the ones shown in Figure 1-3. To enter information, click in the text box to the right of the field name and type. For example, click in the box to the right of Customer ID and type the customer's ID number. Repeat this process by selecting a different set of fields and entering data, as needed until you've recorded everything you know about the contact.

On the Miscellaneous Fields page shown in Figure 1-3, four user-defined fields appear. *User-defined* means you're free to use 'em for whatever you want. When you change from one set of settings to another, some fields may already be filled in; you probably entered the data for these fields on the General or Details pages. In fact, if you want, you can skip the General and Details pages, and enter all your contact data on the All Fields page.

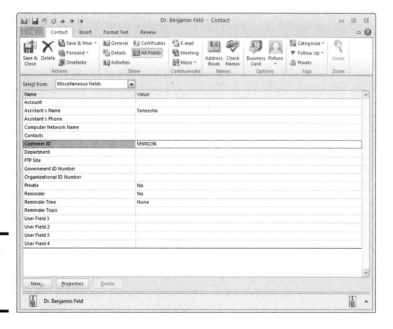

Figure 1-3:
Miscell-
aneous
minutiae.

Basing a Contact on an Incoming E-Mail

Because you mostly use contacts to send e-mail messages, it makes sense to create new contacts by using the information gleaned from messages they send you. After Outlook automatically creates a contact by using what information it can get from a message, you can always fill in the missing blanks manually.

To create a new contact from an e-mail message, follow these steps:

1. **In the header of a message that someone's sent to you, hover the mouse pointer over the name of the person you want to add to Contacts to make the Contact Card appear, as shown in Figure 1-4.**

The name doesn't need to appear in the From field; it can simply be the name of someone the message was also sent to.

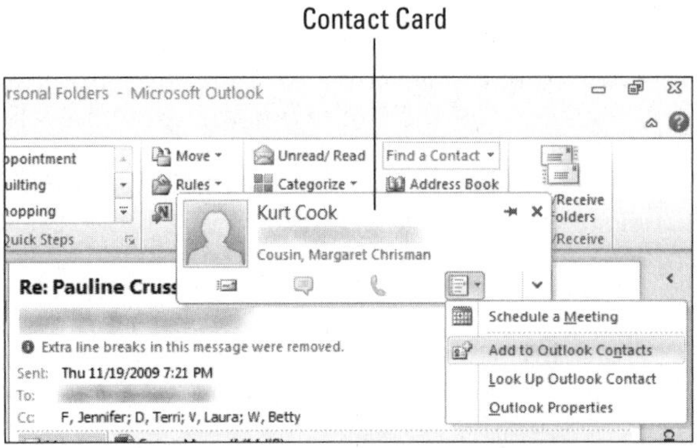

Contact Card

Figure 1-4: Use an e-mail message to create a contact.

2. **Click the View More Options For Interacting With This Person button and select Add to Outlook Contacts from the pop-up menu that appears.**

By the way, the View More Options button looks like a menu. When you select Add to Outlook Contacts from its pop-up menu, a Contact form appears. Outlook creates the new contact and fills in what it knows: Full Name, File As, E-Mail, and Display As. Looks like you're off to a good start, although maybe not: unless the contact already exists in one of your Contact lists, Outlook won't really know what the contact's name is. Instead, it assumes that the first part of the e-mail address represents that person's name, and so it places that information in the Full Name and File As fields. Feel free to change any of these fields and add other information as needed.

If you have multiple e-mail accounts, you may also have multiple Contacts lists. Mostly this depends on how those e-mail accounts were set up, but I can tell you that if you use Exchange, it is typically set up with its own data file, which results in a Contacts list that's separate from your personal e-mail account. In addition, you may have added additional Contacts lists of your own. So when you follow these steps to add a contact, Outlook checks all these Contacts lists for the contact's full name.

3. **Click the Save & Close button on the form's Contact tab to save the new contact.**

Adding a Suggested Contact

Outlook keeps track of the people with whom you communicate and assembles a Suggested Contacts list (for each e-mail account) of people who aren't already in your Contacts list. Assuming you want to take Outlook's suggestion and add one of these people to the Contacts list for that e-mail account, follow these steps:

Actually, Outlook assembles a list of e-mail addresses not in Contacts, so you may want to use the Suggested Contact list as a way of updating existing contact information. If so, see the section, Changing Contact Information," earlier in this chapter, for details on how to do that.

If you have multiple e-mail accounts, you may also have multiple Contacts lists. But not all of these Contacts lists will generate a Suggested Contacts list. If an e-mail account is saved to a new Outlook data file, then a Suggested Contacts list is created for that account. Otherwise, suggestions generated by messages sent to that e-mail account are lumped together with suggestions generated by the other e-mail accounts associated with that data file.

1. **Go to Contacts and select the Suggested Contacts list for one of your e-mail accounts from the Navigation pane.**

   For example, I have an Exchange account with its own data file, and several personal accounts that use a different data file. When I click the Suggested Contacts list for one of those accounts, a list of suggested contacts duly appears, as shown in Figure 1-5.

2. **Double-click the suggested contact that you want to add.**

   A new Contact form appears. (Refer to Figure 1-5.) The E-Mail, and Display As fields are filled in. Also, if the contact is already listed under a different e-mail account (so that Outlook knows the contact's name), then the Full Name and File As fields may also be filled in.

3. **Add any additional information, as needed.**

4. **Click the Save & Close button on the form's Contact tab to save the suggested contact.**

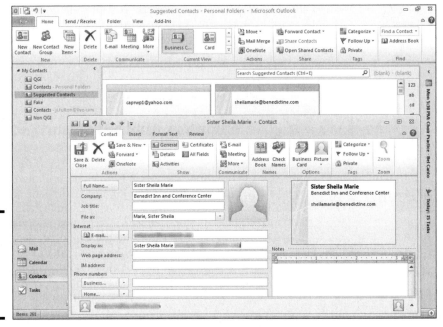

Figure 1-5:
Easily convert a suggestion into a real contact.

The only problem with the Suggested Contacts list is that it just doesn't know when to let go. Your newly modified suggested contact is still stuck in the Suggested Contacts list, and I'm guessing you didn't go to all this trouble just to keep it there. So, drag the entry from the Suggested Contacts list and drop it on the Contacts list in the Navigation pane. That'll make it part of your regular Contacts and thus easier to find and use, when needed.

Creating Another Contact from the Same Company

Quite often, you meet several people from the same company. From a Contacts point of view, you have a lot of duplication going on there — the same company name, phone number (but different extension), address, and so on. You don't need to manually reenter all this duplicate stuff when setting up a series of similar contacts — I mean, this is the digital age, isn't it?

To set up a new contact from the same company as an existing contact, follow these steps:

1. **Go to Contacts and double-click somebody from the same company as the new person you want to add.**

2. **Click the Save & New button on the Contact tab and select Contact from the Same Company from the pop-up menu that appears.**

A new Contact form pops up, containing the company information of the original contact, as shown in Figure 1-6. Outlook copies things such as the Company, Electronic Business Card, Web Page Address, Business Phone, Business Fax, and Business Address.

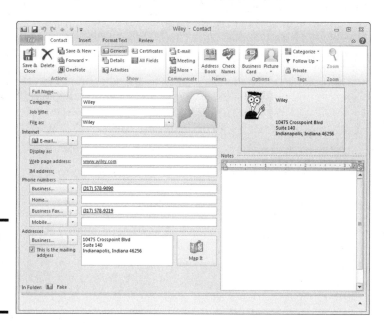

Figure 1-6: Same company, different contact.

Outlook also takes the liberty of entering the company name as the File As field, regardless of whether you used the company name in the File As field on the original contact. However, as soon as you enter a Full Name, the File As field changes. You might, however, want to select Company Name or Company Name (*Last Name, First Name*) from the File As drop-down list (to the right of the text box) to sort the similar contacts together.

3. **Click the Save & Close button on the form's Contact tab to save the new contact.**

Getting Rid of Duplicate Contacts

Well, you gotta give it to Outlook: It tries darn hard to stop you from creating duplicate contacts. When you attempt to, it flashes a dialog box at you, asking whether you really, truly want to create a duplicate. (See Figure 1-7.) This dialog box appears, by the way, whether you're creating the new contact from scratch, an e-mail message, an Electronic Business Card, or an Outlook item, or simply importing a bunch of contacts, one of which happens to be a duplicate.

Outlook stays on the lookout for duplicate contacts because of its Duplicate Detection option. By default, this baby's on, but you can turn it off if it's bothering you. For example, if you're importing a bunch of contacts from some other source, you might want that process to go automatically without prompting you every minute or so about some silly duplicate. If you turn the option off, you have to hunt down and destroy the duplicates yourself manually, but it's a pretty good tradeoff for a few minutes of uninterrupted work. To turn off the Duplicate Detection option, click the File tab to display Backstage, select Options from the list on the left to display the Outlook Options dialog box, and select Contacts from list on the left to display the Contacts options. Then, in the Names and Filing section, deselect the Check for Duplicates When Saving New Contacts check box, and then click OK.

Figure 1-7:
Duplicate
dilemma.

As you can see in Figure 1-7, the Duplicate Contact Detected dialog box shows you which contact Outlook thinks is similar to the one you're trying to add, displaying the old contact's Electronic Business Card. On the right, you can see what's going to change if you continue — the stuff in orange is the new contact info, whereas the stuff that's crossed out is the old info that'll be replaced. The stuff in black is from the old contact; it won't change if you continue because the new contact doesn't contain different information in these fields. You can select the Add New Contact radio button at the top of the dialog box to add the new contact, despite the warning (which you might want to do if this contact just happens to share the same name as someone else you know). Or you can select the Update Information of Selected Contact radio button to update the information in the existing contact by using the information from the new contact.

If you select the Update option, the new contact isn't added. Instead, data from the new contact that's different from the info in the existing contact is changed. A copy of the original contact, before Outlook updated it, appears in your Deleted Items folder, if you need it back.

If you choose to add the new contact, you end up with two entries. You might want to add an initial or something to one of the duplicate contacts to help distinguish the two.

You can, whenever needed, search and destroy any duplicate contacts by following these steps:

1. Change to Contacts, and then select a view that you can use to sort the records and find duplicates most easily.

I tend to choose Phone view because it's one of the list views in which each contact appears on its own line, and you can easily sort the contacts in a manner that helps you identify duplicates, as shown in Figure 1-8. (For more on list views, see Book VIII, Chapter 2.) For example, after changing to Phone view, I clicked the Full Name header to sort the list by Full Name.

Click the Full Name header to sort the view.

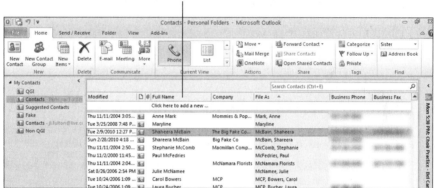

Figure 1-8:
Phone view.

When you find a set of duplicates, you might find it helpful to know which of the two duplicates is older. You can do that by customizing the view to show the Modified column, as shown in Figure 1-8.

2. Click the Add Columns button in the Arrangement group on the View tab.

The Show Columns dialog box peeks out, as shown in Figure 1-9.

3. Select Modified from the Available Columns list on the left and click Add.

The Modified column is added to the bottom of the Show These Columns in This Order list on the right.

4. Click Move Up a few times to move the Modified column up in the Show These Columns in This Order list, where you can easily see it in the Phone view.

5. Click OK to return to Phone view, where a new column has joined the rest.

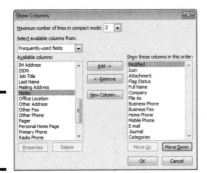

Figure 1-9:
Add the
Modified
column.

The new column is rather skinny, making it pretty useless at its initial size, in my humble opinion. Drag the right edge of the column to make it bigger so that you can read the modified date.

6. **Sort the list by clicking the header at the top of any column.**

   For example, you might want to sort the list by Full Name or by File As. The list shown in Figure 1-8 is sorted by Full Name, as you can tell by the little triangle on the Full Name column header.

7. **Scroll down the list looking for duplicates.**

   I apparently have two Shaheera McBains in my Contact list. (Refer to Figure 1-8.)

8. **When you find a duplicate, compare the two modified dates to see which one is newer (and perhaps more current).**

9. **Select the duplicate that you want to delete, and then click the Delete button on the Home tab.**

Chapter 2: Working with Your Contacts

In This Chapter

✔ Changing your view of the Contacts list

✔ Tracking down a lost contact

✔ Locating a contact's address or Web page

✔ Ringing up a contact through Outlook

✔ Reviewing all the things you've done for a contact

You may find having a long list of people you know and work with useful for more than just sending e-mails. For example, if you really need some tech help and your main contact is out sick, it's helpful to know someone else who works for the same company. You can use several different methods for locating the people you need to contact, such as changing your view of the Contacts list or searching for information that you know exists in a contact's data (such as a company name or city). After you find a contact, you can use its information to help you locate the contact's address on a map or display a contact's Web site in your browser. Assuming your computer has a modem (most do, on their motherboards), you can use your computer to automatically dial the contact. Finally, in this chapter, you can discover how to review the activity associated with a contact, such as recent appointments, tasks, or e-mail messages.

Picking a View That Suits Your Needs

Like with all Outlook modules, the Contacts list can display its information in a lot of different ways. Although I detail the views (and how to customize them) in Book VIII, Chapter 2, I thought I'd mention them here because the card views are rather unique: Business Card and Card views.

Normally, Contacts displays its information in the form of Electronic Business Cards, as shown in Figure 2-1. To change to Business Card view, select it from the Current View palette on the Home tab, or click the Change View button on the View tab and select Business Card view from the palette that appears. In this view, each contact appears as a card — some quite colorful, as you can see in Figure 2-1. See Book IV, Chapter 3 for more information on Electronic Business Cards. To view more or less cards in this view, adjust the zoom by using the Zoom slider located at the bottom of the window.

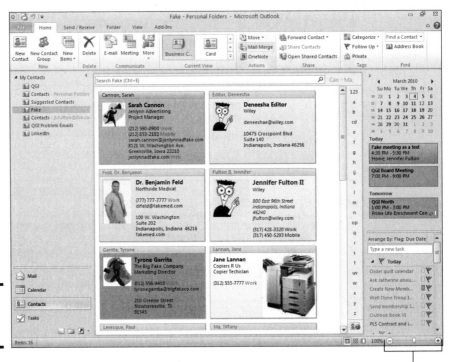

Figure 2-1:
Business
Card view.

Zoom slider

You can choose to view simple address cards by changing to the Card view (see Figure 2-2). This view displays a bit less information on each contact, while allowing you to see more contacts on your screen at a time.

In all the card views, buttons run along the right side of the window; click a button to jump to a contact that begins with that letter. If you need to search using an alternate alphabet, click the Alternate Alphabet button at the bottom of the alphabet buttons and choose an alternate alphabet. Buttons for that alphabet appear just to the left of the original alphabet buttons. Use either set to search your contacts.

The cards appear to be sorted by last name, but in reality, they are actually sorted by the File As field for each contact. Also, in all card views, some view buttons run along the bottom of the window, just to the left of the Zoom slider. (Refer to Figure 2-2.) Here's what those buttons do:

✦ **Normal:** This view displays the Navigation pane, the cards, and the To-Do bar.

✦ **Cards Only:** As you might guess, this view displays just the cards, hiding the Navigation pane and To-Do bar. You can use this view as an alternative to adjusting the zoom to see more cards, since more cards appear automatically when the Navigation pane and To-Do bar are minimized.

✦ **No To-Do bar:** This view sends the To-Do bar into hiding, while displaying the cards and the Navigation pane.

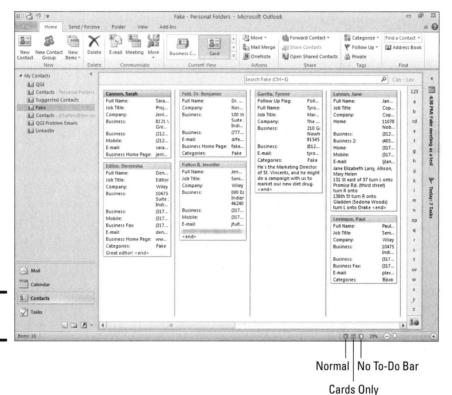

Figure 2-2:
Card view.

Normal | No To-Do Bar

Cards Only

The other views are list views; a list view displays its information in columns, with each contact appearing in a separate row. The List view is shown
in Figure 2-3. List views such as this one (the other is called Phone view) can
group similar information together in collapsible groups. To group items,
select an arrangement from the Arrangement palette on the View tab. In
the view shown in Figure 2-3, I selected Categories from the Arrangement
palette to group the listing by category. Groups can be expanded or collapsed. For example, I could collapse the Doctor group by clicking the black
right triangle thingy in front of the `Categories: Doctor` heading. I could
expand the Book group by clicking the white right arrow in front of the
`Categories: Book` heading.

In the list views, the view buttons that appear at the bottom of the window
are slightly different than what you get with the card views. (See Figure 2-3.)
Here's what those buttons do:

✦ **Normal:** This view displays the Navigation pane, the particular Contact list, and the To-Do bar.

✦ **Reading:** Reading view displays just the Contact list, hiding the Navigation pane and To-Do bar so that you can view more columns.

Click to expand the category.

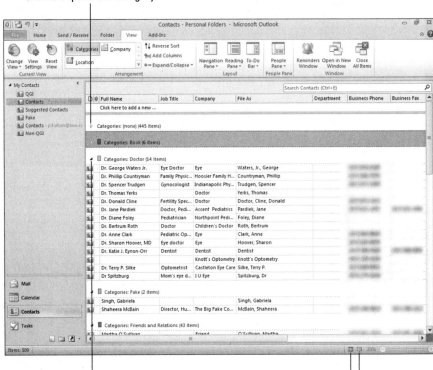

Figure 2-3:
List view.

Click to hide the category.

Normal

Reading

You can sort and customize each view, and even create your own views; see Book VIII, Chapter 2 for the lowdown.

Locating a Contact

Nothing's more frustrating than looking for something you know should be right there because, by goodness, you remember putting it there just a second ago, carefully balanced on the stack of unopened mail and lists of phone calls you need to return. Luckily, Outlook makes it easier to find a lost contact than it is to find your keys, your cell phone, or the remote. In fact, you have as many ways to find a contact as you have to lose your stuff.

You can quickly look up a contact's info while you scan his or her latest e-mail. Just hover the mouse pointer over the sender's address at the top of the Message window to make the Contact Card appear. Click the View More Options button (it looks like a paper with text on it) and select Look Up Outlook Contact from the pop-up menu that appears.

Okay, let the search begin! You can perform these kinds of searches:

✦ **Search within any module.** To search for a contact from any module such as Calendar or Mail, type all or any part of a contact's name (first or last), e-mail address, display name (the name used to resolve e-mail names), or company name in the Find a Contact text box located at the right end of the Home tab, and press Enter. You can also type the File As name, which is typically the first and last name of the contact, but you can make it anything when you create a contact. For example, when I add contractors to my Contacts list, I use the File As text box to list what they do, such as plumber, electrician, or carpenter. That way, when I want to search for the plumber I used last time, I can just type `plumber` and press Enter.

After you press Enter, the matching contact instantly appears. If more than one contact matches your search, the Choose Contact dialog box appears. (See Figure 2-4.) Select one of the contacts listed and click OK.

To relocate a contact that you found recently by using the Find a Contact text box, click the down arrow at the right-end of the text box to display a list of recently found contacts and click the name of the contact you want to redisplay.

✦ **Search for a contact from within Contacts.** If you know a particular contact is out there but can't find that person by searching from within the other modules, you can try searching within the Contacts module. For example, to find the eye doctor whose name you've forgotten because you saw him only once over a year ago, you can type `eye` in the Search Contacts box and, I hope, find the doc (assuming you've typed the word *eye* anywhere in that contact's information). See Figure 2-5. Notice that I said nothing about pressing Enter — Outlook starts its search as soon as you start typing. With each additional letter, you narrow down the search to just those contacts who match everything you've typed. You can enter partial information and even combine stuff to find a contact — for example, you might type `t copier` to find someone named Tom, Tonya, Tyrone, or Ty who sells or fixes copiers.

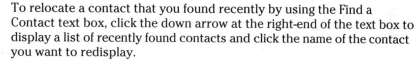

Figure 2-4:
Got him!

Search Contacts box   Close Search

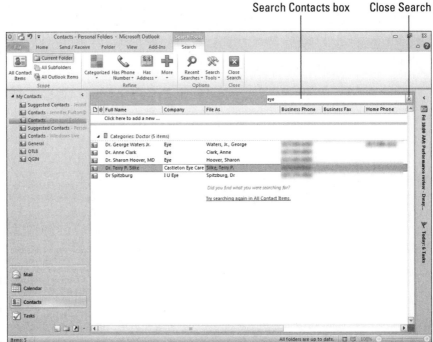

Figure 2-5:
Really, really
search.

After you type something in the Search Contacts box, the display
changes dynamically to display only matching contacts. You get the
details of searching in Book IX, Chapter 4; for now, to return to displaying all contacts, click the Close Search button — it appears both on the
Ribbon's Search tab and next to the Search Contacts text box.

✦ **Group, then search to find a contact.** You might hunt down a lost contact by sorting to group similar ones together. You can find out all about
sorting in Book VIII, Chapter 2, but for now, I can show you some basics.

First, change to a list view in Contacts (such as Phone or List). The
Phone view simply lists everyone alphabetically and doesn't group similar
contacts together, although you can group them quickly by selecting an
arrangement from the Arrangement palette on the View tab, and then
clicking the More button in the Arrangement group and selecting Show
in Groups from the menu that appears. The other list view (which is
called List) automatically groups similar contacts by their company.
Although again, you can select a different grouping by making a selection
from the Arrangement palette on the View tab. You can use these groups
to quickly locate the contact you are looking for. For example, if you
have several contacts at Copiers R Us, you can group the listing by
Company and scan the Copiers R Us group for the contact you want, as
shown in Figure 2-6.

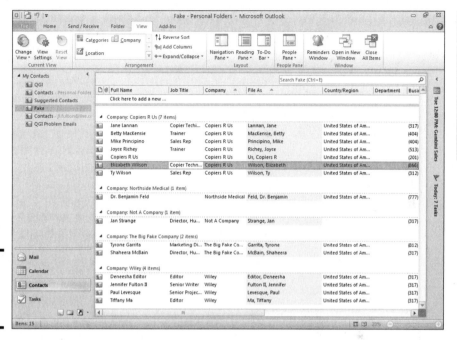

Figure 2-6:
Use groups
to find a
contact.

You can group contacts by category. To find out how to create categories and assign them to contacts, see Book VIII, Chapter 1. You can add a column to a list view and sort by it in order to find a contact. For example, you could add the Assistant's Name column and sort by it to find the name of the new guy who's assistant you've known for a long time. See Chapter 1 in this minibook, for help.

Viewing a Map to a Contact's Address

I do business with a lot of my contacts, so I really need to have an address for them. More important than that, however, I need to know where the silly address is located! Well, not to worry; although cyberspace was almost as uncharted as an ancient sea ten years ago, Internet maps have brought accessibility to those thar-be-dragons areas.

To be able to map someone's address, you must be connected to the Internet.

To display a map of a contact's address, follow these steps:

1. **Double-click the contact whose address you want to find to open it.**

The Business address for the Contact (if any) appears in the Contact form.

2. **If the address that you want to find doesn't appear on the Contact form, click the arrow next to the button in the Addresses area of the Contact form and select the type of address that you want to locate, such as Home or Other.**

Because a contact can have up to three addresses, you need to display the address that you want to find first so that Outlook knows which address to look up.

3. **Click the Map It button, located just to the right of the address box.**

Alternatively, you can click the More button in the Communicate group on the Contact tab and select Map It from the pop-up menu that appears. Whichever method you use, your Web browser opens, displaying the map by using Bing, a Microsoft site. (See Figure 2-7.) The location of the contact address is marked on the map by a pushpin icon.

4. **Adjust the map, as needed, to get the information you're looking for.**

You can change from map view to a photo view by clicking either Aerial (for a satellite view) or Birds Eye (for a view that overlays the road map on top of the satellite view) from the navigation box. Use the Zoom controls to zoom in and out, and use the arrows to move within the map (or just click the map and drag it up, down, left, or right to change the portion of the map that you're seeing).

Zoom In/Out   Navigation control   Change View

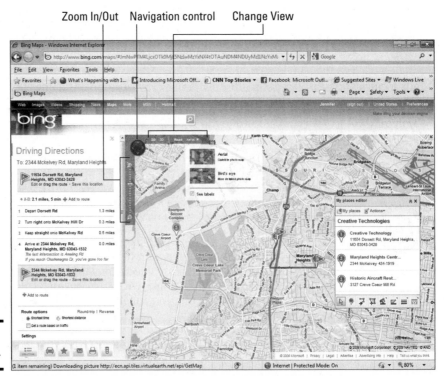

Figure 2-7:
A Bing map.

5. **To get driving directions, hover the mouse over the pushpin icon on the map that marks the location of your address, and select either Drive From Here or Drive To Here from the palette that appears.**

   The Driving Directions pane appears on the left.

6. **Type your location in either the Start or End text box in the Driving Directions pane and click Get Directions.**

   Step by step driving directions to the location you selected appear in the Driving Directions pane.

To send a link to this map in an e-mail, click the Share Your Map button (located at the bottom of the Driving Directions pane). In the Share dialog box that appears, click the E-Mail link. If you are asked whether it's okay to send this information to Outlook, click Allow. An e-mail message appears with the link to your map in the message area. Address the message, edit the Subject (it initially says only Bing Maps), and add explanatory text if you want, by typing that text in the message area. Click Send to send your message.

Browsing to a Contact's Web Page

It seems that just about everyone is on the Web: bookstores, groceries, government offices, car lots, dance studios, libraries, and offices (such as yours). Many people even have their own personal Web sites — especially because so many host sites give you the space for free. The point I'm trying to make here is that a lot of your contacts probably have Web sites associated with them.

After you find the address of a contact's Web site, you can enter it in the Web Page Address text box in the Contact form, as shown in Figure 2-8. To visit the contact's page, click the More button in the Communicate group of the form's Contact tab and select Web Page from the pop-up menu that appears — or better yet, just click the Web page's link in the Contact form's Web Page Address text box. The page instantly appears in your Web browser, as shown in Figure 2-8.

A lot of people include not only their contact information, but their company's Web page address at the bottom of all their e-mails. Typically, this text is presented as a hyperlink that you only need to click to display the page in your Web browser. If the Web page address appears as only text (which it might if the message was sent to you using text format instead of HTML), you can right-click the text, select Copy from the pop-up menu that appears, and then paste the address right into the Web Page Address text box, instead of typing that address manually.

As easy as it might be to record a contact's Web site, I personally don't enter a Web site address into Outlook for someone or some company I don't know. In addition, I typically test the Web site address in my browser before I enter it in Outlook. At the same time, I always exercise restraint, and I make it a point not to visit any ol' Web site some stranger sends me in an e-mail. I look at "official" e-mails with disbelief — especially unsolicited e-mails that threaten to turn off my credit card unless I confirm my private information on what's sure to be a bogus Web site.

In any case, don't fear as far as Web sites addresses and Outlook are concerned — you have to manually add a Web site into a Contact form and then click the link to display that site in your Web browser. So, rest assured that no scam e-mail can enter a Web site address into an existing contact, launch your browser, and force you to order ten tons of chocolate at double the price.

Figure 2-8:
Visit a contact's Web page.

Calling a Contact

E-mail is convenient, and everyone uses it (even for silly things, such as e-mailing a co-worker about lunch, even though she works in the cubicle next to yours). If you e-mail too much (hey, you know whether you have a problem), let me reintroduce you to an old friend — the telephone. Using this old-fashioned-yet-sturdy device, you can call a colleague or friend, and talk *live*.

Okay, you can talk with a person live in another way, and it's a little more hip: instant messaging. Granted, by talking, I mean typing text back and forth, although you can send live video and audio through an instant messenger, if you want. (See Book III, Chapter 2 for more about instant messaging.) You can also use Outlook to send text messages to a cell phone if you don't want to send e-mails, although it might not be as instantaneous as text messaging since you are going through Outlook with its Send/Receive cycles. Again, see Book III, Chapter 2 for help. Now, this talking to a contact thing has a small hitch — it all depends on your computer having a modem (most do these days, often on the motherboard), and also whether you have the modem connected to a phone outlet. Actually, the phone cord from the modem's phone jack in your computer needs to run to your phone, and then another phone cord needs to run from your modem's line jack to the wall jack. I should also mention here that you need to have a working phone service, which these days with the popularity of cell phones is not always a given, and yes, you have to have a standard phone (not wireless) that you can use for the talking to your contact part. If you don't have a modem hooked up and ready to go when you initiate the procedure described here, Outlook may dial the number, but the modem won't be able to make the connection, so you won't have any way of talking to the person. After you get everything hooked up, you can initiate all your phone calls with a simple click, saving those newly manicured hands for more

Now, I know that you're probably thinking, "Gee, that's a whole lot of messing around with the back of my computer for a simple task — dialing a phone." Keep in mind that you can store a whole lot of phone numbers for a contact within Outlook — including home and work numbers, cell phone number, assistant's phone number, pager number, you name it. And because you have to open Outlook to look up the phone number anyway, why not have it do the dialing for you? If you do, you can also create a Journal entry to make a note about the call and its length — which is handy if you bill clients for your time or just want to prove to your boss that yes, you actually *do* work.

Although it looks like Outlook can only store four phone numbers initially, you can select a different phone number type from any of the Phone Number lists and enter an additional phone number without erasing whatever was displayed in that box originally. For example, you could click the Business button, select Assistant, and enter a phone number for the contact's assistant without losing the business number. You can only show four numbers at a time, but you can store up to nineteen.

To phone a contact, follow these steps:

1. **Double-click the contact you want to call to open it.**

The Contact form pops up, as shown in Figure 2-9.

You don't actually need to open a contact to dial his or her phone number. After selecting a contact from the Contacts list, click the More button in the Communicate group on the Home tab and choose select Call from the pop-up menu that appears. The familiar list of phone numbers associated with that contact appears. Click a phone number, and then skip to Step 3 to see what to do next.

Figure 2-9:
Phone a
friend.

2. **Click the More button on the form's Contact tab and select Call from the pop-up menu that appears.**

   A list of all the phone numbers you have for that contact appears. Select one of the numbers on the list. The New Call dialog box jumps up. Refer to Figure 2-9.

3. **(Optional) If you want to create an entry in the Journal that logs this call, select the Create New Journal Entry When Starting New Call option.**

4. **To check that your location has been set up correctly in Windows by whoever installed Windows on your computer, click the Dialing Properties button.**

   In the Phone and Modem dialog box that appears, you can verify that Windows knows what area code you're in — and whether it has to dial a 9 or some other code to get an outside line on your phone. Click OK to return to the New Call dialog box.

5. **Click Start Call.**

   The Call Status dialog box appears.

6. **Click Talk.**

   The modem dials the number. If you started a Journal entry in Step 3, a Journal form appears; type your notes in the Notes area.

7. **When you finish your chat, click End Call.**

8. **Click Close.**

9. **Back in the Journal form (assuming you have one), finish your notes and click Save & Close.**

   For help in viewing the Journal entry of your call, see the following section.

If you get used to your new phone butler, you might want to make having Outlook dial for you even more convenient by setting up a speed-dial list. Follow these steps:

1. **Open the New Call dialog box.**

   Change to Contacts if needed (by clicking the Contacts button on the Navigation pane), select any contact, click the More button in the Communicate group on the Home tab, select Call from the pop-up menu that appears, and select New Call from additional popup menu.

2. **Click Dialing Options.**

   The Dialing Options dialog box jumps out, as shown in Figure 2-10.

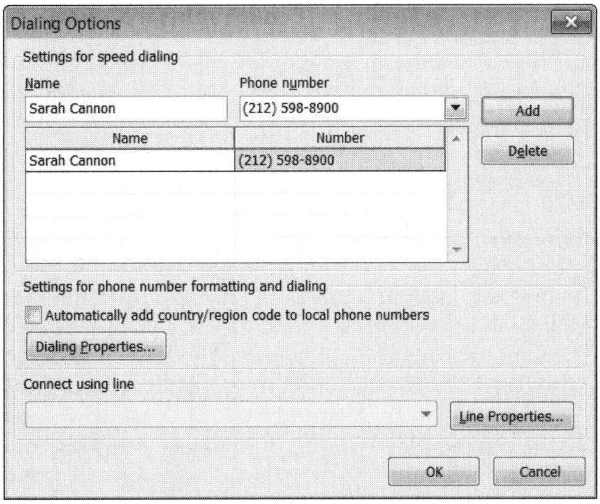

Figure 2-10:
Add the
Favored
Few to your
speed-dial
list.

3. **In the Settings for Speed Dialing section, type the name of a contact in the Name text box and press Tab.**

   The contact's first phone number should appear in the Phone Number text box.

4. **If you want to add a different number, click the arrow on the right of the Phone Number text box and select a phone number from the drop-down list that appears.**

   If, for some reason, a phone number doesn't appear in the drop-down list, type the phone number you want to use in the Phone Number text box.

5. **Click Add to add this person to your speed dial.**

6. **Repeat Steps 3 to 5 to add other speed dial contacts; click OK when you're through.**

To remove a speed-dial contact from the list, redisplay the Dialing Options dialog box, select a speed-dial contact, and click Delete.

To dial one of your speed-dial numbers, change to Contacts, click the More button in the Communicate group on the Home tab, select Call from the pop-up menu that appears, and select Speed Dial from additional pop-up menu. A list of speed-dial contacts appears on yet another pop-up menu; select one of those contacts to bring up the New Call dialog box with that phone number already selected. Opt to start a Journal entry, if you want, and then click Start Call.

Viewing Activity Associated with a Contact

Outlook can track specific activities associated with selected contacts in its Journal, which you can read about in Book I, Chapter 1. Regardless of whether you choose to use the Journal, you can have Outlook instantly scan its records for any items associated with a particular contact.

The Journal tracks activities only for your main Outlook data file. Typically, you only have one data file, and everything is stored in it. However, depending on how e-mail accounts are added to Outlook, you may have more than one. To see if you have more than one data file — and if so, which one is acting as the default (main) file — click the File button to display Backstage, and select Info from the list on the left to display the Account Information options on the right. Click the Account Settings button, and select Account Settings from the drop-down menu to display the Account Settings dialog box. Click the Data Files tab to view your data files; the default file is marked with a checkmark icon. Suppose you have two data files — one for Exchange and one for your personal folders. Assuming Exchange is your default data file, then contacts in Exchange will show the Activities button I talk about in this section, while contacts in your personal folders will not.

When you create an e-mail, receive one, or send or receive a meeting or task request, those items are automatically associated with a contact. You can also associate a new task with a contact without sending out a task request (reassigning a task). Just drag the contact with the right mouse button and drop it onto the Task button on the Navigation pane and select Copy Here As Task with Shortcut from the pop-up menu that appears.

To display a list of items associated with a contact, follow these steps:

1. **Double-click a contact whose activities you want to view to open the contact.**

2. **Click the Activities button in the Show group on the Contact tab.**

Be patient; after a moment or two, a list of activities associated with this contact appears.

3. **Double-click an activity to view it.**

The details for the selected item appear for your inspection.

You can build a comprehensive record of activities related to business contacts by using the Business Contact Manager; see Book VII for details.

Updating a contact through the People pane and its social networks

There's another way in which you might view activities associated with a contact, and that's through the Outlook Social Connector and the People pane. You can learn more about the People pane in Book I, Chapter 1, but for now I can remind you that it's the pane that appears at the bottom of every Outlook form. You may have noticed it more often in Mail, since that's probably where you spend the most time. When you expand the People pane, shown in Figure 2-11, it displays activities that the sender of that message has participated in, such as meetings, tasks, e-mail exchanges and so on. Some of the information you see in the People pane comes from Outlook, while other information comes from social networking sites (such as SharePoint, Facebook, LinkedIn, MySpace, Xing, and so on) that you and this contact both belong to.

In Contacts, you will see a separate folder for each social connector you subscribe to. For example, if you subscribe to LinkedIn and Facebook, you'll see two folders, one for each social network. In these folders, you'll find your contacts for that network. For example, in my Facebook folder, I will find the contacts I've made on Facebook. If I add a new contact to Facebook, that contact automatically appears in the Facebook Contacts folder in Outlook. These contacts may also exist in my main Contacts folder as well, so there might be some duplication going on. If you open a contact, the People pane appears at the bottom of the Contact form. No surprise there, since I just told you that the People pane appears at the bottom of every Outlook form. With the People pane, you can quickly review activity related to the contact, including any recent status updates and postings on his/her social networks. (Again, see Book I, Chapter 1 for more information.)

If you receive an e-mail from someone who's connected to you through one of your social networks, and that person has updated their personal information on that social network, then if you open the People pane in that e-mail, you may see a message on the InfoBar at the top of the pane, telling you that the contact has new information. Whether this message appears depends on the social connector. In any case, by clicking the Infobar on the People pane when you see such a message, you can automatically update that contact's data in your main Contacts folder. If such a message does not appear, you can update your main contact by pressing Ctrl and dragging the updated contact card from its social connector folder, and dropping it onto the main Contacts folder in the Navigation Pane. The Duplicate Contact Detected dialog box appears; select the Update Information of Selected Contact radio button and click Update.

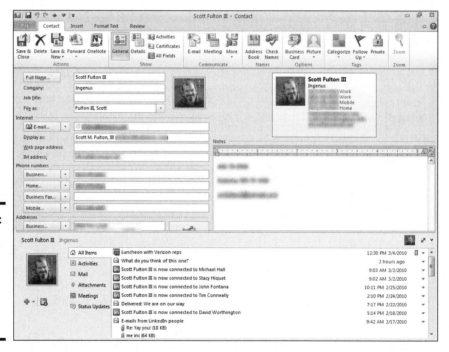

Figure 2-11:
Keep tabs
on your
friends and
colleagues
with the
People
pane.

Chapter 3: Dealing with Electronic Business Cards

In This Chapter

✔ Improving the look of an electronic business card

✔ Using business-card templates

✔ Sending electronic business cards to friends and colleagues

✔ Creating contacts from electronic business cards you receive

✔ Changing how Outlook displays electronic business cards

---

*B*usiness cards are fairly common; even though they're still made with simple paper, they're an easy way to share contact information with another person. And, paper or not, business cards sure beat writing on your arm or the back of a napkin. Electronic business cards are a bit rarer — but even so, they're a great way to share contact information digitally.

When you create a contact, Outlook automatically creates an electronic business card, as well; it's just a conglomeration of basic contact data (name, company, address, e-mail, and so on), arranged in the familiar business-card format.

You can share basic contact information quickly by simply attaching an electronic business card to an outgoing e-mail. Likewise, others can share contact data with you by sending you electronic business cards — either theirs or someone else's. Because you can share electronic business cards — yours, or someone in your Contacts list — it doesn't hurt to make them look pretty. You can find out how to do just that and more in this chapter.

Editing a Contact's Electronic Business Card

You don't actually need to do anything to make an electronic business card; Outlook creates it automatically when you create a contact. You may want to edit the electronic-business-card portion of a new or existing contact, however — especially if you're the contact and you plan on sharing your electronic business card with others.

You can share an electronic business card by attaching it to an e-mail; you can find out how in the section "Sharing Electronic Business Cards and Contacts," later in this chapter. You can also share your electronic business card as part of your *signature file* — a bit of text that appears at the end of every outgoing e-mail message. (See Book II, Chapter 4 for the lowdown on signature files.)

To edit the look of a electronic business card for a contact, follow these steps:

1. **Open or create the contact whose electronic business card you want to change, and then click the Business Card button on the Contact tab.**

   The Edit Business Card dialog box appears, as shown in Figure 3-1.

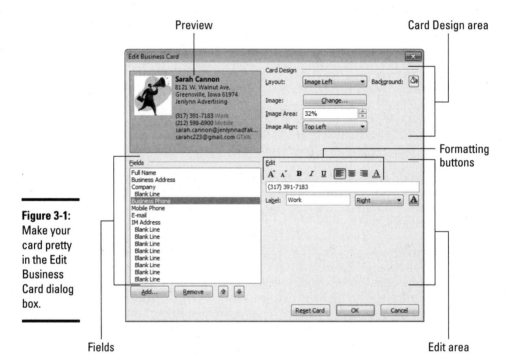

Figure 3-1: Make your card pretty in the Edit Business Card dialog box.

2. **Add, remove, or reorder the fields.**

   A preview of the completed electronic business card appears in the upper-left; just below, the Fields box lists the fields displayed on the card and the order in which they appear. You can add or remove fields or change their order:

- **Add a field.** To add a new field to the card, such as E-Mail 2 or Home Phone, first click in the Fields list above where you want the new field to appear. Click Add, and then select the field you want from the pop-up menu that appears. For example, click the Add button, select Phone from the first pop-up menu that appears, then select Home Phone from the additional pop-up menu that appears.

  The Blank Line field allows you to add a blank line between items on the card.

- **Remove a field.** To get rid of a field that you don't want to appear on the card, select it, and then click Remove.

- **Rearrange fields.** To rearrange the order in which a field appears, select it in the Fields list, and then click the up- or down-arrow button until it's in the position you want it.

You don't normally change contact info in the Edit Business Card dialog box; typically, you just change the appearance of information. To change contact data, use the Contact form. Simply double-click the contact whose information you want to change, make your changes in the Contact form that appears, and click Save & Close. See Chapter 1 of this minibook for more info.

3. **To change how the data in a particular field looks on the card, first click that field in the Fields list.**

   For example, in Figure 3-1, I clicked the Business Phone field. The data in the Business Phone field appears on the lower-right, in the Edit area.

4. **Click one of the formatting buttons in the Edit area.**

   You can use Increase Font Size, Decrease Font Size, Bold, Italics, Underline, Align Text Left, Center, Align Text Right, or Font Color. Click as many buttons as you need to achieve the look you desire. For example, you can click both the Center and Bold buttons.

   Some fields have labels that identify them, and these labels appear below each field in the Edit area (for example, the Business Phone field has a label: Work). This label also appears on the electronic business card.

5. **Change the label's text by clicking in the Label text box and typing a new label.**

   Some fields have a space for a label, but you must type the label you want to use yourself, in the Label text box. Remove the label altogether by selecting the label text and pressing Delete. Removing the label removes the label text from the electronic business card.

6. **Change the label's location relative to the data by selecting an option from the drop-down list to the right of the Label text box (for example, you can select Left or Right).**

   In Figure 3-1, I selected Right, so the label (Work) appears to the right of the business phone number.

7. **Change the label's color by clicking the Font Color button and selecting a color from the palette that appears.**

8. **To include an image on the electronic business card, click the Change button to the right of Image, select an image file from the Add Card Picture dialog box that appears, and then click OK.**

   In Figure 3-1, I chose a small image of a person with a megaphone to denote advertising. If this company really existed, I might have chosen to include their company logo.

   If you've added a picture to a contact — by clicking the Picture button on the Contact tab, as explained in Chapter 1 of this minibook — then that picture appears on the contact's electronic business card. If you choose a different image here (by clicking the Change button), then that image will appear on the electronic business card instead. However, the original contact image you selected with the Picture button remains on the Contact form, and it's the image that's displayed on the Picture pane. This allows you to add a photo of your contact (through the Picture button) that helps you identify that person, while using a different image (such as a company logo) on the contact's electronic business card.

9. **Select the layout you want from the Layout drop-down list in the Card Design area.**

   In Figure 3-1, I chose a small image and placed it to the left by selecting Image Left from the Layout list. (If I wasn't using an image at all, I could choose Text Only from this list, then skip Steps 10-11.) To use the image as the card background, select Background Image from the Layout list.

   Fill the background of the card (the part where the image doesn't show) with a color by clicking the Background button and selecting a color from the palette that appears. Even if you use a background image, you can fill the rest of the card's background (assuming the image doesn't fit edge to edge) with a color if you want. For Figure 3-1, I choose a dark melon color that matched the color behind the person in the image I selected, for a nicely coordinated look.

   If you want to include a background and an image (such as a sunset and a nice photo of yourself), you'll have to merge the background and your photo into a single photo using a photo editor (such as Paint Shop Pro or Adobe Photoshop). Then use your merged photo as the background of your electronic business card.

10. **Adjust the size of the image by changing the value in the Image Area text box.**

    You can either click in the text box and type an Image Area value, or click the up and down arrows to the right of the text box to change the value. In the figure, I set the area to 32%; if I made this larger (say, 45%) the card text would be pushed to the right and the image would be bigger.

Creating a Reusable Electronic Business Card **449**

Book V
Chapter 3

Dealing with
Electronic
Business Cards

11. **Change where the image appears exactly by selecting a position from the Image Align drop-down list.**

The alignment you select from the Image Align list coordinates with the Layout you choose in Step 9 to position the image exactly. For example, in Figure 3-1, I choose Image Left for the layout. This places the image on the left side of the card. From the Image Align list, I choose Top Left, which places the image at the top, left side of the card. I could have chosen Center (to place the image in the middle vertically, along the card's left edge), or Fit to Edge, which would not have stretched the image from the top to the bottom edges, making it a skinny image that fills the left side of the card.

12. **When you're done making changes to the card, click OK.**

The edited electronic business card appears in the Contact form.

13. **To save the card changes permanently, click the Save & Close button on the form's Contact tab.**

If you make changes to the card that you don't like, you can remove them in one step: Click the Reset Card button in the Edit Business Card dialog box, and then click Yes in the warning dialog box that appears to reset the card's formatting and layout to the Outlook default.

Creating a Reusable Electronic Business Card

You may find the electronic business card pretty handy. Not only can you use it to share your information with somebody, but you can also use an electronic business card sent to you to effortlessly create a new contact in your Contacts list. (You get to perform this magic in the section "Creating a Contact from a Electronic Business Card Sent to You," later in this chapter.) In addition, you can use an electronic business card as a template to create similar electronic business cards for several contacts. For example, you might create an electronic business card template for yourself and modify it slightly to create multiple cards for different occasions — business, personal, and simply fun. Or you might create a template to apply to all your top clients, making them easier to spot in Contacts. Your company, meanwhile, might create a template so that employees present a unified appearance through their electronic business cards.

Creating a new electronic business card template

An electronic business card is created when you create a new contact. So if you want to create multiple electronic business cards for yourself, you will need to add yourself to Contacts multiple times. This means you'll be listed in your Contacts list several times. Not that it matters — unless you find multiple entries for one person confusing. Outlook doesn't.

Suppose you want to create a template, and use that template to create simi-lar looking electronic business cards for everyone in your choral group. If you display your contacts using Business Card view, then the people in your choral group will be easy to spot, as their cards will have a similar look. To create this template, you will essentially create a new contact, only that con-tact won't have much in it other than a photo and other elements you want to reuse. Follow these steps to create the reusable electronic business card for your choral group:

1. **Get a template from Microsoft, and use it as your starting point.**

Start by downloading a template from Office Online, located at office. microsoft.com. Search in the Outlook templates section for electronic business cards. (Make sure that you look in the Outlook section of the online templates; otherwise, you may end up browsing templates for creating and printing paper business cards in Word.) Browse through the templates, and when you find one you like, click Download. Poof! The template appears in Outlook as a new contact (see Figure 3-2). I found a clean, black and white electronic business card template online called Spotlights which I thought fit my music theme, so I downloaded it.

Figure 3-2: Microsoft provides some neat templates that you can use.

Since the choral template you are about to make is actually just a new contact, you can create your template from scratch by starting with a new contact, and adding the graphic, colors, and fonts you like. See the "Editing a Contact's Electronic Business Card" section, earlier in this chapter, for help in making your design.

2. **Remove the fake phone numbers, addresses, and other data that you won't need for everyone in the choral group.**

   For example, I selected and deleted the E-mail and Home phone from the template. I replaced the Full Name with `Choral Template` so I'd be able to find this special contact-template again when I want to add the members of my choral group to Contacts. I replaced Company with `Glenbrook Chamber Choir` so I wouldn't have to type that in for each choir member. I replaced the Business Phone and Business Address with the church's address and phone so I would have that handy if I was trying to find a particular choir member. If you want, you can just leave the text in the template you downloaded (as placeholders) for when you create actual contacts from this template.

3. **Make changes to the electronic business card as desired.**

   You don't need to leave the electronic business card the way it comes in the template; if the font doesn't fit your style, or you want some bold text or a different color, follow the steps given in the "Editing a Contact's Electronic Business Card" section, earlier in this chapter, to make changes. For example, the Spotlights template included the business fax number on the electronic business card, and I didn't think I'd need that for my choral group, so I removed it. I wanted to include the choral members' home phone and address on the card, so I added them.

4. **Save the template by clicking Save & Close.**

   The template is saved to your Contacts list as a new contact. I typed `Choral Template` in the Full Name box, and my template got filed under Template, Choral. When I want to find this template to add another choral member, I can simply search the Contacts list for the word **template** or look in the Ts (by clicking the T button on the right side of the window in Business Card or Card view).

Using a template to create a new contact

After you create or download a template (as discussed in the preceding section), follow these steps to create a new contact by using it:

1. **Search your Contacts list for the electronic business card template you want to use, and double-click to open it.**

   I searched in the Ts and found my choral group template.

2. **Click the Save & New button on the Contact tab and select New Contact from the Same Company from the pop-up menu that appears.**

   A new Contact form appears, featuring the data from the template, including the electronic business card. For my template, I typed the member's name in the Full Name text box, and filled out the E-mail, Home Phone, and Home Address boxes.

3. **Type the necessary additional contact information into the form and click the Save & Close button on the Contact tab.**

Applying a new template to an old contact

You can use a template to update an existing contact, but it's a little tricky. For example, suppose I already have a few members of my choral group entered into Contacts, but I really like the look of the new template I've created (especially the electronic business card). I can open the choral group template and follow these steps to apply its design to one of those existing choral group members:

1. **Click the Save & New button on the Contact tab and select Contact from the Same Company from the pop-up menu that appears.**

   A new contact appears, with some of its stuff filled in. This data came from the template. In my case, the new contact has the Company Name (which is the name of the choir), Business Phone (the phone number of the church where we practice), and Business Address (church address).

2. **Remove the template information.**

   Normally, I'd remove most of the data from the template because I typically don't want the template data to override your real contact's stuff. But in this case, I know that what I've entered into the template (for church phone and address) is correct, so I'll just keep that.

3. **Enter the contact's name in the Full Name text box.**

   In my case, I had already entered in Katie Small in Contacts before I decided to get fancy and create this cool choir template. I want to apply the template to her contact data, so I will type Katie Small in the Full Name field. The name must exactly match the Full Name for the contact to which you want to apply this template, so if I'm not sure, I might check the spelling of Katie's name before continuing.

4. **Click Save & Close.**

   Because the name you typed in the Full Name box exactly matches someone else in your Contact's list, the Duplicate Contact Detected dialog box appears, telling you that you're about to add two contacts with the same name.

5. **Select the Update Information of Selected Contact radio button and click Update.**

   Your existing contact is updated with the electronic business card template. Close the template by clicking its Close button; you're done with it until you need it to add another contact in that group.

Sharing Electronic Business Cards and Contacts

One of the chief reasons for creating electronic business cards (besides making your contacts look cool) is to share them. You can also share your own card, either as part of the signature placed at the end of every e-mail or in just a single message. (For help in adding your electronic business card to your e-mail signature, see Book II, Chapter 4.)

When you share an electronic business card, you're sharing just the information that appears on that contact's electronic business card. If you want to be more complete, you can send someone the actual Outlook contact for that person, which contains all the contact's information, not just selected fields. Of course, keep in mind that although most e-mail programs can read electronic business cards, a recipient can't open an Outlook contact file if he or she doesn't have Outlook.

To include an electronic business card or an Outlook contact in an e-mail message, follow these steps:

1. **Change to Contacts if needed by clicking the Contacts button on the Navigation pane, and click the contact you want to share with someone.**

2. **Click the Forward Contact button on the Home tab.**

   A pop-up menu appears.

3. **Select how you want to share the contact.**

   The menu offers you these choices:

   - *As a Business Card:* Send the contact's electronic business card information in vCard format, an electronic business card format which most e-mail programs can use. A new e-mail message appears; the electronic business card is inserted into the text area of the message and attached to the message, as well. (See the background of Figure 3-3.) If you receive an e-mail with an electronic business card attached, you can use it to add that contact to your Outlook. See the next section, "Creating a Contact from an Electronic Business Card Sent to You," for help.

   - *As an Outlook Contact:* Send all the contact's information (and not just the data that appears on his or her electronic business card) in an Outlook Contact file. A new e-mail message appears with the Contact file already attached to the message (refer to the foreground of Figure 3-3). If you receive an e-mail with a Contact file attached, you can use it to add that contact to your Outlook. See the next section, "Creating a Contact from an Electronic Business Card Sent to You," for help.

- *Forward as Text Message:* Sends the contact information as a text message to someone's cell phone. You must have text messaging enabled through an Outlook Service Provider to use this option; see Book III, Chapter 3 for information on how to do that.

4. **Click Send to send the message.**

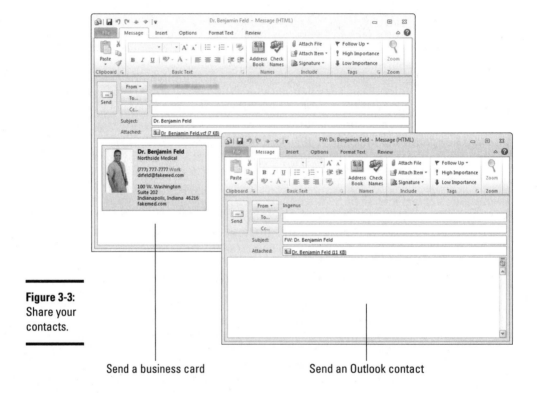

Figure 3-3:
Share your
contacts.

Send a business card   Send an Outlook contact

Creating a Contact from an Electronic Business Card Sent to You

After someone sends you an electronic business card in an e-mail, you probably want to know how to get the contact data out of the e-mail and into Outlook. As the following sections explain, it's all pretty straight-forward. Alternatively, what if someone sent you contact information in the form of an Outlook file? What do you do then? Turns out, the process is also pretty easy.

Using an electronic business card to add a contact

Did you receive an electronic business card for someone who's not on your list of Outlook contacts? Follow these steps to add the contact to Outlook:

1. **If the contact card appears in the e-mail message, right-click the electronic business card, and select Add to Outlook Contacts from the pop-up menu.**

You can't miss it; it looks like a business card, and it's prominently displayed in the message area. You don't have to open the message to right-click the card; you can just view its contents in the Reading pane.

When you right-click the electronic business card, a pop-up menu appears. (See the foreground of Figure 3-4.)

2. **Select Add to Outlook Contacts from the pop-up menu.**

A Contact form appears, with the info taken from the electronic business card displayed (see the background of Figure 3-4).

If the electronic business card is attached to the e-mail, click the cards filename at the top of the Reading pane, and in the Attachments tab that appears, click the Open button to open the Contact form.

3. **Click the Save & Close button on the form's Contact tab to save the new contact.**

If the contact's name happens to match somebody in your Contacts list, a warning dialog box appears — if you continue with the save, you'll lose that old contact. You have a couple of options:

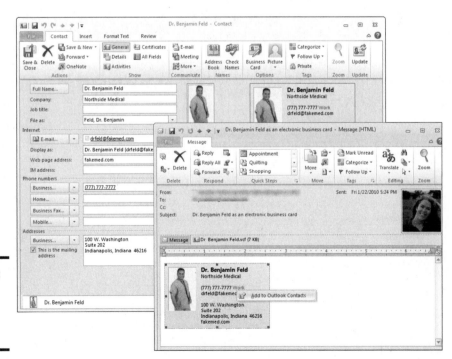

Figure 3-4:
Adding an electronic business card.

- To keep the old and add the new, select the Add New Contact radio button and click Update to create a separate, new contact with the same name.

- To trash the old data and update your existing contact with this new information, select the Update Information of Selected Contact radio button and click Update, instead.

Using an Outlook file to add a contact

Did someone forward a contact to you as an Outlook Contact? Then follow these steps to add that contact to Outlook.

1. **In the e-mail message, click the attachment.**

You don't have to open the message to click its attachment (you can view the message in the Reading pane, and click the attachment, which is listed just above the message area). When you click the attachment, the Attachments tab appears, as shown in the foreground of Figure 3-5, and the contact info appears in the Reading pane or message area.

Open

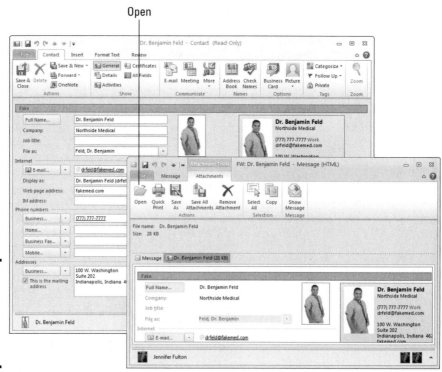

Figure 3-5: Adding an Outlook contact that someone sent to you.

2. **Click the Open button on the Attachments tab.**

   A Contact form appears, featuring all the contact's information (not just the data that's displayed on the contact's electronic business card). See the background of Figure 3-5.

3. **Click the Save & Close button on the form's Contact tab to save the new contact.**

   If the contact's name matches someone in your Contacts list, a warning dialog box appears — if you continue with the save, you'll lose that old contact. Choose one of these options:

   - To keep the old and add the new, select the Add New Contact radio button and click Update to create a new contact with the same name.

   - To update your existing contact with this new information, select the Update Information of Selected Contact radio button and click Update, instead.

Displaying More Electronic Business Cards

When you look at Contacts, by default, each contact appears as an electronic business card in Business Card view. If you make the Navigation pane really skinny, you can display more electronic business cards. But that trick makes the Navigation pane almost too thin to use. You can also click the Cards Only button at the bottom of the Outlook window to hide the Navigation pane, as well as the To-Do bar, to display more cards. Sometimes, you want it all — the Navigation pane, the To-Do bar, and more cards. In that case, click the Normal button on the status bar, and then adjust the zoom by using the Zoom slider. To hide the To-Do bar but display the Navigation Pane, click the No To-Do Bar button on the status bar and then adjust the zoom. (See Figure 3-6.)

A better solution, assuming that you prefer to see more cards when you use Business Card view, is to customize that view. For an intro to customizing Outlook views, check out Book VIII, Chapter 2.

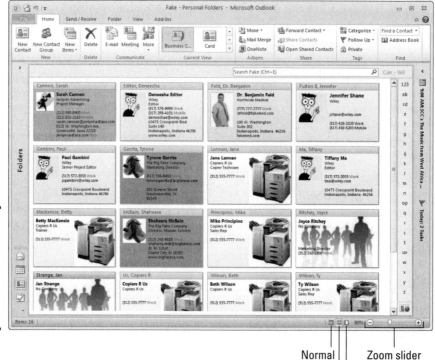

Figure 3-6: Display more electronic business cards, if you want.

Normal

Cards Only

No To-Do Bar

Zoom slider

Chapter 4: Contacts Collaboration

In This Chapter

✓ **Sharing contacts over an Exchange network**

✓ **Restricting access to your contacts**

✓ **Viewing somebody else's contacts**

*I*n your Contacts list, you probably have quite a collection of people: friends, family, and colleagues. In addition, you may have many other contacts you want to share, such as doctors, babysitters, plumbers, electricians, carpenters, and other resources. In addition, your co-workers might want the scoop on your list of new and prospective clients. So, you might want to share your Contacts list for any number of reasons, and in this chapter, you can find out how.

Normal sharing occurs over an Exchange network (a corporate network that uses Microsoft Exchange), between you and your co-workers. However, you can share contacts, even if you're not on an Exchange network. For example, you can e-mail an electronic business card or simply share the contact in Outlook format. (See Chapter 3 of this minibook for help.)

Sharing Your Contacts

Assuming that you work on an Exchange network (the Outlook status bar displays Connected to Microsoft Exchange if you are), you can share your contacts with other people on the network. Like me, you may have contacts in your Contacts list that you don't want to share. Unfortunately, sharing on an Exchange network is mostly an all or nothing proposition — if you share a Contacts folder, you share pretty much everything in it. You can, however, create an additional Contacts folder, place only the contacts you want to share in that folder, and share just that folder and not your main Contacts one. For example, if you're working with a big team on a huge project, you can create a project folder and put all the contacts you need to complete the project — including client contacts — in that folder. Or maybe you can more easily do the reverse: Create a folder and place your private contacts in it. Then, share the main Contacts folder on the Exchange network.

You can mark individual contacts as private so that when someone views the other contacts in a shared folder, he or she doesn't see those private contacts. You may want to use this method if you have only a few contacts you don't want to share. To make a contact private, click the contact to select it, then click the Private button on the Home tab. If you're in the midst of creating a contact (or you have the contact form open for some other reason) click the Private button on the Contact tab.

If you like the idea of creating a new Contacts folder and putting only the contacts you want to share in it (I certainly do), see Book IX, Chapter 1 for step-by-step pointers on how to create the folder and move contacts into it.

Now, when I say all or nothing, I don't mean that you have to open your Contacts list to the world — or, at least, the part of the world that has access to your Exchange network. Nope, you can share your list with Bryan and not with Kelly, if you want. You can also define the level of sharing: For example, you can control whether people can just view contacts, or update and create them, as well.

So, when you share your contacts, you can do one of two things:

✦ **Share the main Contacts folder with basically everyone on the network.** You can designate what everyone can do, such as view only, or view and edit. See the following section.

✦ **Share either the main Contacts folder or a custom Contacts folder with only the specific people you select.** See the section "Sharing contacts with specific people," later in this chapter.

Sharing contacts with everyone

Following the steps in this section, you can share your main Contacts folder. You can't use these steps to share a Contacts folder that you created. Well, okay, you might try — and it may seem to work — but it doesn't work correctly. Basically, Microsoft can't think of a reason why you might create a special Contacts folder and want to share it with *everybody.* If you're determined to share the custom folder with everyone, you're gonna have to follow the steps in the following section — and (unfortunately, but literally) e-mail everyone a sharing invitation. To access a custom folder, you must use a sharing invitation. (Sorry, that's just the way it is.)

To share a main Contacts folder with everyone on the Exchange network, follow these steps:

1. **Click the Folder Permissions button on the Folder tab.**

The Contacts Properties dialog box pops up.

2. **Click the Permissions tab, and in the Name list, click Default, as shown in Figure 4-1.**

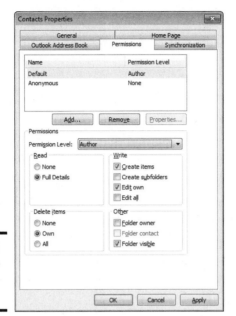

Figure 4-1:
You decide
how much
to share.

3. **From the options that appear in the Permissions Level list, select the level that describes the kind of things you want visitors to be able to do.**

The Permissions options include

- *Publishing Editor:* Lets a user create, edit, delete, and view contacts. Users can also create subfolders within the shared folder.

- *Editor:* Same as Publishing Editor, except the user can't create subfolders.

- *Publishing Author:* Lets a user create and view contacts, create folders, and edit or delete contacts which that user has created him- or herself.

- *Author:* Same as Publishing Author, except that the user can't create subfolders.

- *Nonediting Author:* Same as Author, except that the user can't edit existing contacts, even if he or she created them.

- *Reviewer:* Lets a user view contacts only.

- *Contributor:* Lets a user create and edit new contacts; but the user can't view existing ones unless he or she created them.

- *None:* Prevents all users from accessing the folder at all — a user can't even view the contacts in the folder.

4. **Click OK.**

   Your main Contacts folder appears in the Navigation pane with a special icon that looks like a hand holding a business card. This icon shows everyone that the folder is open for visitors.

As long as everyone knows you're in the sharing mood, they can access your main Contacts folder simply by selecting your name from a list. They don't need an e-mail invitation from you or a secret codeword. All the same, unless you work at the Real Good Psychics Hotline, your colleagues probably don't know that you've suddenly taken to sharing your Contacts list. So, you may want to send an e-mail to the people with whom you want to share this folder, just to let them know. The rest of everybody on your network can just fend for themselves. If you decide to send out e-mails to let people know your Contacts folder is shared, you don't need to send anything special, just a little note from you telling the people you care about most that your default Contacts list is now shared. Check out the section "Viewing Contacts Shared by Others," later in this chapter, for the lowdown on how a person on your network gains access to your Contacts folder after you share it.

Sharing contacts with specific people

Sometimes, you don't want to share with everyone — like when you have only three pieces of pumpkin pie left and eight guests. Yep, better to stash the pie away until they all leave and have it as a midnight snack. (No need to tell the husband, either, because you can't divide three by two. Nope, better that you save everyone the bad feelings of being left out by eating the rest of the pie yourself. Oh, the things you do for your family!)

In the procedure we describe in this section, you share a Contacts folder and send a sharing invitation to the specific people you choose. For custom folders that you've created, you have only two access cards you can hand out to visitors: *Reviewer* (which means they can only view your contacts) or *Editor* (which means they can create, edit, delete, and view contacts, even ones they don't create themselves). If you're sharing your main Contacts folder to a select few (rather than everyone, as described in the previous section) by using this procedure, then you can provide visitors only Reviewer status — at least, initially. After the sharing invitation goes out, you can always change a particular person's access level, as desired — see the section "Changing permissions or stopping sharing," later in this chapter.

To share a Contacts folder with a select few, first select it in the Navigation pane. You can share your main Contacts with just a few people by following these steps, or a Contacts folder you've created. (If you want to share your main Calendar with everyone, see the preceding section.) After selecting a Contacts folder, follow these steps to share it:

1. **Click the Share Contacts button on the Home tab.**

A Message form appears, as shown in Figure 4-2. The form in the background of Figure 4-2 appears if you share your main Contacts folder; the form in the foreground appears if you share a Contacts folder you added yourself.

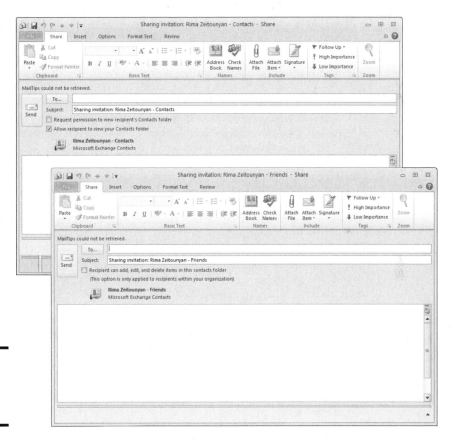

Figure 4-2:
Send your
sharing
invitation.

2. **In the To text box, type the addresses of the people with whom you want to share your contacts.**

3. **Edit the Subject text if you like.**

Normally it shows Sharing invitation: *Your Name – Folder Name.*

4. **(Optional) In the large text box at the bottom of the form, type a short message explaining the invitation, if you want.**

5. **(Optional) If you are sharing your main Contacts folder, select the Request Permission to View Recipient's Contacts Folder check box.**

If you select this check box, you request specific permission to view each addressee's Contacts folder, in return.

6. **If you're sharing your main Contacts folder, make sure that the Allow Recipient to View Your Contacts Folder check box is selected.**

   Otherwise, you won't actually be sharing your Contacts with anyone.

7. **If you are sharing a Contacts folder that you created, and you want to give users Editor access, select the Recipient Can Add, Edit, and Delete Items in This Contacts Folder check box.**

   If you don't select this option, visitors get only Reviewer access, which means they can look but not touch.

8. **Finish the message and click Send.**

   A dialog box appears, asking whether you really want to share this folder. If you do, click Yes. Another dialog box appears, telling you that your Contacts folder is shared.

9. **Click OK.**

   The folder you chose appears in the Navigation pane with a special icon, which looks kinda like a Contacts handout — a hand holding a business card. The icon lets you know that you've shared this folder, just in case you're the forgetful type.

The recipients of your e-mails can click the link in the message to connect to the shared folder. See the section "Viewing Contacts Shared by Others," later in this chapter, for more information.

Changing permissions or stopping sharing

After sharing a main Contacts folder or a Contacts folder you came up with on your own, you don't have to continue sharing it forever. For example, you can change a person's permissions so that he or she can't add or remove contacts anymore, or you can remove his or her permission to even access the folder at all.

When you initially share the main Contacts folder with individual users, they get Reviewer status, which means they can only view contacts. You probably want to give users Reviewer status, anyway, because I'm guessing you don't want to grant someone the ability to add contacts to your main list, or to change or delete contacts.

However, by following the general steps in this section, you can change the access level for anyone you want and grant someone broader access to your Contacts folder. I wouldn't, however. Instead, move the contacts you want to relinquish control over into a different Contacts folder, and then grant a higher level of access to only that new folder. But that's just me — a control freak who doesn't like to think of someone accidentally deleting all the Contacts it took me so long to collect.

To change a user's permission to use a shared folder, follow these steps:

1. **Select the shared Contacts folder in the Navigation pane.**

2. **Click the Folder Permissions button on the Folder tab.**

The *Folder Name* Properties dialog box pops up.

3. **Change permissions, as desired.**

You have two options:

- *To make a change that affects everyone:* Select Default from the Name list. Then, make a selection from the Permissions Level drop-down list or, to completely revoke all access, select None.

- *To make a change to a particular user's permissions:* Select the user's name from the Name list, as shown in Figure 4-3. Then, from the Permission Level drop-down list, select the level of access you want to grant this user.

Figure 4-3:
Change
permissions
to use a
folder.

If you've granted basically the same access to everyone through the Default classification, then you can add a specific user to the list and set the permission level you want for that particular person. To add someone to the Name list, click Add, select the person from the list that appears, and click Add to add him or her. Select more names, if you want, and click Add. After you gather all the names you want to add to the Name list in the Properties dialog box, click OK. Any new user you add gets the Default permission level. Select a name in the Name list and select a different Permission Level, as desired.

4. **Click OK.**

The permissions are changed right away.

If someone is viewing your Contacts folder when you change his or her level of access, that change affects him or her immediately — or as soon as your change filters through the network. If you've removed access from someone, the Contacts list soon disappears from his or her screen.

Viewing Contacts Shared by Others

If someone on your company's Exchange network has been nice enough to share his or her Contacts folder with you, or even a special Contacts subfolder, you can easily gain access to it. After you make the initial contact (pardon the pun), the folder appears in the Navigation pane in the section called Shared Contacts, making it really easy to retrieve those contacts when you need them.

After you gain access to someone's Contacts folder (the main one or a custom Contacts folder), if you don't have editing permissions, you can't make any changes to a contact. If you try to change a contact when you don't have permission to, a dialog box appears, asking whether you want to save a copy of this contact to your Contacts folder. Click Yes to do just that.

Accessing someone's main Contacts folder

To gain access to somebody else's shared, main Contacts folder for the first time, follow these steps:

1. **Click the Open Shared Contacts button on the Home tab.**

The Open Shared Contacts dialog box appears, as shown on the left in Figure 4-4.

2. **Type the name of the person whose calendar you want to view in the Name text box.**

Alternatively, if you don't know the person's name, click the Name button. The Select Name: Contacts dialog box appears. (On the right in Figure 4-4.) Select a name from this dialog box and click OK. You're returned to the Open Shared Contacts dialog box.

3. **Click OK.**

The folder, assuming that it's shared and you have permission to access it, appears in the Shared Contacts list in the Navigation pane. The contacts in the folder appear on the right. If you don't want to display this Contacts folder right now, just uncheck its check box. The next time you want to view this Contacts folder, click the check box.

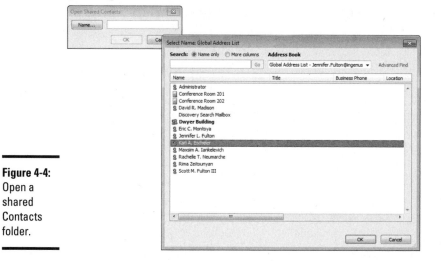

Figure 4-4:
Open a
shared
Contacts
folder.

If the Contacts folder you just tried to open is shared, but not with you, a
dialog box appears, asking whether you want to ask for permission. Click
Yes to make a message form appear, with a nicely typed request to use the
folder. Make sure that the Request Permission to View Recipient's Contacts
Folder check box is selected. If you want to allow access to your main
Contacts folder in return, select the Allow Recipient to View Your Contacts
Folder check box. Click Send to send the request.

You can get rid of a shared contacts folder from the Shared Contacts list if
you don't think you need to view it anymore. Just select the Contacts folder
that you want to remove and click the Delete Folder button on the Folder
tab. By the way, this step doesn't actually delete the Contacts folder from
the owner's system.

Accessing someone's custom Contacts folder

If someone has gone to the trouble of creating a custom group of contacts
they want to share with you, then at some point, you get an e-mail invitation
asking you to come on in. Most likely, you get either Reviewer access (view
only) or Editor access (create, edit, and delete contacts). Regardless of what
kind of access the user decides to grant you, after you add that folder to your
Shared Contacts list, you can easily view its contents any time you want.

To access someone's shared, custom Contacts folder or a main Contacts
shared with a selected few, follow these steps:

1. **Click the Mail button on the Navigation pane to change over to Mail
and then either select the sharing invitation to view it in the Reading
pane or double-click it to view it in a separate window.**

2. Click the Open This Contacts Folder button.

This button appears at the top of the Reading pane, or on the Share tab in the message window. (See Figure 4-5.)

You are automatically switched over to the Contacts module, where the Contacts folder now appears in the Shared Contacts group on the Navigation pane. The contents of the shared Contacts folder is automatically displayed for you, as shown in Figure 4-6.

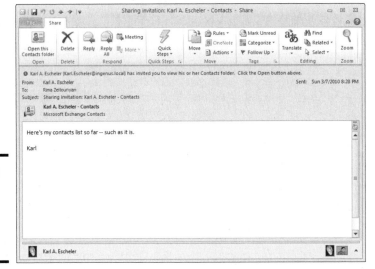

Figure 4-5:
Gaining access to a custom Contacts folder.

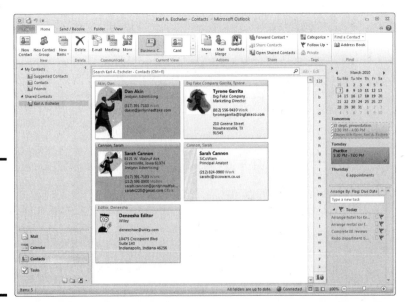

Figure 4-6:
After it's shared, just click a Contacts folder to view its contents.

Book VI

Tracking Tasks, Taking Notes, and Organizing Life with OneNote

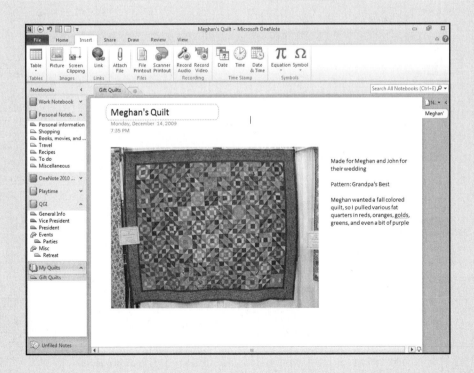

Contents at a Glance

Chapter 1: Creating Simple To-Do Items

In This Chapter

✔ Tracking tasks with the To-Do bar

✔ Adding and adjusting flags

✔ Checking off To-Do items

✔ Finding stuff to do

✔ Making the To-Do bar your own

✔ Working with the Daily Task List

*I*t always seems like I have more than enough to do — in fact, I have so many things on my list, I probably won't be taking a vacation anytime soon. Luckily, I have my nagging buddy Outlook to remind me what to do so that I don't waste valuable time thinking about which impossible task I should tackle next. Outlook presents its list of tasks in several places so that it's nearly impossible for you to say, "Sorry, I forgot to do that." You can find tasks on the To-Do bar, the Daily Task List in Calendar, and the Tasks module (and maybe under the couch). It's not like I think you don't have enough to do, but if you want to find out how to deal with all those nagging tasks, I recommend one more task: reading this chapter.

The To-Do bar normally appears in every module except Calendar, where tasks and To-Do items are displayed on the Daily Task List. However, if the To-Do bar doesn't appear in any module, click the To-Do Bar button on the View tab and select Normal from the pop-up menu that appears to show it. To hide the To-Do bar temporarily, click its Minimize button, or click the To-Do Bar button on the View tab and select Minimize from the pop-up menu. To remove it completely, select Off from the menu, instead.

Using the To-Do Bar to Track To-Do Items

In Book I, Chapter 1, I introduce you to the To-Do bar, with its To-Do items and Tasks list, Date Navigator, and appointment/meeting/event bubbles (see Figure 1-1). That chapter also covers the difference between a To-Do item (which you create from another Outlook item, such as an e-mail, simply by flagging that item) and a task (which is pretty complex, typically including a starting/ending date, status, priority code, and percentage complete). Here are some other differences of note:

Upcoming events/meetings/appointments

Date Navigator

Figure 1-1:
The handy
dandy
To-Do bar.

To-Do items and tasks

✦ You can reassign a task to somebody else on your company network, whereas you can't reassign a To-Do item.

✦ A task can recur at regular intervals, whereas a To-Do item is a one-shot deal.

✦ Both tasks and To-Do items appear on the To-Do bar, the Tasks list, the To-Do list, and the Daily Task List in Calendar, so you usually can't tell one from the other by just looking. When you open them up, however, you can tell right away — tasks open up into a conventional Task form, but To-Do items open into the Outlook item used to create them, such as an e-mail message.

In Book I, Chapter 2, you discover how to create a simple To-Do item using the Type a New Task box on the To-Do bar. In this chapter, I show you how to create To-Do items the way they were meant to be created — from other Outlook items. (For help in creating complete tasks, see Chapter 2 of this minibook; for information on how to add quick tasks by using the Daily Task List, see the section "Creating a Task by Using the Daily Task List in the Calendar," later in this chapter.)

To automatically assign a flag to certain incoming messages, simply design a rule that describes the type of messages you want to flag. Flagged messages appear on the To-Do bar, To-Do list, and Daily Task List. See Book IX, Chapter 2 for help in creating rules.

Turning an incoming e-mail into a To-Do bar item

Because e-mails often contain requests for you to look up something, report on something, or to do some other something, Outlook makes it easy for you to turn an e-mail into a reminder to do that something. To flag an e-mail message for follow-up and add a reminder to the To-Do bar, To-Do list, and Daily Task List, follow these steps:

1. **Locate the e-mail you want to flag, and either select it or open it (your choice).**

2. **Click the Follow Up button on either the Home tab (if you just selected the e-mail) or the Message form's Message tab (if you went ahead and opened the e-mail message), and then select a flag from the pop-up menu that appears.**

Your choices, shown in Figure 1-2, include

Book VI Chapter 1

Creating Simple To-Do Items

Flagged messages   Choose a flag

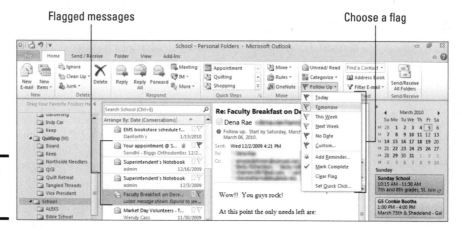

Figure 1-2: Plant your flag.

- **Today:** Sets the due date to today.

- **Tomorrow:** Sets the due date to tomorrow.

- **This Week:** Sets the due date to Friday of the current week (or the last day of your work week, if you've changed in Outlook what you consider "work days" — see Book IV, Chapter 5).

- **Next Week:** Sets the due date to Friday of next week (or whatever the last day of your work week is currently set to).

- **No Date:** Flags an item with an indefinite, get-to-it-when-you-can kind of date.

- **Custom:** Select this option to flag the item with a unique date. When you select Custom from the pop-up menu, the Custom dialog box appears, as shown in Figure 1-3. Normally, when you flag an item such as a message, the Start Date is set to the date on which you set the flag, and the Due Date is based on the kind of flag you select, such as Tomorrow. In the Custom dialog box, you can select any Start Date and Due Date you want. To be reminded about the task, select the Reminder check box and set a Reminder date and time. Click OK.

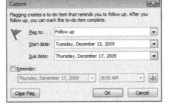

Figure 1-3:
Customize
the flag.

In Figure 1-2, I got a message asking me to help with the Faculty Holiday Breakfast at my daughter's school, so I clicked the Follow Up button and selected Tomorrow from the menu because I can't get to it right now. As you can see in the figure, I already have another message flagged for some kind of follow up action, so I better get cracking on all of them!

After you flag a message, a colored flag appears in the Flag column of the message list in the Mail module, at the right end of the mail header. A notation reminding you that a Follow Up flag has been set also appears in the InfoBar of the message. The flag's color is based on the due date you select from the Follow Up list. In Figure 1-2, one message has a bright red flag because it represents something I need to get done today. After I select the Tomorrow flag for the Holiday Breakfast message, a slightly less red flag appears next to its header. In addition, after you flag a message, a To-Do item appears in the appropriate group in the To-Do bar (for example, the Today group); the same item is added to the Daily Task List and the To-Do list.

You can flag an e-mail message quickly by clicking the Flag column in the message list. The flag that appears is controlled by the Quick Click Flag value, which is usually set to Today. Thus, if you click the Flag column on a message's header, you probably set a Today flag and add that message-task to the To-Do bar in the Today group. You can find out how to change the Quick Click Flag to some other value in the "Setting the Quick Click Flag" section, later in the chapter.

Turning a contact into a To-Do bar item

If you have a special contact you want to get in touch with, you can flag that contact in Outlook. When you do, a To-Do item appears in the To-Do bar as a visual reminder to pick up the phone, write an e-mail, or stop by soon. The To-Do item also appears in the usual places — the To-Do list and the Daily Task List. The flag appears in Contacts in the list views (Phone and List), but not the card views (Business Card and Card). Regardless of the view, a textual reminder appears in the InfoBar if you open the contact, as shown in Figure 1-4.

A textual reminder appears on the Info Bar   Select a flag from the Follow Up list.

Figure 1-4:
Gotta call
soon.

To flag a contact and create a To-Do item, follow these steps:

1. **Locate the contact you want to flag and either select it or open it (your choice).**

2. **Click the Follow Up button on the Home tab (if you select the contact) or the Contact form's Contact tab (if you open the contact, as shown in Figure 1-4), and select a due date from the pop-up menu.**

   You can select Today, Tomorrow, This Week (actually, either Friday of the current week or the last work day), Next Week (that's Friday or the last work day of the following week), or No Date (which flags the item but doesn't create a due date).

Select Custom to set your own specific date and add a reminder, if you want. (See the preceding section for a complete description of each due date type.)

A flag doesn't appear in Contacts unless you use Phone or List view, but you do see the flag — well, okay, the textual equivalent of a flag — if you double-click the contact itself (the text flag is hiding in the InfoBar). The flag — this time a real, honest-to-goodness flag — also appears in the usual places: the To-Do bar, To-Do list, and Daily Task List. If you actually get around to contacting your contact and want to check that task off as completed, see the section "Marking a To-Do item as finito," later in this chapter. If you need to move the item to a later date in the To-Do bar, To-Do list, and Daily Task List, change the flag: See the section "Changing the Flag You've Assigned an Item," later in this chapter.

If the To-Do bar happens to be displayed in Contacts and you currently have its list sorted by either Start or Due Date, you can just drag a contact and drop it on the To-Do list to create a To-Do item. For example, grab a contact you want to get in touch with by the end of the day, drag the contact onto the To-Do bar, and drop it in the Today group. Also, if you are using Phone or List view, you can flag a contact quickly by clicking the Flag column. The flag that appears is controlled by the Quick Click Flag value; see the next section for help with Quick Click Flags.

Setting the Quick Click Flag

You may have already discovered that in Mail, if you click the flag column in the message listing, you set automatic Quick Click Flag for Today. Likewise, if you display Contacts in a list view, you can click the flag column to set a flag for a contact that's set to Today. The Quick Click Flag, as Outlook calls it, is set to Today by default, meaning that if you want to quickly flag an item, Outlook obliges you and sets a flag for Today.

To change the Quick Click Flag value, follow these steps:

1. **Click the Follow Up button on the Home tab and select Set Quick Click from the pop-up menu that appears.**

The Set Quick Click dialog box jumps up, as shown in Figure 1-5.

Figure 1-5:
Just choose
the flag you
use most
often.

2. **From the drop-down list, select the value you want Outlook to assign an item if you quick click that item.**

3. **Click OK.**

As a reminder, to use Quick Click, just click in the Flag column next to a message in the message listing, or a contact in a contact list.

Changing the Flag You've Assigned a To-Do Item

If you don't happen to get your To-Do item done when you thought you would, it doesn't go away. For example, if you assigned a Today flag to an e-mail so that you'd remember to look something up and get back to a client, and you just didn't get that done, then the To-Do item continues to nag you from its place on the To-Do bar, appearing in tomorrow's Today list. It changes color, however, from ordinary black text to a more eye-catching-you-better-really-get-this-done red text. Likewise, the To-Do item appears in red text on the To-Do list if you don't get it done on-time. Red tasks appear above the black tasks originally scheduled for that day.

Book VI
Chapter 1

Creating Simple
To-Do Items

But you don't need to let Outlook get away with its aggressive red-texting behavior: If you know you really can't get something done on the day a flag says you need to and you want to reschedule it for another day, you can change the flag. Follow these steps:

1. **Click the To-Do item whose flag you want to change in the To-Do bar, To-Do list, or Daily Task List.**

   If you click an item in the To-Do bar or Daily Task List, then the Task Tools/Daily Task List Tools tab appears, as shown in Figure 1-6. If you click an item in the To-Do List, click the Home tab before continuing to Step 2.

   If you're changing the flag for a message or contact and you see its flag in the message/contact listing, you can right-click that flag and select a new flag from the pop-up menu that appears.

2. **Select the flag you want to use from the Follow Up section of the Task Tools/Daily Task List Tools/Home tab that appears.**

   For example, if you click the Next Week button, the To-Do item moves to the appropriate group in the To-Do bar/Daily Task List/To-Do List (in this case, the Next Week group) and comes back to haunt you at that time.

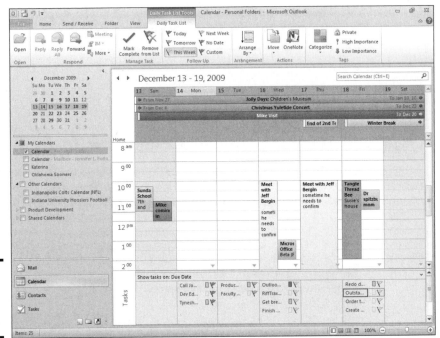

Figure 1-6:
Change the
flag for a
To-Do item.

Changing a To-Do Item's Name

When you create a To-Do item from a message or a contact, the message subject or contact name is used as the To-Do item's name. That name, unfortunately, may not really tell you what exactly you're supposed to do when you glance at that To-Do item. Fortunately, you can change the item's name without affecting the actual message heading or contact name by following these steps:

1. **Click the item whose name you want to change, pause for a moment, and then click it again.**

You can perform this surgery by clicking the item in the To-Do bar, Daily Task List, or To-Do List. If you double-click (two clicks in quick succession), you won't break anything, but you just open the item, which doesn't help you change the item's name. So, watch your trigger finger.

2. **Edit the item name, or simply drag over it to select it and then type a new name.**

3. **Press Enter.**

The new item's name appears in the listing.

Dealing with a To-Do Item You've Finished or No Longer Want to Flag

After you create all your To-Do items, you're probably anxious to check one or two off your list. When you mark a To-Do item as complete, Outlook instantly removes that item from the To-Do bar and the To-Do List, but not the Daily Task List. Check that one off! If you haven't actually completed anything but simply put the item on the To-Do list by accident, you can remove it just as easily by simply removing its flag. We cover both procedures in the following sections.

Marking a To-Do item as finito

Marking off something on your To-Do list can be very satisfying. I sometimes add stupid stuff to my list, such as Get a Cup of Coffee, just so I can experience the satisfaction of checking off something before 10 a.m. If you finish something on your list, you can easily check it off. Just follow these steps:

1. **Change to the appropriate module and locate the item you want to mark off.**

   You can finish off an item by using the To-Do bar, the To-Do list, or the Daily Task List.

2. **Click the item's flag.**

   Outlook immediately removes the item from the To-Do bar and To-Do list. Don't freak; the message or contact from which you created the To-Do item doesn't go away, just the To-Do item.

   If the To-Do item is a message, then the flag on the message's header in the message list changes to a check mark, as shown in Figure 1-7. If the item is a contact, the text in the InfoBar of the opened contact changes to tell you that the Follow Up was completed today.

Removing a flag rather than marking it complete

Sometimes, you just want to remove a flag, not because you got something done, but because you set the flag by accident or it's simply no longer relevant. Or maybe you want to remove a flag because it's become more annoying than helpful. To remove a flag, follow these steps:

1. **In the To-Do bar, To-Do list, or Daily Task List, click the To-Do item that you want to change.**

   If you click an item in the To-Do bar or Daily Task List, then the Task Tools/Daily Task List Tools tab appears (refer to Figure 1-6). If you click an item in the To-Do List, click the Home tab before continuing to Step 2.

Figure 1-7:
Check
another
one off.

A checkmark in the Flag column tells you that this To-Do item is done.

A To-Do item is removed when it is marked complete.

If you're changing the flag for a message or contact and you see its flag in the message/contact listing, you can right-click that flag and select Clear Flag from the pop-up menu that appears.

2. **Click the Remove from List button on the Task Tools/Daily Task List Tools/Home tab.**

   Outlook removes the flag and takes the item off the various To-Do lists: the To-Do bar, To-Do List, and Daily Task List. If you used a message or contact to create the To-Do item, that message or contact simply returns to its normal, boring existence without the flag — Outlook doesn't delete it.

Deleting a To-Do item

Deleting a To-Do item gets rid of it permanently, so this is not something you will normally want to do. But I offer these steps here for the neat freaks out there who just have to throw out something once they are done with it. When you delete a To-Do item, it doesn't go off skulking to the To-Do list or the Daily Task List with a line struck through it — no, the item goes away permanently. Okay, maybe not exactly permanently because the deleted item will still be in the Deleted Items folder until you empty it, but you know what I mean. It's a goner.

In addition, when you delete a To-Do item this way, the message or contact you used to create the To-Do item goes away, too. Don't worry; you get a warning, so you can always talk your way out of it if you didn't actually mean to remove the message or contact, too.

To delete a To-Do item, follow these steps:

1. **In the To-Do bar, To-Do list, or Daily Task List, click the To-Do item that you want to get rid of.**

2. **Press Delete.**

    You see a warning asking whether you really, really want to delete the To-Do item because you'll be removing that message or contact, too.

3. **Click OK to remove the To-Do item and its associated Outlook item.**

Finding Flagged Messages

You can easily flag a message so that you can remember to follow it up. (If you forget how, see the section "Turning an incoming e-mail into a To-Do bar item," earlier in this chapter, for help.) You can even set a flag on an e-mail that you're sending to someone else to help you remember to follow up on it. (See Book III, Chapter 1 for help on that one.)

After flagging all these messages, however, you may simply want to corral them all. Want to find the incoming messages you've flagged for follow-up? No problem. Want to locate the outgoing messages you flagged before you sent them off? No worries. How about finding any responses you've sent to a flagged message? So simple a child could do it. Just follow these steps:

1. **Select an e-mail folder and click inside the Search *Folder Name* box, located at the top of the message list.**

    To locate flagged messages you've sent to others, select the Sent Items folder. (Messages you sent with a flag for the recipient only are treated as un-flagged messages because you didn't set a flag for yourself.)

    When you click inside the Search *Folder Name* box, the Search Tools Search tab appears, as shown in Figure 1-8.

2. **Click the Flagged button on the Search tab.**

    The flagged messages in the current folder appear (refer to Figure 1-8). To display all flagged messages — no matter what folder they're in — click the Try Searching Again in All Mail Items link that appears below the current list of flagged messages.

    Alternatively, you can quickly display all flagged messages by clicking the For Follow Up folder, located in the Search Folders section of the Navigation pane. For more on using Search folders, see Book IX, Chapter 4.

Search *Folder Name* box

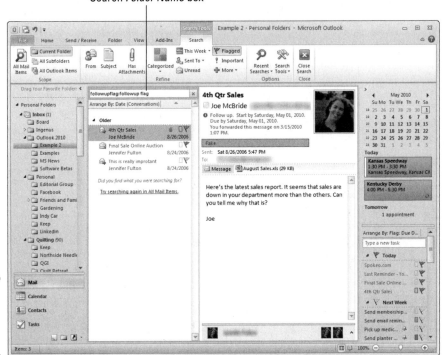

Example 2 - Personal Folders - Microsoft Outlook

Figure 1-8:
Find flagged
messages
quickly.

3. **To arrange messages by their Flag date, select either Flag: Start Date or Flag: Due Date from the Arrangement palette on the View tab.**

   The messages are grouped together by the type of flag they have.

4. **To find responses to messages you flagged, select the message, then click the Close Search button on the Search tab. Then display messages in Conversation order by selecting the Show as Conversations option in the Conversation group on the View tab.**

   All messages and their replies are grouped together; to display the entire conversation string, click the right-pointing arrow on the first message's header. The conversation is expanded, and related messages appear, including any replies you've sent.

Customize the To-Do Bar

I don't know if you use the To-Do bar a lot, but frankly, I find it almost as indispensable as coffee. For example, if I haven't had a second cup of coffee yet, I'm constantly glancing over to the To-Do bar to see what day it is or what month. Okay, maybe I already know the date (despite the lack of caffeine in my system), but I do find that I refer to the To-Do bar all the time to remind me of upcoming appointments and meetings, and things I better get done soon (especially if I want to keep my job and my ability to buy more coffee).

If you're a To-Do bar devotee like me, then you should customize it so that it works and acts exactly the way you want it to:

✦ **To show more or less tasks and To-Do items:** Hide the other To-Do bar parts (the Date Navigator or the Appointments section) or widen the To-Do bar (to display more months on the Date Navigator or more task detail).

✦ **To hide one of the To-Do bar parts:** Click the To-Do bar button on the View tab and select Date Navigator, Appointments, or Tasks List from the pop-up menu that appears to remove that section. If you turn off the Tasks list, for example, more appointments/meetings appear.

✦ **To adjust the width of the To-Do bar:** Position the mouse pointer over the To-Do bar's left edge and drag to the left to make the To-Do bar wider and the viewing area smaller. If you make the To-Do bar wide enough, two months appear in the Date Navigator area.

✦ **To show more than one month on the Date Navigator without making the To-Do bar fatter:** Click the To-Do Bar button on the View tab and select Options from the pop-up menu that appears. The To-Do Bar Options dialog box, shown in Figure 1-9, appears. Type the number of months that you want displayed vertically down the To-Do bar in the Number of Month Rows text box. Click OK.

WARNING!

In order to show more than one month vertically on the Date Navigator, something's gotta give, meaning that you may sacrifice your To-Do List in favor of a multi-month display that you hardly ever use. So feel free to change the Number of Month Rows back to one if displaying multiple months proves to take up too much valuable real estate.

Figure 1-9: Exercise your To-Do bar options.

✦ **To hide the details of appointments or meetings marked as private:** Click the To-Do Bar button on the View tab and select Options from the pop-up menu that appears. In the To-Do Bar Options dialog box, deselect the Show Details of Private Items option and click OK. (Refer to Figure 1-9.)

✦ **To hide events:** Click the To-Do Bar button on the View tab and select Options from the pop-up menu that appears. In the To-Do Bar Options dialog box, deselect the Show All Day Events option and click OK. (Refer to Figure 1-9.)

✦ **To rearrange tasks and To-Do items:** Drag them up or down in the Tasks list area on the To-Do bar and drop them where you want them. For example, if you have several To-Do items staring you in the face for today, you can rearrange them by priority or the order in which you hope to get them done. While you drag, a red line with red arrows on either end guides you so that you know where the item will appear if you drop it right then, as shown in Figure 1-10.

If you drag an item into a different group (moving it from Today to Tomorrow, for example), the item's flag automatically changes.

✦ **To sort your tasks and To-Do items:** Click the Arranged By button at the top of the Tasks list on the To-Do bar and select a sort option from the pop-up menu that appears. Normally, Outlook sorts items by due date, but you can select Date (for Tasks, this is set to None; for To-Do items, this date matches the date the message was sent or the contact was created), Categories, Start Date, Folder, Type (which separates the To-Do items from the tasks), or Importance.

When you create a task (as opposed to a simple To-Do item), you can set a priority to that task, which hopefully lights a fire under you when the time comes. Assuming that you've prioritized your tasks, you can sort the To-Do bar by priority (Importance). You learn to create tasks in Book VI, Chapter 2.

Figure 1-10: Rearrange your tasks.

✦ **To show completed items on the To-Do bar:** When you check off a task or a To-Do item, it's removed from the To-Do bar, although a completed task still appears on the Tasks list and the Daily Task List with a line struck through it to show that you've finished it. You can keep completed items on the To-Do bar if they provide some sense of closure for you. Start by clicking the Arranged By button at the top of the Tasks list area and selecting View Settings from the pop-up menu that appears.

Click the Filter button, click the Advanced tab in Filter dialog box that appears, and then click the Clear All button. Click OK to return to the Advanced View Settings dialog box, and click OK again to return to the main Outlook screen.

Be sure that you want to show completed tasks on the To-Do bar because undoing it is rather complicated. To hide completed tasks and To-Do items once again, you need to click the Arranged By button and select View Settings from the pop-up menu that appears. Click the Filter button to open the Filter dialog box and click the Advanced tab. Now, to add the filters that prevented the completed tasks from appearing, click the Field button, select All Task Fields from the pop-up menu that appears, and select Date/Time Fields from the pop-up menu, and Date Completed from the additional pop-up menu that appears. From the Condition drop-down list that appears, select Does Not Exist and click the Add to List button to add the condition. Click the Field button again, select All Task Fields from the pop-up menu that appears, and select Flag Completed Date from the additional pop-up menu that appears. From the Condition drop-down list that appears, select Does Not Exist and click the Add to List button to add this second condition. Click OK in the Filter dialog box and in the Advanced View Settings dialog box, and vow never to display completed items again.

✦ **To change the color of an overdue item:** When an item is past its Due Date, it appears on the To-Do bar in a red font. If you prefer some other color to alert you when an item's past due, click the Arranged By button at the top of the Tasks list area of the To-Do bar and select View Settings from the pop-up menu that appears to display the Advanced View Settings dialog box. Click the Conditional Formatting button to open the Conditional Formatting dialog box. Select Overdue Tasks from the Rules For This View list and click the Font button. Select the Color you want from the Font dialog box and click OK in the Font, Conditional Formatting, and Advanced View Settings dialog boxes. By the way, this action doesn't change the color of overdue items on the Daily Task List, To-Do list, or Tasks list.

Creating a Task by Using the Daily Task List in the Calendar

If you display your appointments, meetings, and events in the Calendar by using the Normal or Calendar and Tasks buttons on the status bar, a Daily Task List appears at the bottom of the viewing area. (See Figure 1-11.) You can also display the Daily Task List by clicking the Daily Task List button on the View tab and selecting Normal from the pop-up menu that appears.

On the Daily Task List, your tasks and To-Do items appear on the day on which they're due — unless, of course, you don't get them done. In that case, these items move to the next day and appear in frantic-get-it-done red text. You can use the Daily Task List to create a quick, non-detailed task. (To find out how to create a more complete task, see Chapter 2 of this mini-book.) Follow these steps:

1. **In Calendar, display the day on which you want to add a task.**

   You want to see the day on which the task is due, so scroll if you need to until you can see it.

2. **Click an open area within the Daily Task List for the day on which you want to add the task.**

   A white rectangle appears.

3. **Type a name for the task, as shown in Figure 1-11, and press Enter.**

Click here to add a task.   Minimize button

Figure 1-11:
Add a new
task to your
Calendar.

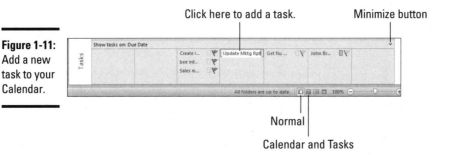

Normal

Calendar and Tasks

If you need to change a task or To-Do item to a different day, you can just drag and drop it within the Daily Task List. You can also rearrange the order in which items appear for a single day by dragging and dropping them within that day.

You can make other changes to the Daily Task List, as well. For example, you can temporarily minimize it by clicking its Minimize button. When the Daily Task List is minimized, Outlook displays the total number of tasks and the number of completed ones on a bar at the bottom of the Outlook window so that you still know you have tasks due that day. Click the bar's Restore button to redisplay the Daily Task List.

You may find it odd, but completed tasks continue to appear on the Daily Task List, even after you check them off. Of course, they appear below the unfinished tasks so that you continue to easily see the things you need to get done. If you'd rather get rid of the tasks you've completed so that they stop cluttering up the Daily Task List, click the Daily Task List button on the View tab, select Arrange By from the pop-up menu that appears, and then dese-lect the Show Completed Tasks check box to toggle that option off.

The tasks and To-Do items on the Daily Task List appear on the day they're due, unless they don't get done, in which case, they appear on the next day. These items keep on moving onto the next day until you get them done (or remove them). If you have multiple tasks or To-Do items on a single day, they're arranged by original due date, meaning that the things you didn't get done yesterday appear at the top of the list. To arrange items by start date, click the Daily Task List button on the View tab, select Arrange By from the pop-up menu that appears, and select By Start Date.

Chapter 2: Dealing with More Complex Tasks

In This Chapter

✔ Creating tasks with detailed information

✔ Making a task repeat

✔ Looking at your Tasks list

✔ Turning tasks into appointments and e-mails into tasks

✔ Having Outlook remind you about a task

In Chapter 1 of this minibook, you can find out how to create quick-just-make-a-note-of-that To-Do items from e-mails, contacts, or scratch. To-Do items are real handy and quick to make. But they aren't so hot when you have more information that you need to record about a task, such as its current status, priority, and the amount of work that's already been completed. With a task, you can record not only all this info, but you can also do fancy stuff such as make the task recur at regular intervals or reassign the task to someone else on your staff while still maintaining some control. You can also set a reminder to complete the task on time, just like the reminders you set for appointments, meetings, and events. If you want to create tasks that have realized their full potential, you're reading the right chapter.

Creating a Detailed Task

If you want to keep track of the little details surrounding something you have to get done, you need to create a task, not a To-Do item. (For more on To-Do items, see Chapter 1 of this minibook.)

To create a task from any module, follow these steps:

1. **Click the New Items button on the Home tab and select Task from the pop-up menu that appears.**

   If you happen to be in Tasks, you can just click that ol' New Task button on the Home tab.

   The Task form appears, similar to the one shown in Figure 2-1.

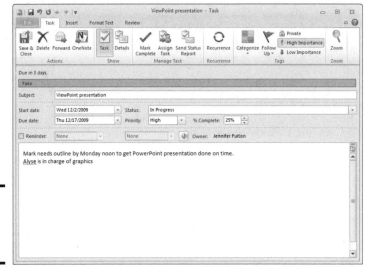

Figure 2-1:
Creating
a detailed
task.

2. **Type a description for the task in the Subject text box and select a due date from the Due Date drop-down list.**

3. **Fill in the information that you want to track.**

   Here are your options:

   • **If you've started the task:** Select a start date from the Start Date drop-down list and select a status from the Status drop-down list. You may also want to make a note of how much you've done by changing the % Complete value (click the up or down arrow, as needed).

   You can't update the % Complete value without changing the Status. If you change the Status to Completed, the % Complete value becomes 100 automatically. If you select In Progress as the Status, you can enter any value below 100; if the Status is Deferred or Waiting on Someone Else, you can enter any value from 0 to 100. If you change the % Completed value to 25% without changing the Status first, the Status is automatically changed to In Progress.

   You can type words in the date text boxes, instead of selecting an actual date. For example, you can type today or tomorrow, or three days from now. Outlook recognizes some holidays, as well, such as Fourth of July, New Year's Eve, or Christmas.

   • **If this task is important:** Click the High Importance button on the Task tab; click the Low Importance button to remind you that although this task has a due date, you may be able to let it slide a little.

- **To prevent you from forgetting the task's due date:** Select the Reminder check box and select a date and time from the Reminder lists.

- **To group this task with similar ones:** Assign it a category or two. Assuming that you've set up categories (see Book VIII, Chapter 1 for help if you haven't), specify as many categories as you want for this task by click the Categorize button on the Task tab and selecting them one at a time.

- **To record any details:** Type them in the large Notes section. Flip over to the form's Format Text tab to format the text, if you want.

4. **To record even more details about a task, click the Details button on the form's Task tab.**

   The Details tab of the Task form, shown in Figure 2-2, appears. Here are some details you can add:

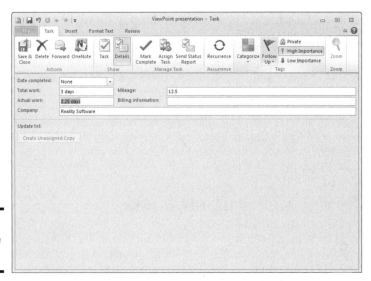

Figure 2-2: It's all in the details.

- **To track the amount of work you've done on this task so far:** Enter the number of hours in general terms in the Total Work text box. If you prefer to mark the time in days, weeks, or months, just type that instead, such as `3 days` or `2 weeks`.

- **If you're keeping track of this information because it's client-related:** Enter the specific billable hours in the Actual Work text box. Enter any other billing info in the Billing Information text box. Type the client or company name in the Company text box.

- **If you're going to be reimbursed for the number of miles you've driven to complete this task:** Enter the number of miles you've driven so far in the Mileage text box.

5. **Click the form's Insert tab and use its buttons (Attach File, Outlook Item, Business Card) to attach any important data.**

   If you have data that's related to this task, such as sales reports, budget info, or the name of that guy who's creating a sample marketing campaign, attach that data to the task so that you can easily access it. See Book II, Chapters 1 and 3 for the lowdown on inserting files, Outlook items, and such.

6. **If you're done, click the Save & Close button on the Task tab.**

   If this task is one that happens again and again at some kind of regular interval, you can easily make it recur. See the section "Scheduling a Recurring Task," later in this chapter.

To make changes to a task you've saved, just click it to display the Home/Daily Task List/Tasks List tab, which has the tools you need to make changes. You can do that from the Tasks list, Daily Task List, or the To-Do bar.

In the following sections, you can figure out how to create a task from an existing e-mail, appointment, or meeting. You can't create a task from an existing contact, however, because Outlook interprets your actions as an attempt to pass that task onto a fellow colleague (see Chapter 3 of this minibook for more on reassigning tasks). If you want to create a task and keep a particular contact's info close at hand, then attach the contact's business card by using the form's Insert tab, as described Book II, Chapter 3.

Turning an e-mail into a task

You can easily turn an e-mail message into a To-Do item by simply flagging it, as explained in Chapter 1 of this minibook. A To-Do item is fine if you need just a simple reminder. But if you want something more detailed, you should create a task. You don't need to start from scratch, however — not if you have an e-mail message that already provides some of the details.

To create a task from an e-mail, follow these steps:

1. **Drag the message to the Tasks button in the Navigation pane and drop it.**

   A new Task form appears.

2. **Select a due date from the Due Date list and set other options, as desired.**

The text of the e-mail message appears in the Notes section; I often scroll through this text to reference the information I need to create the task (such as the date it's due).

The message's subject automatically becomes the subject of the task, although you can change it by editing the text in the Subject text box.

3. **Click the Save & Close button on the Task tab to save the task.**

If you create new tasks from e-mail messages a lot, you can create a Quick Step to help you do that quickly. See Book I, Chapter 2 for the lowdown.

Linking an appointment or meeting to a task

You may want to link a task to an appointment (or vice versa) for several reasons, although I can't think of a single one. No, just kidding. Actually, I often set up appointments or meetings with clients or colleagues, and then think of several things I better do before that appointment or meeting happens. So I find it handy to have the two linked together.

To use an existing appointment or meeting to create a task, follow these steps:

1. **Drag the appointment or meeting to the Tasks button on the Navigation pane and drop it.**

A new Task form appears.

2. **Select a due date from the Due Date list and set other options, as you want.**

The details of the appointment or meeting appear in the Notes section of the task; the subject of the appointment or meeting is used as the subject of the task although you can change it by editing the text in the Subject text box.

3. **Click the Save & Close button on the Task tab to save the task.**

Which happened first, the chicken or the egg? If you created your task first, such as creating a sales demo or a department report, only to later schedule a meeting or appointment in which to present it, you can still use the existing task to create the appointment/meeting you need. Follow these steps:

1. **Drag the task onto the Calendars button on the Navigation pane and drop it.**

A new Appointment form appears.

The details of the task appear in the Notes section; the message's subject becomes the subject of the appointment although you can change it by editing the text in the Subject text box.

2. **Select a start time and date from the Start Time drop-down lists, and an end time and date from the End Time drop-down lists.**

   Set any other options you want to, as well.

3. **To turn this appointment into a meeting, click the Invite Attendees button on the Appointment tab.**

   See Book IV, Chapter 4 for help in creating meetings.

4. **When you finish adding the details of your appointment or meeting, click the Save & Close button.**

Scheduling a Recurring Task

Some tasks just keep on giving. You finish them once, and they return the next day, bearing gifts of multiple reports, endless notes, and recurring demands on your time. If you have a task that you need to complete on a regular basis, such as reviewing a sales report and preparing a chart analyzing its data, you don't have to manually copy it over and over again in your Tasks list. Instead, you can set up the parameters that make it recur.

You can't make a To-Do item that you created from a contact into a recurring one. You can, however, make a To-Do item created from an e-mail, appointment, or meeting (as described in Chapter 1 of this minibook) into a recurring To-Do item. If you want to create a recurring task that's linked to a contact, then start from scratch in creating the task, attach the contact by using the Task form's Insert tab, then follow the steps in this section to make that task recur.

Now, it's time to make your task (or To-Do item) recur. If you're still in the process of creating the task, fine; otherwise, open the task (by double-clicking it in the To-Do bar, Tasks List, or Daily Task List) so that you can make changes. In the Task form, follow these steps:

1. **Click the Recurrence button on the Task tab.**

   The Task Recurrence dialog box appears.

2. **Select the Recurrence Pattern radio button for the basic interval at which you want the task to repeat.**

   You can choose from Daily, Weekly, Monthly, or Yearly.

3. **Set the recurrence options.**

   Depending on the frequency you selected in Step 2, a set of options appears to the right of the Recurrence Pattern radio button list. Set those options to match the pattern of repetition:

- **Daily:** Choose between repeating every day, every other day, and so on, or repeating every weekday and skipping weekends.

  Normally, you want the task to recur at whatever pattern you select, regardless of whether you get each task done on time. If you want Outlook to create a new copy of the task only after you complete the previous one, then select the Regenerate New Task *Number of* Day(s) After Each Task Is Completed radio button and type an interval in the text box. When you select this option, the next recurrence does not appear until you get the previous task done.

- **Weekly:** Select the Recur Every *Number of* Week(s) On radio button and enter a number in the text box to specify how often the item recurs: weekly, every other week, or whatever. Then, select the check box for the day on which that happens. To create a new copy of the task only after you complete the previous task, select the Regenerate New Task *Number of* Week(s) After Each Task Is Completed radio button and enter the interval you want in the text box.

- **Monthly:** You can choose a particular day of the month (or every so many months), such as the 10th of every third month, by selecting the Day *Number* of Every *Number of* Months radio button and entering numbers in the two text boxes. Or you can choose the first, second, third, fourth, or last weekday of every month or so, such as the second Thursday of every other month, by selecting The *Number of Weekday* of Every *Number of* Month(s) radio button and selecting a number from the first list, a weekday from the second list, and typing a number in the text box. Finally, you can select the Regenerate New Task *Number of* Month(s) After Each Task Is Completed radio button and enter the appropriate number in the text box to create a copy of this task only after the previous one is completed.

- **Yearly:** Like Monthly, you can select a particular date (such as October 16) by selecting the Every *Month Day* radio button, selecting a month from the list and typing a day in the text box. You can select a particular day within a certain month (such as the last Friday of November) by selecting The *Number of Weekday* of *Month* radio button, selecting a number from the first list, a weekday from the second list, and a month from the last list. You can also select the Regenerate New Task *Number of* Year(s) After Each Task Is Completed radio button and enter a number in the text box to create a copy of this task only after the previous one is completed.

4. **In the Range of Recurrence area at the bottom of the dialog box, select a date from the Start drop-down list, then select the appropriate radio button.**

   For example, does the task repeat forever? (Probably, if you're Sisyphus.) Then select No End Date. Or does it recur so many times (such as five times, as shown in Figure 2-3) and then stop? Then select the End After *Number of* Occurrences radio button and enter a number in the text box. Or does it repeat until the end of November and then no more? Select the End By radio button and select an ending date from the drop-down list.

5. **Click OK.**

The task form reappears, and the recurrence pattern you selected appears on the form's InfoBar. Click the Save & Close button on the form's Task tab to save the task and its repeating pattern. Recurring tasks appear in the Tasks list with a special Recurrence icon (a small clipboard and check mark with two small bent arrows that signify repetition I guess). The task appears only once in the Tasks list, however. When you mark the first task complete or when its due date passes, the next occurrence of the task appears in the list, like magic (only without the black hat and white doves).

Figure 2-3:
Can you
repeat that?

To skip one occurrence of a recurring task, open that particular occurrence and click the Skip Occurrence button on the open form's Task tab. To end a task recurrence, open the task, click the Recurrence button, and click the Remove Recurrence button in the Recurrence dialog box that appears.

Viewing Tasks

When you switch over to the Tasks module, you see two lists — the To-Do list and the Tasks list. You create To-Do items from e-mails, contacts, or other Outlook items; you create tasks from scratch, using the Task form. The To-Do list contains both To-Do and Task items; the Tasks list contains only tasks. Initially, the Tasks list appears in Simple List view which displays all tasks, completed or not. (See the next section, "Working with Tasks" for help in changing to a view that displays only completed tasks.) The To-Do list uses To-Do List view by default, as shown in Figure 2-4. On the To-Do list, you can tell tasks from To-Do items easily; tasks appear with a clipboard icon with a small checkmark; To-Do items appear with an icon that represents the Outlook item that was used to create them, such as a small envelope (for items created from an e-mail message) or a business card (for items created from a contact).

You can display the Tasks list by using To-Do List view if you want, although typically a list view offers the most useful perspective, such as organizing tasks by category, or listing only the tasks that are due in the next seven days.

To-Do items

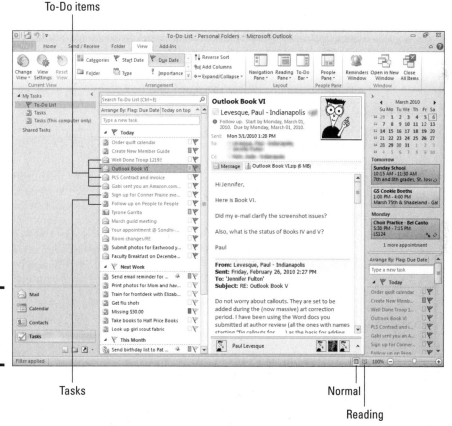

Figure 2-4:
To-Do List
view or not
To-Do?

Tasks   Normal

Reading

There's nothing particularly alarming about To-Do List view, but because it's the only one that's substantially different, I thought I'd talk about it. When you change to To-Do List view, a list of active (non-completed) tasks appears in a column, with a Reading pane on the right, just like in Compact view in Mail. Not surprisingly, the whole thing works just like Compact view; click a task or To-Do item on the left, and its details appear on the right. So, if you want to know how much work you've done on a particular task, you can click it and check out its % Complete value.

This view is also pretty nifty if you routinely create To-Do items from other Outlook items, such as messages, contacts, and appointments. When you use an Outlook item as the basis for a new To-Do item, the contents of that Outlook item are copied to the new To-Do item's Notes section. And you can quickly scan the notes for a selected To-Do item or task in the Reading pane, if you use the To-Do List view.

The Tasks module has two buttons that you can use to quickly display or hide the To-Do bar, which might seem like a pretty useless use of space there. To display the To-Do bar and the Navigation pane, click the Normal button located on the status bar at the bottom of the window (refer to Figure 2-4). To hide the Navigation pane and the To-Do bar, click the Reading button on the status bar.

Working with Tasks

I must confess; sometimes, when I display the Tasks list (not the To-Do list), I can get quite overwhelmed. Not only do I see an almost endless list of things I better get done soon, but for reasons I can't fathom, Outlook also shows all those tasks I've already gotten done. Frankly, I don't need the list to be any longer, but maybe you like seeing all the stuff you've ever done. To each his own.

Fortunately, you can do a number of things to make your Tasks list more user-friendly. For starters, you can:

✦ **Change your view.** One way to get rid of those completed tasks and yet not actually remove them is to change to the Active view by clicking the Current View button on the Home or View tab and selecting Active from the palette that appears, as shown in Figure 2-5. (If you're already on the View tab, clicking the Change View button there and selecting Active from the palette that appears does the very same thing.) Active view displays only, *active tasks* — things you're still working on and haven't completed yet. This view should shorten your list considerably. By the way, you can also use several other views that don't show completed tasks: Next 7 Days, Overdue, and To-Do List. (The To-Do List is a rather special view — the previous section "Viewing Tasks," earlier in this chapter, discusses it in depth.)

If you like one of the other views better, such as Simple List or Prioritized, and you don't want the completed tasks showing up, you can customize the view so that they don't appear. See Book VIII, Chapter 2 for help.

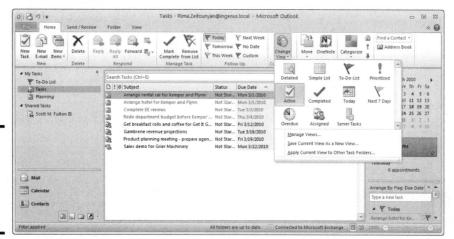

Figure 2-5:
Why stare at a bunch of completed tasks?

✦ **Delete the task.** This step works pretty well because it dumps those completed tasks in the trash. However, if you created a To-Do item by using a message or contact, then deleting the completed To-Do item from your Tasks list/To-Do List also removes the associated message/contact. Probably not the best idea, but hey, you're done with it, right? So why not delete it?

✦ **Remove the flag.** This action is usually reserved for To-Do items that you never wanted to create (for example, you flagged an e-mail by accident), so it's not meant to be used to remove an old task from your Tasks list. However, if you created a To-Do item by using a message or contact, and you've completed the task and want to remove it from your list, then select the To-Do item and click the Remove from List button on the Home tab.

✦ **Change the color of completed tasks.** Frankly, I find the gray color that Outlook uses for completed tasks to be quite fine and unnoticeable. But maybe you want to notice them more, or maybe your eyes are just naturally attracted to gray and won't notice blue or some other color as much. To change the color of completed tasks, click the File tab to display Backstage, and select Options from the list on the left to display the Outlook Options dialog box. Select Tasks from list on the left, and the Tasks options appear on the right. In the Task options section, select a color from the Completed Task Color palette. Click OK. Completed tasks are displayed in the color you selected.

Changing the color of overdue tasks

When you don't complete a task by its due date, Outlook gets really angry and changes the task text to red in a pitiful attempt to get you to sit down, be quiet, and get the task done already. Okay, maybe it's not so pitiful because, frankly, red makes me anxious and actually does make me want to do that task so it'll stop haunting me. But what if red's your favorite color? What if you wait until a task is overdue to complete it, just so that you get to see it change color first? What about that, eh, Outlook?

I guess you can continue to ignore the red color of overdue tasks, or you can change it to a color that'll prompt you to do something, such as finish the silly task. To change the color of overdue tasks on the Tasks list, follow these steps:

1. **Click the File tab to display Backstage, and select Options from the list on the left.**

The Outlook Options dialog box appears.

2. **Select Tasks from the list on the left.**

The Task options appear on the right, as shown in Figure 2-6.

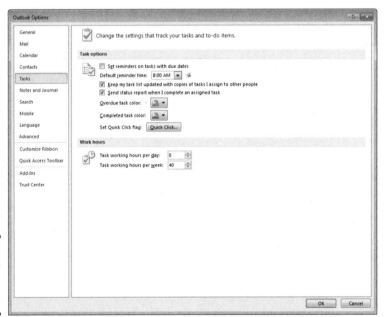

Figure 2-6:
Change how an overdue task looks.

3. **In the Overdue Task Color palette, select the color you want to use to mark tasks not completed on time.**

4. **Click OK.**

Overdue tasks are displayed in the color you selected.

This color change, by the way, affects only how tasks and To-Do items appear on the Tasks list and To-Do list. You can't change the color of over-due tasks in the Daily Task List, which appears in the Calendar. You can, however, change the color of the tasks and To-Do items on the To-Do bar, but not in the manner shown here. See Chapter 1 of this minibook for more on changing To-Do bar colors.

Sorting and rearranging tasks

You can sort and rearrange your tasks however you like. To sort tasks in a list view, simply click the heading above the column you want to use to sort. For example, click the Status column to sort by status. For more tips on sort-ing a list view, see Book VIII, Chapter 2.

Tasks that have the same due date may appear in a rather random order in the listing, typically by the date on which you created them. However, you can rearrange the listing to show the tasks in whatever order you find useful. Just drag and drop tasks to rearrange their order. Doing so also rearranges those tasks on the To-Do bar and the Daily Task List so that you don't have to spend the time you should be using to complete tasks in simply rearranging them.

Wanna keep certain tasks together? You can assign the tasks the same priority, and then use Prioritized view.

Updating what you've done on a task

To update the progress you've made on a task, double-click the task to open the Task form and change what applies:

✦ **Update the status of the project.** Select a new status from the Status drop-down list and enter a % Complete value in the text box.

✦ **Update the amount of work you've done on a project.** Click the Details button on the Task tab and update the values in the Total Work and Actual Work (billable hours) text boxes. If you get reimbursed for mile-age, you can update the value in the Mileage text box, as well.

After you make your changes, click the Save & Close button on the form's Task tab.

Marking a task as complete

Nothing is quite as satisfying as getting something done — except maybe checking it off your impossibly long list of things to do. And I guess the folks at Microsoft understand because Outlook provides a lot of ways in which you can mark off a task after you get it done:

✦ **Click in the Flag column.** Appears next to the task in the Tasks list, the Daily Task List, or the To-Do bar. After you click it, the flag changes to a check mark to indicate that you've finished the task. Completed tasks are removed from the To-Do bar.

✦ **Click in the Complete column.** Appears next to the task in the Tasks list, in most views. The column (when shown) isn't marked as Complete, but a check box appears in the column, as shown in Figure 2-7. When you click the column to mark a task as complete, a small check mark is added to the check box.

Complete column   Flag column

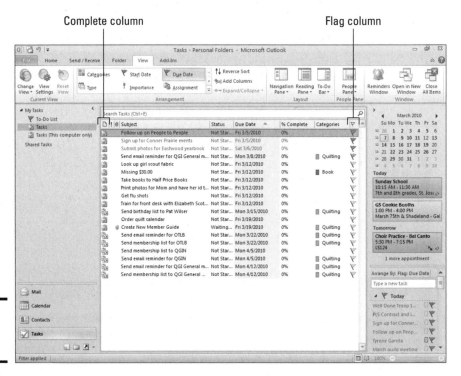

Figure 2-7:
Complete
your task.

✦ **Right-click a task and select Mark Complete from the pop-up menu that appears.** You can right-click a task in the Tasks list, Daily Task List, or To-Do bar to display this menu. Again, completed tasks are marked with a check mark.

✦ **Update the % Complete to 100.** You can make this change from many of the list views in Tasks by simply changing the value in the % Complete column. If the column isn't visible in the current view, you can just open the task and change the % Complete value in the task form that appears.

Setting an Automatic Reminder for Tasks

To ensure that I get something done on time, I make sure that I'm reminded about it again and again. Of course, I can't turn Outlook into my personal task-nagger, but I can turn it into something that's pretty close. To tell Outlook that you want it to remind you to get a task done, follow these steps:

1. **Select the task or To-Do item in the To-Do bar, Tasks list, To-Do list, or Daily Task List.**

2. **Click the Custom button in the Follow Up group on the Tasks list, Daily Task List, or Home tab.**

   The Custom dialog box appears

3. **Select the Reminder check box, then select the date and time you want to be reminded from the drop-down lists, as shown in Figure 2-8.**

   Make sure that you pick a date that allows you enough time to complete the task after Outlook pokes you in the side.

4. **Click OK to save your changes.**

**Book VI
Chapter 2**

**Dealing with More
Complex Tasks**

Figure 2-8:
Set a reminder so that you complete a task on time.

If you set a reminder for a task, then eventually Outlook taps you on the shoulder and asks, "Um, got it done?" See Figure 2-9.

Figure 2-9:
Outlook gently reminds you to get things done.

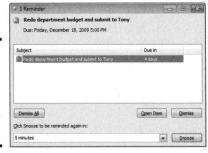

The due date for the task appears at the top of the Reminder window. To review the details of the task or to change them, click Open Item. Click Dismiss to simply get rid of the reminder — after that, you're on your own to get the task done on time. If you want Outlook to remind you again to finish the task, select an interval from the Click Snooze to Be Reminded Again In drop-down list and then click the Snooze button.

To redisplay the Reminders window, click the Reminders Window button on the View tab.

Chapter 3: Spreading the Joy: Task Assignments

In This Chapter

✔ Assigning tasks to others and reclaiming those tasks

✔ Receiving progress reports on a reassigned task

✔ Dealing with tasks someone wants to reassign to you

✔ Sharing your tasks and viewing somebody else's tasks

*L*ately, it seems like everybody has a lot to do. Whether it's writing a report, attending a conference, viewing a new product presentation, or wooing a new client, you always have work to be done. Sometimes, no matter how good a scheduler you are, time simply gets away from you. At such times, it's nice to know that you have co-workers to help share the load — provided you come bearing a good enough bribe.

Because Outlook comes equipped with a nice task master, it should be no surprise that it also includes a nice task delegator. By using Outlook, you can send requests to colleagues to take on a task — basically, reassigning the task to them. Of course, what goes around comes around because they can say, "Right back at ya!" and reassign tasks to you, too. Along the way, both of you can receive regular status reports that let you know just how lousy both of you are at getting anything accomplished.

In addition, just like your other Outlook folders, you can share your Tasks list. You may want to do so if you have a micromanager boss who likes to control every minute of your day or if you simply want to prove to him or her that you really are truly busy right now. In any case, this chapter shows you how to reassign tasks, accept reassignments, and share your Tasks list.

Assigning a Task to Someone Else

When needed — or hey, whenever you feel like it — you can reassign one of your tasks to someone else. At least, you can try. Here's how it works: You create a task, make little progress, and then wake up one day with the brilliant plan of passing it on to someone else before your boss asks you whether you've finished working on it yet. So, you send out a task reassignment, which comes in the form of an e-mail message. Here begins a game I call Pass the Hot Potato.

You can reassign tasks to colleagues — or anyone, for that matter — even if you're not on an Exchange network. The process simply happens via e-mail, rather than automatically, as it does on an Exchange network. Updates even occur, but through e-mail. If you request to be kept updated on a task and someone changes the status of a task or the amount of work completed, you get an e-mail updating you. When you open that e-mail, your copy of the task gets updated automatically.

The recipient of your joy opens the e-mail and gets the potato, which in this game is ownership of the task. Yep, whether he or she wants it, he or she is now the task's owner. And only the owner of a task can make changes to it, so potato-ownership is important when it comes to task management.

As the current potato guy, the recipient can decide to either accept or decline your kindness, depending on his mood. He can also try reassigning the task to someone else, in which case, that someone else becomes the potato owner. Should he accept the task, he becomes the task's current owner, and the task is placed on his Tasks list. Should he decline, the task gets sent back to you, and you become the potato owner once again, although you can't actually update the task until you officially reclaim it. Don't worry; reclaiming a task is simple, but if you don't want to finish the task yourself, you can boot that task over to the next poor sap on your list without reclaiming it.

Now, back to that hot potato. When a task is updated, Outlook hunts down all previous potato owners of the task, all the way back to the task originator, and updates all copies of the task on their systems. When the task is finally completed, a status report is sent to all the prior owners.

To reassign a task, follow these steps:

1. **Create the task request.**

   You can create this request in a couple of ways:

   - *If you haven't created the task yet:* Click the New Items button on the Home tab, select More Items from the pop-up menu that appears, and then select Task Request from additional pop-up menu that appears.

   - *If you've already created a task you want to reassign:* Open the task and click the Assign Task button on the form's Task tab.

   A Task Request form appears.

2. **In the To text box, enter the e-mail address of the person or persons to whom you want to assign the task.**

   The Subject shows the name of the task upon which this task request is based; if it's a new task request, type a description for the task in the Subject text box.

Although you can assign the same task to more than one person, if you do, you aren't automatically updated on the task's status. Instead of assigning one task to several people, you may want to consider breaking up a large job into smaller, more specific tasks and assigning those smaller tasks to different people.

If you attempt to reassign a task to someone who's out of town, no longer with the company, or otherwise incapable of responding, MailTips (along with Exchange) alerts you to that fact prior to you sending off the task request. See Book I, Chapter 1 for more info.

3. **Select the due date for the task from the Due Date list, and if the task is already underway, update its status by selecting one from the Status list, percent complete by typing a value in the % Complete box, and start date by selecting one from the Start Date list, if needed.**

4. **If you want to stay updated on the task status, be sure to select the Keep an Updated Copy of This Task on My Task List check box, as well as the Send Me a Status Report when This Task Is Complete check box, as shown in Figure 3-1.**

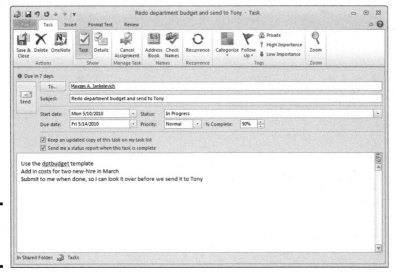

Figure 3-1:
Please take
this task.

If you don't want to be bothered so much, but you want to know when the task is finally finished, deselect the Keep an Updated Copy of This Task on My Task List check box.

You can make a new task recurring, prior to assigning it to someone else. See Chapter 2 of this minibook for help.

If this is a recurring task, the task remains in your Tasks list, even if you don't select the Keep an Updated Copy of This Task on My Task List check box. If you select the Send Me a Status Report when This Task Is Complete check box, you get updates when each occurrence of the task is finished.

5. Type a message for the recipient in the Notes area at the bottom of the form, if you want.

6. Click Send to send the request.

The task is marked in the listing with a handout icon (a hand holding out a task). Now, you just have to wait and see whether your recipient accepts or not. Either way, you get an e-mail message telling you his or her intentions.

Reclaiming a Task You Tried to Reassign

After you send off a task reassignment, you can only twiddle your thumbs until you hear back from the victim (um, I mean recipient). Unless or until he or she officially rejects the task, the recipient retains potato-ownership, and there ain't nuttin' you can do about it. Well, okay, if needed, when the guy or gal is unavailable, clueless, or otherwise indecisive and simply can't be coaxed into at least declining the task so that you can get the potato back, you can give up on him or her entirely and create a copy of the task that you can either finish yourself or attempt to reassign to someone else at the bottom of your People I Like list.

When the recipient chooses to accept or decline your kind invitation to do more work, you receive an e-mail message. On the InfoBar of the message, you see text telling you if the recipient accepted or declined. Also, the small icon that appears to the left of the message header in the message list bears a large red X if the recipient declines (and none if the recipient accepts). If the recipient declines, the task in your Tasks list changes to bold to alert you, just like an incoming message is bold to indicate that you haven't read it yet. Open either one — the task or the message — to return them to normal text. The icon for the task still screams "Take me!": a right arrow pointing towards a small person (sucker). Click the task to view the response in the Reading pane.

Again, if your task request is rejected and you want to reassign the task to someone else, you don't have to officially reclaim it in order to try reassigning it again. See the preceding section for how-to's. If you need to update the task before passing it on or want to simply reclaim a task you tried reassigning that was ultimately rejected, follow these steps:

1. **Double-click the task to open it.**

When it opens, the task displays its information, but not in changeable form. (See Figure 3-2.)

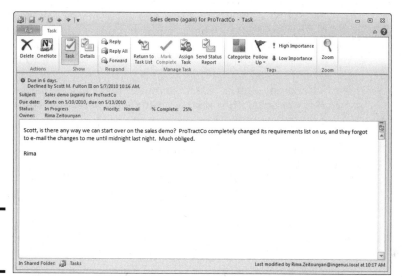

Figure 3-2:
Reclaim
that task.

2. **Click the Return to Task List button on the Task tab.**

The task is converted to an unassigned task.

3. **Click the Save & Close button on the Task tab.**

The task is added back to the Tasks list, with a normal task icon (the simple check mark).

 You can also reclaim a task when the rejection notice comes in without switching over to the Tasks list. Open the e-mail message and simply click the Return to Task List button on the Message form's Task tab and then click the Save & Close button to take that task back.

 You can't reclaim a task after someone has accepted it, but you can make a copy of it for your own purposes. For example, you might want to create a new task that's similar to the one you reassigned, and you want to copy the details from the original task so you don't have to enter them all in yourself. Click the Details button on the form's Task tab and click Create Unassigned Copy. A warning dialog box appears, telling you that you'll own the copy and won't receive updates on the original task. Click OK to create the task copy. Click Save & Close.

Checking the Progress of an Assigned Task

Assuming that all goes well and your victim (er, colleague) accepts the task reassignment request, you're still not completely out of the loop. You receive an update when the task is completed (assuming that you selected that option when you sent the task request), although you can request an update whenever you like by sending off a request e-mail. (See the section "Sending a status report on an assigned task," later in this chapter, for information on how to generate a status report at any time.) In addition, the task automatically updates from time to time (assuming that you selected the Keep an Updated Copy of This Task on My Task List check box when you reassigned the task), while the recipient makes progress on the task and updates his or her copy.

For the I-don't-want-to-do-the-task-but-I-must-maintain-control-over-it-because-I-don't-trust-anyone types, Outlook provides several ways in which you can check up on your reassigned tasks. In addition, you can generate automatic updates for tasks you've taken on. (This setup should also satisfy the I'm-very-busy-so-let's-just-get-this-done types, as well.) Control whether updates are sent automatically (for tasks that are reassigned to you) and whether your Tasks list is automatically updated when progress reports come in on tasks you've reassigned by following these steps:

1. **Click the File tab to display Backstage, and select Options from the list on the left.**

   The Outlook Options dialog box presents itself, as shown in Figure 3-3.

2. **Select Tasks from list on the left.**

   The Tasks options appear on the right.

3. **To automatically update the status of tasks you reassign whenever an update e-mail arrives, select the Keep My Task List Updated with Copies of Tasks I Assign to Other People check box.**

4. **To automatically generate a report when you complete a task that was reassigned to you, select the Send Status Report when I Complete an Assigned Task check box.**

5. **Click OK.**

   From now on, any task requests you send or receive use the options you selected. Of course, for an individual task, you can always override the options that you set as the defaults.

Besides setting the options that affect all task reassignments, you can check up on reassigned tasks periodically, when the mood hits you. For example, if you regularly reassign tasks, you may simply forget which ones you've reassigned and which ones you haven't.

To view a list of all the tasks you've reassigned, follow these steps:

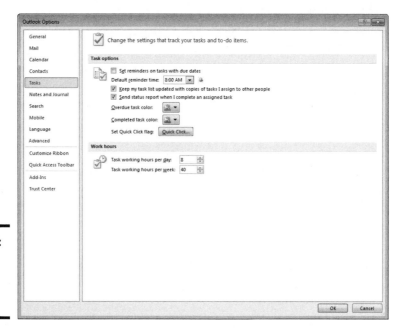

Figure 3-3:
Set task reassign-
ment options.

1. **Click the Change View button on the View tab and select Assigned from the palette that appears.**

You can also click the Current View button on the Home tab to select Assigned view. This view displays only those tasks that you've reas-signed, in a list view, like the one shown in Figure 3-4.Reassigned tasks also appear even if they have not yet been accepted or declined.

You may want to try sorting any view by assignment and then taking the further step of grouping tasks. The approach groups the tasks by their owner and allows you to see both your tasks and any reassigned ones. For example, if you're using Simple List view (which sorts tasks by due date), click the Assignment option in the Arrangement palette on the View tab to sort by task owner. To make this arrangement a bit more obvious, group your tasks by selecting Show in Groups from the Arrangement palette on the View tab.

If you want to compare how many tasks you've reassigned to Betsy and how many to Robyn, you can sort the Assignment list by owner by click-ing the Owner heading at the top of that column. You can sort by status to see how many tasks are nearing completion, or due date to see how many tasks are overdue. Slow down though, Quickdraw McGraw! You might need to add the Owner and Status columns to the view first. See Book VIII, Chapter 2 for more help on sorting and adjusting the view.

2. **After you locate a reassigned task that you want to check up on, simply double-click the task to open it up and view its details.**

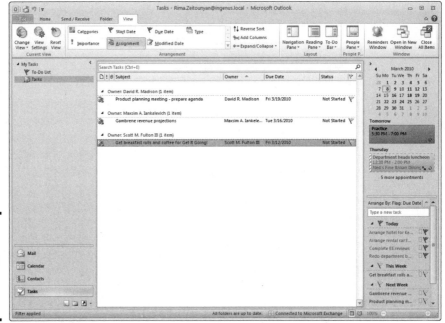

Figure 3-4:
All you
needed was
a different
point of
view.

Dealing with Task Assignments Sent to You

No sense fooling yourself; sooner or later, your boss or somebody else on
your team will read the Outlook manual and figure out that she can automate
a job she loves to do — that is, reassigning tasks to *you*. Oh, well. At least the
process makes it just as easy for you to say, "Uh, no thanks." And when you
find yourself pressured to accept a task, don't despair; you can easily pester
the task giver with status reports and updates. That'll show 'em.

In the rare instance where you accept a task and later discover that completing it on time is simply no longer in the cards, you can try reassigning the
task to someone else. It'll feel a little like regifting a holiday fruitcake that
keeps getting passed around from house to house because nobody wants to
eat it, but then, someone's bound to be hungry enough to try it, right?

Accepting or declining a task

A task request comes to your door disguised as a regular ol' e-mail message.
When you get a task request, you have to accept it before it can be added to
your Tasks list, where you can track it. If you decline the invitation to take on
more work, the person who sent you the task request can then reclaim the task
and either do it him- or herself, or send a task request to some other patsy.

When you receive a task request, you become the task's owner, regardless of whether you actually accept the task. As the owner, you become the only one who can update the task. If you decline the task request, the task giver needs to reclaim the task so that he or she can resume ownership. Ownership is key because only the owner of a task can change it, mark it complete, or delete it. And remember to at least accept or decline the task request; until you do, the original owner can do nothing with the task. To do your part, follow these steps:

**Book VI
Chapter 3**

**Spreading the Joy:
Task Assignments**

1. **Change over to Mail by clicking the Mail button on the Navigation pane and view the task request, either by opening it or selecting it and glancing at the Reading pane.**

   A task request comes at you as a normal e-mail message, which proves once again that you should be careful what e-mails you open.

2. **Click the appropriate button, based on what you've decided to do.**

   You can choose from Accept and Decline. If you are viewing the request in the Reading pane, these buttons appear at the top of the pane, just above the Subject. If you open the request, these buttons appear in the Respond group on the Task tab.

   Either the Accepting Task or the Rejecting Task dialog box appears, depending on which button you click. (I'm a good team player, so I always get the Accepting Task dialog box that appears in Figure 3-5.)

Figure 3-5:
Choices,
choices.

3. **To edit the reply and perhaps explain your response, select the Edit the Response Before Sending radio button and click OK.**

   To simply send your response to the task request without including a message, select the Send the Response Now radio button and click OK. Your response is sent immediately, in the form of an e-mail message; if you accepted the task request, the task is placed on your Tasks list.

4. **If you selected Edit the Response Before Sending in Step 3, type your comments in the message form that appears.**

5. **Click Send to send the message response along.**

   If you accepted the task request, the task is placed on your Tasks list.

Sending a status report on an assigned task

As the new owner of a task, you need to keep everyone updated on your progress. Of course, some things happen automatically. For example, whenever you make changes to a task, such as updating its status or the number of hours you've spent on it, all copies of that task are automatically updated, as well — at least, the copies whose owners asked to be updated periodically when they sent the task request on to you. The task originator, as well as any prior owners who passed the task onto you, all have copies of the task. But all these prior owners are probably not as invested in getting the job done as you are, and so they're most likely not opening the task and looking at it for updates. Nope, they're waiting to hear from you, and the easiest way for you to make that happen is to throw a status report at them.

Don't depend on updates to keep your boss informed of your hard-earned progress on a task. If your boss originally sent the task request to more than one person (regardless of whether they accepted it), your boss's copy of the task is no longer automatically updated. Also, your boss may not have selected the Keep an Updated Copy of This Task on My Task List check box when he or she created the task request. In such a case, your boss depends on your status reports to keep him or her informed, so make sure that you send those reports often!

A status report is automatically generated when you complete a task that you've been assigned, so you don't need to follow these steps to create one after you finish a task.

To generate a status report on a task you've been assigned, follow these steps:

1. **In the Tasks list, double-click the reassigned task on which you want to report to open it.**

   Reassigned tasks appear with a special icon in the Tasks list — a small task icon being held by two hands, one at the top and one at the bottom.

   As silly as it may be, you can send a status report on a task that you reassigned, although you can't edit or update that task at all because you're no longer its owner. I'm not sure what you'd say in such a report, though. Maybe, "Hey, what's going on?"

2. **To send the report to the originator only, click the Send Status Report button on the form's Task tab.**

   Or, if you want to send the report to everyone who's requested one, click the Reply All button on the form's Task tab.

   Whichever button you click, the Mail module jumps into action, and a message form appears, as shown in Figure 3-6. The pertinent details of the task — including its start date, due date, current status, percentage complete, and number of hours spent on the task so far — appear in the body of the message.

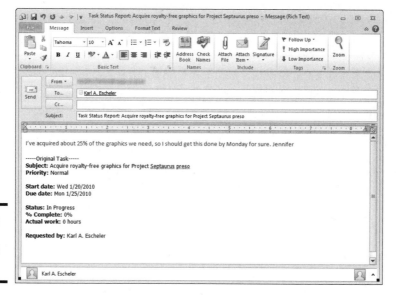

Book VI
Chapter 3

Spreading the Joy:
Task Assignments

Figure 3-6:
Hey, Ma,
look what I
done!

3. **Address the message, if necessary.**

   If the task is assigned to you, the names of everyone who needs to be updated appear automatically in the To box. If you clicked the form's Send Status Report button and you're a former owner of the task (or simply an interested party), you need to enter the addresses of the people you want to update in the To text box.

4. **In the message area, type any comments you want to make about the task and its current status, and then click Send to send the report.**

5. **Click the form's Close button to close the task form.**

Status reports, by the way, show up as regular messages in the Inboxes of whomever you send them to. The copy of the task that the original owner may have in his Tasks list isn't changed or flagged in any way, so hopefully, he sees your status report in his avalanche of e-mail and appreciates the update. Regardless, assuming that the original owner requested an updated task copy, his task updates automatically when you change the task's details — so, that's one way in which he can find out whether you've made progress.

Reassigning a reassigned task

When a task request arrives at your door, regardless of whether you accept it, you're its owner — at least, until the task giver decides to take the poor task back and reclaim it. As the owner, you can update the task and even send periodic status reports. You can also pass on the love, so to speak, by assigning the task to someone else. Follow these steps to assign a task that's been reassigned to you:

1. **In Tasks, open the task you were reassigned that you now want to reassign to someone else by double-clicking it.**

The task form appears.

2. **Click the Assign Task button on the form's Task tab.**

The humble task form transforms itself into a task request, as shown in Figure 3-7.

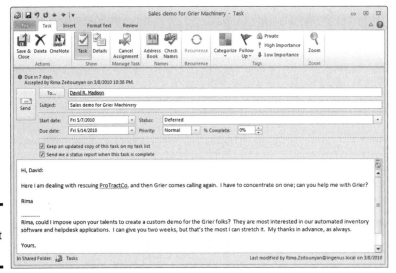

Figure 3-7:
Pass the hot
potato.

3. **In the To box, enter the e-mail address of the person (or people) to whom you want to reassign this task.**

4. **Update the task's status and any other information.**

For example, you may want to change the status to Deferred.

Even though you're passing this task along to somebody else, you can still stay updated on the task's status by selecting the Keep an Updated Copy of This Task on My Task List check box and/or the Send Me a Status Report when This Task Is Complete check box.

5. **(Optional) Type a message for the recipient, if you want.**

Perhaps an offer of money will help.

6. **When you're ready, click Send to send the request.**

You'll know in a little while if he or she accepts — just watch your Inbox for the response message.

Forwarding a Task Rather than Reassigning It

Sometimes, you want to share a task, which may or may not have anything to do with task reassignment. For example, if you create a task that reminds you to get your monthly expense report in and make it recurring, setting all the dates and even including a series of reminders to check over before you turn in the report, you may want to share your fully developed task with another colleague. You're not asking him or her to complete your expense report, so you're not reassigning the task. Instead, you're providing your colleague with the details needed to create a similar task in his or her Tasks list.

You can share a task by forwarding it, just like you might forward a regular e-mail message. The recipient of the forwarded task can then add the task to his or her Tasks list, which saves him or her the trouble of creating this particular task from scratch.

To forward a task to someone, follow these steps:

1. In the Tasks module, select the task you want to forward.

No need to open the task.

You can forward a recurring task, if you want.

2. Click the Forward button on the Home tab.

A new message form is created by the Mail module, listing the task as an attachment, as shown in Figure 3-8.

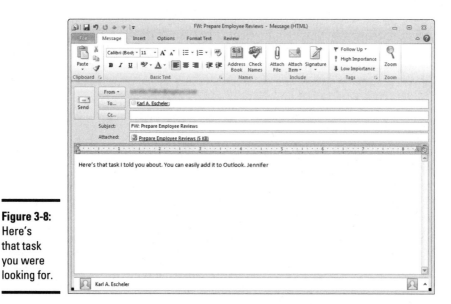

Figure 3-8:
Here's
that task
you were
looking for.

3. **In the To text box, type the address of the person to whom you want to forward the message.**

   The Subject is already provided for you; it's based on the task name. You can change it, if you want, by editing the text in the Subject box.

4. **Type a message in the message area.**

5. **Click Send to forward the task and the message.**

Now, what happens when the recipient gets your little package? Obviously, he or she needs to view the message first. The message includes the task listed as an attachment, as shown in Figure 3-9.

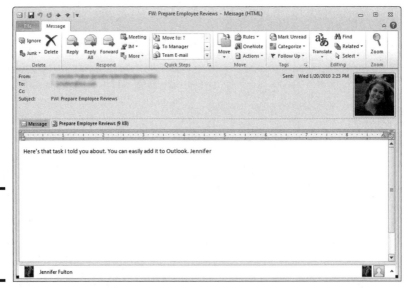

Figure 3-9:
Here's something else I want you to do.

Whether or not you open the message, here's what the recipient can do with the attached task:

✦ **To simply view the task:** If the recipient simply clicks the attachment name (which appears in the message header), then the task details appear in the Reading pane (or message area, if the message is open). If the recipient double-clicks the attachment name, the familiar task form appears, but the task is not editable.

✦ **To add the task to his or her Tasks list:** The recipient doesn't need to open the e-mail, but instead simply drag the attachment from the Reading pane and drop it on the Tasks button on the Navigation pane.

This whole procedure of forwarding a task and then dragging and dropping it on your Tasks list depends, of course, on the person with whom you want to share the task actually having Outlook. True, the outlook for Outlook is pretty good, and so you can probably assume that in most cases, Outlook is what people use, but some people don't, and what do you do then? In such instances, you can just send the task in text form. In an e-mail message, click the Outlook Item button on the form's Insert tab. The Insert Item dialog box appears. Select Tasks from the Look In list, and when your tasks appear in the Items list at the bottom of the dialog box, select the one that you want to share. Before you click OK, however, be sure to select the Text Only radio button. The task details are copied into the message as text.

Sharing Your Tasks List

You can pass on a task to someone else, as described in the section "Assigning a Task to Someone Else," earlier in this chapter. When you reassign a task to a colleague, he or she takes over ownership and becomes the only one who can make updates to the task. You can try reassigning a task to more than one person, but that kinda leaves you out of the loop, update-wise — unless each recipient of the task request manually sends you status reports about his or her progress on the task.

You can also distribute responsibility for particular tasks by simply sharing them. You can share your Tasks list only if you work on an Exchange network. After you share it, your colleagues can view your Tasks list, and depending on what kind of security you establish, they can even add new tasks and update existing ones.

Just because you're in a sharing mood doesn't mean that you have to share everything. When needed, you can designate certain tasks as private, which means that no one can view them but you. You can also approach this problem in a different way. If you want to share only certain tasks, you can create a new Tasks folder and then drag the tasks you want to share into it. Or, if the tasks you want to hide are in fact a smaller group of tasks, you can drag the tasks you want to hide into the new folder and then share your main Tasks folder only.

To make a task private, select it in the Tasks list and click the Private button in the Tags group on the Home tab.

Want to create a new Tasks folder and put either the private or the not-so-private tasks in it? Good idea. Wish I'd thought of it. Oh, yeah, I did — and I put the details you need to know to create just such a folder in Book IX, Chapter 1.

This sharing process lets you be a little bit more picky than just putting up a No Trespassing sign on a few select tasks. You can either:

✦ **Share the main Tasks folder with basically everyone on the network.** You designate what everyone is allowed to do, such as View Only, or View and Edit. See the following section for details.

✦ **Share either the main or a custom task folder almost completely.** You share this folder with only the specific people you select. See the section "Sharing tasks with specific people," later in this chapter.

Sharing tasks with everyone

You can't use the steps described in this section to share a task folder you've created all by your lonesome because you don't send a sharing invitation by using this method, and you need to send a sharing invitation to share a custom folder. I know — what I just said probably doesn't make much sense. I mean, just what is a sharing invitation? (I talk about sharing invitations and sharing custom folders in the upcoming section, "Sharing tasks with specific people".) This section is for people who want to share their main Tasks folder. If you want to share a custom folder instead, you need to jump to the following section.

To share your main Tasks folder with everyone on the network, follow these steps:

1. **Click the Folder Permissions button on the Folder tab.**

The Tasks Properties dialog box pops up.

2. **In the Name list, click Default (see Figure 3-10).**

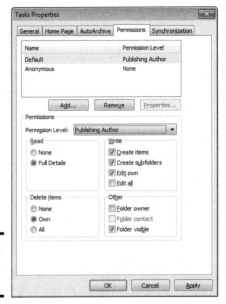

Figure 3-10:
See, it's fun
to share.

3. **From the options that appear in the Permission Level drop-down list, select the one that describes the kind of things you want visitors to be able to do.**

   You have these choices:

   - *Publishing Editor:* Create, edit, delete, and view tasks. The user can also create subfolders within the shared folder.

   - *Editor:* Same as Publishing Editor, except the user can't create subfolders.

   - *Publishing Author:* Create and view tasks, create folders, and edit or delete tasks they've created themselves.

   - *Author:* Same as Publishing Author, except the user can't create folders.

   - *Nonediting Author:* Same as Author, except they can't edit existing tasks, even if they created them.

   - *Reviewer:* Can only view tasks.

   - *Contributor:* Create and edit new tasks, but they can't view existing ones unless they created them.

   - *None:* Prevents the users from accessing the folder at all — they can't even view the tasks in the folder.

4. **Click OK.**

   The main Tasks folder appears in the Navigation pane with a special "Hey, I'm open for business" icon (a hand holding a task), showing that it's now shared.

After you share your main Tasks folder, although it's not required, you may want to send the people you want to share the folder with a general message that you've shared your folder. They don't actually need an invitation, as described in the following section. Nope, all someone on your Exchange network needs to know to access your folder right now is your name and the fact that you've placed a Welcome mat at the door of your main Tasks folder. See the section "Viewing Tasks Shared by Others," later in this chapter, for more info on how your recipient gains access to your main Tasks folder after you grant it.

**Book VI
Chapter 3**

**Spreading the Joy:
Task Assignments**

Sharing tasks with specific people

When it comes to sharing, I'm probably like most people — I mean, most people who also grew up in a family of ten where if you didn't grab, and grab quickly, you were eating your napkin for dinner. Anyway, if you have a Tasks folder to share but you want to be selective about who has access to it, you can share that folder with only certain privileged people.

In this procedure, you share the folder and send a sharing invitation to the specific people you choose. For custom folders that you've created, you have only two access levels you can select from: *Reviewer* (which means they can view tasks only) or *Editor* (which means they can create, edit, delete, and view tasks, even ones they don't create themselves). If you're sharing your main Tasks folder in this way, you may want to provide recipients with only Reviewer status — at least, initially. After the sharing invitation goes out, you can always change a particular person's access level, as desired — see the following section.

To share a Tasks folder with a select few, first select it in the Navigation pane. You can share your main Tasks folder with just a few people by following these steps, or a custom folder you've created. (If you want to share your main Tasks folder with everyone, see the preceding section.) After selecting a Tasks folder, follow these steps to share it:

1. **Click the Share Tasks button on the Folder tab.**

   A message form appears, as shown in Figure 3-11. The form in the background of Figure 3-11 appears if you share your main Tasks; the form in the foreground appears if you share a Tasks folder you created.

2. **In the To text box, add the addresses of the people with whom you want to share this folder.**

3. **Edit the Subject text if you like.**

   Normally it shows Sharing invitation: *Your Name – Folder Name.*

4. **Type a message explaining the invitation, if you want, in the large text area at the bottom of the form.**

5. **If you're sharing your main Tasks folder, select the Request Permission to View Recipient's Tasks Folder check box.**

   By selecting this check box, you request permission to view each addressee's Tasks folder, in return. Again, you're granting them only Reviewer status (look, but don't touch), so you're asking them to grant you that same access in return.

   Using this e-mail message, you can't request permission to access a specific folder within an addressee's main Tasks folder, but you can send your own separate message requesting permission.

6. **If you're sharing your main Tasks folder, make sure that the Allow Recipient to View Your Tasks Folder check box is selected.**

   Otherwise, well, you won't actually be sharing your tasks.

7. **If you're sharing a folder that you created and want users to only view tasks (Reviewer access), deselect the Recipient Can Add, Edit, and Delete Items in This Tasks Folder check box.**

   If you want them to be able to muck things up (by granting them Editor access), select the check box, instead.

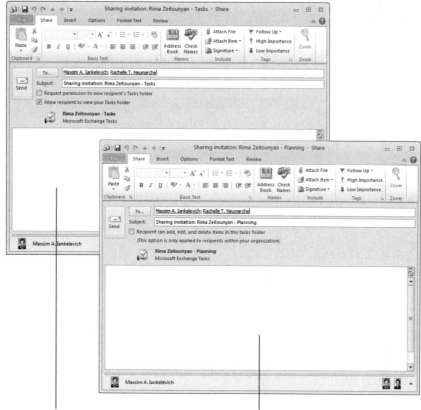

Figure 3-11:
Here, please
share my
workload.

Share your main Tasks folder.   Share a tasks folder you've created.

8. **Click Send.**

   A dialog box appears, asking for confirmation.

9. **Click Yes to confirm the invitation.**

   Another dialog box pops up, telling you that the folder is now shared.

10. **Click OK.**

The folder you chose appears in the Navigation pane with a special icon, showing that it's now shared — a hand holding a task. When the recipient(s) get your invitation, they need to follow up to actually gain access to your Tasks folder. Luckily, that's not a complicated process, as explained in the section "Viewing Tasks Shared by Others," later in this chapter.

Changing permissions or stopping sharing

Just because you were nice enough to share a Tasks folder, you don't have to keep giving and giving and giving. Nope, if you're sharing the folder with select people, for example, you can change what they can do. If you're sharing the folder with basically everyone on the network, you can either just stop sharing it or change the universal access level, or a particular person's access level.

To change permission to use a shared folder, follow these steps:

1. **Select the shared folder in the Navigation pane.**

2. **Click the Folder Permissions button on the Folder tab.**

The Properties dialog box for the selected folder appears, as shown in Figure 3-12.

Figure 3-12:
Change
what a user
can do to
your tasks.

3. **Change permissions, as desired.**

You have two options:

• *To make a change that affects everyone:* Select Default from the Name list and make a selection from the Permission Level list. To completely revoke all access to outsiders, select None.

• *To make a change to a particular user's permissions:* Select the user's name from the Name list and make a selection from the Permission Level list.

4. **Click OK.**

The permissions are changed right away.

If someone is viewing your Tasks folder right now and you change her level of access, it affects her immediately — or, well, almost immediately, as soon as your change filters through the network. If you've removed access, the tasks she's viewing disappear from the screen, and she can't reopen them.

Viewing Tasks Shared by Others

Assuming that someone has given you access to his or her shared Tasks folder (or a special subfolder created just for sharing), you can easily open that folder and view the tasks within. After you open the folder for the first time, it's added to the Navigation pane, making it really easy to view tasks (and edit them, if you have permission) when needed. Shared folders appear in the Shared Tasks group on the Navigation pane, and are labeled with the owner's name.

**Book VI
Chapter 3**

Spreading the Joy: Task Assignments

Accessing someone's main Tasks folder

If someone's shared his or her main Tasks folder with you, follow these steps to open it the first time:

1. **Click the Open Shared Tasks button on the Folder tab.**

The Open Shared Tasks dialog box appears, as shown on the left in Figure 3-13.

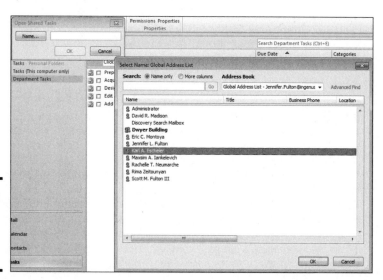

Figure 3-13:
Open a
shared
Tasks
folder.

2. **Type the name of the person whose folder you want to access in the Name text box.**

Alternatively, click the Name button to display the Select Names: Global Address List dialog box, shown on the right in Figure 3-13. Select the person from those listed and click OK to return to the Open Shared Tasks dialog box.

3. Click OK.

The person's main Tasks folder, assuming that it's shared and you have permission to access it, appears in the Shared Tasks group on the Navigation pane. The tasks in that folder appear on the right.

If the folder is shared but you haven't been given access to it just yet, a dialog box appears, asking whether you want to beg for permission.

4. Click Yes.

A message form appears, asking for permission to use the folder.

5. Select the Request Permission to View Recipient's Tasks Folder check box.

If you want to offer access to your main Tasks folder in return, select the Allow Recipient to View Your Tasks Folder check box.

6. Click Send to send the request.

After you gain access to someone's Tasks folder, you can simply click that folder in the Navigation pane at any time to display the tasks within.

You can remove a shared Tasks folder from the Shared Tasks list if you don't think you'll need to open it again. Simply select the shared Tasks folder you want to remove and click the Delete Folder button on the Folder tab. By the way, this action doesn't actually delete the Tasks folder from the owner's system, regardless of your level of access.

Accessing someone's custom task folder

If someone has decided to share only a special Tasks folder that he or she has created, you get an e-mail telling you so. You might also get an e-mail granting just you or a limited number of your colleagues, access to someone's main Tasks folder. Regardless, you can use this e-mail to gain access to the specified folder. The folder's creator determines your level of access; typically, you have either Reviewer (view only) or Editor (create, edit, and delete tasks) access. Regardless of your level of access, after you gain access to the folder, you can easily view its contents any time you want.

To access someone's shared, custom Tasks folder or main Tasks folder, follow these steps:

1. **Change over to Mail by clicking the Mail button on the Navigation pane and either select the sharing invitation to view it in the Reading pane or double-click it to view it in a separate window.**

2. **Click the Open This Tasks Folder button.**

This button appears at the top of the Reading pane or on the Share tab in the message window.

You are automatically switched over to the Tasks module, where the folder now appears in the Shared Tasks group on the Navigation pane with a small sharing icon (a clipboard with a check mark and a blue double-arrow below), as shown in Figure 3-14.

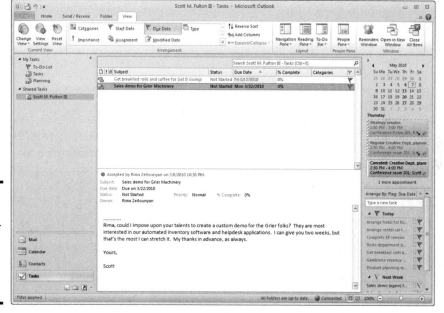

Figure 3-14: The shared Tasks folder appears in the Navigation pane.

Chapter 4: Taking Notes

In This Chapter

✔ **Creating notes with detailed information**

✔ **Organizing notes**

✔ **Changing how notes look**

✔ **Covering the Desktop with reminders**

✔ **Passing notes onto others**

*I*t seems like I keep notes everywhere — in my purse, in my jacket pocket, on the fridge, and all over my desktop. Despite the fact that Outlook lets you keep all your notes in one place, I don't use the feature too often (although I should). By using Outlook, you can not only jot down something important in a place where you can actually find it, but you can also group similar notes together by using categories, stick them on your computer's Desktop (where you can remember to read them first thing each morning), and even share notes with friends and colleagues when you need to. Covering your desk with miscellaneous bits of papers isn't a good option, and creating notes in Outlook is at least organized. But to take your notes to the next level, you need OneNote. By using OneNote, you can gather related notes, graphics, video, audio, Outlook items, and more in one spot. See Chapter 5 of this minibook for more info.

I have to admit it, I do like the Notes feature in Outlook, but maybe not for the reasons you'd expect. I most often create notes on my smartphone, and then import them into Outlook to use as reference, rather than the other way around.

Creating a Complete Note

You can create notes from just about any Outlook item, and when you do, the contents of that item appear in the note where you can add additional comments. For example, you can create a note from an appointment. To do so, just drag and drop the appointment on the Notes icon on the Navigation pane. I almost never use this approach, however, because I can just open the appointment and type my notes in that large white text box that's provided for just that purpose. But if you like this drag-and-drop stuff, see Book I, Chapter 2 for more ideas on how to use it.

Nope, when I get around to actually recording a note in Outlook, I do it the old-fashioned way — which only takes a second, as it turns out. Follow these steps:

1. **Click the New Items button on the Home tab, select More Items from the pop-up menu that appears, and select Note.**

If you're in the Notes module, you can click the New Note button, instead.

A new, blank note window jumps out, and your cursor appears within it, ready for you to write something.

2. **Type the note.**

That's right, just type to record your note, as shown in Figure 4-1. The first line of the note is important because it acts as a kind of note title and, in some cases, may be all you see prior to reopening the note. So, make that first line count. (By the way, you can copy stuff to the Clipboard and paste it into the note if you need to.)

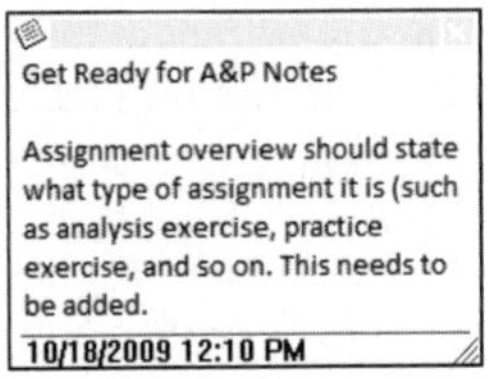

Figure 4-1:
Make a note
of that.

Get Ready for A&P Notes

Assignment overview should state what type of assignment it is (such as analysis exercise, practice exercise, and so on. This needs to be added.

10/18/2009 12:10 PM

3. **To resize the note window, click an edge or corner, and then drag.**

While you type, text automatically wraps within the note frame. However, if your note is really long, you may want to resize the note window so that you can see its text more easily.

4. **Format the note text, if you want.**

You can't format a note, but you can create a kind of bulleted list by preceding each item with an o or a *. You can also change the text font, color, and size for all notes. See the section "Making Notes Look the Way You Like," later in this chapter, for more information.

5. **When you're done with the note, close it by clicking its Close button (the X).**

You can keep the note open as long as you want — while you keep working, adding more information when you finish that phone call, e-mail exchange, or meeting. Even if Outlook is minimized, you still can see your note because it's in its own window.

After you close a note, it appears on the right in the Notes pane, as a small adhesive-note-type icon. To see the contents of a particular note, just double-click it to open it right up. You can maximize the note window by double-clicking the blue title bar that runs along the top of the window.

Organizing Notes with Categories

As you probably noticed, by default, notes are yellow. You can change this default color, although I don't mind the yellow myself; if you do, see the section "Making Notes Look the Way You Like," later in this chapter. You can also change a note's color by assigning a category to it. Categories have the advantage of allowing you to group similar notes together.

To assign a category to a note, follow these steps:

1. **Move the note outside the Outlook window.**

If the note's still open, you don't need to close it, but you should move it outside the perimeter of the Outlook window before continuing to Step 2. If you don't move the note, then it will be overlaid by the Outlook window when you use the Ribbon to apply the category and you won't be able to see how the new color looks.

2. **Click the Categorize button on the Home tab and select the category you want to assign this note from the list that appears.**

The note changes to the color of the category you applied. You can repeat this step to apply more than one category to the note; the note will take on the color of the last category you applied. Wanna know how to create categories so that you can organize notes? I know I do! See Book VIII, Chapter 1.

**Book VI
Chapter 4**

Taking Notes

After you assign a category to a note, the note's icon changes to that category's color. That way, you can easily see which notes belong together. You can also arrange notes by category, as you can see in the following section. In addition, when you open the note, the note's color changes, too. You may think that assigning a dark purple category to a note would make it impossible to read, but Outlook automatically changes the text to white in such cases, so you can read your note text easily.

Selecting a Notes View

Like all the Outlook modules, the Notes module lets you change the arrangement of its items (notes) to make finding stuff easy. By default, Outlook shows you all your notes, as icons, arranged much more neatly than notes typically appear on my desk, let me tell you. To change to a different view, click the Change View button on the View tab and select a view from the pop-up menu that appears, or select the view you want from the Current View palette of the Home tab (you can also click the Change View button on the View tab and select a view from the palette that appears). Figure 4-2 shows the Notes List view. Here's the lowdown on the various views:

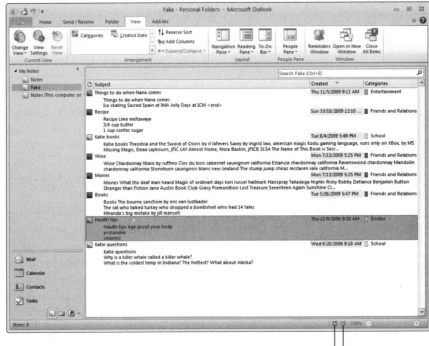

Figure 4-2:
It's up to
your point of
view.

Reading

Normal

- ✦ **Icon:** Displays notes as small sticky notes, arranged in the order in which the notes were created, with the newest notes appearing at the top of the window.

- ✦ **Notes List:** Displays a long list of your notes, in a kind of AutoPreview, where the contents of each note appear below the note's title. Notes are displayed in the order in which they were created, with the newest notes appearing at the top of the window.

- ✦ **Last 7 Days:** Lists your notes similar to Notes List view, except that you see only the notes you've created recently. Notes are arranged in the order in which they were created, with the newest notes appearing at the top of the window.

Regardless of which view you choose, you can quickly sort your notes so that you can easily work with them. I wish sorting through my pile of notes jotted down on the back of envelopes, scrap paper, and napkins was as easy. Simply select the sort order that you want to use from the Arrangement section of the View tab. Your options change depending on the current view, but you can choose sort orders such as Date, Categories, and Created Date.

If you're using a list view (Notes List or Last 7 Days view), you can sort the list by a particular column by simply clicking that column's header. For example, to sort the notes alphabetically by title (the first line of each note), click the Subject column header.

Like the other Outlook modules, Notes has a default (Normal) view, which displays the Navigation pane on the left and the To-Do bar on the right. To change to this Normal view, click the Normal button on the status bar. If you have a lot of notes to browse through, you might want to make more room for them by clicking the Reading button, which minimizes the Navigation pane and the To-Do bar. The Reading button shows up on the status bar when you're in Notes List or Last 7 Days view. If you're using Icon view, then you can click the Normal button (to display the Navigation pane and the To-Do bar) or the Icons Only button (to display the notes icons and hide the Navigation pane and To-Do bar).

Making Notes Look the Way You Like

Notes are kinda fun, and handy — when you remember to use them, that is. We all make a lot of notes all day long, and if you're at your computer, you may as well put them in Outlook, where they won't fall out of your pocket.

After spending some time creating notes, you'll be happy to know you can modify the way they work and look. For example, if you're bored with that dull yellow color, you can start off your notes with a jazzy blue or a pristine white. If you're playing the ol' eye trombone thing, like me (moving closer to the screen one minute and then farther back the next to keep things in focus), you can increase the default font size or select a more readable font so that you can more easily use notes. You can change the note's default size, as well, perhaps saving you time resizing note windows.

To change the default color, size, or font for all your notes, follow these steps:

1. **Click the File tab to display Backstage, and select Options from the list on the left.**

The Outlook Options dialog box appears.

2. **Select Notes and Journal from the list on the left.**

The Notes and Journal options appear on the right, as shown in Figure 4-3.

3. **Select the defaults you want.**

You have these options:

- *To select a default note color:* Select a color from the Default Color palette. You may want to choose a color not associated with a category so that you can easily tell which notes don't have a category assigned to them.

- *To change the default note size:* Select a size from the Default Size drop-down list. You can choose from Small, Medium (the default), or Large.

- *To change the default note text's font, size, or color:* Click the Font button. In the Font dialog box that appears, select options for Font, Font Style (such as bold or italic), Size, and Color. Click OK.

- *To include the modified date and time at the bottom of the note window:* Select the Show Date and Time That the Note Was Last Modified check box. The date and time still appear in list views even if you turn off this option.

4. **Click OK to save your changes.**

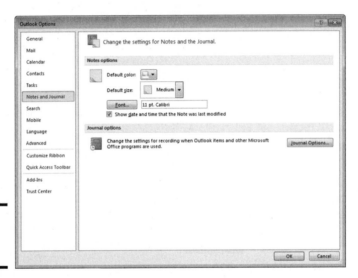

Figure 4-3:
Set note
defaults.

Sticking Notes to Your Desktop

If you have a note that you need to see tomorrow morning, bright and early, you can stick the note on your computer's Desktop, rather than leave it in Outlook. This handy trick also works for notes that you need to see often, such as "Lay off the donuts — the reunion is this summer!"

To put a note on your Desktop, drag and drop it there. A note on your Desktop looks just like it does in Outlook — an icon that looks like a small adhesive note. To open the note, double-click the icon. You can even make changes, if you like, and then close the note by clicking its Close button. If you delete the note on the Desktop, it's removed from the Desktop but not Outlook.

The note still appears in Outlook, too, so if you happen to be working in Outlook, you can find your note there, as well as on the Desktop.

Passing Notes

Hopefully, you have something useful to record in a note — other than this week's grocery list, your gym locker combination, or your favorite laugh from Comedy Central. If so, you can easily share your pearls of wisdom with colleagues and friends. Follow these steps:

1. **Select the note you want to share.**

   The note is highlighted.

2. **Click the Forward button on the Home tab.**

   A new message form opens, with the note shown as an attachment (see Figure 4-4).

3. **Address the message, edit the Subject (if you want), and then type a message in the large text box.**

   The default Subject comes from the title of your note.

4. **When you finish your message, click Send to send the message with its note attachment.**

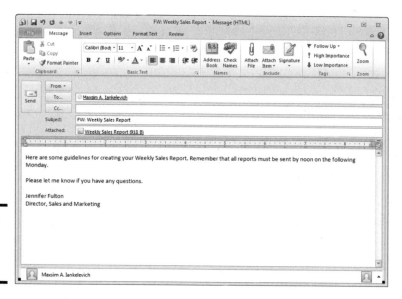

Figure 4-4:
Hold the
salt, pass
the note.

The recipient, assuming that he or she has Outlook, can open the attachment and read it or print it. He or she can also drag the attachment to the Notes icon and drop it, copying the note to his or her system.

Chapter 5: Taking Notes in Overdrive: OneNote

In This Chapter

✔ Discovering a whole new way to organize your notes

✔ Adding notebooks, new pages, and sections

✔ Creating note content

✔ Inserting files and links in your notes

The idea behind OneNote isn't new — it's as old as writing itself. From the dawn of time, whenever man had something important to remember, he wrote it down — that is, after he invented paper, a writing system, ink, and an eraser. By using OneNote, you, too, can cover your cave with important bits of information — for example, a meeting agenda, a map to the meeting site, flight info, things to do for the meeting, sales charts, images taken at a meeting or class lecture, and meeting/lecture/conference notes. OneNote can gather all sorts of notes, graphics, audio and video files, Outlook items, and other stuff all in one spot where you can find it. And instead of letting you dump all this glorious information in one big heap, OneNote directs you in various ways in which you can *organize it.*

OneNote is now included with all versions of Office, so if you haven't used it before, give it a try! You start OneNote as you might any other Office program — click the Start button, then select All Programs, Microsoft Office, and finally Microsoft OneNote 2010 from the pop-up menus that appear. You can also start OneNote by clicking its button in the system tray (which is located at the right side of the Windows taskbar): Click the up arrow at the left edge of the system tray, and click the OneNote button on the palette that appears.

You can add Outlook items directly to OneNote by clicking the item to add (such as a meeting request with details about the meeting) and clicking the OneNote button on the Home tab. Link information in any Office document (such as the meeting agenda, meeting notes, or a meeting presentation) to a OneNote page by clicking the Linked Notes button on the Review tab. You can create links to other stuff as well, such as pages you browse on the Internet. See the section, "Creating a Linked Note," later in this chapter, for more information on creating these links.

OneNote really helps you organize your life. For example, suppose you've just snapped some photos, taken notes, and recorded audio by using your cell phone during an important meeting. What should you do with all this related data? Consider offloading it all to the hard drive and then importing that data into OneNote, where you can group it logically.

Organizing in OneNote

OneNote is like a bunch of electronic notebooks. You can organize each notebook into sections by using tabs, like you might insert tabs into a school binder full of notebook paper. You can add as many note pages in each section of a notebook as you need. Each page in a notebook is just like a piece of paper; you can click anywhere on the page, and then type text or insert a graphic, screen clip, audio file, Outlook item, or bits of wisdom from the Web. (See Figure 5-1.) If you have a pen tablet or a tablet PC, you can write or draw on it to add information to a page. Stuff that you add to a page, such as a note, gets placed inside a box onscreen that's called a *container.* You use these containers to move stuff around on a page.

A pen tablet is an accessory that you can connect to your computer. By dragging a pen-shaped stylus over its flat surface, you can write, select, and draw with amazing ease. A Tablet PC is a lightweight computer whose size may range from that of a checkbook to a legal pad. Typically, each tablet PC is equipped with a touchscreen that enables the user to write, select, or draw by dragging a finger or a pen-shaped stylus across the front of it.

You start out by picking a page on which to put some stuff. (You can find out more about how to navigate around OneNote and locate a page in the following section.) However, if you just have to write something down right now, and you don't want to think about which notebook or section it should go into, you can place it in the Unfiled Notes section until you can find or create a place for it. Click the Unfiled Notes button at the bottom of the Navigation bar to jump to that section.

Even after you put something on a page, you can still reorganize it however you want, dragging and dropping directions next to a map, or moving a picture of a digital camera next to a bulleted list you're compiling of Web sites that offer the camera and various accessories for sale. To move a note or other object, click the top border of its container to select the object, and then drag it around on the page until you find its new home.

Collapsed Navigation bar

Expand Navigation Bar button

Section tab

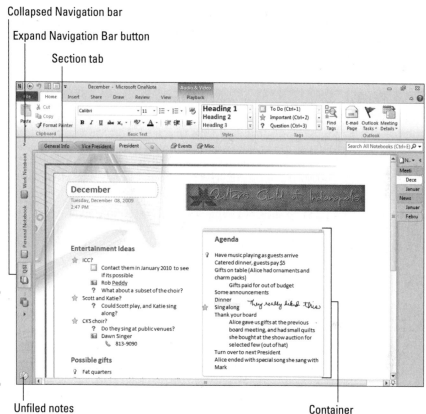

Figure 5-1:
OneNote
helps you
get a handle
on your life.

Unfiled notes

Container

So that you can more easily add or move objects around on a page, you
might want to temporarily hide all the tabs and the Navigation bar by clicking the Full Page View button on the View tab. To return to regular view,
click the Normal View button. To work in OneNote alongside some other
application (such as Outlook), click the Dock to Desktop or New Docked
Window button on the View tab, which pushes the OneNote window to
the right, and displays the last active window (the window that was active
just prior to you switching to OneNote) to the left. This makes the Dock to
Desktop view perfect for working in OneNote side-by-side with your other
programs. You can also adjust the view by using the Zoom buttons on the
View tab: Zoom In, Zoom Out, 100%, 75%, or Zoom (where you select a different percentage from its drop-down list, or type one into the text box). By the
way, the Full Page View and Dock to Desktop buttons appear on the Quick
Access toolbar at the top of OneNote's main window.

One thing you don't see on your tour of OneNote is a Save button. In
OneNote, you don't need to save anything you do; it takes care of saving
automatically while you work.

Navigating in OneNote

OneNote has a simple structure. Each notebook is divided into tabbed sections, which are further divided into separate pages. Here's how to get around OneNote:

✦ **To open a particular notebook, click the notebook's button on the Navigation bar.** For example, click the Personal button to open the notebook that's installed with OneNote. You will find this notebook useful, as it acts as both a help guide and a working teaching tool that you can play around with as you learn to use OneNote. As you add other notebooks, click one of your notebooks' buttons to open the notebook and work with it.

✦ **You can minimize the Navigation bar and expand it, when needed.** The expanded bar lists all your notebooks. (See Figure 5-2.) When a notebook is expanded, each page in that notebook appears in a list. You can collapse a notebook's list by clicking its Collapse button; you can then expand it again so that it shows all the notebook's pages by clicking the Expand Navigation Bar button. To minimize the Navigation bar, click the Collapse Navigation Bar button. On a minimized Navigation bar (refer to Figure 5-1), each notebook appears as a simple icon; section pages don't appear. To expand the Navigation bar again, click the Expand Navigation Bar button.

✦ **To change to a different section of a notebook, click that section's tab.** The section tabs run along the top of the window. You can jump directly to a specific section in a notebook (even in a different notebook) by clicking that section's name in the expanded Navigation bar listing.

✦ **To change to a different page within a section, click that page's tab.** Page tabs appear in a list on the right. The Page Tab area is normally rather skinny; if you want to expand it so that you can more easily read long page tab names, click the Expand Page Tabs button (it looks like a left arrow [<]). Go ahead — I know you want to.

Each section of a notebook contains at least one page, but a section can contain a lot more than one page. You can create subpages, as well, in order to organize certain pages under a main page. You can find out how to create pages in the section "Adding a New Page," later in this chapter.

After you put together a page in OneNote, you can send it to Word if you want to take advantage of that program's superior word-processing capabilities: In OneNote, click the File tab to display Backstage, select Send from the list on the left to display the Send options on the right, and then select Send to Word.

Expand Notebook list

Collapse Navigation Bar button

Section tabs

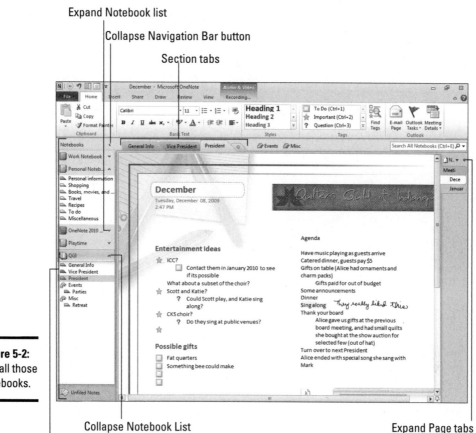

Book VI
Chapter 5

Taking Notes
in Overdrive:
OneNote

Figure 5-2:
List all those
notebooks.

Collapse Notebook List

Expand Page tabs

Navigation bar

Creating a Notebook

OneNote starts you out with one notebook for the best part of your life:
Personal. You don't have to use the Personal notebook, but it makes
sense to use it— at least, until you feel comfortable enough to create your
own notebooks. To change to a particular notebook, click its icon on the
Navigation bar. The Personal notebook is already divided into sections, with
little tabs marking each section. You can rename the section tabs or remove
them and add your own sections (see "Adding a Section" and "Renaming
or removing sections" later in this chapter, for help with sections). You
can also create your own notebooks, regardless of whether you keep the
Personal notebook.

To create a new notebook, follow these steps:

1. **Click the File tab to display Backstage, and select New from the list on the left.**

   The New Notebook options appear on the right, as shown in Figure 5-3.

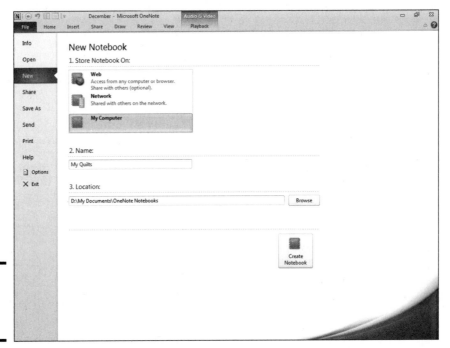

Figure 5-3:
Create
a new
notebook.

2. **Select where to store the new notebook from the Store Notebook On list.**

   You have several options:

   - *Web:* Allows you to share the notebook with others or just your-self, through Windows Live SkyDrive Located at skydrive.live.com, Windows Live SkyDrive is a place where you can keep your documents so you can access them from anywhere with in Internet connection, You can also share the documents on Windows Live SkyDrive with your Live contacts (or with the public), making it a perfect place for collaborating on OneNote notebooks, Office docu-ments, and anything else you can think of. You need to register for a Windows Live ID to use this service, but it's free.

   - *Network:* Allows you to share the notebook with your work col-leagues through the office network

   - *My Computer:* Probably the most common option, which stores the notebook close to home, on your computer

3. **Type a name in the Name text box.**

4. **Specify where you want to create the notebook in the Location text box.**

   How you specify location depends on what storage area you selected in Step 1:

   - *On the Web:* The Web Location (Windows SkyDrive) is already selected for you, so with this option you don't need to do a thing.

   - *On your company network:* Click Browse and select a shared folder from Select Folder dialog box that appears, then click Select.

   - *To store on your computer:* Click Browse and select a folder from the Select Folder dialog box that appears. Click Select.

To quickly create a new shared notebook, click the New Shared Notebook button on the Share tab. The New options in Backstage appear, with the Web option selected, but if you prefer to share this new notebook through your company's network, you can select Network from the Store Notebook On list if you like.

5. **Click the Create Notebook button.**

   The new notebook pops open in OneNote, as shown in Figure 5-4. A button for the new notebook appears on the Navigation bar, below all the other notebooks. The name on this button matches the Name you typed in Step 3. You can move the Notebook button up in the Navigation bar, if you like, by simply dragging and dropping it. The current notebook is represented by an open book icon on the Navigation pane; when the notebook is not active, it appears as a closed book icon.

When you create a new blank notebook, it has one section (called New Section 1) that contains a single, blank page. Give the section tab a name by double-clicking the tab and replacing the New Section 1 text. To name the new page, type something in that little oval-looking thing that you see at the top of the page. The page title then appears on the right, on the page's tab. Until you type a page title, the page tab says Untitled. If you don't type any title in the oval, OneNote just uses the first sentence that you type on the page itself as the page title and displays that text on the page tab. After you add more pages to this section, you can click this tab to jump right back to this page at any time. You're probably itching to get something down on that nice, empty page. Go ahead; all you have to do is click anywhere you want on the blank page and start typing.

Each item on a page is saved within its own container. So, if you start typing on the page, a box forms around what you type. Text automatically wraps within the box, and the box expands to fit the width of the page and the depth of your text, so you have no sizing problems there. The containers surround every object — not just text, but also graphic images, Outlook items, drawings, and so on. You can use these containers to move things around; click the top of a container to select everything in it, and then drag the container to move it.

Inactive notebook   Type your page title here

Section tab

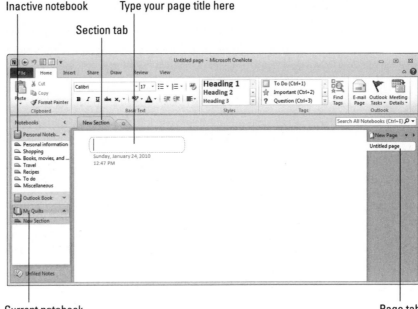

Figure 5-4:
Voilà! New
notebook.

Current notebook   Page tab

Each notebook appears on the Navigation bar with its own colored icon. These colors are assigned automatically by OneNote, but you can change them to be more meaningful to you. To change the color of a notebook's icon, right-click it on the Navigation pane, and select Properties from the pop-up menu that appears. The Notebook Properties dialog box appears. Select the color you want from the Color palette and click OK. You can also change the notebook's name, location, and format (converting it from OneNote 2010 format to OneNote 2007 format when needed, for example) in this dialog box.

Adding a New Page

Each section starts off with one page. It doesn't take long to fill it, but even before you do, you may want to create a new page, instead of dumping every-thing on the same page. No problem; adding a new page to a section is easy — just click the New Page button on the right (just above the page tabs).

After the page is added, click in the oval bubble at the top of the page and type a page title. The title appears on the page's tab on the right. You can change this title as often as you feel like it, until you finally get a title that makes sense to you and describes the contents of the page. (If you don't type a title, the text from the first note appears on the page tab.)

Next, you can add content to the page. That content can be in the form of text, audio, video, graphic images, charts, tables, bulleted or numbered lists, and just about anything else you can think of. Throughout this chapter, I show you how to add stuff to a page, but to add a quick note, see the section "Taking a Note," later in this chapter.

Renaming, rearranging, or removing pages

After creating a few pages, you might want to make some changes such as these:

✦ To rename a page, edit the text displayed in the oval at the top of the page.

✦ To remove a page (or subpage) and its contents, right-click its tab over there on the right, and choose select Delete from the pop-up menu that appears.

> You can restore a page you've deleted by accident (and its contents too), as long as you haven't emptied the Recycle Bin for this notebook. See Book VI, Chapter 6 for more information on the Recycle Bin.

✦ To rearrange the order of the pages in a section, click a page's tab, drag it up or down the list of page tabs, and drop it where you want it. To move a page to a different section, drag the page tab onto a section button on the Navigation bar and drop it, or drag and drop it on a section tab at the top of the window.

Adding subpages

If you just want to continue what's on a page, you can stretch out the current page or add a *subpage*. A subpage has its own title and appears as a small page tab on the right, below the main page's full tab. You can move, copy, delete, and e-mail a page and its subpages like they're one unit.

To create a subpage, follow these steps:

1. **Click the down arrow on the New Page button.**

2. **Select New Subpage from the pop-up menu that appears.**

A new subpage is created, and its tab appears below the current page's tab in the page list, as shown in Figure 5-5. A subpage is just like any other page — you can put whatever you want on it.

Here are some tips for working with subpages:

✦ **To select a main page and all its subpages:** Double-click the main page's tab. You can then move, copy, delete, or e-mail all the pages in the group.

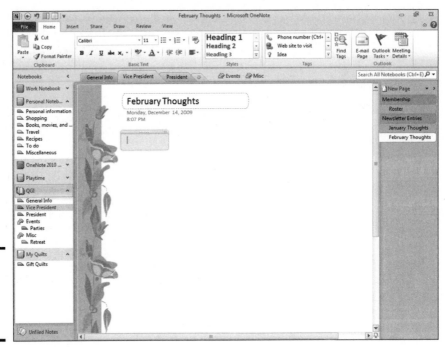

Figure 5-5:
A subpage
appears
below the
main page.

✦ **To make an existing page into a subpage:** Right-click the page tab and select Make Subpage from the pop-up menu that appears. You can use this command on a main page (to create a subpage) or on a subpage (to create a sub-subpage).

✦ **To return a subpage to main page status (or to raise a lowly sub-sub-page into a subpage):** Right-click the subpage's tab and select Promote Subpage from the pop-up menu that appears.

✦ **To temporarily hide the subpages below a main page:** Right-click the main page's tab and select Collapse Subpages from the pop-up menu that appears. Right-click the main page's tab and select Expand Subpages from that same pop-up menu to redisplay the subpages once again.

Adding a New Page by Using a Template

Instead of adding a boring white page to a notebook, you can jazz things up by adding a new page that has a fancy background or some sample structure. You simply need to apply a template when you create the page. Some templates include text sections to get you started on that page. For example, a Project Overview page has a place for the project name and description, and a bulleted list for the project goals. To add a new page to a notebook by using a template, follow these steps:

1. **Click the down arrow on the New Page button and select Page Templates from the pop-up menu that appears.**

The Templates pane makes a guest appearance on the right (see Figure 5-6).

New Page button

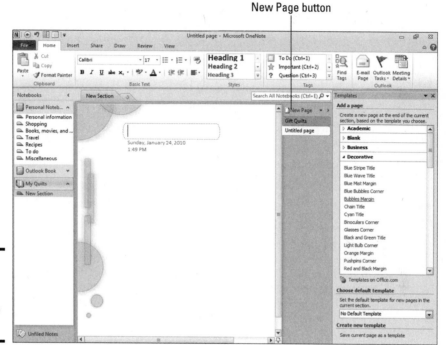

Book VI
Chapter 5

Taking Notes
in Overdrive:
OneNote

Figure 5-6:
No reason
why a new
page has to
be boring.

2. **Select a template from the Templates pane.**

Click the right arrow in front of a category to display its templates. For example, click the right arrow in front of the Business category to see its templates. Click a template in the listing to create a new page using that template. If you don't like what you see, you can click a different template — the different template you select is applied to the new page instead of the original template.

You can keep trying out templates in this manner, as long as you don't switch to something else. If you do, then selecting a template from the list will create another new page. To view even more templates, click the Templates on Office.com link at the bottom of the Templates pane to visit Microsoft's Web site and download a template.

3. **Close the Templates pane by clicking its Close button (X).**

After you select a template for a new page, that template is added to the New Page drop-down list. So later on, if you click the down arrow on the New Page button, you can select a template you've used before from the drop-down list, and skip the whole process of displaying the Templates pane.

Adding a template to an existing page

You can't apply a template to an existing page, but you can create a new page by using a template and then copy the stuff from the other page onto it. Follow these steps:

1. **To copy everything on the page, click outside the borders of the object containers so that you don't select just one, and then press Ctrl+A.**

2. **Click the Copy button on the Home tab to copy everything you've selected.**

3. **Click the page tab of the new, templated page to display it.**

4. **Click on the page, and then click the Paste button to paste it all.**

Designating a favorite template

Hey, gotta template you like a lot? Then designate it as your favorite template, and then when you click the New Page button *in this same section of the notebook*, a new page using that template will be created instantly. You see, you can designate a different favorite template for each section of a notebook, and of course, you can designate different favorites in each notebook you create.

Here's how to designate a favorite template for new pages created in the current section of this notebook: Display the Templates pane by clicking the New Page button and selecting Page Templates from the pop-up menu that appears. Select the template that you want to use most of the time from the Choose Default Template list.

Adding a Section

Notebooks in OneNote are divided into little sections marked by tabs that run along the top of the window. (See Figure 5-7.) Each section (and its associated tab) gets its own color, which helps you identify sections with a particular purpose. For example, you might create a new section for each class you're taking, for each major client you handle, or for each person on your team.

Change the color of a section's tab by right-clicking the tab, selecting Section Color from the pop-up menu that appears, and then selecting a color from the additional pop-up menu that appears. You don't have to make each tab a different color; you can use the colors to visually group similar sections, for example.

Show the Rest of the Sections button

Section Tabs

Click here to add a new section.

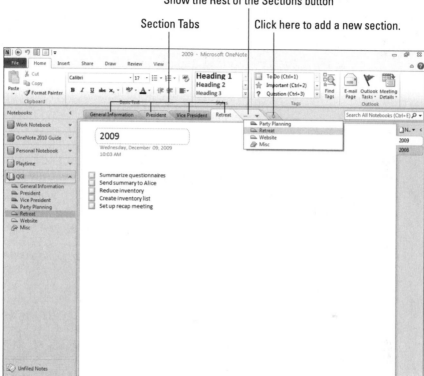

Figure 5-7:
Divide your
notebook
into
sections.

Each section is stored as a separate file in whatever folder you choose to
create the notebook in.

To create a new section in the current notebook, follow these steps:

1. **Click the Create a New Section tab at the end of the section tabs.**

A new section is added to the notebook, and its tab appears at the top
of the window at the end of the list of tabs. The new section tab is highlighted; OneNote is waiting for you to name your new baby.

2. **Type a name for the section and press Enter.**

To move from section to section, click a section's tab. The first page in that
section appears. To move to a different page, click the page tab you want
to view from the tabs listed on the right. If a notebook has a lot of sections,
they may not all be displayed. In such a case, click the Show the Rest of the
Sections button to display a menu of the missing sections and/or section
groups. Select the section or section group from this menu to display it.
(You learn about section groups in the upcoming section, "Adding a Section
Group".)

Renaming, rearranging, or removing sections

After you create sections in a notebook, you can play around with them as much as you like. Here are some things you can do:

✦ To rename a section, right-click the section tab and select Rename from the pop-up menu that appears. The current section name is highlighted; simply type the new name or edit the existing text, then press Enter.

✦ New sections are added to the end of the tab list, on the right. You can reorder the sections by dragging a section's tab along the line of tabs. A black downward triangle marks the spot; when the triangle is located where you want the section tab to be, release the mouse button to drop it. To move a section to another notebook, expand the Navigation bar and then drop the tab within the notebook list.

✦ To remove a section (and its contents), right-click the section tab and select Delete from the pop-up menu. A dialog box warning you that you are about to lose the contents of the section appears. Click Yes to remove the section and all its pages.

You can restore a section you've removed by accident (and of course, all of its pages), as long as you haven't emptied the Recycle Bin for this notebook. See Book VI, Chapter 6 what you need to know about the Recycle Bin.

Adding a Section Group

You can create a section group and fill it with as many sections as you like. A section group is still part of a notebook, but it appears to the right of the section tabs as a button. When you click the button, it's as if you're opening a new notebook. You can put one section here, or several. Section groups give you a way to put a few pages together in an easy-to-get-to place that's away from the main section.

To create a section group, follow these steps:

1. Right-click the section tab area and select New Section Group from the pop-up menu that appears.

A new group is created and added to the right of the tabs. The new section group button is highlighted; it's waiting for a name.

2. Type a name for the new group and press Enter.

Pick a name that makes sense to you. (Figure 5-8 shows you that I added an Events group and the ever-popular Misc.)

3. Click the section group button that you just created and named.

A gray page appears, which tells you that there are no sections (or pages for that matter) in this particular section group yet.

Section Group buttons

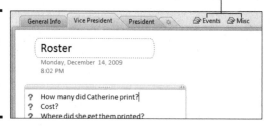

Figure 5-8:
Add section
groups to
a notebook
for ancillary
material.

4. **Click the gray, empty page to create a section.**

   A section tab is added. The placeholder name for the section is high-lighted; type a name for the section and press Enter. The section contains one page. Add whatever you want to this new page. Add pages and sections to this new section group, if you want.

   Drag an existing section onto the Section Group button and drop it to move that section into your new group.

5. **Click the Navigate to Parent Section Group button (see Figure 5-9) to return to the main sections.**

Click here to return to the main sections.

Figure 5-9:
Return
ticket.

Taking a Note

To add text to a page, just click and type. (Okay, you might take one second to change to the notebook, section, and page on which you want to store the note.) Text is stored instantly in a little container with cute borders that cause the text to wrap within it. The container automatically widens to the width of the page and keeps expanding height-wise while you add more text.

If you're not sure where you want to file your new note, you can change to the Unfiled Notes notebook by clicking its icon on the Navigation bar, and then create the note.

You can also resize or move the container:

+ **Resize the container to keep the text in a specific area.** Move the mouse pointer over the right side of a container, and when it changes to a two-sided arrow, click. Drag the right edge of the container left or right to make the container larger or smaller as needed. Similarly, you can drag a container's bottom edge up or down to resize it.

+ **Move the container around on the page.** Move the mouse pointer over the top edge of the container and when it changes to a four-headed arrow, click and drag the container wherever you want on the page. To move the container to a different page, section, or notebook, you need to cut and paste it.

Creating a Linked Note

By using OneNote 2010, you can now create automatic links to Web pages, Word documents, PowerPoint presentations, and even other pages within OneNote. So, while you're browsing through the latest sales report in Word, you can take notes in OneNote on the latest sales figures and create an automatic link back to the report file. Later, when you scan through your notes in OneNote and notice a link icon, you can hover the mouse pointer over the link icon to reveal a small thumbnail of the Web page or document the link points to, as shown in Figure 5-10. As you learn in this section, you use this thumbnail to jump to the Web page or document the link points to.

Link icon

Figure 5-10: Link Web pages, documents, and presentations to the notes you take.

To create a linked note, follow these steps:

1. **Turn on linked note-taking.**

   You can turn on this feature in one of several ways:

   - Put OneNote in a docked window by clicking the Dock to Desktop button on the View tab. (See the section "Organizing in OneNote," earlier in this chapter, for more info.)

   - Click the Linked Notes button on the Review tab in OneNote, Word, or PowerPoint. You can also click the OneNote Linked Notes button on the Command bar in Internet Explorer to begin linked note-taking.

   - Click the New Docked Window button on the View tab to open a second OneNote window just for linked note-taking.

   The window you initiated linked note-taking from (IE, Word, PowerPoint, or OneNote) is moved over to the left, and the OneNote window containing your current page is placed on the right, as shown in Figure 5-11.

   If OneNote was running when you initiated linked notes, then you have two OneNote windows open — the docked window you now see on the right, and your original working window which is either shown on the left (if you started linked notes from OneNote) or hidden (if you started linked notes from a different program).

**Book VI
Chapter 5**

Taking Notes
in Overdrive:
OneNote

Link icon

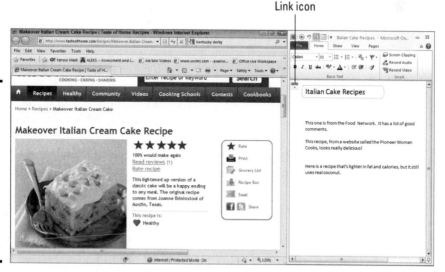

Figure 5-11: After you start linked note-taking, OneNote creates links to the Web pages or documents you browse.

2. **Select the OneNote page to which you want to link, if needed.**

   - If you clicked the Linked Notes button in IE, Word, or PowerPoint, the Select Location in OneNote dialog box may appear; if so, Select the OneNote page on which you want to create links from the Pick a Section or Page in Which to Put the Item list and click OK. The page you select appears in the OneNote window on the right.

   - If you clicked the Dock to Desktop or New Docked Window button in OneNote, linking is typically automatically enabled; look at the Link Icon (chain link) at the top of the OneNote page to be sure — it should not have a circle with a red diagonal line through it. If linking is not turned on, click the Link Icon and select Start Taking Linked Notes from the pop-up menu that appears.

3. **View whatever you want to link to in the window on the left.**

4. **In the docked OneNote window, start taking a note.**

   Whatever Web page, Word file, PowerPoint presentation, or OneNote page (in the main window) you were just looking at is automatically linked to the note you type. A small icon representing the program to which the link points appears to the left of the link — for example, in Figure 5-11, you see a small Internet Explorer to the left of the note I'm typing in OneNote. That tells me that a link to the Web page I'm currently viewing was created by OneNote.

   When you link to Word, PowerPoint, or some other page in OneNote, OneNote records the exact cursor position within the file (the current paragraph or slide), as well, so when you use the link later, you're taken to that exact spot. In Internet Explorer, the position on the page affects the thumbnail image that's captured, but it doesn't affect the link that's created because when you use the link to return to IE, it displays the top of the Web page you linked to.

5. **When you finish taking linked notes, click the Link icon at the top of the page and select Stop Taking Linked Notes from the pop-up menu that appears.**

   The Link Icon looks like a chain link when it's on (refer to Figure 5-11), and a chain link with a red "Do Not" circle on it when linked notes is not on (refer to Figure 5-10).

6. **If needed, close the docked OneNote window by clicking its Close button.**

   If you initiated linked note-taking while OneNote was already running, you have an extra OneNote window open, and it's the docked window. Unless you think you'll be turning Linked Notes on again soon, give yourself some working room by closing that extra window. Remember, the main OneNote window is still open on the left, so you're not closing OneNote completely.

If OneNote was not running when you initiated linked note-taking, then there is only one OneNote window open. You can close it if you don't want to continue to use OneNote, by clicking its Close button.

If you keep this docked window open, you can start linked note-taking again by clicking the Link icon in the docked window and selecting Start Taking Linked Notes from the pop-up menu that appears.

After you create linked notes, you can use them pretty easily. As you can see in Figure 5-10, just hover the mouse pointer over a one of the small Word, PowerPoint, or Internet Explorer icons that appear to the left of a linked note to open a thumbnail image of the Web page or file (also shown in Figure 5-10) so that you can verify this is the link you want to view. Click the icon instead of hovering to open the related file or Web page in a separate window. Easy as that!

Adding Links to Other Pages, Files, or the Internet

Because you can automatically link Word docs, PowerPoint presentations, and Web pages to OneNote, you might be wondering why I'd suggest the manual method of inserting hyperlinks yourself. *Hyperlinks* — or just links, as their closest friends call them — allow you to jump to some other bit of information with a single click. In OneNote, a link may take you to a different section, a different paragraph on the same page, or to another page altogether. Hyperlinks can also link you to documents and other files, whether they're located on your computer or the network. You can also link to a page out on the Internet. Unlike their automatically inserted cousins, manually inserted hyperlinks allow you to link to other parts of a OneNote notebook; files not created by Word or PowerPoint; or Web pages, Word, or PowerPoint files you're currently not viewing (and don't feel like opening just so that you can create a link).

Linking to other notebook pages

You can create any number of pages in a notebook, in the same section or a different section. Of course, you *can* jump from page to page by just clicking the section tab and then clicking the page tab, but that method always seemed like the long way round to me, so I started looking for a shortcut. Turns out that you can insert a hyperlink on a page that, when clicked, jumps you right to some other page. Actually, you create a link to a specific paragraph on a page, which can be the first paragraph at the top of the page or a paragraph somewhere else, if that suits you better. If you don't want to link to a particular page, but to a whole section, you can do that, too.

You can use page hyperlinks to create a table of contents for a notebook that a lot of people are going to use (or hey, maybe just you). You can also use page links to point to pages on any kind of list, such as a list of favorite restaurants, key concepts, or special terms.

To create a page or section link, follow these steps:

1. **Copy the hyperlink.**

   How you copy the hyperlink depends on what you want to link to, exactly:

   - *To link to a specific paragraph:* Move the mouse pointer to the left of that paragraph and right-click. Select Copy Link to Paragraph from the pop-up menu that appears.

   - *To link to a specific page:* Right-click the tab of the page to which you want to link, and from the pop-up menu that appears, select Copy Link to Page.

   - *To link to a particular section:* Right-click the section tab, and then select Copy Link to Section from the pop-up menu that appears.

   A link to the paragraph, page, or section is created and placed on the Clipboard.

2. **Change over to the page on which you want to add the link, and click on the page where you want the link to appear.**

3. **Click the Paste button on the Home tab.**

   The hyperlink appears on the page as blue, underlined text; if you linked to a paragraph, the first few words of that paragraph are used as the link text, otherwise, the name of the page or section is used. Click this link, and the paragraph, page, or section you selected in Step 1 appears.

To create a new page instantly and add a link to that new OneNote page on the current page, first type a phrase to use as the link. For example, you might type Tablet PCs. Next, select this phrase by dragging over the text. Click the Link button on the Insert tab to display the Link dialog box. Select your new page from the Pick a Location in OneNote list. The new page has been named using the text you just selected, and you'll find it in the Create New Page section located at the bottom of the Pick a Location in OneNote list. Click OK to create the link and the new page at the same time.

Linking to files, documents, or Web pages

To create a link to a page on the Internet, you can just type that page's address anywhere on a note page. OneNote recognizes the format of a Web link (the www. part is usually a dead giveaway) and turns your text into a clickable link. If the Web address does not include the traditional "www" part, you must type the entire address, as in http://skydrive.live.com for OneNote to recognize the text as a Web page address. You can also copy the link from your browser and paste it onto the page. When linking to a file or other document, you can simply drag and drop the file from Windows Explorer onto a page and create an instant link.

Another way to create a link is a bit slower, but it allows you ↴
text on the page that points to a Web page or document withou↴
actual Web address or file path on the page.

To insert a link in OneNote that links to a Web page or file on your ↴
or network, follow these steps:

1. Click the Link button on the Insert tab.

The Link dialog box jumps up. (See Figure 5-12.)

Browse for file

Browse the Web

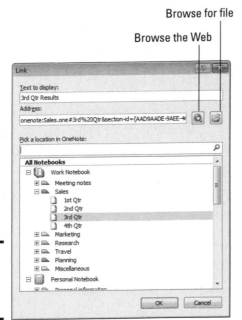

Figure 5-12:
Create your
own links
manually.

2. Type the text you want to appear as the link in the Text to Display text box.

This text appears in blue underline on the OneNote page, and when the mouse moves over it, the pointer changes to a hand to indicate that the text is really a link.

3. Select the item to which you want to link.

You can perform this step in several ways, depending on what you're linking to:

> *… link to a Web page:* Click the Browse the Web (globe) button. A browser window opens. Browse to the page you want to link to and copy the page address. Paste that address in the Address text box in the Link dialog box.

- *To link to a file on your computer or network:* Click the Browse for File (folder) button, select the file, and click OK.

- *To link to a OneNote page:* Select that page from the Pick a Location in OneNote list.

4. **Click OK to insert the hyperlink.**

   You can change the hyperlink later (either its address or the link text itself) by right-clicking the link and selecting Edit Hyperlink from the pop-up menu that appears.

Inserting a Document or File

It may seem kind of silly to attach a document or a file to a note because you can often readily access that document or file, and a link to a document is so much simpler and takes up less room inside the note. (To find out how to link to a document or file, see the section "Adding Links to Other Pages, Files, or the Internet," earlier in this chapter.)

However, what do you do if you're away on a trip or working at home, and a critical piece of information you need is on the office network? A link to a document on a network to which you can't connect doesn't do you much good. If you want to make sure that you always have access to a particular file or files, you can attach them to a page. Follow these steps:

1. **Click the Attach File button on the Insert tab.**

   The Choose a File or a Set of Files to Insert dialog box appears.

2. **Change to the folder that contains the file(s) you want to attach, and then in the file listing, hold down Ctrl and click each file you want to attach.**

3. **Click Insert.**

   The file(s) are attached to the current note page. Icons that represent each file appear on the page, as shown in Figure 5-13.

If you double-click one of these icons, the associated file opens. A warning dialog box may appear, telling you not to open the file if you don't trust its source. (Good advice under any circumstances.) Click Yes to close the dialog box and open the file.

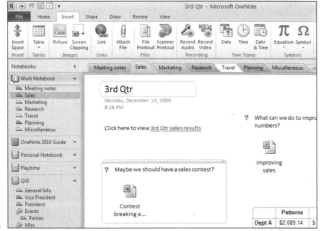

Figure 5-13:
Insert files
that you
may need to
reference
on the road.

OneNote attaches a copy of the file(s) you selected to the page. If someone updates the original file(s) later, the file(s) that you view through OneNote will not be current. A link, on the other hand, always points to the actual, updated file, but it does require that you have access to the folder in which the linked file is located. See the section "Adding Links to Other Pages, Files, or the Internet," earlier in this chapter, for help.

Inserting a Picture of a Document

Besides linking and attaching files, you have another option, and it involves inserting a picture of the document's contents. Instead of calling the result a picture, however, OneNote calls it a *printout,* but you get the idea. You can type text over the top of a picture-page or add notes next to a picture-page, which makes this option good for inserting digital copies of handouts from a lecture or meeting so that you can annotate them. For example, if you receive a presentation in PowerPoint format, you can insert it as a printout in OneNote and add your own thoughts while you review the slides. You can also use the drawing tools to circle or highlight important information. See the sections "Writing and Drawing by Hand" and "Drawing Lines, Arrows, and Shapes" for more info.

To insert a picture of a document's contents, follow these steps:

1. **Click the File Printout button on the Insert tab.**

   The Choose Document to Insert dialog box appears.

2. **Change to the folder that contains the file(s) you want to attach, and then in the file listing hold down Ctrl and click each file you want to attach.**

.Insert.

..e application associated with the file(s) you selected starts, and
..neNote loads each file and then adds it to the page in the form of a picture, as shown in Figure 5-14, which shows the first slide in a PowerPoint
presentation I inserted.

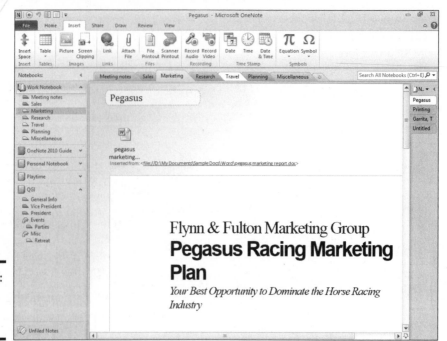

Figure 5-14:
Insert a
photo of a
document.

TIP

If you're in a program (such as PowerPoint or Excel, although it can be any
program, even a non-Office one) and want to send the document to OneNote
so that you can annotate it, select the Print command, and then select Send
to OneNote 2010 from the Name list. The result is the same as inserting a file
printout, as discussed in this section. By the way, you can select a section
of a Web page or document prior to sending it along to OneNote if you want
to insert only part of that page or document — just be sure to select the
Selection radio button in the Print dialog box to indicate that you want to
send just the current selection to OneNote.

An icon that represents the file appears; use it to open the actual file, if
needed (assuming that you have access). A notation appears below the
icon, reminding you that you inserted this data as a printout from a file and
including a clickable link to the file. (I guess OneNote wants to make really
sure that you can call up the file if you want to.) Below the icon and the
link, you finally see a picture of each page of the document's contents. Yes,

if the document has more than one page, you see more than one picture. And yes, they're pictures, which means that you can drag them around and resize them just like you can any other picture on a notebook page. (See the section "Inserting Images," later in this chapter, if you need help with that process.)

OneNote can search the text of a picture-page and help you find something in it if you need to. This feature is real handy when you insert as a printout some lecture handouts or some kind of technical document that you need to reference. See Chapter 6 of this minibook for help.

Suppose someone sends you a copy of a note page from OneNote, and you see one of these funky picture-pages on it. You can double-click the icon or click the link to open the document so that you can print or edit it. If you don't have access to the file's location, however, don't despair. You can still copy the contents of the picture-page and paste it into a document to create a file of your own that you can edit, print, or do anything else with. Just right-click the picture-page and select Copy Text from This Page of the Printout from the pop-up menu that appears. If the document is a series of picture-pages in the notebook, rather than just one page, then select Copy Text from All the Pages of the Printout, instead.

Inserting an Image from a Scanner or Digital Camera

You can scan a document and place it directly into OneNote as a picture-page, if you like. You can also insert an image directly from your digital camera. Follow these steps:

1. **Click the Scanner Printout button on the Insert tab.**

   The Insert Picture from Scanner or Camera dialog box appears.

2. **Select the scanner or camera to use from the Device list.**

3. **Select the quality you want in the scan (Web or Print) by clicking either the Web Quality or Print Quality radio button in the Resolution section of the dialog box.**

   Web Quality is 72 DPI, and Print Quality is 300 DPI. The more dots per inch, the higher the quality, so if you plan on printing your OneNote pages, select Print Quality. Otherwise, Web Quality (which works for on-screen display purposes) should do just fine.

4. **To add the scanned image to the Clip Organizer in Office, select the Add Pictures to Clip Organizer checkbox.**

5. **Click Insert (to insert a scanned document) or Custom Insert (to insert an image from a camera or to set options for a scan).**

- If you clicked Insert, the document is scanned and inserted into the current OneNote page.

- If you clicked Custom Insert, and you are scanning a document, the Scan using *Scanner Program* dialog box appears where you can set options for the scan. The options available to you vary by scanner, but generally you can choose between a full-color or black and white scan. After you click Scan, the document is scanned and inserted into the current OneNote page.

- If you clicked Custom Insert and you are inserting images, the Get Pictures from *Pictures Location* dialog box appears. Select the images you want to insert by pressing Ctrl and clicking the image thumbnails in the large box at the bottom of the dialog box. Click Get Pictures and the image(s) you selected are inserted into the current OneNote page.

Creating a Quick Side Note from Any Program

You can gather information from various locations, such as Web sites and documents, by using a side note. A *side note* is like an adhesive note; you can use it to jot down a quick thought about a telephone conversation, e-mail message, something you saw on the Web, or whatever. The beauty here is that you can create side notes when you're not in OneNote, but instead working in some other program. Side notes are placed in the Unfiled Notes notebook in OneNote, where you can view them later and move them into a more appropriate place. Use side notes to gather your thoughts while you work; use OneNote to organize them.

Side notes aren't just for text; oh, no. You can drag and drop anything you like into them, including images. You can also select something, copy it to the Clipboard, and paste it into a side note. In fact, you can do anything with a side note you might do with a regular note, including recording audio or video, tagging, creating a task, capturing a screen shot, or drawing with a pen tablet or tablet PC.

To create a side note, follow these steps:

1. **Click the Open New Side Note (a big N) button on the Windows task-bar.**

   The Open New Side Note button does not appear on the Windows task-bar until you use OneNote for the first time.

   A side note window appears, as shown in Figure 5-15. You can also press Windows+N to create a side note.

Figure 5-15:
Jot down a
quick note.

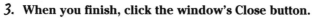

2. **Add data to your side note.**

You can type or write (by using a pen tablet or tablet PC), drag and
drop, copy and paste, or otherwise use your clever imagination (and the
help in this chapter) to put data in the side note.

You can use many of the OneNote tools to create your side note, such
as formatting, screen clipping, drawing, and adding more pages. You can
find out how to do all these things and more in this chapter.

3. **When you finish, click the window's Close button.**

New page(s) are added to the Unfiled Notes notebook, where you can
view or relocate them later.

Formatting Text

I get bored pretty easily, so I format my text to jazz it up, using the buttons
conveniently placed on the Home tab. Of course, you can just type a note
and leave it at that. But if you have time, adding formatting may help you
more easily find certain information on a page. (Check out Figure 5-16 to see
what I mean.)

I won't bore you with too many details — if you've used other Office programs, you already know how to format: just drag over existing text and
click a button on the Home tab, such as Bold or Italics to apply that format.
To format all the text in a container, click the container's upper border to
select everything inside, and then apply your formatting. You can also click
buttons on the Home tab to select formats, and then type.

Bulleted list   Numbered list

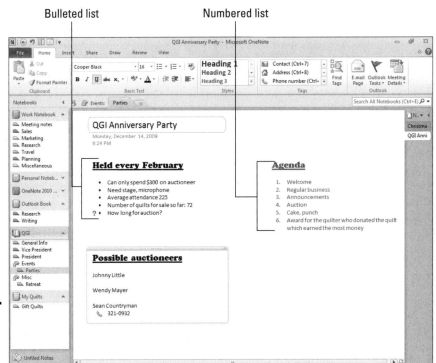

Figure 5-16:
Make that
text pretty.

A lot of my note-taking involves making lists, so if you're like me, you make
lists like crazy. Here's how:

✦ **Create a bulleted list.** Click where you want to start the list, click the
arrow on the Bullets button, and then select a bullet style from the
pop-up menu that appears. Type each item on its own line; press Enter
to create the next item.

✦ **Create a numbered list.** Click where you want the list to appear, click
the arrow on the Numbering button and select a number style from the
pop-up menu that appears, and then type each item, pressing enter to
add the next item.

Rather than a bulleted or numbered list, you can create a list of To-Do items
by applying the To-Do tag, which inserts a check box in front of the items
you apply the tag to. The check boxes allow to you check off items in such a
list when you get them done. Alternatively, you can create tasks in OneNote
that appear in Outlook's Tasks list. See Chapter 6 of this minibook for more
info on using tags or creating Outlook tasks.

Creating a table

I seem to create a lot of tables — mine are like long lists that just happen to like standing in neat columns. If you're not sure what a table is, take a look at Figure 5-17. To create a table, follow these steps:

1. **Click the Table button on the Insert tab.**

   When you click the Table button, a palette of squares appears

2. **Drag over the squares to select the number of columns and rows you want for your table.**

3. **Type column headings, one per square *(cell)*, across the first row.**

   If you plan to add row headings down the first column, then start in the second cell in the first row with your column headings, as shown.

4. **After entering headings, type the data in the empty cells.**

   To move from cell to cell in a row, press Tab. You can also just click in each cell.

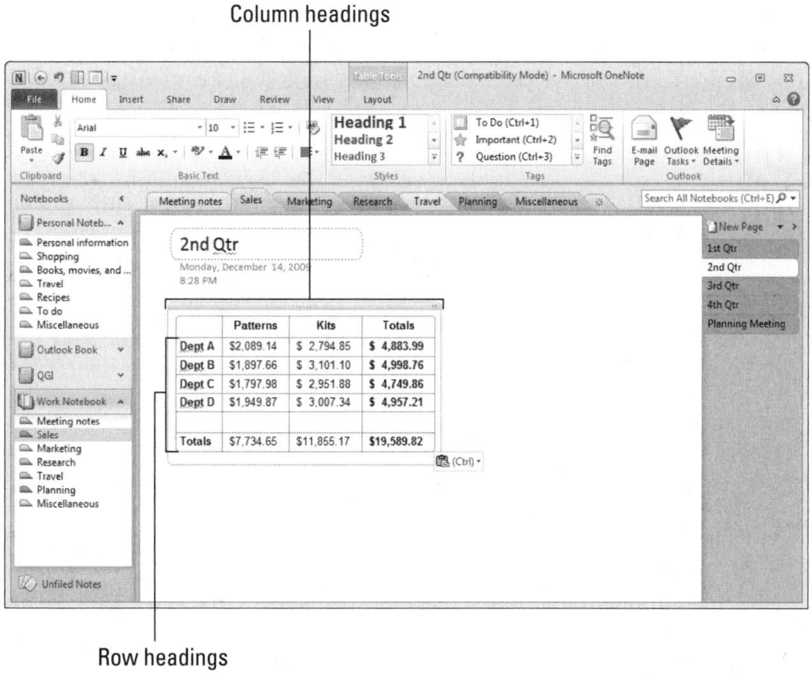

Column headings

	Patterns	Kits	Totals
Dept A	$2,089.14	$ 2,794.85	$ 4,883.99
Dept B	$1,897.66	$ 3,101.10	$ 4,998.76
Dept C	$1,797.98	$ 2,951.88	$ 4,749.86
Dept D	$1,949.87	$ 3,007.34	$ 4,957.21
Totals	$7,734.65	$11,855.17	$19,589.82

Figure 5-17:
Table that
idea.

Row headings

You can copy a table directly from an Excel worksheet in order to collect its data together with other notes and material on the same client, project, or job. Just open the Excel worksheet you're interested in, drag over the cells in the worksheet to select them, and then click the Copy button on the Home tab. Switch over to OneNote, click in the page where you want the Excel data to appear, and click the Paste button on the Home tab. The Excel data appears in a table, and a link to the Excel workbook appears just below the data on the page.

After creating a table in OneNote, you can make changes to it however you want, using the buttons on the Table Tools Layout tab:

✦ **To insert a column:** Click inside the table, and then click either Insert Left or Insert Right to add a column to the left or right of the current cell.

✦ **To add a new row at the end of the table:** Simply click in the last column of the last row, and then press Enter.

✦ **To add a new row somewhere in the middle of a table:** Click in any row and click either Insert Above or Insert Below to add a row above or below the current cell.

✦ **To delete a column or row (and everything in it):** Click in that column or row, and then click either Delete Columns or Delete Rows.

Borders appear around each cell in the table, but you don't have to stare at them. To turn borders off, click the Hide Borders button on the Table Tools Layout tab.

Adding space to a page

After you type a bunch of notes or add graphics, audio files, and such, you may want to add extra space to the bottom of a page. You can do so easily by clicking the Scroll Down by Half Page button at the bottom of the vertical scroll bar. To add space between notes or any object, click the Insert Space button on the Draw or the Insert tab. Then, click and drag to expand the space between objects, as shown in Figure 5-18.

Updating the date or time

A date and time normally appear below the page title (although they can be removed if desired). This date and time are set when you create the page, and they don't change, even if you update the page with new information. To change the date or time that appears at the top of a page, follow these steps:

1. **Click the date or the time that you want to change.**

A Calendar or Clock icon appears just to the right of the date or time you clicked.

Insert space

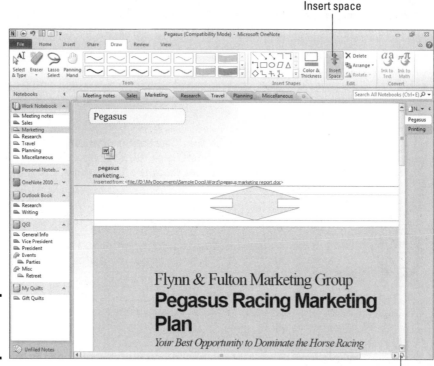

Figure 5-18:
Wide open
spaces.

Scroll down by a half-page

2. **Click the icon that appears to the right (the calendar or the clock).**

3. **Change the date or time.**

   - If you are changing the date, a calendar appears when you click the calendar icon, displaying the current month. Change to a different month if desired by clicking the arrows to the left or right of the month name. Then click the day you want to insert. To insert today's date, simply click the Today button. The date on the page is immediately changed.

   - If you are changing the time, the Change Page Time dialog box appears when you click the clock icon. Select the time you want to insert from the Page Time drop-down list, or type the time in the Page Time box. Click OK, and the time on the page is immediately updated.

If you want, you can insert a date and time elsewhere on the page by clicking the Date, Time, or Date & Time button on the Insert tab.

Writing and Drawing Notes by Hand

If you have a pen tablet attached to your computer or you use a tablet PC, you don't have to be confined by a keyboard when collecting your thoughts in OneNote. Working in conjunction with a touch-enabled operating system, such as Windows 7, OneNote allows you to write your notes freehand and draw, doodle, circle something, or highlight an important idea by including a star or arrow. Follow these steps:

1. **To activate the pen so that OneNote doesn't treat it as just another mouse, click the More button in the Tools group on the Draw tab and select a pen or highlighter from the Tools palette that appears, as shown in Figure 5-19.**

This palette offers a variety of thick and thin pens, along with some wide highlighters that use semitransparent digital ink.

You can design your own pen by selecting Color & Thickness Options and selecting a color/thickness from the dialog box that appears.

Tools palette

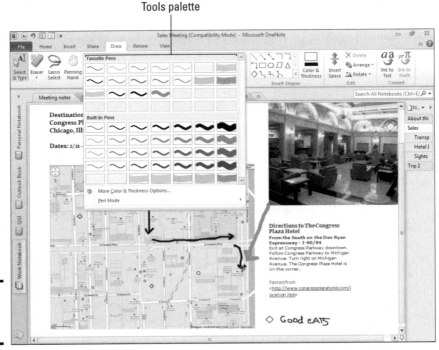

Figure 5-19:
Choose a pen.

2. **Draw on the tablet surface to create text or a doodle.**

You can also write a math equation, if you want.

3. **To return to a regular mouse, click the Select & Type button on the Draw tab.**

If you don't have a pen tablet or a tablet PC, you can draw with just a regular old mouse by selecting a pen or highlighter to activate the drawing feature. However, drawing with a mouse, rather than a pen tablet or tablet PC, is pretty difficult because a mouse isn't really designed for drawing.

If you make a mistake while drawing or writing with the pen, you can use an eraser, located on the Draw tab, to get rid of any stray marks. Click the arrow on the Eraser button to display a list of eraser size options, and then select the size you want. The Stroke eraser can remove an entire pen stroke with one click, so it's handy (but dangerous if that's not what you wanted to do).

Set drawing options

You can set options to help you use the pen more intuitively, if you want. Click the File tab to display Backstage, and select Options from the list on the left to display the OneNote Options dialog box. Select Advanced from list on the left to display the Advanced options on the right. In the Pen section, set these options:

+ Deselect the Disable the Scratch-Out Gesture while Inking check box if you want to be able to erase pen strokes by scratching back and forth over them three times.

+ Select the Use Pen Pressure Sensitivity check box to allow you to make the line fatter by simply pressing harder with your pen. This option does tend to make the notebook file larger, though, so keep that in mind.

+ Select the Automatically Switch between Inking, Selecting, Typing, and Panning check box to allow OneNote to change the pen tool to a pointer when you start doing something that seems more mouse-like, such as clicking a container.

If you want to select anything you've handwritten, click the Select & Type Text button on the Draw tab, and then drag over any text you want to select. You can also draw around the text by using the Lasso Select tool on the Draw tab to select all the text. To select a single word, double-click that word, just like you do in Word.

It's touching

If you have a touch screen, you can use simple gestures in OneNote to scroll and draw:

+ **Scroll.** Drag up or down with your finger, instead of scrolling with the mouse.

+ **Pan.** Drag left or right with your finger.

✦ **Zoom.** Pinch your fingers together and expand them slowly to zoom out. To zoom in, reverse the gesture and slowly bring your fingers together.

Adding rules to a page

When I try to write notes, frankly, they come out a little awkward, even when I use a pen tablet or tablet PC. Having ruled paper seems to help me write more legibly, though. If you're planning to draw, having a grid might help you draw straight lines more accurately.

You can't display rules or a grid on the part of a page that's decorated with a background graphic. So, if you created the page by using a decorative template, you can't show the rules or grid. But you can extend the page, and then display the rules or grid in the extended area, if you want. To display the rules or grid on a page, follow these steps:

1. **Click the Rule Lines button on the View tab and select a rule or grid type from the palette that appears.**

2. **If you want the rules or gridlines to appear in a different color, click the Rule Lines button again, select Rule Line Color from the bottom of the palette, and then select the color you want from pop-up menu.**

3. **Extend the page, if needed, by clicking the Scroll Down by Half Page button at the bottom of the vertical scroll bar.**

   On a page that's not designed for rules (because it uses a background graphic), you need to extend the page to see the rules.

Converting handwriting to editable text or an equation

Here's something that's pretty neat — a way to turn your handwritten scribbles into neat, editable text or into a math equation that looks like you typed it. Having editable text or an equation gives you an advantage (besides the fact that no one will know what sloppy handwriting you have) because you can format it, as well.

You can convert only handwritten text or math that OneNote recognizes as such. To create convertible handwritten text, you need a tablet PC — basically, a laptop that includes a swivel monitor that allows you to write on it with a stylus, or some kind of similar handheld device that also runs the tablet PC operating system.

To convert text, follow these steps:

1. **Select the text to convert.**

   How you make this selection depends on what you want to select:

- *The entire page:* Click the page's tab.

- *A note container:* Click the top border of the note's container.

- *Within a note container:* Click the Select & Type button on the Draw tab, and then drag over just the text you want to convert or double-click a single word to select just that word.

2. **Click the Ink to Text button on the Draw tab.**

   The selected handwritten text is converted to editable text.

3. **If OneNote converts a handwritten word to something other than what you want, then edit it, as needed.**

To convert an equation, follow these steps:

1. **Select the math to convert.**

   What you want to select decides how you select it:

   - *The entire page:* Click the page's tab.

   - *A note container:* Click the top border of the note's container.

   - *Within a note container:* Click the Select & Type button on the Draw tab, and then drag over the math equation that you want to convert or double-click a portion to select just that part.

2. **Click the Ink to Math button on the Draw tab.**

   OneNote turns your written equation into a text one.

3. **Make corrections, as needed.**

   The equation appears in the Insert Ink Equation dialog box, as shown in Figure 5-20. You can make these corrections:

Book VI
Chapter 5

Taking Notes
in Overdrive:
OneNote

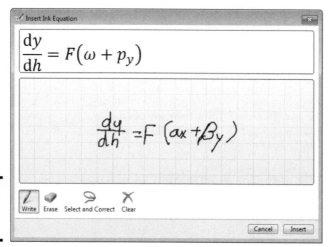

Figure 5-20: Correct the math.

- *To erase a part of the equation:* Click the Erase button and drag over the parts of the equation that you want to remove.

- *To rewrite part of the equation after you remove the incorrect portion:* Click the Write button and write it over.

- *To have OneNote reconsider and reconvert a section of the equation:* Click the Select and Correct button, and draw a lasso around that part. A menu of options appears; select the correct interpretation.

4. **Click Insert to insert the equation.**

   The original drawn equation remains; drag over it and press Delete to remove it.

Drawing Lines, Arrows, and Shapes

You can draw with your pen. To draw straight lines, though, you may want to use the Insert Shapes tools on the Draw tab, shown in Figure 5-21. You can control these tools by using a regular mouse or a pen tablet/tablet PC, so don't feel left out if you don't have one.

Figure 5-21: Draw lines, arrows, and such.

To select an Insert Shapes tool, click the More button in the Insert Shapes group on the Draw tab to display the Insert Shapes palette. Then, click the tool you want. You can choose from three basic types of tools: Line, Basic Shape, and Graph tools. Here's how to use them:

✦ **To create a line:** Select one of the line tools, click the page, and then drag to create the line. If the line has an arrow, it points in the direction you drag.

✦ **To create a basic shape, such as a rectangle, oval, parallelogram, triangle, or diamond:** Click the appropriate button. Then, click the page to establish the upper-left corner of the object and drag downward and to the right to create the object.

✦ **To create a graph:** Select one of the graph tools, click the page, and then drag to create the graph. If the line has an arrow, it points in the direction you drag.

✦ **To change an object's line color or width:** Click the Select & Type button — if needed to change from the drawing pointer to the regular mouse cursor — then click the object to select it. *Handles* (light blue squares) appear around the object's perimeter to show that it's selected. Click the Color & Thickness button and select the color and thickness you want from the pop-up menu that appears, then click OK.

From this point forward, objects you draw use the color and thickness you just selected. To remind you of your selections, they appear on the Color & Thickness button.

✦ **To create more than one of a certain kind of object:** Click the More button in the Insert Shapes group on the Draw tab to display the Insert Shapes palette, then Lock Drawing Mode option. This feature allows you to use over and over again the line or shape button that you select without having to click it repeatedly. When you're through creating that type of object, click the Lock Drawing Mode button again to turn it off.

✦ **To rotate an object or line:** Select it first by clicking it. Click the Rotate button on the Draw tab and select a rotation from the pop-up menu that appears. For example, select Rotate Left 45°. You can also flip an object over its vertical or horizontal axis by selecting Flip Vertical or Flip Horizontal.

✦ **To get rid of an object:** Click it to select it, and then click the Delete button on the Draw tab or just press Delete.

✦ **To resize an object:** Click it to select it, and then drag a handle outward or inward; drag a corner handle to resize an object proportionately.

To select multiple objects, just lasso them. Click the Lasso Select button on the Draw tab and drag to draw a circle around the objects you want to select. You may also find this tool helpful when you need to select a single object that's in a container along with several other objects.

Inserting Images

Notes in OneNote aren't just text — they can contain a lot of stuff, including tables, audio and video files, and (well, at least according to the heading here) images. Why would you add an image to a note? Well, you can use an image to dress up the note, making the image a background or just a piece of art on the page. You may also want to add photos to help you identify things, such as a new client, your kids, or a digital camera you're looking to buy.

Not every image has to be a photo; nope, you can include a piece of clip art or maybe an Internet map that shows the fastest route from your hotel to the convention center. You can insert images directly from your computer, digital camera, or scanner (as you can read about in the section "Inserting an Image from a Scanner or Digital Camera," earlier in this chapter) You can also grab them right off a Web page or steal them from your computer screen — see the following section for help.

When you have an image in OneNote (whether it's a screen shot or an inserted image file), you can search its text. Yep, OneNote does a pretty good job of reading the text in an image, helping you locate that image again, based on your search text. See Chapter 6 of this minibook.

To insert an image file, follow these steps:

1. **Click the Picture button on the Insert tab.**

The Insert Picture dialog box appears.

2. **Browse to the image file, select that file from the file list, and then click Insert.**

After the image is added to a page, as shown in Figure 5-22, you can do what you'd normally do in any other program with an inserted image:

Handles

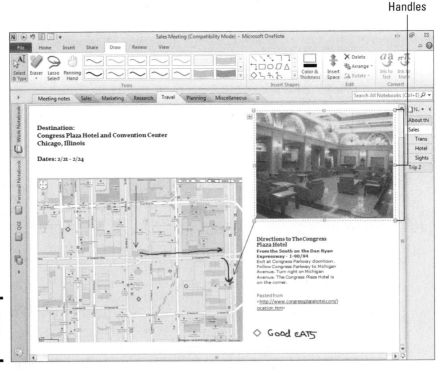

Figure 5-22:
Add images
to a note.

✦ **To resize the image:** Click its border to display the *handles* (those small squares that surround the image). Drag a handle inward to make the image smaller or outward to make it larger. I recommend using a corner handle to keep the image from getting thrown out of proportion.

✦ **To move an image on the page:** Click the image to select it, and then drag and drop the image where you want it to live.

✦ **To add text over top of the image (as a kind of image caption):** Click in the image, and then just type. You can format the text like you format any other text you add to a note (see the earlier section, "Formatting Text," for help. The text appears on top of the image, in its own container that you can move, as needed. (Click the container and drag.) You can add as many text captions as you like by just clicking the image and typing.

If you want to turn your newly inserted image into the page background, right-click the image and select Set Picture as Background from the pop-up menu that appears.

Inserting a Screen Shot

You can add an image to a page by simply grabbing it. Without the help of OneNote's screen capturing tool, you might normally grab an image by using a screen-capture program or a graphics editor that has screen-capturing capability. That's what I used to get the images for this book. You're not going to need either one, though, because OneNote has screen-capturing capability built right in.

For you Windows 7 or Vista users out there, OneNote's screen clipper works similarly to the Windows' Snipping tool, except the screen shots are saved automatically in OneNote (rather than within the Snipping Tool window).

To grab a picture of something you see on your screen, follow these steps:

1. **Display the window that you want to capture.**

   If you want to grab something from a Web page, start your browser and display the Web page. If you want to take a picture of a new program or some error message, then display that.

2. **Change back to OneNote by clicking its icon on the Windows taskbar.**

3. **Click the note page where you want the image to appear after you capture it.**

4. **Click the Screen Clipping button on the Insert tab.**

   OneNote minimizes itself, and the window you selected in Step 1 comes into view, although it's dimmed. You are about to select the exact area of the screen you want to capture, and as you do, that area will become un-dimmed.

5. **Click in the upper-left corner of the area you want to capture, and then drag downwards and to the right, creating a rectangle.**

While you drag, the area you select changes to full color and the unselected area remains dim. The area inside the selection rectangle is the area OneNote captures, as shown in Figure 5-23.

After you release the mouse button, OneNote comes back to the forefront and shows you the image you captured on the page where you clicked. At the bottom of the image, OneNote automatically places a note to remind you that you captured this image yourself, and when. This note helps you easily distinguish captured images from images you've saved on the computer and inserted manually, or images brought in from your camera or scanner (see the sections "Inserting an Image from a Scanner or Digital Camera" and "Inserting Images" earlier in this chapter.) If you captured a portion of a Web page, a link to that Web page appears, as well, so you can revisit the page later, if needed.

If you didn't capture the correct area, just delete the image (by clicking it and pressing Delete) and redo the preceding steps.

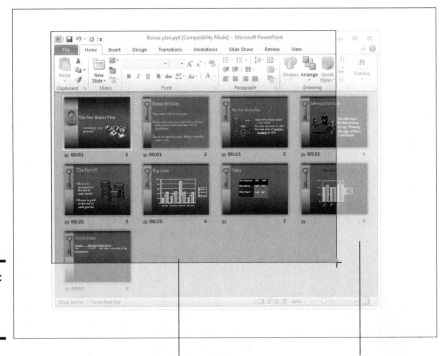

Figure 5-23:
Capture an
on-screen
image.

Select the area you
wish to capture.

The area of the screen you are
not capturing remains dimmed.

The image you just captured, by the way, is placed on the Clipboard so that you can paste it into another program. You can, for example, paste the image into a graphics editor so that you can save the image permanently in a file that you can edit.

You can grab a quick image from anywhere by just pressing Windows+S. Drag to define the area that you want to capture, and OneNote displays a dialog box so that you can decide where to place the captured image.

Adding Audio or Video

**Book VI
Chapter 5**

Taking Notes in Overdrive: OneNote

Sometimes, the written word just doesn't tell the whole story; in such cases, you may want to record your thoughts about a note, image, drawing, or other bit of information and store it on a page. Or perhaps you'd find typing along while someone's talking inconvenient, especially if you're trying to listen and think of questions and comments at the same time. In other cases, trying to create a typed note while someone's talking may be considered rude. But if you record someone else speaking, then you don't need to worry that you'll miss the important parts of a lecture or meeting — you can always just play it back.

OneNote provides the recording capabilities; you just have to look pretty (or talk pretty, if you're recording audio). Well, okay, you do need to supply a few things for OneNote to perform its magic. To record audio, your computer is gonna need a microphone. (Laptops typically have one built-in, so if your computer is a laptop, you may have just lucked out.) To record video, you need a Webcam.

After you install all the necessary equipment, follow these steps to record audio or video:

1. **Click in the note page where you want the recording to appear when you are through.**

2. **Click the Record Audio or Record Video button on the Insert tab.**

The current date and time appear on the page, along with an icon representing the recording. The Recording tools appear.

If OneNote isn't currently running, you can start an audio recording by right-clicking the OneNote icon at the right end of the Windows taskbar and selecting Start Recording Audio from the pop-up menu that appears.

3. **Record the audio/video that you want.**

If you want to mark a particular place in the recording or make a comment about it, simply type a note. In Figure 5-23, I typed my notes just below the recording, but you can actually type them anywhere — they'll still be linked. Notes that you create during a recording are linked to that spot in the recording.

4. **When you finish, click the Stop button on the Recording tab.**

OneNote creates an audio (`.wma`) or video (`.wmv`) file. The icon on the page represents this file.

To play the recording, double-click its icon.

A dialog box may appear, asking if you want to allow OneNote to search the text spoken in the audio or video recordings. If so, click Enable Audio Search, although doing so is not always a guarantee that OneNote will find what you're looking for when you search for this same recording at a later time because OneNote may not understand each word in the recording (and thus may not be able to find that word when searching). See Chapter 6 of this minibook for help in searching.

If you select the See Playback button on the Playback tab, then while the recording plays, notes you may have typed during that recording are high-lighted at the same point in the recording at which you made them origi-nally. In Figure 5-23, for example, the note Thom – Great Idea for Market Rollout is highlighted when the part where Thom describes his idea for the upcoming rollout is played in the audio file. If you want to jump directly to a spot at which you made a note, hover the mouse pointer over the note to make a Play button appear just to the left of the text. (Again, see Figure 5-24.) Click this button to start the recording.

Figure 5-24:
Play your
recording
back.

The recording stops automatically, although you can stop it early by clicking the Stop button on the Playback tab. Click the Pause button on the Playback tab to pause the playback temporarily; click the Pause button again to resume.

Chapter 6: Maximizing the Power of OneNote

In This Chapter

✔ Adding (or importing) details to OneNote

✔ Creating Outlook items from within OneNote

✔ Sharing notes in all sorts of ways

✔ Protecting your notes from prying eyes

✔ Reorganizing and searching your note pages

✔ Tagging important items

*O*neNote is a fairly simple application, on the surface; click a page and type to create a note. Organize notes on different pages, sections, and notebooks. But it turns out that under this unassuming package lies a pretty powerful assistant. While creating notes and collecting images, charts, and documents, you can create a quick reminder in OneNote to do something. You can also add a quick contact, appointment, or meeting in Outlook, all without leaving the comfort of your little note-taker. If you've already set up a meeting or appointment, you can insert the details on a note page so that you have everything in one place: OneNote.

After you gather a lot of stuff in OneNote, you don't need to keep it all to yourself. OneNote lets you easily share your thoughts, whether you choose to e-mail them, blog them, or simply share a file. You can even share pages in a live session in which everyone contributes at the same time. On the other hand, if sharing isn't your thing, you can keep your notes safe and secure with a super-secret password (and optional decoder ring).

Whether you choose to share your notes or keep them all to yourself, you can tag important information to make it easier to find later. And OneNote certainly gives you a lot of ways to search for data, including searching not only text notes, but also the text in audio and video files and photos, too.

Although if you've read Chapter 5 of this minibook you're probably a OneNote expert by now, it bears repeating that stuff you add to a OneNote page is saved automatically for you. So don't go wasting your time looking for a Save button; you don't need one.

Inserting Details of an Appointment or Meeting on a Page

OneNote and Outlook are good buds, working very closely with each other. When needed, you can insert the details of an Outlook appointment or meeting into a note, where you can refer to it while you gather the materials for that appointment or meeting. Okay, it's not a glamorous feature — but, hey, it beats typing the details manually or, worse yet, forgetting the appointment or meeting altogether.

To insert the details of an appointment or meeting on a OneNote page, follow these steps:

1. **Make sure that Outlook is running, then in OneNote, click on a note page where you want the details of a meeting or appointment to appear.**

2. **Still in OneNote, click the Meeting Details button on the Home tab.**

A list of today's appointments and meetings appears in a drop-down list.

3. **Select the appointment or meeting that you want to insert.**

You can do one of two things:

- Click an appointment or meeting in the list.

- Click Choose a Meeting from Another Day to display the Insert Outlook Meeting Details dialog box, as shown in Figure 6-1. Change to the date of the appointment or meeting by clicking the Previous Day or Next Day button, or by clicking the Calendar button in the upper-right corner and selecting a date from the calendar that appears. Select the appointment or meeting that you want, and then click Insert Details.

The details of the appointment or meeting — its time, date, location, and agenda items, as well as a list of the attendees — are inserted onto the page in a text container. ***Note:*** This data isn't connected to Outlook, so if you change something in the OneNote copy, don't expect Outlook to notice.

If you happen to be in Outlook's Calendar module, you can send an appointment/meeting from there to OneNote without switching programs. Just select the appointment or meeting and click the OneNote button on the Calendar Tools tab. The Select Location in OneNote dialog box appears; select the page on which you want to insert the meeting or appointment, and then click OK. This method inserts the same info as using the Meeting Details button in OneNote does, but it also creates a link to the item in Outlook so that you can easily open it from OneNote to check for any updates.

Previous Day

Next Day

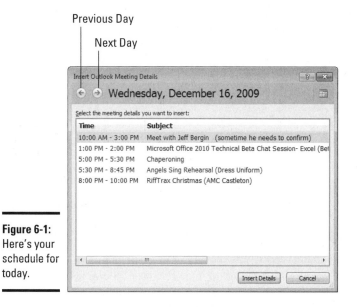

Figure 6-1:
Here's your
schedule for
today.

Creating an Outlook Task on a Page

You can create a task on a note page in OneNote, which also adds that task
to the Outlook Tasks list. If you check off the task in OneNote, it's checked
off on the Outlook Tasks list, too. If you spend a lot of time in OneNote, you
don't need to switch back and forth just to check on a task.

If you don't want to involve Outlook in tracking tasks that you create in
OneNote, you can tag an item with a To Do tag, which creates a check box
that you can use to track things to do. See the section "Tagging Important
Information," later in this chapter.

To add a task to a OneNote page and Outlook's Task list, follow these steps:

1. Type the task on a OneNote page.

For example, click a page and type `Update slide #4 in Sales`
`presentation` or `Send meeting notes to Alice`. You don't have
to select the text, but just keep the cursor in the note container.

**2. Click the Outlook Tasks button on the Home tab. From the submenu
that appears, select a due date, such as Today or Next Week.**

A task flag appears next to the description that you typed in Step 1. You
can view the task details by hovering the mouse over the description.
(See Figure 6-2.)

Figure 6-2:
Jot down
those things
to do.

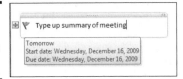

If you're in Outlook, no need to switch to OneNote to record a task. Start by selecting the task or To-Do item in the Tasks module, To-Do bar, or Daily Task List, then click the OneNote button on the Calendar Tools/Tasks List/ Daily Task List tab. The Select Location in OneNote dialog box appears; select the page you want to insert the task on and click OK.

Marking an Outlook Task as Done

Assume that at some point, you'll get this task done. If you're in Outlook, no problem; just mark that task off in the usual manner. If you're in OneNote, you don't have to switch programs just to check something off your Great Big Jobs list:

✦ **To check off a task on a page:** Click the flag to change it to a check mark.

✦ **To change the due date:** Click the description, click the Outlook Tasks button on the Home tab, and then select a different date from the pop-up menu that appears.

✦ **To remove the task from the note page and Outlook:** Right-click the description, click the Outlook Tasks button on the Home tab, and select Delete Outlook Task from the pop-up menu that appears. The task icon is removed, but the text you typed remains on the page. Select it and press Delete.

Don't select the task text and press Delete without first removing the task from Outlook because otherwise, the task is removed from only OneNote, not Outlook.

✦ **To open the task in Outlook so that you can add more details or assign it to someone:** Click the description, click the Outlook Tasks button on the Home tab, and select Open Task in Outlook from the pop-up menu that appears.

Inserting an Outlook Contact or E-Mail on a Page

Because Outlook and OneNote are such buddies, it shouldn't surprise you that you can call up OneNote from Outlook and make it take notes about an important message or contact. I mean, what are friends for, right? In fact, in earlier sections of this chapter, I explain how to insert the details of an Outlook appointment or meeting onto a page, and how to link a task in OneNote to Outlook's task list. The process for capturing the details of a contact or e-mail are roughly the same: Basically, you just send a selected e-mail or contact from Outlook over to OneNote, and OneNote creates a nice little page for that e-mail or contact on which you can take notes. A link is created in OneNote so that you can flip back to Outlook and take a look at the original item.

To create notes about an Outlook contact or e-mail, follow these steps:

1. In Outlook, select the item on which you want to take notes.

You don't have to open the item, although if it's already open, you don't have to close it.

2. Click the OneNote button on the Home tab.

The Select Location in OneNote dialog box appears (see Figure 6-3).

3. Select a page on which you want to insert the e-mail or contact, then click OK.

The information in the e-mail or contact is added to the page you selected. If you selected a section, then a new page is created. (Refer to Figure 6-3.)

4. Add whatever notes you want to the page.

If you sent a contact to OneNote, click the Link to Outlook Item link that appears on the OneNote page to open the contact in Outlook.

If you sent an e-mail to OneNote, you can click the link that's provided to create a new e-mail to the sender.

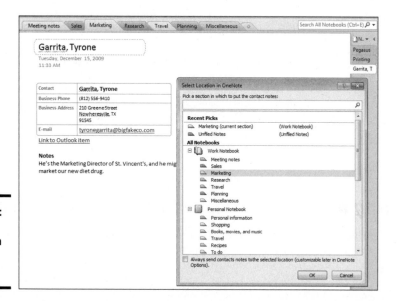

Figure 6-3:
Send
OneNote a
nice little
package.

Sending a Page to Someone

One of the reasons why it's so great to gather a lot of information in OneNote is that you can share it. And the simplest way to share your notes is to send them in an e-mail message. Best of all, the recipient doesn't need to have OneNote installed to be able to view what you're sending because each page you include in the e-mail message is sent as a picture.

To send notebook page(s) in an e-mail message, follow these steps:

1. **Select the page(s) that you want to send.**

   The procedure varies, depending on what you want to send:

   - *To select a page:* Click its page tab.

   - *To select a page and all its subpages:* Double-click the main page's tab.

   - *To select more than one page:* Hold down Ctrl while you click each tab.

   You can't send less than one page. If you select a note container, you end up sending the entire page. If you want to send only part of a note, copy that part to a new page and send that page.

2. **Click the E-Mail Page button on the Share tab.**

   An e-mail form jumps up, as shown in Figure 6-4. The page(s) you selected are copied into the message area of the e-mail as individual pictures of each page.

3. **Address the e-mail.**

   The Subject is based on the first page you choose, but you can change it, if you want.

4. **Type a message above the page text, if you want.**

5. **Click Send.**

   The e-mail is sent in HTML format in order to display the pictures properly within the message area. The recipient can copy the pictures into OneNote if he or she wants to.

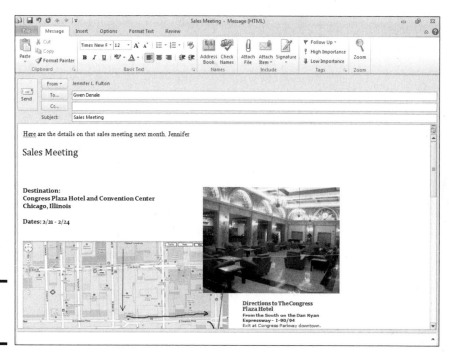

Figure 6-4:
Send it
along.

When you send a note in an e-mail, everything's sent, including the audio or
video recordings you may have created, and any files you've embedded on
the page. You can't do much if you don't want to send such files along with
a OneNote page, except manually selecting and deleting the files listed in the
Attached box in the message form. But if you're sure you never want to send
such files when e-mailing pages from OneNote, you can tell OneNote that
you prefer not to do that. In OneNote, click the File tab to display Backstage,
select Options from the list on the left to display the OneNote Options dialog
box, select Advanced from list on the left to display the Advanced options
on the right, and then in the E-mail Sent From OneNote section, deselect the
Attach Embedded Files to the E-Mail Message as Separate Files check box.
Click OK.

E-mailing a OneNote or PDF Version

You can make it easier for recipients to use your OneNote pages if they also
use OneNote by including a OneNote file with the pages you send. If the
recipient doesn't use OneNote, you can send a version in PDF, a file format
that displays text and graphics exactly as you see them on-screen, without
those crazy adjustments that some programs make before they display data.
In addition, PDF files are editable when needed.

PDF is so prevalent on the Internet that using this format almost guarantees that the recipient can view what you send.

To e-mail a OneNote or PDF version of a page, follow these steps:

1. Select the page(s) that you want to send.

How you make this selection depends on what exactly you plan to send:

- *To select a page:* Click its page tab.

- *To select a page and all its subpages:* Double-click the main page's tab.

- *To select more than one page:* Hold down Ctrl and click each tab.

You can't send less than one page — even if you select a note container, you send the entire page. To send part of a note, copy just the part you want to a new page and send that page.

2. Click the File tab to display Backstage and select Send from the list on the left.

The Send options appear on the right.

3. Select the format that you want to use from those listed on the right.

You have these options:

- *To send the page(s) in OneNote format:* Select the E-Mail Page as Attachment option.

- *To send the page(s) in PDF format:* Select the E-Mail Page as PDF option.

An e-mail is created, and the page(s) are attached in the appropriate format. In addition, if you send the page(s) in OneNote format, then a picture of each page is inserted in the message area of the e-mail.

4. Address the e-mail.

The Subject is based on the first page you choose, but you can change it, if you want.

5. Type a message and click Send.

If you prefer to e-mail pages in OneNote format, you can tell OneNote to always include an attachment when you use the E-Mail Page button (as explained in the preceding section). Click the File tab to display Backstage, select Options from the list on the left to display the Outlook Options dialog box, select Advanced from the list on the left to display the Advanced options on the right, and in the E-mail Sent From OneNote section, select the Attach a Copy of the Original Notes as a OneNote File check box. Click OK.

Sending Your Notes to Word

After collecting various data in OneNote, you can import your notes into Word. There, you can use Word's broader set of tools to polish your notes and make them presentation-ready, if needed. Follow these steps:

1. **Select the page(s) that you want to send.**

How you select pages depends:

- *To select a page:* Click its page tab.
- *To select a page and all its subpages:* Double-click the main page's tab.
- *To select more than one page:* Hold down Ctrl while you click each tab.

You can't send less than one page. To send a single note from a page, copy the note to a new page and send that page.

2. **Click the File tab to display Backstage, and select Send from the list on the left.**

The Send options appear on the right.

3. **Click Send to Word.**

The page(s) appear in Word.

4. **Edit them however you like, then click the Save button on the Quick Access toolbar to save the result.**

Sharing Some of Your Notes

OneNote loves to share. In fact, it provides many ways in which you can share your OneNote information. For example, you can zip off a quick e-mail message and send along a few note pages, if you want; see the section "Sending a Page to Someone," earlier in this chapter. You can also publish your notes in a shared folder and make them available to your colleagues, regardless of whether they also use OneNote. If you're a blogger, you can add your notes directly to your blog. You can also share a whole notebook and let everyone contribute their ideas.

Instead of sending note pages in an e-mail, if you want to share them with colleagues on your network, why not publish them to a shared folder? Follow these steps:

1. **Select what you want to share.**

   How you select depends on what you want to share:

   - *To select a page:* Click its page tab.

   - *To select a page and all its subpages:* Double-click the main page tab.

   - *To select more than one page:* Hold down Ctrl while you click each tab.

   - *To select a section:* Click its section tab.

   Although you *can* share a notebook by following these steps, you can use a much simpler way, which I describe in the following section.

2. **Click the File tab to display Backstage and select Save As from the list on the left.**

   The Save As options appear on the right, as shown in Figure 6-5.

3. **From the Save Current list, select what you want to include.**

   Select Page, Section, or Notebook to include the page(s), section, or notebook that you selected in Step 1.

4. **From the Select Format list, select the format you want to use.**

   Select a format that you know the recipient(s) can open and use. OneNote format is probably the most useful for sharing because you can see the changes that each individual makes and even return to an earlier version of your notes before those changes were made. You can also select Word, PDF, XPS (a kind of XML format), or Web Page format. As soon as you select the format, a Save As dialog box appears.

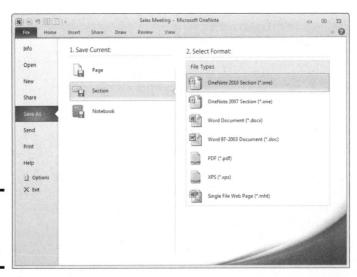

Figure 6-5:
Save your notes to share them.

5. **From the folder list, select the shared folder in which you want to save the file.**

    The name of the file is taken from the page, section, or notebook that you selected in Step 1, so you don't have to change it (although you can).

6. **Click Save to save the file.**

Sharing Notebooks

You can share OneNote information by sharing a notebook. Typically, you designate a notebook to be shared when you create it. (See Chapter 5 of this minibook.) You can, however, suddenly share an already existing notebook, if the Ghost of Notebooks Past pays you a visit and unlocks your miserly heart. For example, you can share a notebook you've been using for a new project that you're involved in and use the newly shared notebook to gather everybody's ideas, notes, suggestions, and (when people have time) actual work on the project.

Users of a shared notebook can all work at the same time; changes are merged together automatically. If you use the Web to share the notebook, users can work in their browsers to make changes if they don't have OneNote. Follow these steps to share one of your OneNote notebooks:

1. **Click the Share This Notebook button on the Share tab.**

    The Share Notebook options appear. See Figure 6-6.

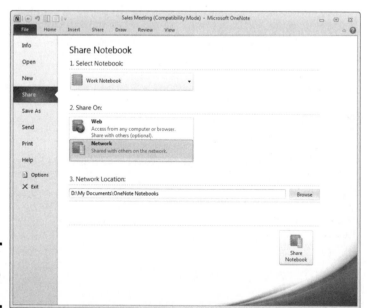

Figure 6-6:
Share entire notebooks.

Book VI
Chapter 6

Maximizing the
Power of OneNote

The current notebook appears in the Select Notebook list.

2. **If you want to share a different notebook, open the Share Notebook drop-down list and select the notebook you want to share.**

3. **From the Share On list, select where to store the shared notebook.**

   You have several options:

   • *Web:* Allows you to share the notebook with others through Windows Live SkyDrive. Located at skydrive.live.com, Windows Live SkyDrive is a place where you can keep your documents so that they can be accessed from anyplace with an Internet connection, Based on the location on Windows Live SkyDrive that you select to store this notebook (see Step 4), the notebook is either shared with your Live contacts only or with the public. You need to register for a Windows Live ID to use this service, but it's free.

   • *Network:* Allows you to share the notebook with your work colleagues through the office network.

4. **Specify where you want to share the notebook.**

   How you specify location depends on what storage area you selected in Step 3:

   • *On the Web:* The Web Location (Windows SkyDrive) is already selected for you, so with this option you don't need to do a thing.

   • *On your company network:* Click Browse and select a shared folder from Select Folder dialog box that appears, then click Select.

5. **Click the Share Notebook button.**

   A dialog box appears, telling you that OneNote is synching the shared copy with the original. This means that OneNote is ensuring that the copy you are sharing has the same contents as your original.

6. **Click OK to dismiss the dialog box.**

7. **Right-click the shared notebook's icon in the Navigation bar and select Copy Link to Notebook from the pop-up menu that appears.**

   This step lets everyone know where your shared notebook is located so that they can open it in their copies of OneNote.

8. **Start a new e-mail message in the Mail module of Outlook, paste the link into the text, and send it off to the people with whom you want to share the notebook.**

The people you invite to share your notebook must have access to the shared folder.

Synchronizing changes

If you get an e-mail notifying you of a shared notebook, just click the link in the message to open that notebook in OneNote. When more than one person has access to a shared network, OneNote has quite a job keeping up with all the simultaneous changes. What it does to resolve this sticky situation is to periodically synchronize the changes being made by a particular user with the data stored in the file. Even so, conflicts may arise — but at least OneNote gives you a way to resolve them.

If you want to see who made changes to a note and when, right-click the note and look at the bottom of the pop-up menu that appears.

First, to see whether a shared notebook contains all the latest and greatest, check out its icon on the Navigation bar, shown in Figure 6-7. If the synchronization can't be completed, it's probably because you're not connected to the shared folder where the notebook is kept. That doesn't mean you can't keep working, though; your changes are updated the next time you connect. If you're connected but the notebook just isn't synchronized yet, you can force OneNote to synchronize it now: Right-click the notebook's icon on the Navigation bar and select Sync This Notebook Now from the pop-up menu that appears, or press Shift+F9.

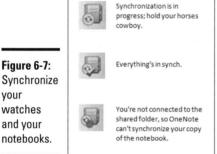

Figure 6-7:
Synchronize
your
watches
and your
notebooks.

Sometimes, when you happen to be working on the same note that somebody else is working on in a shared notebook, an error message appears in the yellow information bar at the top of the window. To see how your changes are in conflict with someone else's, click the information bar to create a new page. The new page lists the conflicting changes in red. For example, two people might have edited the same paragraph in different ways. Change back to the real page, make the changes manually, if you want, and then delete the Conflicts page.

From time to time, OneNote may run across a section that it needs to update, but another user has moved or deleted the section. Oops! In such cases, OneNote lists the little lost section in the Misplaced Sections list, along with odd socks and pens without caps. OneNote keeps the data in the lost section in the notebook until it finds where that data should go. A button for the Misplaced Sections list appears on the Navigation bar, just above the All Notebooks button. Click the button to see the list; right-click a section and select Delete from the pop-up menu that appears to remove it permanently. You can also move the lost section to a permanent location by dragging it from the Misplaced Sections section on the Navigation bar to some other section or notebook on the Navigation bar, and dropping it.

Reviewing changes

You can easily tell when someone else makes a change to a shared notebook because the section that contains the change appears in bold on the Navigation bar. In that section, the page that contains the tab also appears in bold over on the right. Click the page tab and view the change, which is highlighted for you on the page so that you can quickly spot it. After you review a change (by viewing the page), the highlighting is removed.

You can also locate recent changes in a notebook by following these steps:

1. **Click the Recent Edits button on the Share tab and select a time period from drop-down list.**

For example, select Today. A list of changes made today appears in the Search Results pane, seen in Figure 6-8.

2. **Select a page from the Search Results pane to view that page.**

The page appears on the left. The changes on a page are highlighted with a dark yellow highlight, as shown in Figure 6-8, with the text at the top of that page. In addition, the tabs of pages that contain changes also appear in dark yellow. Review them at your leisure and select a different page to review, if you want.

Figure 6-8:
Review
changes
one by one.

3. **Repeat Step 2 to review a different page's changes.**

4. **Close the Search Results pane by clicking its Close button — the little X.**

The highlights are removed, along with the Search Results pane.

You can also view changes by author. Follow these steps:

1. **Click the Find by Author button on the Share tab.**

   The Search Results pane displays the names of the people who've made changes to the notebook.

2. **Click the right-pointing arrow in front of a user's name to expand the listing for that user and view his or her changes.**

3. **Select a page in the Search Results pane to view that page.**

   The page appears on the left, with changes made by the selected user highlighted in dark yellow. Review them, and then select a different page to review from the Search Results pane, if you want.

4. **Repeat Steps 2 and 3 to review a different user's changes.**

5. **Close the Search Results pane by clicking its Close button.**

   The highlights are removed, along with the Search Results pane.

If you click the Hide Authors button on the Share tab to turn it off, then the initials of the user who made a change on the page appears to the right of that specific change.

Dealing with different versions of a page

With several users making changes to the same notebook, it's not impossible to imagine that they might make changes to the same page. What you see when you view a notebook, however, is the latest edition. To review previous versions of the current page, follow these steps:

Previous versions of pages are not saved unless the history for a notebook is activated, which it normally is. You can, however, save a lot of storage space by not saving this history. To deactivate the history function for a notebook, click the Page Versions button on the Share tab and select Disable History for This Notebook from the pop-up menu that appears.

1. **Click the Page Versions button on the Share tab and select Page Versions from the pop-up menu that appears.**

   The versions for the page are listed like page tabs (but with the date of that version) on the right, below the page tab.

2. **Select a version tab to view it.**

   The selected version of the page appears on the left.

3. **(Optional) Click the yellow InfoBar at the top of the page to restore or delete this version of the page.**

   A drop-down menu appears. You have several options to choose from:

- *Delete Version:* Don't keep this version.

- *Restore Version:* Replace the current version of the page with this version.

- *Copy Page To:* Copy this version of the page to another location within this notebook or another one.

4. **To hide the different versions again, click the Page Versions button on the Share tab and select Page Versions from the pop-up menu that appears.**

You can remove unneeded page versions in the current section, section group, or the entire notebook by clicking the Page Versions button on the Share tab and making a choice from the drop-down menu that appears: Delete All Versions in Section, Delete All Versions in Section Group, or Delete All Versions in Notebook. In dialog box that appears, click Yes to confirm the deletion.

Using the Recycle Bin to restore a deleted page

You may love the fact that you can review versions of a page in case some-one makes a change to the notebook that turns out to be a mistake. But what if someone removes a page altogether? Well, the page isn't lost — it's simply hiding in the Recycle Bin. You probably already know a lot about the Recycle Bin, in general, but here are a few tips for dealing with the Recycle Bin in OneNote:

- ✦ **Display the Recycle Bin.** Click the Notebook Recycle Bin button on the Share tab and select Notebook Recycle Bin from the pop-up menu that appears. The deleted pages in the current notebook appear in a tempo-rary section called Deleted Pages. Tabs for each deleted page appear on the right.

- ✦ **Restore a deleted page.** Right-click the page in the Recycle Bin and select Move or Copy from the pop-up menu that appears. In the Move or Copy Pages dialog box that pops up, select the section into which you want the page moved, then click Move.

- ✦ **Empty the Recycle Bin for the current notebook.** Click the Notebook Recycle Bin button on the Share tab and select Empty Recycle Bin from the pop-up menu that appears.

- ✦ **Hide the Recycle Bin.** Click the Notebook Recycle Bin button on the Share tab to toggle it off. The temporary section, Deleted Pages, is removed from the notebook, and the page you were on prior to display-ing the Recycle Bin reappears.

Deleted pages are automatically removed from the Recycle Bin 60 days after they're deleted, so don't feel like you have to empty the trash if you don't want to.

Blogging Your Notes

If you have your own blog, you can publish your notes directly to that blog so that you can share them with your readers. Common places where you might set up a blog include Windows Live Spaces, Blogger, Community Server, TypePad, WordPress, and SharePoint.

This task assumes that you also have Word 2010 installed, which I bet you do.

Follow these steps:

1. **Select the page(s) you want to blog.**

How you select depends on what you're selecting:

- *To select only part of a page:* Drag over the text and images that you want, or hold down Ctrl while you click the top border of various note containers.

- *To select a page:* Click its page tab.

- *To select a page and all its subpages:* Double-click the main page tab.

- *To select more than one page:* Hold down Ctrl while you click each page's tab.

2. **Click the File tab to display Backstage, and select Send from the list on the left.**

The Send options appear on the right.

3. **Select the Send to Blog option.**

If you haven't already entered your blog information somewhere in Office, the Register a Blog Account dialog box appears. If you have entered this info before, skip to Step 4.

4. **Click Register Now, and then follow the wizard to enter the information Office needs to post to your blog.**

You can, if hard-pressed for time, skip the process of registering your blog and just create the blog page now by clicking Register Later.

Whether you've already registered your blog, are registering now, or plan to register later, Word launches and creates a Word document, such as the one in Figure 6-9, by using the page(s) you selected. All pages that you selected in Step 1 appear in a single Word document.

5. **Edit the Word document (if desired), and then click the Publish button on the Blog Post tab in Word, and select Publish from the pop-up menu that appears.**

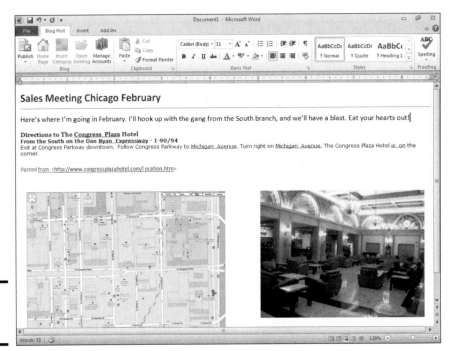

Securing Your Notes

You can keep all kinds of notes in OneNote: lecture notes, conference notes, or the daily bits of everyday life. Most of it would probably never cause a fuss, even if it got posted to the Internet. But some of it may be company information that's proprietary, credit information that you need to kept private, or personal bits of trivia that you don't want just any old nosy body to know.

Audio or video recordings aren't protected when you protect a section because they're stored in separate files and aren't part of the notes file. If you need to protect the contents of such recordings, do not share OneNote pages that contain them.

To password-protect a section of a notebook, follow these steps:

1. **Right-click the section tab, or the section name in the Navigation bar, and select Password Protect This Section from the pop-up menu that appears.**

   The Password Protection pane appears, as shown in Figure 6-10.

2. **Click the Set Password button.**

   The Password Protection dialog box appears (see Figure 6-10).

Set Password button

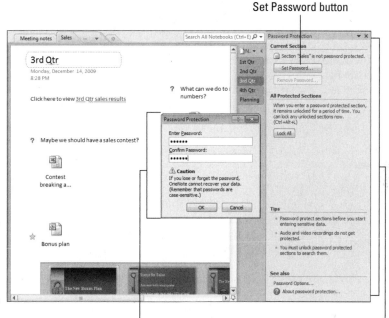

Figure 6-10:
Protect your
notes from
prying eyes.

Password Protection dialog box

Password Protection pane

3. **Type the password that you want to use in the Enter Password box.
Type the same password in the Confirm Password box and click OK.**

If you're going to use a password to protect something, you may as well use
one that's difficult to guess. Be sure to mix upper- and lowercase letters, as
well as a few numbers, into your passwords to make them more secure.

A dialog box may appear, asking about backup copies. If this section has
existed for awhile, OneNote has probably backed up the section and, if so,
that backup file is unprotected. You can click Delete Existing Backups to
remove these unprotected copies, or you can click Keep Existing Backups to
keep them until you can move the files to a protected folder.

The section you password-protect by following the preceding steps is actually not protected right away. It remains open for you to use for awhile (by
default, this courtesy period is ten minutes, although you can change that,
as you learn in the next section). If you want to lock the section immediately,
click the Lock All button on the Password Protection pane.

Remember the password you use, or you can't view the contents of this
section again.

Unlocking a protected section

To unlock a password-protected section, follow these steps:

1. Click the section's tab.

When a section is password-protected and you click its tab, you're not shown the contents of that section, but instead see a sad, gray page that informs you that the section is protected with a password.

2. Click the locked page.

The Protected Section dialog box appears.

3. Type your password in the Enter Password box and press Enter.

After you unlock it, a section should stay unlocked, right? Well, depending on your options, a section may stay unlocked only while you work on it, and then, after a certain amount of time or right after you switch to another section, it may lock itself again. To view the stuff in that section, you need to reenter your password. Believe it or not, this seemingly crazy behavior actually protects you, if you walk away from your computer and forget to secure a section you're working on. Follow these steps to set those options:

1. Click the File tab to display Backstage, and select Options from the list on the left.

The OneNote Options dialog box appears,

2. Select Advanced from the list on the left.

The Advanced options appear on the right, as seen in Figure 6-11.

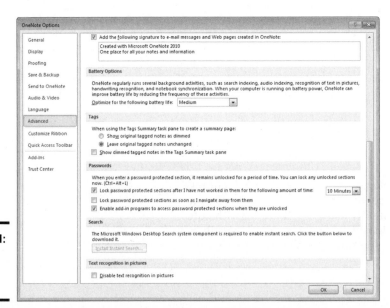

Figure 6-11:
Set your password options.

3. **Select the security options that you want.**

   The security options appear in the Passwords section. You have a few options from which you can choose:

   - *To lock a section again after a certain amount of time passes:* Select Lock Password-Protected Sections After I Have Not Worked in Them for the Following Amount of Time check box, and then set the amount of time you want from the drop-down list.

   - *To lock a section immediately after you change to a different section:* Select the Lock Password-Protected Sections as Soon as I Navigate Away From Them check box.

   - *To allow other applications to access data in unlocked sections:* Select Enable Add-On Programs to Access Password Protected Sections When They Are Unlocked check box.

4. **Click OK.**

If you have to leave your computer for a moment and want to lock all your password-protected sections so that no one can access them, right-click one of those sections, select Password Protect This Section from the pop-up menu that appears, and in the newly-visible Password Protection pane, click Lock All.

Removing the password protection

You can remove a password from a section, if it becomes too much of a bother. To remove a password, follow these steps:

1. **Change to the section whose password you want to remove by clicking the section's tab, or selecting that section's name in the Navigation bar.**

   If the section is locked, type your password to unlock the section.

2. **Right-click the section tab, or the section name in the Navigation bar, and select Password Protect This Section from the pop-up menu that appears.**

   The Password Protection pane appears.

3. **Click the Remove Password button.**

   The Remove Password dialog box appears. To remove the password, you have to prove you know it.

4. **Type the password in the box provided and click OK.**

Changing the password

You can change a password, something you may want to do if you suspect that your password is no longer that secure. To change a password, follow these steps:

1. **Right-click the section tab, or the section name in the Navigation bar, and select Password Protect This Section from the pop-up menu that appears.**

The Password Protection pane makes an appearance on-screen.

2. **Click Change Password.**

The Change Password dialog box appears, as shown in Figure 6-12.

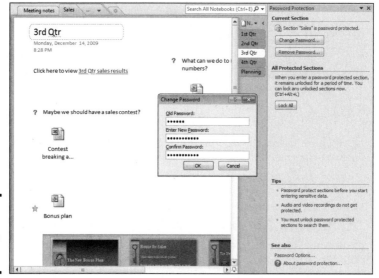

Figure 6-12:
Change a
password, if
needed.

3. **In the Old Password text box, type the current password for this section. Then, in the Enter New Password text box, type the new password that you want to use.**

4. **Type the new password again in the Confirm Password box and click OK.**

Reorganizing Your Notes

The whole point behind OneNote is organization. Face it, OneNote's the one stop informationarama. So you probably can't imagine anything more frustrating than discovering, after you work hard to gather a lot of data together, that your notes are less than organized.

Selecting pages

The first step in cleaning house is to select what you want to move. Here's how:

✦ **Select a page.** Click its tab to jump to it, and then click it again to select the page.

✦ **Select a main page and all its subpages.** Change to the main page in the group, and then double-click its tab.

✦ **Select several unrelated pages.** Hold down Ctrl while you click each page tab.

✦ **Select consecutive page tabs.** Click the first page's tab, hold down Shift, and click the last tab in the group.

The tabs of selected pages are grayed so that you can tell they're selected.

Moving pages and notes

Pages don't have to stay in the order they were born. Nope, if a page turns out to be more important than you originally thought it might be, after you get some content on it, you can move the page up in the page tab listing. Likewise, you can move less important pages down in the listing. You can also move a page into a different section altogether.

**Book VI
Chapter 6**

**Maximizing the
Power of OneNote**

To move a page up or down the page listing, while keeping it in the same section, follow these steps:

1. **Select the page(s) to move.**

You can move more than one page at a time if you want. See the preceding section for help.

2. **Drag the selected page(s) up or down the page tab list.**

A small black triangle appears to the right of the tabs while you drag.

3. **When that triangle is where you want the page(s) to be, release the mouse button to drop them.**

You can also move page(s) to a completely different section when that suits you by following these steps:

1. **Select the page(s) to move.**

For help, see the preceding section.

2. **Drag the selected page(s) over to the section tab in which you want them located and drop them.**

To move the page(s) to a section in a different notebook, expand the Navigation bar so that you can see the notebook listing. Drag the selected page(s) over to the Navigation bar on the left, as shown in Figure 6-13. If the sections for that notebook are listed, then simply drop the page(s) on the proper section. If the sections aren't shown, don't panic; just hover the mouse over the notebook in which you want to place the page(s). After a moment, the notebook opens, showing you its various sections; drop the page on the section in which you want it to appear. You can then click the tab to display that section and drag the page up or down the page tab listing on the right to put it where you want it in that section.

Figure 6-13:
Move pages
around.

You can put notes on a page anywhere you want, but they don't have to stay there. Every object on the page has its own container. Each text note, for example, is surrounded by a little box.

Here are a few tricks of the trade:

✦ **To move a note somewhere else on the page:** Move the mouse pointer over the top edge of the box (container) that contains the note (the mouse changes to a four-headed arrow), then click and drag.

✦ **To move a paragraph within a note:** Move the mouse pointer to the right of the paragraph until it changes to that four-headed hydra-pointer thingy and drag.

✦ **To merge two note containers so that only one box surrounds them both:** Drag one note container over the other while holding down Shift and rubbing your tummy. (Okay, tummy rubbing is optional.)

When you drag and drop notes, they seem to snap into place, almost as if invisible lines are on the page, magically causing stuff to line up against them. Well, aliens haven't just landed, but there really are, magic invisible lines on the page that *do* force stuff to line up. If you want something to stay right there and not move, you can override the magic lines by holding down Alt while you drag and drop.

Moving sections

You don't have to let pages and notes have all the fun. If you're rearranging the furniture, why not rearrange sections in a notebook to better suit the way in which you use them? Here are some techniques you can use to move sections:

✦ **To move a section within the same notebook:** Drag its tab along the tab listing and then drop it. While you drag, a little black down arrow follows your movement; when the arrow is located where you want the section tab to appear, release the mouse button to drop it.

✦ **To move the section to a different notebook:** Drag its tab over to the expanded Navigation bar and hover over the notebook in which you want the section to appear. If the notebook's sections aren't currently displayed, then after a bit, the notebook wakes up enough to show you its list of sections. Drag the mouse down the list until you reach the place where you want the section to appear, and then release the mouse button to drop it.

You can also drag sections up or down within the listing on the Navigation bar — within the same notebook, or into a different notebook.

Tagging Important Information

The whole idea behind OneNote is that it gives you a great place to keep track of a lot of related stuff — notes, images, tables, charts, and audio and video data. But what good is it to collect your things in one place if you can never find them again? In the following section, I show you how to search for a specific bit of information based on the text it contains. In this section, I show you another way in which you can make important information stand out: by using tags.

OneNote comes with a bunch of tags that you can use to highlight whatever you want. You can find an Important tag (a star), a Question tag (a question mark), an Idea tag (a light bulb), and many more. When you tag an item, the icon associated with that tag appears to the left of the object's container. The To-Do tag is kind of unique because it puts a check-box icon in front of the item that you can actually check off when you get that item done.

What's the difference between adding an Outlook task to a page (as explained in the section "Creating an Outlook Task on a Page," earlier in this chapter) and simply tagging something with the To Do tag? Well, first of all, the To Do tag item doesn't appear in Outlook, like an actual task does. Also, you can apply a To Do tag to any container, not just text, which makes it different from an Outlook task. Both, however, present you with a way in which you can check off the item after you get it done.

To apply a tag, follow these steps:

1. **Select an object that you want to tag by clicking the top border of the object's container.**

   You can select a note, a picture, a drawing, anything.

2. **Select a tag from the Tags drop-down list on the Home tab.**

   The most frequently used tags are listed first; click the More button to display the rest of the tags. The icon for the tag you selected instantly appears to the left of the selected object, as shown in Figure 6-14.

Create your own tags

Why go with only the tags that OneNote suggests? Create your own tags that you can attach to your notes by clicking the More button in the Tags group, and selecting Customize Tags from the drop-down list that appears. The Customize Tags dialog box appears. Click the New Tag button and, in the New Tag dialog box that appears, type a name for the tag in the Display Name box. Select a symbol to represent that tag from the Symbol palette, a font color for tagged text from the Font Color palette, and a highlight color (if desired) to highlight tagged text from the Highlight Color palette. The font color and highlight color you select are applied to any note text that uses this tag. A preview of your choices appear in the Preview pane.

You can modify an existing tag that you don't plan to use as it currently is; just display the Customize Tags dialog box, select a tag, and click the Modify Tag button. Then, make any changes you want (for example, change the tag's name) and click OK. By the way, if you want to move a tag that you use frequently up in the Tags list, select that tag in the Customize Tags dialog box and use the up- or down-arrow buttons to the right of the list to move it.

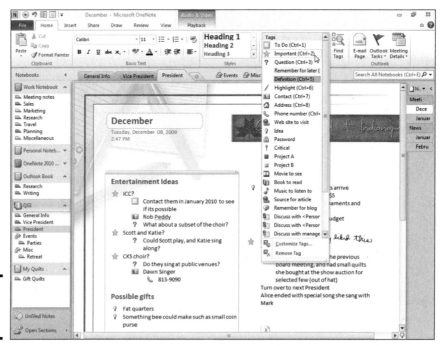

Figure 6-14:
Tag,
you're it.

Searching for Data

One of the advantages of using OneNote over, say, tons of tiny bits of paper scattered across your desk, snuggled in your pockets, and tucked into the corners of every room in your home is that you can *find your notes when you need them.* And finding them has never been easier because you can actually let OneNote do the finding for you. Yep, just type some words, and OneNote goes searching through your haystack of notes and finds that missing needle.

If some of the pages you want to search are password-protected, you need to unlock them by entering your password before OneNote can search them.

Follow these steps to search for OneNote text:

1. **Type some search text in the Search All Notebooks text box at the top of the OneNote window, as shown in Figure 6-15.**

   For example, type sales or economics in the Search All Notebooks text box. While you type, results appear in a list.

   Here are some search tips:

   - Use quotes to find some exact phrase, such as "metal stress".

   - Upper- and lowercase, it's all the same to OneNote. Don't worry about typing John Doe — if you type john doe instead, OneNote still finds a match.

   - Use OR when you have several search criteria. For example, if you type metal OR stress, notes that contain either word, or both, appear. If you type metal stress, items that contain both words, although not necessarily together or in that order, appear.

   - Use NEAR to look for two words within a few words of each other in the text. For example, type Joe NEAR cell to search for Joe's cell phone number.

   - To find an audio recording, you can try typing just audio or video, but that may pick up notes, too. If you type audio recording started or video recording started, you get only audio or video files because OneNote marks them with a note that contains the date on which you made the recording, something like Audio Recording Started 3:59 PM Wednesday, January 15th, 2010. You can also type audio Wednesday to find a recording that you made Wednesday, although you may find a note that contains a reference to that recording.

Search All Notebooks   Results List

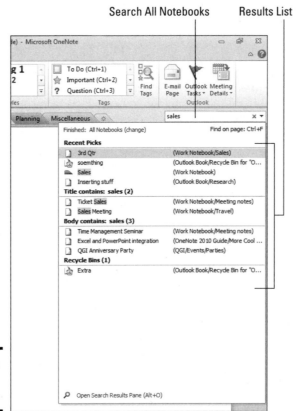

Figure 6-15:
Search for
sales.

OneNote may skip an audio file that matches your search text simply because Windows hasn't had time to index that file. (Windows "listens" to the audio file and creates a list of the words in it.) Basically, you just need to give Windows time because this indexing business occurs in the background while you do real work. If the audio file is a long one, it may take a while to index it, but if OneNote skips a file because that file isn't indexed, a message appears telling you so. In such a case, you can always try the search again or simply listen to the audio files that were skipped and see for yourself whether one of them is the one you wanted.

2. **(Optional) Adjust the search criteria by clicking the down arrow at the right end of the Search All Notebooks and selecting where you want OneNote to search from the drop-down list that appears.**

   By default, OneNote searches all open notebooks. When you click the down arrow in the Search All Notebooks box, a drop-down list appears. You have several choices:

   • *To search the current page:* Select Find on This Page.

   • *To search the current section:* Select This Section.

- *To search the current section group (the current section and all open sections in that group):* Select This Section Group.

- *To search the current notebook only:* Select This Notebook.

The search results list is automatically changed to include only the search results that match the search area you just selected.

OneNote remembers the scope of the last search you did, so if you want to search that same area (such as This Section), you don't need to select the search area in Step 2. If you want to set the current selection as your default for all searches, select Set This Scope as Default.

3. **Scan down the search results list and click the page you want to view.**

The list remains open (until you click something on a note page or change to a different program such as Outlook) so you can click a different page in the search results list if the first one you selected isn't the one you want to view.

Using the Search Results pane

At the bottom of the search results list, an Open Search Results Pane link appears. Click this link to display the pane if you want to keep your search results open even after you click on a note page or switch to a different program for a moment. After you display the Search Results pane (see Figure 6-16), text and page tabs that match the current search criteria are highlighted in dark yellow to help you find what you're looking for quickly. The results list in the Search Results pane is arranged by date (the date associated with the page the note is on). You can sort the results by section or title by selecting that option from the Sort By drop-down list. Display whatever sort you use in reverse alphabetical order by clicking the Sort Descending button.

Sort Descending

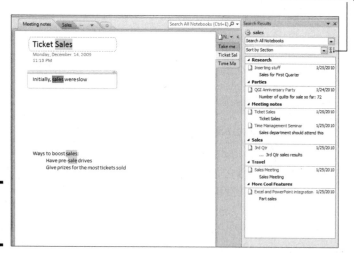

Figure 6-16:
Search for
sales.

Click a page in the Search Results pane to display it on the left. After you finish reviewing the search results, click the Close button on the Search Results pane to make that pane go away.

Finding tagged items

OneNote provides you with a set of *tags* (icons) that you can use to mark items that are important to you in some way. You can add a To Do tag, a Critical tag, and a Remember for Later tag. (See the section "Tagging Important Information," earlier in this chapter.) After tagging various items, you can use those tags to locate the items later.

To search for tagged items, follow these steps:

1. **Click the Find Tags button on the Home tab.**

The Tags Summary pane appears, listing all the tagged items in the current notebook, grouped by tag, as shown in Figure 6-17. To change how items are grouped, select an option from the Group Tags By drop-down list. For example, rather than Tag Name, you can select Date or Title (which means the page title).

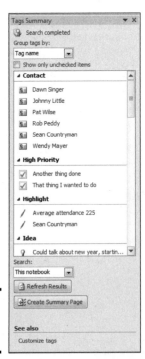

Figure 6-17:
Find tagged
items.

2. **Open the Search drop-down list at the bottom of the pane and select the area you want to search.**

   For example, select This Section or This Week's Notes.

3. **If you change the scope of the search in Step 2, click Refresh Results to have OneNote search this newly defined area.**

4. **Click an item in the list to display it on its page on the left.**

If you click the Create Summary Page button at the bottom of the task page, a new page is added to the current section, behind the existing pages in the section. The page that's created simply contains a copy of the items in the task pane, in their current order.

Book VII

Working with Business Contact Manager

The 5th Wave   By Rich Tennant

"Hold on, Barbara. Let me launch Outlook and
see if I can find a newsgroup on this."

Contents at a Glance

Chapter 1: Minding Your Business Contact Manager

In This Chapter

✔ Looking at Business Contact Manager, versus Outlook

✔ Figuring out whether BCM can work for you

✔ Using Business Contact Manager

✔ Importing contacts into BCM

While Microsoft was creating the world of personal computing, it realized the use of cool software could prevent disorganization, and so the company created Outlook. Computer users everywhere rejoiced because Outlook helped them organize their contacts and calendars.

But hark! Microsoft soon heard rumblings about a new type of software — Customer Relationship Management, or CRM. The newly organized wanted to become even more organized. Business people wanted to manage their relationships with their customers (or prospects or leads or vendors) so that all their employees could see who's done what to whom, what the business has promised and delivered, what money the business owes, and what receivables the business has coming in. Even nonprofit organizations and soccer moms felt a need to share contact and calendar information with other people.

Enter Business Contact Manager (BCM). BCM is the entry-level CRM program that Microsoft has integrated into the Microsoft Office Professional Plus 2010 suite version of Outlook. BCM is built right into that version of Outlook as another Address Book.

Comparing BCM and Outlook

You're probably wondering what the difference is between Outlook and Business Contact Manager. We like to think of BCM as Outlook on steroids. Here's a list of the main power features in BCM:

✦ In addition to Contact Records, you can create Account Records in BCM. Think of an Account Record as a master record that contains information about a company, rather than an individual.

REMEMBER

You can easily link BCM Contact Records to BCM Account Records to help keep track of all the individuals who work at the same company.

✦ BCM allows more flexibility if you need to add fields to help keep track of your business.

✦ You can use BCM to set up marketing campaigns and track their effectiveness.

✦ You can set up Opportunities (as in "sales opportunities") in BCM to help you track your company's sales process.

✦ BCM can help you keep track of your client-based projects..

✦ You can share BCM across a network so that everyone in the office sees the same data. You can even let co-workers take a subset of your BCM database with them when they leave the office and synchronize their changes back to yours when they return.

✦ BCM comes equipped with a lot of reports and dashboards that can help you keep better tabs on your business.

✦ Because it stores its data in a SQL database, BCM can hold more contacts than can Outlook.

Knowing Who Should Use BCM

Although anyone can use Business Contact Manager, certain kinds of organizations and individuals are better suited to BCM.

So, just who would benefit the most by using BCM? Here are a few folks who come to mind:

✦ A CEO who needs to know what his salespeople are doing and how they're treating his customers.

✦ An administrative assistant who wants to automate routine tasks and keep a schedule of various tasks and activities.

✦ A salesperson who wants to make sure that she's following up on all her prospects.

✦ A disorganized person who wants to become more organized.

✦ A smart person who realizes that he'll have more time to play if he works more efficiently.

✦ Anyone who wants to separate her personal contacts from business contacts or keep track of multiple sets of contacts.

✦ Anyone who needs to track money through a process — whether it's a pledge or donation to a charity.

✦ A lazy person who knows it's more fun to play than to work.

So, all kinds of businesses are ideal BCM candidates:

✦ Businesses that want to improve communication among employees

✦ Small businesses that have to rely on a small staff to complete a multitude of tasks

✦ Businesses of all sizes that are looking for software that can automate their business functions and make them more productive in less time

✦ New businesses that want to grow by marketing to their prospects

✦ Existing businesses that want to retain their current customers by providing an excellent level of customer service and developing lasting relationships

Getting Started in BCM

BCM comes as a part of Outlook 2010 when you purchase Outlook in the Microsoft Office Professional Plus 2010 suite.

You can access the various BCM components by using one of the following methods:

✦ Click the Business Contact Manager icon on the Navigation pane (or press Ctrl-9).

✦ Expand the Business Contact Manager folder in the Folder List.

In addition, a Business Contact Manager folder appears below the My Contacts folder when you click the Contacts icon on the navigation bar. This folder will contain the new BCM contacts and accounts that you add.

Creating a database

When you first install BCM, the cheerful Startup and Welcome to BCM Wizard appears, which allows you to create your BCM database. Although the Welcome Wizard doesn't hand out coupons like the Welcome Wagon does, it does help you create your all-important database. However, if you miss this wizard or want to create another database, follow these steps:

1. **From Outlook, click the File tab, and then choose Business Contact Manager.**

The Business Contact Manager window appears, as shown in Figure 1-1.

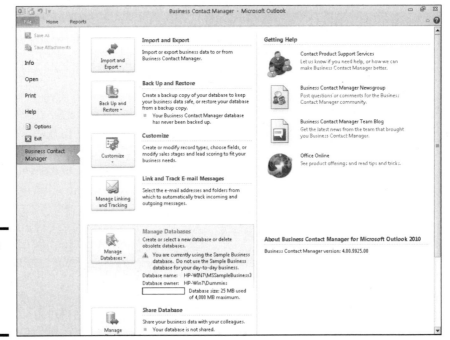

Figure 1-1:
The
Business
Contact
Manager
window.

2. **Click the Manage Databases icon, and then choose Create or Select a Database from the options that appear (see Figure 1-2).**

   The Create or Select a Database Wizard opens.

3. **Click the Create a New Local Database option.**

   The Create a New Local Database Wizard advances to the Create a New Local Database window, shown in Figure 1-3.

4. **Enter the name of the new database into the text field, and then click Create.**

   You may want to name your database something that you can pick out of a crowd, such as CoolBeans or LetsMakeMoney. You also should avoid spaces in the name, as well as characters such as @#$%^&*, especially if you don't want your computer to think you're swearing at it. If you don't suggest a name, Business Contact Manager suggests one for you: MSSmallBusiness.

   After you click Create, BCM creates your database and takes you to the Business Contact Manager Dashboard window.

When you create a database, it opens automatically. Don't sweat when your old one disappears. You can find out how to switch between databases in the following section.

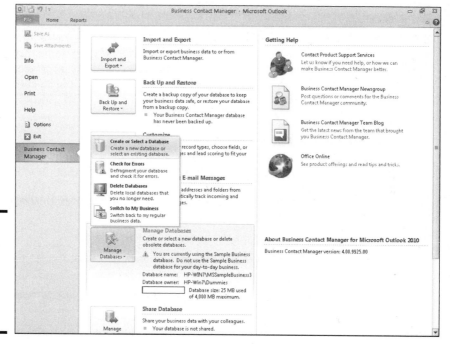

Figure 1-2:
Creating a new Business Contact Manager database.

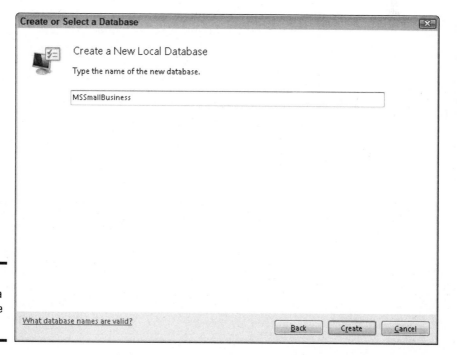

Figure 1-3:
Assigning a name to the database.

BCM uses SQL as its database engine. When you create a new database, two data files are actually created: one with an `.mdf` extension and the other with an `.ldf` extension. You can find those files somewhat buried alive deep in the bowels of your computer — in the Users\User Name\App Data\Local\ Microsoft\Business Contact Manager folder. If you want to rename those files, you can stop the SQL service, navigate to that folder, and rename the two files in question.

Opening a database

After you create a database, you may actually want to use it. Follow these steps to switch back and forth between your databases:

1. **From Outlook, click the File tab, and then choose Business Contact Manager.**

   The Business Contact Manager window appears.

2. **Click the Manage Databases icon and select the Create or Select a Database option.**

   The Create or Select a Database dialog window opens, revealing two choices:

   - **Connect to a Local Database:** Allows you to navigate to a database that's stored on your computer

   - **Connect to Remote Database:** Allows you to navigate to a database that's stored on someone else's computer

   For our example, we use the Local Database option. If you prefer to connect to a Remote Database, you have to supply the name of the other computer before you can proceed to Step 4.

3. **Click Connect to Local Database.**

   The Connect to a Local database window that you see in Figure 1-4 springs to life.

4. **Select the name of your database, and then click Connect.**

   BCM stores its data in a SQL database, which simply means that the database must be connected to SQL in order to work. (Make sure that you throw in a comment about how you "had to connect your database to SQL" the next time you go to a cocktail party.)

   If you want, you can tap your fingers on the desk for a minute while your computer makes a bit of noise and ultimately returns to the Business Contact Manager Dashboard window.

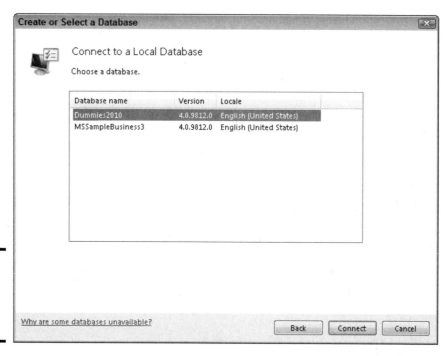

Book VII
Chapter 1

Minding Your Business Contact Manager

Figure 1-4:
Selecting a previously created database.

Finding your current database

Nothing's worse than getting lost in an endless maze of databases. Okay, worse things happen, but not knowing which database you're using can be extremely frustrating — especially if you've spent the day entering tons of contact information, only to discover that you entered it into the *wrong* database.

To get the M.O. on a database that may be MIA, simply click Outlook's File tab, and then choose Business Contact Manager. The Business Contact Manager window appears, with the Database area smack dab in the middle of the screen. In addition to seeing the name of your current database, you also see the name of the computer, the owner of the database, and the size of the database.

Deleting a database

Life changes, things happen, and it's time to bid your database adieu. Maybe you created a database for the leads that you purchased, and you now find that you no longer need them. Or maybe you created a database in error and want to get rid of the evidence before the boss sees it. Whatever the reason, you can just as easily delete a database as create it in the first place. Just follow these steps:

1. **From Outlook, click the File tab, and then choose Business Contact Manager.**

   The Business Contact Manager window makes an appearance.

2. **Click the Manage Databases icon and then select Delete Databases.**

   The Delete Databases dialog box opens, displaying a list of your databases. As a safety precaution, the database you currently have open appears grayed out and can't be deleted.

3. **Highlight the database that you want to delete, and then click Delete Database.**

   A warning dialog box appears, asking whether you're of sound mind and body. Okay, the warning doesn't actually prompt you for your current state of mental health, but it does give you a chance to halt the deletion process.

4. **Click Yes if you really want to get rid of the database in question.**

   BCM doesn't believe in lengthy goodbyes. Wham, it removes your database, permanently (meaning forever) — so think carefully before clicking that Yes button.

Importing Contacts into BCM

The only thing worse than doing a bunch of work is having to redo it all. With that thought in mind, BCM has thoughtfully included an Import Wizard that can magically transform your old database information into a shiny, new BCM database. If you're using a program such as ACT! or Access, and you decide to switch to BCM, you can do so without losing — or retyping — your data. If you're currently using QuickBooks, you can import your various lists of customers and vendors into BCM. Even if you use an Excel spreadsheet to keep track of your contacts, not to worry — BCM helps you move those contacts easily and painlessly into BCM.

If you have multiple users — salespeople, for example — who have been keeping their own individual lists of contact data, you can import those lists into one new BCM master database for your company. You can even import one BCM database into another BCM database, if that floats your boat.

Determining your data type

So, what specific data types can you bring into BCM? A couple of the options that the wizard offers carry the .bcm handle because they involve bringing existing BCM data into your database:

+ **Business Contact Manager data (.bcm):** Imports all the good stuff, including business contacts, accounts, opportunities, and communication history. It also imports your customizations, such as user-defined fields, form layouts, project templates, and custom reports. Use this option if you accidentally create two separate databases and want to merge them together, or if someone else in your organization already uses an existing BCM database. You can also use this option to collect data from remote guys; you can import their data into the company database at regular intervals.

✦ **Business Contact Manager Customizations (.bcmx):** Allows you to import just your customizations, including any user-defined fields that you created for your database. Use this option if you need to create an empty clone of your original database.

✦ **Comma Separated Values (.csv):** The one-size-fits-all option for importing data. Basically, if you can get your Comma Separated Values (CSV) information *out* of a program, you can get it *into* BCM. CSV is also the format of choice for organizations that run trade shows or that sell prospect lists. You just have to ask someone, "Can you send me those names in a CSV format?" BCM's Import function allows you to map incoming fields from the CSV file into the fields that BCM stores in its database, which allows you to get the right data in to the right place.

Most software programs allow you to export data to a text file. Even if you're using a (gasp!) DOS-based program, you can probably find a Print to File option that creates an ASCII or text file. You can then open that text file in Excel and save it as a .csv file.

✦ **Excel Workbook (.xls or .xlsx):** Bring in your business contacts or accounts.

✦ **Access database (.mdb or .accdb):** Depending on the tables that you use in Access, use this option to bring in business contact or account information.

✦ **Outlook Contacts folder:** Bring in any of your Outlook contacts and plunk them into your BCM business contacts.

If you plan on building your database by using information that another user keeps in Outlook, you need to get your hands on a copy of his or her .pst file and open it on your machine. Only then can you import all his or her contacts.

Book VII
Chapter 1

**Minding Your
Business Contact
Manager**

The rest of the import choices actually involve a two-pronged attack: BCM converts your data into a BCM database, and then you need to import that BCM database into your existing database. After you convert the information, BCM automatically prompts you to import it into your existing database. You have the following choices:

✦ **ACT!:** Actually one of the coolest import options. BCM can capture your existing contacts, companies, groups, opportunities, notes, and histories.

✦ **QuickBooks:** Although you may want to use this option if you currently use QuickBooks, it doesn't work if you're using a fairly recent edition of QuickBooks. The newest version that BCM supports is QuickBooks 2005.

Importing data

To import data, you have to follow quite a few steps along the way, but the effort is worth it when you think of all the time saved! BCM comes equipped with an Import Business Data wizard that guides you through the process and guarantees that you don't get lost along the way.

Don't be surprised if your data appears a bit scrambled when you import your information from a different software program into Business Contact Manager. Because the format of these programs differs quite a bit from BCM, your data might not import flawlessly.

Follow these steps to import existing information into BCM:

1. **From Outlook, click the File tab, and then choose Business Contact Manager.**

   The Business Contact Manager window appears.

2. **Click the Import and Export icon.**

   A dropdown list opens that offers three different import options:

   • **Import from a File:** Imports `.bcm`, `.bcmx`, `.csv`, `.xls`, `.xlsx`, `.mdb`, and `.accdb` files.

   • **Import Outlook Contacts:** Imports your Outlook contacts.

   • **Import from Other Applications:** Imports `.pad`, `.dbf`, and `.IIF`, files.

3. **Select the type of data that you're going to import.**

   For our example, we are importing an Excel file, so click the Import from a File selection. The Import Business Data dialog box appears, as shown in Figure 1-5.

   Not sure which type of data to import? We explain the different data choices in the preceding section.

4. **Click Browse and navigate to the location of your data source import file.**

5. **Select the data file you want to import and click Open.**

   The file you selected now appears in the Import Business Data window's File to Import text box.

6. **Click Next and select your Duplicate handling import option.**

   You're given two options here:

   • Do not import duplicate records

   • Import duplicate records as new records

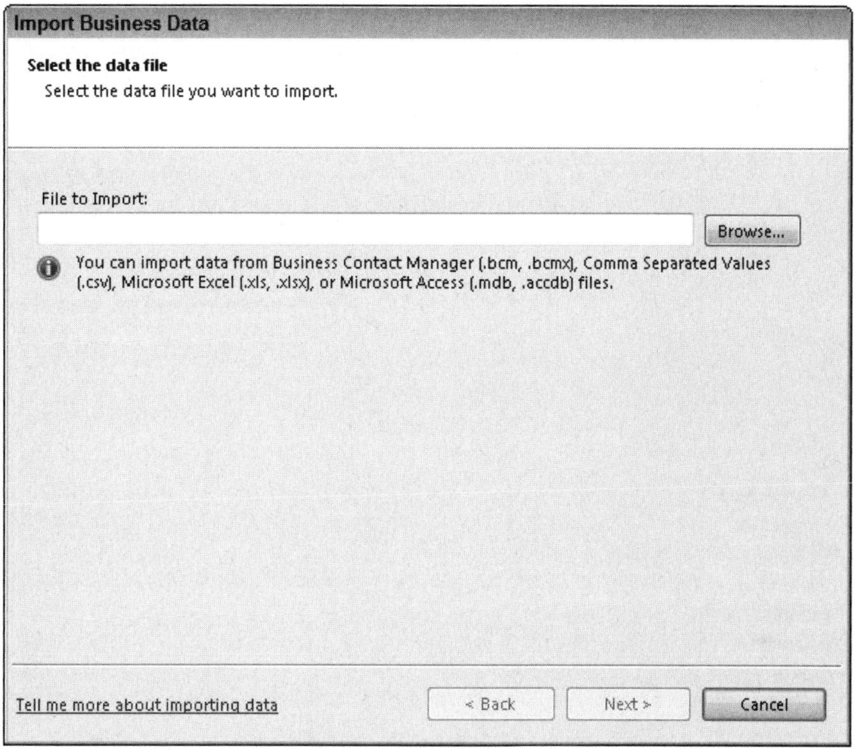

Figure 1-5:
The Import
Business
Data
dialog box.

Decide whether you want to import duplicates into your database. For
example, when you import contacts from various sources, those sources
may have overlapping contacts. In some cases, you might want to include
the duplicates to make sure that you don't lose any notes or other pertinent
information associated with a contact in only one source.

7. **Click Next to continue.**

The Select Record Types and Map Fields screen of the Import Business
Data wizard appears that you see in Figure 1-6.

8. **Make a selection from the Record Type drop-down list to indicate the
type of records that you want to create in Business Contact Manager.**

You can import your information as Accounts, Business Contacts,
or Leads.

9. **Click the Map button.**

Holy guacamole! The Map Fields dialog box (which you can see in
Figure 1-7) springs to life. At first, this dialog box seems way too confusing,
but after you analyze the options, it all makes sense:

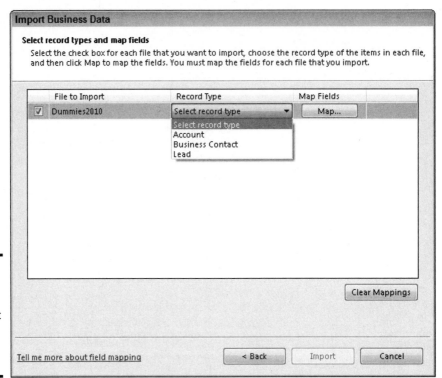

Figure 1-6:
Deciding
the kind of
records that
you want to
create
in BCM.

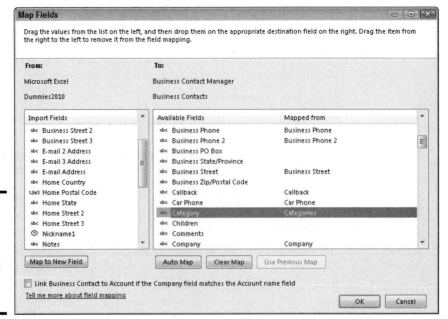

Figure 1-7:
Mapping
the import
file fields
to the BCM
contact
fields.

- **Auto Map:** If you click the Auto Map button, any fields from your import file that identically match a BCM field appear in the Mapped From column. (The import fields are on the left, and the BCM fields are on the right.)

- **Manual mapping:** Map an Import Fields entry to the Available Fields in BCM by dragging the entry from the From column to the To column. Figure 1-7 shows several examples of manually mapped fields. We mapped the Import Fields entry Categories to the Available Fields entry Category. When you map fields, those entries disappear from the Import Fields list.

- **Map to New Field:** To import information into your database for which BCM doesn't have a field, click an Import Fields entry and click the Map to New Field button. Fill in the necessary field information in the Add a Field dialog box that opens, and then click OK.

10. **Click OK, and then Import, to continue to the end of the Import Business Data Wizard.**

    You get to sit back and watch a moving graphic that illustrates how your data information is flying from your import file into the arms, er, fields of BCM. When your data finishes flying through cyberspace, you're treated to a congratulatory message. Too bad it doesn't include champagne and bon bons!

11. **Click Close when the Importing Complete message appears.**

    Give yourself a really big pat on the back — you deserve it!

Moving contacts from Outlook

Entering new contact data into BCM can be a drag — but not if you can *drag* that data into your database from Outlook. For your next trick, you can magically transform Outlook contacts into BCM Business Contacts or Accounts. Just drag yourself through the following steps:

1. **Click the Contacts folder on Outlook's folder list.**

   You'll be able to view your Outlook contacts in Outlook's main screen.

2. **Select the contacts that you want to transform into Business Contacts or Accounts.**

   You have a couple of options for selecting contacts:

   - To select all contacts, hold down the Ctrl key and press the A key on your keyboard.

   - To select only some contacts, hold down the Ctrl key and click the contacts that you want.

3. **Right-click and then drag the selected contacts to either the BCM Business Contacts or Accounts folder.**

If you simply drag a contact from the Outlook Contacts folder to a Business Contact Manager folder, the contact disappears from Outlook and appears in BCM. However, if you press and hold the Ctrl key as you drag the selected contact to a Business Contact Manager folder, the contact stays in the Outlook Contacts folder and a copy of the contact appears in BCM. If you accidentally move a contact from the Outlook Contacts folder when you meant to copy it, press Ctrl-Z to undo the move and try again. When you drag a Contact or Account from BCM to the Outlook Contacts folder, the record appears in both places.

The contact(s) now reside happily among the rest of your BCM Business Contacts or Accounts.

Chapter 2: Introducing the Basic Business Contact Manager Elements

In This Chapter

✔ **Creating and using BCM Business Contacts**

✔ **Adding Accounts**

✔ **Linking Outlook and BCM**

✔ **Working with Business Projects**

You have Outlook Business Contact Manager (BCM) up and running, and you're anxious to dive right in to it. Well, you've headed to the right chapter! In this chapter, you can find out how to create Business Contacts — those people with whom you do business. You'll add in a few Accounts (sort of super contacts) that represent the main companies that those Business Contacts associate with. If you already have contacts in Outlook, this chapter shows you how to move, copy, and link those contacts to Business Contact Manager. Finally, if you're interested in project management, this chapter covers that, as well.

Working with Business Contacts

No tour of BCM can be complete without locating your Business Contacts; after all, BCM does stand for Business Contact Manager. As the name Business Contact Manager implies, contacts are the heart and soul of the program. A contact is one person, and BCM comes with many fields that can store information about that person. You can have all types of contacts — prospects, customers, friends, enemies, vendors — and each contact has information that's specific to him or her.

You can find your BCM Contacts in a number of places:

✦ Click the arrow to the left of Business Contact Manager on Outlook's Folder list on the Navigation pane, and then click the arrow to the left of Business Records.

✦ Click the Business Contact Management icon on the bottom of the Navigation pane (or press Ctrl-9) and then select Business Contacts from the top portion of the Navigation pane.

Adding a new Business Contact

BCM comes configured out of the box with more than 50 fields of data that you can store about each contact. You can add more fields if you want to customize BCM to better fit your needs. In addition, BCM provides you with forms to use when you enter either a Business Contact or a Lead. You can also add additional forms to create specific types of Business Contacts records, such as Employees or Enemies.

Follow these steps to add a new Business Contact:

1. **Click the Business Contacts folder in the Folder list.**

2. **Click the New Business Contact icon on the Home section of the Ribbon.**

   Alternatively, you can click the New Items icon in the Home section of the Ribbon, select Business Contacts from the pop-up menu that appears, and then select either Business Contact or Lead.

   Either way, a blank Business Contact record form opens to the General tab. Enter all the pertinent info for your new contact in this area, as shown in Figure 2-1.

   If you added your own Business Contact forms, you might also see choices such as Employee or Enemy.

3. **Start filling in your tidbits of information.**

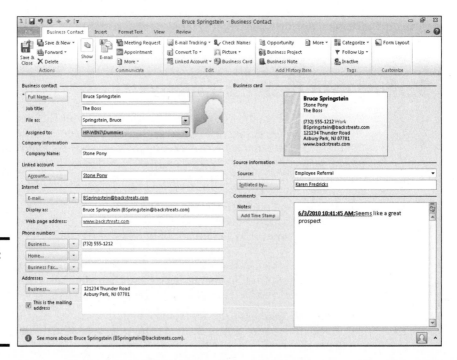

Figure 2-1: Adding a new Business Contact record.

The only field you must enter is the Full Name field. However, this field is just the proverbial tip of the BCM Contact iceberg. A few things aren't apparent to the naked eye, so we want to point them out:

- **Full Name button:** Click this button to bring up a dialog box in which you can enter a contact's title (Mr., Mrs., and so on); first, middle, and last name; and suffix (Jr., Sr., and so on). You can see what we mean by giving Figure 2-2 a gander.

You might notice the Show This Again checkbox at the bottom of the Check Full Name dialog box. Check this if you'd like to have BCM automatically prompt you any time there is a confusion as to a contact's first, last and middle name.

- **File As:** Outlook uses this field to sort the name in list views of contact names.

- **Company**: You might want to avoid this one. The Account field serves the same purpose and gives you the added benefit of linking all the same contacts with the same Account together.

- **Account button:** Opens all the Account records if you need to link the Business Contact record to an Account record. In addition, if you input the name of an existing Account in the Account field, BCM automatically creates a link between the Contact record and the Account record.

**Book VII
Chapter 2**

Introducing the
Basic Business
Contact Manager

Figure 2-2:
The Check
Full Name
dialog box.

- **E-mail button:** BCM stores up to three e-mil addresses per Contact. Just click the drop-down arrow to switch between the addresses.

- **Web Page Address:** A hyperlink; fill in your contact's Web site, give it a click, and your browser will open to the site.

- **Phone Numbers:** BCM has room for more phone numbers than you can shake a stick at — or at least nearly 20 of them, including everything from mobile phone to assistant's direct line. And, if you need more, you can add them. If you click the down arrow to the right of one of the phone field labels, you can select which number you want to use. Although you can store 19 phone numbers, you can display only three numbers at a time. Clicking the phone label also allows you to change the country code for that contact in case the contact is located somewhere other than in the United States.

- **Addresses:** This field works the same way as the Phone fields. Clicking the drop-down arrow lets you select a different set of address fields — Business, Home, or Other.

  Several of the other fields include drop-down arrows so that you can select a value from the drop-down list, thus ensuring that you enter your information consistently. If you're familiar with the options in the drop-down list, you can simply type the first letter or so of your intended info, and poof! BCM fills in the rest of the information automatically.

- **Picture:** Click this field to call up a dialog box that you can then use to search your hard drive for a photo (or icon or logo) of that person to include as part of the Business Contact record. This picture is also sent to your smartphone when you sync.

- **Initiated By button:** Click this button to link this contact to another Contact, Account, or Marketing Activity. You can use this button to keep track how this contact came into your world.

- **Comments**: Use this field to add any pertinent comments you might have about the contact such as "he's really a nice guy" or "don't mention his ex-wife." You can even click the Add Timestamp button if you'd like to record the exact date and time of your comment.

4. **Click the Details icon in the Show section of the Ribbon.**

   You can fill in a few more fields about the Contact, including job info; personal stuff, such as birthdays and anniversaries; and communication preferences. You can view these options in Figure 2-3.

5. **(Optional) Fill in additional information on any custom-defined tabs that you or someone else in your organization might have created.**

   The object of the game is to paint as vivid a picture of your Contact as possible.

6. **Click the Save & Close icon when you finish entering your contact information.**

   Or click the Save & New button if you had so much fun adding one Contact that you just can't wait to do it again. Outlook saves the record you entered and presents you with a new, blank Business Contact screen so that you can start working on your next victim.

Making changes to a Business Contact

You've worked really hard at adding all sorts of new contacts to your database. Life is good. The birds are singing. Time to go try out that new putter. However, even the best-laid plans of mice, men, and golf carts can get messed up. Perhaps one of your clients has the audacity to change his e-mail address, and another one changes her phone number. You may even have a lowdown, nasty former client decide to take his business elsewhere — and you can't wait to remove all remnants of him from your database.

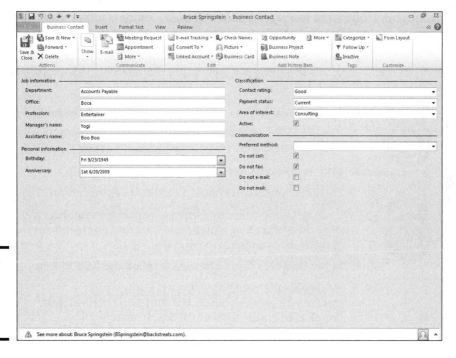

Figure 2-3:
Adding a
few more
contact
details

Fear not — stuff happens, and BCM makes it really easy to deal with change. Simply double-click the name of the Business Contact that you want to change, make your changes, and click the Save & Close button on the Ribbon.

Not seeing your Business Contacts? You'll find Business Contact Manager in the Folder list of Outlook's Navigation pane. From there, you can click the arrow next to BCM to expand your Business Records and then click the arrow next to Business Records to reveal your Business Contacts.

Adding a Business Contact from an Account record

You may want to think of a BCM Account like it's a super-sized Business Contact. In an Account, you can enter information about an organization or large company with lots of employees. In general, you create a Business Contact for a single individual and an Account for a bunch of individuals who all work together and attend the same holiday party.

In many cases, if you're dealing with a BCM Account, you're probably dealing with a group of individuals who share several things in common: the same address, main phone number, and signature on the bottom of their paychecks. If you want, you can enter all those Business Contacts individually, get a migraine, and storm into your boss's office complaining that you're overworked or underpaid. Or you can use the following method to enter a bunch of Business Contacts, sneak out to the driving range for an hour, and then storm into your boss's office complaining that you're over-worked or underpaid. Follow these steps:

1. **Click the Accounts subfolder on the Folder list under the Business Records folder of the Business Contact Manager section of the Navigation Pane.**

2. **Find the Account to which you want to add a Business Contact.**

   Haven't set up any Accounts yet? If you're not sure how to create a new Account take a look at the next section "Getting the 411 on Accounts."

3. **Double-click the Account to open it.**

   The Account record should swing open at this point.

   You right-clickers in the crowd may prefer to right-click an Account record and choose Create⇨New Business Contact from the menu that appears, then skip to Step 6.

4. **In the Business Contacts section, click the Add button.**

   The Business Contacts section appears way at the bottom of the Account screen. When you click the Add button, a list of all existing Business Contacts who aren't already linked to an Account record appears.

5. **Click the New button.**

   A new Business Contact record opens, just like magic. And, just like magic, the address and phone information are already filled in. The Account name appears in the Account field, and the Web site address is in the Web page field. Talk about automation!

6. **Fill in the Business Contact's name, phone extension, and any other information that's pertinent just to him or her.**

   BCM is pretty good, but it's not psychic. You have to add these tidbits of information on your own.

7. **Click Save & Close to save your entries.**

Getting the 411 on Accounts

Accounts are the way to organize several Contacts into their company affili-ations. You have another entire record of data that you can customize sepa-rately from a Contact. It can contain fields that are specific to the company, rather than the people working at the company. An Account is quite handy if you work with multiple people at the same company — the purchasing manager, the production manager, and the accounting department, for example. Each contact at that company has his or her own Business Contact record, in which you can enter notes about conversations and appointments with that person. All that data rolls up into an Account view so that you or anyone else in your organization can see what's going on with that Account at a higher level.

You may find yourself relying on Accounts, even if you're not using BCM to manage a business. You can use Accounts to group all sorts of people together. Perhaps you want to keep track of a soccer team, a PTA, or your kid's homeroom class. You can make these groups your Outlook Accounts.

Face it: Bureaucracy is alive and well and living in most civilized countries. Actually, it probably lives in *un*civilized ones, as well. Your database may contain the names of the head honcho (also known as The Decision Maker), your main point of contact, the person who signs the checks, and the person who actually does all the work (the Administrative Assistant). It seems easy at first, until the head honcho gets fired, the check signer takes off for Brazil — and new people replace both of them.

If you deal with really large companies (generally, those that have their own cafeteria and a lot of cubicles), you're probably dealing with numerous Business Contacts, as well. The question then becomes, "Which do you create first: the Business Contact or the Account?"

In Business Contact Manager, you can

Book VII Chapter 2

Introducing the Basic Business Contact Manager

✦ Create an Account and add new Business Contacts to it at the same time.

✦ Create a new Business Contact and add a new Account to it at the same time.

✦ Link a new or existing Account to existing Business Contact records.

✦ Link a new or existing Business Contact to an existing Account record.

You may be tempted to create either a Business Contact or Account for every new person you meet. If you decide to use Accounts, you're much better off entering both the Account and first Business Contact record at the same time. You can create them on the fly much, much more easily than you can hunt them down and link them later.

You may have a slight feeling of déjà vu if you read through the following sections. No, you're not having a flashback to the '60s — you probably just read the section above, Adding a new Business Contact, which focuses on adding a Business Contact record. Working with Business Contacts and working with Accounts is a pretty similar process.

Entering Accounts

Follow these steps to create a new Account:

1. **Click the Accounts folder in the Folder list.**

2. **Click the New Account icon on the Home section of the Ribbon.**

Alternatively, you can click the New Items icon in the Home section of the Ribbon and then select Account⇨Account from the pop-up menu that appears.

A blank Account record form opens to the General tab, like the one you see in Figure 2-4.

The only field you must fill out is the Account Name field. However, you may want to take an extra gander at a few other areas:

- **Office:** Use this field to designate different locations or divisions within the company.

- **E-Mail, Phone Numbers, and Addresses:** The drop-down arrows to the right of some of these field labels indicate that more fields are lurking behind those innocent-looking arrows. For example, click the E-Mail arrow, and you can add a second or third e-mail address; unfortunately, you can see only one of them at a time.

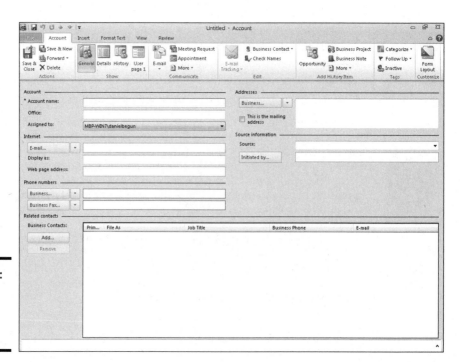

Figure 2-4:
The Account record window.

- **Initiated By:** Click this button to see a list of all your Business Contacts, Marketing Campaigns, Opportunities, and Business Projects. Select an item from the list so that you can associate the name of an existing Account, Contact or Lead to the new Account. This will help you track the source of all your new business. You can see how to make this association in Figure 2-5.

Figure 2-5:
Selecting an
Initiated By
source.

- **Business Contacts:** Link to a new or existing Business Contact. Simply click the Add button and select the name of the Business Contact that you want to associate with this Account from the Select the Business Contacts to Link to the Account dialog box. If you hold down the Ctrl key while selecting those critters, you can associate multiple Business Contacts to the Account at the same time.

Can't find the Business Contact that you're trying to associate with the Account? Click the New button on the Select the Business Contacts to Link to the Account dialog box. BCM snaps to attention and presents you with a brand-new Business Contact form and the keys to the city.

- **Categories:** If you associate a category with an Account (see Book VIII, Chapter 1), the category (or categories) appears at the top of the Account screen.

Several fields have a drop-down arrow to the right of them; using these drop-down lists helps ensure the consistency of the database. If you type the first letter or so of a drop-down item, BCM completes the rest of the word for you. If you add in a value that doesn't appear in the drop-down list, BCM asks whether you want to add that item to the drop-down list; if you decline the invitation, BCM prevents you from adding it into the field.

3. **Click the Details icon in the Show section of the Ribbon.**

   At this juncture even more fields appear, in which you can add additional information about the new Account, including revenue and employee information.

4. **(Optional) Click any user-defined tabs that appear in the Show section of the Ribbon and fill in the pertinent information.**

5. **Click the Save & Close icon on the Ribbon to record your changes.**

Creating an Account from an existing Business Contact

For generations, people have pondered that age-old question: Which came first, the Account or the Business Contact? Okay, maybe that's not the age-old question, but it's one that we can attempt to answer. In the preceding section, you can create the Account first. In this section, you create the Business Contact first and use that Contact to create a new Account.

To create a new Account from an existing Business Contact, follow these steps:

1. **Open a Business Contact record.**

2. **Click the Account button. (Refer to Figure 2-1.)**

   A list of all your existing Accounts appears.

3. **Click the New button.**

   The Account window appears. The form is already partially filled out with information from the Business Contact screen. (The Account form should look a lot like what you see in Figure 2-4.)

4. **Fill in any additional Account information.**

5. **Click Save & Close when you finish.**

Editing an existing Account

After you have a few Accounts under your BCM belt, you need to know a little about their care and feeding — or, at least, about their editing and deleting. These tasks may seem painfully easy, but we want to make sure that you know what to do if a company moves to Podunk Junction or decides to permanently shutter its doors. You may even be staying up late worrying that you might have misspelled the name of an Account by accident. Go back to sleep — BCM has your back covered!

Changing data in an Account record is simple. Just follow these steps:

1. **Click the Accounts subfolder on the Folder list under the Business Records folder of the Business Contact Manager section of the Navigation pane.**

All your Accounts magically appear on the main Outlook screen.

2. **Double-click the Account record that you want to change.**

The Account window appears, displaying the info for that record.

You can delete information by pressing Delete or Backspace, or you can fill in information for fields that you originally left empty.

3. **Click Save & Close to save your changes.**

If you decide that you don't want to save the changes, either press the Esc key or click the X in the upper-right corner of the form; when a dialog box appears, asking whether you want to save changes, click No.

Linking Outlook to BCM Records

You can find a lot of good — and great — software on the market. Unfortunately, if you purchase several pieces, you may face the word that strikes terror in the heart of computer users everywhere: incompatibility. You know the drill — you install one piece of software only to find that another piece of software stops working. And a call to tech support generally ends with you feeling like a human ping pong ball. Outlook combines its power as an e-mail client and basic calendar with the contact management functionality of BCM so that you get two very powerful programs combined into one piece of software. No problems with compatibility here because the programs are designed to work together seamlessly.

Linking existing Outlook activities to a BCM record

The previous chapter of the book shows you how you can take existing Outlook contacts and "convert" them to BCM Business Contacts or Accounts by simply dragging an Outlook Contact record to the appropriate BCM folder. And, if you have existing Outlook calendar items and/or tasks, you can link them to a BCM record. Linking activities to a BCM record increases Outlook's basic calendaring function by creating a history of all the interactions you've had with a specific Business Contact or Account.

Here's all you need to do to link your existing activities to a BCM record:

1. **From Outlook, select the Calendar or Tasks folder from the Navigation pane.**

2. **Double-click the appointment or task that you want to link to a record.**

   The corresponding activity opens up. It's quite a bit simpler than the one you use to schedule appointments in BCM. However, in Figure 2-6, you can see that a special Business (BCM) area appears on the Ribbon.

3. **Click Link to Record on the Business tab of the Ribbon.**

   The Link to Business Contact Manager Record dialog box opens.

Business tab

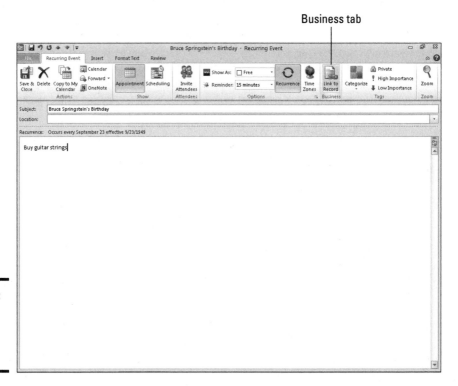

Figure 2-6:
Linking an
Outlook
appoint-
ment.

4. **Select the record type that you want — Accounts, Business Contacts, Leads, Opportunities, or Business Projects — from the Item Type drop-down list.**

5. **Type the name of the record that you want to attach to the activity in the Search box or select the name from the list.**

   You can link multiple records to an appointment by holding down the Ctrl key while you select the records.

6. **Click the Link To button to add the selected Account, Business Contact, Lead, Opportunity, or Business Project record to the Linked Records box.**

7. **Click OK to close the Link to Business Contact Manager Record dialog box, and then click Save & Close to save the appointment.**

   From this point forward, you'll be able to view the activity directly from the BCM record by clicking History on the Show tab of a record's Ribbon. More importantly, you'll be able to see in an instant an entire history of all the interactions you've had with the record.

Linking a BCM record to a new Outlook item

Just as you can link an existing Outlook item to BCM, you can also create a new Outlook appointment, e-mail message, or task that's automatically linked to the open BCM record. Follow these steps:

1. **Create or select an Account, Business Contact, Opportunity, or Business Project record.**

   If you've already created the BCM record, you can simply select the record — you don't have to open it.

2. **Click the desired action in the Communicate section of the Ribbon.**

   For example, you might want to schedule a Meeting with an Account, or send an e-mail to a Contact. You can see a sneak preview of the BCM Ribbon in Figure 2-7.

Book VII Chapter 2

Introducing the Basic Business Contact Manager

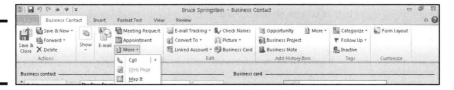

Figure 2-7: The BCM Ribbon.

3. **(Optional) Click More.**

   In addition to the options that are visible on the Ribbon you'll find even more options lurking in the More drop-down list such as Call and Map It.

Once you've selected an activity, the corresponding Outlook form opens and you can proceed to fill in the form as usual. This process in BCM has only one crucial difference than when you're creating those items in Outlook: The new items now link back to a BCM record.

Turning Your Business into a Major Project

While you delve into the various features of Business Contact Manager, you may start thinking of BCM as a super-sized version of Outlook. Everyone knows (or should know) that Outlook allows you to create tasks and appointments. BCM takes the concept one — or three — steps further by allowing you to group together all the tasks and appointments that relate to a single project. Even better, you can assign the various project tasks to an authorized user of your Business Contact Manager database.

Projecting your Business Projects

The first step in working on a project is to create it. Okay, that step seems a bit obvious, but using BCM can help you break a huge undertaking down into smaller, bite-sized pieces. In BCM, a Business Project, such as a trade show or conference, can include several project tasks that you need to delegate to various people in your organization, who need to complete those tasks. When you think of completed tasks — or think of new ones — you can enter them in BCM, where you can track their progress. Alternatively, you can put all your tasks on sticky notes, but then you're going to have to spend a lot of your time praying that no one turns on the paddle fan!

To create a Business Project in BCM, follow these steps:

1. **Click Business Projects in the BCM area of the Outlook Folder list on the Navigation pane.**

2. **Click the New Business Project icon in the New section on the Home tab of the Ribbon.**

Alternatively, you can click the New Items icon in the Home section of the Ribbon and select Business Project.

Not surprisingly, the Business Project form appears, and it looks exactly like the one in Figure 2-8.

3. **Fill in the pertinent details of the project.**

You can start by adding as much — or as little — information as you want. Here are a few of your options:

- *Project Name:* You can't tell a book by its cover, and you can't keep track of your projects without a good title.

- *Project Type:* If you have a whole lot of projects going on, you can group them together according to type.

- *Link To:* If your project revolves around one of your big Business Contacts or Accounts, you can link to it so that you can cross-reference your projects by Account or Business Contact.

- *Status Information:* Fill in a couple of the important details in this section of the form, including the start and due dates, the status, and the priority of the project.

- *Related Accounts and Business Contacts:* In this section, you can add the entire cast of characters who will be working on your project with you.

- *Project Tasks:* Add as many new tasks to the project as you want — and assign them to whomever you want!

4. **Click Save & Close in the Actions section of the Ribbon when you finish creating the Business Project.**

   You'll now see a list of all your projects when you click the Business Projects folder in the Business Contact Manager section of the Navigation pane.

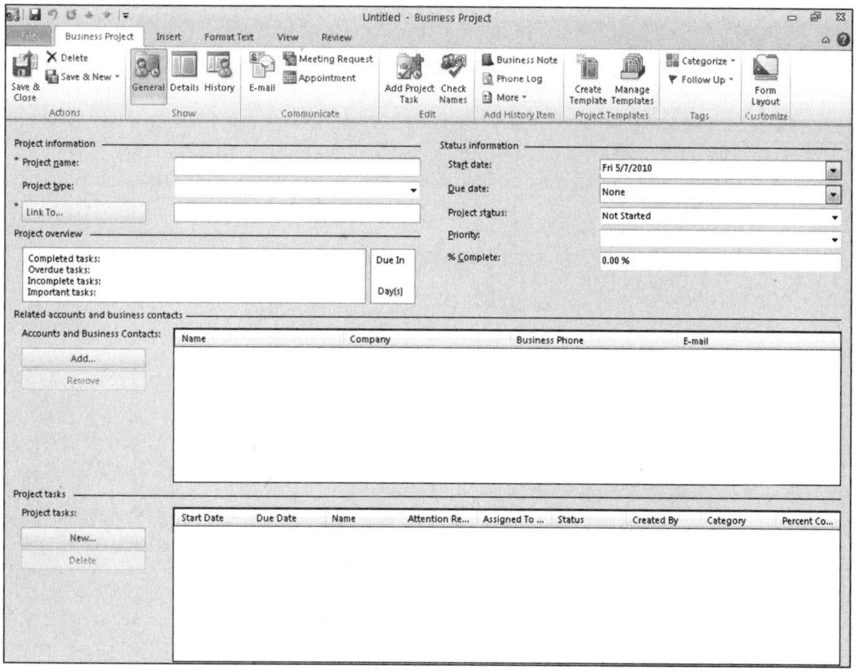

Figure 2-8:
Creating a
Business
Project.

Chipping away at a Business Project

A Business Project can contain multiple tasks assigned to multiple victims. When a project task is assigned to you, rise to the occasion and complete the task. When you complete your tasks, you can record that information in Outlook so that everyone involved in the project can track the progress of the project.

You can access your project-related tasks in two ways:

✦ Double-click the task from the Project Tasks folder in the Business Contact Manager area of the Navigation Pane. You can see what a list of tasks looks like in Figure 2-9.

✦ Click the Business Projects folder in the Business Contact Manager area of Outlook's Navigation pane and then double-click one of the Business Projects. Double-click a task in the Project Tasks area on the General tab of the Business Project.

After you've changed the Status field to Completed and saved the task, the latest information from the task appears in the linked Business Project form. If you complete the task, you can recognize that important milestone because Outlook crosses off the task in your Project Tasks folder, and the status appears as Completed in the Project Tasks section of the Project record.

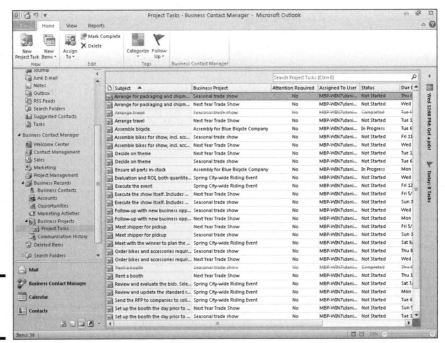

Figure 2-9:
Accessing
BCM tasks.

Tracking your project progress

If you're the owner of a business, you probably sleep better at night knowing that your project is progressing its way to completion. Or, if you're an overworked and underpaid employee, you may sleep better at night knowing that you're job is a bit more secure because you've organized your various Business Projects extremely well. In either case, we assume that you're the project manager for this project and that you need to make sure that you keep the project on track.

When you see that the assigned person has (or people have) completed various tasks within a Business Project, update the overall progress of the Business Project itself by following these steps:

1. **Open the Business Project that you want to edit.**

You can find all your Business Projects neatly arranged in the BCM section of Outlook's Folder list. When you double-click one of them, the Business Project form springs to life.

2. **Change the Project Status and % Complete entries in the Status Information section of the Business Project record.**

Typically you'll want the Project Status to reflect a major milestone such as In Progress or Deferred. The % Complete is your best-guess estimate of how far along you are on the project. Figure 2-8 shows the Project Status field, where you can track the status of the project.

3. **View the important information about the status in the Project Overview section.**

BCM keeps a running tally of where you stand in each of your projects. As you change the status of a task, BCM will automatically update the Project Overview area to reflect how many tasks are overdue, and how many you still have left to complete — and how many days remain until your final deadline! You even get a large countdown number reminding you of how many days are left until the due date.

4. **Click Save & Close when you finish editing the project.**

Bidding your project adieu

If you feel that old news is . . . well . . . old news, you may want to remove your Business Projects from BCM when you complete them.

When you delete a Business Project, you also lose all the content of that project. You may want to keep completed projects on file and not delete them so that you can refer back to them if you find yourself dealing with a similar project again in the future.

You can archive your old information, instead of deleting it.

To delete a Business Project do one of the following:

+ Open the Business Project and click Delete from the Actions section of the Ribbon.

+ Select the Business Project on the Folder list and then click the Delete icon on the Home section of the Ribbon.

+ Right-click the Business Project on the Folder list and select Delete from the pop-up menu that appears.

Just in case you accidentally deleted the *wrong* Business Project — or if you just plain changed your mind — you can easily recover the deleted Business Project by dragging it out of the BCM Deleted Items folder back to the Business Projects folder or by selecting it in the Deleted Items Folder and clicking the Restore button from the Home section of the Ribbon. Whew! Alternatively, you can delete the Business Project from the Deleted Items folder if you're really positive you never want to look at that project again!

Chapter 3: Working with Opportunities

In This Chapter

✔ **Creating an opportunity**

✔ **Tweaking existing opportunities**

✔ **Working with products and services**

*I*n this chapter, you can discover how to use BCM to work with your sales process. You can find out how to create an initial opportunity and update the sale while it makes its way through the sales funnel. For good measure, we even show you how to add new products and services into the mix.

Creating a New Opportunity

In BCM, an *Opportunity* is a potential sale to a Business Contact or Account, and you must associate each opportunity with either a Business Contact or Account. When you create an opportunity, you're actually creating a new item in much the same way that you create a new Business Contact or Account. (You can flip back to Chapter 2 of this minibook for more details on how exactly you go about doing those particular tasks.) When you create an opportunity, you can include the names of your products or services, specify a sales stage and forecasted close date, and even add your own user-defined fields. If you prefer, you can create a new opportunity directly from a Business Contact or Account record.

After creating an opportunity, you can go to the Opportunity folder, where your Opportunities are listed together, or view the Business Contact's or Account's History tab. As if that isn't enough, you can choose from a slew of Opportunities reports or access one of the neat Opportunities dashboards that, like your car's dashboard, shows you graphical representations about what's going on in your business.

You can make your first million — and track it in BCM — in a number of ways:

✦ From either the Business Contacts or Accounts folder, right-click a Business Contact or Account and choose Create➪New Opportunity from the menu that appears.

✦ While adding or editing a Business Contact or Account record, click History in the Show area of the Ribbon, and then choose New➪Opportunity.

✦ Click the drop-down arrow on New Items icon on the Outlook Ribbon, and then select Opportunity from the drop-down list.

Whatever your method, you're immediately transported to the opportunity's General tab, shown in Figure 3-1.

If you didn't know better, you'd think that you're looking at a Business Contact or Account record, and you enter some very similar information. Here's a rundown of the information to add. These fields hang out together in organized bundles:

✦ **Opportunity Information area:** Contains pretty much the must-have fields that you need to fill in:

    • *Opportunity Title:* This field is mandatory, we suppose, so that you can keep your opportunities apart. Feel free to name the opportunity with an important tidbit of information, such as "This one will finance my kids' education."

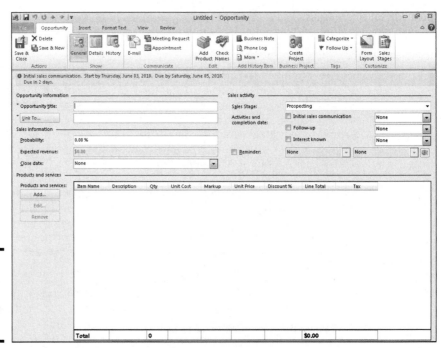

Figure 3-1:
Entering a new Opportunity record.

- *Link To:* This required field links the opportunity to a Business Contact or Account. Click the button, and a window appears. In this window, you can select an account, click the Link To button, and then click OK to attach the Account to the opportunity. If you prefer, change the Item Type drop-down list to Business Contacts and link one of your Business Contacts to the new opportunity. (Keep in mind that an Opportunity can only be linked to one record.)

✦ **Sales Information and Sales Activity areas:** Where you track a deal while it moves through the sales process. These areas contain a number of fields:

- *Sales Stage:* A sales stage helps you track the progress of your Opportunity. You can select a sales stage, such as Prospecting or Proposal/Price Quote from the drop-down list.

- *Probability:* As an Opportunity moves through the sales process, you can update the Probability that the sale will be completed. For example, an Opportunity in the Needs Analysis stage might only have a 50% chance of closing whereas an Opportunity that is in the Negotiation/Review stage could have a 75% chance of closing.

- *Dates:* At different sales stages, you have a number of different dates that you can use to help you track where you are in the sales process — and where you need to be. You can, for example, indicate the Close Date that you think your red-hot opportunity will convert into cold hard cash; the Delivery Date reminds you of when your client should receive your product; and even a reminder date that will cause Outlook to sound an alarm on the given date.

TIP

You may want to set a reminder to follow up with the people who are trying to give you some of their hard-earned money. The Reminder field consists of Date and Time drop-down lists, and an Alarm button. Click the Alarm button to open a dialog box, where you can select the alarm sound of your choice — a loud ka-ching is certainly appropriate.

✦ **Products and Services areas:** This will show you a list of all the products that you are trying to sell, their dollar amount, and the total value of the Opportunity. You can learn how to add products to an Opportunity later in this chapter in the Adding Products and Services to an Opportunity section.

Click Save & Close when you finish entering the basic opportunity information. Or, if your business is really on a roll, click Save & New to forge on to your next opportunity.

Finding More Opportunity in Your Opportunities

At times, your head may be swimming with all the BCM information that you're attempting to cram into it. Don't get discouraged if you don't feel like you're mastering all the bells and whistles immediately. One of the fun parts of Outlook is delving deeper and deeper into its features.

Book VII
Chapter 3

Working with Opportunities

The preceding section walks you through the creation of a basic opportunity. The following sections show you how you can take the opportunity and run with it. Who knows, you may even score a touchdown — or, at least, a really large sale!

Wrapping a ribbon around an opportunity

Just like in other records in BCM, the Ribbon at the top of the window gives you a few more places to store your data, as well as a few more functions to help keep track of your opportunities. A few of the areas are specific to opportunities, including

✦ **Details:** You can add a few more pertinent notes to the Opportunity by clicking Details in the Show area of the Ribbon. We're not quite sure why this window is called Details when the only thing it contains is a huge area in which you can add time-stamped comments.

✦ **Categorize:** The Categorize button (found in the Tags section of the Ribbon) isn't specific to opportunities; you see its identical twins throughout Outlook. However, the concept of using categories is so important that it deserves an extra mention. You can learn more about Outlook's categories by taking a look at Book VIII, Chapter 1.

Editing an opportunity

You may want to edit an opportunity for two main reasons:

✦ You forgot to add some information the first time, or some of your original information requires a bit of tweaking. (That's an official computer term.)

✦ You want to track the progress of the opportunity while it makes its way from freezing cold to super hot.

Follow these steps to make a change to an existing opportunity:

1. **Click Opportunities from the Business Contact Manager area on the Navigation pane.**

The Opportunities list opens. (See Figure 3-2.)

2. **Double-click the opportunity that you want to edit.**

The opportunity record appears.

Not sure how to find the opportunity you're looking for? You can type your search criterion into the Search box at the top of the Opportunity list and then click the Search (magnifying-glass) button.

3. **Update information, as necessary.**

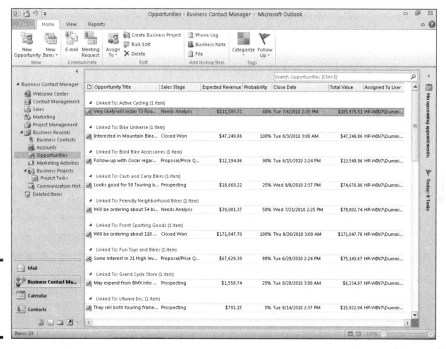

**Book VII
Chapter 3**

Working with Opportunities

Figure 3-2:
BCM's Opportunities list.

In addition to adding information that you omitted the first time, you want to make sure that you change the information in the Sales Stage field. This update helps keep you on top of the opportunity while it makes its way along the path of your sales pipeline. Also, while you work your way through the stages, the probability of closing becomes higher and higher.

4. **Click Save & Close when you finish making all your changes.**

Closing the deal

And now the moment you've waited for — drum roll, please — it's time to close the deal. All those hours of sweat chasing that prospect are going to (hopefully) pay off in spades.

You close a deal in the exact same way that you edit one — by opening an existing opportunity. At that point, you select either Closed Won (yippee) or Closed Lost (gasp!) from the Sales Stage drop-down list. When you make this change, notice the following:

✦ All existing fields go gray, which means that you can no longer enter any additional information into them.

✦ The probability changes to 100% if you selected Closed Won and 0% if you selected Closed Lost.

✦ The boss either greets you with a cigar and a slap on the back, or a pink slip.

Deleting an opportunity

In general, you're better off marking an opportunity as Closed Lost instead of just deleting it. You can often gain valuable insight from a lost opportunity: Maybe one of your competitors is offering a new product, or someone else is selling a comparable product for half the price. Other times, you may just want to get rid of the evidence: Perhaps the company you were selling to closed its doors for good, or maybe you inadvertently entered in the same opportunity twice. Whatever the reason, the procedure for removing unwanted opportunities is as simple as choosing one of these methods:

✦ Right-click the Opportunity record from the Opportunities Folder list and select Delete from the pop-up menu that appears.

✦ Double-click the Opportunity record to open it, and then click the Delete button on the Ribbon.

✦ Highlight the Opportunity record in the Opportunities Folder list and press Ctrl+D.

As soon as you perform one of the preceding operations, your opportunity disappears. Quickly. Without further warning.

Make a mistake? Fortunately, when you delete an opportunity, it's gone, but certainly not forgotten. It's sitting in the Business Contact Manager's Deleted Items folder, just waiting to be rescued. To do so, just drag it back to the Opportunities folder or select the item in the Deleted Items Folder and click the Restore button from the Home section of the Ribbon. To delete it permanently, give it a right-click in the Deleted Items folder and select OK from the pop-up menu that appears.

Adding Products and Services to an Opportunity

After you create an opportunity, you can add specific products and services to it. If you're like most people, this part is fun because those products and services come with a price tag — which hopefully translates into money in your pocket.

In an existing Opportunity record, the Product and Services area runs along the bottom of the Opportunity window when the General button selected. In this area, you get to count the cash, bill for the beans, dream of the dollars. . . . In any event, the Products and Services portion of this tab is where you get to add all the line items for your opportunity and sit back while BCM crunches the numbers for you.

Follow these steps to start counting those beans:

1. Click the Add button in the Products and Services area, or click Add Product in the Edit section of the Ribbon.

The Add Product or Service dialog box, shown in Figure 3-3, appears.

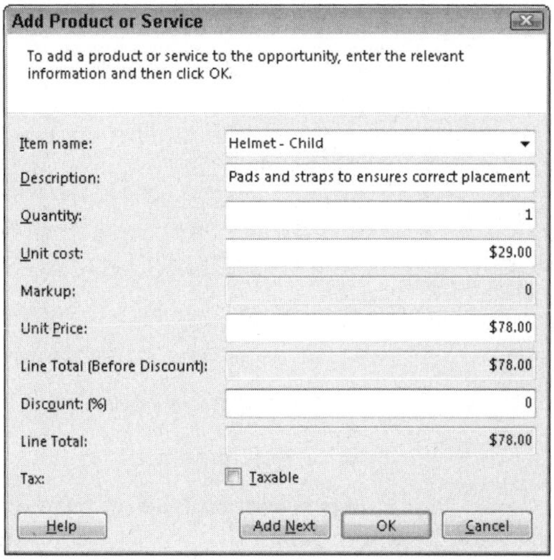

Figure 3-3:
The Add Product or Service dialog box.

Book VII Chapter 3

Working with Opportunities

2. Click the Item Name drop-down arrow and select the name of the product from the list of existing products.

Alternatively, you can simply type the first several letters of a product name if you're already familiar with the items in your product list.

3. (Optional) Scroll to the bottom of the Item name list and select Edit This List if you don't see the product that you need; if you don't need to add a product, skip to Step 8.

The Products and Services dialog box appears. Amazingly, it looks just like Figure 3-4.

All the products and services that you've created in BCM are proudly displayed in the Products and Services window.

4. Click the Add button to make the Add Product or Service dialog box appear.

It looks very much like the Add Product or Service dialog box shown in Figure 3-3, except that this one has no place to add a discount.

5. Fill in the juicy details, and then click Save.

You'll return to the Products and Services dialog box.

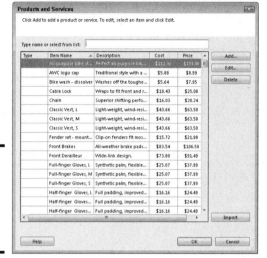

Figure 3-4:
The
Products
and
Services
dialog box.

6. **Click OK to close the Products and Services dialog box.**

   The Add Product or Service dialog box appears.

7. **Click the Item Name drop-down arrow and select the name of the product you just added from the list.**

8. **In the Quantity field of the Add Product or Service dialog box, enter the quantity that you're going to sell of the item.**

   When you set up your product list, you can set up a default quantity. Feel free to change it each time you create a new opportunity. When you change the quantity, the Line Total (Before Discount) field changes, as well. You doubting Thomases in the crowd may want to grab a calculator and check the math — don't worry, it's correct!

9. **(Optional) Change the Unit Cost and the Unit Price values.**

   You can't enter anything in the Markup field because BCM is doing the math for you.

10. **(Optional) Type a Discount percentage.**

    Ooh and aah when the Line Total totals up for you. Okay, you don't have to ooh and aah — or if you do, do it quietly so that the rest of the office doesn't think you have a stomach ache.

11. **Click OK if this product is the only one you're entering.**

    Click Add Next if you want to add another product, and then repeat Steps 2 to 11. Once you click the OK button you will end up back at the Opportunity where you'll be able to admire all the products and services that you've added.

After you add products to an Opportunity, you can

✦ Highlight a line item and click the Edit button if you need to modify one of the products.

✦ Highlight a line item and click the Remove button if you want to remove an item from the Opportunity record. A dialog box appears, asking whether you're sure you want to remove the item — the answer is Yes, so click that button.

Also, at the bottom of the Products and Services table, you can find the grand total for Quantity and Line Total. In addition, BCM calculates the Expected Revenue field based on the probability percentage and the total of all your line items.

Editing or Deleting a Product or Service

You can edit or delete a product or service in the Product and Services dialog box. By now, you probably don't need a road map because you found your way there when you added new products. However, just in case you spilled coffee on your map, here are the necessary directions.

1. **Click Opportunities from the Business Contact Manager Folder list.**

2. **Open an existing opportunity by double-clicking it.**

3. **Click Add in the Products and Services area.**

The Add Product or Service dialog box opens.

4. **Click the Item Name drop-down list, scroll to the bottom of the list, and select Edit This List.**

The Products and Services dialog box springs to life.

5. **Click a product or service to select it.**

6. **Click Edit to open the Edit Product or Service dialog box, where you can change the item name, description, default quantity, unit cost, or unit price of a product of service. Click Save to save your changes.**

Alternatively you can click Delete to remove a product or service.

7. **Click OK to close the Products and Services dialog box, and then Cancel to close the Add Product or Service dialog box.**

When you delete a product, it doesn't end up in the Deleted Items folder. If you choose to Delete rather than Edit a product a rather ominous warning appears; take heed — the product disappears permanently from the product list.

Chapter 4: Reports and Dashboards

In This Chapter

✔ Meeting the BCM reports

✔ Using a BCM report

✔ Modifying the format of a report

✔ Making changes to information in a report

✔ Working with Dashboards

After you fill your Business Contact Manager database with lots of records, activities and opportunities, you can do the fun part — sitting back and using it. In this chapter, you can find out about the various BCM reports and Dashboards. I also include basic information on editing report templates.

Knowing the Basic BCM Reports

BCM comes with a menu of over 70 basic reports right out of the box. At least one of the basic BCM reports can probably give you exactly the information that you're looking for, so you don't even have to customize it.

You can access the BCM reports from any of the BCM folders on the Navigation pane. After you click on a folder, you'll see the Reports tab on the Ribbon. As Figure 4-1 shows you, the BCM report tab is divided into four sections; these sections reflect four of the most valuable areas of BCM:

Figure 4-1:
BCM's
Reports tab

+ **Contact Management:** Microsoft knows that your BCM Accounts and Business Contacts drive your business, so BCM comes equipped with 13 Accounts reports, 15 Business Contacts reports, and two Leads reports. The title of most of these reports reflects how the Accounts are grouped together in the body of the report. For Example, Figure 4-2 shows you a sample of the Accounts by Rating report, which groups Accounts by the rating (ranging from Poor to Excellent) that you assign to them.

Leads reports give you different ways to view the new leads that are coming into your database. If you aren't tracking leads, these reports don't mean much to you. However, if you're paying a lot of money to get new leads for your database, you may find these reports invaluable.

If you're the boss, you may be wondering exactly what your employees are doing all day. If you're the employee, you may want to prove to your boss that you are indeed up to good things in your on-duty time. Either way, the Business Contact Activity Summary report might fit the bill. Or, you might find the birthday and anniversary reports helpful, such as the Business Contacts by Birthday report in Figure 4-3, if you want to send cards on those red letter days.

✦ **Sales:** BCM provides you with a variety of Sales reports, including nine Opportunities and two Top Customers reports. You can also find reports for Top Products, Top Referrers, and Dormant Customers in the Sales area.

The Opportunity reports use information that you entered into an Opportunity record. If you don't use the Opportunities feature, you also don't use these reports. An opportunity sales funnel or sales pipeline is an important part of the sales process; you can see BCM's version in Figure 4-4.

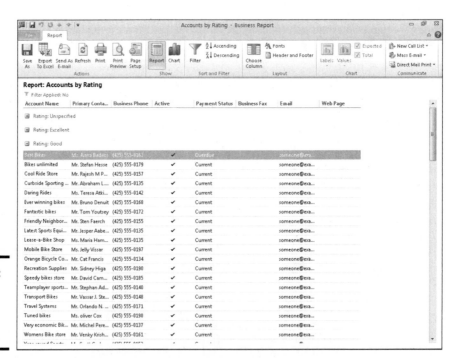

Figure 4-2:
The Accounts by Rating report.

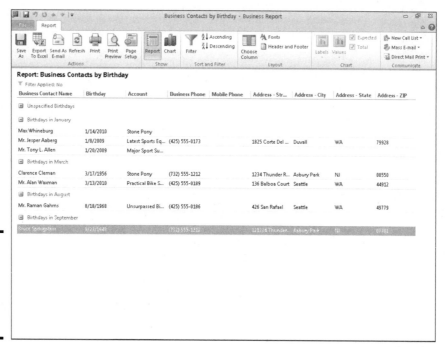

Figure 4-3:
The Business Contacts by Birthday report.

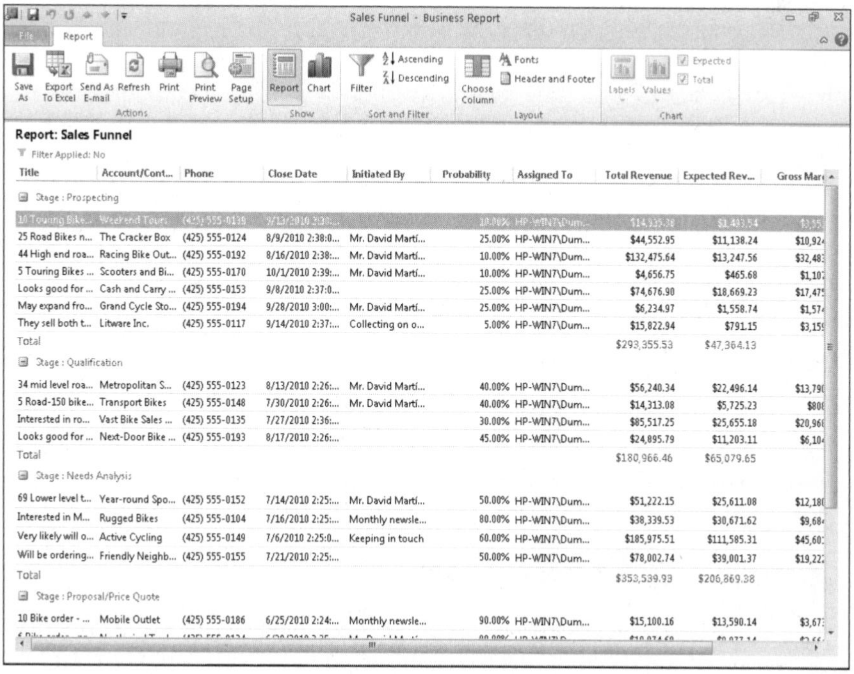

Figure 4-4:
The Sales Funnel report.

Chapter 3 of this mini-book tells you everything you need to know about Opportunities — and then some!

✦ **Marketing:** We think that we can safely make one major assumption about your marketing campaigns: If they don't result in new business, they're not worth the time and money you spend on them. The BCM Marketing reports give you a handle on your marketing campaigns.

✦ **Project Management:** One of the strengths of Outlook has always been its ability to help you schedule and follow up on tasks. BCM runs with that concept and takes it to a whole new level. You can think of a project as a super-sized task. Whereas a task involves one chore that one individual needs to do, a project involves a multitude of tasks that, in general, several individuals need to do over a period of time. BCM offers ten Business Projects and five Project Tasks reports to help you keep track of your projects. Figure 4-5 shows you an example of the Business Projects by Status report.

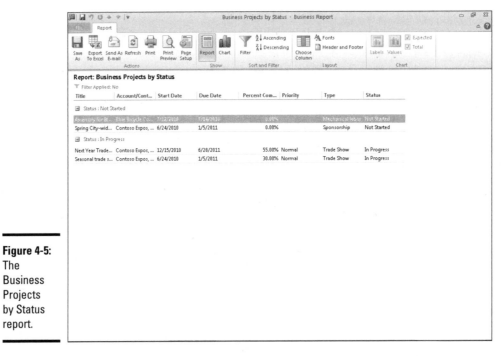

Figure 4-5: The Business Projects by Status report.

Running a BCM Report

You can create a BCM report ridiculously easily — just select a report by clicking it. Follow these steps to run any one of the out-of-the-box BCM reports:

1. **From Outlook, click the Business Contact Manager folder, and then click the Reports tab.**

   The Ribbon now reflects the report options. (Refer to Figure 4-1.)

2. **Click the drop-down arrow of the report category that you want to run.**

   Here's the fun part — you get to pick which type of report you want. For the purpose of the rest of this chapter, we use an Account report.

3. **Select the specific report that you want from the drop-down list.**

   In a flash, your report springs to life.

4. **Click a column heading to re-sort your report.**

   By default, most of the BCM reports appear in alphabetical order. If you're left-handed — or just enjoy seeing your reports sorted in Z-to-A order — you can reverse the sort order with a single click of any column heading.

5. **Change the order of the columns by dragging them to a new location.**

   If you're not thrilled with the order in which the columns appear in the report — or if you just like to exercise a bit of control — drag a column to a new location by holding down your left mouse button on a column head, move it to the left or right, and then release the button when you have the column positioned where you want it.

6. **Save, export, e-mail, or print your report.**

   **Book VII
Chapter 4**

   You can see all the options on the Ribbon in Figure 4-5. Click the one that you want and sit back while BCM does all the work. The Export to Excel option works well if you want to share the report with a non-BCM user. The Send As E-mail option has to be one of the neatest of the report features; BCM thinks about it momentarily and then opens a new e-mail message with your report already attached as an Excel attachment.

   **Reports and
Dashboards**

   Don't forget to save your report prior to closing it because BCM doesn't prompt you to save the report when you close it.

   You can easily convert many of the reports into graphical charts by clicking the Chart icon on the Show area of the Ribbon. (Again, refer to Figure 4-5.) After your report morphs into a chart, you might want to make a few changes by selecting one of the Chart options that appear on the Chart area of the Ribbon.

7. **When you finish working with the report, simply press the Esc key to close it.**

Giving Your Reports a Facelift

You probably want to modify a basic report somewhat — or even give it a complete makeover. If that sounds like you, then start by tweaking some of the fields already on your report template. You can remove one or two of the existing columns and replace them with columns that are more to your liking. You may decide to make the font a wee bit larger to accommodate your 40-something eyes. The more ornery members of the crowd may not be happy with the order in which the fields appear in one of the reports, so you might want to move them around. These changes are simple if you know the tricks.

Modifying an existing report

You probably first want to decide which fields will — or won't — appear in your report. Being familiar with the structure of your existing database can prove helpful during this process. Thus, you need to know the field names that you're working with. For example, if you want to include the name of a company, you must know that the field containing that information is called Account.

After you make the momentous decision of determining which fields you want to appear in your report, follow these steps to get the job done:

1. **Open the report that's closest to what you're looking for.**

With more than 70 reports to choose from, why choose a report that's not even close to what you want when another report can almost do the trick? For this example, we use the Quick Accounts List report.

2. **Click Choose Column in the Layout area of the Ribbon. (Refer to Figure 4-5.)**

At this juncture, the Customize Report: Choose Column dialog box, shown in Figure 4-6, snaps to attention. The dialog box allows you to determine which columns end up appearing in the report.

Figure 4-6:
The
Customize
Report
dialog box.

3. **Click the plus sign (+) to the left of one of the column types to display more field choices.**

   You probably first want to modify your report by adding or removing the columns that you see in the existing database. Each column of a BCM report is based on a field in an Account, Business Contact, Opportunity, or Business Project record.

   Depending on the report you select, you have different column types available to you:

   - *Basic:* Contains the basic record fields. Your choices vary, depending on the type of report you're running. For example, an Account report displays Account fields, and an Opportunity report displays Opportunity fields.

   - *Business Address:* Provides you with postal address fields, including City, State, and Zip Code, for reports on your Business Contacts and Accounts.

   - *Contact:* Helps you contact an Account or Business Contact, including fax, phone, Web address, and e-mail address.

   - *Mail:* Shows the recipient, sender, and date of an e-mail message; these options appear only on reports that provide information about e-mail activity.

   - *Tracking:* Shows the date that an Account or Business Contact was created or modified, as well as the person who did the creating or modifying.

   - *Custom:* Allows you to use the customized fields that you added to your Account, Business Contact, Opportunity, or Business Project records.

4. **Select the check box to the left of any field that you want to add to your report.**

   You can check as many fields as you want; BCM adds the fields that you check as new columns at the end of the report.

5. **Deselect the check boxes to the left of any columns that you don't want to appear in your report.**

   Sorry to be the bearer of bad news, but most paper holds only a finite number of columns. If you add a bunch of columns, you probably want to remove a few, as well.

6. **Rearrange the columns on your report by clicking on a column heading and then dragging it to the left or right.**

   You'll be amazed at how easily you can drag a column — and all the information that it contains — to a new spot on your report.

7. **(Optional) Click the Save As icon on the Actions area of the Ribbon.**

If you've made lots of customizations BCM cheerfully saves your report for future use. Want to use the report again? You can find it by clicking the Saved Reports icon in the Open area of the Ribbon. (Refer to Figure 4-1.)

8. **Press the Esc key to close the report.**

Filtering out the bad stuff

You can modify your BCM reports by changing the content of the report. You can create filters to determine what data you want to appear in your report. For example, you might want an Opportunities report to only include Opportunities for a specific sales person, or a Business Contact report that only includes contacts in specific states. Although you can create complex queries, the process that you follow is quite simple. Follow these steps:

1. **Open the report to which you want to add filters.**

2. **Click the Filter icon in the Sort and Filter area of the Ribbon. (Refer to Figure 4-5.)**

   The Filter Accounts dialog box, shown in Figure 4-7, appears.

   For this example, we use the Quick Accounts List report. The options in Figure 4-7 may be slightly different than the ones you see if you filter a different report. No problem — the concepts work exactly the same.

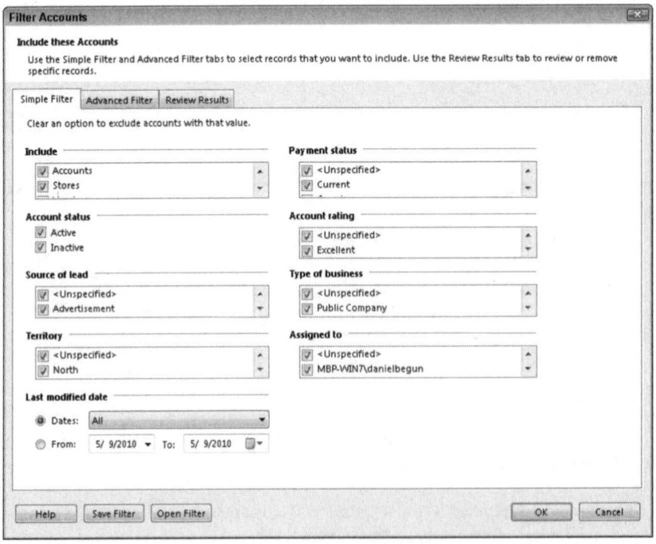

Figure 4-7:
Filtering a
BCM report.

3. **Check the options for the data that you want to appear in your report.**

If you're one of those people who have trouble deciding what flavor you want at the local ice cream shop, then you may have problems in this dialog box because you have a lot of choices. However, if you believe the more the merrier, then you should have a field day.

Each option represents one of the fields in the Account, Business Contact, Opportunity, or Business Project on which you're reporting. The choices within the option appear in the drop-down list for that field. In our example of the Quick Accounts List report, the option Account Status, which represents one of the Account record fields, includes the option choices of Active or Inactive.

You really have a lot of information to choose from when filtering a report — and not all of it's readily visible. Scroll bar indicators appear to the right of many of the fields, which means that you have more field choices to choose from. If you're interested in seeing — or not seeing — information from a given field, give those scroll bars a scroll.

4. **(Optional) Click the Advanced Filter tab.**

    After you conquer the Simple Filter tab, you might want to create advanced filters that find data within a given range. For example, an advanced filter can help you find all your top-rated Accounts in the cities of Chicago, New York, and Los Angeles.

5. **(Optional) Click the Review Results tab.**

    A list of the records that meet your filtering criteria appears as well as a physical count of the number of records found.

6. **(Optional) Click Save Filter.**

    The only thing worse than doing work is having to do the same work over again. After you slave over the various filter options, you may want to save your work so that you don't have to reapply all the changes that you've made. BCM assigns your saved query the .bcmq extension.

    If you already saved a query, you can click Open Filter to open an existing filter.

7. **Click OK to apply the filter.**

    At this point, you can print the report, save it, or just close it.

Drilling for Dollars in Your Reports

The entire purpose of a BCM report is to provide you with accurate, up-to-the-minute information. And, before you hit that Print button, review your report to make sure that all the report information is correct. For example, you might notice that the report doesn't have a phone number for one of your best clients, or it lists that client as inactive.

BCM's ability to edit information on the fly from within a report is a great way to both modify incorrect and add missing information.

Giving your reports a helping hand

Drill is the official computer term for the ability to zoom into report information in order to view and/or edit it. Follow these steps to drill into your report:

1. **Move your mouse over the area of your report where you see inaccurate or missing information.**

2. **Double-click that report item.**

   Zoom! You're transported to the BCM record that stores the information. For example, if you're looking at a Business Contact report and notice that a phone number is missing, give that contact a double-click. The corresponding Business Contact record appears.

3. **Make your changes.**

   In this case, more is more. In addition to missing a phone number, you might notice that the City and State fields are also blank. You may as well make as many corrections as you want.

4. **Click the Save & Close icon to save any changes you've made and to close the record.**

   Double zoom! You land with a thump back in your report.

Having a refreshing look at your report

After you change the information that appears in your report, you probably want to gaze fondly at the new data. But wait. What happened? The new information didn't magically appear! Typically, you first blame yourself and redo the steps you followed to correct information. And it still doesn't work! At this point, you're probably composing a nasty letter to Microsoft in your head complaining about the BCM reports.

In order to speed up the works, BCM doesn't *refresh* the report information until you tell it to do so. BCM includes this delay to allow you to correct many items in your report without having to wait for the report to reappear on your screen.

You can get that new information to appear by clicking the Refresh icon (it looks like two arrows on top of one another) in the Actions section of the Ribbon.

Whew! Problem solved.

Creating an Excel-ent report

As hard as it may be to believe, not everyone you deal with uses BCM, and you have to get the report to them in a manner that they can use. As usual, BCM provides you with two solutions for transporting your report from Point A to Point B, both of which you can access from the BCM Reports menu:

✔ Click the Export To Excel icon in the Actions area of the Ribbon to create a spreadsheet version of the current report.

✔ Click the Send As E-mail icon in the Actions area of the Ribbon to create an e-mail message that includes your report as an attached Excel spreadsheet. You can see an example in this figure.

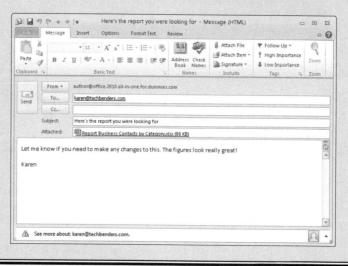

**Book VII
Chapter 4**

**Reports and
Dashboards**

Working with Dashboards

A *dashboard* is a panel below the windshield of a vehicle that contains dials, compartments, and instrument controls. In case you're wondering why a book about Outlook is talking about car parts, it's because *Dashboards* in computer software are very cool areas that contain several graphical snapshots of your information. A *Gadget* is the official name for the various graphics that you find on a Dashboard. In BCM, you can determine which of the Gadgets you want to view on a Dashboard.

Figure 4-8 shows a sample of a Dashboard that displays several Gadgets.

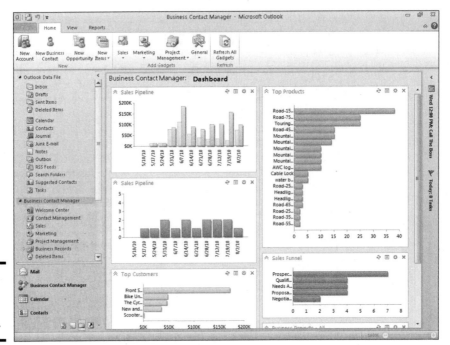

Figure 4-8:
A sample
of a BCM
Dashboard.

You can view a BCM Dashboard by clicking the Business Contact Manager, Contact Management, Sales, Marketing, or Project Management folders on the Navigation pane.

Now comes the best part — you can easily customize your Dashboards and filter the Gadgets to change the information that they show. Just follow these steps:

1. **Click Business Contact Manager on the Outlook Folder list.**

Several Gadgets appear on this Dashboard. See how easy it is to figure out the lingo?

2. **Right-click a Gadget-less area in the Dashboard pane.**

A pop-up menu of the Dashboard options appears. When viewing most of the Business Contact Manager folders, the choices look like what you see in Figure 4-9.

- **To close the Dashboard:** Select the Hide Gadgets option. (The Hide Gadgets option isn't available as an option, however, when you are viewing the Dashboard on the Business Contact Management folder.)

- **To add more Gadgets to the Dashboard:** Select one of the Gadget categories (Sales, Marketing, Project Management, or General), and then select a Gadget from the contextual menu. You have a total of 16 Gadgets to choose from.

3. **To move any Gadget to a new spot on the Dashboard, just hold the left mouse button down on the Gadget's title and drag the Gadget to its new position.**

   You can move the Gadget up or down, or even to a different column.

4. **Double-click a Gadget to edit or view more detailed information.**

   For example, you might be looking at the Top Products Gadget and have a burning desire to know exactly who's buying one of your products.

5. **Right-click a Gadget to open a pop-up menu that includes the Gadget's options.**

   As usual, BCM loves variety so you have a few choices here:

   - *Refresh:* Updates the information on the Gadget to reflect any changes you might have made.

   - *Open Report:* Displays more detailed information.

   - *Options:* Opens a menu, where you can define filters for the information in the Gadget. For example, you might want the Sales Funnel Gadget to reflect only information for the next 30 days.

   - *Remove:* Removes the Gadget from the Dashboard.

**Book VII
Chapter 4**

**Reports and
Dashboards**

Figure 4-9:
The Add
or Hide
Gadgets
menu.

Book VIII

Customizing Outlook

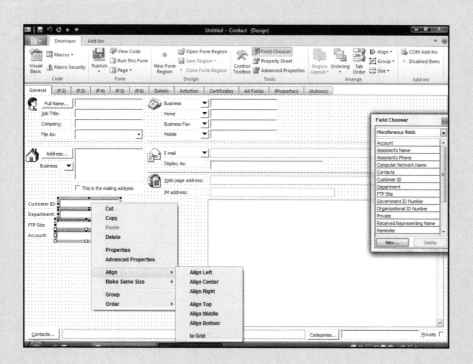

Contents at a Glance

Chapter 1: Organizing Items with Categories

In This Chapter

✓ Grouping similar items together by category

✓ Using Quick Click categories

✓ Adding and removing categories from an item

✓ Renaming, creating, and deleting categories

You can easily get overwhelmed with the amount of data that Outlook contains. A normal person probably receives dozens of e-mails a day, maintains hundreds of contacts, and tracks thousands of appointments per year. And some of that stuff should be grouped together somehow because it deals with the same project, company, or special segment of your life — such as your children. But with everything in Outlook organized by type (appointments in the Calendar and people in the Contacts list), how can you show that two dissimilar items belong together? The answer is by using *categories*.

After you assign a category to a group of items, you can search for them easily. See Book IX, Chapter 4 for help in searching.

Adding a Category to an Open Outlook Item

Outlook comes with six color categories, all with clever names such as Red Category, Green Category, and so on. The first time you choose a color category to assign to an item, you're prompted to rename it to something meaningful, such as the Salmon-Colored Category. No, actually you can supply a real name, such as ABC Company, Marketing Department Stuff, Personal, or Kids. If you have more than one brat (uh, kid), you can create a separate category for each one so that you can more easily see what Sadie, Anya, and Joey have scheduled for after school.

First, you name your categories and assign them to various Outlook items. Then, if you happen to find yourself looking in a Mail folder or viewing your Calendar, you can use the colors to quickly identify what category a particular item belongs to. So, if a marketing meeting conflicts with an appointment you have scheduled with an important client, you know which one you need to attend (the one with the better food, of course). You can even arrange items in a folder by category so that you can quickly group all e-mails related to the ABC account, for example. And if you run out of color categories, you can create more.

But first, you need to start assigning categories to items so that you can group similar things together visually. If you've opened an item, such as an e-mail message or an appointment, the Ribbon at the top of the form provides you with a quick way to assign a category. Follow these steps:

1. **In the open item, click the Categorize button in the Tags section of the form's Ribbon.**

   A menu listing all your current categories appears, like the one shown in Figure 1-1.

Figure 1-1:
Assigning
a category
when
reviewing
an item.

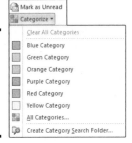

2. **Select a category.**

   If you have more than 15 categories and the one you want to use isn't listed, select All Categories from the list. The Color Categories dialog box appears. Select the category you want to assign and click OK. The listing that appears when you click the Categories button on the Ribbon contains the 15 most recently used categories, by the way; so, if you start using a certain category often, it shows up on the list.

   If this is your first time assigning this category, a dialog box appears prompting to rename it.

3. **Type a name for the category in the Name field of the Color Categories dialog box, and then click OK.**

   The color you chose in Step 2 appears in a band at the top of the form.

When you use a category for the first time, you can change the color assigned to the category and assign a shortcut. See the section "Managing Your Categories," later in this chapter, for help.

You can assign multiple categories to an item by simply repeating the preceding steps. For example, you might assign both the Key Client and ABC Company categories to the same appointment. All the categories you select will appear in the band on the top of your form.

When you close the item, the color appears in the Categories column in most list views, such as the Messages view in Mail. In the Calendar, meetings, appointments, and events appear as little colored rectangles. In some views, the colors don't appear at all, although you can modify a view so that it displays categories. See Book VIII, Chapter 2 to find out how to customize a view.

Adding a Category to an Item without Opening It

You don't have to bother opening an item to assign a category to it. Sure, when you're reading an e-mail or creating a new appointment, you may find it convenient to take the time to categorize each one by using the Categorize button on the form's Ribbon. But when you assign categories after the fact, you can much more easily just grab a bunch of messages and, boom, assign a category to them all.

Follow these steps:

1. **Select the item(s) that you want to categorize.**

To grab a bunch of items, press and hold Ctrl while you click each one. If the items are grouped together, hold down Shift and click the first one in the group, then click the last item in the group.

You can sort items so that you can easily select a bunch of them. See Chapter 2 in this minibook for more info.

2. **Right-click any of the selected items and select Categorize from the pop-up menu that appears.**

Alternatively, feel free to click the Categorize button in the Tags section of the Ribbon's Home tab.

3. **Select a category from the drop-down list that appears.**

If the category you want isn't on the list, select All Categories, select the category from the longer list that appears, and click OK.

If this is your first time assigning this category, a dialog box appears, asking whether you want to rename it.

4. **Unless you think Red Category fits the category's purpose, type a better name in the Name text box.**

Change the color for the category, if you like, and assign a shortcut (see the section, "Managing Your Categories," later in this chapter, for more info).

5. **Click OK.**

The color you chose appears in the Categories column next to the chosen items (assuming that the Categories column is included in the current view).

Assigning a Quick Click Category to an Item

Outlook offers a cool trick so that you can easily assign a frequently used category to any item you want (assuming the Categories column is displayed in the view you're using). First, you have to set the Quick Click category; then, you use it (with a quick click of the mouse) to assign that category to an item.

Follow these steps to set the Quick Click category:

1. **Click the Categorize button in the Tags section of the Ribbon's Home tab and select Set Quick Click from the pop-up menu that appears.**

The Set Quick Click dialog box, shown in Figure 1-2, appears.

Figure 1-2:
Select which category you use the most.

2. **Select the category you want to be able to assign with a single click, and then click OK.**

If this is the first time you're using a Category, Outlook asks you whether you want to rename the category.

3. **Fill in the new name for the Quick Click category.**

You'll notice that the previous name is now highlighted in blue. Simply start typing in the new, improved name and the old one will be replaced by your new one.

To assign the Quick Click category to an item, the Categories column must be displayed in the current view. It so happens that the Categories column appears in Messages view, the most common view in Mail. It also appears on the To-Do bar, which you can make appear in any module you want by selecting the View tab and then clicking the To-Do icon. You can even find the Categories column in most list (column-type) views in Calendar and Contacts. After the Categories column is displayed, just click to the right of your item in the Categories column to assign the Quick Click category to that item, as shown in Figure 1-3.

Figure 1-3:
Your
favorite
category
is a click
away.

One at a time not your thing? No problem, just select multiple items (by holding down Ctrl while you click each one). Then, click once in the Categories column to assign your favorite category to each of the selected items.

You can change the Quick Click category as often as you want; it doesn't affect items you've already categorized by using Quick Click.

Removing a Category from an Item

You can so easily assign categories to your Outlook items that it can sometimes get out of control. Kind of like a small tattoo — one might be okay, even tasteful. But 20 are just downright hard to look at. Follow these steps to remove a category from an item:

1. Select the item or items you want to change.

To remove a category from one item, select that item. If you want to remove the same category from several items, select all the items at the same time. Press and hold Ctrl while you click each item to select it; or click the first item, press and hold Shift, and click the last item in that group. Got 'em selected? Good.

2. Select the category to remove.

Yep, you remove categories from an item one at a time. You can do any of the following:

- *Click the Categorize button in the Tags section of the Ribbon's Home tab, and then select the category you want to remove from the pop-up menu that appears.* See Figure 1-4. Categories assigned to an item are highlighted in the Categories list (they appear with an orange border around the color block on the menu).

You can remove a category from an item that's open; just click the Categorize button on the form's Ribbon and, from the pop-up menu that appears, select the category that you want to remove.

**Book VIII
Chapter 1**

**Organizing Items
with Categories**

- *Click the Categories column to remove the Quick Click category if the Categories column happens to be showing.* Change to a list view, if needed, to display that column. In Mail and on the To-Do bar, however, you can remove any category (and not just the Quick Click category) by clicking in the Categories column. See Figure 1-4.

- *Right-click to remove a category.* To remove a single category from an item without making a trip to the Ribbon, right-click the item, select Categorize from the pop-up menu that appears, and then click the category you want to remove.

- *To remove all the categories from an item, click the Categorize button in the Tags section of the Ribbon's Home tab, and then select Clear All Categories from the pop-up menu that appears.* All the previously assigned categories will disappear.

Figure 1-4: Remove unwanted categories from an item one at a time.

Managing Your Categories

Outlook starts you off with six categories, but you can easily add more. You can also remove categories that you don't need any more and revisit existing categories at any time to rename them or assign them their own shortcut key.

Renaming a category

When you first used any one of Outlook's six categories, Outlook asked whether you wanted to rename the category. If you were sick that day or if you feel that the name you gave a category (even one you created yourself) simply doesn't work for you now, you can change it. Follow these steps:

1. Click the Categorize button in the Tags section of the Ribbon's Home tab, and then select All Categories from the pop-up menu that appears.

The Color Categories dialog box appears, as shown in Figure 1-5.

If you happen to have an item open and it has a category assigned to it, then a color bar (or bars, if more than one category has been assigned) appear near the top of the form window. Double-click this color bar to display the Color Categories dialog box.

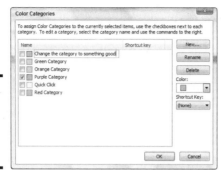

Figure 1-5:
Refine your
categories
with this
dialog box.

2. **Select the category that you want to change and click Rename.**

3. **Type a new name into the Name field, and then press Enter.**

4. **If you want to assign the category you're renaming to the currently selected item(s), click the check box in front of the category.**

5. **Click OK.**

   When you view any item that has this category assigned to it, you see the new category name, even if the category was assigned before you changed the name.

Assigning shortcut keys to categories

When you used any one of the original categories for the first time, Outlook gave you a chance to assign a shortcut key to the category. You probably didn't do that unless you had an inkling at the time that you were going to use this category often. In any case, after you discover which categories you use most often, you can assign shortcut keys to them so that you can easily use them.

A *shortcut key* is typically two keys, such as Shift+B or Ctrl+V, which you press at the same time to activate a command without making a side trip to the Ribbon. To prevent you from creating a key combination for a color category that Outlook already uses to activate some other command, Outlook limits you to a short list of key combos from which you can choose. So, assign a shortcut key only to the categories you use frequently. You don't typically need one for the Quick Click category because it's so easy to apply.

You can add a shortcut key to your category by following these steps:

1. **Click the Categorize button in the Tags section of the Ribbon's Home tab, and then select All Categories from the pop-up menu that appears.**

   The Color Categories dialog box rears its pretty little head.

2. **Select the category to which you want to assign a shortcut key.**

**Book VIII
Chapter 1**

**Organizing Items
with Categories**

3. **Select a shortcut key from the Shortcut Key drop-down list, as shown in Figure 1-6, and then click OK.**

   If you accidentally choose a combo that another category is using, a warning dialog box appears asking you if you'd like to reassign the shortcut to a new category. Just click the No button in the dialog box and make a different choice.

   The combination you select appears in the Shortcut Key column.

4. **Make all your shortcut assignments by repeating Steps 2 and 3.**

5. **When you're through, click OK to close the Color Categories dialog box.**

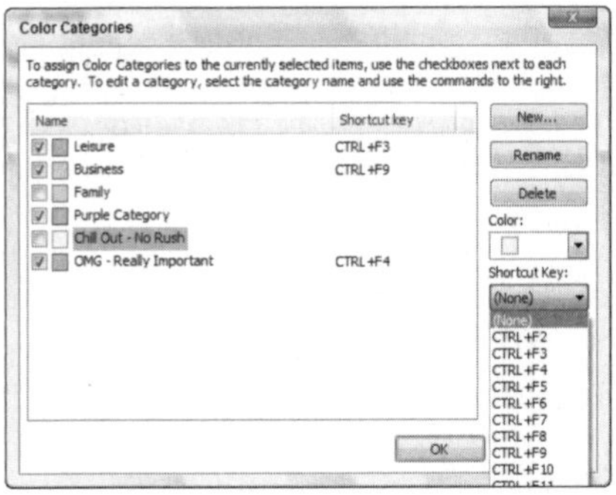

Figure 1-6:
Make
assigning
a favorite
category
easy.

To assign a color category to an item by using a shortcut key, select the item first. You can select more than one item if you want: Press and hold Ctrl while you click each item; or press and hold Shift, click the first item in a group, and then click the last item. After you select the items that you want to categorize, press both keys in the shortcut combination at the same time to assign the category.

Assigning new colors to categories

When you created your initial categories, you probably didn't give much thought to the color used by a category — until you discovered the color was a bit drab or didn't match your office decor. No problem; you can just substitute a more suitable color. To change the color assigned to a particular category, follow these steps:

1. **Click the Categorize button in the Tags section of the Ribbon's Home tab, and then select All Categories from the pop-up menu that appears.**

   The Color Categories dialog box appears.

2. **Click the category to which you want to assign a new color.**

3. **Select the new color that you want to assign to the category from the Color drop-down list.**

   You have 25 colors to choose from, so knock yourself out. The color you select appears next to the category in the list.

4. **If you want to change the colors assigned to other categories, repeat Steps 2 and 3.**

5. **Click OK when you finish redecorating your categories.**

After you assign a new color to a category, items that already use that category are instantly changed to the new color. You don't have to do a thing.

Creating new categories

You quickly begin to outgrow the six measly categories that Outlook provides. For example, maybe you added a Business category and now want to divide it into Clients and Prospects. Not to worry; you can add new categories anytime you need to. Items can have multiple categories assigned to them, so even though you identify something as Business, you can also further identify it as belonging to Clients or Prospects. Follow these steps to create a brand new, never before seen, category:

1. **Click the Categorize button in the Tags section of the Ribbon's Home tab, and then select All Categories from the pop-up menu that appears.**

   The Color Categories dialog box pops up once again. Guess you might consider it a one size does all kind of box.

2. **Click the New button.**

   The Add New Category dialog box appears, as shown in Figure 1-7.

Figure 1-7:
Add your own categories.

3. **Type a name for the new category in the Name field.**

4. **Using the handy drop-down lists, select a color and assign a shortcut key, if you want.**

   Outlook suggests the next color in its list as the color you should use for this new category. If you don't happen to like that color, you can open the Color drop-down list and select a different color for the category.

5. **Click OK.**

If you accidentally select a key combo that another category is using, a warning similar to what you see in Figure 1-8 appears. Click the No button if you don't want to reassign this key combo, and then make a different choice.

Figure 1-8: Outlook won't let you make a wrong choice.

Microsoft Outlook

You already created a category called "Blue Category". Select another category name.

OK

The category you just created appears in the category list of the Color Categories dialog box. You can make adjustments to the new category (such as selecting a different color) — for example, if it turns out that your original choice is too similar to another category that you use a lot. You can also create another category by clicking New and repeating the preceding steps. When you've exhausted yourself, click OK to close the dialog box.

Before you close the Color Categories dialog box, be sure to look at what's checked. Any categories that have a check mark are applied to the currently selected item(s), regardless of whether that's what you intend.

Removing a category

Occasionally, clothes go out of style. Take bell bottoms, peasant blouses, and tie-dyed T-shirts, for example. No wait — those things are back in again. Well anyway, occasionally categories go out of style, and you find that they just aren't useful anymore. You can keep an unused category in your Outlook closet (for sentimental reasons or in case your children can find some use for it 20 years from now), or you can remove the category by following these steps:

1. **Click the Categorize button in the Tags section of the Ribbon's Home tab, and then select All Categories from the pop-up menu that appears.**

The Color Categories dialog box opens.

2. **Select the category you want to get rid of.**

3. **Click Delete.**

A warning dialog box appears, asking whether you really, really want to delete this poor little category that's never done anything to you.

4. **Click Yes.**

   The warning dialog box closes, and the category is removed from the list shown in the Color Categories dialog box.

5. **Click OK to close the Color Categories dialog box.**

When you delete a category, Outlook removes it from the Categories list, and you can't use it anymore. However, deleting a category doesn't affect any items that you had previously assigned to the now-defunct category. You can either leave the old category attached to the items, or you can manually remove the deleted category from any items that you want to. See the section "Removing a Category from an Item," earlier in this chapter, for help.

**Book VIII
Chapter 1**

**Organizing Items
with Categories**

Chapter 2: Changing Your View on Outlook

In This Chapter

✔ **Working with views**

✔ **Arranging your items**

✔ **Using the Reading pane**

✔ **Looking for unread e-mail**

A common ailment among computer users is screen envy. Generally, this disease strikes you when you observe someone else's computer screen and notice that things look a bit different than what you're used to seeing. Unfortunately, some people assume that *different* means *better* and start to worry that the other computer is somehow better than their own.

There are two known cures for screen envy:

✦ Realizing that different isn't necessarily better

✦ Mastering the art of customizing your computer screens

This chapter is devoted to changing the basic Outlook look and feel. You can explore the ways in which you view the various Outlook items, and even how you can change those views if the notion strikes you. The chapter also shows you a few tricks to get the most out of your existing views and how to group your Outlook items together.

Viewing Outlook in a Whole New Light

Every Outlook folder displays the items it contains in a layout, or *view*. Views give you different ways to look at the same information in a folder by putting it in different arrangements and formats. Outlook offers several standard views for a folder that you can choose from, or you can create custom views. You can switch between views or stick to your tried-and-true favorite view. In fact, Outlook is so proud of the various view options that it devoted an entire tab — the View tab — to the various Outlook views.

This chapter relies a bit more on your personal taste than do most of the rest of the areas of this book. If you're not happy with the view you create, simply click the Reset View button in the Current View section of the Ribbon's View tab to reset your view to the factory default.

Changing views

Like with anything else, start simply and proceed to fancier maneuvers after you conquer the basics. Those of you with inquiring minds can start by checking out the existing Outlook views. Follow these steps to change your view (in Outlook):

1. Click the Ribbon's View tab and head on over to the Current View section.

The nice thing here is that the sky is the limit. You can change the view for any of the Outlook folders by following the same procedure.

2. Click the Change View button and select Manage Views from the pop-up menu that appears.

The Manage All Views dialog box, which you see in Figure 2-1, appears on-screen. In this example we're changing the Inbox views; if you're making changes to other Outlook folders the dialog box will look a bit different.

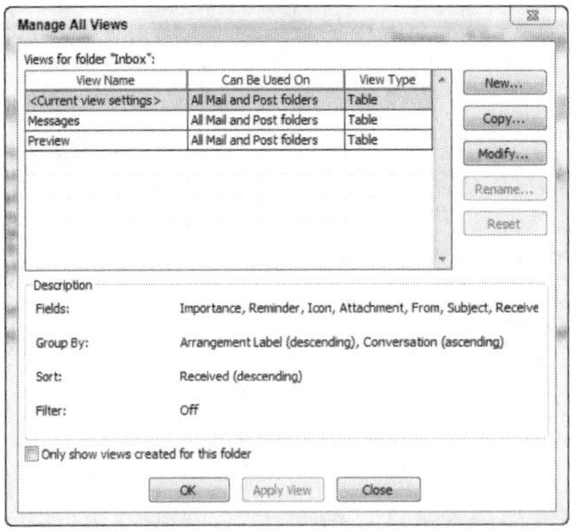

Figure 2-1:
Managing
your views.

3. Select a view from the Views for Folder *Name* list, and then click the Apply View button.

Although the Apply View button is grayed out in Figure 2-1, it becomes active after you select a view.

The dialog box closes, and your Outlook items now reflect the view that you selected.

Tweaking an existing view

You may have realized that you can customize the various Outlook views in countless ways. But wait! With the purchase of the knife set, you can get even more customizations. And, if you order now, we'll even let you keep those customizations at no extra charge!

Okay, we're not actually running an infomercial, but the thought of taking a piece of software and totally reformatting it might get you excited. After you have a chance to investigate the existing Outlook views, you might decide to spice them up a bit. To modify an existing view, follow these steps:

1. **Click the Ribbon's View tab, then click the Change View button in the tab's Current View section.**

2. **Select Manage Views from the pop-up menu that appears.**

   The Manage All Views dialog box opens.

   You can follow these steps to modify any of the Outlook modules.

3. **Select the view that's closest to your desired goal, and then click Modify.**

   Although you can start from scratch, if you prefer, you can generally tweak an existing view more easily. If you're not sure exactly what the current view looks like, you can read a description of it in the Description area of the Manage All Views dialog box.

   The Advanced View Settings dialog box that you see in Figure 2-2 opens. (This particular Advanced View Settings dialog box is devoted to Messages.)

4. **For each type of change that you want to make, click a button and select the options you want from dialog box that appears.**

   Options that are grayed out aren't available with the view you're currently using. Consider switching to another view if you want to use those options. For example, you can't add columns to the Business Cards view, but you can add fields to the Cards view.

   We cover the first three options in the section "Tabling the Table View," later in this chapter. But if you want to modify other views, such as a card view, here's your chance to do so. Clicking these buttons lets you make the associated modifications:

   - *Columns:* Add more columns to any layout.

   - *Group By:* Group all similar items together.

Book VIII
Chapter 2

Changing Your
View on Outlook

- *Sort:* Sort the current layout in the manner of your choosing.

- *Filter:* You can create a filter to include only those items that match a certain criteria. Perhaps you want to quickly access only your hot prospects in California, or your e-mail that came in from six key contacts. Figure 2-3 shows you an example of a filter.

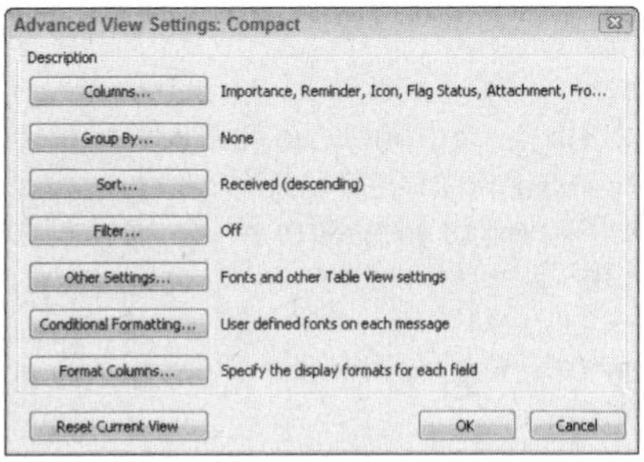

Figure 2-2: The Advanced View Settings dialog box.

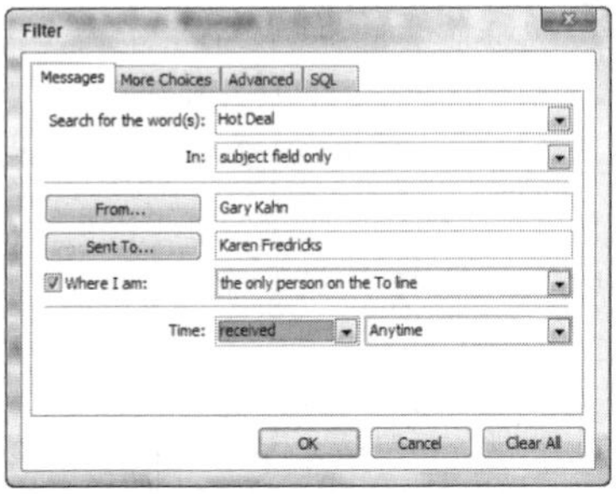

Figure 2-3: Creating a custom filter.

- *Other Settings:* Pick the font that you want to use and other settings pertinent to the current view. (Figure 2-4 shows you the kinds of options that you can change for the Inbox Message view.)

- *Conditional Formatting:* Select a font for specific items. For example, you can have all your unread e-mail show up in magenta or the contracts in your distribution list in chartreuse.

- *Format Columns:* If you're working in a Table view, you can have each of your columns formatted in a different way. You can even rename the column headings, if you so desire.

5. **Click OK to close the current dialog box, and then click OK in the Advanced View Settings dialog box to close it.**

6. **Click OK to close the Manage All Views dialog box.**

Figure 2-4:
Other view settings that you can tweak.

Resetting a standard view

After you customize the current view, you can sit back and admire your handiwork. If you're less than totally thrilled with your masterpiece, however, you can easily reset the view back to its original, pristine form. Follow these steps:

1. **Select the Ribbon's View tab, and then click the Reset Views button in the tab's Current View section.**

A dialog box appears asking you if you'd like to reset the view back to its original settings.

If you're a real Outlook power user and routinely use more than one view, you'll have to first change your view by following the steps outlined in the "Changing views" section, earlier in this chapter.

While you access the various views, sometimes the Ribbon's Reset View button is grayed out. That's your tip that the view has never been tinkered with.

2. **Click Yes to revert your settings back to their original shape.**

Changing the name of a view

Ironically, although you can customize a view in more ways than you ever dreamed possible, one thing you can't do is to rename a predefined view. Try as you might, you can't change Business Card to Really Important Address Card. You can, however, copy a predefined view, give it a name, and then customize it. Follow these steps:

1. **Select the Ribbon's View tab, and then click the Change View button in the Current View section.**

2. **Select Manage Views from the pop-up menu that appears.**

The Manage All Views dialog box opens.

3. **Select the view that you want to rename in the View Name list and click Copy.**

   The Copy View dialog box opens.

4. **Enter the name of the new view in the Name of New View text box and click OK.**

   The Copy View dialog box closes.

5. **Click OK to close the Manage All Views dialog box.**

Creating a view from scratch

Considering that Outlook comes equipped with myriad views, and that you can customize all those views from here to Podunk Junction and back, you may wonder why you'd want to create a view from scratch. As the saying goes, different strokes for different folks. And, if you happen to be one of those people who's stroking along differently from the rest of the world — or maybe if you have an adventurous side — here's your opportunity to explore uncharted waters. Follow these steps to create a brand-new view:

1. **Click the Ribbon's View tab and head for the tab's Current View section.**

2. **Click the Change View icon and select Manage Views from the pop-up menu that appears.**

   The Manage All Views dialog box makes an appearance.

3. **Click the New button.**

   The Create a New View dialog box that you see in Figure 2-5 appears.

Figure 2-5:
Creating a new Outlook view.

4. **Enter a name in the Name of New View field.**

   After all, creating something new is only half the fun. The other half comes in being able to *find it* again later — and know what it's for.

5. In the Type of View box, select a view type.

Your choices are

- *Table:* Probably the most common view, a table displays your information as rows, with columns representing the various fields of information for each record.

- *Timeline:* Available only with the Inbox and Tasks folders, the Timeline displays each of your items appear at the appropriate date on the timeline. Think back to elementary school and you'll know exactly what an Outlook timeline looks like; if you can't remember back that far, see Figure 2-6.

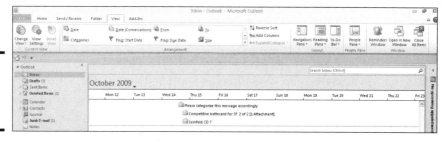

Figure 2-6: The Timeline view.

- *Day/Week/Month:* Available with the Calendar folder, this view allows you to flip back and forth between a Daily, Weekly, and Monthly view of your calendar.

- *Card:* Most commonly used with the Contacts folder, a Card view allows you to look at your information in the form of a business card. This view is most often used by Outlook users who are mourning the passage of the Rolodex.

- *Icon:* Generally used with Notes, Icon view displays your information as a series of sticky notes.

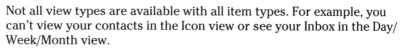

Not all view types are available with all item types. For example, you can't view your contacts in the Icon view or see your Inbox in the Day/Week/Month view.

6. Select a radio button in the Can Be Used On area.

Your options are to share the view with anyone that you share your Outlook with, horde the view for only your own usage, or apply the view to all folders that can be used with that particular view type.

7. Click OK.

The Manage All Views dialog box appears again. Try to contain your excitement at finding yourself in old, familiar territory.

8. **Click OK to close the Manage All Views dialog box.**

   Wonder of wonders! Feel free to pat yourself on the back knowing that you have taken another giant step towards becoming an Outlook power user!.

Deleting a custom view

After you have a chance to fool around creating new views, you may realize that the out-of-the-box views are really just what the doctor ordered, and you want to simplify your life — and Outlook — by getting rid of your custom views. Not a problem — just follow these simple steps:

1. **Click the Ribbon's View tab and head for the tab's Current View section.**

2. **Click the Change View button and select Manage Views from the pop-up menu that appears.**

   The Manage All Views dialog box opens. (Refer to Figure 2-1.)

3. **Select the view that you want to delete in the View Name column.**

   No Delete button appears when you select a predefined view because you can't delete predefined views. When you click a view that you created all by yourself, though, the Delete button *does* appear.

4. **Click the Delete button, and click Yes when the dialog box appears, asking you if you're sure you want to delete the view.**

   Bye, bye view.

5. **Click OK to close the Manage All Views dialog box.**

Tabling the Table View

The Table view is one of the most popular views in Outlook. Its popularity is based in part on the fact that the Table view is highly customizable. You can master several neat table tricks so that you, too, can be popular. Okay, these tricks may not make you the life of the party, but they do make you popular around the water cooler if you pass them on to your co-workers.

Adding a column to a table

One of the most common things you'll want to do is add another column to the current List view. You can accomplish that feat by following these steps:

1. **Open any folder in Table view.**

   You can recognize Table view because the folder information will be arranged in a list. If you'd really like to double-check that you're in Table view, follow the instructions from the "Changing views" section above and verify that the view you are in does in fact have the View Type as Table listed in the Manage All Views dialog box.

2. **Click the Ribbon's View tab, and then click the Add Columns button in the tab's Arrangement section.**

   The Show Columns dialog box opens, as shown in Figure 2-7.

Figure 2-7:
Adding new columns to a List view.

3. **Select the column that you want to add from the Available Columns list, and then click the Add button.**

4. **(Optional) Click the Frequently-Used Fields text box and select a different set of fields from the drop-down list that appears if you don't see the field you're looking for.**

5. **(Optional) Select a field from the Show These Columns in This Order list, and then click the Move Up or Move Down button to change the order that the columns will appear in the Table view.**

6. **Click OK when you finish adding new fields.**

Removing columns

You might decide that one or more of the columns in the Table view contain information that you don't need. You can remove those columns by following these two easy steps:

1. **Right-click the column heading that you want to remove.**

2. **Select Remove This Column from the pop-up menu that appears.**

Worried that you won't be able to get your column back again? Don't be — just read the preceding section about adding columns.

Moving a column

You may think it's a drag if your columns aren't in the order that you want them to be. A drag is a *good* thing when it comes to column arranging because that's just how you're going to do your arranging. Hover the mouse pointer over the column heading you want to move, and then click and drag the column to your preferred destination. Outlook helps you by flashing two red arrows, indicating the spot where your new column will end up.

Resizing a column

If you feel like you're seeing spots before your eyes when you gaze at a list of Outlook items, you need to either see your doctor immediately or widen your columns a smidge. When a column isn't wide enough to contain all the data, Outlook *truncates* it by placing four little dots at the end of the column.

If you've worked with Excel spreadsheets in the past you're probably already an old pro at this, but just in case you haven't, here's the drill:

1. **Move the mouse pointer to the right edge of the column that you want to widen until the cursor morphs into a two-headed arrow.**

2. **Drag the edge of the column until the column is the desired width.**

 If you're a real column perfectionist and, like Goldilocks, want to have your columns sized *just right,* you can double-click the right edge of the column header when you see the double-headed arrow. Outlook automatically sizes your column to fit the largest entry in that column.

Arranging for a Different View in Outlook

You can group similar E-Mail, Contact, Task, and Project items together so that you can view them more easily. For example, Outlook automatically groups items by date. The default Inbox groups are Today, Yesterday, Last Week, Last Month, and Older. If you often find yourself buried under a mountain of e-mail, you'll probably like this feature because the newest mail automatically appears in the top of your e-mail heap, while the older mail sinks to the bottom. Figure 2-8 shows this feature in action.

Figure 2-8:
An Inbox grouped by date.

Getting in with the in group

You can group items together in ways other than by date. You can also group your Outlook items by using several predefined grouping scenarios. If you take a gander at the Arrangement section of the Ribbon's View tab, you can see some of the predefined groupings. You can also click the More button (see Figure 2-9) to reveal more grouping choices (see Figure 2-10).

Figure 2-9:
Finding more ways to arrange your data using the More button.

Figure 2-10:
Some more options for grouping your data.

Grouping your e-mail by date or by using one of the predefined group schemes is probably more than sufficient to keep you happy, healthy, and well organized. But you may just feel the urge to do things a bit differently. For example, you may want to see all your contacts grouped by categories or your tasks grouped by priority.

Follow these steps to group your items together by virtually any field in your database:

1. **Click the View Settings button in the Current View section of the Ribbon's View tab.**

   The Advanced View Setting dialog box opens. (Refer to Figure 2-2.)

2. **Click the Group By button.**

   The Group By dialog box appears, looking very much like the one shown in Figure 2-11.

**Book VIII
Chapter 2**

**Changing Your
View on Outlook**

Figure 2-11:
Creating
custom
groups for
your Outlook
items.

3. **Deselect the Automatically Group According to Arrangement check box.**

   The various Group By options now come to life — or, at least, aren't grayed out like they were before.

4. **Select a field to group by from the Group Items By drop-down list.**

   Outlook presents the most frequently used fields for that item type in this list. If you're grouping contacts, for example, the drop-down list includes choices such as Company, Categories, and State. If you're grouping e-mail, the list shows choices such as Importance, Subject, and Received Date.

5. **(Optional) Select a different field set from the Select Available Fields From drop-down list in the bottom-left corner of the dialog box if you don't see the field you're looking for.**

   Perhaps you added a new field to track a product preference for all your contacts. If you select User-Defined Fields in Folder from the Select Available Fields From drop-down list, you can group items by product preference.

6. **Select the Ascending or Descending radio button for the sort order of the group headings.**

7. **(Optional) Select the Show Field in View check box if you want to display the field by which you're grouping items.**

8. **(Optional) Select a field in the Then By drop-down list to divide each group into subgroups.**

   For example, you may want to group your contacts by category, and subdivide each category into states. (You have the same options to do a secondary sort in Ascending order and to include the name of the column.)

9. **Select the way you want to view your groups in the Expand/Collapse Defaults drop-down list.**

   By default, you can select All Expanded to show all items, All Collapsed to show just the group headings, or As Last Viewed to keep your groups exactly the way they were the last time you looked at them.

10. **Click OK to close the Group By dialog box, and then click OK in the Advanced View Settings dialog box to close it.**

    After you close the dialog boxes, you can expand groups by clicking the plus sign that appears to the left of the group name and collapse a group by clicking the minus sign that appears to the left of the group name.

Sorting Your Data

Outlook always displays your data in some kind of order. Unfortunately, that order may not be exactly what you had in mind. For example, you might want a list of your contacts sorted alphabetically by state, but Outlook shows the contacts sorted by last name by default.

Sort of sorting your column

You may cringe when a salesperson tells you that something can be done with the click of a button, but when it comes to sorting an Outlook column, he's right. Click the column heading of the column that you want to sort by, and Outlook responds by sorting your table based on that column. Want your contacts in Zip-code order? Click the Postal Code field. Change your mind and want your contacts listed alphabetically by company? Click the Company field.

If you want to reverse the order of the sort, click the column a second time. After you sort your data, you can tell which field your data is sorted by: If you look carefully at the column headings, one of them has a tiny up-pointing arrow indicating that the data in that column is sorted in ascending order. If the arrow points downward, your data is in descending order.

What sort of sort do you want?

You can easily click a column heading, but you may want to sort your information by more than one criterion; for example, you might want to see your contacts sorted first by state and then by the cities within each state. Or you may be looking at your contacts in one of the views and wondering how in the world you can sort those cards because you don't have any column headings to click.

To take your sorting skills up to the next level, follow these steps:

1. **Click the Ribbon's View tab, and then click the View Settings button in the tab's Current View section.**

The Advanced View Settings dialog box opens. (Refer to Figure 2-2.)

2. **Click the Sort button.**

The Sort dialog box opens, as shown in Figure 2-12.

Figure 2-12:
Creating a
custom sort.

3. **Select the first field that you want to sort by from the Sort Items By drop-down list.**

4. **(Optional) If you don't see the field you're looking for, select another set of fields from the Select Available Fields From drop-down list down in the lower-left corner of the dialog box.**

5. **Select the Ascending or Descending radio button, depending on whether you want your fields sorted from A to Z or from Z to A.**

6. **Repeat Steps 3 through 5 with the Then By lists, which appear below the Sort Items By list, if you want to create secondary sorts within the main sort.**

7. **Click OK to close the Sort dialog box.**

Outlook, always eager to please, opens a dialog box, warning you if one of the fields you chose doesn't appear in the current view. It asks whether you'd really like to sort in the manner you indicated even though you won't be able to see the contents of the sort column.

8. **If you want to use the sort , click the Yes button.**

The warning dialog box closes.

9. **Click OK to close the Advanced View Settings dialog box.**

Reading Can Be a Pane

The Reading pane allows you to preview various Outlook items without having to actually open them. Although you may associate the Reading pane with viewing the e-mail in your Inbox, you can also use the Reading pane to preview items in the Drafts, Calendar, Contacts, Tasks, Notes, and Journal views. The Reading pane also allows you to open attachments, follow hyperlinks, use voting buttons, and respond to meeting requests. Figure 2-13 shows the Reading pane for a selected e-mail item.

Security isn't an issue when it comes to using the Reading pane. You can safely preview your e-mail in the Reading pane without fear of encountering a virus. Previewing an e-mail message doesn't run any potentially dangerous scripts that the e-mail may contain.

Reading is a turn-on

You may want to experiment with the Reading pane to see whether the feature is for you. Here are a few of the ways that you can customize the Reading pane:

✦ **Location:** Depending on your preference, the Reading pane can appear to either the right or bottom of the item that's currently selected. Select the Ribbon's View tab, click the Reading Pane button in the tab's Layout section, and then select Right or Bottom from the pop-up menu that appears.

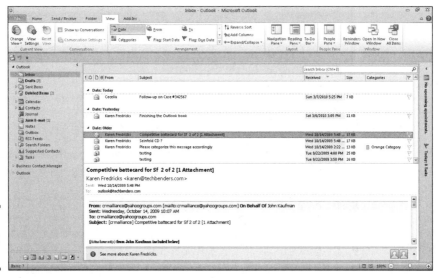

Figure 2-13:
The Reading pane.

**Book VIII
Chapter 2**

**Changing Your
View on Outlook**

✦ **Side-view size:** If the Reading pane runs along the right side of Outlook, you can change its size by hovering the mouse pointer on either the left or the right border of the Reading pane and, when the pointer becomes a double-headed arrow, dragging the border to the left or right.

✦ **Bottom-view size:** If the Reading pane runs along the bottom side of Outlook, you can change its size by hovering the mouse pointer over the top of the Reading pane and, when the pointer becomes a double-headed arrow, dragging the border higher or lower.

✦ **Removing the pane altogether:** If you feel that the Reading pane is a pain, you can turn it off completely by clicking the View tab's Reading Pane button, and then selecting Off from the pop-up menu that appears.

Reading in the Reading pane

Outlook lets you keep track of your unread messages by both displaying unread messages in bold and keeping a count of them by default for each of your Inboxes. In turn, you need to send a signal to Outlook that you've read a message, which you can do in a number of ways. The most obvious way is by opening a message; Outlook takes the cue and automatically marks the message as read.

Manually marking messages

If you prefer, you can send the signal to Outlook manually that you've finished reading a message by following these steps:

1. **Select the messages that you want to change in one of your Inbox folders.**

How you select the messages depends on which ones you want to select:

• *To select adjacent items:* Click the first item, then Shift-click the last item.

• *To select nonadjacent items:* Click the first item, and then Ctrl-click additional items.

• *To select all items:* Click one item, then press Ctrl+A.

2. **Right-click the selected message(s) and select either Mark as Read or Mark as Unread from the pop-up menu that appears.**

Displaying All the Messages in a Folder

So that you can easily find your unread messages, Outlook displays them in bold text in your Inbox. An unopened envelope appears next to the message in Table view. In addition, the number of unread messages appears next to the name of each of your Inbox folders.

If you prefer, you can display the total messages in the folder, rather than just the unread ones. Follow these steps:

1. **Right-click the folder and select Properties from the pop-up menu that appears.**

The Properties dialog box appears before your eyes, just like the one in Figure 2-14.

Figure 2-14:
The
Properties
dialog box
for Outlook's
Inbox.

2. **Select the Show Total Number of Items radio button.**

3. **Click OK to close the Properties dialog box.**

Chapter 3: Customizing Outlook Forms

In This Chapter

✔ **Customizing the Quick Access toolbar**

✔ **Customizing an Outlook form**

✔ **Creating custom fields**

✔ **Making a form the default**

*I*f variety is the spice of life, this chapter is certainly one of the spicier ones because it's all about customizing Outlook. You can start by exploring the mysteries of the Quick Access toolbar and move on to creating custom forms. You can find out how to add a custom field or two, and get a few tips on how to give your form a bit of extra pizzazz. Finally, you can find out how to make your new form the default one that Outlook uses each time you create a new item.

Making Quick Changes to the Quick Access Toolbar

The Quick Access toolbar is a customizable toolbar that appears below the Ribbon for most Outlook items. Although the Ribbon lists all the functions that are currently available, the Quick Access toolbar contains only those commands that you're most likely to use. For example, if you categorize all your contacts, you can add the Categorize icon to the Contact module's Quick Access toolbar. Or, if you routinely schedule follow-ups directly from incoming e-mail messages, you may want to add the Follow-Up icon to Mail's Quick Access toolbar.

Each of the various Outlook items has its own unique Quick Access toolbar, so you use one Quick Access toolbar when you add or edit a contact record and another Quick Access toolbar when you send or receive e-mail.

You can see the Quick Access toolbar in all its glory below the Ribbon in Figure 3-1.

Figure 3-1:
Outlook's
Quick
Access
toolbar.

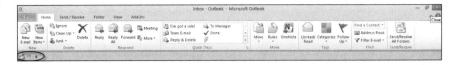

It turns out that you can find the Quick Access toolbar hanging out in one of two places:

✦ The upper-left corner of an opened item above the File tab

✦ Directly below the Ribbon

If you don't want the Quick Access toolbar to appear in one of these locations, you can move it to the other one fairly easily. Right-click the Ribbon and select Show Quick Access Toolbar Below the Ribbon from the pop-up menu that appears. If you've already moved it, you pick the Show Quick Access Toolbar Below the Ribbon option.

 You may find that the Ribbon takes up a bit too much real estate on the various Outlook forms. If this is the case, consider adding the key features that you use to the Quick Access toolbar and hiding the Ribbon by giving it a right-click and selecting Minimize the Ribbon from the pop-up menu that appears.

Adding a Quick Access toolbar command from the Ribbon

You can add any one of the commands displayed on the Ribbon to your Quick Access toolbar, which you can do if you want to hide the Ribbon but still access various Ribbon commands, with the click of a button. Add a command to the Quick Access toolbar by following these steps:

1. **Right-click the command that you want to add to the Quick Access toolbar.**

A shortcut menu springs to life, like the one you see in Figure 3-2.

Figure 3-2:
Adding a
command
to the Quick
Access
toolbar.

> Add to Quick Access Toolbar
>
> Customize Quick Access Toolbar...
>
> Show Quick Access Toolbar Above the Ribbon
>
> Customize the Ribbon
>
> Minimize the Ribbon

2. **Click the Add to Quick Access Toolbar option on the shortcut menu.**

   Miraculously, the new command takes a place of honor at the rightmost location of the Quick Access toolbar.

Yet another way to quickly add Quick Access toolbar commands

You can find as many commands available to add to the Quick Access toolbar as there are flavors at your local ice cream parlor. Follow these steps to add the main ones:

1. **Click the Customize Quick Access Toolbar icon at the end of the Quick Access toolbar.**

   The Customize Quick Access Toolbar menu opens, displaying a list of the most popular functions. As you can see in Figure 3-3, the items that already appear on the Quick Access toolbar have check marks next to them.

Figure 3-3:
Quickly
adding more
items to
the Quick
Access
toolbar.

2. **Click the item you want to add to the Quick Access toolbar.**

   If you want to *remove* an item, click a checked item to deselect it.

Adding yet more Quick Access toolbar commands

You may feel that choosing one of the more popular functions will work just fine. However, if you're a power user who won't be content to just follow the crowd, you probably want to forge your own way. Follow these steps to include even more options in the Quick Access toolbar:

1. **Open the Quick Access Toolbar Editor.**

   You can use one of the following methods:

   • Right-click the Ribbon and select Customize Quick Access Toolbar from the pop-up menu that appears.

   • Click the Customize Quick Access Toolbar icon at the end of the Quick Access toolbar and select More Commands from its pop-up menu.

Both methods lead you to the Quick Access tab of the Outlook Options dialog box. If you want to see it for yourself, take a look at Figure 3-4.

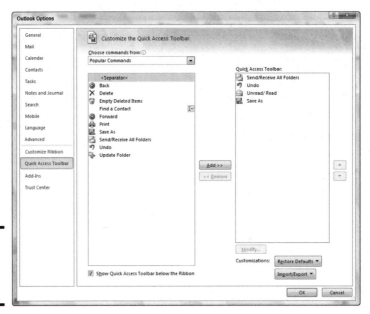

Figure 3-4:
The Editor
Options
dialog box.

The commands that appear on the left side of the screen (in the Choose Commands From area) represent all the commands from which you can choose. The commands on the right, in the Quick Access Toolbar area, are all the commands that currently appear on the Quick Access toolbar.

2. **Select a command from the left side of the screen and click the Add button to move it to the Quick Access toolbar commands on the right side of the screen.**

   For example, you may want to add the Print button if you routinely print some of your e-mail messages.

3. **Select another list of commands by clicking the drop-down arrow to the right of Popular Commands.**

   Baby, you ain't seen nothing yet! As its name implies, the commands listed under Popular Commands are the most popular commands that you may want to add to the Quick Access toolbar. However, they represent only the tip of the iceberg. You can select Commands Not in the Ribbon or All Commands to see a lot more choices.

The <Separator> command may leave you wondering. A *separator* is a vertical line that appears between the various commands on your Quick Access toolbar. You can use a separator to help you organize the various commands into groups. Feel free to add as many separators as you need.

4. **(Optional) Select a command in the Quick Access Toolbar section, and then click the up or down arrow to change the order of your commands.**

5. **(Optional) Select a command in the Quick Access Toolbar section, and then click the Remove button to remove a command from the Quick Access toolbar.**

You may find that you're not sure how a command will work. If you're not sure, go ahead and add the command to the Quick Access toolbar — you can always remove it later.

6. **(Optional) Click the Restore Defaults button to reset the Quick Access toolbar to the way it was originally.**

7. **Click OK after you finish adjusting the commands on the Quick Access toolbar.**

Figure 3-5 shows you a sample of a new and improved Quick Access toolbar.

Figure 3-5:
A
customized
Quick
Access
toolbar.

Playing with Forms

Every time you click New in Outlook, a form opens, ready and willing to hold your new information. Although you may be more than happy to use the existing forms that come with Outlook, you might just be one of those people who has to have it his (or her) way.

Creating a new form by using existing fields

If you just gotta have your own customized form, your first item of business is to find an easy way to get to the Custom Forms area. Because you probably need to go back and tweak your custom form a few times before you get it just right, add the Custom Forms command to the Quick Access toolbar. You can do that by following the directions in the preceding section, "Adding yet more Quick Access toolbar commands."

Outlook comes equipped with hundreds of standard fields that are ready and waiting to hold your information. You can add any of them to an existing form by following these steps:

1. **Click the Custom Forms button on the Quick Access toolbar, and then select Design a Form from the pop-up menu that appears.**

   The forms of the Standard Forms Library appear in the Design Form dialog box. These forms appear when you create a new item, such as a new contact, message, or appointment. You can see the dialog box in Figure 3-6.

Figure 3-6:
The Design
Form dialog
box.

   You may have noticed that most things in life can be done in one of two ways: the hard way and the easy way. Frankly, if I'm given the option, I generally vote to try the easy route first. That rule applies to Outlook, as well — you can design a form from scratch, or you can modify an existing form.

   Unfortunately you can't edit all the Outlook forms. A few of the forms include <Hidden> after their names, which means that you can't edit these specially protected forms.

2. **(Optional) Select another folder from the Look In drop-down list.**

   For example, if you've already created some custom forms, you find them hanging out in the Personal Forms Library.

3. **Select a form to modify, and then click Open.**

   I use the Contact form for this example. Some of the Outlook forms are more conducive to customizing than others. I recommend that you begin by tinkering with the standard Contact form because this form holds all the key contact information whereas the standard e-mail form doesn't have as many fields available to add to it.

   The Contact Design window — or the window associated with that other form you went with — opens. You can see what the Contact Design window looks like in Figure 3-7.

   At first glance, this window looks almost identical to the window that you see when you create a new contact. It has, however, a few notable differences:

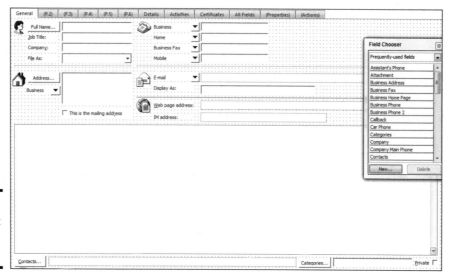

Figure 3-7:
The Contact
Design
window.

- The title bar includes (Design).

- The pretty blue background is replaced by a series of boring gray dots.

- The Field Chooser button tools you'll need on order to open and close the Field Chooser palette will appear on top of the form. (By default, the Field Chooser palette is open.)

In Figure 3-7, a large white text box takes up a lot of the area of the form. In this area, you generally type notes.

4. (Optional) Click the notes text box so that little grab-able handles appear around the box. Then, click one of those handles and drag the box borders.

You can resize the notes text box so that it takes up less space on your form.

5. Click the File tab and select Save As.

The Save As dialog box opens.

6. Navigate to the folder where you want to save the form.

By default, Outlook buries it in a Templates folder, which is as good a place as any to save your template.

7. In the Save As text box, enter a brand-new name.

If you save the form by using a new name, you can go back to the original form just in case something goes wrong.

8. Select the extension type `.oft` **in the Type drop-down list.**

You have a few other file extension choices, but using the `.oft` extension ensures you that you can use the template in Outlook.

**Book VIII
Chapter 3**

Customizing
Outlook Forms

9. **(Optional) Add a new page to the form.**

Figure 3-7 shows that the form comes with five additional tabs or pages labeled P.2 to P.6. Also, the page numbers surrounded by parentheses indicate that these pages aren't currently displayed. Follow these steps to add these pages to your form (if you need them):

a. *Click the tab for the page you want to add.*

b. *Click the Page button in the Form section of the Ribbon.*

c. *Select the Display This Page option from the pop-up menu that appears to display the page.* You'll notice that the parenthesis disappear after the page number. Alternatively, a page is automatically displayed if you drag a field onto it.

d. *Click in the Rename This Page field and supply a new name for the page.*

e. *Click OK to close the Rename Page dialog box.*

Not all things are created equal, which is certainly the case with Outlook's pages. Don't be upset if you click a page and find that you can't rename it. Some of the pages are system pages, which you just can't rename.

10. **Select the field that you want to add to the form from the Field Chooser and drag that field to the appropriate spot on the form.**

While you drag the field, both the field and the corresponding label move together to the new location on your form. Unlike some graphic programs, Outlook tries to line up the fields perfectly for you.

The same field can appear multiple times on a form. However, all the fields contain the same piece of information. For example, you can add the phone number on several pages of your form, so you can view the same phone number from various areas of your form.

Can't find the Field Chooser? Many users close it when it's in their way. To bring it back, simply click the Field Chooser icon on the Tools section of the Form Designer's Ribbon.

Can't find the field you need? Click Frequently-Used Fields at the top of the Field Chooser and select All Contact fields from the drop-down list that appears.

11. **(Optional) Click a field and press the Delete button in the Field Chooser to remove a field from the form.**

12. **Click the File tab and then click Save to save your form.**

13. **Click the Publish button in the Form section of the Ribbon and select Publish Form As from the pop-up menu that appears.**

When you *save* a form, you're saving it to your hard drive or network. When you *publish* a form, you're saving it to one of your Outlook folders so that you can use it when you create a new item.

14. **In the Publish Form As dialog box that appears, select the Outlook folder from the Look In drop-down list, give the form a name in the Display name field, and click Publish.**

    You probably want to use the same name that you used when you saved the form in Step 13. You can see what that display name would look like in Figure 3-8.

15. **Click the File tab and click Close to close your newly customized form.**

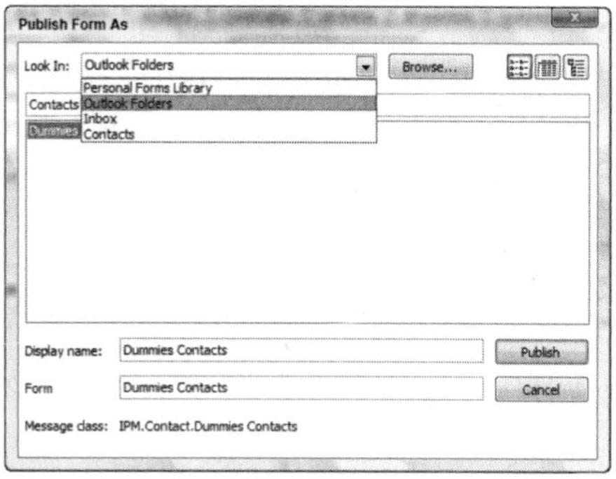

Figure 3-8:
Publishing a
new Outlook
form.

Form Beautification 101

If you followed the steps in the preceding section, you're now the proud owner of a new, customized form. You can master a few cool party tricks, however, to provide your form with a little more polish. Although they're not mandatory, they lead to a more professional-looking form — and help you find an avenue for the artistic side of your personality. To do a bit of advanced renovation to a form, follow these steps:

1. **Click the Custom Forms icon on the Quick Access toolbar and select Design a Form from the pop-up menu that appears.**

    The Design Form dialog box opens.

2. **Select User Templates in File System from the Look In drop-down list.**

    If you were creative in choosing the file location when you created the form, you have to click the Browse button, navigate to the location of your saved form, and click Open.

    From this point forward, all the steps are optional, albeit fun.

3. **Select the form you want to tweak, and then click Open.**

    True to its word, Outlook opens your form.

4. **Add a colorful background to your form.**

Although you may be delighted with the silvery blue background of the basic Outlook form, you may want to coordinate your form with the office décor. Follow these steps to change your background:

a. *Right-click the form background and select Advanced Properties from the menu that appears.*

Alternatively, you can click Advanced Properties on the Tools portion of the form's Ribbon.

The Properties palette opens.

b. *Click BackColor (short for background color) on the Properties dialog box.*

You'll notice a new string of somewhat nonsensical text appear in the Apply field at the top of the Properties palette.

c. *Click the ellipsis button (the three little dots) at the right of the Apply field.*

d. *Select a color from the color dialog box, and then click OK.*

You'll notice that a new set of cryptic letters now appears in the Apply field — and that the form's background has changed to the color you just selected.

5. **Add a colorful background to a specific field.**

For example, you may want emphasize a field by coloring it yellow. Just follow these steps:

a. *Right-click a field and select Advanced Properties from the pop-up menu that appears.*

The Properties palette opens.

b. *Click BackColor on the Properties dialog box.*

Once again you'll see a slight change in the contents of the Apply field.

c. *Click the ellipsis button (the three little dots) to the right of the Apply field.*

d. *Select a color from the color pallet and click OK.*

Again you'll notice a change in the rather cryptic contents of the Apply field but more importantly you'll notice that the fields on the form have changed to the new color.

6. **Make two or more fields the same size.**

When you move fields onto your form, those fields aren't all exactly the same size. Although this size difference doesn't affect your data input, you may find it annoying — and you can easily correct it by following these steps:

a. *While holding down your Ctrl key, click fields that you want to resize.*

b. *Still holding down the Ctrl key, select the field that's the correct size and then let go of the Ctrl key.*

This last field you select becomes the anchor field and now has white handles.

    c. Right-click any of the selected fields and select Make Same Size from the pop-up menu that appears, then select Both from the submenu. The selected fields are now the exact same size as the anchor field.

7. **Align two or more fields.**

When you customize a form, a series of dots appear on the Form Designer. These dots represent the *snap-to grid;* ideally, any new field you place on a form snaps to these dots so that your new fields line up with each other. If for some reason the fields seem slightly out of whack, you can line them up manually, as well, by following these steps:

    a. While holding down your Ctrl key, click any field(s) that you want to line up with your anchor field.

    b. Still holding down the Ctrl key, select the field that's in the correct location and then let go of the Ctrl key.

    This field becomes the anchor field and now has white handles.

    c. Right-click any of the selected fields and select Align from the pop-up menu that appears.

    d. Select one of the Align options. Although typically forms contain fields that are aligned along the left side, you might want the fields to align along the right, or have the tops of two fields align to the anchor field.

You can get an idea of what it's like to align fields in Figure 3-9.

8. **Group several fields together.**

Although you can easily drag a field to a new spot on the form, the process becomes tougher if you have to drag a whole bunch of fields at the same time because you have to select them all first. To solve this problem — or, at least, to make life a wee bit easier — you can group several fields together and then move them around your form en masse so that you can keep their alignment in tack. For example, you may have added fields for the names and birthdates of your contact's kids; grouping them enables you to move those multiple fields around with a click and drag. Move a bunch of fields at one time by following these steps:

    a. While holding down the Ctrl key, click all the fields you want to group together.

    Alternatively, you can hold down your left mouse button and lasso all the fields by drawing a box around them.

    b. Right-click any of the selected fields and select Group from the pop-up menu that appears.

A selection box appears around the group of fields. From now on, anytime you move one member of the group, the whole group tags along.

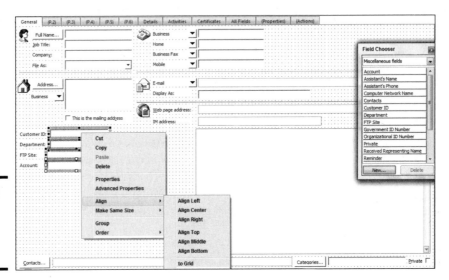

Figure 3-9:
Aligning
fields on
a custom
form.

9. **When you complete your beautification project close and save the form by clicking the Close button in the top right corner of the form (the red X) and then clicking Yes when prompted to save your changes.**

When you're ready to actually start using your spiffy new form, you'll have to publish it. To publish a modified form, follow the directions in the preceding section ("Form Beautification 101") to open the form and then click the Publish button on the form's Ribbon.

Adding custom-defined fields

I'm a firm believer that a little knowledge is a dangerous thing. Although you can easily add a field to Outlook, you should still make it a well-thought-out decision and plan it in advance. Planning prevents you from adding thousands of contacts to your database, only to find that you have to modify each record to include information that you omitted the first time around.

To add new fields by returning to the scene of the crime — or, at least, the place where you created your custom form — follow these steps:

1. **Click the Custom Forms button on the Quick Access toolbar, and then select Design a Form from the pop-up menu that appears.**

   The Design Form dialog box opens, showing a list of the basic Outlook forms.

2. **Select the name of the form you want to edit and click Open.**

   Theoretically, it doesn't matter which form you choose because your mission here is to add new fields to the database. In any event, the Form Designer opens with the Field Chooser dialog box prominently displayed.

3. **Click New on the Field Chooser dialog box.**

The New Column dialog box opens, as seen on stage, screen, and in Figure 3-10.

4. **Type the name of the new field in the Name text box.**

5. **Select the type of field that you want to add from the Type drop-down list (refer to Figure 3-10).**

Let the games begin! You have a number of field type choices here. If your field is going to contain a numeric value, you can designate the field as a Number, Percent, Currency, or Integer field. If you're tracking time, you can use a Date/Time or Duration field.

You may notice Yes/No listed as one of the data types. Just in case you're wondering, a Yes/No field is what most people would consider a check-box field.

6. **Select a format from the Format drop-down list.**

You have a variety of format options that depend on the data type you selected in Step 5. If you chose Date/Time, you can now select the data format that you want to use, as shown in Figure 3-11. If you chose Number, you can decide how you want to deal with everything from commas and decimal points to negative numbers.

7. **Click OK to close the New Column dialog box and add your new field to Outlook's repertory of forms.**

If you happen to give the field a name that's already in use, Outlook presents you with a dialog box telling you that the field name is already in use and that you need to come up with a different one before continuing.

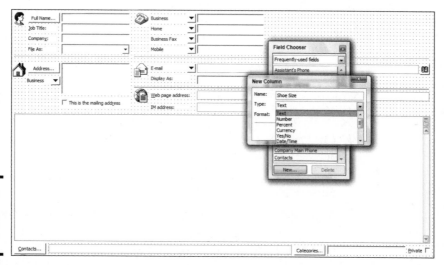

Figure 3-10:
Adding a new field to Outlook.

Figure 3-11:
Opening
the Format
drop-down
list.

8. **Select the User-Defined Fields in Folder option in the Field Chooser dialog box to track down your new field so that you can add it to your own form.**

Using Custom Forms

After you create your custom forms, the hard part is over. Now, you get to pretty much rest on your laurels. However, before you head to the pool with drink in hand, you may want to give a bit of thought to what you're going to do with the forms now that you have them.

One thing you might want to do with your new custom form is associate that form with a specific Outlook folder. Associating a form with a folder can unleash an entirely new aspect of Outlook. For example, say that you've divided your contacts folder into three subfolders: one for friends, one for customers, and one for vendors. The information that you enter for a customer may be quite different from what you enter for a friend. Although keeping credit card information on file may seem like a no-brainer for your customer contacts, your friends may not be as willing to give you that important tidbit of information. Conversely, you may want to keep the names of your friends' children in Outlook, but you may not need this information for your customers and vendors.

Associating a form with a folder is a two-step process: First, you make the form available in the folder, and then you make that form the default form when you add new items to that folder. Follow these steps:

1. **From Outlook's Folder list, right-click the folder that you want to associate with the customized form and select Properties from the pop-up menu that appears.**

   The Properties dialog box associated with the kind of form you're dealing with springs to life, just like the one you see in Figure 3-12.

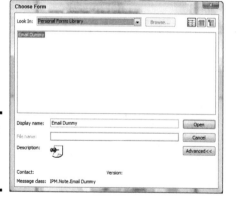

Figure 3-12:
The
Properties
dialog
box for a
Contacts
form.

2. **Select the form in the When Posting to This Folder, Use drop-down list.**

   Select Forms from the When Posting to This Folder, Use drop-down list if you don't see the form you want to associate with the current folder.

   The Choose Form dialog box that you see in Figure 3-13 opens; select the location of your form and click Open. The form now appears in the When Posting to This Folder, Use drop-down list, so you can actually follow this step.

Figure 3-13:
The Choose
Form dialog
box.

3. **Click OK to save your changes.**

Book IX

Managing All Your Outlook Stuff

The 5th Wave   By Rich Tennant

"My spam filter checks the recipient address, http links, and any writing that panders to postmodern English romanticism with conceits to 20th-century graphic narrative."

Contents at a Glance

Chapter 1: Finding a Place for Your Stuff

In This Chapter

↙ **Organizing your Outlook files**

↙ **Cleaning up Outlook**

↙ **Archiving old data**

As George Carlin said, "All you need in life is a little place for your stuff." If this is your first foray into Outlook, you're probably wondering how it could ever get messy and disorganized. When you come to rely on Outlook for each and every aspect of your busy life, however, you accumulate more and more stuff. This chapter shows how to create folders to hold your stuff. You can see how to use the Organize feature and reduce the size of your stuff. You can even find out how to put stuff into storage — or in this case, archival folders.

Developing an Outlook Filing System

Out of the box, Outlook comes with a variety of folders aimed at storing your stuff:

✦ Inbox

✦ Drafts

✦ Sent Items

✦ Deleted Items

✦ Calendar

✦ Contacts

✦ Tasks

✦ Notes

✦ Journal

✦ Outbox

When you first use Outlook, these folders are sufficient for storing your various Outlook items. While your life becomes more complicated, however, so does Outlook. If you want to save some of your thousands of incoming messages, for example, you may want to subdivide your Inbox into folders for each of your clients. Keeping your personal contacts in separate folders from your business contacts can also make your life easier, so you may want to subdivide your contacts, as well.

So, how many folders can you create? The sky's the limit. You really can't outgrow Outlook. You can add new folders when the need arises without worrying that you're going to run out of room in your filing cabinet.

If data management isn't your forte, stop worrying. If you swing open any of the file drawers in your desk, you probably find that you put your insurance information into a folder labeled Insurance, and your tax information into a folder labeled Taxes. That same sense of order applies to Outlook — except you don't have to invest in a bunch of folders and worry about creating neat little labels!

Creating a new folder

The hardest part about creating a new folder is deciding what to name it. The easy part is creating the folder. Follow these steps to get started:

1. **Right-click any of the existing Outlook folders and select New Folder from the pop-up menu that appears.**

The Create New Folder dialog box opens, as shown in Figure 1-1.

Figure 1-1:
Creating a
new Inbox
folder.

2. **Enter a name for the new folder in the Name text box.**

3. **Select the folder location from the Select Where to Place the Folder list box.**

If a subfolder or two exists within a folder, a plus sign appears to the left of the main folder. Click that plus sign to make the subfolders appear.

You might be wondering what to select from the Folder Contains drop-down list. Actually, you don't have to concern yourself with that drop-down list because it defaults to the folder type that you selected in Step 1.

4. **Click OK to close the Create New Folder dialog box.**

Sigh happily, knowing that you're well on the way to organizational bliss. Figure 1-2 shows a Folder list that has been customized to include new folders.

Figure 1-2:
An Outlook
Folder
list that
contains
new folders.

Moving an item to another folder

You can most easily move an item to another folder by dragging it from one folder to the next. Follow these steps:

1. **Select the item(s) that you want to move.**

Although you can move your items one by one, you can much more easily drag a bunch of items at the same time. You can select multiple items in several ways:

- *To select adjacent items:* Click the first item, hold down the Shift key, and then click the last item.

- *To select nonadjacent items:* Click an item, hold down the Ctrl key, and then click each additional item.

- *To select all items:* Click an item, and then press Ctrl+A.

2. **Drag the selected item(s) to the destination folder.**

   When you drag the items, they disappear from the first folder and find a permanent home in the new folder — unless you move the items again.

   Sometimes, you may want an item to appear in both the original and the new folder. For example, you might store all your contacts in the Contacts folder but want to copy select contacts into a new folder to make them easier to access. Select the item(s), as outlined in Step 1, drag them by using the right-mouse button to the new folder, and then select Copy from the pop-up menu that appears.

3. **Ponder how you can go about organizing your closets that easily.**

Rearranging your folders

When you create new folders in Outlook, they appear alphabetically in the Folder list. Drag as you might, you can't change the order. However, you can drag your folder in order to make it a subfolder of another folder. Alternatively if a folder is a subfolder of another folder, you can drag it up to the top of the Folder list to promote it to being a full-fledged folder of its own.

Giving folders the heave-ho

If you've ever attempted to redo an office file system, you know that it can be a lesson in futility; some drawers are filled to overflowing, and others sit empty. Fortunately, Outlook makes manipulating files easy. If you identify a folder that you no longer need, you can easily delete it. Just give the folder a right-click and select Delete Folder from the pop-up menu that appears. A dialog box appears, in which Outlook prompts you to click Yes if you really want give the folder (and all its contents) the heave-ho. (See Figure 1-3.)

Figure 1-3:
Bidding
adieu to a
folder.

Just like you wouldn't walk the tightrope without a net, Outlook comes equipped with a safety net of its own. Don't panic if you accidentally delete a folder. Run, don't walk, to your deleted folders; you'll find any folders that you deleted sitting patiently in the Deleted Items folder on Outlook's Navigation pane. If you want to salvage your folder, simply drag it back to where it belongs.

Moving an item to a different type of folder

Outlook has all kinds of neat party tricks up its sleeve. If you move an item to a different type of folder, for example, all kinds of cool things happen:

✦ If you drag an e-mail item to the Contacts folder, Outlook attempts to create a new Contact Record from the e-mail message. It fills in the name and e-mail, and the body of the message appears as a note on the Contact Record.

✦ If you drag an e-mail item to the Calendar, Outlook creates an appointment. The New Appointment dialog window will open showing the current date and time; change the date and time, if necessary, and you're ready to go.

✦ Drag an e-mail item to the Tasks folder, and you're ready to follow-up on an e-mail. Outlook creates a new task — the details of the e-mail become the details of the task, as shown in Figure 1-4.

✦ If you love sticky notes, drag an e-mail message to the Notes folder. A new note will open with the contents of the e-mail; optionally, you can fill in any other details that you'd like to record at the top of the note.

✦ Drag a Calendar activity to the Inbox to remind someone about an appointment. Fill in the contact's e-mail address, and you're ready to send the reminder off.

✦ Drag a contact to the Inbox to have Outlook create a new e-mail message addressed to the contact.

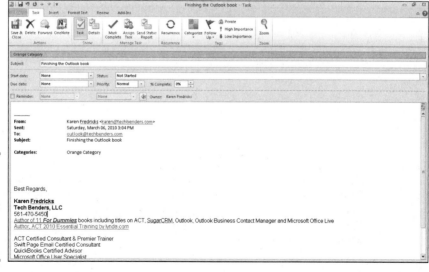

Figure 1-4:
Creating a
Task from
an incoming
e-mail
message.

Cleaning Up Your Mess

Needless to say, while you create and receive more and more Outlook items, your Outlook file gets bigger and bigger. Having a bloated data file slows down your search when you try to find an item or, even worse, makes Outlook slow to open. You may also find that creating a backup of a large data file takes a lo-o-o-ng time.

Most people have at least a few tools to help keep up with housekeeping at their homes. Similarly, Outlook has several cleanup tools up its sleeve.

Cleaning up your folders

For many people, the best part of watching *The Jetsons* cartoon was watching the various robots whisking around, taking care of their human counterparts. Outlook's Clean Up feature is kind of like one of those robots. The Clean Up option scours your folders for all duplicate messages and removes them.

Follow these steps to make Outlook get you cleaned up in a jiffy:

1. **Select the folder that needs TLC (tender loving cleaning).**

2. **Click the Folder tab on Outlook's Ribbon, and then click the Clean Up Folder button in the Clean Up section.**

3. **From the drop-down menu select Clean Up Folder to clean up your currently selected folder or Clean Up Folder & Subfolders if the currently selected folder contains sub-folders that you'd like to clean.**

The Clean Up Folder dialog box appears. (See Figure 1-5.)

Figure 1-5:
The Clean Up Folder dialog box.

4. **Click the Settings button to indicate your cleaning preferences.**

The Outlook Options window for the kind of folder you selected in Step 1 appears. If you sniff really hard, you might catch a whiff of disinfectant. As you can see in Figure 1-6, you have a number of options. For example, you can opt to create a folder for all those messy messages, just in case Outlook is a bit too zealous in its cleaning effort. Or you might prefer to have Outlook ignore any messages that you haven't had a chance to read yet.

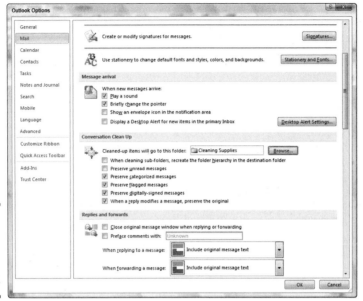

Figure 1-6:
Changing
your
cleaning
preferences.

5. **Click OK to save your preferences and return to the Clean Up Folder dialog box; after the dialog box appears, click the Clean Up Folder button.**

   Outlook cheerfully provides you with a recap of what, if anything, it removed.

Giving Outlook a bit of spring cleaning

Having an excessive amount of e-mail is probably the biggest culprit of Outlook data bloat. Theoretically, you could skim through every one of your Outlook folders and start cleaning them either manually or by using the Clean Up Folder tool. The Clean Up tool will clean up existing e-mail messages based on their date and/or size.

Outlook's Mailbox Cleanup tool gives you a bit more direction if you follow a two-step process:

✦ Evaluate the size of each of your Outlook folders so that you know which ones you want to start pruning.

✦ Search for items that match specific criteria so that you can apply some logic to exactly which items you get rid of.

Follow these steps to start the cleanup process:

1. **Click the File tab, then click the Cleanup Tools button on the Info area of the Navigation pane and select Mailbox Cleanup from the pop-up menu that appears.**

The Mailbox Cleanup dialog box opens, as shown in Figure 1-7.

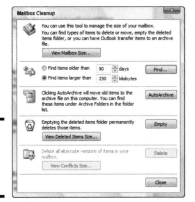

Figure 1-7:
Cleaning up your mailbox.

2. **Click the View Mailbox Size button.**

The Folder Size dialog box opens. (See Figure 1-8.) This dialog box allows you to get a handle on which of your folders are manageable and which ones need to be put on a diet. Oddly enough, even though you clicked the View Mailbox Size button to arrive at this dialog box, you can view the size of *all* your folders.

Figure 1-8:
Viewing the size of your Outlook folders.

3. **Make note of any of the folders that need to go on a quick weight-loss plan, and then click the Close button.**

Although the Folder Size dialog box doesn't let you reduce the size of your folders immediately, it allows you to decide which of your folders you want to prune, archive, or delete entirely.

4. **Back in the Mailbox Cleanup dialog box, select one of the Find radio buttons and enter a value.**

   You have the following options:

   • *Find Items Older than* Number of *Days:* Enter a number between 1 and 999 in the text box.

   • *Find Items Larger than* Number of *Kilobytes:* Enter a number between 1 and 9,999 in the text box.

5. **Click the Find button.**

   The Advanced Find dialog box opens. (See Figure 1-9.) By default, you see all the e-mail that matches the criteria you entered.

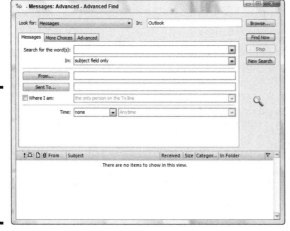

Figure 1-9: Being specific about the Outlook items that you want to clean up.

6. **Click the Browse button to open the Select folders dialog box.**

7. **Select the Outlook folders that you want to clean by placing a check-mark in front of each folder, and then click OK.**

   The detective work that you did in Step 3 comes into play in this step. You probably want to browse to the folders that you feel are in the most need of cleaning. After you click OK, the Advanced Find dialog box reappears.

8. **(Optional) Refine your search by filling in additional information in the various search fields of the Advanced Find dialog box.**

   You can create a very targeted search by looking for specific keywords and indicating where to look for them. For example, you might look for the word contract in the subject line of e-mail messages. You can even search for messages that were sent from or to a specific individual.

9. **Select items from the Advanced Find results pane and give them a right-click, then select which cleanup option you want from the pop-up menu that appears.**

   You have these options:

   • *Delete:* Get rid of the selected items permanently.

   • *Move to Folder:* Relocate the selected items to another Outlook folder.

10. **Click the Close button (the X) in the upper-right corner of the Advanced Find dialog box to close it, or click New Search to hunt down more items to clean up.**

    No one said that cleaning up your data would be an immediate process. You may need to hunt through a whole lot of folders, cleaning while you go. By doing a bit of advanced scouting in Step 3, however, you can get a good idea of where to start.

Emptying the trash

When you delete Outlook items, they're moved to the Deleted Items folder. This is a good thing; if you've ever thrown out a piece of clothing only to find a day later that you really wanted it, you'll know what I mean. However, you can't hold on to all your deleted items forever. You can get rid of them in one fell swoop by following these steps:

1. **Right-click the Deleted Items folder and select Empty "Deleted Items" Folder from the pop-up menu that appears.**

   A stern warning dialog box appears, asking you whether you're 100-per-cent positive that you want to delete the items in your Deleted Items folder on a permanent basis.

2. **Click Yes in the scary warning dialog box.**

   Say *sayonara* to the contents of your Deleted Items folder because they're now gone — permanently.

If you prefer, you can have Outlook empty your Deleted Items folder each time you exit Outlook. To empty the Deleted Items automatically, click the File tab, and then select Options to open the Options dialog box. Click the Advanced tab and select the Empty the Deleted Items Folder when Exiting Outlook check box and then click OK to close the Options dialog box.

If you set the option to allow Outlook to empty the Deleted Items folder every time you close Outlook, you should be aware of one thing: Outlook deletes the entire contents of your Deleted Items folder permanently without stopping to take prisoners. You can't reverse this process, so choose this option carefully!

This is one for the archives

Outlook's Personal Folder file (`outlook.pst`) contains all your current data. However, Outlook also allows you to create another file (`archive.pst`) that holds all the items that you no longer use but still want to keep close at hand. Best of all, you can put the archive file in set-it-and-forget-it mode, which means that Outlook periodically moves items from your current Outlook file to your archive file. Talk about speed cleaning!

When you archive a folder, all the items in that folder which match your criteria are moved into an archival folder. Generally, you move old items so that you can more easily work with the latest and greatest information. If you happen to need to look at some of your older items, you can easily access them by looking at the archival folders.

Turning AutoArchive on autopilot

The first thing you need to know is how to check to see whether AutoArchive is working and, if so, how you can shut it off, if necessary. After you turn on AutoArchive, you can specify which folders you want to have Outlook archive for you. To verify the status of AutoArchive, follow these steps:

1. **Click the AutoArchive Settings button in the Properties section of the Ribbon's Folder tab.**

The Inbox Properties dialog box opens.

2. **Select the Archive Items in This Folder Using the Default Settings radio button, and then click the Default Archive Settings button.**

The AutoArchive dialog box opens. (See Figure 1-10.)

Figure 1-10: Setting up AutoArchive to archive old information automatically.

3. **Select your AutoArchive options.**

As you can see from Figure 1-10, Outlook can archive your data in a variety of ways. You have these options:

- Run AutoArchive Every *Number of* Days

  Deselect the Run AutoArchive Every *Number of* Days check box if you don't want Outlook to automatically archive your data.

- Prompt before AutoArchive Runs

- Delete Expired Items (E-Mail Folders Only)

- Archive or Delete Old Items

- Show Archive Folder in Folder List

You can also indicate the time frame used to identify old items and whether you want to move items to the archive folders or delete them permanently.

4. **Click OK to close the AutoArchive dialog box, and then click OK in the Inbox Properties dialog box to close it.**

Removing AutoArchive from individual folders

By default, the AutoArchive feature archives all your data folders. In general, the whole idea behind archiving is to keep the really important stuff around for posterity. When Outlook archives your data, it moves it into separate archive folders and creates an entirely new .pst file.

You may not think you really need to archive the Deleted Items folder. On the other hand, you may have a few folders that are so important, you don't want any of the items in them moved into an archival folder. Therefore, Outlook provides you with a way to turn archiving on — or off — on a folder-by-folder basis. Follow these steps:

1. **Right-click the folder that you want to AutoArchive, and then select Properties from the pop-up menu that appears.**

   The Properties dialog box for the chosen folder appears.

   Unfortunately, you have to do this procedure for each folder individually.

2. **Click the dialog box's AutoArchive tab.**

   As shown in Figure 1-11, you have several archival options whose radio buttons you can select:

   - Do Not Archive Items in This Folder

   - Archive Items in This Folder Using the Default Settings

   - Archive This Folder Using These Settings

     The options you fill in if you select this radio button include moving the archived items to a new folder or deleting them completely.

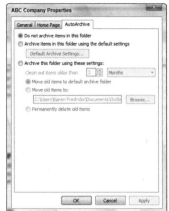

Figure 1-11:
Changing
the Archive
options for
an individual
folder.

3. **Select the radio button for the option you want to apply.**

If you select Archive This Folder Using These Settings, you also have to specify the setting options that appear below it.

4. **Click OK to close the selected folder's Properties dialog box.**

From this point forward, the folder is governed by the rules you set in Step 3 each time Outlook runs AutoArchive.

Archiving items manually

As nice as the thought of archiving your information automatically may be, you might feel more comfortable doing it on your own schedule, rather than on an automated one. Outlook is cool with that. Follow these steps:

1. **Click the File tab on the ribbon, click the Cleanup Tools button in the Info area of the Navigation Pane and select Archive from the popup menu that appears.**

The Archive dialog box opens, as shown in Figure 1-12.

Figure 1-12:
Choosing
the archive
options
manually.

2. **Select the radio button for the folders you want to archive.**

   You have these options:

   - *Archive All Folders According to Their AutoArchive Settings:* This option archives all the folders for which you're set archiving options.

   - *Archive This Folder and All Subfolders:* This option archives only the folder(s) you select in the list box below the radio button.

3. **(Optional) Select a date in the Archive Items Older Than drop-down list to specify which items you consider old enough to archive.**

4. **(Optional) Select the Include Items with "Do Not AutoArchive" Checked check box if you want to archive information you'd previously decided *not* to archive.**

5. **(Optional) Enter a different filename in the Archive File text box if you want to archive your items to a file other than the default archive file.**

   You can click the Browse button and navigate to the proper location in the Open outlo0ok Data Files dialog window to specify this file, if you want.

6. **Click OK to archive your data or Cancel to exit without archiving.**

7. **Click the Home tab to return to the main Outlook view.**

   Outlook now moves any items that match the archiving criteria into the archival folder. No need to panic; you can still access them, as I describe in the following section.

Looking into the archives

The cool thing about archiving your Outlook data is that the information you archived is still right at your fingertips — you don't have to go through a lengthy restore procedure to get to it.

To get a peek at your archived data, follow these steps:

1. **Click the File tab, select the Open from the list on the left, and then click the Open Outlook Data File icon in the main pane.**

   The Open Outlook Data File dialog box appears.

2. **Select `archive.pst` (or whatever you named your archive file) from the Open Outlook Data File dialog box, and then click OK.**

   You return with a thump to the main Outlook view. Discerning eyes, however, will notice a new addition at the bottom of the Folder List: Archives.

3. **Click the plus sign to the left of Archives.**

   The folders you've archived are all listed there, as shown in Figure 1-13.

4. **Click the archive folder that you want to access.**

The contents appear in the main Outlook pane. The contents of the archive folders are somewhat dated because, after all, they contain only those items you deemed old enough to archive.

Figure 1-13:
Looking
at the
Archives.

Restoring from an archive

Don't panic if you accidentally archive too much data and find that you're missing critical information from your regular Outlook folders. You can drag items from an Archive folder back to a regular folder manually, or you can copy the contents of all your Archive Folders back to their original state by importing the `archive.pst` file back into your main `outlook.pst` file.

In order to import the `archive.pst` file into the `outlook.pst` file, you need to close the archive file by right-clicking it and selecting Close "Archives" from the pop-up menu that appears.

Follow these steps to restore a file from the archive:

1. **Click the File tab, select Open on the Navigation pane, and then click the Import icon.**

Outlook's Import and Export Wizard opens. The Import from Another Program or File item should already be highlighted in the Choose an Action to Perform list box, as shown in Figure 1-14.

2. **Click Next to continue.**

The Import a File dialog box opens; see Figure 1-15.

3. **Select Outlook Data File (.pst), and then click Next.**

The next screen of the wizard (Import Outlook Data File) appears; see Figure 1-16.

Figure 1-14:
Importing
your
archived
information
back into
Outlook.

Figure 1-15:
Selecting
the file type
to import
into Outlook.

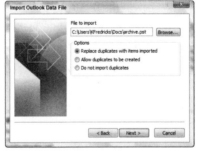

Figure 1-16:
Dealing with
duplicates
when
importing an
archive file.

4. **Use the Browse button to locate your archive file, and then select the appropriate Options radio button.**

   You can replace any duplicates with the imported items, allow duplicates to be created, or not import duplicates. Replacing duplicates with the imported items is probably your safest bet so that you don't end up with a lot of duplicate information.

5. **Click Next to continue.**

   The next screen of the wizard (also labeled Import Outlook Data File) appears. (See Figure 1-17.)

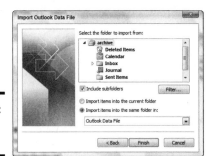

Figure 1-17:
Select a
folder.

6. **In the Select a Folder to Import From list box, navigate to and select the appropriate folder.**

   Select the Include Subfolders check box if you want to include all the subfolders, as well.

7. **Select the Import Items into the Current Folder radio button if you want to restore your archive to one folder; select the Import Items into the Same Folder In radio button and select an Outlook file from the drop-down list if you want the archival items to return to a different Outlook file.**

8. **Click Finish to close the Import and Export Wizard and place all the archived items back to the location you selected.**

Chapter 2: Playing by the Rules

In This Chapter

✔ **Creating basic e-mail rules**

✔ **Creating advanced rules**

✔ **Managing the rules**

*I*t's always nice to play by the rules — at least, that's probably what your mother told you when you were little. As an adult, it's even more fun to play by the rules when you get to create them yourself. This chapter shows you how to transform Outlook into a smart mail clerk that grabs all your incoming e-mails and sorts them automatically for you. Best of all, if your life changes, you can easily change the rules to better suit your new status without the risk of having several game pieces thrown back into your face.

Making Up the Rules as You Go

You can probably visualize a typical mailroom in your mind: Someone with a huge basket of new mail diligently sorts through the pile and places each piece of mail into the appropriate mailbox. That's the very same concept behind the rules that you can have Outlook follow. While your incoming e-mail pours in, Outlook can sort that mail and place it into the appropriate folder.

Creating the basic game plan

The main purpose of an Outlook rule is to make sure that nothing gets lost in the shuffle. Many situations can arise in which a rule can make your life — or, at least, your e-mail — much more manageable.

In case you're wondering whether these rules apply to moving junk mail — yes, they do. If you take a peek at Chapter 3 of this minibook, you can find out how Outlook makes mincemeat out of spam.

Follow these steps to create a basic rule:

1. **Click the Inbox in Outlook's Folder list.**

The rules you're creating work with your e-mail, so it's only fitting that your Inbox becomes your starting line.

2. Click the Rules button in the Move section of the Ribbon's Home tab and select Create Rule from the pop-up menu that appears.

The Create Rule dialog box appears, as shown in Figure 2-1.

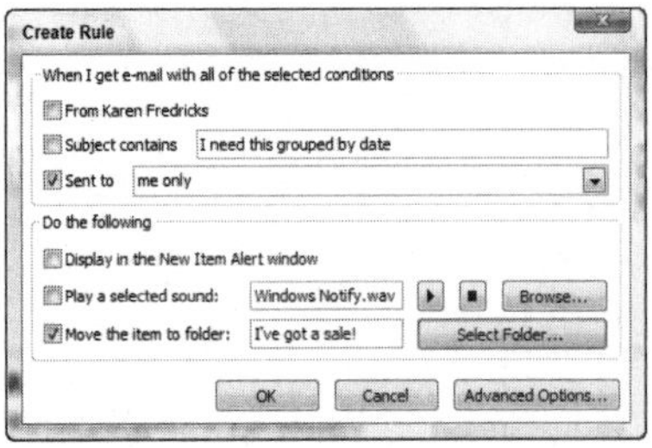

Figure 2-1:
The Create
Rule dialog
box.

3. Select your rule condition(s) and fill in the appropriate content.

Select these check boxes and fill in the appropriate information, if you want:

- *From:* Make sure that all e-mail from a particular person gets sent to a specific folder and/or flagged for follow-up.

- *Subject Contains:* Have all incoming e-mail that contains specific words in the subject line, which you type in the Subject Contains text box, to end up in a specified folder.

- *Sent To:* Move mail that you've sent to particular people (whom you select from the Sent To drop-down list) to specific folders.

4. Select your rule action(s).

You can select any of these check boxes and fill in the appropriate information:

- *Display in the New Item Alert Window:* A pop-up window appears when your boss, for example, sends you a message.

- *Play a Selected Sound:* Outlook sounds an alarm anytime a message arrives from your spouse, or someone else who has high placement on the food chain. Click the Browse button and, in dialog box that appears, click the sound you want to play.

- *Move the Item to Folder:* Move any e-mail that you receive from a specific person to a specific folder. Click the Select Folder button and, in the dialog box that appears, click the folder you want to use.

5. Click OK to save your rule.

If the powers that be — in this case, Outlook — approve your rule, the dialog box you see in Figure 2-2 appears.

Figure 2-2:
Success!
You've
created a
new rule.

Taking rules the whole nine yards

By now you're probably thinking that you have customized your rule in every way possible. But wait. In several situations, you may need an even more sophisticated rule:

✦ You want only those e-mails from Mr. Big that are set at a certain priority level to be transferred to another folder.

✦ You're tracking multiple e-mail addresses and want the mail clerk (in this case, Outlook) to sort your messages into corresponding folders.

✦ You want to move all the bounced e-mail that's returned to you into another folder so that you can take further action later.

✦ You want to be on the lookout for e-mail that contains specific words or phrases.

You can handle all these situations by using Outlook rules. And, even though you might need a very complex and complicated rule, Outlook comes equipped with a handy dandy wizard to guide you through the process. Have it help you by following these steps:

1. **Click the Inbox in Outlook's Folder list.**

   Rules are associated with a specific Inbox. If you've subdivided your Inbox into subfolders, you can create a rule for anyone of those subfolders.

2. **Click the Rules button in the Move section of the Ribbon's Home tab and select Create Rule from the pop-up menu that appears.**

   The Create Rule dialog box appears.

3. **Click the Advanced Options button.**

   If all systems are go, the Rules Wizard (as shown in Figure 2-3) appears.

   Although the Rules Wizard looks a bit daunting at first, it's relatively easy to master. The Which Condition(s) Do You Want to Check page (the first page of the wizard) is divided into two areas: The Step 1 area offers a selection of conditions, and the Step 2 area gives you a description of the selected condition(s).

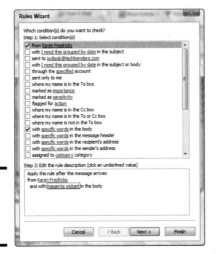

Figure 2-3:
The Rules
Wizard
dialog box.

4. **Select the conditions in the Step 1 area that apply to your rule.**

   You can think of this area as your favorite Chinese restaurant — feel free to select as many items as you want from column A. A description of each item you check appears in the Step 2 area at the bottom of the Rules Wizard dialog box.

5. **Fill in the details for each condition that you selected by clicking the underlined words in the Step 2: Edit the Rule Description area.**

   Figure 2-4 shows an example of the dialog box that opens when you click the Specific Words link.

Figure 2-4:
Adding
specific
words to
the rule's
searching
criteria.

6. **Fill in the criteria that you're looking for, and then click OK.**

   For example, you might have selected the With Specific Words in the Body condition, and you want to indicate that you're looking for messages that contain the phrase *magenta widget*.

7. Fill in the criteria for any of the other conditions that you selected in Step 4, and then click Next to continue to the next page of the Rules Wizard.

After you specify the criteria of the messages that you're looking for, you need to tell Outlook what you actually want to *do* with the messages that meet the criteria. The What Do You Want to Do with the Message page that appears is divided into two areas — the actions and the rule description — in much the same way as the first page of the Rules Wizard.

8. Select the desired actions from the Step 1: Select Action(s) area.

You can take several courses of action. Here are a few that you might find particularly useful:

- Assign the e-mail to a category.

- Forward the e-mail to someone else.

- Flag the message or mark it as important.

- Print the message.

When you select each action, a corresponding rule description appears in the Step 2: Edit the Rule Description area of the Rules Wizard dialog box, as you see in Figure 2-5.

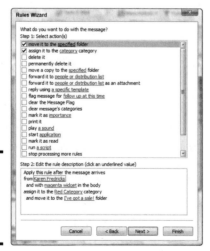

Figure 2-5:
The second
step of
the Rules
Wizard

9. Edit the rule description by clicking the underlined values, filling in the appropriate information in the dialog box that appears, and then clicking OK.

For example, if you selected Assign It to the *Category* Category as one of your actions, you click Category in the rule description area and select one of your categories from the listing.

10. **Click Next to continue.**

Most — if not all — rules have exceptions, and as Figure 2-6 illustrates, the third page of the Rules Wizard (the Are There Any Exceptions page) is exactly the place to define them. For example, you might want to run a rule, except when the message comes from a specific person or already has been assigned a category. Once again, the dialog box is divided into two areas: the exceptions and the description. When you select each action, a corresponding rule description appears in the Step 2: Edit the Rule Description area.

Figure 2-6:
Adding an exception to the rule.

11. **Select any exceptions to the rule, then edit the rule description by clicking the underlined value, filling in the appropriate information in the dialog box that appears, and then clicking OK to return to the wizard.**

For example, you may not want to have a rule apply to incoming mail that's marked as High Importance.

12. **Click Next to continue.**

Finally! You've arrived at the last page of the wizard (the Finish Rule Setup page). You can see it first hand in Figure 2-7.

Figure 2-7:
The final
step of
the Rules
Wizard.

13. **You have a few more simple choices to make.**

The page includes these settings:

- Specify a name for the rule.

- Indicate whether you want to run the rule on existing messages in your Inbox.

- Indicate whether you want to turn on the rule.

You might also give your rule the once-over for accuracy by reviewing the description in the Step 3: Review Rule Description area.

14. **Click Finish to close the Rules Wizard, and then click OK in the Create Rule dialog box to close it.**

15. **(Optional) Give yourself a high five while you think about how organized you've become!**

Adding bells and whistles to your rules

When you were little, you probably made up games with your friends. After a while, you might have decided to tweak the rules of the game a bit — so that they were more in your favor. The preceding section shows you how to create a basic rule. In this section, you can find out how to bend those rules so that they keep you even more organized.

Return to the scene of the crime — or, at least, of your original rule — to tweak an existing rule. Follow these steps to change a rule:

1. **Click the Inbox in Outlook's folder list.**

2. **Click the Rules button in the Move section of the Ribbon's Home tab and select Manage Rules & Alerts from the pop-up menu that appears.**

The Rules and Alerts dialog box appears.

3. **Select an existing rule, and then click the Change Rule button to reveal the Change Rule pop-up menu shown in Figure 2-8.**

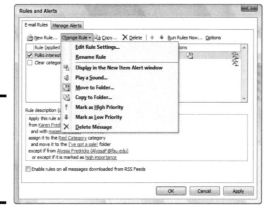

4. **Click a rule option.**

The first two choices are fairly straightforward:

•   *Edit Rule Settings:* If your rule just isn't doing the trick, this option allows you to revisit your rule and change it accordingly.

•   *Rename Rule:* When you originally create a basic rule, Outlook gave it a catchy title. You might decide to give your rule a different name down the road.

The remaining options work on a toggle basis; the first time you click an option, you're prompted to fill in the required information. The next time you click that option, whatever you entered as your preference is removed. The details for each option are as follows:

•   *Display in the New Item Alert Window:* Select this option if you're just dying to know when you receive an e-mail from someone. You receive a special alert, just like the one you see in Figure 2-9; you can even assign a name to the alert, such as Holy Guacamole.

- *Play a Sound:* Assign a sound to play when the special e-mail arrives, such as Beethoven's Fifth or an eloquent Ta-Da.

- *Move to Folder:* Here's your chance to change the folder to which your e-mail moves if you're not happy with the location you originally selected for storage.

- *Copy to Folder:* If you want to be doubly sure that your e-mail doesn't get lost in the crowd, you might consider copying it to a new folder and leaving it in your Inbox until you can follow up on it.

- *Mark as High Priority:* Automatically flag an important incoming e-mail as a high priority.

- *Mark as Low Priority:* Tired of your nagging mother or a high-maintenance client? You can have Outlook mark their messages as low priority items.

- *Delete Message:* Automatically delete an e-mail that arrives from a specific person; this option works especially well when dealing with ex-spouses.

Bending the Rules

Although you may not agree that rules are meant to be broken, you might want to bend them a bit. You can temporarily turn off a rule or use one of your rules for the basis of another rule.

Running with the rules

After you create your rule, you may find that it's not working. You go back to double-check the rule for accuracy, following the steps in the section "Adding bells and whistles to your rules," earlier in this chapter, to no avail. In life, the best solution is often the simplest solution. This idea is particularly true in the computer world. Your rule might not be working because you've never run it on your existing e-mail — or maybe you just haven't turned on the rule. If your rules aren't behaving like you want them to, the following sections can tell you how to remedy the situation.

Teaching old e-mail new rules

When you create a rule, it applies to all the new e-mail that pours into your Inbox. But how about all the e-mail that's sitting in your Inbox waiting for you to take action? When you create a new rule from scratch, Outlook gives you the option to run the rule on existing e-mail. But what if you didn't choose that option? You need to run the rule on your Inbox to take care of all your existing e-mail.

Follow these steps to run your rule on existing mail:

1. **Click the Inbox in Outlook's Folder list.**

2. **Click the Rules button in the Move section of the Ribbon's Home tab and select Manage Rules & Alerts from the pop-up menu that appears.**

   The Rules and Alerts dialog box appears, as shown in Figure 2-10.

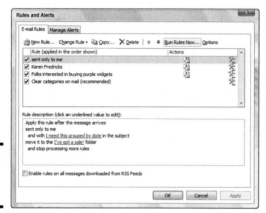

Figure 2-10:
Running a
rule.

3. **Click the Run Rules Now button.**

   The Run Rules Now dialog box, shown in Figure 2-11, appears before your very eyes.

Figure 2-11:
Applying a
new rule
to existing
e-mail.

4. **Select the check boxes for the rules that you want to run.**

5. **(Optional) Select a different Inbox folder by clicking the Browse button to the right of Run in Folder and selecting a different folder from the dialog box that appears.**

6. **(Optional) If you want to include the subfolders of the folder that you selected in Step 5, select the Include Subfolders check box.**

7. **In the Apply Rules To drop-down list, select the type of messages on which you want to run the rule.**

You can run the rule on all messages, unread messages, or read messages.

8. **Click Close to close the Run Rules Now dialog box, and then OK in the Rules and Alerts dialog box to close it.**

Your rules go off to do their thing.

Stop the rule, 1 want to get off

Over a period of time, you might find that your rule works too well, and you want to turn it off for a while so that you can think about what you want that rule to accomplish.

Follow these steps to turn a rule off — and back on again:

1. **Click the Inbox in Outlook's Folder list.**

2. **Click the Rules button in the Move section of the Ribbon's Home tab and select Manage Rules & Alerts from the pop-up menu that appears.**

The Rules and Alerts dialog box appears (refer to Figure 2-10). A slight feeling of déjà vu may be coming over you because you've definitely been here before!

3. **Deselect the check box in front of the rule that you want to turn off.**

When you want to turn the rule back on again, make sure that you place a check mark in front of the rule once again.

4. **Click OK to finish.**

Cheating with the Rules

Over the years, you've probably discovered a whole bunch of computer shortcuts. Most people love shortcuts because they help you get more things accomplished in less time. The same theory holds true with rules. After you spend hours slaving over a rule (or, at least, tell your boss that you've spent hours), you might want to clone your rule. Maybe you set up a cool rule to move all the e-mails that come from Mr. Big to the Mr. Big folder, mark them as important, and categorize them as green for money. Now, you want to do the same thing for Mr. Grande. Or maybe one of your co-workers is so impressed by your Inbox organizational skills that he or she is willing to trade you a large plate of chocolate chip cookies for your list of rules.

Copying a rule

In general, you can more easily tweak an existing rule rather than start over again from scratch. Copying a rule enables you to take an existing rule, clone it, and then make minor modifications to it. Just follow these steps:

1. **Click the Inbox in Outlook's Folder list.**

2. **Click the Rules button in the Move section of the Ribbon's Home tab and select Manage Rules & Alerts from the pop-up menu that appears.**

The Rules and Alerts dialog box makes an appearance.

3. **Select the rule that you want to clone from the Rules and Alerts dialog box.**

4. **Click the Copy button.**

The Copy Rule To dialog box opens (see Figure 2-12). By default, the new rule applies to your Inbox.

Figure 2-12:
The Copy
Rule To
dialog box.

5. **Click OK to close the Copy Rule To dialog box.**

6. **Click OK in the Rules and Alerts dialog box to finish.**

Your cloned rule now appears in your list of rules with a snappy name like Copy of Mr. Big Rule. At this point, you can modify the rule following the steps in the section "Creating the basic game plan," earlier in this chapter.

Importing and exporting a list of rules

Every office generally has two types of computer users: those who can figure out most things and those who ask for help from the ones who can figure out most things. Because you're reading this book, you probably are (or will be) in that first group of computer users. Being in the know has a decided advantage: You can use your power to extract payment from the other, less-computer-literate members of the crowd.

If one of the computer-challenged members of your office compliments you on your rules, you can export your list of rules, and then import them into his or her copy of Outlook. Not only does this process save a great deal of time, but you also look like a hero.

Exporting a list of rules

You can easily export a list of rules, if you follow these steps:

1. **Click the Inbox in Outlook's Folder list.**

2. **Click the Rules button in the Move section of the Ribbon's Home tab and select Manage Rules & Alerts from the pop-up menu that appears.**

   The Rules and Alerts dialog box appears.

3. **Click the Options button.**

   The Options dialog box, just like the one shown in Figure 2-13, opens.

Figure 2-13:
Exporting a
list of rules.

4. **Click the Export Rules button.**

   The appropriately named Export Rules dialog box appears.

5. **Using the dialog box, give the Export file a name, save it to the location of your choice, and then click the Save button.**

   Outlook automatically assigns the `.rwz` extension to the file.

   The Options dialog box reappears.

6. **Click OK to close the Options dialog box, and then click OK in the Rules and Alerts dialog box to close it.**

It never hurts to have a backup. If you save the export file to an external source, you have a backup of your Outlook rules, just in case something wacky should happen in the future.

Importing a list of rules

After you successfully create an export file, you can import your rules to another computer. The rules in the import file are added to existing Outlook rules.

The going rate for a good list of Outlook rules is one large plate of cookies!

Import your rules by following these steps:

1. **Click the Inbox in Outlook's Folder list.**

2. **Click the Rules button in the Move section of the Ribbon's Home tab and select Manage Rules & Alerts from the pop-up menu that appears.**

3. **Click the Options button on the Rules and Alerts dialog box that opens, and then click the Import Rules button in the Options dialog box that opens.**

4. **Using the Import Rules dialog box, navigate to the location of the rules' export file, select the file, and then click Open.**

5. **Click OK to close the Options dialog box, and then click OK in the Rules and Alerts dialog box to close it.**

Although importing doesn't remove or override any of your previously created Outlook rules, importing adds duplicate rules of the same name. For example, if you have a Mr. Big rule and import another Mr. Big rule, you're left with two Mr. Big rules. Although the math is simple, you have to decide which rule you want to keep and which one you want to delete.

Throwing your rules out the window

Easy come, easy go. Over a period of time, you may no longer need a particular rule; maybe you're no longer running that great special on magenta widgets or working with that big client. In any event, you can break those rules — and not get into any trouble!

Follow these steps to delete a rule:

1. **Click the Inbox in Outlook's Folder list.**

2. **Click the Rules button in the Move section of the Ribbon's Home tab and select Manage Rules & Alerts from the pop-up menu that appears.**

3. **Select the rule you want to delete in the Rules and Alerts dialog box that opens, and then click the Delete button.**

   Outlook, always the epitome of a helpful software program, opens a dialog box that politely asks whether you're really sure that you want to delete, remove, and permanently obliterate the selected rule.

4. **Click Yes to delete the rule, and then OK in the Rules and Alerts dialog box to close it.**

Chapter 3: Making Mincemeat Out of Spam

*L*ike it or not, spam has become a way of life for anyone using e-mail. Outlook tries its very best to help you manage the seemingly endless piles of junk mail that are delivered right to your door — or, actually, your Inbox. This chapter shows you how Outlook sorts through your incoming e-mail and moves any suspicious messages to the Junk E-Mail folder. You can also find out how to protect yourself from any phishing scams designed to bilk you out of your hard-earned money. Finally, we talk about the Outlook Postmark that offers you another level of e-mail protection.

Maintaining Your Junk

If the problem weren't so serious, the thought of "maintaining" your junk mail would almost sound humorous. ("What do you want to do when you grow up, Tommy?" "Well, my dream is to someday be able to maintain junk mail.") All humor aside, though, you should do a few things to ensure that Outlook's e-mail filter gives you the level of protection that you need.

Changing the level of protection in the junk e-mail filter

By default, the junk e-mail filter in Microsoft Office Outlook 2010 is turned on, and the protection level is set to Low, which is the setting that's designed to catch only the most obvious spam. You can make the filter more aggressive or turn it off completely by changing the level of protection. Follow these steps:

1. **Right-click any of the e-mail messages in your Inbox and select Junk⇨ Junk E-Mail Options from the menu that appears.**

   The Junk E-Mail Options dialog box opens, as shown in Figure 3-1.

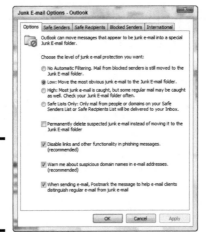

Figure 3-1:
The Junk
E-Mail
Options
dialog box.

2. **Select the radio button for the level of protection that you want on the Options tab.**

   You can choose from

   - *No Automatic Filtering:* Turns off the automatic junk e-mail filter. However, Outlook continues to move messages from people on your Blocked Senders list to the Junk E-Mail folder.

   - *Low:* Filters out only the most obvious junk e-mail messages — generally those trying to lower your mortgage rate, sell you prescriptive medication or make changes to your bank account.

     Microsoft uses an evaluation process that is based on several factors to determine which e-mail will be sent to the Junk E-mail folder. The filter does not look for specific senders, but rather the content of incoming messages, including the time when the message was sent. Although the filtering processes uses some sort of advanced analysis known only to the detectives at Microsoft, the process is far from perfect. Consequently, expect to have some spam slip through the cracks and land in your Inbox while the message from your best friend might end up in the Junk folder.

   - *High:* Use this option if a lot of spam is still appearing in your Inbox with the Low setting. Just make sure that you check your Junk E-Mail folder very carefully because chances are pretty good that Outlook is going to send some legitimate e-mail there.

   - *Safe Lists Only:* Select this option if you only receive e-mail from a limited number of people and your Inbox is flooded with spam. Outlook delivers only messages from your Safe Senders list to your Inbox; the rest are neatly deposited in your Junk E-Mail folder.

3. **(Optional) Select the Permanently Delete Suspected Junk E-Mail Instead of Moving It to the Junk E-Mail Folder check box.**

   Unless you receive e-mail from only a very limited number of people, you probably don't want to use this option. Outlook automatically — and permanently — deletes any messages that it perceives to be spam.

4. **Select the Disable Links and Other Functionality in Phishing Messages check box.**

   Graphics can give an ordinary e-mail message a bit of extra pizzazz. Legitimate e-mailers often link to graphics on their Web sites to avoid embedding a large graphic in the body of an incoming e-mail. Unfortunately, spammers often embed links in graphics that send a signal to the spammer when you open a graphic, making you a prime candidate for more spam. Selecting this option makes you a less likely target for spam.

5. **Select the Warn Me about Suspicious Domain Names in E-Mail Addresses check box.**

   A warning dialog box appears when an incoming e-mail arrives from a domain name (the part of the e-mail address that appears after the @) that's similar to a well-known company. For example, you might receive a message that tries to fool you into thinking that it was sent by your bank.

6. **Select the When Sending E-Mail, Postmark the Message to Help E-Mail Clients Distinguish Regular E-Mail from Junk E-Mail check box.**

   You can find out more about this feature in the section "Giving Your Mail a Postmark," later in this chapter.

7. **Click OK to save your changes and close the Junk E-Mail Options dialog box.**

Giving senders your seal of approval

Although you might often think that a lot of garbage is landing in your Inbox from your boss or one of your co-workers, you'd probably prefer to take a look at it before Outlook banishes it to the Junk E-Mail folder. Outlook's junk e-mail filter is fairly accurate; however, that e-mail from one of your VIPs might be mistakenly marked as junk. To be on the safe side, you can add names to the Safe Senders list. E-mail addresses that appear in the Safe Senders list are never treated as junk. Follow these steps to designate senders who are always welcome in your Inbox:

1. **Right-click any of the e-mail messages in your Inbox and select Junk⇨ Junk E-Mail Options from the pop-up menu that appears.**

   If you look very carefully at the Delete section of the Ribbon's Home tab, you'll find a tiny Junk icon. Clicking it will immediately send the currently selected e-mail message to the Junk folder. If you do feel compelled to use this button, make sure you only click its drop-down

arrow so that you can specify how you want to handle the current message. Simply clicking the icon might inadvertently send an important message to the Junk folder.

The Junk E-Mail Options dialog box springs to attention.

2. Click the Safe Senders tab.

You can see what it looks like in Figure 3-2.

Figure 3-2:
Adding Safe Senders to the junk e-mail filter.

3. Click the Add button.

The Add Address or Domain dialog box appears (see Figure 3-3).

Figure 3-3:
The Add Address or Domain dialog box.

In the Enter an E-Mail Address or Internet Domain Name to Be Added to the List text box, enter the e-mail address or domain name that you want to accept e-mail from. (By typing *@domain.com* or simply *domain.com*, where *domain* is the domain name of, say, a company you do business with, you include all the e-mail addresses from that company in your Safe Senders list.)

4. **Click OK to close the Add Address or Domain dialog box.**

   Outlook returns you to the Junk E-Mail Options dialog box.

5. **(Optional) Select the Also Trust E-Mail from My Contacts check box if you want to consider all the Contacts in your Outlook Address Book as safe senders.**

6. **(Optional) Select the Automatically Add People I E-Mail to the Safe Senders List check box if you want to add people that you e-mail who might not be included among your contacts.**

7. **(Optional) Select a name and then click the Remove button to remove a name from the Safe Senders list.**

8. **(Optional) Select a name and then click the Edit button to change a name on the Safe Senders list.**

9. **Click OK to close the Junk E-Mail Options dialog box.**

Ensuring that your recipients make the list

Rest assured that you're not the only one out there battling e-mail demons. Your friends, colleagues, and your enemies are all dealing with spam — and hoping that their messages are reaching you. There are times when you are not the only person on the To line — or maybe your name doesn't appear in the To line at all. For example, the sender might put your name in the Cc or Bcc line, or include your name on a distribution list. Outlook often filters those messages as junk. In these cases, you'll want to add the sender's name to the Safe Recipient list. By doing so, you can ensure that their mail, at least, reaches you unscathed.

Add a name to the safe recipients list by following these steps:

1. **Right-click any of the e-mail messages in your Inbox and select Junk⇨Junk E-Mail Options from the pop-up menu that appears.**

   The Junk E-Mail Options dialog box springs open.

2. **Click the Safe Recipients tab.**

   You might be yawning about now because the routine for adding a Safe Recipient is pretty similar to that of adding a Safe Sender. For added excitement, take a peek at the Safe Recipients tab, shown in Figure 3-4.

3. **Click the Add button.**

   The Add Address of Domain dialog box opens.

4. **Enter the name or address that you want to add in the Enter the E-Mail Address or Internet Domain Name to Be Added to the List text box.**

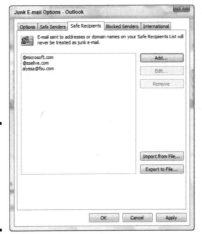

Figure 3-4:
Adding safe
recipients
to the Junk
E-Mail
options.

5. **Click OK to close the Add Address or Domain dialog box and click OK in the Junk E-Mail Options dialog box to close it.**

Blocking a name from your Inbox

You can easily block messages from a specific sender by adding the sender's e-mail address or domain name to the Blocked Senders list. Messages from addresses or domain names in this list are always treated as junk. When you add a sender to the Blocked Senders list, Outlook moves any incoming message from that sender to the Junk E-Mail folder, regardless of the content of the message. Follow these steps to add a sender to your blocked senders list:

1. **Right-click any of the e-mail messages in your Inbox and select Junk⇨Junk E-Mail Options from the pop-up menu that appears.**

   The Junk E-Mail Options dialog box opens.

2. **Click the Blocked Senders tab.**

   Just in case you're wondering, you can see the Blocked Senders tab in Figure 3-5.

3. **Click the Add button.**

   The Add Address or Domain dialog box opens.

4. **Enter the name or address that you want to add in the Enter an E-Mail Address or Internet Domain Name to Be Added to the List text box.**

   You can add specific e-mail addresses, such as `spammer@junk.com`, or an entire domain name, such as `junk.com`.

Figure 3-5:
The Blocked
Senders
tab.

5. **Click OK to close the Add Address or Domain dialog box and click OK in the Junk E-Mail Options dialog box to close it.**

6. **Smile devilishly to yourself while you think of all those nasty spammers who have now been permanently denied entrance to your Inbox.**

Putting Junk in Its Place

Outlook comes equipped with a junk e-mail filter that evaluates incoming messages and moves anything that it thinks might be spam to a special Junk E-Mail folder. By default, Outlook's e-mail filter is set to Low, which means that it finds only the most obvious junk e-mail. After the junk is captured, you can read all these suspicious messages at a later time. If you prefer, you can manually relegate a message to the Junk E-Mail folder.

Relegating a message to the junk pile

No spam filter system is perfect, and Outlook's is no exception. Although Outlook finds the most blatant spam, you may still find a wayward message in your Inbox that wants to help you decrease your mortgage and increase your — well, you can fill in the blank on that one!

If you spot a piece of spam lurking in your Inbox, follow these steps to get rid of it:

1. **Right-click the suspicious message in the Inbox folder and select Junk from the pop-up menu that appears.**

The Junk E-Mail options that you see in Figure 3-6 appear.

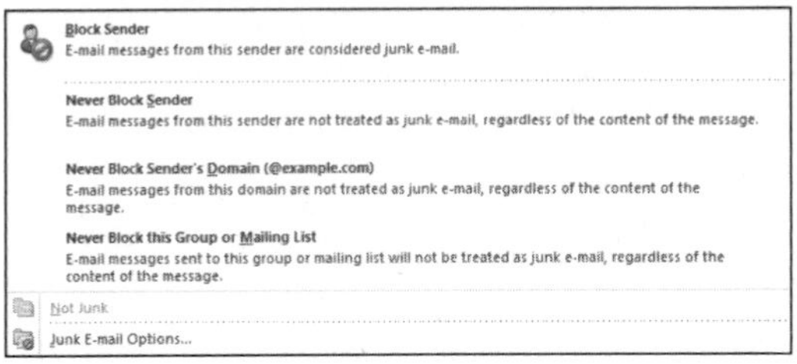

Figure 3-6:
The Blocked
Sender
options.

2. **Select an option.**

   The options are pretty self-explanatory:

   - *Block Sender:* Adds the sender to the Blocked Senders list
   - *Never Block Sender:* Adds the sender to the Safe Senders list
   - *Never Block Sender's Domain:* Adds the sender's domain to the Safe Senders list
   - *Never Block This Group or Mailing List:* Adds the sender to the Safe Recipients list

   If you select the first option, the dialog box you see in Figure 3-7 appears. Like the message says, the e-mail from that sender is zapped to the Junk E-Mail folder. In addition, any new messages that you receive from the same sender will move immediately to the Junk E-Mail folder, leaving you with at least one less piece of spam to deal with!

Figure 3-7:
Dealing
with spam
that lands in
your Inbox.

Sorting through your junk mail

Any message that the junk e-mail filter catches is moved to the special Junk E-Mail folder. You can find the Junk E-Mail folder on Outlook's Folder list, right above the Outbox. You can recognize it by the red circle with the diagonal line running through it, indicating that you can't delete the folder.

Because no spam filter is foolproof, you might want to skim through the messages in your Junk E-Mail folder from time to time to make sure that Outlook didn't mistake something really important for a piece of junk mail. If a message is legitimate, you can move it back to the Inbox or any other folder, and mark it as not junk.

Not sure if any new spam has found its way to the Junk E-mail folder? Outlook will keep track of any new, unread messages and place the total in parenthesis to the right of the Junk E-mail folder.

You can pretty easily sort through your messages and take the appropriate action. Just follow these steps:

1. **Right-click a message in the Junk E-Mail folder and choose Not Junk in the menu that appears.**

   The options you first saw back in Figure 3-6 appear.

2. **Select an option.**

   At this point, you see the same exact options you see when you identify messages in your Inbox as spam (as we describe in the preceding section). However, because you're working with messages that Outlook has marked as spam, concentrate on the three options that can ensure Outlook won't block those messages:

   • Never Block Sender

   • Never Block Sender's Domain

   • Never Block This Group or Mailing List

   In addition, the Not Junk option isn't grayed out. This option provides you with two features for the price of one. It moves the e-mail back to your Inbox, and it adds the sender to the Safe Senders list.

Taking out the trash — permanently

When you delete a message, Outlook automatically moves it to the Deleted Items folder. At that point, you have to delete the message from the Deleted Items folder if you want to permanently remove it. The same process holds true for the Junk E-Mail folder; when you delete one of the messages, it moves to the Deleted Items folder, where you have to deal with it once again. (Alternatively, you might decide to simply delete the entire contents of the Junk E-mail folder and save yourself a drip to the Deleted Items folder.)

After you skim through your Junk E-Mail folder and pick out anything salvageable, you might want to get rid of the true junk once and for all. Follow these steps to do just that:

1. **Right-click the Junk E-Mail folder in the Folder list.**

   A pop-up menu, like the one you see in Figure 3-8, opens.

2. **Select Empty "Junk E-Mail" Folder from the pop-up menu that appears.**

   A warning dialog box appears, asking you whether you're sure that you want to permanently delete all the items in the Junk E-Mail folder.

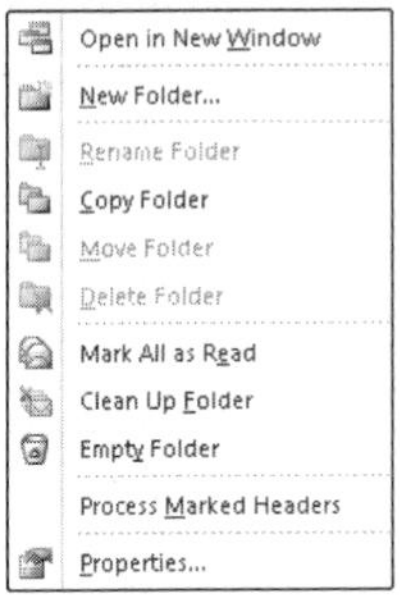

Figure 3-8:
The Junk
E-Mail
folder's
right-click
menu.

3. **Click Yes to remove those annoying junk messages from your life permanently.**

Protecting Yourself from Phishing Attacks

Phishing is a particularly dangerous type of spam. A phishing message tries to get personal information, such as your bank account number and password. Phishing messages sometimes include links to fake Web sites that urge you to enter and submit your personal information; these Web sites may look exactly like the real McCoy.

Because you might have trouble distinguishing a phishing e-mail message from a legitimate one, the junk e-mail filter evaluates each incoming message to see whether it contains suspicious links or was sent by a spoofed e-mail address. Like a protective mother, Outlook tries its best to keep you safe from danger if it suspects phishing by

✦ Sending the message to the Junk E-Mail folder and converting it to plain text

✦ Disabling the links in the message

✦ Preventing you from replying to the message

✦ Blocking any attachments in the suspicious message

✦ Showing you a scary warning if you try to open a link inside the e-mail message

Changing the phishing options

To adjust Outlook's phishing options, follow these steps:

1. **Right-click any of the e-mail messages in your Inbox and select Junk⇨ Junk E-Mail Options from the pop-up menu that appears.**

   You end up on the Options tab of the Junk E-Mail Options dialog box. If you're dying to know what it looks like, take a peek back at Figure 3-1.

Ten tips on how to help reduce spam

This chapter talks about using Outlook's spam filter tools. However, you can do a few other things to reduce your risk of spam:

✔ **Block pictures in HTML messages.** By default, Outlook blocks automatic picture downloads if the content is linked to a server. If you open a message that contains a graphic that links back to a server, and you have this feature turned off, the server is notified that you're downloading a graphic — and that your e-mail address is a valid one.

✔ **Turn off read and delivery receipts and automatic processing of meeting requests.** Spammers sometimes resort to sending meeting requests and messages that include requests for read and delivery receipts. Responding to meeting requests and read receipts helps spammers verify that your e-mail address is a real one.

✔ **Limit the places where you post your e-mail address.** Be cautious about posting your e-mail address on public Web sites, such as newsgroups, chat rooms, bulletin boards, and so forth. When visiting public sites, you might want to use an e-mail address that's different from your main e-mail address. Remove your e-mail address from your personal Web site.

✔ **Review the privacy policies of Web sites.** When you sign up for any online service or newsletter, review the privacy policy of the site carefully before you reveal your e-mail address or other personal information. If the Web site doesn't explain how it plans to use your personal information, consider not using the services at that site.

✔ **Watch out for check boxes that are already selected.** When you shop online, companies sometimes add a check box that's already selected, which indicates that you don't mind if the company sells or gives your e-mail address to other businesses. Clear that check box!

✔ **Don't reply to spam.** Never reply to an e-mail message — not even to unsubscribe from a mailing list — unless you know and trust the sender, such as when the e-mail message comes from a service, an online store, or a newsletter that you've signed up with.

✔ **If a company uses e-mail messages to ask for personal information, don't respond by sending a message.** Most legitimate companies don't ask for personal information to be sent in e-mail. Be suspicious if they do.

✔ **Don't contribute to a charity in response to a request sent in e-mail.** Unfortunately, some spammers prey on your goodwill. If you receive an e-mail appeal from a charity, treat it as spam.

✔ **Don't forward chain e-mail messages.** Besides increasing overall e-mail volume, you lose control over who sees your e-mail address.

✔ **Create a secondary e-mail address that you use when filling out Web forms and making purchases.** Hotmail, Google, and Yahoo! all provide e-mail addresses free of charge. Use an address through one of these services when making an online purchase or accessing a Web site that requires an e-mail address.

2. **Make sure the Disable Links and Other Functionality in Phishing Messages (Recommended) check box is selected.**

   By default, this option is checked, but it never hurts to double-check.

3. **Select the Warn Me about Suspicious Domain Names in E-Mail Addresses (Recommended) check box.**

   This enables Outlook to warn you when it detects a fake domain.

Enable or disable links in phishing e-mail messages

The annoying thing about spam is that it's just so hard to detect. If you set the filter too low, your spam might start to outnumber the good stuff. If you set your filter too high, some legitimate mail very probably gets sent off to the Junk E-Mail folder. If that happens, you need a way to salvage the e-mail so that you can once again access the links that appear in the messages.

If you want to resurrect an e-mail that's been falsely identified as part of a phishing operation, follow these steps:

1. **Move the message back to your Inbox.**

   Either simply drag the message from the Junk E-Mail folder to the Inbox, or right-click the message and select Junk then Not Junk from the pop-up menu that appears.

2. **Open the message and click the InfoBar at the top of the message on the text that says Click on the InfoBar to Enable Functionality (Not Recommended).**

   You can now use any of the links in the e-mail.

Giving Your Mail a Postmark

The Outlook E-Mail Postmark is a new technology from Microsoft designed to help stop junk e-mail. Outlook assigns a Postmark to any e-mail you send that another computer might consider junk mail. Most users don't notice the time it takes to create a single Postmark. However, because spammers generally send thousands of e-mail messages at a time, the process slows down spammers quite a bit. When another user of Outlook 2010 receives your message, his or her version of Outlook recognizes the postmark and makes sure that your message is delivered.

Before sending a message, the junk e-mail filter in Outlook evaluates whether the (legitimate) message has spam characteristics that mean the recipient's spam filter will likely categorize it as spam. If the message has spam characteristics that might prevent it from reaching its destination, Outlook adds a Postmark to the message, which ultimately slows down the time it takes to send the e-mail. If the outgoing e-mail doesn't look like spam, Outlook doesn't add the Postmark and the message is sent immediately.

Outlook E-Mail Postmarking is turned on by default. If you decide that you don't want the feature turned on because you feel it's slowing you down, you can turn it off by following these steps:

1. **Right-click any of the e-mail messages in your Inbox and select Junk⇨Junk E-Mail Options from the pop-up menu that appears.**

   The Junk E-Mail Options dialog box opens.

2. **Click the Options tab.**

3. **Deselect the When Sending E-Mail, Postmark the Message to Help E-Mail Clients Distinguish Regular E-Mail from Junk E-Mail check box.**

4. **Click OK to close the Junk E-mail Options dialog box**

Chapter 4: Seek and Ye Shall Find

In This Chapter

- ✔ Using an Instant Search
- ✔ Searching with a Search folder
- ✔ Finding someone quickly in the Address Book
- ✔ Tweaking the Folder list
- ✔ Playing with Quick Steps

Creating information is only half the fun; after you create it, you want to be able to find it again. Figuring out how to use Outlook is like driving a new car — it takes you a while to find where all the buttons are, but after you do, using them becomes second nature. This chapter shows you how to find anything instantly by using the Instant Search pane. You can create Search folders if you're constantly hunting down the same items over and over again. The Address Book enables you to find that one special contact in a heartbeat. You can master the Navigation pane so that everything you need is right there at your fingertips, and you can even start to use short-cuts as a super-fast way to arrive at your intended destination.

Getting Instant Gratification with Instant Searching

As its name implies, Instant Search is an Office 2010 feature that helps you find items instantly. When you first ran Outlook, you might have noticed a prompt asking if you want to *index* Outlook; presumably, you clicked Yes — even if you didn't really know what that meant. Creating an index of your Outlook content means that, ultimately, you can find things a bit faster. Instant Search in Outlook works by accessing indexed content. Outlook indexes all your items — even the attachments. After the initial indexing takes place, Outlook continues to index your new content in the background.

You can access the Instant Search pane in Outlook's Mail, Calendar, Contacts, Tasks, Notes, Folder List, and Journal views. When you click any of these folders, the Instant Search bar appears prominently at the top of your list of items.

Enabling Instant Search

Instant Search requires certain Microsoft Windows search components in order to function. If you're using Microsoft Windows Vista or Windows 7, you're in luck: They already come equipped with Windows Desktop Search, so Instant Search is enabled automatically.

If you don't already have the Windows Desktop Search component installed, the first time you run Outlook, a dialog box prompts you to download the software. Go ahead and do so. The dialog boxes walk you through saving and installing the Search component. After you download the software, you must restart Outlook in order for Instant Search to function. If you don't enable Instant Search, you can still search — but not as quickly as you can with Instant Searching enabled.

Fiddling with the Instant Search options

To change the Instant Search options, click the File tab, click the Options button, and then, in the Outlook Options dialog box that appears, select Search in the listing on the left. The Search tab opens, as shown in Figure 4-1.

Figure 4-1:
Changing the Instant Search options.

The Search Options dialog box is divided into two sections:

✦ **Sources:** The main reason that Instant Search works so quickly is that Outlook indexes all your Outlook data when you originally install Instant Search, and then retains information about the contents of the various items. When you perform an Instant Search, Outlook uses this information to speed up the searching process.

You can choose the accounts you want Outlook to *index,* or store in its memory. By default, your default is already selected; however, if you really want to make sure, click the Indexing Options button in the Sources section. As you can see in Figure 4-2, the dialog box displays the locations that are indexed.

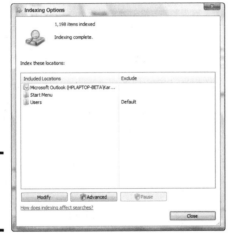

Figure 4-2:
The Search
Options
dialog box.

If you choose not to index any of your Outlook accounts, in essence, you're disabling Instant Search. Although the Instant Search pane still appears, Instant Search no longer works because it doesn't have anything indexed.

✦ **Results:** The Results area allows you to determine how the results of a search will look by setting the following options:

• *Include Results Only From:* By default, an Instant Search searches through only your currently selected folder; after you see the results, you can choose to search your other folders by clicking the Try Searching Again in All Mail Items option, as described in the following section. If you select the All Folders radio button, Instant Search looks through all your Outlook folders without prompting you. Typically, if you have a rough idea of where an item might be lurking, the default setting of Only the Currently Selected Folder is fine.

- *Include Messages from the Deleted Items Folder in Each Data File when Searching in All Items:* Select this check box to have Outlook look through your Deleted Items folder if you select the All Folders radio button. By default, Outlook assumes that you don't want to search through your deleted items; however, if you frequently delete various items without also deleting them from the Deleted Items folder, you might want to select this check box.

- *When Possible, Display Results as the Query Is Typed:* By default, the search results appear in the Instant Search pane while you type; the more you type, the shorter the list of results becomes. If you prefer not to see search results until you press Enter or click the Search button, you can deselect this check box.

- *Improve Search Speed by Limiting the Number of Results Shown:* Speed up your searches by limiting the number of results shown in the Instant Search pane. When your search returns an extremely large number of results, if you select this check box, Outlook limits the number that appear by displaying only the most recent items.

- *Highlight Search Terms in the Results:* If color isn't your thing, you can deselect this check box. Or if yellow isn't your color, you can select a different color for Instant Search to use from the Highlight Color drop-down list.

- *Notify Me when Results Might Be Limited Because Search Indexing Is Not Complete:* In case you jump the gun by trying to perform an Instant Search before Outlook has had a chance to index your information, you can ask Outlook to let you know by selecting this check box.

Searching instantly

Although you can search through any Outlook folder, probably one of the best uses of Instant Search is for searching your e-mail. To find a certain message, follow these steps:

1. **Select the Inbox folder that you want to search from Outlook's Navigation pane.**

2. **Type your search text in the Instant Search text box.**

   Not sure where to find the Instant Search text box? It appears directly below the Ribbon. You can identify it by the word Search emblazoned across it and the snappy magnifying glass.

   Let your imagination run wild! You can search for a specific sender, a phrase in the subject line, or a word in the body of an e-mail. The results of your search appear instantaneously, as soon as you type the first couple of letters of your search string.

Your results appear in the Instant Search Results pane, with the search text highlighted. You don't need to click the Search button to start the search. While you type more characters, your results narrow to reflect your search criterion. Also, a new Search Tools tab appears on the Ribbon, featuring a lot of additional search options. You can see the results of an Instant Search in Figure 4-3.

Figure 4-3:
The results of an Instant Search.

3. In the Instant Search pane results, double-click the item you want to open it.

4. (Optional) Click the Try Searching Again in All Mail Items link at the bottom of the Search Results pane if you want to include all your mail folders in the search.

5. (Optional) Click the X in the Instant Search pane to clear the search.

   You can start a new one by repeating these steps.

Refining your Instant Search

You can most likely find exactly what you're looking for the first time you use an Instant Search. However, you might find that the Instant Search works too well and returns more items than you need. If you find that you have to filter through a long list of items, add a few more criteria to your search so that the Instant Search provides you with a short list of possibilities. Follow these steps:

1. **Click in the Instant Search text box.**

   The Search Tools tab arrives on the Ribbon.

2. **Click the icon that best suits your purposes and fill in the desired results.**

If you're looking for an e-mail from a specific person, for example, click the From button and fill in his or her name in the dialog box that appears.

3. **(Optional) Click additional buttons to display the selected search fields in the Instant Search text box.**

   When you enter information into the search fields or click on a search option, the Instant Search box displays your selections. Talk about having it *your* way! You can search for just about anything your little heart desires, from attachments and categories to sent dates. And, if you don't see the exact field you're looking for, click the More icon to display even *more* fields.

4. From the search results that appear in the list below the Instant Search pane, double-click the item you want to open it.

Although you can't save your Instant Searches, Outlook does display up to ten of your most recent searches. You can find them by clicking the Recent Searches button on the Ribbon's Search Tools tab, and then selecting the search that you want from the list that appears.

Finding what you're looking for with Advanced Find

By now, you might equate the searching options with Goldilocks — you have several good options, and it's up to you to find the best one.

If the search options you've tried aren't working for you — or if you just have an overriding desire to view a few more search options — you might want to check out the Advanced Find feature.

Like its name implies, Advanced Find lets you find an item based on advanced criteria. Follow these steps to find what you're looking for using Advanced Find:

1. **Click in the Instant Search text box.**

   The Search Tools tab magically appears on the Ribbon.

2. **Click the tab's Search Tools button and select Advanced Find from the pop-up menu that appears.**

   The Advanced Find dialog box opens. Advanced Find offers you more search criteria choices, like the ones you see in Figure 4-4.

3. **Fill in the details for the search.**

   For example, you might be looking for any messages containing the word *ka-ching* that your big client sent to you.

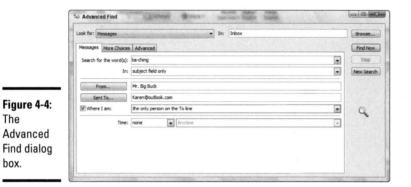

Figure 4-4:
The
Advanced
Find dialog
box.

4. (Optional) Click the More Choices tab.

The More Choices tab appears, as shown in Figure 4-5. As its name suggests, the More Choices tab gives you a few more choices in your search criteria, including read status, importance, and flagging status. You can also search for e-mails that have attachments or that are a certain size.

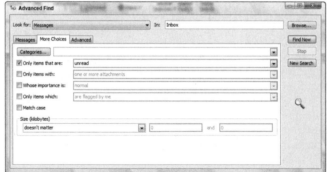

Figure 4-5:
Further
refining your
search.

5. (Optional) Click the Advanced tab to include customized fields as part of your search criteria.

The Advanced tab appears, as shown in Figure 4-6. Not surprisingly, you can get really advanced in this tab. For example, you might be looking for everyone who has a fax number, but not an e-mail address, so that you can create a list of everyone who needs to receive your monthly newsletter by fax. When you select a field from the Define More Criteria area, your query starts to build in the Find Items That Match These Criteria area.

Figure 4-6:
Adding
customized
fields to
your search
criteria.

6. **Click Find Now.**

Outlook cheerfully lists any items that match your search criteria at the bottom of the Advanced Find dialog box. Or, if your search criteria filter out a bit too much, Outlook displays the "There are no items to show in this view" message at the bottom of the Advanced Find dialog box.

Searching through the Search Folders

A Search folder is a virtual folder that contains all e-mail items that match specific search criteria. The information in a virtual folder appears there automatically; you can't move information manually into a virtual folder. For example, the Unread Mail Search folder allows you to view all unread messages from one neat and tidy location — the Unread Mail Search folder — even though the messages may be physically located in different Mail folders. The Unread Mail Search folder is updated automatically; the next time you access it, any messages that you've read since you last opened it no longer appear in this folder.

As you can see in Figure 4-7, these virtual Search folders appear at the bottom of the Outlook Folder list.

By default, Outlook already includes the Unread Mail Search folder that compiles e-mail you've never read from all your Inboxes.

In addition to the default Search folder, Outlook includes several other predefined Search folders. You can customize a predefined Search folder with your own search criteria, or you can create your own custom Search folder by defining specific search criteria. See the following sections to find out how to do all these nifty (and useful) things.

Figure 4-7:
Viewing
Outlook's
Search
folders.

Adding a predefined Search folder

You can add a ton — or, at least, over a dozen — predefined Search folders to your Folder list at the drop of a hat. Just follow these steps:

1. **Right-click Search Folders in the Folder list and select New Search Folder from the pop-up menu that appears.**

The New Search Folder dialog box opens, as shown in Figure 4-8.

Figure 4-8:
Creating a
predefined
Search
folder.

2. **Make a selection in the Select a Search Folder list box.**

You have a bunch of options for creating Search folders, including ones in these categories:

- *Reading Mail:* Unread, flagged for follow-up, or important e-mail

- *Mail from People and Lists:* E-mail sent to or from specific people or distribution lists

- *Organizing Mail:* Categorized, large, or old e-mail; or e-mail that contains attachments or specific words

3. **(Optional) Select Custom in the Select a Search Folder and then click the Choose button in the Customize Search Folder section.**

   This will open the Custom Search Folder dialog window. From here you have two options:

   - Click the Criteria button: This will open the Search Folder Criteria dialog window which is identical to the Advanced Find dialog window displayed in Figure 4-6. At this juncture you can build as fancy of a query as you need.

   - Click the Browse button: This opens the Select Folders dialog window where you can specify which of your mailboxes you'd like to include in the search.

   Figure 4-8 shows an example of a Search folder that includes all the e-mail categorized as a Hot Prospect.

4. **Click OK to close the New Search Folder dialog box.**

   The new Search folder now appears, in all its glory, with the rest of your Search folders. Its name reflects the criterion that Outlook uses to move e-mail into it.

5. **(Optional) Right-click the folder and select Customize This Search Folder from the pop-up menu that appears to rename the search folder or select different search criteria.**

   The Customize *Folder Name* dialog box opens. As shown in Figure 4-9, you can give your Search folder a new name, change the criteria, or associate the Search folder with a different mailbox.

Figure 4-9:
Renaming
a Search
folder.

Tweaking a Search folder

You may find Outlook's capability to perform tasks in multiple ways very endearing. Keep in mind, however, that you don't have to use all of Outlook's search features; you can find the one that makes the most sense for your needs and stick with it.

As an alternative to performing an Instant Search (see "Getting Instant Gratification with Instant Searching," earlier in this chapter) or using one of the predefined Search folders, you may want to create your very own personalized Search folder. Follow these steps:

1. **Right-click Search Folders in the Folder list and select New Search Folder from the pop-up menu that appears.**

The New Search Folder dialog box opens. (Refer to Figure 4-8.)

2. **Select Create a Custom Search Folder all the way at the bottom of the Select a Search Folder list box, and then click the Choose button to the right of the Show Mail with These Categories text box.**

The Customize Folder Name dialog box opens; it's similar to the one in Figure 4-9.

3. Type a name for your custom Search folder in the Name text box.

4. Click Criteria to select the criteria for the Search folder.

The Search Folder Criteria dialog box (quite similar to the Advanced Find dialog box in Figure 4-4) appears.

5. Fill in the search criteria, click OK to close the Search Folder dialog box, and then click OK in the New Search Folder dialog box to close it.

You're little bit of effort will pay off in spades. From now on, any time you access your new Search Folder, it will contain all the items that match your search criteria.

If you're not sure how to define your custom Search folder, check out the steps in the "Finding what you're looking for with Advanced Find" section, earlier in this chapter.

Deleting a Search folder

Because Search folders are virtual folders, deleting a Search folder doesn't delete the e-mail messages collected by a Search folder from their original locations. However — and this is a *big* however — although the Search folders are virtual ones, the e-mail they contain are real, live e-mail messages. So, if you open the folder and delete a *message* contained in that folder, the message is deleted from both the Search folder *and* the Outlook folders where it's stored.

You can most easily delete a Search folder by giving it a right-click and selecting Delete *Search Folder Name* from the pop-up menu that appears. A dialog box appears, prompting you one last time to verify whether this is really your intention; click Yes to remove the folder from your life. If you change your mind and decide you really do want to use that Search folder, feel free to create it again. You may, however, receive some annoyed looks from your computer.

Searching 101 — Finding Names in the Address Book

The preceding sections of this chapter focus primarily on searching through your e-mail. You can also use the Address Book to look up names when you address messages.

A contact must have either an e-mail address or a fax number in order for his or her name to appear in an Address Book search.

To search through your Address Book, follow these steps:

1. **Open the Address Book.**

   You can accomplish this feat in a number of ways:

   - Click the Address Book button in the Find section of the Ribbon's Home Tab.

   - Click the To, Cc, or Bcc button on a new e-mail message.

   - Click the Address Book button in the Names section of a new message form's Ribbon.

   You can see the results of your efforts in Figure 4-10.

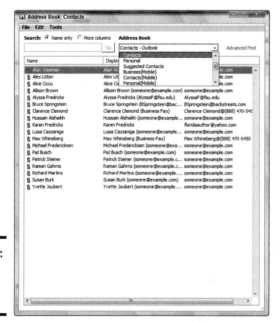

Figure 4-10: Outlook's Address Book.

2. **Select the address book that you want to search from the Address Book drop-down list.**

    Typically, if you're using Business Contact Manager, you have address books for your Accounts and Business Contacts, as well as your Outlook Contacts. (See Book II, Chapter 1 for more on address books.)

3. **Type the name you're searching for in the Search text box.**

    By default, Outlook looks for contacts on a first-name basis. If you have several Susans in your address book, you can continue typing a few of the first letters in the last name. While you type, the contact that matches your search becomes highlighted.

4. **(Optional) Select the More Columns radio button above the Search text box, type your search criteria in the text box, and click Go if you can't find the person you're looking for.**

    You can search for a person by just about any tidbit of information: last name, title, city, and so on. You can search by more than one criterion if you include a comma after each criterion.

5. **Right-click the highlighted name in the Address Book and select Properties from the pop-up menu that appears to view the contact record of the person you found.**

    You can now edit the contact information however you see fit.

Fiddling with the Folder List

The Folder list enables you to view all your folders, including your Inbox and any subfolders you create. The Folder list displays all Outlook items, including the Calendar, Contacts, Notes, and Tasks. This view might become one of your favorites because you can navigate it extremely easily.

Access the Folder list by clicking the Folder List button at the bottom of the Navigation pane. If you want to keep the Folder list as your main view in the Navigation pane while you're working, don't click the other buttons at the bottom of the Navigation pane. If you want to move around in your various Outlook items, click the appropriate folder, icon, or name in the Folder list itself. To view subfolders, click the plus sign to the left of the folder.

Working with Quick Steps and Quick Step Groups

Everyone loves a shortcut, and Outlook is no exception. If you want to be able to accomplish several tasks at the click of a button — and the

Navigation pane buttons just don't do the trick — then you can create a Quick Step to really take care of your e-mail quickly.

You can organize your Quick Steps into groups and arrange the Quick Steps groups on the Ribbon so that you can easily find them. When a message comes in, you can simply highlight the message in your Inbox and click the appropriate Quick Step — and watch while Outlook quickly gets you organized!

Tweaking a Quick Step

Figure 4-11 shows a sample of the type of Quick Steps that appear in Outlook. If you hover your mouse over any of the items, Outlook displays a tooltip, which provides you with a better description of what the Quick Step actually accomplishes. For example, the I've Got a Sale! Quick Step in Figure 4-11 moves an e-mail message to a specific folder and marks the e-mail as read.

Figure 4-11:
Outlook's
Quick Steps.

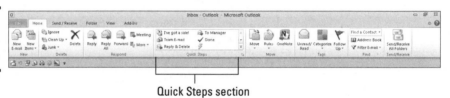

Quick Steps section

You can customize any of the Quick Steps in a jiffy by following these steps:

1. **Click the More button in the bottom-right corner of the Quick Steps section of the Ribbon.**

The Quick Steps pane opens.

2. **Click Manage Quick Steps . . .**

The Manage Quick Steps dialog box opens.

3. Select the Quick Step you want to modify and then click Edit

The Edit Quick Step dialog box opens.

4. **Change the Quick Step options.**

The options vary, depending on which Quick Step you're modifying. The example in Figure 4-12 allows you to rename the Quick Step, move the e-mail message to another folder, and mark the message as read.

5. **Click Save to save the modified Quick Step and then OK to close the Manage Quick Steps dialog box.**

Figure 4-12:
Modifying a
Quick Step.

Creating your own Quick Steps

Because a Quick Step is designed to save you time, it only stands to reason that you can create one quickly. Follow these steps to quickly add a Quick Step to the Ribbon:

1. **Click the More button on the bottom-right corner of the Quick Steps section of the Ribbon.**

2. **Select Create new from the pop-up menu that appears (see Figure 4-13).**

   The Edit Quick Step dialog box opens, which is just like the one shown in Figure 4-12.

Figure 4-13:
Creating a
new Quick
Step.

3. **Give your new Quick Step a name in the Name field and indicate the steps you want the Quick Step to accomplish by making a selection from the Actions drop-down list.**

For example, you might want your Quick Step to move a message to another folder, or automatically schedule a task when a message with a specific subject line appears in your Inbox.

4. **(Optional) Click the Add Actions button.**

What could be better than having someone else do your work for you? Although you can't demand that Outlook dust your living room and clean your windows, you can expect Outlook to keep you ridiculously well-organized at the click of a button. The dialog box for your new Quick Step (Figure 4-14 shows one for Flag and Move options) allows you to add additional actions to a Quick Step, or delete or modify existing actions. For example, you might want Outlook to mark any messages that contain the words *place order* as important, move them to the Sales folder, and forward them on to the flunky who's in charge of order fulfillment.

Figure 4-14: Assigning a few more steps to a Quick Step.

5. **Click Save to save your options.**

Wait for a message to arrive that matches your Quick Step criteria, and then quickly click the appropriate Quick Step, which now appears in the Quick Step section of the Ribbon. You might even want to do a bit of the Texas Two Step to celebrate the success of your Quick Step!

Arranging your Quick Steps

If you're a real Quick Step junkie and create a lot of Quick Steps, you may want to change the order of the Quick Steps. Or, if you develop a borderline case of Quick Step obsession, you might need to create groups within the Quick Step area of the Ribbon to help organize your numerous Quick Steps. Follow these quick steps to organize your Quick Steps:

1. **Click the More button in the bottom-right corner of the Quick Steps section of the Ribbon and then click Manage Quick Steps from the pop-up menu.**

   The Manage Quick Steps dialog box opens. You can see what this dialog box looks like in Figure 4-15.

Figure 4-15:
Adding a bit of order to your Quick Steps.

2. **Select a Quick Step from the Quick Step area, and then click the down-arrow button to move the step lower on the list or the up-arrow button to move it higher.**

3. **(Optional) Select a Quick Step from the Quick Step area, and then click the Group button.**

   A drop-down menu appears, offering you a few options:

   - Move to New Group
   - Rename *Group Name*
   - Delete *Group Name*
   - Move *Group Name* Up or Down

Outlook is so thoughtful that it even provides you with quick ways to deal with your Quick Steps!

Chapter 5: Securing Outlook E-Mail

In This Chapter

✓ Giving Outlook a password

✓ Working with the Microsoft Outlook Trust Center

✓ Addressing security issues

✓ Using digitally signed e-mail

*Y*ou may want to put on a dark trench coat and don a pair of sunglasses while reading this chapter because it deals with ways you can protect yourself from e-mail spies. Adding a password is a simple way to ensure that others aren't accessing your e-mail. You also need to know about security alerts and what to do if you receive one. Your espionage toolkit won't be complete without information on digitally signed and encrypted e-mail. And, of course, remember that your martinis should be shaken, not stirred.

Working with Passwords

Probably the simplest way to protect your Outlook information is by giving it a password. A password prevents intruders from opening your Outlook and sneaking a peek at your entire life, including all your contacts, appointments, and e-mail. However, it can't prevent someone from grabbing your password if you write it down on a sticky note and put it on your monitor.

To add a password to your Outlook file, follow these steps:

1. **Click the File tab, and then select Account Settings from the Account Settings drop-down list.**

The Account Settings dialog box opens, like the one you see in Figure 5-1.

2. **On the Data Files tab, select the Outlook account for which you want to create a password, and then click Settings.**

The Outlook Data File dialog box opens.

Figure 5-1:
The
Account
Settings
dialog box.

3. **Click the Change Password button.**

   The Change Password dialog box opens, as shown in Figure 5-2.

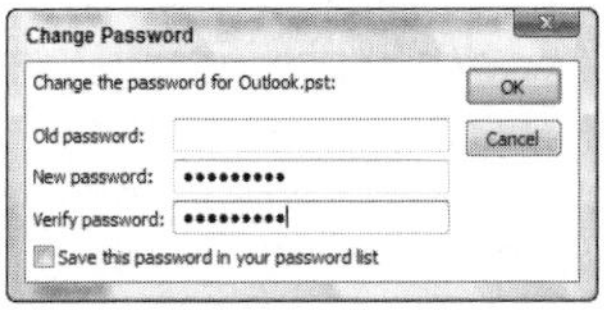

Figure 5-2:
Changing
an Outlook
password.

4. **(Optional) If you already have a password and want to change it, fill in the existing password in the Old Password text box.**

5. **Type your new password in the New Password text box.**

6. **Type your new password in the Verify Password text box, just to be sure you spelled the new password correctly.**

   Outlook doesn't reveal your password while you type it, just in case someone with a set of high-powered binoculars is trying to read what you're typing from across the room. Unfortunately, that means you also can't see what you're typing. If you happen to make a typo and the New Password doesn't match the Verify Password, Outlook prevents you from changing your password.

7. ***Don't* select the Save This Password in Your Password List check box.**

   I guess it kind of seems funny to give a non-instruction, but this one is worth mentioning. If you check this box, you don't have to fill in your password when you open Outlook because Outlook remembers it for you. But if you don't have to enter a password, what's the point of having one in the first place? By checking this box, any spy or questionable person can access your Outlook file without having to supply a password because you've already supplied it for him or her!

8. **Click OK to close the Change Password dialog box, click OK in the Outlook Data File dialog box, and then click Close in the Account Settings dialog box to close it.**

The next time you open Outlook, you're greeted with the cheerful message you see in Figure 5-3. Okay, maybe it's not such a cheerful dialog box; but if you type your password and click OK, you gain admission into the exciting world of Outlook — which is cause for celebration, right?

Figure 5-3:
Entering
your
password.

Remember your password! If you forget your password, you're pretty much up the proverbial creek. If you have a lot of passwords to remember, consider purchasing password wallet software that will store all of your passwords in one secure place and help you to organize your passwords. Or, at the very least, jot that password down in a *very* safe place!

You might rest easier at night knowing that your Outlook is password-protected. No one can open your Outlook if he or she doesn't have the password. However, nothing prevents an intruder from walking off with all your data if you don't close Outlook when you aren't using it!

Trusting the Trust Center

You might snicker at the thought of wearing a trench coat and sunglasses when you use your computer, but allowing a stranger access to your computer is no laughing matter. You need to know about the information that Outlook is sending to the outside world. You can find these options in Outlook's Trust Center.

Microsoft developed the Trust Center to handle security and privacy settings for all the Microsoft Office programs. Microsoft designed the Trust Center to work in the background. In previous versions of Office, warning dialog boxes that asked you to take some form of action frequently popped up while you were working. Unfortunately, you might not have understood the question — much less the answer. Hopefully, the Trust Center automatically provides you with the best level of protection without having to nag you to change various settings.

Getting the lowdown on downloads

The amount of information coming at you through e-mail is astounding. And, if you're a trusting person, you assume that it's coming from a legitimate source. Unfortunately, that's not always the case. Even those seemingly innocuous kitty pictures that you think your spinster aunt sent you might actually come from some nasty person who has a deep desire to set a virus loose on the cat lovers of the world.

Many instances of *malware* — software that is designed specifically to damage or disrupt a computer system — come in the form of pictures that are embedded in HTML e-mail. And you, the trusting recipient, may inadvertently let the malware in by clicking a link — or the picture of a kitty. Rest assured that just like a mother prevents her child from touching a hot stove, Outlook does its darnedest to prevent you from downloading a file that arrived embedded in an incoming e-mail.

Follow these steps to give Outlook the go-ahead to watch your back:

1. **Click the File tab, and then choose Options⇨Trust Center⇨ Trust Center Settings.**

   The Outlook Trust Center opens to the Automatic Download tab.

2. **Select your download options.**

   As you can see in Figure 5-4, Outlook has already set the ground rules by permitting you to download items that come from Web sites in your Trusted Zone, RSS feeds or SharePoint Discussion Boards that you've subscribed to, or from folks in your Safe Senders and Safe Recipients lists. At the same time, Outlook prevents the automatic downloading of pictures and issues a warning if you try to download something from an e-mail message.

3. **Click OK to close the Trust Center and then click OK in the Outlook Options dialog box to close it.**

Guarding your privacy

A lot of criticism has been thrown at Microsoft lately — especially by the cute guy in the Mac ads! Much of this criticism has focused on the lack of security in the Microsoft products. Ironically, Outlook allows you to not only tinker with your security settings as they pertain to your incoming messages, but also to the information that you send — or don't send — to Microsoft.

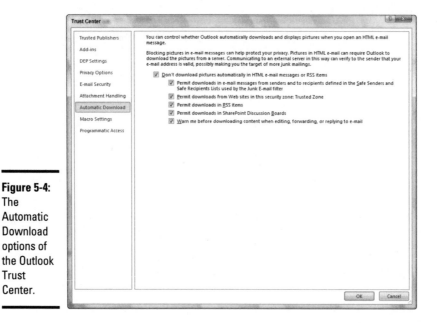

Figure 5-4:
The
Automatic
Download
options of
the Outlook
Trust
Center.

Some folks would argue that Microsoft is trying to obtain information from your computer system so that they can improve the effectiveness of their products. However, some people feel that Microsoft is a bit overly intrusive, and they don't want to give Microsoft access to any of their data.

So, should you give Microsoft full access to your computer? Although you have to be the judge of that decision, after you decide yea or nay, you can follow these steps to voice your opinion:

1. **Click the File tab, and then choose Options⇨Trust Center⇨
Trust Center Settings.**

The Outlook Trust Center opens to the Automatic Download tab.

2. **Click the Privacy Options tab.**

3. **Select the check boxes for the privacy options you want.**

The Privacy Options tab offers these choices:

- *Connect to Microsoft Office Online When I'm Connected to the Internet.* Allows you to get the latest and greatest Help articles hot off the presses — or, in this case, the Web site.

- *Download a File Periodically That Helps Determine System Problems.* You've probably seen the message that pops up periodically telling you that your computer has just thrown a hissy fit and asking you whether you want to be a tattletale and tell Big Brother Microsoft all about it. Checking this option sends that information automatically.

- *Sign Up for the Customer Experience Improvement Program.* The jury is still out on this option. Basically, you're allowing Microsoft to monitor your computer to make sure you're happy. You might wonder what your computer is gossiping to Microsoft about — I know I sure am!

- *Automatically Detect Installed Office Applications to Improve Office Online Search Results.* Lets Microsoft know which Office products you've installed so that they can send you the most appropriate help when you ask for it online.

- *Allow the Research Task Pane to Check for and Install New Services.* Armed with the details about your computer, Microsoft decides which software updates you need and sticks them on your computer.

4. **Click OK to close the Trust Center.**

Grappling with Macros

A *macro* is a tiny program that automates a series of tasks. Typically, programmers write macros to run various commands on your computer. Unfortunately, some macros can put you and your computer at serious risk. For example, a hacker could write a macro to run a virus on your computer.

Handling a macro security warning

If the Trust Center detects a macro in one of your documents, it calls the FBI and runs a background check. Okay, the Trust Center doesn't really call the FBI, but it does check out the macro pretty thoroughly to ensure that a *trusted publisher* created it. If the Trust Center detects a potential problem, it disables the macro by default, and a dialog box appears to notify you of a potentially unsafe macro.

You might be wondering how Microsoft determines whether a macro is from a trusted publisher. Most software vendors that have worked directly with Microsoft are trusted publishers. However, thousands of lesser-known software programs are quite trustworthy — even though a trusted publisher didn't create them. The bottom line is that if you receive a security warning, make sure that you know the publisher.

When a security dialog box appears, you have the option to enable the macro or leave it disabled. Enable the macro only if you're sure it's from a trustworthy source. You can click the Trust All Documents from This Publisher link in the security dialog box if you're sure the macro is from a trustworthy source. Outlook adds that publisher to your Trusted Publishers list in the Trust Center.

Changing the macro settings in the Trust Center

You might want to change the macro settings in the Trust Center to set the level of protection that you're the most comfortable with. You can open the Trust Center and fiddle with the macro settings by following these steps:

1. **Click the File tab, and then choose Options⇨Trust Center⇨ Trust Center Settings.**

The Outlook Trust Center opens to the Automatic Download tab.

2. **Click the Macro Settings tab, as shown in Figure 5-5.**

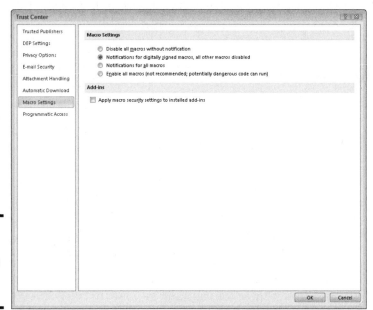

Figure 5-5:
The Macro Settings tab of the Trust Center.

3. **Select the radio button for the macro security option that you want.**

The Macro Settings tab offers these choices:

- *Disable All Macros without Notification.* Outlook disables all macros and doesn't open macro warning dialog boxes.

- *Notifications for Digitally Signed Macros; All Other Macros Are Disabled.* The recommended setting. Outlook allows a macro to run if it's digitally signed by a trusted publisher. If the publisher doesn't appear on the Trusted Publisher list, Outlook disables the macro and notifies you.

- *Notifications for All Macros.* Outlook disables all macros but sends you an alert if it finds one.

- *Enable All Macros (Not Recommended; Potentially Dangerous Code Can Run).* The option here pretty much speaks for itself. Don't choose this option — unless, of course, you have a death wish.

4. **Check the Add-ins checkbox if you'd like the same macro settings to apply to any Outlook add-ins that you are using.**

   For example, you might have purchased an add-in product that allows you to manage .pdf files from within Outlook; checking this option will require the product to follow the same rules that apply to the rest of Outlook.

5. **Click OK to close the Outlook Trust Center.**

Help! Someone's Sending E-Mail on My Behalf

You might be happily working away one day when, out of the blue, one of the following security-warning dialog boxes appears:

✦ A program is trying to access e-mail address information stored in Outlook. If this is unexpected, click Deny and verify that your antivirus software is up-to-date.

✦ A program is trying to send an e-mail message on your behalf. If this is unexpected, click Deny and verify that your antivirus software is up-to-date.

✦ A program is trying to perform an action that may result in an e-mail message being sent on your behalf. If this is unexpected, click Deny and verify that your antivirus software is up-to-date.

Needless to say, these warnings can be quite traumatic. Many recent viruses attacked Outlook, took over the Address Book, and started sending e-mail to all contacts. Small wonder that Outlook feels compelled to issue a warning!

One of two harmless situations can occur that prompt these warnings:

✦ **A program that uses Outlook to send e-mail messages started automatically.** For example, your accounting software might interface with Outlook.

✦ **You started a program that's designed to send automatic e-mail.** For example, you might be using a program to send e-mail newsletters to your entire client base.

When a malicious program makes its way into your Outlook it will begin sending messages out in your name. Those messages might be harmless spam, or they might contain viruses that will in turn cause harm to the recipients of your e-mail messages. In general those message will be sent to the contacts in your Address Book and or the folks whose messages happen to be currently residing in your Inbox.

Answering the security warning

When you receive one of these security warnings, the dialog box offers you two options:

✦ **Deny:** Click this button if you didn't expect a program to access Outlook or if you're at all unsure as to what program is attempting to access Outlook. You probably have a virus knocking on your door — or, more accurately, trying to gain entry to Outlook.

✦ **Allow:** Click this button if you clicked a command or started a program that you know is supposed to access Outlook data or send e-mail messages by using Outlook. For example, you might be using a marketing product that automatically sends out e-mail at pre-assigned time intervals.

Preventing future security warnings

Installing an antivirus program and keeping it up-to-date may prevent a security warning from appearing again. However, be sure of a few things:

✦ Update your antivirus software regularly. Most antivirus programs enable you to get automatic updates when you're online. Unfortunately, some computer users never bother to update their virus protection.

✦ Many new computers come bundled with antivirus software. Unfortunately, this software usually requires a yearly renewal; typically, if you don't pay for the renewal, you're not protected from the latest and greatest — or nastiest and most lethal — viruses. If your antivirus software subscription expires or has been inactive, you may get the security warning again when a program attempts to access Outlook. Guess you might consider this a case of pay now or pay later!

✦ Check with the manufacturer of the antivirus software before you purchase it to makes sure that it works with Outlook so that all incoming e-mail is automatically scanned for viruses.

Outlook's Trust Center actually checks for the presence of antivirus software and determines when Outlook should issue a warning. To view these settings, follow these steps:

1. **Click the File tab, and then choose Options⇨Trust Center⇨ Trust Center Settings.**

Outlook's Trust Center plays Open Sesame.

2. **Click the Programmatic Access tab.**

To see it live, take a peek at Figure 5-6.

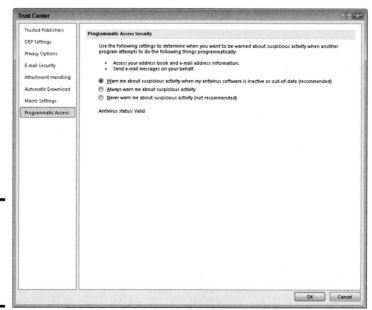

Luckily, you only have to click the tab; you don't have to try to pro-
nounce the darn thing. The bottom of the tab displays the status of your
antivirus software.

3. **Select one of the Programmatic Access security settings.**

   The tab offers these options:

   - *Warn Me about Suspicious Activity when My Antivirus Software
     Is Inactive or Out-of-Date (Recommended).* The default setting in
     Outlook. If your antivirus software isn't working, Outlook warns you
     if something tries to tinker with your e-mail or Address Book.

   - *Always Warn Me about Suspicious Activity.* The most secure setting.
     You're always prompted when a program tries to access Outlook.

   - *Never Warn Me about Suspicious Activity (Not Recommended).* For
     those of you who love jumping out of airplanes without first checking
     to see whether your parachute is operational. That's probably why
     it's not a recommended setting.

4. **Click OK to close the Trust Center and breathe a big sigh of relief.**

Kicking the HTML out of Your E-Mail

In the Middle Ages, e-mail was limited to plain old black and white. With the
dawning of the Age of Enlightenment — or HTML, anyway — e-mail took on

all the colors of the rainbow. Everyone tried to outdo each other by including a lot of gorgeous graphics in their electronic missives. Unfortunately, hackers also saw the advantages of HTML and started embedding links to evil Web sites in seemingly innocent graphics. And yes, you could infect your computer just by opening or previewing an e-mail.

Unfortunately, viruses are part of a vicious circle that's, well, very vicious. As soon as a new virus arrives on the scene, programmers scramble to plug up the hole that let the virus in. In the meantime, the unscrupulous virus creator finds *another* security breach and creates *another* virus. And so it goes.

If you're concerned that reading HTML-formatted messages can put you at greater risk for contracting a virus, you can have Outlook automatically display the messages that you open in plain text. Although it's not a guarantee, you're at somewhat less of a risk. Follow these steps:

1. **Click the File tab, and then choose Options⇨Trust Center⇨ Trust Center Settings.**

Outlook's Trust Center opens.

2. **Click the E-Mail Security tab.**

You can check it out for yourself in Figure 5-7.

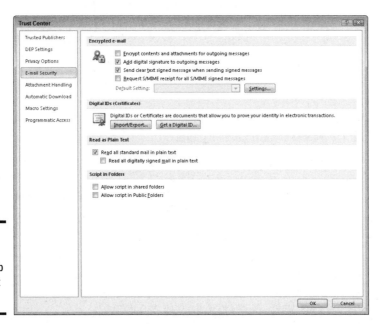

Figure 5-7:
The E-Mail
Security tab
of the Trust
Center.

3. **Select the Read All Standard Mail in Plain Text check box in the Read as Plain Text area.**

   Optionally, you can include all messages signed with a digital signature in the plain-text hamper by selecting the Read All Digitally Signed Mail in Plain Text check box.

4. **Click OK to close the Trust Center.**

Bored with dull text e-mail? If you want to view a plain-text message in its full glory, click the message's InfoBar and select either the Display as HTML option or the Display as Rich Text option.

Sending via Certified E-Mail

Outlook uses e-mail certificates to make the transmission of e-mail a more secure process. In order to use an e-mail certificate, you obtain a digital ID from a certificate authority by paying a fee. After the authority you use certifies your message, your certificate is sent along with that message to prove to your recipient that you're exactly who you say you are. A digital ID also verifies your identity if someone asks you to "sign" a document electronically.

Getting a digital ID from a certifying authority

Although the thought of obtaining a digital ID may strike you as being more high-tech than you bargained for, it's actually a pretty easy process if you follow these steps:

1. **Click the File tab, and then choose Options⇨Trust Center⇨ Trust Center Settings.**

   You find yourself smack in the middle of the Trust Center.

2. **Click the E-Mail Security tab.**

   You probably hate reruns as much as I do, but if you look at Figure 5-7, you can follow along here quite nicely.

3. **Click the Get a Digital ID button in the Digital IDs (Certificates) area.**

   At this point, you take a trip out to the Internet. You can select from a number of providers. After you sign up for the service, you receive your digital ID and instructions via e-mail.

Although this service usually includes a slight fee, the price is certainly worth it. You can't overstate the gratification of a good night's sleep knowing that you have good security on your system.

Putting your digital ID to work

After you obtain a digital ID, you can start using it for all your outgoing e-mail. Follow these steps:

1. **Click the File tab, and then choose Options⇨Trust Center⇨ Trust Center Settings.**

The Trust Center opens.

2. **Click the E-Mail Security tab.**

You're back at Figure 5-7.

3. **Click the Settings button in the Encrypted E-Mail section.**

The E-Mail Security dialog box opens. At this point, you have one of two options:

- If you have a digital ID, the settings to use the digital ID are automatically configured for you. Click OK to close the E-Mail Security dialog box.

- If you don't have a digital ID, click the Get Digital ID button. You then hurtle through the Internet and land in a Microsoft Web site that explains how to get a digital ID.

4. **(Optional) Select the Encrypt Contents and Attachments for Outgoing Messages check box in the Encrypted E-Mail area.**

Selecting this option encrypts all your outgoing messages to any of your contacts who also have a digital ID.

5. **Select the Add Digital Signature to Outgoing Messages check box.**

Selecting this option adds your digital ID to all your outgoing messages.

6. **Check the Send clear text signed message when sending signed messages option.**

This option is checked by default. This will allow recipients who don't have additional security options to be able to read your messages.

7. **(Optional) Select the Request S/MIME Receipt for All S/MIME Signed Messages.**

S/MIME offers you another layer of protection by encrypting your e-mail (making it harder for the bad guys to intercept) and adding a special coding to your e-mails letting your recipients' e-mail programs know that you're one of the good guys and that your e-mail should be treated accordingly.

8. **Click OK to close the Trust Center.**

Exchanging e-mail certificates

You must exchange certificates in order to send encrypted messages to someone. The section "Getting a digital ID from a certifying authority," earlier in this chapter, explains that these certificates are issued by a certification authority. Like a driver's license, they can expire or be revoked. (Fortunately, these certificates aren't influenced by your driving habits.)

You can exchange certificates in a number of ways:

✦ **Send a digitally signed message.** When the recipient adds your e-mail name to his or her contacts, your certificate is added, as well.

✦ **Send an e-mail with your certificate attached.** Certificates are actually special files with the `.cer` extension. So, you can send them with each e-mail like you would any other file — by sending them as an attachment. The recipient can then import the certificate into your contact record.

✦ **Burn the** `.cer` **file to a CD and deliver it to your intended recipient.** You might want to meet in a dark corner of a neighborhood bar when you exchange `.cer` files.

✦ **If you work on the same network, post the certificate somewhere where your recipient can access it.** Once the recipient finds it he can import the certificate into your contact record.

✦ **Create a contact card that includes your** `.cer` **file and send the recipient your card.** The recipient can then open and save the card when they receive your message — and be the proud new owner of both a new contact and your certificate!

Arranging for the clandestine exchange of certificates is the hard part. After you receive a certificate into your nervous, sweaty hands, you add it to the recipient's contact record. You can accomplish this secret exchange of information in one of two ways, as described in the following sections.

Adding a certificate from a digitally signed e-mail

If someone sends you an e-mail that has a digital signature, it's a snap to add the sender's certificate to his or her contact record. Just follow these steps:

1. **Open a message that's been digitally signed.**

2. **Right-click the name in the From box, and then select Add to Outlook Contacts from the pop-up menu that appears.**

3. **(Optional) Select Update Information of Selected Contact button if the Duplicate Contact Detected dialog box appears.**

The certificate is now stored in the contact's record, meaning that you can now send encrypted e-mail messages to this person.

Adding a certificate from a .cer file

If you receive a certificate on a CD or another format — and have sworn on a stack of Outlook bibles that you won't share the confidential information with anyone else, under penalty of death — you can easily add the certificate to an existing contact record. Follow these steps:

1. **Select the Contacts folder on the Folder list.**

2. **Open the contact record to which you want to add the certificate.**

   With any luck, the contact record form springs open. If you need help opening the contact record, see Book IV, Chapter 2.

3. **Select Certificates from the Show drop-down list on the form's Ribbon.**

   The Contact form is replaced by a new, fairly blank, contact page for the currently selected contact.

   If you already have a certificate for the contact, it appears in this list, so you don't need to add one. If one doesn't appear in the list, continue to Step 4.

4. **Click the Import button on the side of the form.**

   The Locate Certificate window opens showing you all the folders that exist on your computer.

5. **Navigate in the Locate Certificate window to the secret location of the certificate; select it and click Open.**

   The certificate is now attached to the contact record.

Book X

Out and About: Taking Outlook on the Road

Contents at a Glance

Chapter 1: Managing Your Company E-Mail

In This Chapter

✓ Letting Outlook handle e-mail while you're out of the office

✓ Getting someone else to handle your e-mail and appointments

✓ Managing Mail and Calendar for someone else

*O*utlook makes handling life's little nuisances pretty easy. For example, Outlook can automatically organize and categorize incoming mail, remind you to leave early for a dentist's appointment, and even nag you to pick up your laundry. But what about vacations or business trips, when you're out of the office for several days in a row? Do you just let e-mail flood the Inbox, or can Outlook help you there, as well, and notify people that you're out of town so that they won't expect an immediate response?

Perhaps you're a busy professional, and you have a nice assistant who not only keeps track of where you need to be *right now,* but even stops drop-in clients at the door so that you can get to that important appointment on time. As nice as that may sound, the system tends to break down every now and then, especially when you make an appointment and forget to tell your assistant, or vice versa. Can Outlook help you keep your appointments in one place, where both you and your assistant can access and make changes to those appointments? The answer to all these questions is a resounding, "Yes!" as you can see in this chapter.

Exchange 2010 now provides MailTips that stop people up short before they send you e-mail while you're out of town. You just have to let Outlook know. Then, if someone from your company addresses an e-mail to you while you're gone, Outlook pops up a MailTip that displays the message you've left behind so that they know when you get back. Of course, MailTips won't stop someone from sending that e-mail, anyway, but it should slow them down a little.

Letting Automatic Replies Handle Mail While You're Gone

Every time I leave the office for even just the afternoon, I return to find my Inbox full of messages. Some are junk, and some are important. But I don't know which until I take the time to go through them all. Wouldn't it be nice to have someone sitting in for you while you're out, deleting the junk, forwarding the stuff that's important to a colleague so that he or she can act on it in a timely manner, and letting everyone else know that you're not ignoring them, you're just out of the office until tomorrow? Well, actually, you do have someone who can sit in at a moment's notice — the "Out of Office Assistant," which in Outlook 2010 has renamed Automatic Replies.

You can use Automatic Replies only if you work on an Exchange network. If you don't, you're not totally out of luck. You can still do some things to get Outlook to help you with e-mail management. See the section "What to do if you have a POP3 or IMAP e-mail account," later in this chapter.

You can use Automatic Replies to send an instant reply to anyone who e-mails you while you're away. What the reply says is up to you: "I'm out of the office; see Bill if you need immediate assistance" or "Leave me alone. I'm on vacation, you bug!"

You can set up rules to process your e-mail automatically, too. For example, you may want e-mails from particular people passed on to someone in your company, and you may want junk newsletters and such automatically deleted.

Turning Automatic Replies on or off

To turn Automatic Replies on, follow these steps:

1. **Click the File tab to display Backstage, and then select Info from the list on the left.**

   The Account Information options appear on the right.

2. **Click the Automatic Replies button.**

   The Automatic Replies dialog box jumps up to help, as shown in Figure 1-1.

3. **Select the Send Automatic Replies radio button.**

4. **To have Automatic Replies send replies during a set period of time, select the Only Send During This Time Range check box, then, select dates and times from the Start Time and End Time drop-down lists.**

If you want to limit the time when Automatic Replies is active (for example, you want to set it up to work while you're on vacation next week, but not actually turn it on right now), then set the appropriate dates and times for Start Time and End Time.

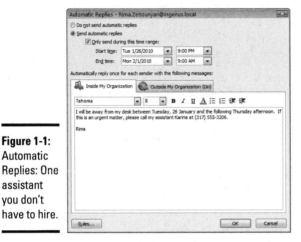

Figure 1-1:
Automatic
Replies: One
assistant
you don't
have to hire.

5. **To create a message for e-mail received from people you work with, click the Inside My Organization tab located in the middle of the dialog box, and then click inside the text box and type a message.**

6. **To create a message for e-mails received from people you don't work with, click the Outside My Organization tab, as shown in Figure 1-2, and then click inside the box and type your message.**

   Make sure that the Auto-Reply to People Outside My Organization check box is selected.

   You can format the text for your outgoing message(s) however you like by using the buttons just above the text boxes on each tab.

7. **Decide which non-colleagues you want to receive this message.**

   Select one of these radio buttons:

   - *My Contacts Only:* Use this auto reply only with people outside your company who are listed in your Contacts.

   - *Anyone Outside My Organization:* Use this auto reply with anyone who sends you an e-mail who doesn't work in your company — even if he or she isn't in your Contacts list.

If you select the My Contacts Only radio button, the contact who e-mails you must appear in your Exchange Contacts list — either the main list or one that you create. The contact can't appear only in a Contacts list in an offline folder or a personal folder you're using with a POP3, IMAP, or HTTP account.

8. **Click OK to finalize your choices and turn Automatic Replies on.**

Figure 1-2:
Create a
message
for people
outside your
company.

When Automatic Replies is functioning, Outlook will present you with a persistent reminder: a big, non-ignorable, yellow bar like police tape that's strapped across the top of the Outlook window in the Mail module that reads, "Automatic Replies are being sent for this account." You can turn off Automatic Replies simply by clicking the Turn Off button that appears on this yellow stripe, nothing else. Or if you feel like going through the motions, here's the formal steps:

1. **Click the File tab to display Backstage, and select Info from the list on the left.**

    The Account Information options appear on the right.

2. **Click the Automatic Replies button.**

    The Automatic Replies dialog box appears.

3. **Select the Do Not Send Automatic Replies radio button.**

4. **Click OK to turn Automatic Replies off.**

Letting rules control mail while you're away

By using the Rules Wizard, you can create a set of rules to handle your e-mail while you're out — for example, you can move e-mail from one folder to another, forward it to a colleague, or delete it. These rules are different from the ones I discuss in Book IX, Chapter 2, in that they come into effect only when you turn on Automatic Replies.

To create a rule that limits what Automatic Replies can do with certain e-mails when you're at the spa (or wherever), follow these steps:

1. **Click the File tab to display Backstage, and select Info from the list on the left.**

The Account Information options appear on the right.

2. **Click the Automatic Replies button.**

The Automatic Replies dialog box jumps up to help. (Refer to Figure 1-1.)

3. **Click the Rules button.**

The Automatic Reply Rules dialog box appears (jump ahead to Figure 1-5), showing a list of currently active rules determining the conditions for which e-mail senders receive replies while you're away.

4. **Click the Add Rule button.**

The Edit Rule dialog box pops up, as shown in Figure 1-3.

Figure 1-3:
You make
the rules.

5. **In the When a Message Arrives That Meets the Following Conditions pane, select the conditions that define the kind of e-mail with which you want to do something special.**

For example, maybe you want to do something special when an e-mail arrives from your boss or one that has a Subject line that includes *Blackford account,* or just *Blackford.*

For the lowdown on how to select conditions that define the e-mail you want to affect and to set advanced rules options, see Book IX, Chapter 2.

6. **If necessary, you can get nitpicky about which e-mails you want to affect by clicking Advanced and specifying additional conditions.**

   In the Advanced dialog box that appears (see Figure 1-4), you can further define the e-mails you want this rule to apply to. For example, you might want to do something special with large e-mails, e-mails received on a particular day or days, e-mails that include attachments, and so on.

7. **After making your selections, click OK to close the Advanced dialog box.**

   The Edit Rule dialog box reappears. (Refer to Figure 1-3.)

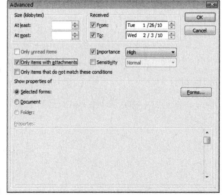

Figure 1-4:
Set more
options
to define
which
e-mails you
want to rule.

8. **If you want this particular rule to be applied last, after all other rules, then select the Do Not Process Subsequent Rules check box.**

   Normally, Outlook applies rules in the order in which they're listed, until every rule has been applied, but turning on this option changes that behavior.

9. **In the Perform These Actions pane, select the action(s) you want to occur with the e-mails that match the conditions you've set.**

   If you're creating a rule that deletes specific e-mail, then for obvious reasons, after that rule is applied, Outlook doesn't go looking at the rest of the rules to see whether any more might apply to the e-mail. You can change the order of rules so that Outlook does something to the e-mail before its deleted, if you want. See the following section for help.

10. **Click OK.**

The rule is added to your other Out of Office rules, and you're returned to the Automatic Reply Rules dialog box.

11. **To create more rules, just click the Add Rule button, and then rinse and repeat Steps 4 to 9.**

12. **To finish adding rules, click OK to dismiss the Automatic Reply Rules dialog box, then click OK again to dismiss the Automatic Replies dialog box.**

Changing the rules

Just because you created some rules doesn't mean you're stuck with them. You can modify rules to make them work the way you want them to work. You can also delete rules that you don't need.

To modify an existing rule, follow these steps:

1. **Click the File tab to display Backstage, and select Info from the list on the left.**

The Account Information options appear on the right.

2. **Click the Automatic Replies button.**

The Automatic Replies dialog box appears.

3. **Click the Rules button.**

Your rules are displayed in a list in the Automatic Reply Rules dialog box, as shown in Figure 1-5.

Figure 1-5:
Select the
rule you
want to
change.

4. **Select a rule and click Edit Rule.**

The Edit Rule dialog box appears. (See Figure 1-6.)

5. **Make changes, click OK to close the Edit Rule dialog box, click OK to finalize changes to Automatic Reply Rules, and then click OK in the Automatic Replies dialog box to close it.**

In other words, OK, OK, OK, enough already.

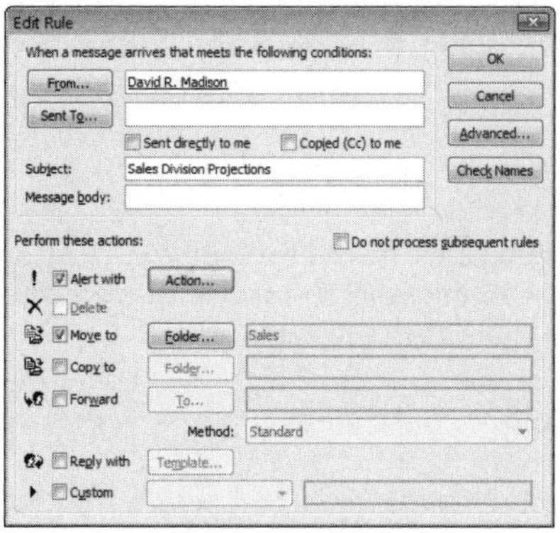

Figure 1-6:
Rules aren't
set in stone.

To change the order in which rules are applied, follow these steps:

1. **Click the File tab to display Backstage, and select Info from the list on the left.**

The Account Information options appear on the right.

2. **Click the Automatic Replies button.**

The Automatic Replies dialog box appears.

3. **Click the Rules button.**

The Automatic Reply Rules dialog box appears. Refer to Figure 1-5.

4. **Select a rule that you want to move up or down in the list.**

Rules are applied in the order in which they appear in the list, so moving a rule up means that it's applied before the rules below it. Moving a rule down means that it's applied after other rules that appear above it.

5. **Click the Move Up or Move Down buttons.**

6. **Repeat Steps 3 and 4 to adjust the order of other rules. When you're done, click OK, then click OK again.**

To remove a rule completely, follow these steps:

1. **Click the File tab to display Backstage, and select Info from the list on the left.**

The Account Information options appear on the right.

2. **Click the Automatic Replies button.**

The Automatic Replies dialog box appears.

3. **Click the Rules button.**

The Automatic Reply Rules dialog box appears. Refer to Figure 1-5.

4. **Select a rule that you want to delete.**

5. **Click the Delete Rule button.**

Why not remove other bothersome rules, such as that red stoplight thing? I mean, why do I have to let others go first just because they have a green light? I like red.

6. **Click OK when you finish.**

What to do if you only have a POP3 or IMAP e-mail account

Well, okay, not everyone has an Exchange network. So, not everyone can just wiggle their fingers and call the Feature Formerly Known as the Out of Office Assistant to take over when they're away from their desks. If you don't have an HTML account, you probably at least use POP3 or IMAP, so you can at least do *something* to handle e-mail when you're away.

Some HTML (Web-based) e-mail accounts provide simple ways to handle incoming e-mail, so you might be able to use a Web interface to set up a system.

Here's the basic plan: You create a plain text message and save it as a template. Then, you create a rule that uses the template to generate outgoing messages while you're out of the office.

Follow these steps to create the template:

1. **From within Mail, click the New Items button on the Ribbon's Home tab and select E-mail Message from the pop-up menu that appears.**

A new mail message form pops up (see the background of Figure 1-7).

2. **Click the Plain Text button on the form's Format Text tab.**

The message is changed to plain text, rather than HTML format. By using plain text, you can't apply any formatting. But you can at least get your message out, especially for folks sending you messages from their mobile phones.

3. **Type the message that you want people to receive while you're gone.**

Looking ahead, remember that Outlook, being a bit of a control freak, keeps track of each and every e-mail you receive while you're gone and sends the reply only once to each address, even if somebody sends you a bunch of e-mail. So keep that in mind when you design your message.

You do not need to enter anyone's address in the To: text box, since you're not sending this message to anyone in particular just now.

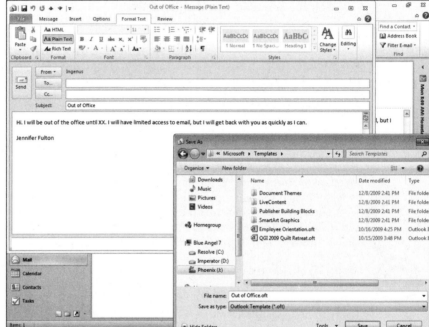

Figure 1-7: Create the message that you want to send when you're out of the office.

4. **To save the message as a template, click the File tab to display Backstage, and select Save As from the list on the left.**

The Save As dialog box pops up. (Refer to the foreground of Figure 1-7.)

5. **In the Save As Type drop-down list, select Outlook Template.**

6. **Enter a name for your template, such as** `Out of Office`, **in the File Name text box and click Save.**

7. **Click the close box ("X") in the form to close the message.**

Because you saved your message as a template and don't want to send it to anyone just now, don't save any changes to the message. In the dialog box that appears, click No.

After you create a template for your out-of-office replies, follow these steps to create a rule to use that template:

1. **(Optional) To base your rules on the recipients or contents of a certain e-mail message you've already received, change to the Mail module by clicking its button on the Navigation pane, and then click that message in the message list.**

For example, if you want to create a rule about the sender or the other recipients of a message, or about a meeting whose invitation appears in the message, or about an attachment that appears in a message, then you can select that message first. The Rules Wizard you'll use in a moment will automatically generate possible rules and criteria for you to choose from, based on the message that currently appears in Mail.

2. **Click the Rules button in the Move group on the Home tab and select Create Rule from the pop-up menu that appears.**

The Create Rule dialog box appears.

3. **Click Advanced Options.**

The Rules Wizard jumps up. (See Figure 1-8.)

4. **Select which types of messages get replies.**

For example, you can send replies only to messages sent directly to you and no one else by selecting the Sent Only to Me check box.

You can set more limiting conditions if you want, or select none at all if you want this rule to apply to all incoming e-mail.

5. **Click Next.**

If you haven't chosen any criteria here at all, Outlook will bring up a dialog box asking you if you mean to apply this rule to every message (no conditions to be checked here whatsoever). If that's what you meant, click Yes; otherwise, click No to return to the conditions list.

The What Do You Want to Do With the Message? Rules Wizard page appears.

6. **In the What Do You Want to Do With the Message? list, select the Reply Using a Specific Template check box, as shown in the background in Figure 1-9.**

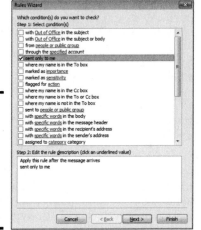

Figure 1-8:
The Rules
Wizard
steps you
through the
process of
creating an
e-mail rule.

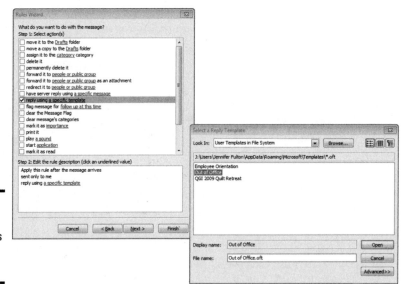

Figure 1-9:
Send out
auto-replies
using a
template.

7. **Click the A Specific Template link that appears in the bottom of the page.**

   The Select a Reply Template dialog box opens. (See the foreground in Figure 1-9.)

8. **Select User Templates in File System from the Look In drop-down list.**

9. **In the list box, select the template you just created and click Open.**

The Select a Reply Template dialog box closes.

10. **Click Next.**

The Are There Any Exceptions? page of the Wizard appears.

11. **Select any exceptions from the Are There Any Exceptions list.**

For example, you might not want to send replies to messages that are actually newsletters, or that you know are newsletters because they're flagged with their titles in their subject lines. To choose an exception, click its check box — just as you did for rules/conditions — and then click the hyperlink in the newly created line at the bottom under "Step 2" to select the item that triggers the exception.

12. **Click Next.**

The Finish Rule Setup page of the Wizard appears.

13. **Type a name for the rule in the Specify a Name for This Rule text box, check the Turn On This Rule check box, and then click Finish.**

Okay, you don't have to turn the rule on right now if you're not heading out of town. To turn your rule on after you create it, click the Rules button on the Home tab, select Manage Rules & Alerts from the pop-up menu that appears, then select your Out of Office rule to turn it on.

14. **When Outlook gives you the warning that it can only run while Outlook is running, click OK.**

The Rules Wizard is dismissed.

Now, if you leave Outlook (and your computer) on, and you have Outlook set up so that it automatically checks for e-mail every once in a while, then when you get an e-mail, Outlook automatically creates a reply by using your template.

When you get back into the office, you'll need to turn off your rule. Here are the steps to follow for that:

1. **Click the Rules button in the Move group on the Home tab and select Manage Rules & Alerts from the pop-up menu that appears.**

The Rules and Alerts dialog box appears.

2. **In the rules list, click the check box beside the rule you want to turn off.**

3. **If you no longer need the rule for any other purpose in the future, then to delete it, click Delete, and respond to the dialog box by clicking Yes.**

4. **Click OK to save your changes.**

Assigning a Delegate to Handle E-Mail and Appointments While You're Gone

If you work on an Exchange network, you can designate someone to act as your delegate, meaning that he or she can take over your day-to-day Outlook operations, including sending e-mails, accepting meeting requests, canceling appointments, and so on. Whether you can get him or her to do your laundry and walk the dog is another story.

In Outlook, you can do a different kind of sharing, which is typically more equal, and involves simply sharing folders. For example, you can share your calendar with someone, and he can share his with you. This sharing might involve only being able to view items in the folder, or it can involve various permission levels all the way up to being allowed to not only view, but create, change, and delete items in the folder. See Book IV, Chapter 3 for how to do this kind of sharing with Calendar; Book V, Chapter 4 for the same for Contacts; and Chapter VI, Chapter 3 for Tasks. Although you can use these same techniques to share an e-mail folder, typically, you use delegate access to allow them to perform certain tasks, acting as you, as described in the following sections.

For delegate access to work, both you and your personal workhorse must not only be on the same Exchange network, but also using the same version of Outlook. Typically, the network administrator makes sure that everyone has the same software, so you probably don't have to worry about compatibility issues. For someone to have access to the e-mails you want him or her to answer, those e-mails must arrive in your regular Exchange mailbox — either the Inbox or some custom folder, not in a personal folder you've created (a completely different data file, which has a .pst extension).

Assigning a delegate

When you assign a delegate to take over some of your Outlook Calendar duties, he or she can not only respond to meeting and task requests (by accepting, declining, or tentatively accepting them), but also receive meeting and task responses (responses to meeting or task requests that you've sent). When people get these meeting/task replies, however, the From field reads something like *Delegate Name* on behalf of *Manager Name*. That way, people know you're not actually responding, but someone acting on your behalf is. For very special delegates, you can adjust the permissions to allow them to do even more — basically acting as your replacement. Don't worry; no matter how many tasks you allow him or her to perform for you, your delegate can't take over your corner office.

To assign a delegate, follow these steps:

1. **Click the File tab, to display Backstage, and select Info from the list on the left.**

The Account Information options appear on the right.

2. **Click the Account Settings button, and then select Delegate Access from the drop-down menu that appears.**

The Delegates dialog box appears.

3. **Click the Add button.**

The Add Users dialog box jumps up, as shown in Figure 1-10.

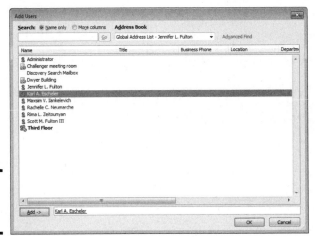

Figure 1-10:
Add a
delegate.

If that ol' Add button isn't active (if it appears grayed out, in other words), you may not be connected to the Exchange network. Check the status bar to make sure that you're connected properly and that the network isn't down for some reason.

4. **From the list of people, select a workhorse (uh, delegate) whom you want to take over your job while you're gone. Click Add, and then click OK.**

The Delegate Permissions dialog box appears.

5. **Choose the modules (such as Calendar or Tasks) you want to delegate to the people you've chosen, and change their level of access as needed by selecting a permission level from the appropriate drop-down list.**

By default, a delegate can reply to meeting requests, and process meeting replies that you receive. He or she can also respond to task requests and task replies. You can allow a delegate to do more, if you want, by changing settings in the Delegate Permissions dialog box, shown in Figure 1-11.

Even though the Inbox permission level is set to None, if you select the Delegate Receives Copies of Meeting-Related Messages Sent to Me check box, your delegate automatically receives your meeting requests and replies in her Inbox. She doesn't need a higher level of permission for your Inbox unless you want her to read, send, or delete e-mails on your behalf. The Calendar and Tasks permission level is set to Editor to allow the delegate to read and respond to task/meeting requests and task/meeting replies and do other stuff. Here's what each permission level allows your delegate to do:

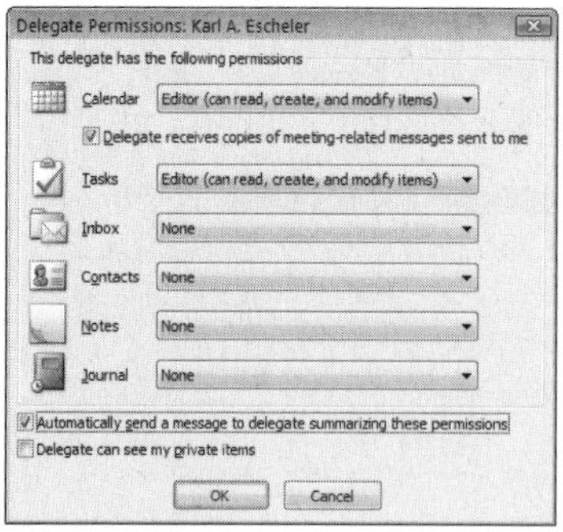

Figure 1-11:
You can
allow your
delegate
to do more
for you.

- *Reviewer:* Delegate can only read items.

- *Author:* Delegate can read any item, create new items, and change or delete only the items he or she creates.

- *Editor:* Delegate can read any item, create new items, and change or delete any item, even if the delegate didn't create the item.

6. **To create a message to your delegate that summarizes the permissions you've just set, select the Automatically Send a Message to Delegate Summarizing These Permissions check box.**

7. **To allow your delegate to see items that you've marked as private, select the Delegate Can See My Private Items check box.**

   This option allows a delegate to see all private items in your Exchange data file, regardless of the folder they're in.

8. **When you're through setting options and having fun, click OK.**

   You're returned to the Delegates dialog box. See Figure 1-12.

9. **Select to whom you want copies of meeting requests sent.**

   Select the radio button for the option that you want:

   • *My Delegates Only, But Send a Copy of Meeting Requests and Responses to Me:* Get copies of the meeting requests and replies that arrive while you're gone.

   • *My Delegates Only:* Allow meeting requests and replies to go to your delegate's Inbox only.

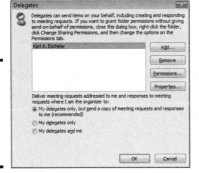

Figure 1-12:
Set
additional
options
for your
delegate.

   • *My Delegates and Me:* Place the original meeting requests and replies in both your delegate's Inbox and yours so that you can also reply to them.

   The problem with this option is that the two of you might reply differently, and who knows what Outlook would do in that situation.

10. **Click OK.**

If you select the Automatically Send a Message to Delegate Summarizing These Permissions option in Step 6, your delegate gets an e-mail letting him know his duties and the permission levels you set. Your delegate can now take over the tasks (replying to meeting requests, for example) that you've assigned.

See "Managing Someone Else's E-Mail and Calendar," later in this chapter, for help with what to do if you've been made someone else's delegate.

Changing a delegate's permission levels

To change what a delegate can do for you, follow these steps:

1. **Click the File tab, to display Backstage, and select Info from the list on the left.**

The Account Information options appear on the right.

2. **Click the Account Settings button, and then select Delegate Access from the drop-down menu that appears.**

The Delegates dialog box jumps up. (Refer to Figure 1-12.)

3. **Select the delegate you want to change and click the Permissions button.**

The Delegate Permissions dialog box peeks out (see Figure 1-13).

4. **To change the access level for one of your Outlook modules, such as Contacts or the Calendar, make a selection from the appropriate drop-down list.**

Your options include Editor, Author, Reviewer, or None. (For more on the mechanics of setting permission levels, see the "Assigning a delegate" section, earlier in this chapter.)

Figure 1-13:
Changing
the
permissions
that you
gave a
delegate.

5. **Repeat Step 3 for other modules, as desired.**

6. **Click OK to close the Delegate Permissions dialog box, and then click OK to close the Delegate dialog box.**

You can also remove a delegate altogether, which you may want to do after you get back to work, by following these steps:

1. **Click the File tab, to display Backstage, and select Info from the list on the left.**

   The Account Information options appear on the right.

2. **Click the Account Settings button, and then select Delegate Access from the drop-down menu that appears.**

   The Delegates dialog box jumps up. (Refer to Figure 1-12.)

3. **In the list, select the delegate you want to remove.**

4. **Click the Remove button.**

   The delegate is removed from your Permissions list and can no longer access your various Outlook folders. Your delegate doesn't get any e-mail letting her know that she's now off the hook, so you might want to drop an e-mail yourself to thank her for her hard work and to tell her to stop reading your mail.

5. **Click OK to close the Delegates dialog box.**

Managing Someone Else's E-Mail and Calendar

You might be given access to somebody else's Outlook folders in several ways. If someone wants to control exactly what you can do and doesn't want you acting on his or her behalf, you were probably given access to a shared folder. You can find help managing these folders in Book IV, Chapter 3 (for Calendar); Book V, Chapter 4 (for Contacts); and Book VI, Chapter 3 (for Tasks).

The following sections discuss what to do when you receive delegate access to someone's folders. With this kind of access, when you create items, you do it by acting on the other person's behalf. If you send a task request, for example, everyone knows that it came from you, but on behalf of someone else. So, no, you can't plan an eight-hour "doing nothing" meeting just to get some time off, without your boss eventually catching on.

Displaying somebody else's folders

When someone sets you up as a delegate, you get an e-mail that details exactly which folders you have access to and what you can do in them. You probably want to display that person's folders in your Outlook right away so that you can keep an eye on them.

Although delegate access is great, unless the person designated as the delegate also makes his or her mailbox visible, you can't access it through the Navigation pane. And if that designee is you, then unless you make the folder visible, you're just no good as a delegate, are you? To make a mailbox visible on the Exchange network, you need to change to Mail, select your Exchange account in the Navigation pane, and click the Folder Permissions button on the Folder tab. The Outlook Today Properties dialog box appears. Click the Permissions tab, and select your delegate from the list of names at the top of the tab. Under Other, select the Folder Visible option and click OK. Then, you can tell your delegate that everything's set.

To add somebody's folders to Outlook so that you can see them each time you start Outlook, follow these steps:

1. **Click the File tab to display Backstage, and select Info from the list on the left.**

The Account Information options appear on the right.

2. **Click the Account Settings button and select Account Settings from the drop-down menu that appears.**

The Account Settings dialog box appears.

3. **Select your Exchange account from those listed at the bottom of the E-Mail tab, and click Change.**

The Change Account Wizard appears. See the background of Figure 1-14.

4. **Click the More Settings button, click the Advanced tab in the Microsoft Exchange dialog box that appears, and then click the Add button.**

The Add Mailbox dialog box opens, as shown in the foreground of Figure 1-14.

5. **Enter the name of the person whose folders you want displayed in your Outlook, and then click OK.**

The Add Mailbox dialog box closes, and the person's name appears in the list at the top of the Advanced tab in the Microsoft Exchange dialog box.

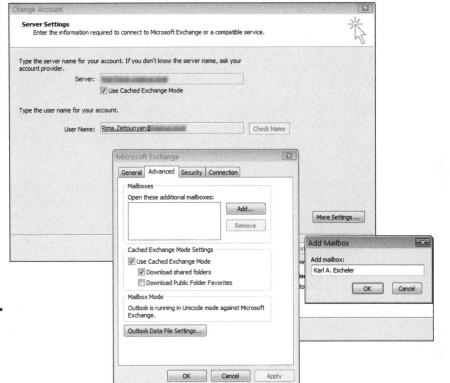

**Book X
Chapter 1**

**Managing Your
Company E-Mail**

Figure 1-14:
The Change
Account
Wizard.

6. **Click OK to dismiss the Microsoft Exchange dialog box.**

   You return to the Change Account Wizard.

7. **Click Next.**

   Outlook has a little message of congratulations for you in this last page
   of this most flamboyant wizard.

8. **Click Finish.**

   The Account Settings dialog box peeks back out.

9. **Click Close and restart Outlook.**

   The name of the mailbox you added will appear in the Navigation pane,
   typically below your own Exchange account. If you've been delegated
   access already, then you'll start to see contents right away. If you
   haven't, the message list on the right will be grayed out and you'll see
   an ominous looking warning that says the object cannot be found. Once
   delegation comes through, this warning will go away.

If the person whose name you typed has granted you access to some or all of her folders, you can access her folders from the Navigation pane within the appropriate module. For example, if you have Editor access to the calendar so that you can handle meeting requests and replies, you also have permission to view that person's calendar and to make appointments and events. After following the preceding steps conveniently provided here by *moi,* you can now access that person's calendar easily, as shown in Figure 1-15, in which I've switched over to my calendar and clicked the calendar for Karl A. Escheler (I found it in the Shared Calendars category) to view his calendar side-by-side with mine. You can repeat this process in any other module to which you have access, such as Tasks, to view its items and perform your duly designated duties as delegate.

When you gain access to someone's Contacts folder, you can click only that folder in the Navigation pane at any time to display its contacts.

If you don't want to see somebody's folders hanging out with yours, causing you to accidentally add your appointments to their calendars or vice versa, you can display their folders just when you need them. When you change to a different module or exit Outlook, another user's folder disappears from view, and you need to repeat the following steps to see it again. To temporarily display someone's folder in Outlook (assuming you have permission), follow these steps:

1. **Click the File tab to display Backstage, and select Open from the list on the left.**

The Open options appear on the right.

2. **Select Other User's Folder.**

The Open Other User's Folder dialog box appears, as shown on the left in Figure 1-16.

3. **In the Name box, type the name of the person whose folder you want to open temporarily.**

Alternatively, you can click the Name button, select that person from a list displayed in the Select Names: Global Address List dialog box (refer to right in Figure 1-16), and then click OK to return to the Open Other User's Folder dialog box.

4. **From the Folder Type drop-down list, select the type of Outlook module that you want to open, then click OK.**

The dialog box closes, and the folder you chose appears in the Navigation pane.

5. **Click that folder to display its contents.**

For example, in the office setup in Figure 1-16, I changed to Calendar and clicked Rima Zeitounyan in the My Calendars area of the Navigation pane to display her calendar next to yours.

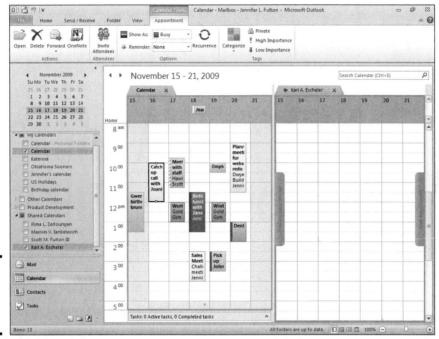

Figure 1-15:
Now you
can access
the folders.

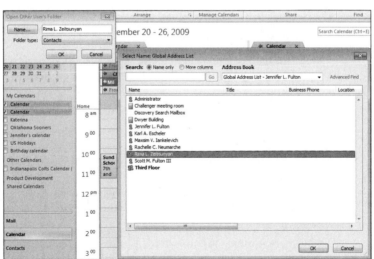

Figure 1-16:
Spying on
another
user, kinda.

If, for some reason, you don't have access to the folder that you want to open, a message dialog box appears, asking whether you want to request access. Click Yes, and Outlook will open up a message form showing the formal request for access sharing. The recipient only needs to accept your request automatically, and the sharing process will begin immediately. (Don't you wish Congress worked like that?)

Dealing with meetings and tasks as a delegate

After you have the folders for that special someone who's stuff you promised to take care of appearing right there in your Outlook, all nice and ready to go, you just need to sit back and wait for a meeting or task request or reply to come in (if that's what you're taking care of). If you're in charge of other things, as well, such as adding or canceling appointments, well, just go ahead and take care of that, too.

Follow these steps to deal with meeting or task requests that come in for the person you're covering for:

1. **Open the task or meeting request to which you want to reply.**

   If the colleague whose stuff you're handling left the Delegate Receives Copies of Meeting-Related Messages check box selected, any incoming meeting requests appear in your Inbox, where you can easily deal with them. If your colleague didn't select this option when he or she set you up as a delegate, then you need to actually check that person's mailbox for the requests (you need at least Reviewer access, as opposed to None, to open the person's mailbox).

2. **When the task or meeting request comes in for the person who made you a delegate, double-click the request to open it, as shown in Figure 1-17.**

   The InfoBar reminds you that this request is actually for someone else.

Unless you were given at least Reviewer access to your colleague's Inbox, you need to do some digging to find and reply to task requests because they don't appear automatically in your Inbox. With Editor access to Tasks, you can use the steps in the preceding section to display your colleague's Tasks folder, and then, when task requests come in, they appear amid the other tasks in your own Tasks list in bold (until you open them, that is).

To help you quickly identify task requests, sort your colleague's Tasks list by person responsible. Click the Change View button on the View tab and select Assigned from the pop-up menu that appears.

Here is where you see the request's true recipient.

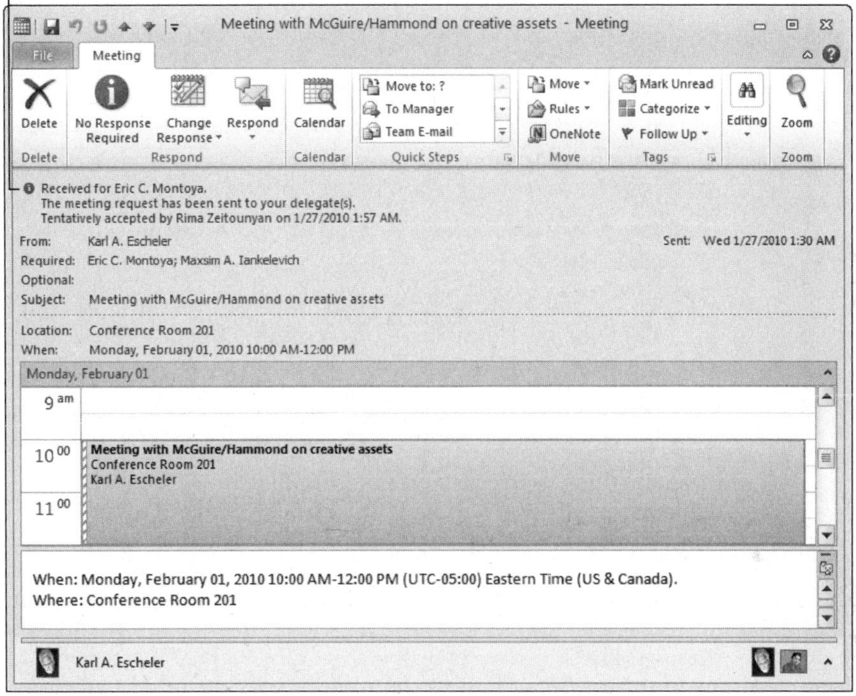

Book X
Chapter 1

Managing Your
Company E-Mail

Figure 1-17:
As delegate,
you can
open up
somebody
else's
requests.

3. **To see the subject of the meeting request on the calendar, double-click the meeting in the request.**

   Outlook switches to the Calendar module. There, the requested time shows up in a calendar specifically marked for the other person, not for you. In case it's still confusing, the other person's name also appears in the meeting box as one of the invited attendees.

4. **Click the meeting box to select it, click the Accept, Decline, or Tentative button on the Meeting tab to respond on the recipient's behalf.**

   As the delegate, hopefully you've been given some guidelines on how to determine whether to accept a meeting or task request. If not, you can always turn to the Magic 8 Ball. In the pop-up menu that appears when you click one of these buttons, you can send your choice now by selecting Send the Response Now. But since you're the delegate, you may prefer to select Edit the Response Before Sending — this way, you can explain to people that you believe, on behalf of that other person, that he or she is definitely, certainly not sure. You could also select Do Not Send a Response, which doesn't send any response to the request at all, but just how friendly is that?

If you selected Edit the Response Before Sending from the pop-up menu, then a message form appears; type a response in the large text box and click Send to send the message. The From box clearly says that this message is from you, on behalf of someone else, so no worries there.

If you want to propose a different time to meet, skip this step and continue to Step 5;

5. **To suggest a different meeting time on the other person's behalf, click the Propose New Time button on the Meeting tab.**

   In the pop-up menu, select Tentative and Propose New Time to accept on the other person's behalf, for now; or Decline and Propose New Time, to reject the current proposition. You'll see the Propose New Time dialog box, which gives you a cool way to select an alternative time from a separate calendar. You can make your suggestion in a number of ways:

   - *To manually select a time:* Click in your row on any time slot that's open. The proposed time is flanked by green and red bars on the left and right, respectively. You can also select a new Meeting Start and Meeting End date and time from the drop-down lists provided.

   - *To have Outlook propose a new time:* Click the AutoPick Next button. Outlook finds the first available free time slot for all attendees. Click the << button to locate the first free time slot available in the vicinity of the original appointment, usually later, within the same day if possible. The suggested meeting time is flanked by green and red bars.

   - *To reset the suggested time to the current meeting time:* Click Current Meeting Time.

   After selecting a new time, click Propose New Time. A meeting reply (message) is created. The InfoBar of the message form displays the current meeting time and the one you're proposing. Type a reason for your proposed new time in the large text box if you want, and click Send to send the message. The From box clearly says that this message is from you, on behalf of someone else, so again, there's no confusion here.

To create a meeting request or task request on behalf of someone else, follow these steps:

1. **Open the other person's Calendar or Tasks folder.**

   See the preceding section for help accessing someone's folders.

2. **Click the New Items button on the Home tab and select either Meeting or Task from the pop-up menu that appears.**

   Create the meeting or task request in the way you would for a meeting or task of your own. For help in creating meeting requests, see Book IV, Chapter 4. For help with task requests, see Book VI, Chapter 3.

3. **Click Send.**

   When a colleague receives the meeting or task request, he sees that you created it, but on behalf of someone else. He knows exactly who's asking the favor and who owes him one if he ultimately accepts.

When meeting replies come in, you simply need to open the messages to have Outlook add that person's Accept, Decline, or Tentative response to the meeting total. For task replies, you need to open the message so that you can at least see whether the person you sent it to accepted the task.

Dealing with e-mail as a delegate

Managing a few meeting replies or task requests that come in while someone's on vacation should probably amount to very little work on your part. Of course, if it's your full-time job to manage someone's schedule, that's another matter altogether. Still, dealing with appointments, meetings, and a few stray task requests is nothing compared to dealing with a steady stream of incoming e-mail. I mean, I know how much e-mail I get on any given day, and if I had to double that by taking on someone else's e-mail, I'd probably never be able to leave the office.

To send out a new e-mail on someone's behalf, follow these steps:

1. **Click the New Items button on the Home tab, and then select E-mail Message from the pop-up menu that appears.**

   A message form jumps up.

2. **In the InfoBar of the message form, if you don't see a button marked From with your account name beside it, then you need to add it to your form.**

   Click the Options tab, and under Show Fields, click From. The From button and your account name will immediately appear in this form, as well as the forms for all other messages you create later until you decide to turn this option off.

3. **In the InfoBar, click the From button and select Other E-Mail Address from the pop-up menu that appears.**

   The Send From Other E-Mail Address dialog box opens, as shown in the background of Figure 1-18.

4. **In the From box, type the name of the person for which you're creating the e-mail .**

   Alternatively, click the From button and select the name from the Choose Sender dialog box by selecting a name from the list and clicking OK. See the foreground of Figure 1-18. After you click OK, you're returned to the Send From Other E-Mail Address dialog box. Yes, you can choose any name from this list, and you may even think you're sending a message as that person. But if you try to send a message as someone who hasn't given you permission to do so, Exchange will send you back a nasty letter scolding you. And there'll be an audit trail on the admin's system as well.

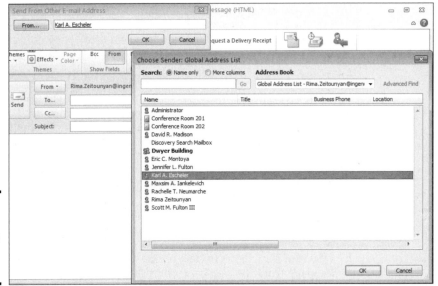

Figure 1-18:
Sending an e-mail that's not from you.

5. **Address the e-mail, type a subject in the Subject text box, and enter your message (or rather, your colleague's message) in that big white text box at the bottom of the form.**

   If you need help creating the e-mail, see Book II, Chapter 1.

6. **When you finish creating the e-mail, click Send.**

   If you were very explicit in your e-mail, then the recipient will know that you sent the e-mail, but he or she also knows that the message was ultimately from someone else. Exchange gives away the secret: Your colleague's name automatically appears in the From text box. (Refer to Figure 1-19.)

To reply to somebody else's e-mail for whom you're acting as delegate, you need to be able to view the contents of his or her Inbox first. See the section "Displaying somebody else's folders," earlier in this chapter, for help. After you display his or her Inbox, follow these steps to reply to messages:

1. **In your colleague's Inbox, select the message to which you want to reply.**

2. **Click Reply.**

A message form appears, as shown in Figure 1-19. Your colleague's name automatically appears in the From text box.

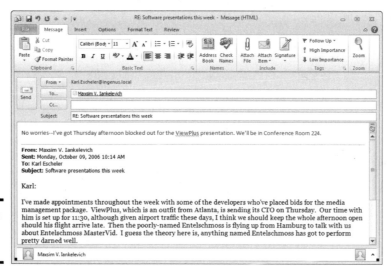

Figure 1-19:
Ghost
writer.

3. **Type the reply in the message text box and click Send.**

The message arrives in the recipient's mailbox, clearly addressed from you (with your name in the message's InfoBar), acting on the behalf of your colleague.

You can follow these same basic steps to forward a colleague's e-mail to someone else, on his or her behalf.

Dealing with appointments as a delegate

As a delegate, if you have access to somebody's calendar, you can not only reply to meeting requests and open meeting replies, but you can also add appointments and events.

Follow these steps to deal with someone else's appointments:

1. **Select your colleague's calendar in the Navigation pane to make it active.**

   If the calendar doesn't appear on the Navigation pane, see the section "Displaying somebody else's folders," earlier in this chapter, for more info.

2. **Click the New Appointment button on the Home tab.**

   An appointment form appears.

3. **Complete the appointment like you would for your own appointment: Add a subject, location, start time and date, end time and date, and so on.**

   If you need help in creating an appointment, see Book IV, Chapter 1.

4. **Click Save & Close to save the appointment.**

   The appointment appears in your colleague's calendar, and it doesn't appear in yours.

Follow these same basic steps to add an event to somebody else's calendar. For help in creating a meeting on behalf of someone else, see the section "Dealing with meetings and tasks as a delegate," earlier in this chapter.

Chapter 2: Turning Your E-Mail Accounts into Roadies

In This Chapter

✔ Keeping in touch, even when you're out of the office

✔ Going live with Windows Live Mail

✔ Making your company's Exchange e-mail vacation-friendly

*O*nce e-mail is set up and working properly, the process of getting e-mail is pretty much a forget about it" kind of thing. You drive to work, get a cup of coffee, sit down at your desk, and start slogging through all the messages that Outlook has downloaded from the e-mail server. At the end of the day, you go home, get another cup of coffee, sit down at your desk, and start slogging through your personal messages. But when you break the routine, trouble starts. You go on vacation, but you want to check whether your boss has responded to your request for more personnel. Or you go on a business trip and need to check e-mail every day. You can't exactly drag your desktop computer with you on that trip, even if you wanted to. And taking your laptop along doesn't take your e-mail with it — or, at least, not your e-mail connection.

So, what's a person to do? I have to assume everybody has this problem because solutions abound everywhere you look. With a smartphone, for example, you can get your e-mail from any location. With a 3G modem, you can easily connect your laptop to the Internet and get e-mail. These two solutions, however, assume that you have a cooperative e-mail account, such as Web mail, that allows you to connect through the Internet and grab your messages. But most corporate accounts aren't Web-mail–based, so it's tough to take them along with you on a trip. And personal e-mail isn't always much better, depending on the kind of account you have. In this chapter, I discuss various options and what you can do to get your e-mail from the road.

Getting Personal E-Mail on the Road

For most of us, e-mail desire doesn't stop when we leave work. Nope, we all have personal e-mail accounts, and most of us use those accounts quite a lot to stay in touch with friends and family. For personal e-mail, you face two problems when trying to check it while on vacation or otherwise away from home:

✦ How to access e-mail that's basically setup to be retrieved at home using Outlook

✦ How to keep all your e-mail on your home computer, even if you use a hotel PC or a friend's computer to view some of it while on vacation

Problem one

To address how to get e-mail on a computer that doesn't have Outlook, you have several options in today's Gotta Get My E-Mail world:

✦ If your e-mail account provides a Web interface, you can access your e-mail by using a Web browser. Don't want to haul along your PC while on vacation? No problem — most hotels provide a computer you can use to do just that. Public libraries provide computers, too, and your cell phone probably has a Web browser, so research your options before you head out.

The problem with using a Web interface with your normal e-mail account is that you typically don't have access to your Outlook contacts. So, if you want to e-mail someone, you have to manually address the message. Bummer. Some Web-based e-mail accounts allow you to import your contacts from Outlook, but if you add new contacts, you have to manually import contacts again to get everything in synch. (See the upcoming section, "Importing Outlook Contacts into a Web-Based E-Mail Account" for help on this one.) This process, however, is just too manual for me, but it may work for you. If you want to find out about a more convenient solution in which everything stays in synch automatically, see the section, "Solutions for a Modern World: Using Windows Live," later in this chapter.

✦ Speaking of cell phones, smartphones provide e-mail access as a matter of course. For example, I can get my e-mail through my BlackBerry easily. It doesn't use Outlook; instead, BlackBerry provides a simple e-mail interface and a way for me to synch my contacts, tasks, and notes with Outlook. iPhones and Palms are similar — instead of providing Outlook, they offer a different interface for sending and receiving e-mail. Depending on the make and model, your cell phone may or may not synch with Outlook's contacts, notes, and tasks, so check that with your service provider.

Windows smartphones come with Outlook Mobile, a kind of miniaturized version of Outlook. Using Outlook Mobile basically eliminates the problems you might have with another phone and synching it with Outlook. But Outlook Mobile requires Microsoft Exchange, which pretty much limits its use to business e-mail.

You may be thinking, "What's the big deal if my phone doesn't synch with Outlook? I can still get e-mail." You sure can, cowboy — but what about your contacts? Without Outlook synching, you end up manually adding or updating your contacts on your cell phone, and that process is pretty tedious, I can tell you.

Suppose you've decided to bypass the whole "What computer can I use while on vacation?" problem by toting a notebook computer with you. You still have to answer the "How do I connect to the Internet?" question, but you can do that fairly easily using a Wi-Fi connection (found in tons of places, from your hotel to coffee houses to public libraries). Outside of Wi-Fi hotspots, you might plug a 3G modem (purchased through your cell-phone provider) into the notebook's USB slot and use your cell-phone service to connect. If, however, the notebook you take on vacation doesn't use Outlook, you need to use its Web browser to get e-mail (assuming your e-mail provider has a Web-mail interface). If the notebook does have Outlook, you face only one possible problem: If the notebook isn't your main computer, then you need to figure out a way to leave e-mails on the server so that you can download them onto your main computer after you get home so that you can keep everything all together.

And that brings us to the second issue concerning getting e-mail while on the road.

Problem two

You can sum up this problem thus: "Doctor Jennifer, I normally get my e-mail on my home computer, and now I'm going on vacation and want to be able check e-mail by using Outlook while I'm gone. But I really like the idea of keeping all my e-mail in one place — my home computer. What do I do?"

Yes, Virginia, there is a Santa Claus — it's Outlook and its ability to beat your e-mail server into submission. In most cases, when you get your e-mail by using Outlook, the e-mail is deleted from the server, and it ain't comin' back, baby. So, how do you tell the server, "Look, I wanna get these e-mails, but I wanna save 'em too so when I get home, I can download them into Outlook and keep all my e-mails together." Luckily, you can tell Outlook to do just pretty easily. (See the upcoming section, "Controlling E-Mail" for help setting that up.) After you tell Outlook what you want, it tells the e-mail server to keep your messages even after Outlook downloads them.

The lowdown on e-mail accounts

Many e-mail accounts wear more than one hat, meaning that you can connect to them by using a variety of protocols. Most personal accounts, for example, use either POP3 or HTTP protocols to retrieve and post e-mail. When you use POP3, it gets the mail from the server and then deletes it. HTTP is a whole different animal. With HTTP, you bypass Outlook and use your Web browser to manage e-mail. The Web interface allows you to look at e-mail and delete it from the server when you want; otherwise, that e-mail stays on the server. So, if you mostly use POP3 to dump your e-mail into Outlook, you can go on vacation and use the hotel's computer and its Internet connection to check e-mail by using HTTP. As long as you don't delete messages, you can get them again by using Outlook when you get home. Also,

when you use a smartphone, you can view your e-mails without deleting them because that's how a smartphone is normally set up.

Some personal accounts use IMAP to retrieve and post e-mail messages. With IMAP servers, the e-mail remains on the server and gets copied to Outlook. When you delete a message in your Inbox, it's marked for deletion from the IMAP server, and the next time you connect, that message is deleted permanently.

You can change how POP3 and IMAP accounts normally act and get Outlook to leave the messages on the server when desired, so you can download them into a more permanent location (such as your home computer) when you're ready.

Solutions for a Modern World: Using Windows Live

Now that we've defined the two problems you face when trying to get your personal e-mail while on the road, let's talk about solutions. For problem one: How to get e-mail without using Outlook, we talked about using a cell phone or a Web browser to access your e-mail. For a gal or guy on the go, Web mail (an HTTP account) is the way to go in style. Because Web mail is HTTP-based, you can access it from anywhere that you can find an Internet connection. Sounds like heaven, right? Well, it's not bad, but it's not Outlook. Web-mail accounts often have clumsy interfaces that make it difficult to scan through your messages quickly and get rid of the ones you no longer want. And Web mail accounts typically don't interface with Outlook, so if you're using Web mail while on a trip, you may have to enter e-mail addresses manually to send any messages (assuming you even know the addresses to use).

If you plan to get your e-mail through your smartphone, make sure that the phone synchs with Outlook, or you won't be able to access your contacts to send new e-mails rather than replies.

Don't get me wrong — my home account comes with an HTTP interface, and I don't care how clumsy the thing is, it's really convenient because I can use it basically anywhere. I just wish it had all my e-mail addresses so that I didn't have to remember them when I go on a trip. Of course, after I enter e-mail addresses manually into the Web interface of my home e-mail account, they stay there — but I'm just not into manual stuff anymore.

So, what's a gal to do? I went hunting for a Web account that does interface with Outlook — and, wouldn't you know, I found one. It's called Windows Live Mail.

Adding a Windows Live Mail account to Outlook

Here's the lowdown, in manager-speak: You're going to leverage the power of your existing Web-based e-mail (specifically, Windows Live Mail, Office Live Mail, Windows Live Hotmail, Hotmail, MSN e-mail, or whatever Microsoft is calling it this week), along with the Microsoft Office Outlook Connector add-in, to create a richly featured Web-mail–Outlook experience. In other words, with the help of a magic gizmo called Microsoft Office Outlook Connector, you download your Web-based e-mail into Outlook. You also can send e-mail through the Web account, using the Outlook interface and its valuable list of contacts.

Book X
Chapter 2

Turning Your
E-Mail Accounts
into Roadies

First, you need to install the Connector and configure it to work with your Web-based e-mail account by following these steps:

1. **Click the File tab to display Backstage, and select Info from the list on the left.**

   The Account Information options appear on the right.

2. **Click the Add Account button.**

   The Auto Account Setup page of the Add New Account Wizard appears, as shown in the background of Figure 2-1.

3. **Enter your Windows Live Mail account info into appropriate fields of the Auto Account Setup page.**

   As shown in Figure 2-1, you need to type in stuff such as your name, e-mail address, and password.

4. **Click Next.**

   The Microsoft Outlook dialog box, shown in the foreground of Figure 2-1, appears. Outlook uses a program called the Outlook Connector as a go-between for linking up Windows Live Mail's Web mail interface and its own e-mail program. You need to install it before Outlook can configure your Windows Live Mail account.

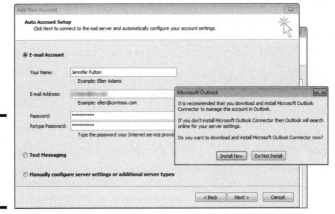

Figure 2-1:
Add a
Windows
Live Mail
account.

5. **Click the Install Now button to download Outlook Connector.**

6. **After the program is downloaded, a dialog box appears telling you so. Click Run to run the setup program for Outlook Connector.**

7. **A dialog box appears, displaying the license agreement for Outlook Connector. Read and accept the license agreement, and click Install.**

   After Outlook Connector is installed, the Auto Account Setup page of the Add New Account Wizard reappears.

8. **Click Next.**

   Outlook logs onto your account, sends a test message, and then displays the last page of the Add New Account Wizard.

9. **Click the Finish button.**

   Your Windows Live Mail account is added to the Navigation pane.

You can now create e-mail messages within Outlook and send them through your Web account (Windows Live Mail). You can also download your Windows Live Mail Web mail into Outlook. To change to your Windows Live Mail account, so you can view its mail, just select it in the Navigation pane in Outlook.

If you have more than one e-mail account set up in Outlook, normally, everything is sent through the main account. So, if someone gets an e-mail from you and clicks Reply, his or her reply goes to your main e-mail address. If you're using Outlook to help you send and receive e-mail for a Web-based account, you might want replies to any messages you send to go back to that e-mail address. To send an e-mail from Outlook by using your Web account, you need to select that account from the From drop-down list in the message form, as shown in Figure 2-2. (See Book III, Chapter 5 for more information on using multiple accounts in Outlook.)

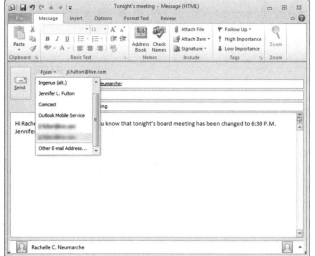

Figure 2-2:
Sending an
e-mail from
your Web
account.

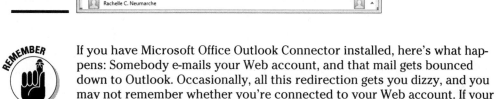

If you have Microsoft Office Outlook Connector installed, here's what happens: Somebody e-mails your Web account, and that mail gets bounced down to Outlook. Occasionally, all this redirection gets you dizzy, and you may not remember whether you're connected to your Web account. If your Web account happens to be Windows Live Mail, lucky you, because you can easily check its status from within Outlook. First, on the Navigation pane, click any folder in your Web account, such as the Inbox, then look at the status bar. Mine tells me that it's Connected to Windows Live Hotmail, so it's all good (except that Microsoft apparently can't decide whether to call it Windows Live Mail or Windows Live Hotmail).

Outlook contacts and Windows Live Mail

After you add your Windows Live Mail account to Outlook, any contacts you may already have in that account on the Web are automatically downloaded into Outlook, and placed in a new Contacts folder called something like `Contacts - jenfakeaddress@live.com`.

If you want to add any of your Outlook contacts to your Windows Live Account so they are available through its Web interface as well, just press Ctrl and drag and drop those contacts into this new Contacts folder.

Importing Outlook Contacts into a Web-Based E-Mail Account

If you have a Windows Live Mail account, contacts you add to the Windows Live folder in the Contacts module in Outlook are automatically added to the Contacts list in Windows Live on the Web. In addition, any changes you make to the contacts in the Windows Live folder in Contacts are synched automatically with your Windows Live contacts out on the Web, and vice-versa.

If you do not want to use Windows Live, you can import the e-mail addresses in your Outlook Contacts list into the Contacts list for most Web-based accounts, so that you don't need to retype them in that account should you need to use its Web interface to send a message. For example, if you have a Yahoo! account, you can import your Outlook contacts and make them available to you whenever you use that account. Need to go on a trip? No problem — if your Outlook contacts are up on Web in your Yahoo! account, you can log in from anywhere that has an Internet connection and send e-mail to anyone you need without all that manual-e-mail-address-typing nonsense.

Basically, you need to complete a two-part process to get your Outlook Contacts up on the Web and into your Web-based e-mail account. In the first part of the process, you export your Outlook Contacts into a special kind of file known as CSV file. You can export all of your contacts, but if you know that you will only want certain contacts on the Web, you can collect the contacts that you want and place them in a separate Contacts folder in Outlook before exporting contacts (see Book IX, Chapter 1 for help in creating folders).

CSV is short for Comma Separated Values, and it's basically a long list of data with commas between each item. It's a pretty common format, and one that both Outlook and most Web-based e-mail accounts support.

To export your contacts to a CSV file (whether from a separate folder or the whole thing), follow these steps:

1. **Click the File tab to display Backstage, and select Open from the list on the left.**

   The Open options appear on the right.

2. **Click the Import option.**

   The Import and Export Wizard appears.

3. **From the Choose an Action to Perform list, Select Export to a File and click Next.**

   The Export to a File Wizard appears.

4. **From the Create a File of Type list, select Comma Separated Values (Windows) and click Next.**

The Select Folder to Export From page of the Wizard appears.

5. **From the Select Folder to Export From list, select the Contacts folder you want to export from and click Next.**

The Save Exported File As page of the Wizard appears.

6. **Click Browse, and in the Browse dialog box that appears, select the folder in which you want to save the CSV file, type a name for the file in the File Name box, and click OK.**

You're returned to the Export to a File Wizard.

7. **Click Next.**

The last page of the Wizard appears.

8. **Click Finish.**

The Contacts folder you selected is exported to a CSV file.

Now that you have created a CSV file with your Outlook contacts in it, it's time to import them into your Web-based e-mail account's Contact list out on the Web. Follow these steps:

1. **Log on to your Web-based e-mail account using a Web browser.**

2. **Change to the Contacts folder for your account.**

For example, in Yahoo! and Google, I clicked the Contacts folder which was listed on the left side of the screen. Your contacts list appears.

3. **Look for an option for importing contacts and click it.**

For example, in Yahoo! I clicked the Tools button and selected Import from the menu that appears. In Google, I clicked the Import link at the top of my contacts list. Anyway, after you click the option for importing contacts into your Web-based e-mail program, some kind of Import Contacts page appears. You use this page to select what to import into your Web-based e-mail account. (See Figure 2-3.)

4. **Select the option that allows you to import CSV files.**

For example, in Yahoo! I clicked the Others option. In Google, the Import page was set up to import CSV so I didn't need to do a thing.

5. **Click Browse to open the Choose File to Upload dialog box, and then locate the Outlook CSV file you just created.**

6. **After you locate your file, select it and click Open.**

You're returned to the Import Contacts page.

7. **Click the Import (or similar) button.**

Your Web-based e-mail program imports the contacts, then displays how many contacts were added or updated during the import process.

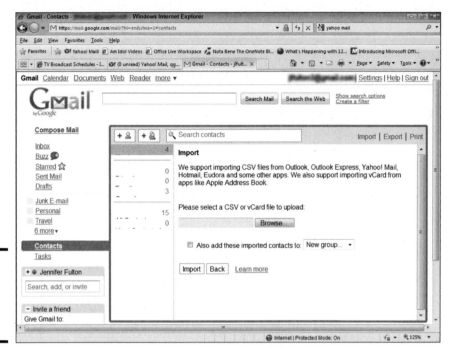

Figure 2-3:
Importing
those
Outlook
contacts.

Controlling E-Mail

Earlier in this chapter, we defined the two problems you face when trying
to get your personal e-mail while on the road. You learned how to solve
problem one, so let's talk about problem two: How to view your e-mail while
on vacation, and still download the messages into Outlook from the server
when you get home.

If you use a Web-mail interface to check your mail, you don't have a problem
because the mail stays on the server until you download it into Outlook. The
same thing typically happens when you use a smartphone to check e-mail —
e-mail stays put until you download and then delete it by using Outlook (you
could have set up your smartphone to delete the messages it receives — but
that's your business, not Outlook's). But if you have one of those cute lightweight notebooks that has Outlook installed, why not cart it along on vacation or wherever— because what could be easier than using Outlook? Those
little notebooks are pretty small, though, so perhaps you have a main PC
on which you prefer to keep most of your personal e-mail. Or maybe you're
actually toting your office laptop with you so that you can check business
and personal e-mail while you're away. In such a case, you might want your
e-mails left on the server so that when you get back home, you can download them to your home PC. If that sounds like your situation, read on.

Getting e-mail messages on a second computer without deleting them

Follow these steps to tell Outlook to retrieve e-mail from a POP3 server without deleting the messages:

1. **Click the File tab to display Backstage, and select Info from the list on the left.**

The Account Information options appear on the right.

2. **Click the Account Settings button, and select Account Settings from the drop-down list.**

The Account Settings dialog box jumps up, with the E-Mail tab displayed. See Figure 2-4.

**Book X
Chapter 2**

Turning Your
E-Mail Accounts
into Roadies

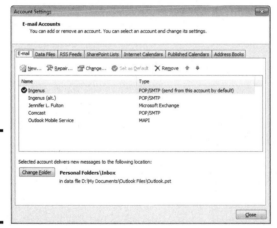

Figure 2-4:
The
Account
Settings
dialog box.

3. **Select the account that you want to change from the list.**

Refer to Figure 2-4.

4. **Click the Change button.**

The Change Account Wizard appears (see the background of Figure 2-5).

5. **Click the More Settings button.**

The Internet E-Mail Settings dialog box pops out. (See the foreground of Figure 2-5.)

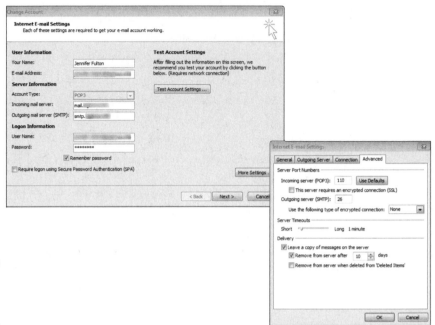

Figure 2-5:
Keep a copy
for yourself.

6. **Click the Advanced tab and select the Leave a Copy of Messages on the Server check box (refer to Figure 2-5).**

   This feature tells Outlook to leave your messages alone.

7. **Set deletion options.**

   With POP3 accounts, your ISP is only going to be so patient; typically, you can keep only so many megabytes of messages on its server before it either sends you an evil e-mail telling you to fix it, cancels your account, or charges you a lot of extra money for going over the limit. Well, you can stop the problem before it starts by setting a limit on the messages Outlook leaves on the server. Here are your options:

   - *To remove the messages after a set period of time:* Select the Remove From Server After *Number of* Days check box. Then, specify the actual number of days that you want messages left on the e-mail server by clicking the up or down arrow keys to the right of the text box or by typing a value.

   - *To remove messages from the e-mail server when you empty them out of your Deleted Items folder:* Select the Remove From Server When Deleted From "Deleted Items" check box.

8. **Click OK to close the Internet E-Mail Settings dialog box.**

   The Change Account Wizard appears.

9. **Click Next.**

   The last page of the Wizard appears.

10. **Click Finish.**

    You're returned to the Account Settings dialog box.

11. **Click Close to close the Account Settings dialog box.**

Downloading only message headers

You can deal with the problem of checking e-mail while you're away from your main computer by just checking message headers. The message header, or Subject, should tell you whether an e-mail is important enough to bother downloading. After downloading a message, you can tell Outlook to remove it from the server or keep it there, depending on your needs.

Message headers appear in the Inbox, looking just like normal e-mail. When you click a message header, though, its content doesn't appear in the Reading pane. In addition, message headers are marked with a special icon, which looks like a telephone and envelope. (See Figure 2-6.)

Message Header icon

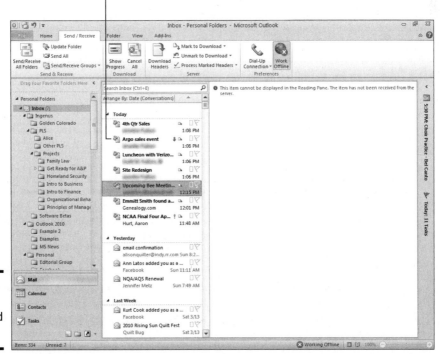

Figure 2-6:
Message headers and their icons.

You can, when needed, tell the server to stop deleting messages that you download, keeping them around for a while on the server. For help, see the preceding section.

Viewing headers has some advantages. You can delete junk mail and spam without downloading those messages to your system and possibly infecting it. You can keep most e-mail on the server for later downloading (possibly at your main computer) and get only the messages you need now. Also, by scanning headers, you can process e-mail more quickly and get back to that well-deserved vacation.

To download just the message headers, leaving the actual messages on the server for a particular account, follow these steps:

1. **Click the Send/Receive Groups button in the Send & Receive group on the Send/Receive tab.**

2. **Select the e-mail account whose message headers you want to get from the pop-up menu that appears.**

   A submenu appears, listing commands that are valid with that e-mail account.

3. **Select Download Inbox Headers.**

   Outlook checks the e-mail server for that account and downloads just the message headers.

You can set up a Send/Receive Group that downloads just the message headers all the time for a particular e-mail account. To find out how to do it, see Book III, Chapter 5.

To download only headers for all of your accounts, click the Download Headers button on the Send/Receive tab.

Working with message headers

After downloading headers, you need to mark the ones you want to act on, and then process them. For example, if you want to view the contents of a particular message, you need to mark it for download. You can also mark headers for deletion, if you've already decided that you don't need to read a particular message. Follow these steps:

1. **Select the message headers to mark.**

   Message headers are marked with a telephone and envelope icon (refer to Figure 2-6.) To tell Outlook which messages you want downloaded from the server, you have to mark them. You start by selecting the headers you want to mark.

Click a single message header to select it. To select several message headers, hold down Ctrl and click each header that you want to select; or hold down Shift, select the first header in a group, then select the last one in the group.

2. **Mark the message headers.**

You follow a different procedure, based on what you want to do with the header:

- *To mark a header for download to your computer and removal from the server:* Click the Mark to Download button on the Send/Receive tab and select Mark to Download from the pop-up menu that appears. These headers are marked with a download icon like the Upcoming Bee Meeting header shown in Figure 2-7.

- *To mark a header for downloading while leaving it on the server:* Click the Mark to Download button on the Send/Receive tab and select Mark to Download Message Copy from the pop-up menu that appears. These headers are marked with a download copy icon, like the Emmitt Smith header shown in Figure 2-7.

- *To mark a header for deletion:* Right-click the header and select Delete from the pop-up menu that appears. You can also select a header and press Delete. The header appears in strikethrough to indicate that it's set for deletion. In addition, these headers are marked with a delete icon, like the NCAA Final Four header shown in Figure 2-7.

Messages marked for deletion aren't removed from an IMAP server until you say "Boo!" Well, actually, the items are deleted only when you physically yank them from the server's greedy hands by issuing a purge command. Select the e-mail folder that contains the items you want to delete from the server, and then click the Purge button on the Folder tab and select Purge Marked Items in *Folder* from the pop-up menu that appears. Click Yes to confirm.

3. **To process the marked headers for a particular account, click the Send/Receive Groups button on the Send/Receive tab, select an account name from the pop-up menu that appears, and then select Process Marked Headers from additional pop-up menu that appears**.

To process marked headers for all e-mail accounts, click the Process Marked Headers button on the Send/Receive tab and select Process Marked Headers from the pop-up menu that appears.

You can't process message headers if they've been moved from the Inbox to another e-mail folder.

After you process them, message headers marked for downloading appear in your Inbox. Message headers that you marked for deletion are removed from the server.

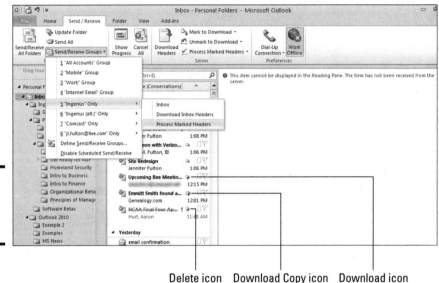

Delete icon   Download Copy icon   Download icon

Figure 2-7:
Ready, set,
mark your
header!

Taking Microsoft Exchange on the Road

It seems a little funny to be talking about taking Exchange on the road because it's designed to be used on a company network. But the reality is, even though you may have a desk downtown, you probably spend very little time at it. Or, even if you do keep your desk chair warm from 8 a.m. to 5 p.m., your work probably doesn't stop just because you're sitting in your living room. So, what should you know about taking Outlook out on the road? The following sections help you fill in the blanks.

Some additional ways in which Exchange can help you when you're out of the office include giving you the ability to view a text transcription of voice messages left on your phone. Pretty cool, right? Yep, you can set up Exchange Server 2010 to transcribe voice messages that someone leaves on your office phone into text messages that are sent to your Inbox, along with a copy of the actual voice recording. You can read the message on your smartphone or through a Web interface without having to listen to the voice recording itself.

Another way in which Exchange can come to your out-of-office rescue is through the Outlook Web App, which provides a pared-down version of Outlook that runs on the Exchange Server. You access Outlook Web App through a Web browser, which makes it the perfect out-of-office partner. With it, you can view e-mails, instant messages, text messages, contacts, and your calendar, although it does not offer all the rich tools (such as Quick Steps, complex searching, and customizable views).

What to do when you're out of the office

Normally, you connect to Exchange over your company's network. If you need to connect to Exchange when you're out of the office, your system administrator has several options. In a lot of cases, he or she sets up a VPN, or *virtual private network,* that you can use to connect via the Internet. Connecting through a VPN typically gives you access to the complete network, so it's really just like being in the office. But connecting to Exchange through a VPN, in order to maintain high security, is often a complicated and time-consuming process.

Another alternative that your system administrator may use is Outlook Anywhere (if your company network uses Exchange Server 2010). This option also connects you to the company's network by using the Internet, but it provides access only to e-mail and nothing else on the network. You can connect to your work e-mail through Outlook Anywhere fairly painlessly and fast, so if you and your colleagues need only e-mail access when you're out of the office, it's a good way to go. Typically, if your network system administrator decides to go the Outlook Anywhere route, he or she also does the setup on your office computer. But if you're using your personal laptop or home computer to connect to Outlook Anywhere so you can check your work e-mail, don't expect him or her to pay you a house call.

To turn on the Outlook Anywhere option for your home computer, click the File tab to display Backstage, select Info from the list on the left to display the Account Information options on the right. Click the Account Settings button, and select Account Settings from the pop-up menu that appears to display the Account Settings dialog box. Select your Exchange account from the list, and click the Change button to display the Change Account Wizard. Click the More Settings button to open Microsoft Exchange dialog box and click the Connection tab. Still with me? Good. In the Outlook Anywhere section, select the Connect to Microsoft Exchange Using HTTP check box. Click the Exchange Proxy Settings button to open the Microsoft Exchange Proxy Settings dialog box, and then type the Internet address that your system administrator told you to use in the Use This URL to Connect to My Proxy Server for Exchange text box. If the administrator babbled something about a secure sockets layer, select the Connect Using SSL Only check box. Set other options as instructed by the administrator, and be sure to make a selection from the Proxy Authentication Settings drop-down list (ask your administrator for the setting you need). Click OK twice to close dialog boxes and return to the Change Account Wizard where you click Next to advance to the last page of the Wizard, and Finish to complete the job.

Downloading the Offline Address Book

For Exchange users, the Global Address List is king. It contains a list of everybody in the corporation; their e-mail addresses; and other information such as employee IDs, department names, and phone numbers or extensions. While you're connected to Exchange, Outlook resolves e-mail addresses by looking them up in the Global Address List. If you use Exchange in Cached Exchange mode, Outlook looks up addresses in the offline address book in order to reduce network traffic and the number of times it has to run back to the server to check stuff.

The offline address book contains only the most basic information needed to resolve e-mail addresses and get messages on their way. Because Outlook refers to the offline address book whenever it needs to check up on somebody, it becomes even more important if you're working offline (temporarily disconnected from the company network) or trying to get some e-mail composed while you're between connections at the airport. As you might imagine, you need to have an offline address book that's at least kinda up-to-date if you want to be able to work offline effectively.

To ensure that your offline address book is updated regularly, follow these steps:

1. **Click the Send/Receive Groups button on the Send/Receive tab and select Define Send/Receive Groups from the pop-up menu that appears.**

   The Send/Receive Groups dialog box appears, as shown on the left in Figure 2-8.

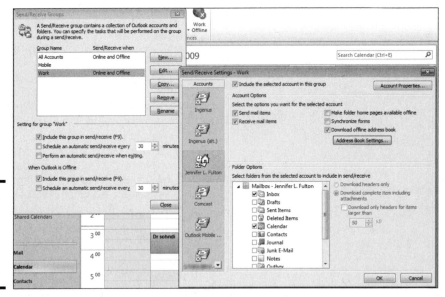

Figure 2-8: Keep that offline address book up-to-date.

2. **Select the group associated with your Exchange account.**

   If you have more than one Send/Receive group, be sure to select the one that includes your Exchange account. For me, that's my Work group.

3. **After you select the correct account, click Edit.**

   The Send/Receive Settings dialog box appears, as shown on the right in Figure 2-8.

4. **Select the Download Offline Address Book check box.**

   It appears in the Account Options section of the dialog box.

5. **Click the Address Book Settings button.**

   The Offline Address Books dialog box appears, as shown in Figure 2-9.

6. **Select the Full Details or No Details radio button, depending on how much detail you want to store in the offline address book.**

   Typically, you want to go with Full Details so you'll be able to access the information you need on a contact, even if you're offline.

7. **Select the address book you want to use from the Choose Address Book drop-down list.**

   If you're part of a really, really, super-big organization, you may have more than one address book to choose from.

8. **Click OK about a billion times to step your way back through all the dialog boxes.**

Figure 2-9:
Set your
offline
address
book
options.

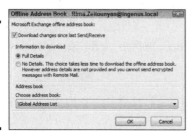

If you have the Download Offline Address Book option turned on, Outlook automatically updates the offline address book about once a day or so. You can get Outlook to update the offline address book immediately by following these steps:

1. **Click the File tab to display Backstage, and select Info from the list on the left.**

   The Account Information options appear on the right.

2. **Select your Exchange account from the Account Information list, click the Account Settings button, and then select Download Address Book from the pop-up menu that appears.**

   The Offline Address Book dialog box appears. (Refer to Figure 2-9.)

3. **In the Information to Download section, select either the Full Details or No Details radio button, depending on how much data you want to download right now (and how long you want to wait for it).**

4. **Click OK.**

   Outlook downloads the updated offline address book.

Changing the Cached Exchange mode settings to download only headers

Normally, when you use Outlook on an Exchange network, it works just like any other e-mail account. At regular intervals, Outlook checks the server for new mail, and when it finds new mail, Outlook places that new mail in your Inbox. If you have a slow network connection or get tons of e-mail that you can easily ignore, you may want to tell Outlook to download only message headers to your computer so that you can mark the ones you want to read.

In the section, "Controlling E-Mail," earlier in this chapter, you can learn how to manually download the message headers for an account, instead of retrieving actual messages. That method is useful, but you have to repeat the process each time you want to retrieve just headers rather than full messages. With Exchange, you can automate the process by telling Outlook that you want to retrieve only message headers for awhile. Outlook responds by grabbing message headers only until you tell it you want to return to full message downloading. Follow these steps:

1. **Click the Download Preferences button on the Send/Receive tab.**

   A pop-up menu appears.

2. **Select a download option.**

   The menu includes these options:

   - *Download Full Items:* Have Outlook download complete messages.

   - *Download Headers and Then Full Items:* Have Outlook download message headers only, and then download the message content when you click a header.

   - *Download Headers:* Have Outlook download only message headers. When you click just a header, a short preview of the message appears in the Reading pane, as shown in Figure 2-10.

Headers for messages that have not yet been downloaded appear with an envelope icon. (See Figure 2-10.) When you click one of these headers, the contents of the message is downloaded automatically if you selected the Download Headers and Then Full Items option. If you selected the Download Headers option, then part of the message appears. Click the Download the Rest of This Message Now button (refer to Figure 2-10) to download the actual message.

To have Outlook download only headers when the network connection is slow, select either the Download Full Items or the Download Headers and Then Full Items option from the menu, and then click the Download Preferences button again and select On Slow Connections Only Download Headers from the menu.

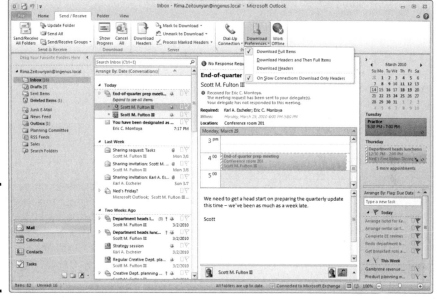

Book X
Chapter 2

Turning Your
E-Mail Accounts
into Roadies

Figure 2-10:
Click a
header
to see a
preview of
your e-mail.

You can also take yourself offline (where you don't receive any messages or even check for them) by clicking the Work Offline button on the Send/Receive tab. Working offline allows you to speed up your computer to do other work, instead of letting it constantly check for e-mail over a slow network. It also prevents you from sending any messages you're creating from going out, until you are completely sure you want the world to see them.

Chapter 3: Printing Your Stuff and Taking It with You

In This Chapter

✔ Printing messages so that you can refer to them

✔ Printing the documents attached to a message

✔ Printing an entire list of items

✔ Printing a blank calendar so that you can mark it up

*I*n today's electronic age, where everyone has more electronic gizmos hanging off their body than a space-age robot, it seems almost quaint to think of printing something on paper. "Look Jimmy, in that museum case over there. That's a paper calendar. Grandpa used to carry one just like that, to and from school, through the snow, in bare feet, just so he could keep track of his homework assignments."

But let's face it. As much as we'd like to pretend we live in the 21st century (oh, that's right, we do), there are times when paper is a happy sight. For example, when you suddenly discover that a new client's office isn't where you thought it was, you're really glad to see that little piece of paper sitting there on the passenger seat — the printout that contains the directions to the client's office, which they sent to you anyway, even though you reassured them a thousand times that you knew exactly where they were located. Yep, it was a lucky thing your assistant printed that message for you because she knows you couldn't find a tree in a forest. Or the printer connected to your computer.

You might want to print out other things from Outlook, for times when you can't use your smartphone or notebook computer. If you're heading into a meeting of company bigwigs, for example, you might want to have everybody's name right there in your pocket, in case you suddenly can't recall who the VP of Marketing is this week, and there he is, heading right across the room at you. When you travel, you might prefer to whip out a piece of paper that contains your schedule, rather than squeeze out of your economy-class airplane seat, retrieve your notebook computer from the overhead compartment, and wait five minutes for it to start up. This chapter shows you practical and creative ways that you can have fun with paper.

The tasks in this chapter assume that you have your computer attached to a printer, either directly or through a network, and that the printer has paper, ink, and a valid driver's license.

Printing Items and Any Attached Documents

If you receive a message that contains important information, which you need to carry with you when you're not at your computer, you can just print that message out. For example, the message may contain directions to an off-site meeting, your itinerary for a business trip, your flight number and confirmation information, and other important data.

In addition, sometimes a message comes to you, dragging some of its buddies (attachments) along with it. When you want, and without much fanfare, Outlook can print out the message's attachments, too. Of course, you don't have to print the attachments just because they're there.

By the way, you don't have to limit yourself to simply printing messages. Oh, no; if you want to print the details of a task, contact, or appointment, you certainly can, along with any attachments. If you just want to print a list of items (similar to the list views available in each module), see the next section, "Printing a List of Items" for help.

Although Outlook tries hard to print an item's attachments, it has its limits. If the attachment is zipped, for example, Outlook can't print it. Also, you must have a program compatible with the attachment installed on your computer in order for Outlook to print it. In addition, if the file is a non-Office file, even if you have a compatible program installed, the attachment may only *open* in that program and not automatically *print.*

To print selected items and (optionally) any attachments, follow these steps:

1. **Select the message(s), appointment(s), meeting(s), contact(s), task(s), or note(s) that you want to print.**

If you select a single item, don't open it if you want to be able to print attachments. You can select multiple items; not all of them have to have attachments for you to be able to print the ones that do. Here's how to select multiple items:

- *To select noncontiguous items:* Hold down Ctrl and click each item.

- *To select contiguous items:* Hold down Shift, click the first item in the group, then click the last item.

If you're in Calendar and using one of the Day/Week/Month views, you can select individual appointments/meetings if you want to print just them and their attachments. If you're not interested in attachments so much as the details of your appointments/meetings, and you only want to print a week or month's worth, then don't worry about selecting anything. Instead, you limit your calendar printout by specifying the range of dates to print, as shown in Step 9.

2. **Click the File tab to display Backstage, and select Print from the list on the left.**

   The Print Settings options appear on the right, as shown in Figure 3-1.

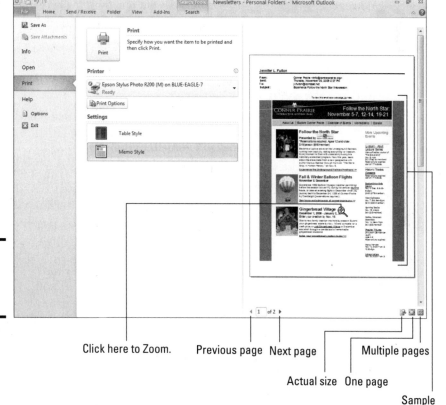

Figure 3-1:
The Print
Settings
options.

Click here to Zoom.   Previous page Next page   Multiple pages

Actual size One page

Sample

3. **Select the printer that you want to use from the Printer drop-down list.**

4. **Select a print style in the Settings pane.**

   You must select Memo Style (which is specifically designed to print the contents of an item) or Calendar Details Style if you want to print any attached files. If you are not interested in printing attachments, there are many styles you can choose from. Here's a brief explanation of each style:

To learn the best way to print a list of items, see the next section, "Printing a List of Items," for help — here, I assume that you are not printing a list of items and so I will not discuss the options that appear when you do that.

For messages, tasks, and notes, you have these two print style options:

- *Table Style:* Prints items in a long list, which is discussed in detail in the next section

- *Memo Style:* Prints the contents of each item — select this style if you want to print attachments

There are several Calendar print styles:

- *Daily Style:* Prints Calendar items one day per page (work hours only), including a Daily Task List.

- *Weekly Agenda Style:* Prints Calendar items in a Weekly view that resembles a day planner.

- *Weekly Calendar Style:* Prints Calendar items in a Weekly view that resembles the Outlook Weekly Calendar view.

- *Monthly Style:* Prints Calendar items in a Monthly view.

- *Tri-Fold Style:* Prints Calendar items with each page divided into three sections. The detail for a single day appears on the left, the Daily Task List appears in the middle, and a weekly summary of the week appears on the right. (See Figure 3-2.)

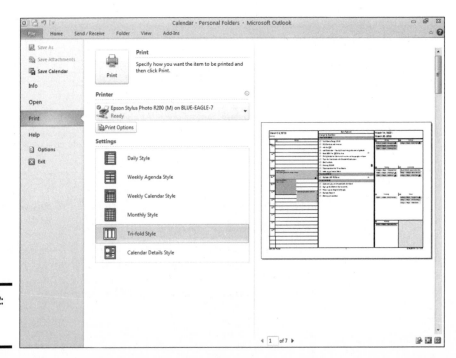

Figure 3-2:
A triple threat.

- *Calendar Details Style:* Prints Calendar items one after the other, with full details, grouped by day.

- *Memo Style:* Prints the contents of each item — select this style if you want to print attachments.

There are several Contacts print styles:

- *Card Style:* Prints the information that you see on the address cards in alphabetical order. (See Figure 3-3.)

- *Small Booklet Style:* Prints the names and addresses like a small book. Outlook prints on both sides of each piece of paper, and when you put the papers in order, you can create a little address book. The font is a bit small — but still readable.

  To print by using Small Booklet or Medium Booklet Style, your printer must be set up for double-sided printing.

- *Medium Booklet Style:* Similar to Small Booklet Style, but this style creates a booklet in a larger font. It's a bit more readable than the Small Booklet Style, although it's also bulkier because it takes more pages to print the same number of contacts.

- *Memo Style:* Prints the contents of each item — select this style if you want to print attachments.

- *Phone Directory Style:* Prints only contact names and phone numbers in a long list.

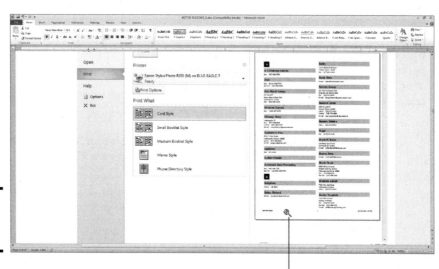

Figure 3-3:
Pick a card,
any card.

Click here to zoom.

If you don't need to print attachments, multiple copies, a limited selection of items, or to customize the page setup, you can skip all the way to Step 27.

After selecting a style, you might want to examine the printout to make sure it's what you want. Click the sample on the right side of the Print Settings page to zoom in on it; click again to zoom back out. Several buttons appear below the sample that you can use to view the item in actual size, one page at a time, or in groups of multiple pages. Click the Next Page button to view the next page of the printout; click the Previous Page button to view the previous page.

5. **Click the Print Options button.**

   The Print dialog box, shown in Figure 3-4, appears. The options that appear in this dialog box vary, based on the print style you selected from the Settings pane in Step 4. I discuss these options in the next steps.

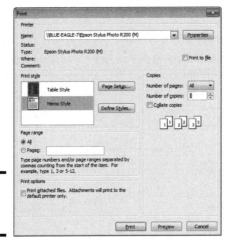

Figure 3-4:
The Print
dialog box.

6. **To produce multiple copies of your printout, enter the number of copies you want in the Number of Copies text box.**

7. **(Optional) If you print more than one copy, you might want to give that Collate Copies check box a click and save yourself the trouble of putting the pages in order after they're printed.**

   If you don't select the Collate Copies option, then Outlook prints multiple copies of page one, and then the copies of page two, and so on. With the Collate Copies option selected, Outlook prints one set: page one, two, and so on, and then it prints the next set.

8. **(Optional) Change the Page Range if desired.**

You can limit the printout, even if you didn't select anything, by selecting the Pages radio button and typing the page numbers that you want to print in the Pages text box. For example, if you only want to print the pages 2, 3, and 4 of a very long message, type 2-4 in the Pages text box. To print pages 2, 5 and 6, type 2, 5, 6.

9. **(Optional) Change the Print Range if desired.**

If you are printing contacts:

- Despite what you might have selected in Step 1, you can print all the contacts in the current folder by selecting the All Items radio button.

- To print only the selected contacts from Step 1, select the Selected Items radio button instead.

If you're printing Calendar items:

- Specify the portion of your Calendar to print by entering a start date in the Start text box, and an end date in the End text box.

- Hide the details of items marked as private by selecting the Hide Details of Private Appointments checkbox.

10. **If you want to print attachments, select the Print Attached Files check box.**

Again, you must select the Memo Style in Step 4 to be able to print attached files.

11. **Click Page Setup to open the Page Setup dialog box.**

12. **Click the Format tab, as shown in Figure 3-5.**

The Format Options shown on the left side of this tab vary depending on what you are printing (for example, contacts) and the print style you select (for example, Card Style), as shown in Figure 3-5.

13. **(Optional) Change Format Options.**

If you are printing contacts, you may see these options, depending on the print style you selected in Step 4:

- *Sections*: Select the Immediately, Follow Each Other radio button to have each group of contacts (the As, Bs, Cs, and so on) follow each other on the page with no breaks. Select the Start On A New Page radio button to start each group of contacts (the As, Bs, Cs, and so on) on a new page.

- *Number of Columns:* Select the number of columns to print per page of the booklet or directory from the Number of Columns drop-down list.

- *Blank Forms at End:* Select how many blank contact pages to add to the back of the booklet from the Blank Forms at End drop-down list.

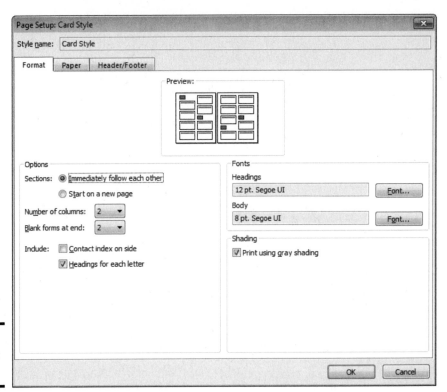

Figure 3-5:
The Format
tab.

- *Contact Index on Side:* To display the alphabet along the side of the booklet, with the letter(s) of the last names of the contacts on that page highlighted (for example, F might be highlighted to indicate that the contacts on that page all have last names that begin with F), select the Contact Index on Side check box.

- *Headings for Each Letter:* To display a letter heading at the top of each contact group, select the Headings for Each Letter check box.

If you are printing calendar items, you may see these options, depending on the print style you selected in Step 4:

- *Arrange Days:* Select the Top to Bottom radio button to arrange days vertically; select the Left to Right radio button to arrange days horizontally.

- *Layout:* Select the layout to use such as 2 Pages/Week from the Layout drop-down list.

- *Tasks:* Choose whether to include tasks with your calendar information, and which tasks layout to use (To-Do bar or Daily Tasks List), from the Tasks drop-down list.

- *Include:* Select the Notes Area (Blank) check box to add an unlined notes section at the bottom of the calendar; select the Notes Area (Lined) to add a lined notes section instead.

- *Print From/Print To:* To limit the hours for which appointments and meetings are included in the printout, select the first hour of the day to include from the Print From drop-down list. Select the last hour of the day to include from the Print To drop-down list.

- *Only Print Workdays:* Select the Only Print Workdays check box to include only items in your calendar that occur on workdays.

- *Print Exactly One Month Per Page:* Select the Print Exactly One Month Per Page check box to reduce the font if needed to fit each month from your calendar on a single page.

- *Left Section/Middle Section/Right Section:* With the Tri-Fold Style, you can select what you want to print (such as Daily Calendar, Weekly Calendar, Monthly Calendar, Daily Task List, To-Do bar, or a notes section) in each of the three columns of the printout by making selections from the Left Section, Middle Section, and Right Section drop-down lists.

- *Start a New Page Each:* Select how much information you want to include on each page of the printout by selecting Day, Week, or Month from the Start a New Page Each drop-down list.

- *Print Attached Files:* With the Calendar Details Style, select the Print Attached Files check box to print any file attached to the selected calendar items.

14. **Click the Font button next to Title, Fields, Date Headings, Appointments, or Body to change the font for that element of the printout.**

    The Font dialog box appears.

15. **Select a font from the Font list, font attributes (such as bold) from the Font Style list, and font size from the Size list; then click OK.**

    The Page Setup dialog box reappears.

16. **To remove the gray shaded areas of the printout, deselect the Print Using Gray Shading check box.**

17. **Click the Paper tab in the Page Setup dialog box, as shown in Figure 3-6.**

18. **Select a paper size from the Type list box.**

    For example, for 8.5-x-11-inch paper, select Letter.

19. **From the Size list box, select how you want that paper size utilized.**

    For example, you might choose Franklin Day Planner Classic to print out your calendar for your Franklin Day Planner.

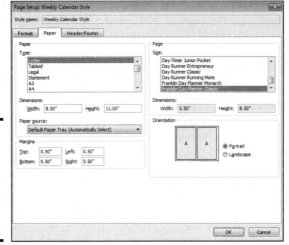

Figure 3-6:
With page
setup, you
can change
the format
of the
printout.

20. **To change the page orientation, select either the Portrait or Landscape radio button.**

The sample changes to show what your choice means.

21. **Make any other changes you want in the Paper tab.**

In the Dimensions pane, you can enter custom dimensions for some paper type you can't find in the Type list, for example. You can also adjust the margins in the Margins pane.

22. **Click the Header/Footer tab, shown in Figure 3-7.**

A *header* prints at the top of every page in a printout, and a *footer* prints along the bottom, so adding a header or footer only makes sense if you're printing something that's more than a single page.

23. **In the Header or Footer pane, click in the text box where you want the header to appear on the page.**

For example, to have your name appear on the upper left of the printed page, click in the left text box in the Header pane.

24. **Either type what you want to appear or click a button to insert an option.**

These buttons appear at the bottom of the dialog box:

- *Page:* Displays the current page number on each page
- *Total Pages:* Inserts the total number of pages in the printout
- *Date:* Inserts the current date
- *Time:* Inserts the current time
- *User Name:* Inserts your name

25. **Select the Reverse on Even Pages check box to reverse the order of the header or footer items on even-numbered pages.**

For example, if you inserted your name on the left, your name prints on the right on page two (and page four, page six, and so on).

26. **Click OK to close the Page Setup dialog box.**

The Print dialog box appears.

27. **In the Print dialog box, click Preview to view your changes.**

The original Print Settings page appears. Check out the printout to make sure it's going to look the way you want to before you print. See Step 4 for help with browsing.

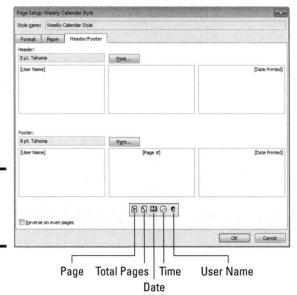

Figure 3-7: Adding a header or footer.

Page   Total Pages | Time   User Name
Date

28. **Click Print.**

The item(s) you selected in Step 1 are immediately printed. If you choose to print attachments, you might see a message reminding you to open only attachments you know came from a trusted source, and therefore probably don't contain any viruses. (Outlook must open the attachments in a compatible program to print them.)

29. **If a warning message appears (and you're sure the attachments are safe), click Open to continue.**

The attachments are printed.

Printing a List of Items

Sometimes, you don't need the contents of an item printed; you just need a list. You can print your Tasks list, for example, or you can print a list of contacts at a client's company so that you can take it with you on a business trip. The process is fairly simple. First, select a view that displays the items you want to print, and then begin the print process. Outlook offers a lot of options along the way, so put your decision cap on.

To print a list of items, follow these steps:

1. **Change to the module that contains the items you want to print by clicking its button on the Navigation pane.**

   Want to print tasks? Well then, change over to the Tasks module. Appointments more your worry? Then change to Calendar.

2. **Select the folder you want to print.**

   For example, in Mail, you might have many folders in which you organize incoming mail. In Contacts, you might have a New Clients folder in which you keep all your new client contacts. If the module you are in contains multiple folders, select the folder you want to print.

3. **Click the Change View button on the View tab and select a list view from the palette that appears**

   In Mail or Tasks, you can select any view as they are all essentially list views. In Calendar, select either the List or Active views; in Contacts, select either Phone or List view.

4. **(Optional) Rearrange the order of the items before printing by simply clicking the column header of the column you want to sort by.**

   For example, click the Due Date column to sort a list of tasks by their due date.

5. **Select the items you want to print.**

   You don't have to print all the items in the current folder, although Outlook prints everything it sees unless you make a selection:

   - *To select noncontiguous items:* Hold down Ctrl and click each item.

   - *To select contiguous items:* Hold down Shift, click the first item in the group, then click the last item.

   Some views automatically hide certain items, so by choosing one of them, you can limit the size of your printout without having to select anything. For example, the Active view in Tasks displays only the active tasks, and not the completed ones. Another way to limit the view is to search for the items you want to print. See Book IX, Chapter 4, for the lowdown.

If you display a list by using some kind of grouping, such as categories, you can collapse the groups you don't want to print so that they're not visible by clicking the down arrow in front of the group.

6. **Click the File tab to display Backstage, and select Print from list on the left.**

   The Print Settings options appear on the right.

7. **Select the printer you want to use from the Printer drop-down list.**

8. **Select Table Style from the Settings pane.**

9. **(Optional) Click the Print Options button.**

   The Print dialog box shown in Figure 3-8 appears. (If you don't need to make any changes to how your items print, skip to Step 11.)

   The Print dialog box offers you a bunch of choices; I explain most of those choices in the section "Printing an Item and Any Attached Documents," earlier in this chapter. When using Table Style, however, you have a few unique options that deserve explanation:

   - You can print the entire list of items in the current folder (despite what you might have selected in Step 5) by selecting the All Rows radio button.

   - To print only your selected items, you must select the Only Selected Rows radio button, instead.

10. **After selecting options in the Print dialog box, click Preview to preview your list of items.**

    The Print Settings page reappears.

Before printing, you might want to examine the printout to make sure it's what you want. Click the sample on the right side of the Print Settings page to zoom in on it; click again to zoom back out. Several buttons appear below the sample that you can use to view the item in actual size, one page at a time, or in groups of multiple pages. Click the Next Page button to view the next page of the printout; click the Previous Page button to view the previous page.

11. **Click Print.**

    The item(s) you selected in Step 5 are immediately printed in a long list.

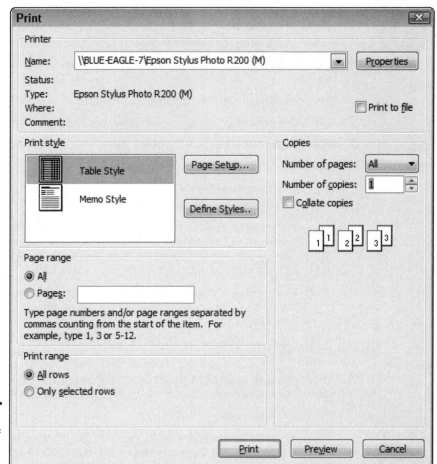

Figure 3-8:
Print a list of items.

Printing a Blank Calendar

Sometimes, you may find having a blank calendar printout handy, especially if you're out of the office (or away from home) and need to jot down an appointment or meeting. To print a blank calendar, however, you need to create one first. Thankfully, that's not difficult.

To create and print a blank calendar, follow these steps:

1. **Change to Calendar by clicking its button on the Navigation pane.**

2. **Click the New Calendar button on the Folder tab.**

The Create New Folder dialog box appears, as shown in Figure 3-9.

Figure 3-9:
Creating
a blank
calendar.

3. **In the Name text box, type a name for the new folder.**

I typed the name `Blank` so that I could remember never to fill it. That way, I always have a blank calendar for printing.

4. **From the Folder Contains drop-down list, select Calendar Items, select Calendar from the Select Where to Place the Folder list box, and then click OK to create the blank calendar.**

The calendar appears in the My Calendars list on the Navigation pane.

5. **In the My Calendars section of the Navigation pane in Calendar, select the check box for the new, blank calendar you just created.**

The blank calendar appears.

6. **Click the File tab to display Backstage, and select Print from the list on the left.**

The Print Settings options appear on the right.

7. **Select the printer that you want to use from the Printer drop-down list.**

8. **In the Settings pane, select the print style you want to use.**

See the earlier section, "Printing Items and Any Attached Documents" for help in selecting a print style.

9. **Click the Print Options button.**

The Print dialog box appears. Specify the portion of the calendar to print by entering a start date in the Start text box, and an end date in the End text box. Set any other options you want. See the section "Printing Items and Any Attached Documents," earlier in this chapter, for help with making selections.

10. **After selecting options in the Print dialog box, click Preview to preview the layout for your blank calendar.**

The Print Settings page reappears.

Before printing, you might want to examine the printout to make sure it's what you want. Click the sample on the right side of the Print Settings page to zoom in on it; click again to zoom back out. Several buttons appear below the sample that you can use to view the item in actual size, one page at a time, or in groups of multiple pages. Click the Next Page button to view the next page of the printout; click the Previous Page button to view the previous page.

11. **Click Print.**

The blank calendar is immediately printed.

Index

B

F

M

Q

R

T

Notes

Business/Accounting & Bookkeeping

Bookkeeping For Dummies
978-0-7645-9848-7

eBay Business
All-in-One For Dummies,
2nd Edition
978-0-470-38536-4

Job Interviews
For Dummies,
3rd Edition
978-0-470-17748-8

Resumes For Dummies,
5th Edition
978-0-470-08037-5

Stock Investing
For Dummies,
3rd Edition
978-0-470-40114-9

Successful Time
Management
For Dummies
978-0-470-29034-7

Computer Hardware

BlackBerry For Dummies,
3rd Edition
978-0-470-45762-7

Computers For Seniors
For Dummies
978-0-470-24055-7

iPhone For Dummies,
2nd Edition
978-0-470-42342-4

Laptops For Dummies,
3rd Edition
978-0-470-27759-1

Macs For Dummies,
10th Edition
978-0-470-27817-8

Cooking & Entertaining

Cooking Basics
For Dummies,
3rd Edition
978-0-7645-7206-7

Wine For Dummies,
4th Edition
978-0-470-04579-4

Diet & Nutrition

Dieting For Dummies,
2nd Edition
978-0-7645-4149-0

Nutrition For Dummies,
4th Edition
978-0-471-79868-2

Weight Training
For Dummies,
3rd Edition
978-0-471-76845-6

Digital Photography

Digital Photography
For Dummies,
6th Edition
978-0-470-25074-7

Photoshop Elements 7
For Dummies
978-0-470-39700-8

Gardening

Gardening Basics
For Dummies
978-0-470-03749-2

Organic Gardening
For Dummies,
2nd Edition
978-0-470-43067-5

Green/Sustainable

Green Building
& Remodeling
For Dummies
978-0-470-17559-0

Green Cleaning
For Dummies
978-0-470-39106-8

Green IT For Dummies
978-0-470-38688-0

Health

Diabetes For Dummies,
3rd Edition
978-0-470-27086-8

Food Allergies
For Dummies
978-0-470-09584-3

Living Gluten-Free
For Dummies
978-0-471-77383-2

Hobbies/General

Chess For Dummies,
2nd Edition
978-0-7645-8404-6

Drawing For Dummies
978-0-7645-5476-6

Knitting For Dummies,
2nd Edition
978-0-470-28747-7

Organizing For Dummies
978-0-7645-5300-4

SuDoku For Dummies
978-0-470-01892-7

Home Improvement

Energy Efficient Homes
For Dummies
978-0-470-37602-7

Home Theater
For Dummies,
3rd Edition
978-0-470-41189-6

Living the Country Lifestyle
All-in-One For Dummies
978-0-470-43061-3

Solar Power Your Home
For Dummies
978-0-470-17569-9

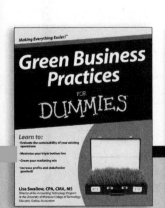

Internet

Blogging For Dummies,
2nd Edition
978-0-470-23017-6

eBay For Dummies,
6th Edition
978-0-470-49741-8

Facebook For Dummies
978-0-470-26273-3

Google Blogger
For Dummies
978-0-470-40742-4

Web Marketing
For Dummies,
2nd Edition
978-0-470-37181-7

WordPress For Dummies,
2nd Edition
978-0-470-40296-2

Language & Foreign Language

French For Dummies
978-0-7645-5193-2

Italian Phrases
For Dummies
978-0-7645-7203-6

Spanish For Dummies
978-0-7645-5194-9

Spanish For Dummies,
Audio Set
978-0-470-09585-0

Macintosh

Mac OS X Snow Leopard
For Dummies
978-0-470-43543-4

Math & Science

Algebra I For Dummies,
2nd Edition
978-0-470-55964-2

Biology For Dummies
978-0-7645-5326-4

Calculus For Dummies
978-0-7645-2498-1

Chemistry For Dummies
978-0-7645-5430-8

Microsoft Office

Excel 2007 For Dummies
978-0-470-03737-9

Office 2007 All-in-One
Desk Reference
For Dummies
978-0-471-78279-7

Music

Guitar For Dummies,
2nd Edition
978-0-7645-9904-0

iPod & iTunes
For Dummies,
6th Edition
978-0-470-39062-7

Piano Exercises
For Dummies
978-0-470-38765-8

Parenting & Education

Parenting For Dummies,
2nd Edition
978-0-7645-5418-6

Type 1 Diabetes
For Dummies
978-0-470-17811-9

Pets

Cats For Dummies,
2nd Edition
978-0-7645-5275-5

Dog Training For Dummies,
2nd Edition
978-0-7645-8418-3

Puppies For Dummies,
2nd Edition
978-0-470-03717-1

Religion & Inspiration

The Bible For Dummies
978-0-7645-5296-0

Catholicism For Dummies
978-0-7645-5391-2

Women in the Bible
For Dummies
978-0-7645-8475-6

Self-Help & Relationship

Anger Management
For Dummies
978-0-470-03715-7

Overcoming Anxiety
For Dummies
978-0-7645-5447-6

Sports

Baseball For Dummies,
3rd Edition
978-0-7645-7537-2

Basketball For Dummies,
2nd Edition
978-0-7645-5248-9

Golf For Dummies,
3rd Edition
978-0-471-76871-5

Web Development

Web Design All-in-One
For Dummies
978-0-470-41796-6

Windows Vista

Windows Vista
For Dummies
978-0-471-75421-3

Available wherever books are sold. For more information or to order direct: U.S. customers visit www.dummies.com or call 1-877-762-2974.
U.K. customers visit www.wileyeurope.com or call (0) 1243 843291. Canadian customers visit www.wiley.ca or call 1-800-567-4797.